BLONDIE®

THE BUMSTEAD FAMILY HISTORY

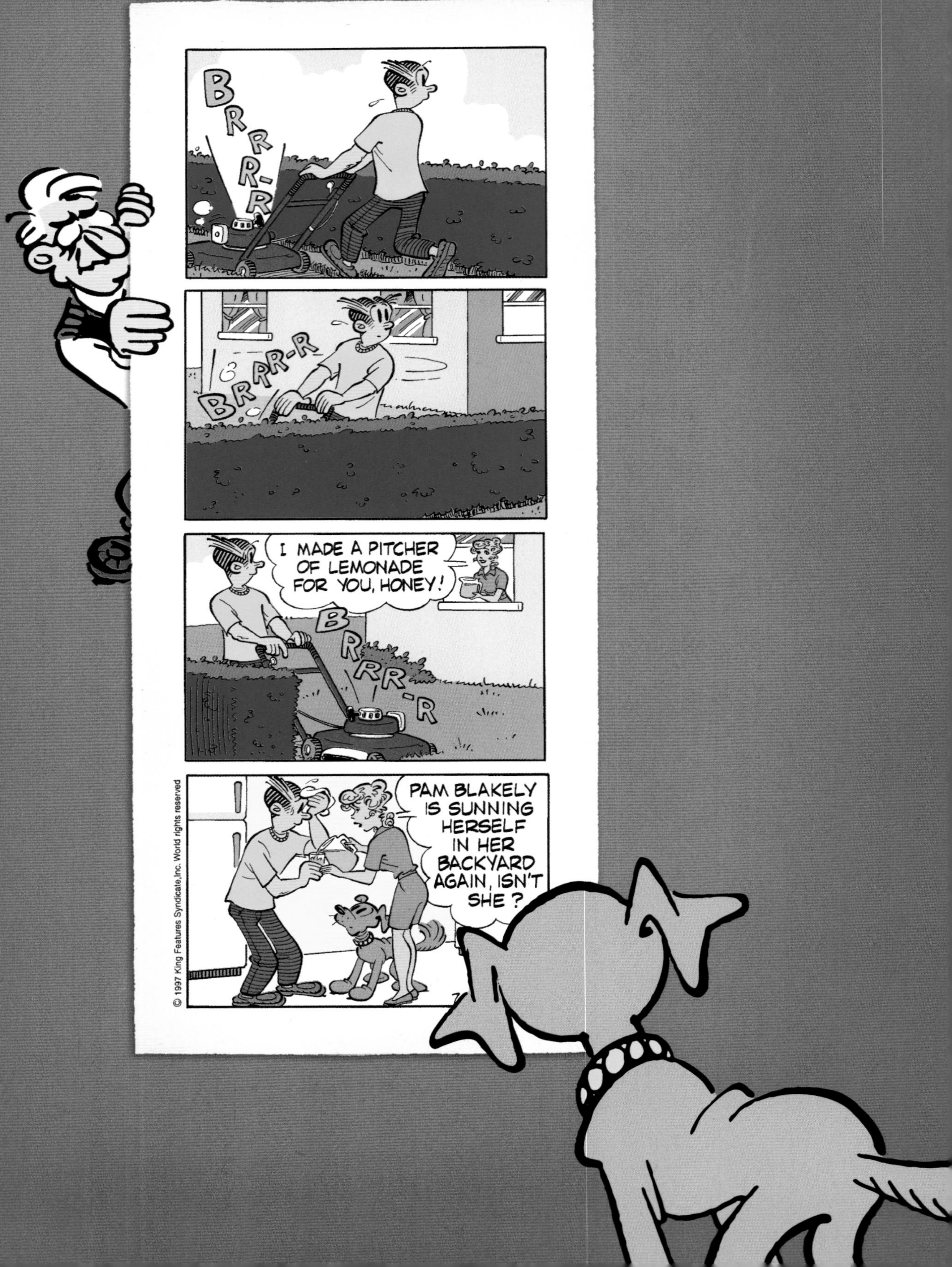
BRRR-R
BRRR-R
I MADE A PITCHER OF LEMONADE FOR YOU, HONEY!
BRRR-R
PAM BLAKELY IS SUNNING HERSELF IN HER BACKYARD AGAIN, ISN'T SHE?
© 1997 King Features Syndicate,Inc. World rights reserved

BLONDIE®

THE BUMSTEAD FAMILY HISTORY

DEAN YOUNG

&

MELENA RYZIK

WHAT MAKES YOU THINK THAT ?

THOMAS NELSON

Since 1798

NASHVILLE DALLAS MEXICO CITY RIO DE JANEIRO BEIJING

Dedicated to the memory of
Jay Kennedy (1956-2007),
editor-in-chief of King Features Syndicate and scholar of the arts.

Published in Nashville, Tennessee, by Thomas Nelson. Thomas Nelson is a trademark of Thomas Nelson, Inc.

Thomas Nelson, Inc. titles may be purchased in bulk for educational, business, fundraising, or sales promotional use. For information, please email SpecialMarkets@ThomasNelson.com

Library of Congress Cataloging-in-Publication Data

Young, Dean, 1938-
Blondie: the Bumstead family history / Dean Young and Melena Ryzik.
p. cm.
ISBN-13: 978-1-4016-0322-9 (alk. paper)
ISBN-10: 1-4016-0322-X (alk. paper)
1. Blondie (Comic strip) I. Ryzik, Melena. II. Title.
PN6728.B55Y584 2007
741.5'6973--dc22

2007012830

Printed in China

07 08 09 10 11 – 9 8 7 6 5 4 3 2 1

TABLE OF CONTENTS

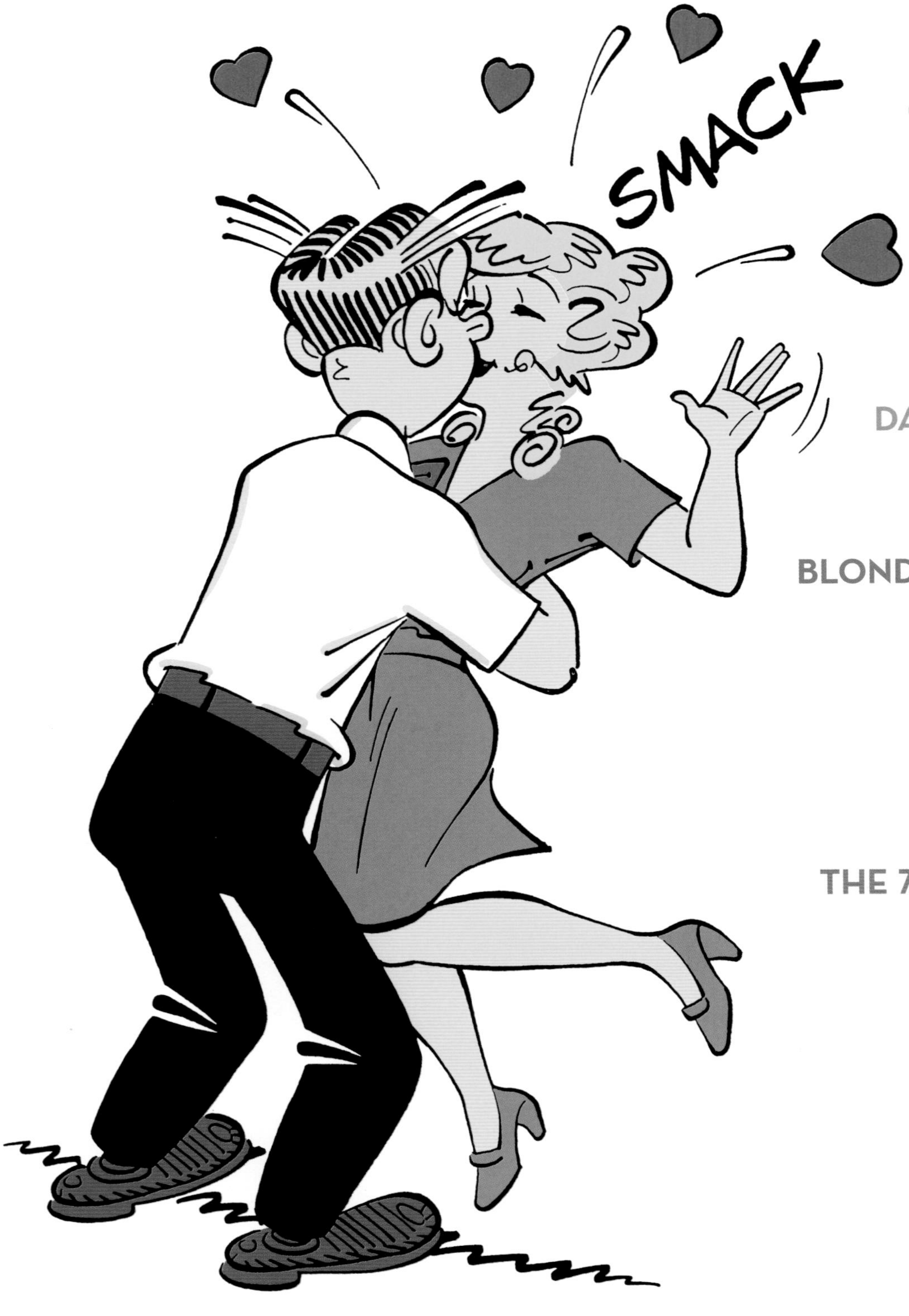

SMACK

Over the years I have often wondered what my father, Chic Young, would have to say about the amazing durability of the characters that he created almost eight decades ago. I'm sure he would be thrilled to know that the world is still enjoying a daily dose of his wacky creation.

And every day, I thank my lucky stars for this magical menagerie of zany comic strip characters that became my responsibility to protect, honor, and keep funny. What a thrill it is to work with characters that literally explode like chemicals when they come in contact with one another. Sometimes I just turn them loose and let them do whatever they want. It's almost like the strip could write itself. With this cast of characters, even a monkey could do it!

My dad taught me all the nuances of how to run a big-time comic strip during the twelve years I worked with him. It was a great father-son relationship and a great working relationship. One day toward the end of working together was particularly memorable when he told me never to worry about the comic strip. "If it seems funny to you, just do it, and the comic strip will take care of itself," he said. I wasn't so sure when 300 newspapers dropped the comic strip immediately after his death. In the years that followed, however, we got all of those newspapers back, plus hundreds more — proof enough that his words were remarkably prophetic, and the characters that he created more enduring than he could have ever imagined.

The strips on the pages ahead are some of my personal favorites. I hope you enjoy them as much as I have enjoyed the privilege of creating them for you.

DEAN YOUNG

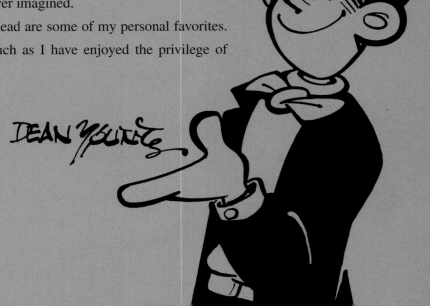

CHAPTER 1

THE BUMSTEAD FAMILY ALBUM

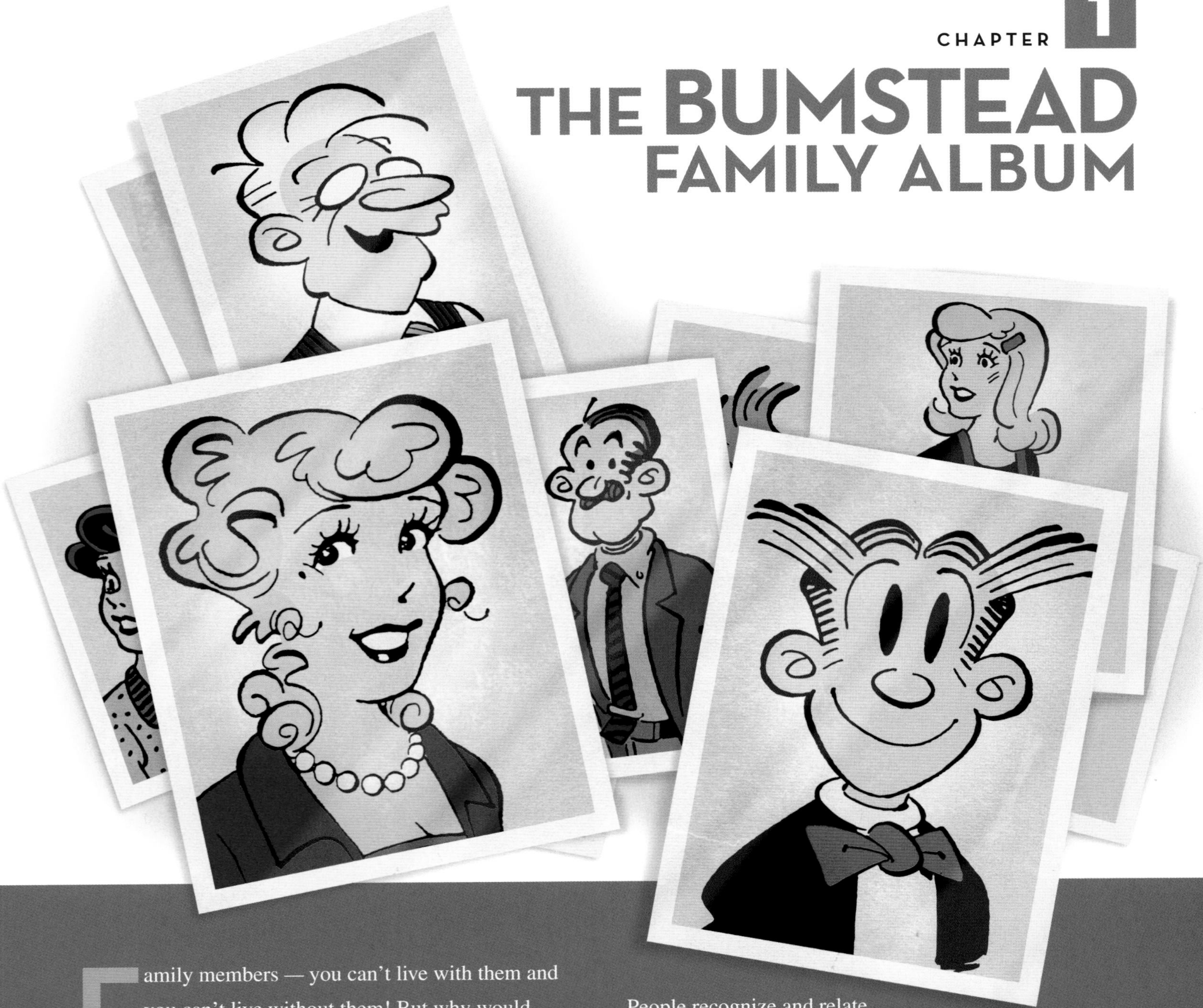

Family members — you can't live with them and you can't live without them! But why would anyone want to live without the Bumsteads? Since 1930, Dagwood and Blondie Bumstead, along with their children Cookie and Alexander, have brought humor and joy into the homes of millions of *Blondie* fans around the world.

This enduring domestic comedy continues to make an indelible impression in the hearts and minds of *Blondie* fans who connect with the Bumsteads' ability to cope, without losing sight of the little things that count. People recognize and relate to the Bumstead family because they see themselves and their loved ones reflected inside the paneled walls of this adored comic strip.

The Bumstead Family Album is a celebration of family at its most genuine. As you thumb through the pages of this book, take pleasure in the book's most simple and universal truth: "home is truly where the heart is." So, sit back, relax and enjoy some treasured quality time with family.

BLONDIE

Blondie was born on September 8, 1930, and she was already a knockout. With wavy golden tresses, pouty lips, long-lashed eyes, and a sensational shape, this one-of-a-kind cartoon figure quickly enchanted millions. The original doyenne of domesticity, she eventually grew to symbolize the myriad changes in American womanhood. With a relentlessly can-do spirit, a husband, two kids, a dog, a job, and a house in the suburbs, Blondie epitomized that combination of pluck, humor, and passion that drove the American Dream at a time when the nation needed it most – and we loved her for it.

But it wasn't always so. The pretty woman in the ruffled dress arrived in the nation's newspapers as a two-dimensional—as in pancake-flat—stereotype of a character that had already captured the public's imagination: the flapper.

A symbol of women's growing independence in the years following the Nineteenth Amendment, the flapper was a rebellious risk-taker and a free spirit. In the jubilant post–World War I years, she was a perfect subject for the pages of the daily and weekly comics, which could chronicle her adventures, and misadventures alike. As a fun-loving, man-chasing young lady with the perfectly comic surname Boopadoop, the early Blondie displayed a decidedly screwball sensibility. Yet her creator, Chic Young, recognized something more than a newsprint-ready blonde joke. She wasn't a dizzy blonde as much as she was a dizziness-inducing blonde, embodying the whirlwind lifestyle that the "It" girls of the era seemed to suggest.

But the Depression put a damper on this party-heavy image. As Blondie's real-life counterparts were evolving, so was she. First she traded ditziness for a diploma as she became a student, then a slew of boyfriends for the eternal Dagwood Bumstead—of the J. Bolling Bumsteads, rail industry titans and the funny page answer to the Vanderbilts.

Blondie and Dagwood's first date wasn't depicted in newsprint, but it probably involved a soda, a sandwich (pastrami on rye) and a chaste kiss—if Dagwood was lucky (about the kiss, that is—he definitely got the sandwich). Preternaturally awkward, he was nonetheless a millionaire, the beneficiary of his father's riches. Blondie, on the other hand, was beautiful but decidedly lower middle class; she

WHAT'S WRONG, HONEY?
I CAN'T LOG IN ON MY COMPUTER BECAUSE I FORGOT MY NEW PASSWORD
MY MIND IS A COMPLETE BLANK!
THINK, DEAR... YOUR PASSWORD MUST BE SOMETHING OR SOMEONE THAT YOU LOVE!
pastrami
YOU'RE RIGHT! I'VE GOT IT!
© 2005 by King Features Syndicate, Inc. World Rights reserved
www.Blondie.com
6-28

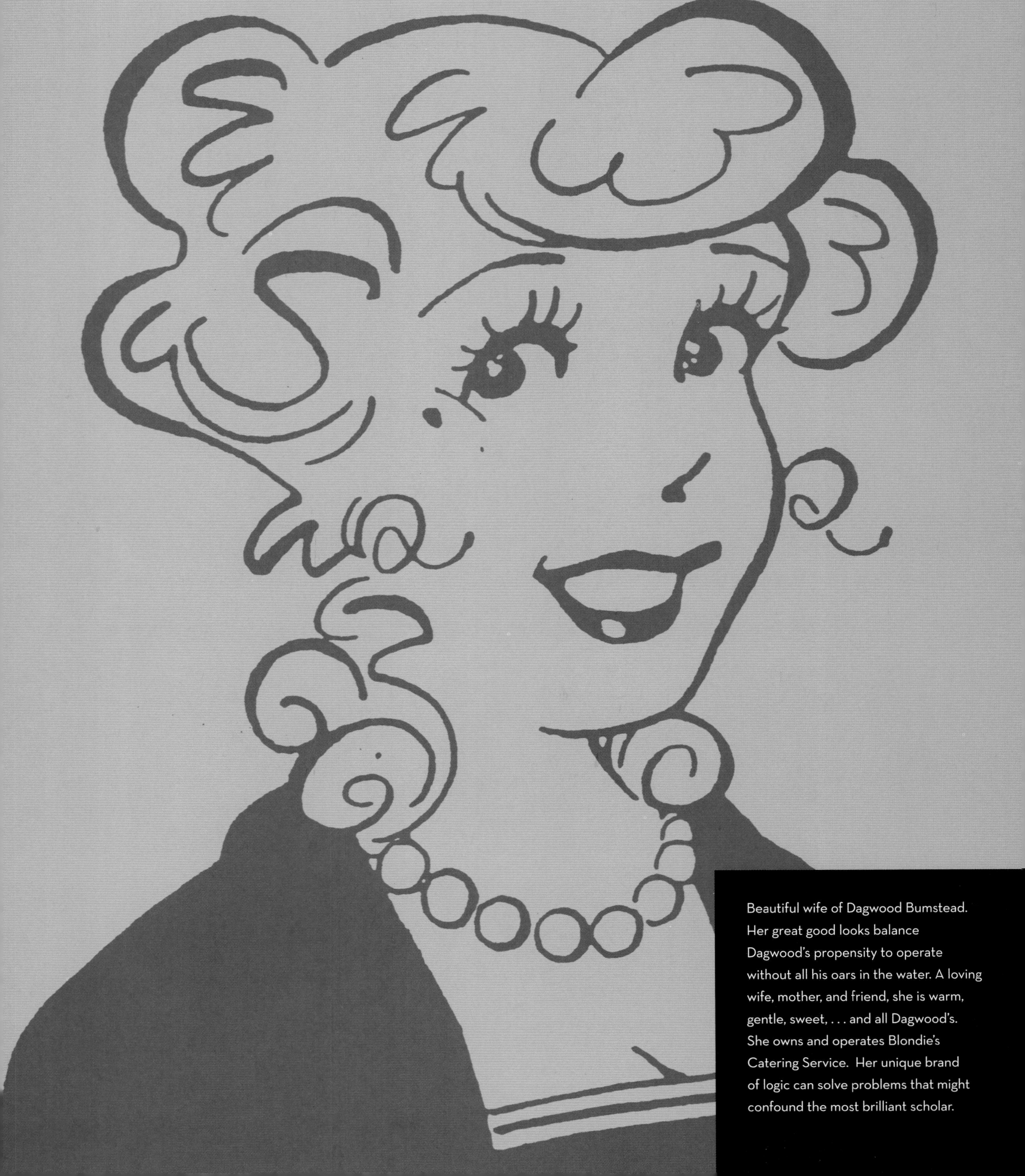

Beautiful wife of Dagwood Bumstead. Her great good looks balance Dagwood's propensity to operate without all his oars in the water. A loving wife, mother, and friend, she is warm, gentle, sweet, . . . and all Dagwood's. She owns and operates Blondie's Catering Service. Her unique brand of logic can solve problems that might confound the most brilliant scholar.

had graduated from student to secretary and still lived with her mother. Nonetheless, Chic Young quickly realized that it was a match made in newspaper heaven—the pathetic playboy and the gorgeous, suspiciously good-hearted, blonde. Was she a gold-digger? Was he handsome enough to keep her attention? Would their affection survive the perils of real life? Like any industrialists worth their rep, the J. Bolling Bumsteads didn't care for reality. They disinherited their only son, inadvertently paving the way for a historic, ever-expanding relationship between Blondie and Dagwood and the nation, which quickly fell for this unlikely couple. It's a love affair that's lasted more than seventy-five years, and counting.

Blondie has remained beautiful for every one of those seventy-five years. Without the benefit of plastic surgery, Botox, or even, seemingly, diets or exercise, she has managed to retain her increasingly sensational figure and luminous skin. (If only real life were as kind as newsprint!) Her clothing, though, has undergone a makeover—where once Chic Young lifted her fashions out of the Sears, Roebuck catalog, now she is devoted to Bloomingdale's.

Cartoonist Dean Young, who took over the comic strip after his father Chic's death in 1973, actually does all of Blondie's shopping, picking her wardrobe out of catalogs and fashion magazines (not *Vogue*—the middle-class Bumsteads *are* on a budget) for artist John Marshall to illustrate. Working together, Dean and John—and all the artists before him, including Jim Raymond, Stan Drake, and Denis LeBrun—have taken pains to keep the characters, especially Blondie, up-to-date with today's trends and technologies. They use cell phones and computers. Blondie's iconic curly flapper 'do has become more relaxed, and her personality more astute. In the 1990s, she entered the workforce with her very own catering business. Now in her mid-thirties, where she'll likely—and enviably—stay, Blondie has evolved from a frivolous good-time gal to a modern, accomplished businesswoman. In the process, she's cemented her status as America's favorite blonde.

Read by hundreds of millions of people the world over, adored by all, Blondie has overseen an empire that has spanned newspapers, books, radio shows, TV, (a 1957 series starring Arthur Lake, another series from 1968 to

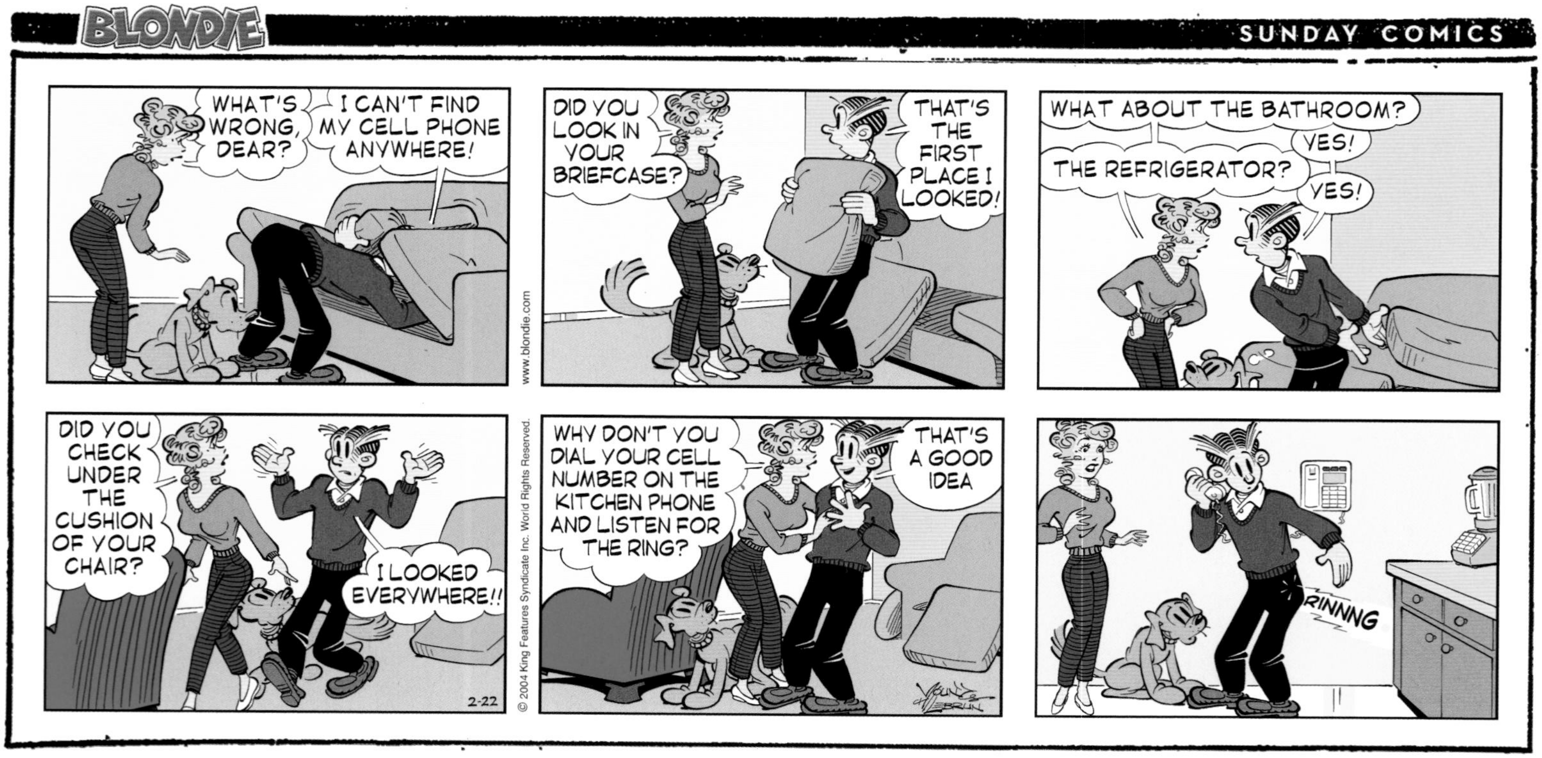

BLONDIE
SUNDAY COMICS
WHAT'S WRONG, DEAR?
I CAN'T FIND MY CELL PHONE ANYWHERE!
DID YOU LOOK IN YOUR BRIEFCASE?
THAT'S THE FIRST PLACE I LOOKED!
WHAT ABOUT THE BATHROOM?
YES!
THE REFRIGERATOR?
YES!
DID YOU CHECK UNDER THE CUSHION OF YOUR CHAIR?
I LOOKED EVERYWHERE!!
WHY DON'T YOU DIAL YOUR CELL NUMBER ON THE KITCHEN PHONE AND LISTEN FOR THE RING?
THAT'S A GOOD IDEA
RINNNG
www.blondie.com
© 2004 King Features Syndicate Inc. World Rights Reserved.
2-22

BLONDIE
SUNDAY COMICS
Z
Z
HA!
Z
IS ANYTHING WRONG, DEAR?
I JUST THOUGHT OF A SNAPPY COMEBACK FOR HERB'S FUNNY MESSAGE ON HIS ANSWERING MACHINE
YOU'RE REALLY SOMETHING, DO YOU KNOW THAT?
DARN RIGHT I AM
www.blondie.com
© 2004 King Features Syndicate Inc. World Rights Reserved.
2-8

1969, and an animated version in 1987, starring Loni Anderson as the voice of Blondie and Frank Welker as Dagwood), and twenty-eight full-length Columbia Motion Picture movies. From 1938 to 1950, Penny Singleton and Arthur Lake brought Blondie and Dagwood to life on the big screen. Today, even a Broadway musical is in the works.

The *Blondie* cast has appeared in nearly every medium that's fit to print, including greeting cards, towels, figurines, light switch plates, lunch boxes, and cookie jars. Appearing at pop culture auctions and on eBay, *Blondie* paraphernalia is considered very collectible. As one of only a few comics to survive the political, social, and economic upheaval of the thirties and come out stronger for it, *Blondie* is not just a comic strip; it's a phenomenon.

Through all the changes she's seen and undergone, though, the character Blondie has maintained a consistent voice and presence in American culture. Above all, she is a loving wife, mother, and friend. Her devotion to Dagwood is one of the founding principles of the strip. In fact, Blondie is in many ways an idealized woman.

"A fantasy," says Dean Young, "for every guy in the world."

The Bumsteads' long and loving relationship gives hope to misfits everywhere, and the comic's success is no doubt based partly on the idea that a woman like Blondie could go for a guy like Dagwood.

But Blondie is much more than the sum of her (very substantial) parts. In fact, one of her most important roles is never mentioned, though it's evident in every panel. Blondie is, in fact, the strip's "straight (wo)man," the Hardy to Dagwood's Laurel, the Ricky to his Lucy. Whenever he flails through a situation, it is Blondie's reaction—the smile, the surprise, or, let's face it, the long-suffering sigh—that gives heft to the humor.

Blondie is in many ways an idealized woman – "a fantasy," says Dean Young, "for every guy in the world."

Dagwood may be the funny one, but Blondie is the constant—the backbone of the strip. No wonder it's named for her.

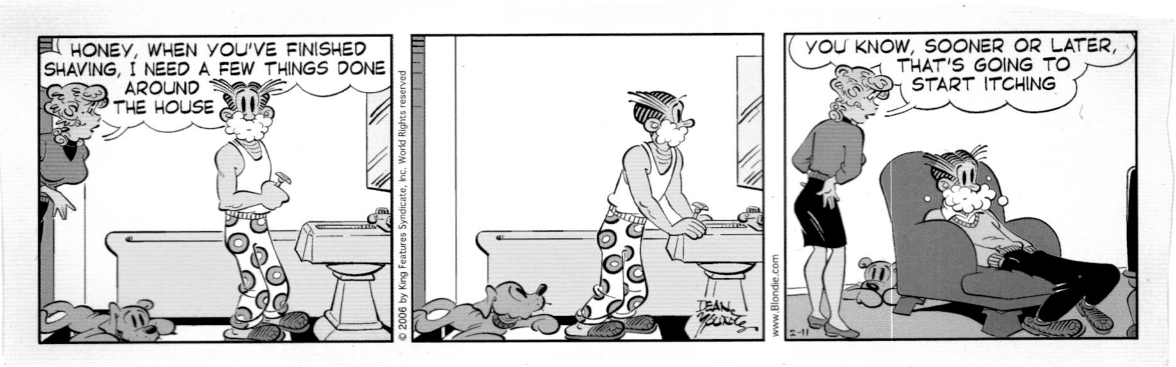
HONEY, WHEN YOU'VE FINISHED SHAVING, I NEED A FEW THINGS DONE AROUND THE HOUSE
YOU KNOW, SOONER OR LATER, THAT'S GOING TO START ITCHING
© 2006 by King Features Syndicate, Inc. World Rights reserved
www.Blondie.com

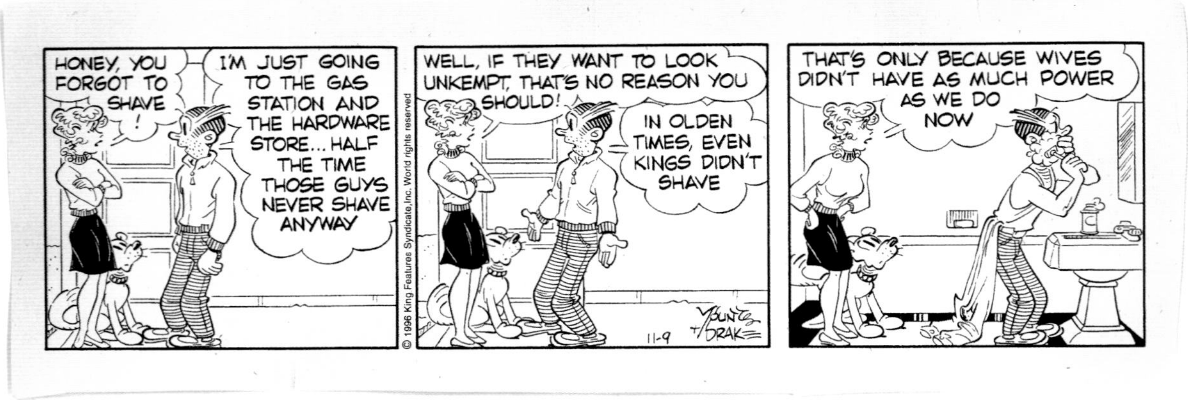
HONEY, YOU FORGOT TO SHAVE!
I'M JUST GOING TO THE GAS STATION AND THE HARDWARE STORE... HALF THE TIME THOSE GUYS NEVER SHAVE ANYWAY
WELL, IF THEY WANT TO LOOK UNKEMPT, THAT'S NO REASON YOU SHOULD!
IN OLDEN TIMES, EVEN KINGS DIDN'T SHAVE
THAT'S ONLY BECAUSE WIVES DIDN'T HAVE AS MUCH POWER AS WE DO NOW
© 1996 King Features Syndicate, Inc. World rights reserved

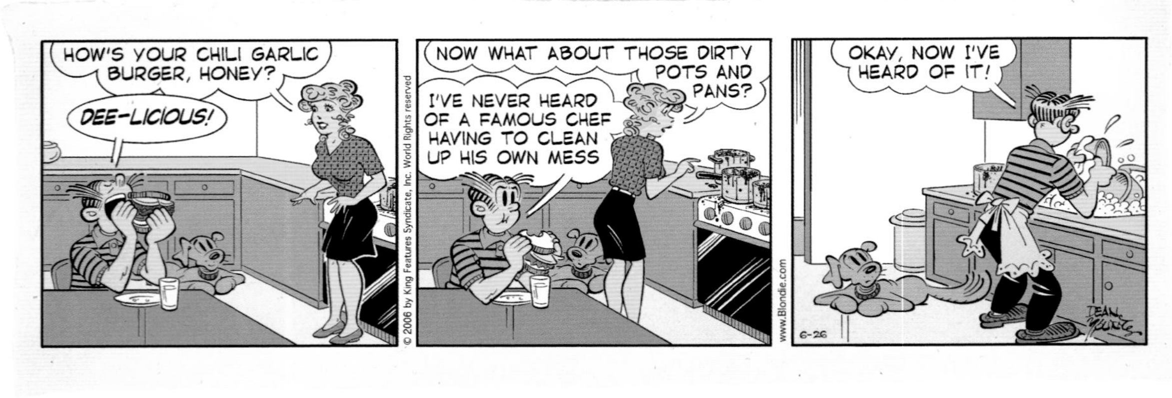
HOW'S YOUR CHILI GARLIC BURGER, HONEY?
DEE-LICIOUS!
NOW WHAT ABOUT THOSE DIRTY POTS AND PANS?
I'VE NEVER HEARD OF A FAMOUS CHEF HAVING TO CLEAN UP HIS OWN MESS
OKAY, NOW I'VE HEARD OF IT!
© 2006 by King Features Syndicate, Inc. World Rights reserved
www.Blondie.com

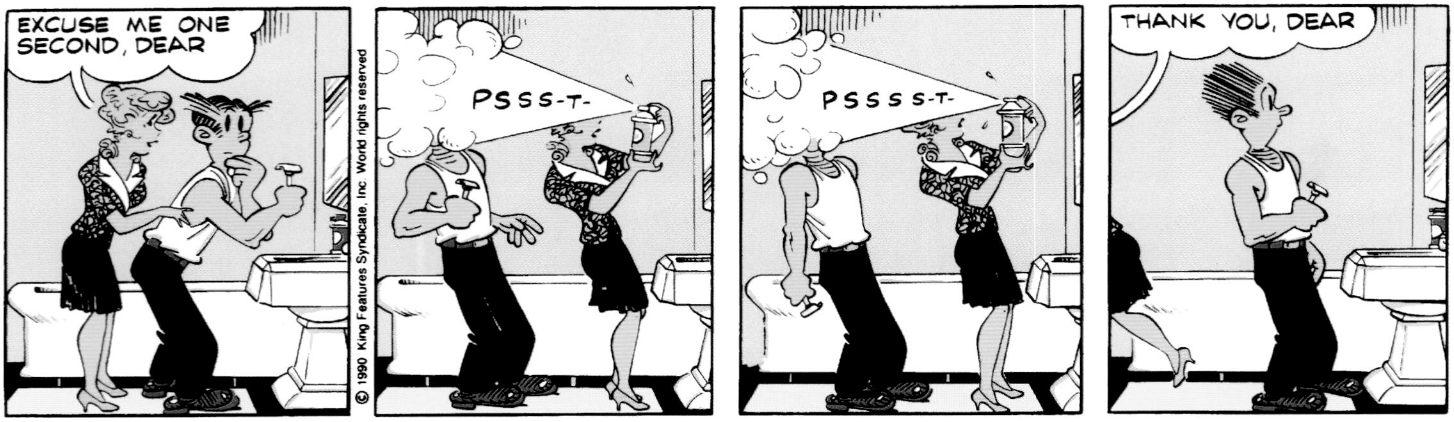
EXCUSE ME ONE SECOND, DEAR
PSSS-T-
PSSSS-T-
THANK YOU, DEAR
© 1990 King Features Syndicate, Inc. World rights reserved

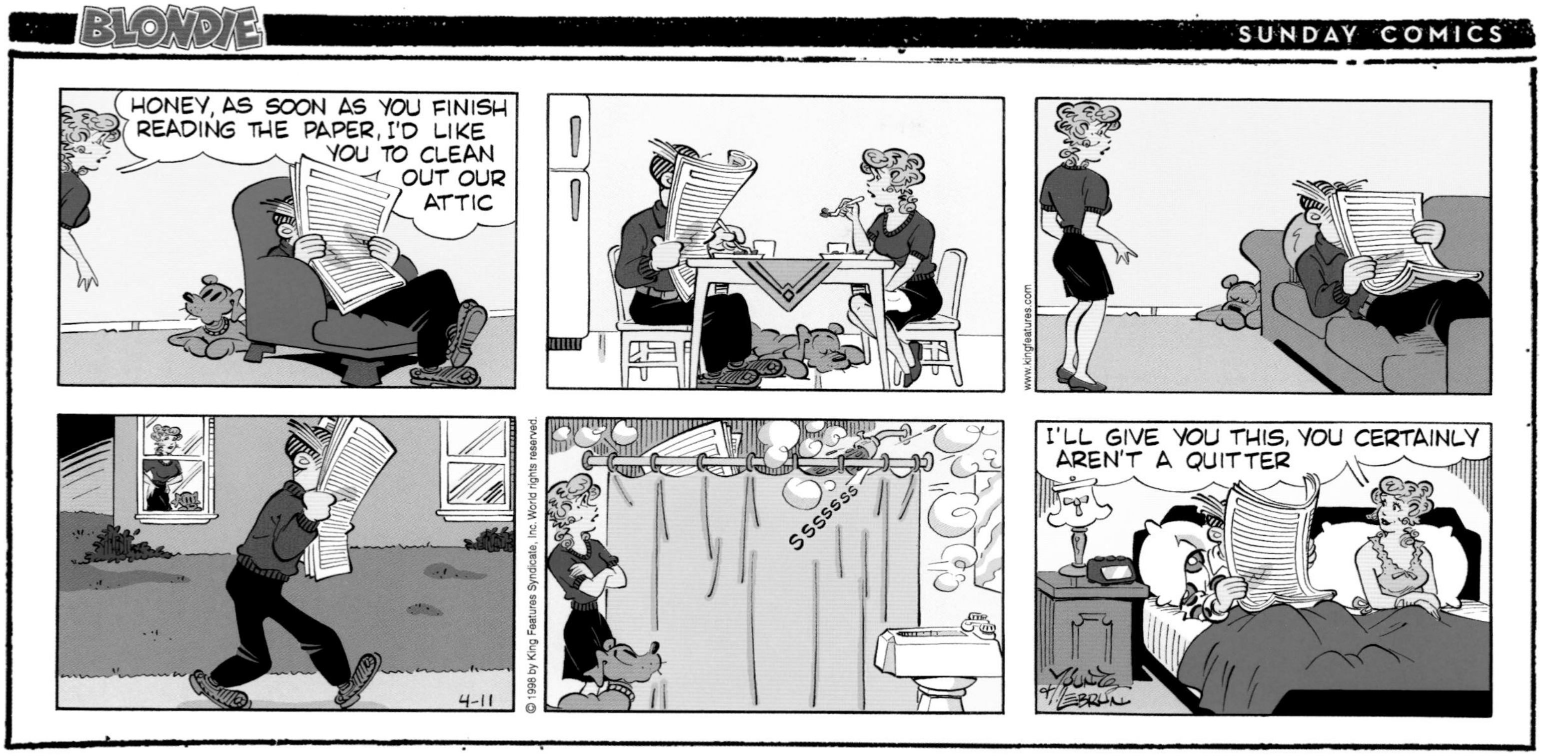
BLONDIE
SUNDAY COMICS
HONEY, AS SOON AS YOU FINISH READING THE PAPER, I'D LIKE YOU TO CLEAN OUT OUR ATTIC
www.kingfeatures.com
4-11
© 1998 by King Features Syndicate, Inc. World rights reserved.
SSSSSSS
I'LL GIVE YOU THIS, YOU CERTAINLY AREN'T A QUITTER

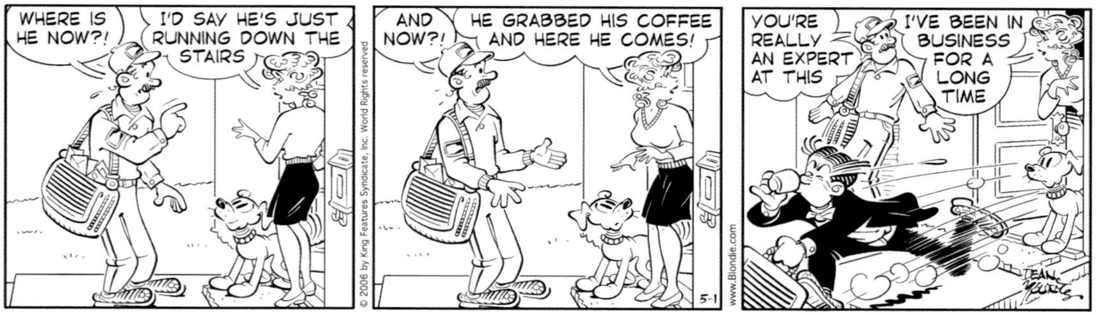
WHERE IS HE NOW?!
I'D SAY HE'S JUST RUNNING DOWN THE STAIRS
© 2006 by King Features Syndicate, Inc. World Rights reserved.
AND NOW?!
HE GRABBED HIS COFFEE AND HERE HE COMES!
5-1
www.Blondie.com
YOU'RE REALLY AN EXPERT AT THIS
I'VE BEEN IN BUSINESS FOR A LONG TIME

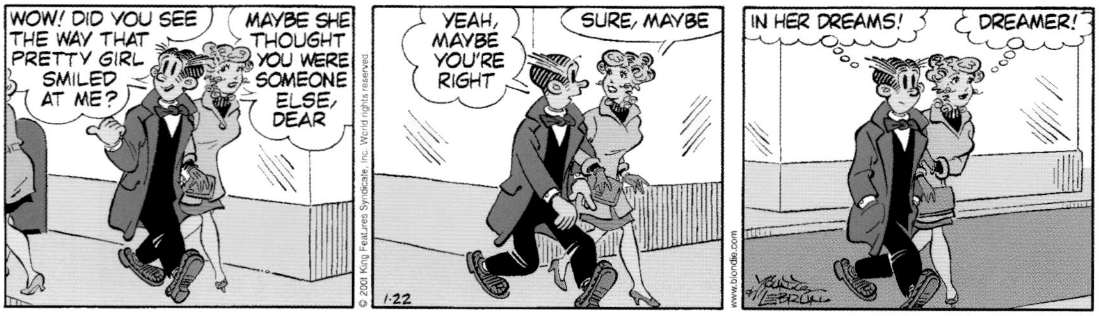
WOW! DID YOU SEE THE WAY THAT PRETTY GIRL SMILED AT ME?
MAYBE SHE THOUGHT YOU WERE SOMEONE ELSE, DEAR
© 2001 King Features Syndicate, Inc. World rights reserved.
YEAH, MAYBE YOU'RE RIGHT
SURE, MAYBE
1-22
www.blondie.com
IN HER DREAMS!
DREAMER!

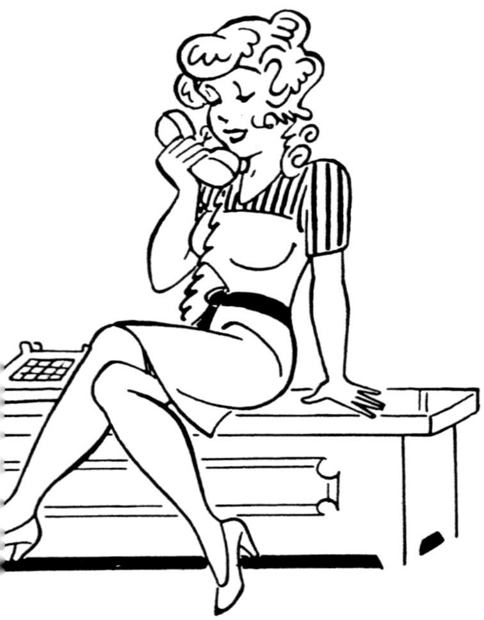

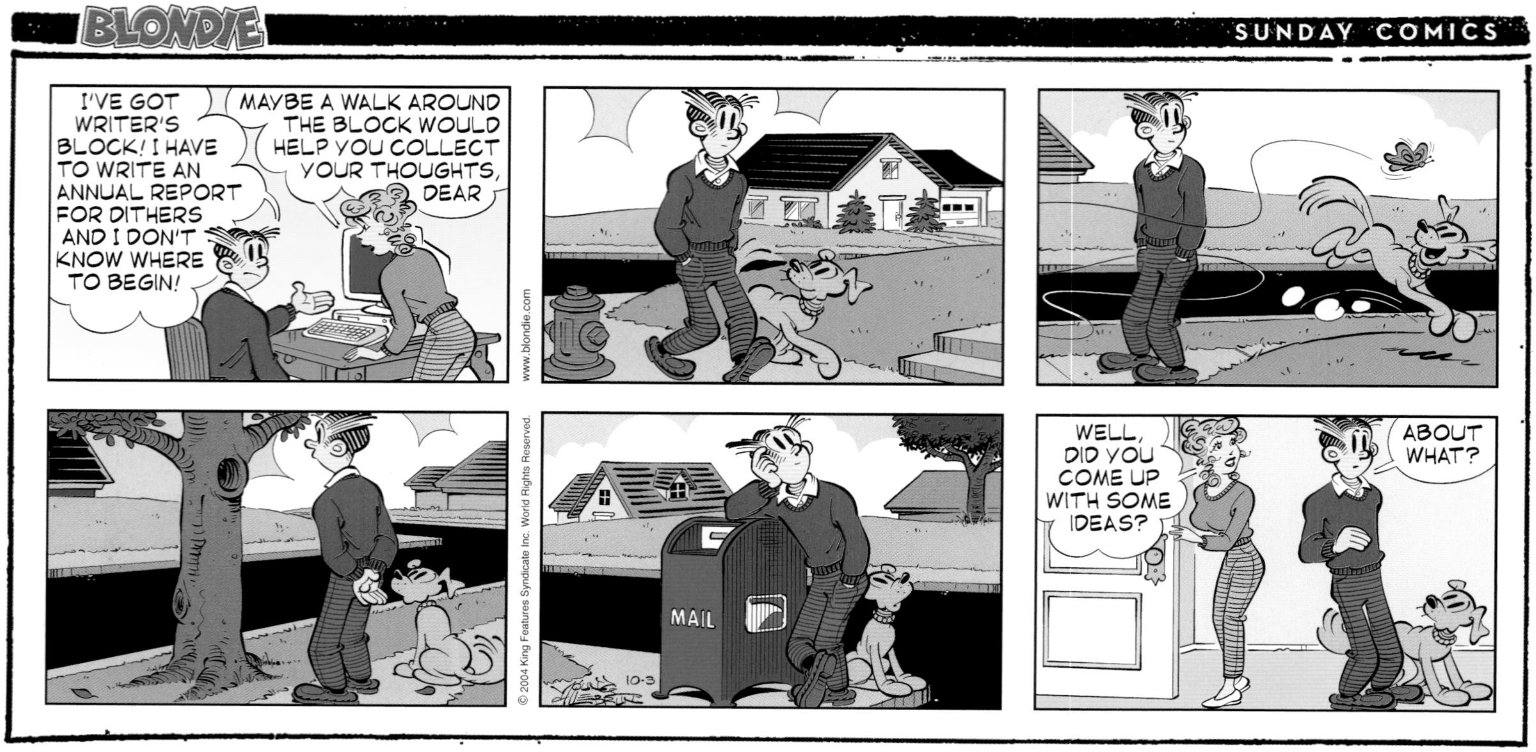
BLONDIE
SUNDAY COMICS
I'VE GOT WRITER'S BLOCK! I HAVE TO WRITE AN ANNUAL REPORT FOR DITHERS AND I DON'T KNOW WHERE TO BEGIN!
MAYBE A WALK AROUND THE BLOCK WOULD HELP YOU COLLECT YOUR THOUGHTS, DEAR
www.blondie.com
© 2004 King Features Syndicate Inc. World Rights Reserved.
MAIL
10-3
WELL, DID YOU COME UP WITH SOME IDEAS?
ABOUT WHAT?

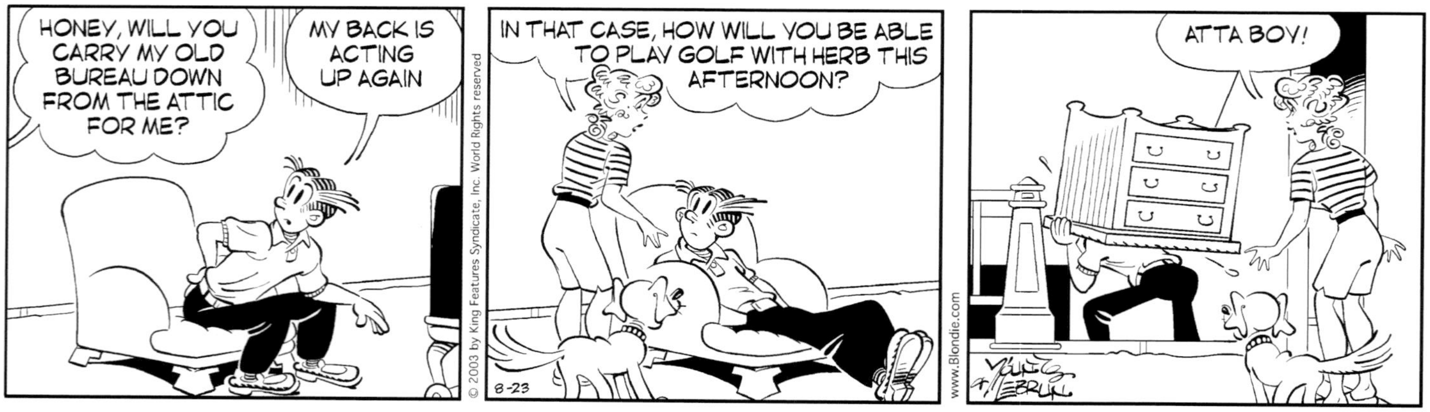
HONEY, WILL YOU CARRY MY OLD BUREAU DOWN FROM THE ATTIC FOR ME?
MY BACK IS ACTING UP AGAIN
© 2003 by King Features Syndicate, Inc. World Rights reserved
IN THAT CASE, HOW WILL YOU BE ABLE TO PLAY GOLF WITH HERB THIS AFTERNOON?
8-23
www.blondie.com
ATTA BOY!

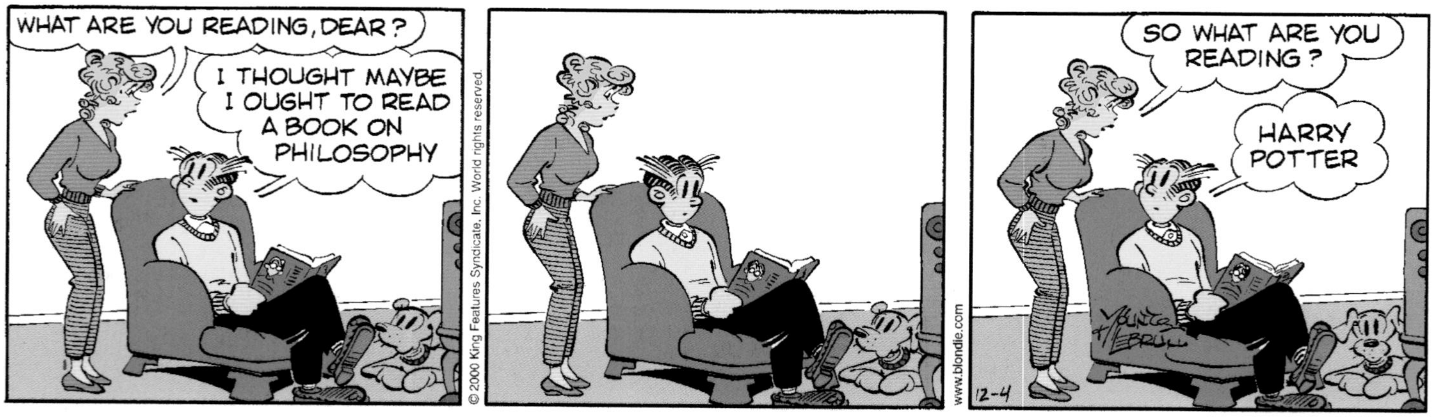
WHAT ARE YOU READING, DEAR?
I THOUGHT MAYBE I OUGHT TO READ A BOOK ON PHILOSOPHY
© 2000 King Features Syndicate, Inc. World rights reserved.
www.blondie.com
SO WHAT ARE YOU READING?
HARRY POTTER
12-4

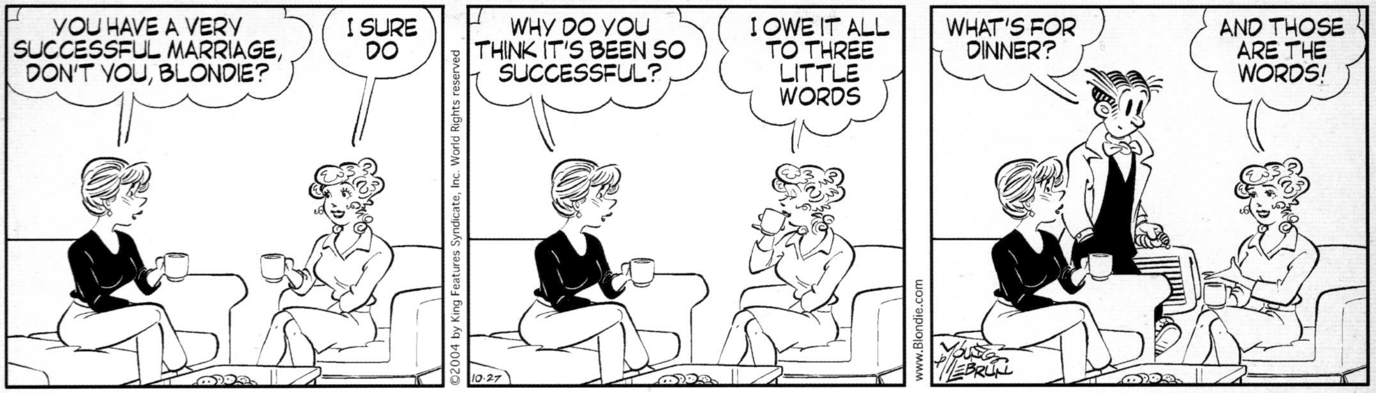
YOU HAVE A VERY SUCCESSFUL MARRIAGE, DON'T YOU, BLONDIE?
I SURE DO
©2004 by King Features Syndicate, Inc. World Rights reserved
10-27
WHY DO YOU THINK IT'S BEEN SO SUCCESSFUL?
I OWE IT ALL TO THREE LITTLE WORDS
www.Blondie.com
WHAT'S FOR DINNER?
AND THOSE ARE THE WORDS!
YOUNG LEBRUN

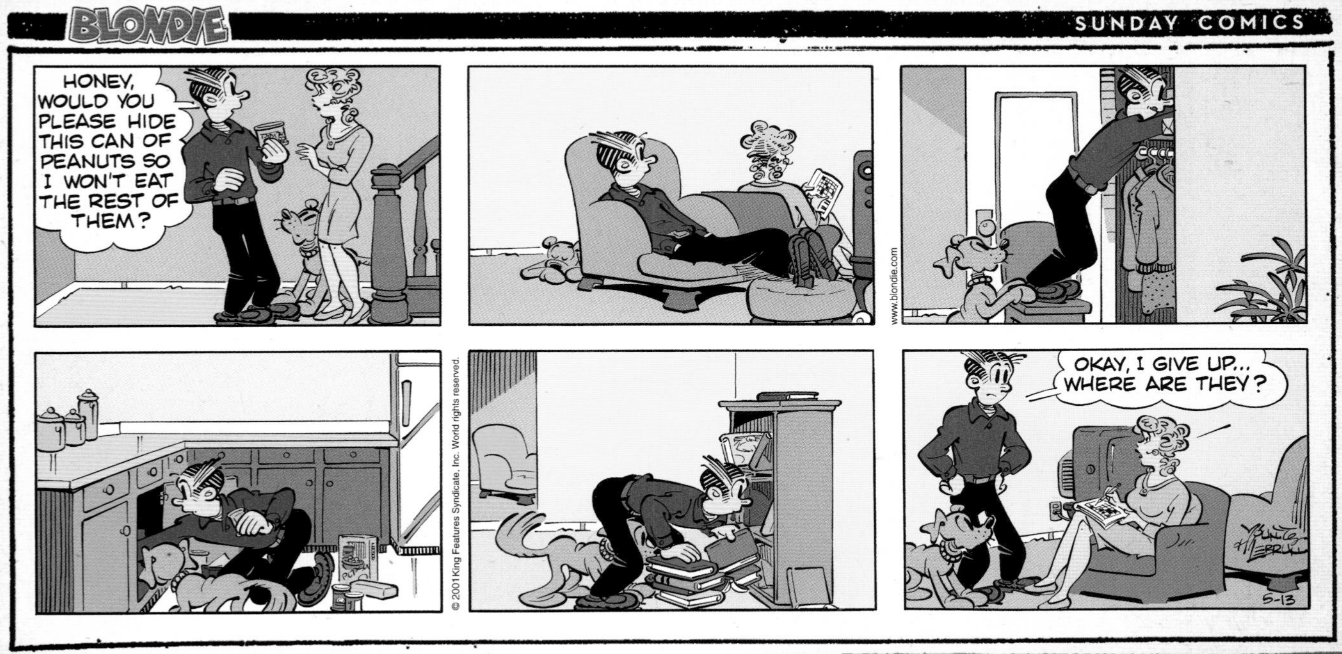
BLONDIE
SUNDAY COMICS
HONEY, WOULD YOU PLEASE HIDE THIS CAN OF PEANUTS SO I WON'T EAT THE REST OF THEM?
www.blondie.com
© 2001 King Features Syndicate, Inc. World rights reserved.
OKAY, I GIVE UP... WHERE ARE THEY?
YOUNG LEBRUN
5-13

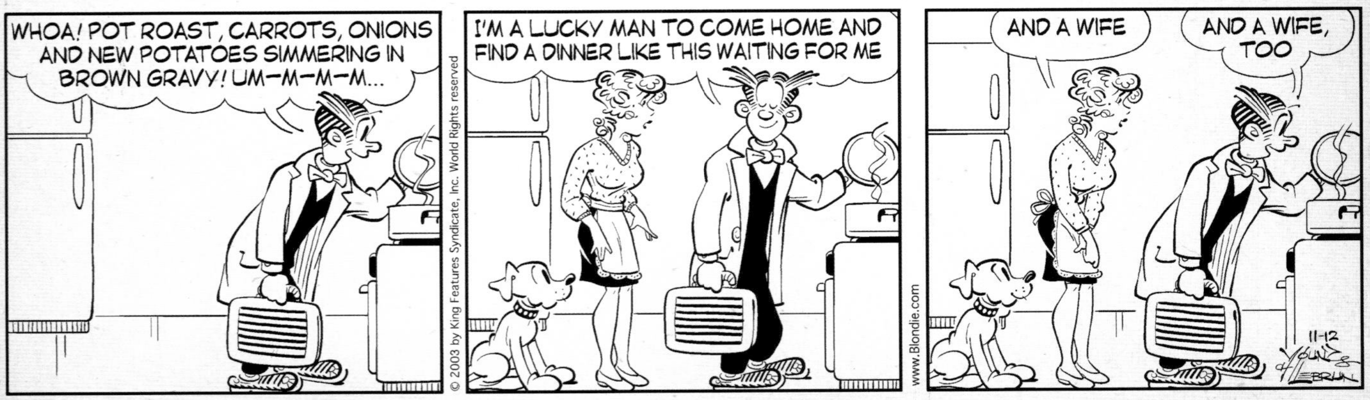
WHOA! POT ROAST, CARROTS, ONIONS AND NEW POTATOES SIMMERING IN BROWN GRAVY! UM-M-M-M...
© 2003 by King Features Syndicate, Inc. World Rights reserved
I'M A LUCKY MAN TO COME HOME AND FIND A DINNER LIKE THIS WAITING FOR ME
www.Blondie.com
AND A WIFE
AND A WIFE, TOO
11-12
YOUNG LEBRUN

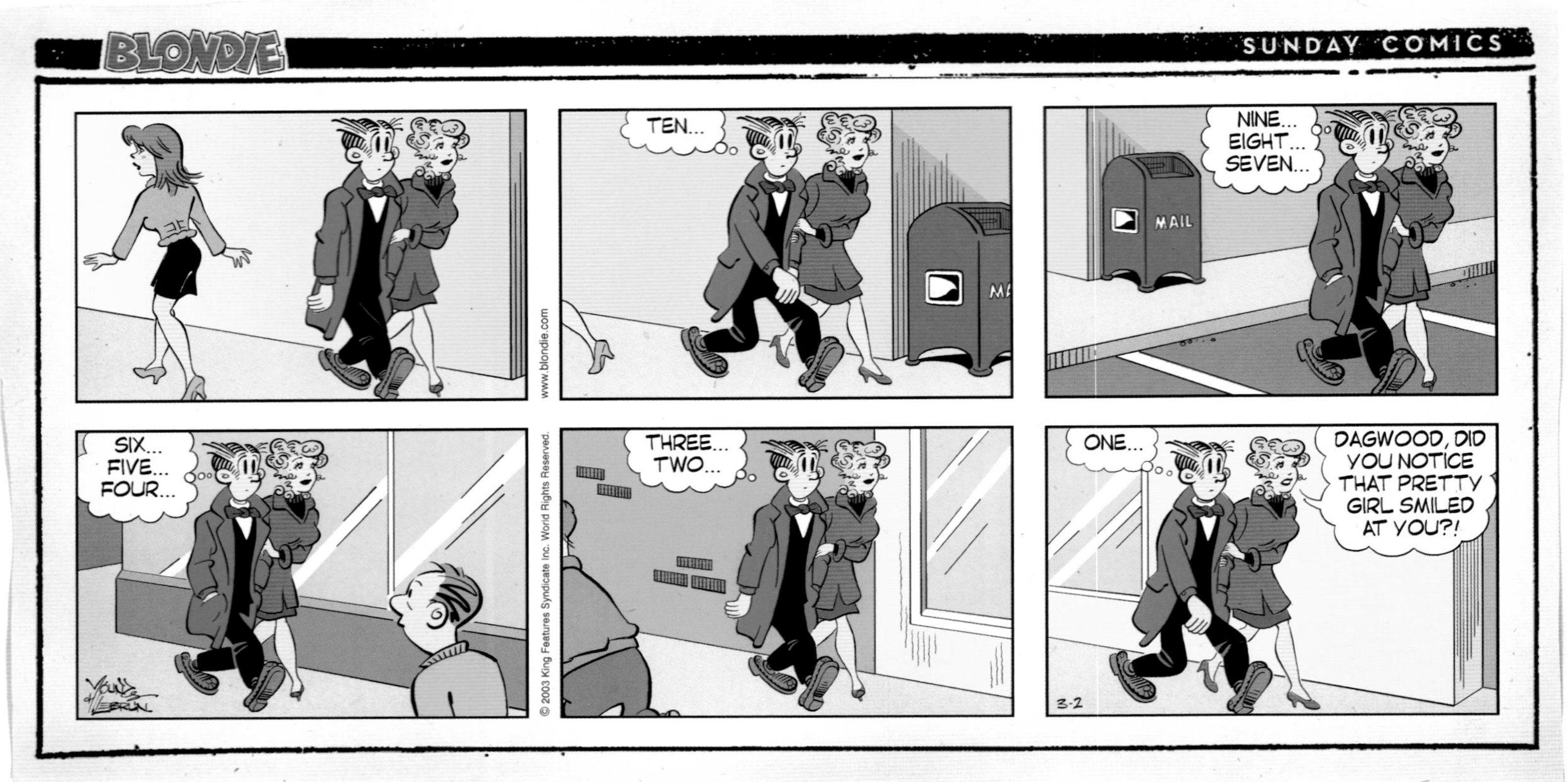
BLONDIE
SUNDAY COMICS
www.blondie.com
© 2003 King Features Syndicate Inc. World Rights Reserved.
TEN...
NINE... EIGHT... SEVEN...
MAIL
SIX... FIVE... FOUR...
YOUNG LEBRUN
THREE... TWO...
ONE...
DAGWOOD, DID YOU NOTICE THAT PRETTY GIRL SMILED AT YOU?!
3-2

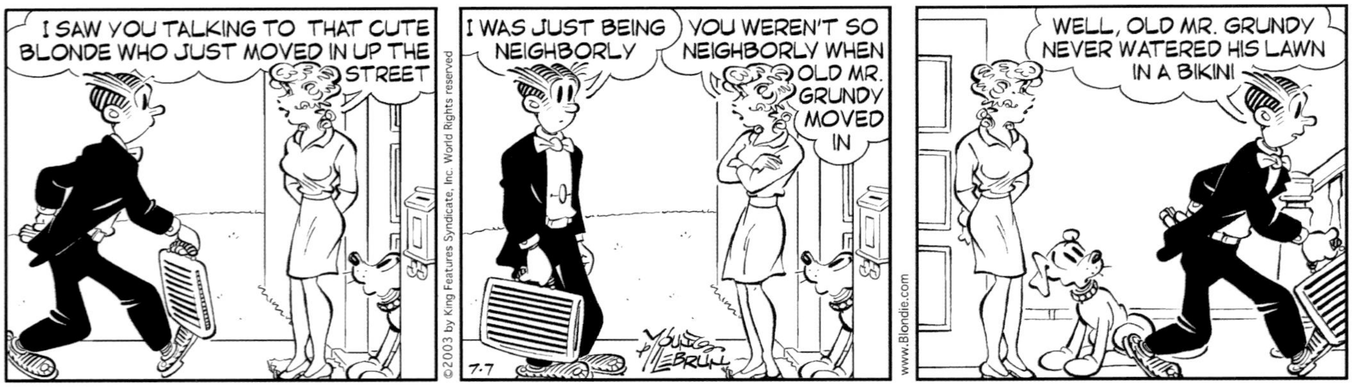
I SAW YOU TALKING TO THAT CUTE BLONDE WHO JUST MOVED IN UP THE STREET
© 2003 by King Features Syndicate, Inc. World Rights reserved
I WAS JUST BEING NEIGHBORLY
YOU WEREN'T SO NEIGHBORLY WHEN OLD MR. GRUNDY MOVED IN
7-7
YOUNG LEBRUN
www.Blondie.com
WELL, OLD MR. GRUNDY NEVER WATERED HIS LAWN IN A BIKINI

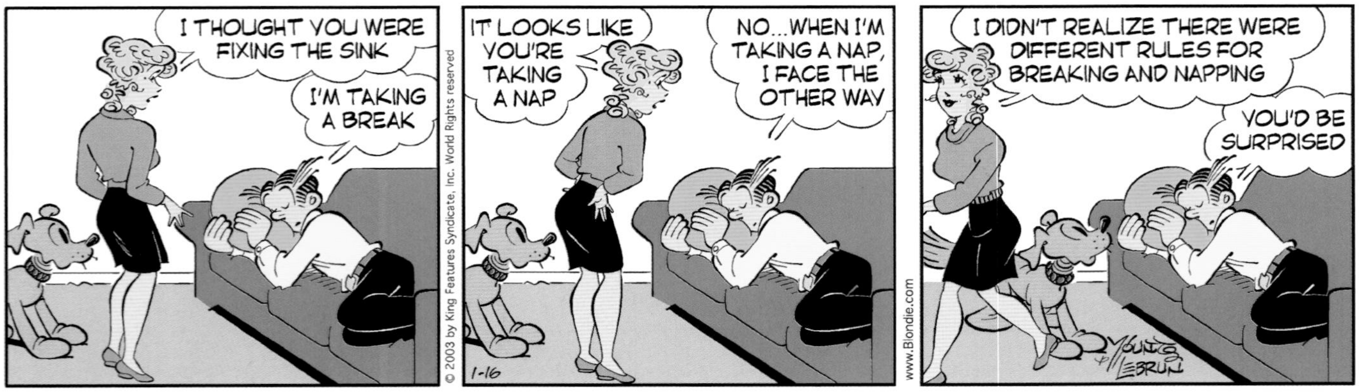
I THOUGHT YOU WERE FIXING THE SINK
I'M TAKING A BREAK
© 2003 by King Features Syndicate, Inc. World Rights reserved
IT LOOKS LIKE YOU'RE TAKING A NAP
NO...WHEN I'M TAKING A NAP, I FACE THE OTHER WAY
1-16
www.Blondie.com
I DIDN'T REALIZE THERE WERE DIFFERENT RULES FOR BREAKING AND NAPPING
YOU'D BE SURPRISED
YOUNG LEBRUN

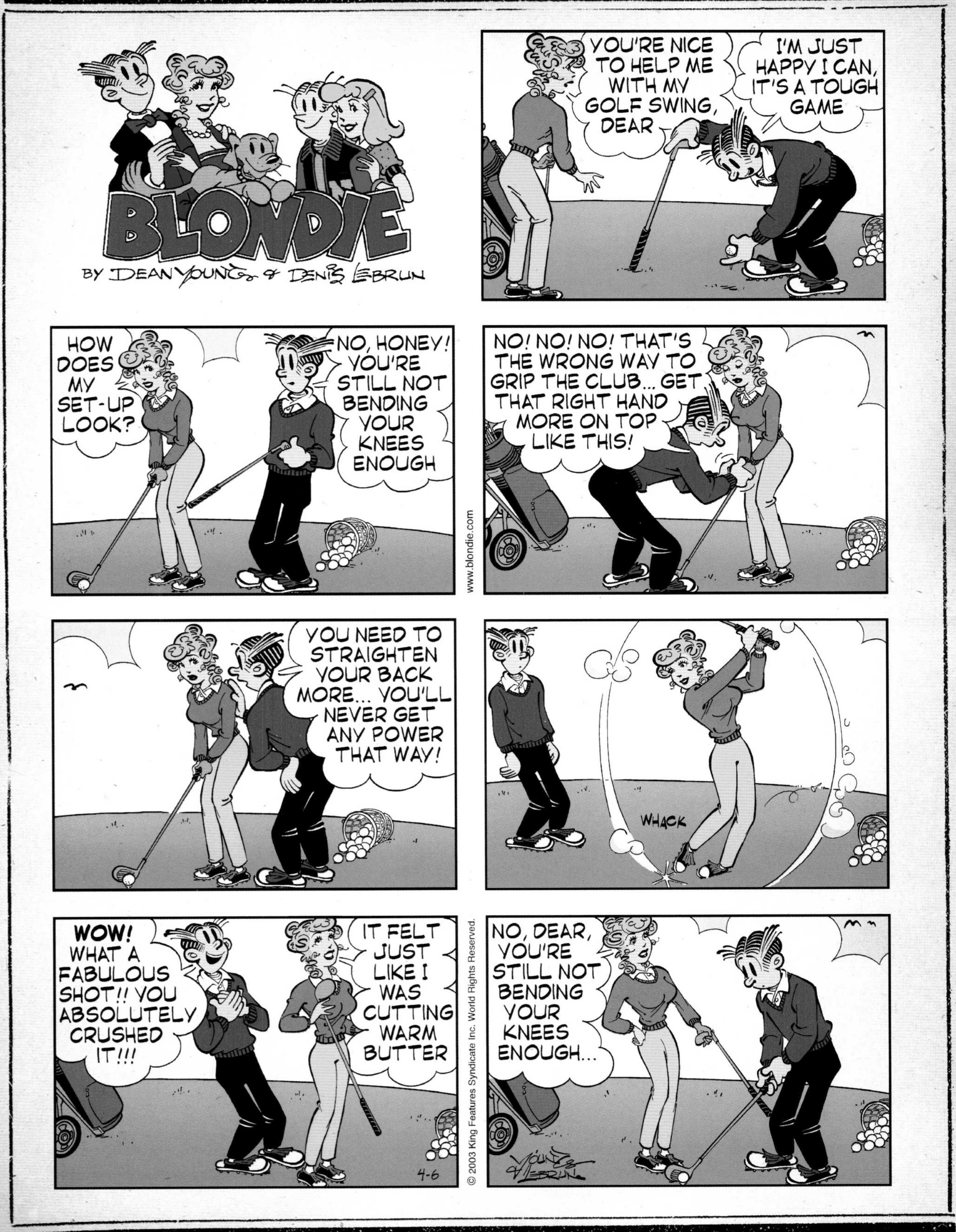
BLONDIE
BY DEAN YOUNG & DENIS LEBRUN
YOU'RE NICE TO HELP ME WITH MY GOLF SWING, DEAR
I'M JUST HAPPY I CAN, IT'S A TOUGH GAME
HOW DOES MY SET-UP LOOK?
NO, HONEY! YOU'RE STILL NOT BENDING YOUR KNEES ENOUGH
NO! NO! NO! THAT'S THE WRONG WAY TO GRIP THE CLUB... GET THAT RIGHT HAND MORE ON TOP LIKE THIS!
YOU NEED TO STRAIGHTEN YOUR BACK MORE... YOU'LL NEVER GET ANY POWER THAT WAY!
WHACK
WOW! WHAT A FABULOUS SHOT!! YOU ABSOLUTELY CRUSHED IT!!!
IT FELT JUST LIKE I WAS CUTTING WARM BUTTER
NO, DEAR, YOU'RE STILL NOT BENDING YOUR KNEES ENOUGH...
4-6
YOUNG LEBRUN
www.blondie.com

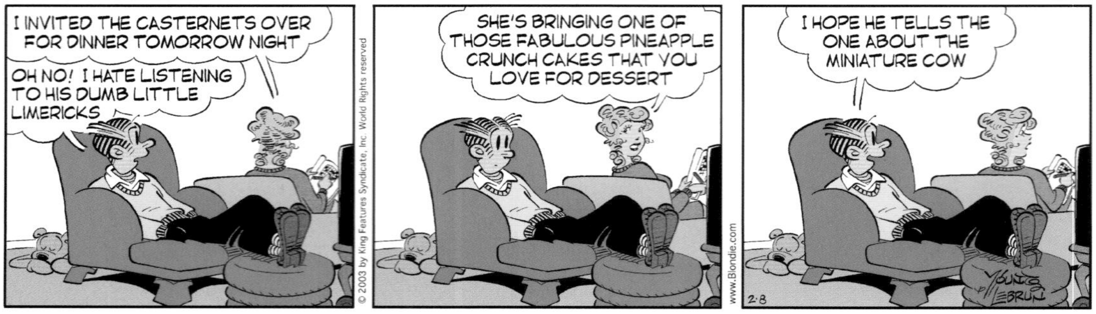
I INVITED THE CASTERNETS OVER FOR DINNER TOMORROW NIGHT
OH NO! I HATE LISTENING TO HIS DUMB LITTLE LIMERICKS
SHE'S BRINGING ONE OF THOSE FABULOUS PINEAPPLE CRUNCH CAKES THAT YOU LOVE FOR DESSERT
I HOPE HE TELLS THE ONE ABOUT THE MINIATURE COW
© 2003 by King Features Syndicate, Inc. World Rights reserved
www.Blondie.com
2-8

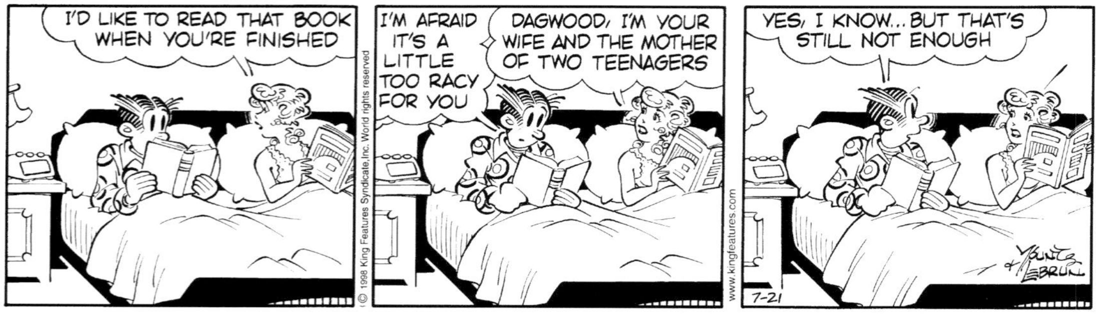
I'D LIKE TO READ THAT BOOK WHEN YOU'RE FINISHED
I'M AFRAID IT'S A LITTLE TOO RACY FOR YOU
DAGWOOD, I'M YOUR WIFE AND THE MOTHER OF TWO TEENAGERS
YES, I KNOW... BUT THAT'S STILL NOT ENOUGH
© 1998 King Features Syndicate Inc. World rights reserved
www.kingfeatures.com
7-21

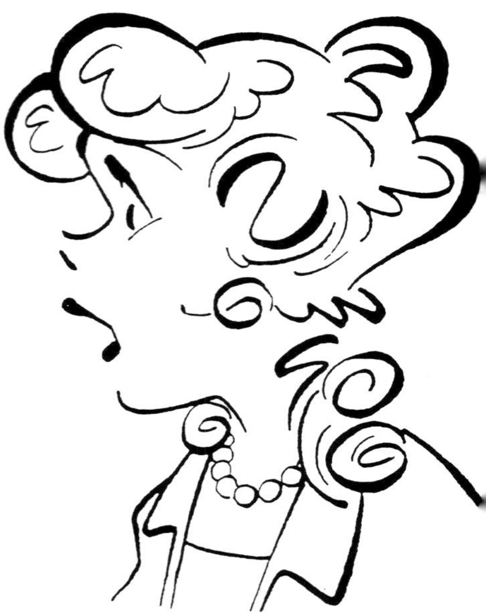

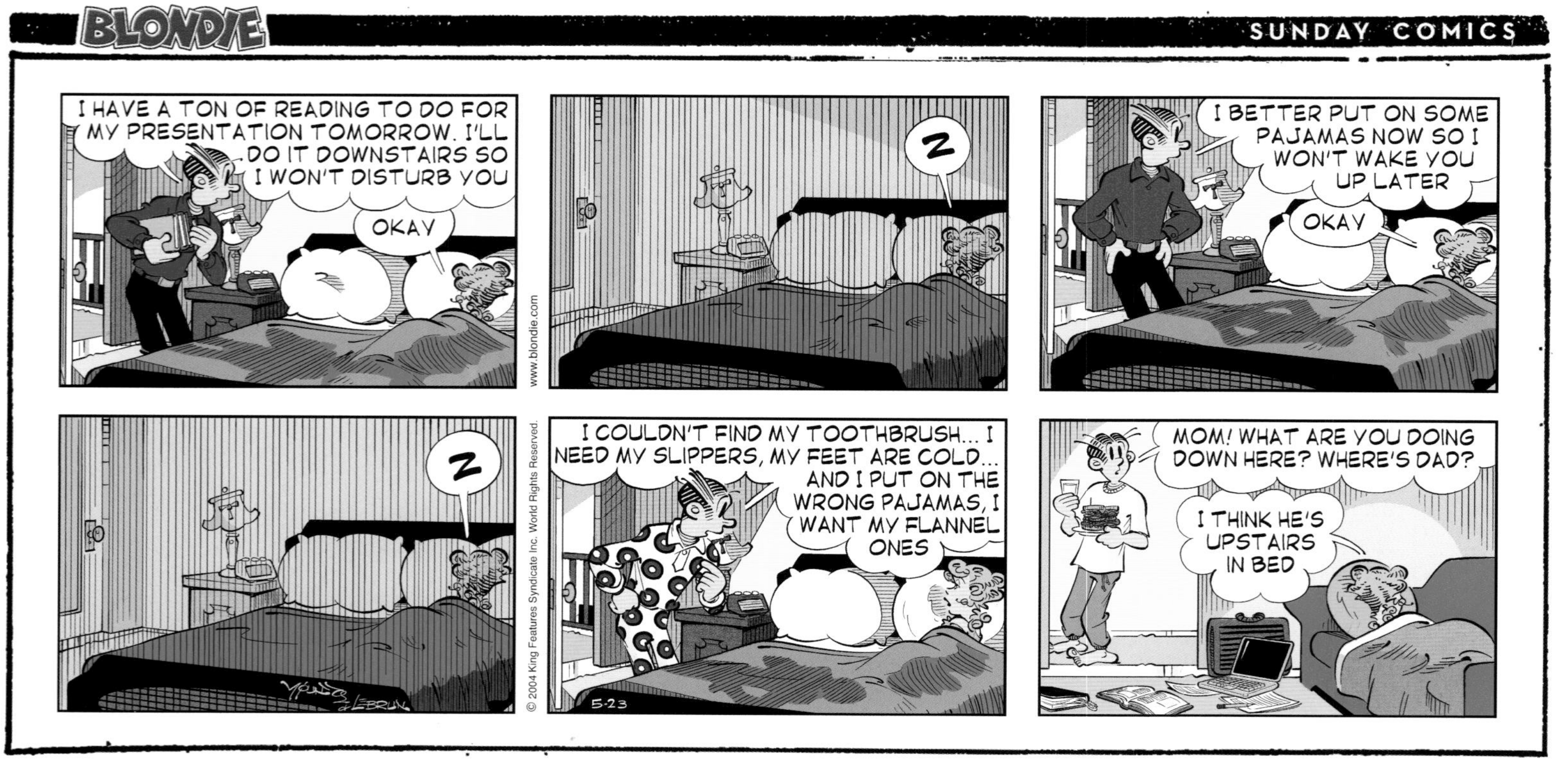
BLONDIE
SUNDAY COMICS
I HAVE A TON OF READING TO DO FOR MY PRESENTATION TOMORROW. I'LL DO IT DOWNSTAIRS SO I WON'T DISTURB YOU
OKAY
Z
I BETTER PUT ON SOME PAJAMAS NOW SO I WON'T WAKE YOU UP LATER
OKAY
Z
I COULDN'T FIND MY TOOTHBRUSH... I NEED MY SLIPPERS, MY FEET ARE COLD... AND I PUT ON THE WRONG PAJAMAS, I WANT MY FLANNEL ONES
MOM! WHAT ARE YOU DOING DOWN HERE? WHERE'S DAD?
I THINK HE'S UPSTAIRS IN BED
www.blondie.com
© 2004 King Features Syndicate Inc. World Rights Reserved.
5-23

HONEY, THE FAUCET IN THE LAUNDRY IS LEAKING
I'M WAY AHEAD OF YOU
© 2006 by King Features Syndicate, Inc. World Rights reserved
YOU MEAN YOU ALREADY FIXED IT?
www.Blondie.com
NO, I MEAN I ALREADY NOTICED IT
2-7

WHAT KIND OF KISS DO YOU CALL THAT?
PECK
© 1998 King Features Syndicate, Inc. World rights reserved
SMACK
www.kingfeatures.com
THAT WAS MUCH BETTER
1-26

IT FEELS STUFFY IN HERE, DEAR
© 2003 by King Features Syndicate, Inc. World Rights reserved
I'M GOING TO OPEN THE WINDOWS!
www.Blondie.com
BLON-DIEEEEE!!!

SURPRISE!!
ROSES?! THEY'RE BEAUTIFUL!!
© 2004 by King Features Syndicate, Inc. World Rights reserved
SMACK
8-24
www.Blondie.com
YOU BOUGHT THAT NEW GOLF CLUB YOU'VE BEEN RAVING ABOUT, DIDN'T YOU?
IT'S A BEAUT, TOO! WAIT'LL YOU SEE IT!!

DAGWOOD

"Dagwood Bumstead," Dean Young is fond of saying, "is the greatest victim of circumstance in the world."

It didn't start out that way. As envisioned by Dean's father, Chic, the creator of *Blondie*, Dagwood was a loser, but a rich one—he stood to inherit his family's rail industry fortune. But when a certain blonde intervened, Dagwood chose love over money, and the trajectory of the strip was forever cast.

Dagwood himself remained largely unchanged, although a few million dollars poorer. Physically, he's been the same wild-haired string bean since 1930, when Blondie debuted. Though he's lost the old-fashioned sock garters, Dagwood's workday uniform—slacks, bow tie, and white shirt with one giant button (a convenience device Chic Young invented to avoid drawing rows of tiny fasteners)—has stayed intact. Ditto his quarter-slot eyes and, of course, trademark locks.

"If Dagwood didn't have that hair, he'd look like Archie," says Dean Young. "If you change those cowlicks sticking out, you're in the wrong business. It's like the tinsel on a Christmas tree!" While Blondie looks like a real woman—our hero Dagwood looks more like "an alien from the planet Zork," avers Dean (he means it in a loving way).

Still, the guy has managed to hang on to one of the most attractive women in the funny pages for more than three-quarters of a century, so he must be doing something right. But it's difficult to tell what it is. A walking, talking, tumbling comedy of errors, Dagwood Bumstead is hard-pressed to get through even one day of life unscathed—or not hungry.

His morning begins, like most of ours, with the buzzing of an alarm clock. Except—and here come the circumstances—his morning is somehow perpetually ten minutes behind. By the time he's up, he's already substantially late for work. To save precious moments, his family has engineered a clothing-coffee-breakfast routine that would leave NASA's efficiency experts agog. With clothing on, coffee gulped, and briefcase in hand, our hero makes a mad dash out the door and past—or more likely into—the hapless mailman. No time to spare for apologies, sorry! Dagwood races on.

WHEN THE MOON HITS YOUR EYE LIKE A BIG
© 2001 King Features Syndicate, Inc. World rights reserved.
www.blondie.com
HEY, HONEY!
I JUST ORDERED ONE, DEAR
3-10

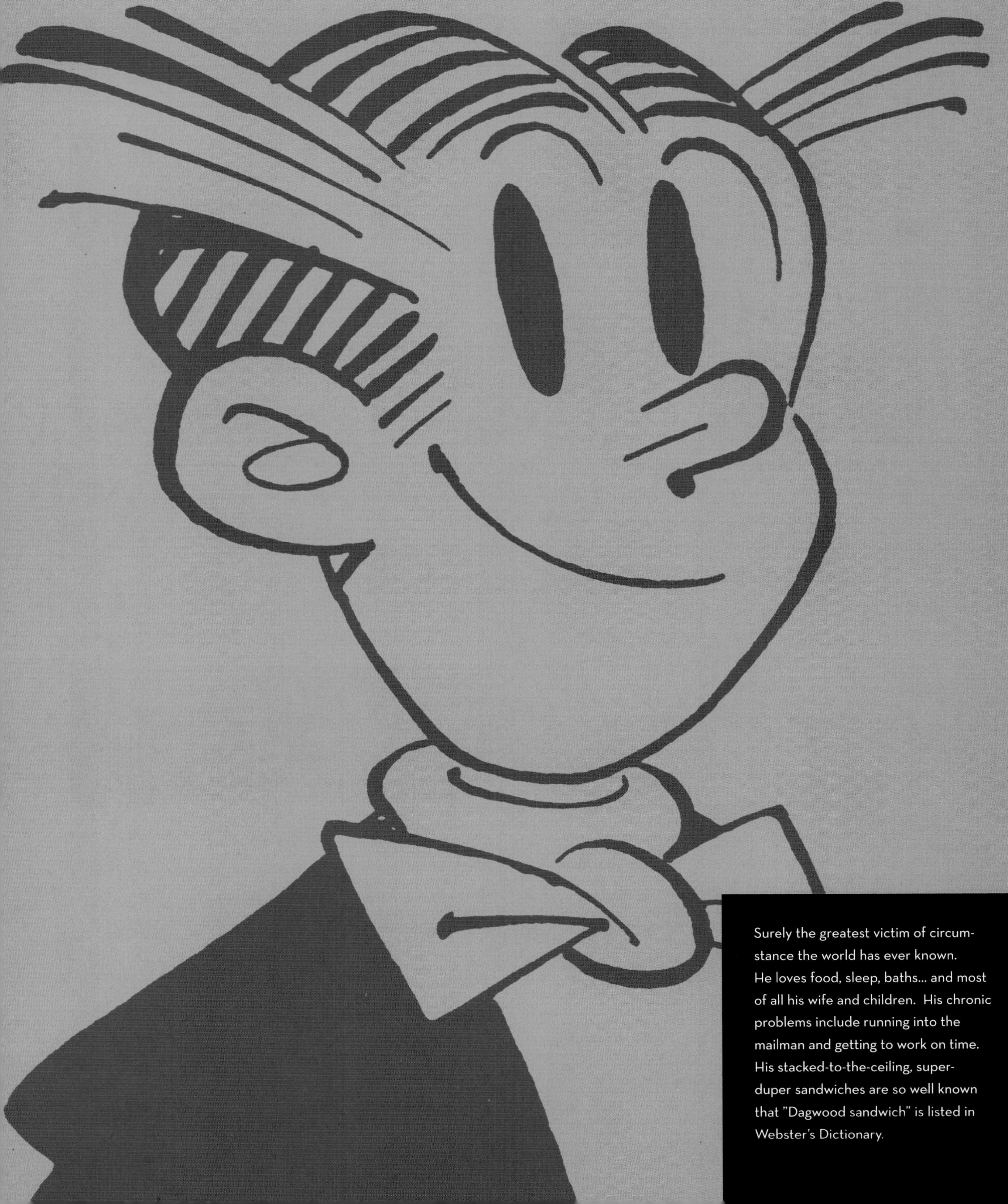

Surely the greatest victim of circumstance the world has ever known. He loves food, sleep, baths... and most of all his wife and children. His chronic problems include running into the mailman and getting to work on time. His stacked-to-the-ceiling, super-duper sandwiches are so well known that "Dagwood sandwich" is listed in Webster's Dictionary.

BLONDIE
SUNDAY COMICS
OKAY, THIS SHELF IS THE PERFECT SPOT FOR THE CARAMEL CORN AND PEANUTS
AND THESE CHOCOLATE-COVERED PRETZELS CAN GO IN THIS DRAWER NOBODY EVER USES
I'LL STASH THESE CHEESE DOODLES AND TWINKIES UNDERNEATH THE SOFA
AND THIS BOOKSHELF IS A GREAT SPOT FOR THESE CHIPS
CHIPS
BY THE WAY, HONEY...
YOU KNOW THAT DIET I PROMISED YOU I'D GO ON? I THINK I'M JUST ABOUT READY
www.blondie.com
© 2006 King Features Syndicate Inc. World Rights Reserved.

If he hasn't missed his car pool (a modern-day upgrade from the bus he used to take to work), Dagwood can regale them with tales of his exploits—otherwise known as his favorite TV programs—or simply stare off, his mind occupied with more pressing matters, like lunch. At the office, he begins a long day of avoiding work, napping, and alternately cowering from and arguing with his boss, who has not seen fit to give him a raise in decades. (Circumstance again.)

Another car pool ride, and it's home to Blondie, and his favorite part of the day: the passionate kiss hello. Scratch that—his favorite part of the day is dinner. Then lunch, then breakfast. Wait, how do the midnight snacks rank? Dagwood's appetite is as legendary as the sandwiches he creates to satisfy it.

"He's got a black belt in buffet," crows Young, who is no slouch in the gustatory arts himself. Still, Young is no match for Dagwood, whose metabolism must run at super-cartoon-human speeds to account for all the calories he's consumed over the years. A running gag since the beginning of the strip, Dagwood's monster multilevel sandwiches—

Sleeping, eating, working — these are the essential ingredients of Dagwood's life.

made of every ingredient available in the fridge, from cheese to sausage to sardines to onions (for "authority") slapped between two paltry pieces of bread—are an art form. (In 2006, life began to imitate art when Dean created Dagwood's Sandwich Shoppes, a chain of fast-food restaurants famous for—what else?—overstuffed sandwiches. Happily, the shops' sandwiches taste better than Dagwood's sound.)

But man is not destined for lunch-meat love alone. In Dagwood's case, he's also fond of sleeping, napping, and resting—the holy triumvirate of male behavior. If his sandwiches are renowned, so is his ability to snore through almost any situation, personal or professional. He's a champion sofa surfer, a crown prince of couch potatoes, and a king among slouchers.

Sleeping, eating, working—these are the essential ingredients of Dagwood's life. Anything else? Yes, the most important thing—family. His children, and especially his wife, are his most important companions and audience.

"Without them, he would be, in a word, a loser," says Dean. "Having a wife like Blondie allows him to operate the way he does. She validates his existence."

A bumbling, fumbling slacker, with a weird look and weirder tastes (seriously, sardines?), Dagwood would be confined to the back lots of the funny pages were it not for his wife. Not only is she fun to look at, she's the epitome of class, grace, and decorum—all the things that Dagwood is not. Just as there would be no day without night or salt without pepper, the Dagwood we know and love, the source of so much humor and joy throughout the years, would not exist without Blondie. She defines him in a way that's more than just circumstantial. She was his choice, and it was the smartest choice he ever made.

MOM, WE CAN'T DO OUR HOMEWORK WITH DAD SINGING LIKE THAT
©1979 King Features Syndicate, Inc. World rights reserved.
THERE'S A SHIP LIES RIGGED
AND WAITING IN THE HARBOR
9-10
HE'S STILL SINGING, MOM··· I CAN SEE HIS LIPS MOVING!

BLONDIE
SUNDAY COMICS
THAT DRIPPING FAUCET DOWNSTAIRS IS DRIVING ME NUTS
I CAN'T HEAR IT
www.blondie.com
WELL, I'M GONNA DO SOMETHING ABOUT IT
THERE, THAT'S BETTER!
WHAT DID YOU DO?
© 2005 King Features Syndicate Inc. World Rights Reserved.
I HAD A HAM SANDWICH
3-27

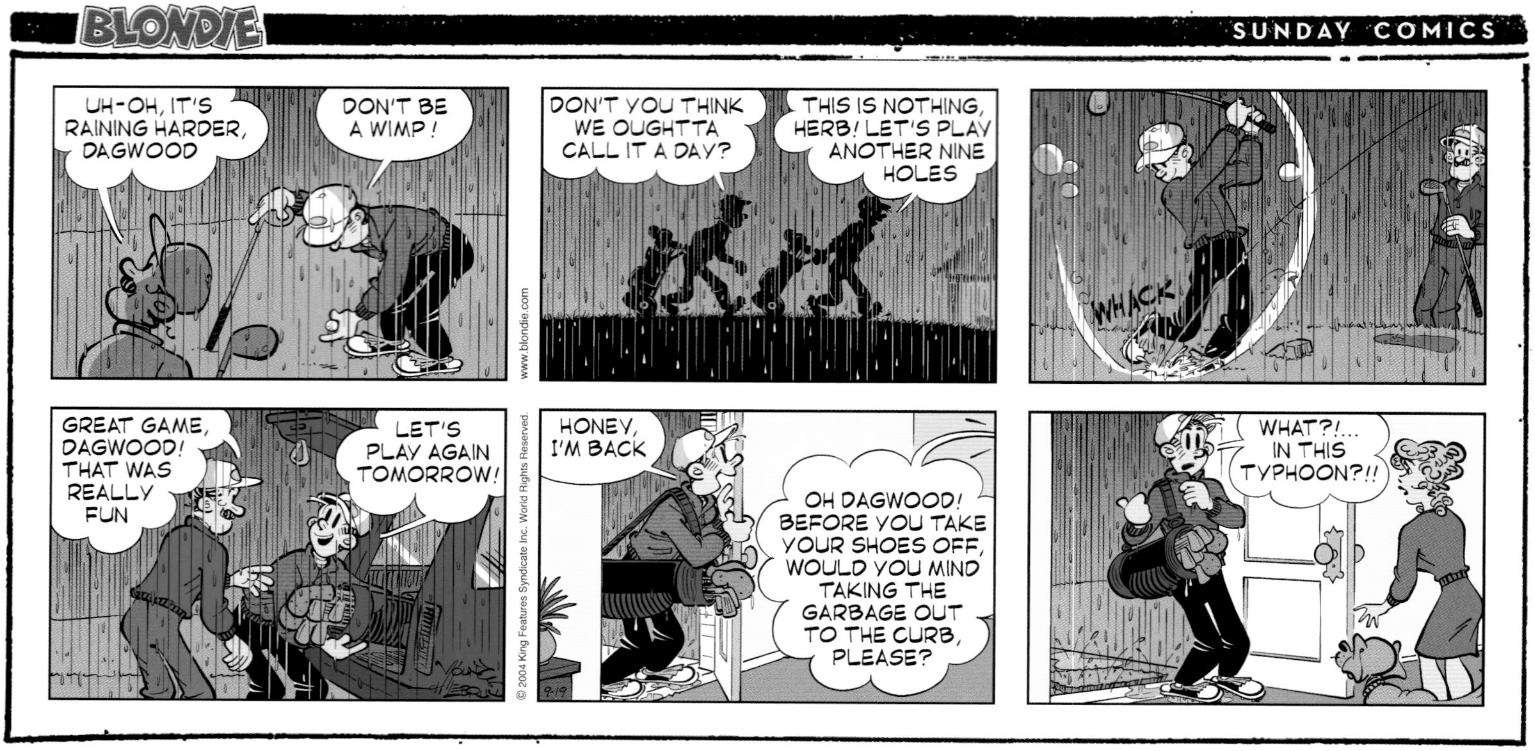
BLONDIE
SUNDAY COMICS
UH-OH, IT'S RAINING HARDER, DAGWOOD
DON'T BE A WIMP!
DON'T YOU THINK WE OUGHTTA CALL IT A DAY?
THIS IS NOTHING, HERB! LET'S PLAY ANOTHER NINE HOLES
WHACK
GREAT GAME, DAGWOOD! THAT WAS REALLY FUN
LET'S PLAY AGAIN TOMORROW!
HONEY, I'M BACK
OH DAGWOOD! BEFORE YOU TAKE YOUR SHOES OFF, WOULD YOU MIND TAKING THE GARBAGE OUT TO THE CURB, PLEASE?
WHAT?!... IN THIS TYPHOON?!!
www.blondie.com
© 2004 King Features Syndicate Inc. World Rights Reserved.
9-19

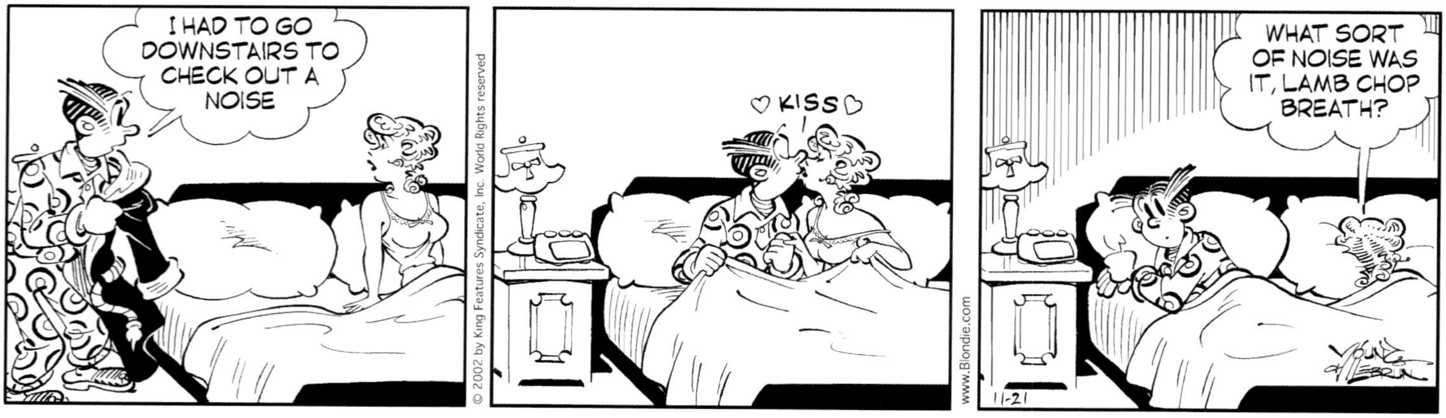
I HAD TO GO DOWNSTAIRS TO CHECK OUT A NOISE
KISS
WHAT SORT OF NOISE WAS IT, LAMB CHOP BREATH?
© 2002 by King Features Syndicate, Inc. World Rights reserved
www.Blondie.com
11-21

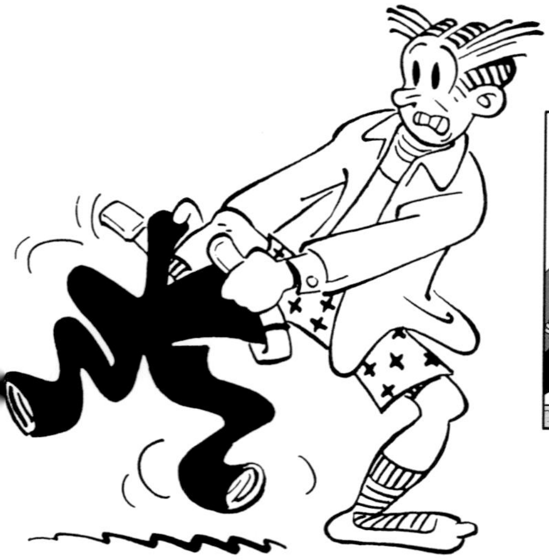

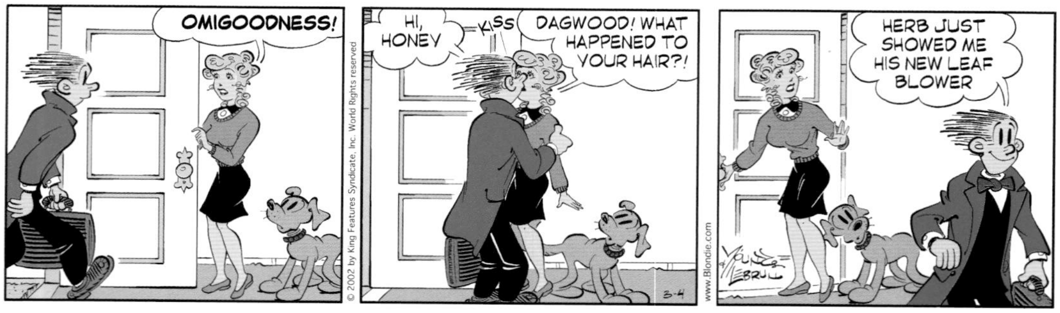
OMIGOODNESS!
HI, HONEY
KISS
DAGWOOD! WHAT HAPPENED TO YOUR HAIR?!
HERB JUST SHOWED ME HIS NEW LEAF BLOWER
© 2002 by King Features Syndicate, Inc. World Rights reserved
www.Blondie.com
3-4

WHAT ARE YOU WATCHING, HONEY?
THIS IS GREAT!
IT'S AN OLD-FASHIONED MOVIE
WHEN THE COWBOY ONLY KISSED HIS HORSE
© 2006 by King Features Syndicate, Inc. World Rights reserved
www.Blondie.com
5-15

LOOK AT THIS NEW HIGH-TECH ELECTRIC TOOTHBRUSH I BOUGHT!
IT BEEPS WHEN IT'S TIME TO STOP BRUSHING...
IF I DON'T BRUSH LONG ENOUGH, IT E-MAILS THE AMERICAN DENTAL ASSOCIATION!
© 2003 by King Features Syndicate, Inc. World Rights reserved
www.Blondie.com
12-1

EXCUSE ME, I DON'T MEAN TO STARE, BUT ARE YOU A MALE MODEL?
NO
THAT'S A SHAME... YOU'D MAKE A REALLY GREAT ONE
DAGWOOD, WHAT TOOK YOU SO LONG?
DID YOU KNOW THAT THEY MAKE COSMETICS FOR MEN?!
TUDBURY'S
© 2001 King Features Syndicate, Inc. World rights reserved
www.blondie.com
2-5

I FIGURED OUT WHAT'S WRONG WITH THE FRONT HALL LIGHT SWITCH
I MUST'VE FOULED IT UP WHEN I WAS FOOLING AROUND WITH IT
CAN YOU FIX IT?
ISN'T IT ENOUGH THAT I FIGURED OUT WHAT WAS WRONG WITH IT?
© 2006 by King Features Syndicate, Inc. World Rights reserved
www.Blondie.com
2-13

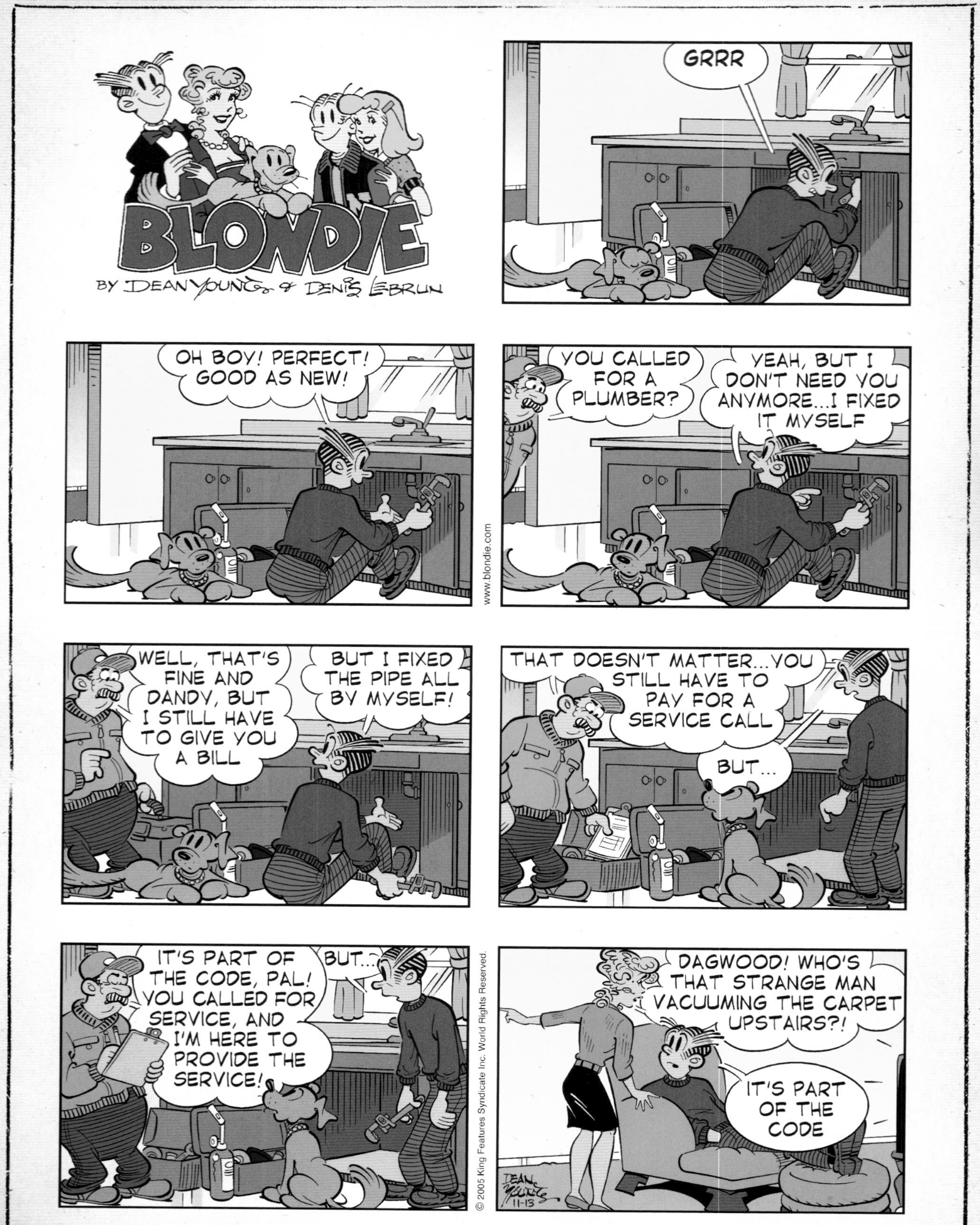
BLONDIE
BY DEAN YOUNG & DENIS LEBRUN
GRRR
OH BOY! PERFECT! GOOD AS NEW!
YOU CALLED FOR A PLUMBER?
YEAH, BUT I DON'T NEED YOU ANYMORE...I FIXED IT MYSELF
www.blondie.com
WELL, THAT'S FINE AND DANDY, BUT I STILL HAVE TO GIVE YOU A BILL
BUT I FIXED THE PIPE ALL BY MYSELF!
THAT DOESN'T MATTER...YOU STILL HAVE TO PAY FOR A SERVICE CALL
BUT...
IT'S PART OF THE CODE, PAL! YOU CALLED FOR SERVICE, AND I'M HERE TO PROVIDE THE SERVICE!
BUT...
© 2005 King Features Syndicate Inc. World Rights Reserved.
DAGWOOD! WHO'S THAT STRANGE MAN VACUUMING THE CARPET UPSTAIRS?!
IT'S PART OF THE CODE
DEAN YOUNG 11-13

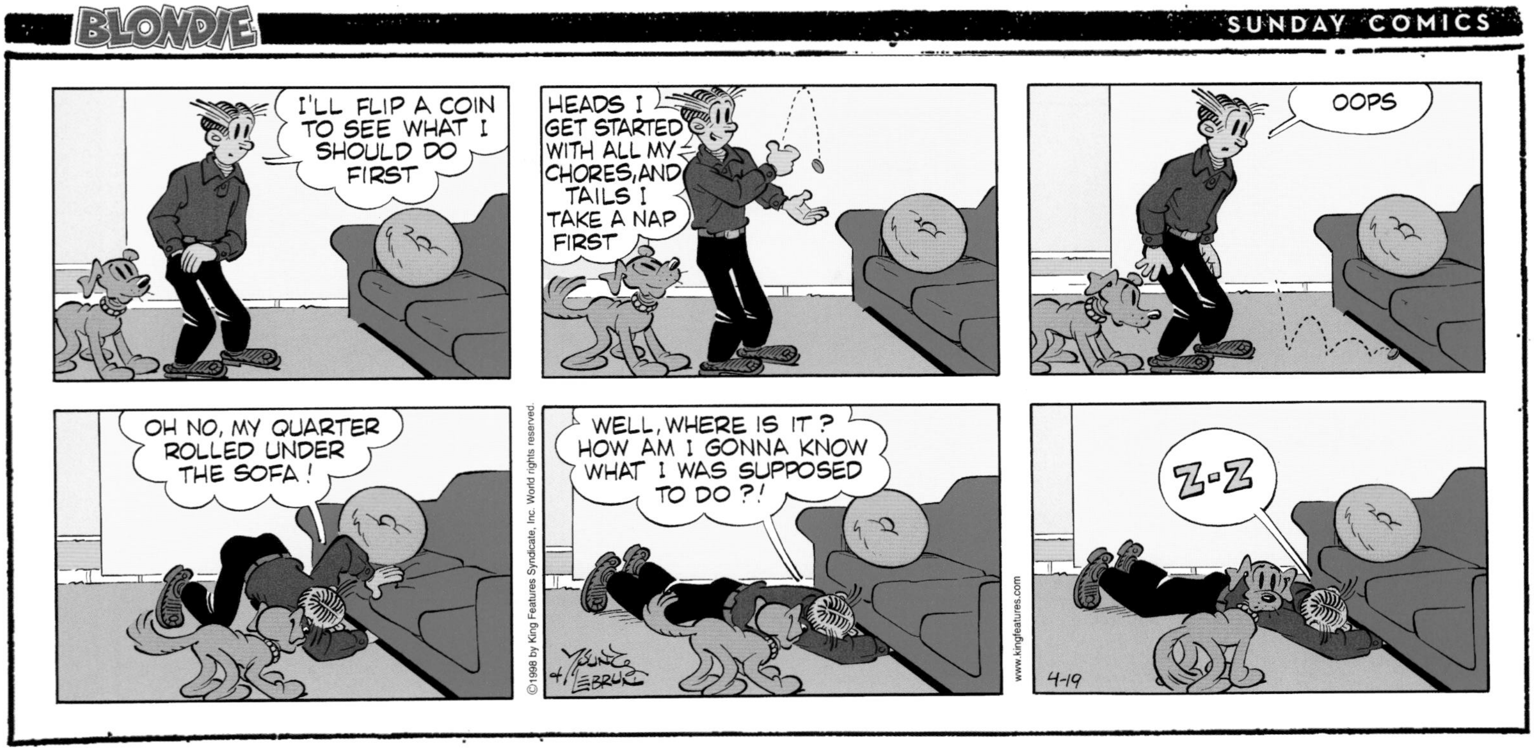
BLONDIE
SUNDAY COMICS
I'LL FLIP A COIN TO SEE WHAT I SHOULD DO FIRST
HEADS I GET STARTED WITH ALL MY CHORES, AND TAILS I TAKE A NAP FIRST
OOPS
OH NO, MY QUARTER ROLLED UNDER THE SOFA!
WELL, WHERE IS IT? HOW AM I GONNA KNOW WHAT I WAS SUPPOSED TO DO?!
Z-Z
© 1998 by King Features Syndicate, Inc. World rights reserved.
www.kingfeatures.com
4-19

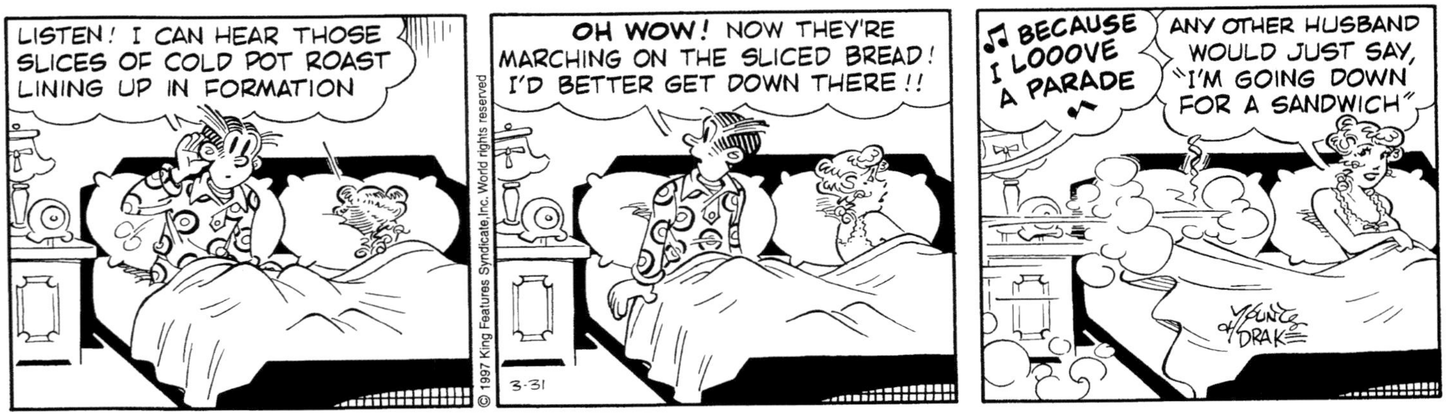
LISTEN! I CAN HEAR THOSE SLICES OF COLD POT ROAST LINING UP IN FORMATION
OH WOW! NOW THEY'RE MARCHING ON THE SLICED BREAD! I'D BETTER GET DOWN THERE!!
♫ BECAUSE I LOOOVE A PARADE
ANY OTHER HUSBAND WOULD JUST SAY, "I'M GOING DOWN FOR A SANDWICH"
© 1997 King Features Syndicate, Inc. World rights reserved
3-31

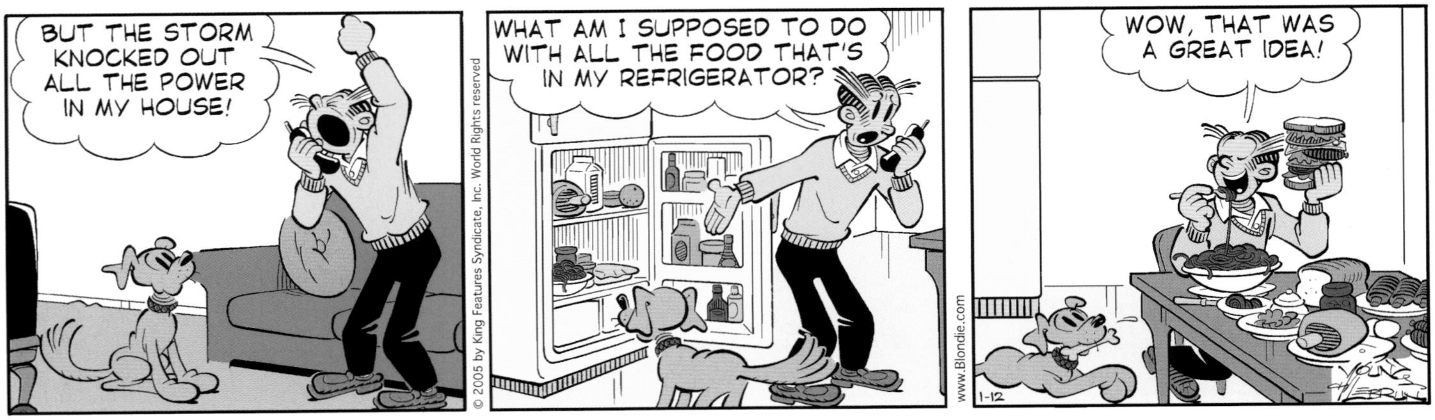
BUT THE STORM KNOCKED OUT ALL THE POWER IN MY HOUSE!
WHAT AM I SUPPOSED TO DO WITH ALL THE FOOD THAT'S IN MY REFRIGERATOR?
WOW, THAT WAS A GREAT IDEA!
© 2005 by King Features Syndicate, Inc. World Rights reserved
www.Blondie.com
1-12

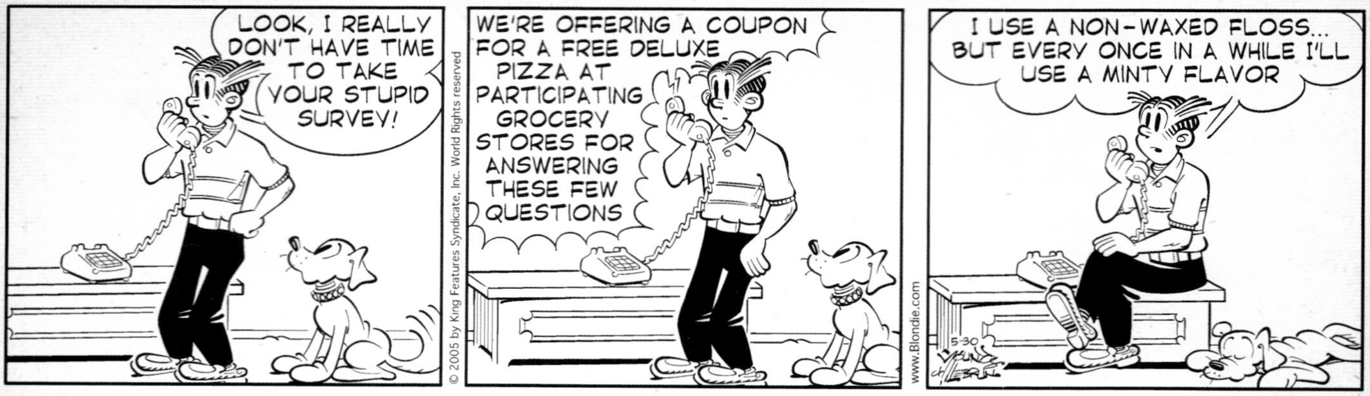
LOOK, I REALLY DON'T HAVE TIME TO TAKE YOUR STUPID SURVEY!
© 2005 by King Features Syndicate, Inc. World Rights reserved
WE'RE OFFERING A COUPON FOR A FREE DELUXE PIZZA AT PARTICIPATING GROCERY STORES FOR ANSWERING THESE FEW QUESTIONS
www.Blondie.com
I USE A NON-WAXED FLOSS... BUT EVERY ONCE IN A WHILE I'LL USE A MINTY FLAVOR
5-30

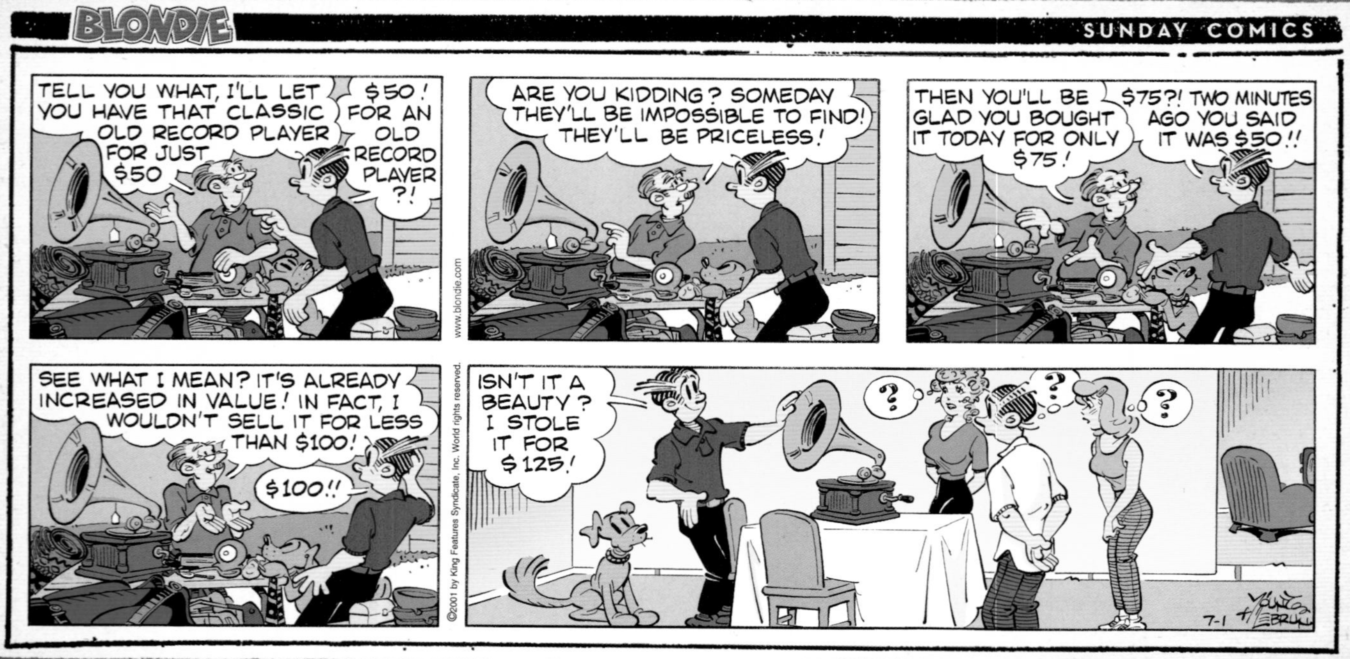
BLONDIE
SUNDAY COMICS
TELL YOU WHAT, I'LL LET YOU HAVE THAT CLASSIC OLD RECORD PLAYER FOR JUST $50
$50! FOR AN OLD RECORD PLAYER ?!
www.blondie.com
ARE YOU KIDDING? SOMEDAY THEY'LL BE IMPOSSIBLE TO FIND! THEY'LL BE PRICELESS!
THEN YOU'LL BE GLAD YOU BOUGHT IT TODAY FOR ONLY $75!
$75?! TWO MINUTES AGO YOU SAID IT WAS $50!!
SEE WHAT I MEAN? IT'S ALREADY INCREASED IN VALUE! IN FACT, I WOULDN'T SELL IT FOR LESS THAN $100!
$100!!
©2001 by King Features Syndicate, Inc. World rights reserved.
ISN'T IT A BEAUTY? I STOLE IT FOR $125!
?
?
?
7-1

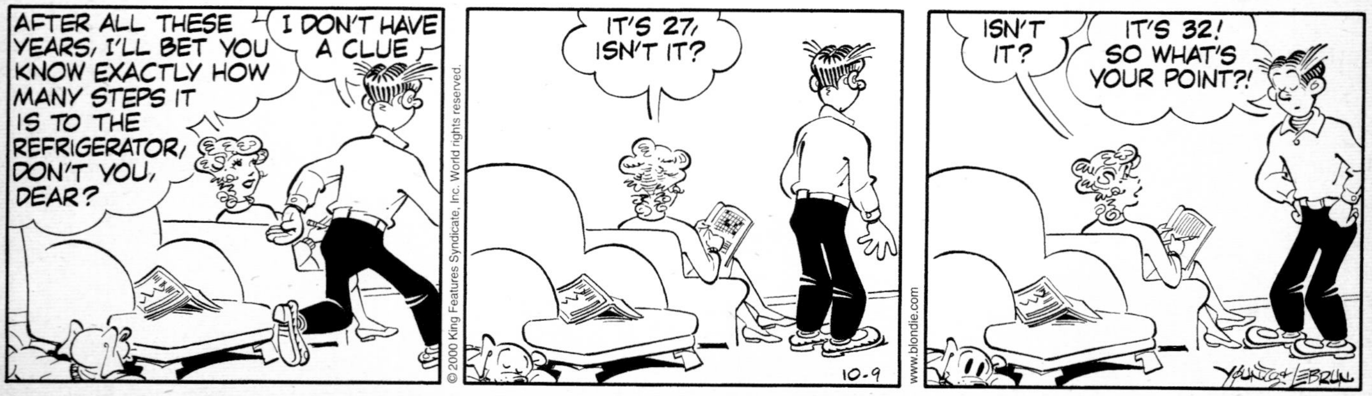
AFTER ALL THESE YEARS, I'LL BET YOU KNOW EXACTLY HOW MANY STEPS IT IS TO THE REFRIGERATOR, DON'T YOU, DEAR?
I DON'T HAVE A CLUE
© 2000 King Features Syndicate, Inc. World rights reserved.
IT'S 27, ISN'T IT?
10-9
www.blondie.com
ISN'T IT?
IT'S 32! SO WHAT'S YOUR POINT?!

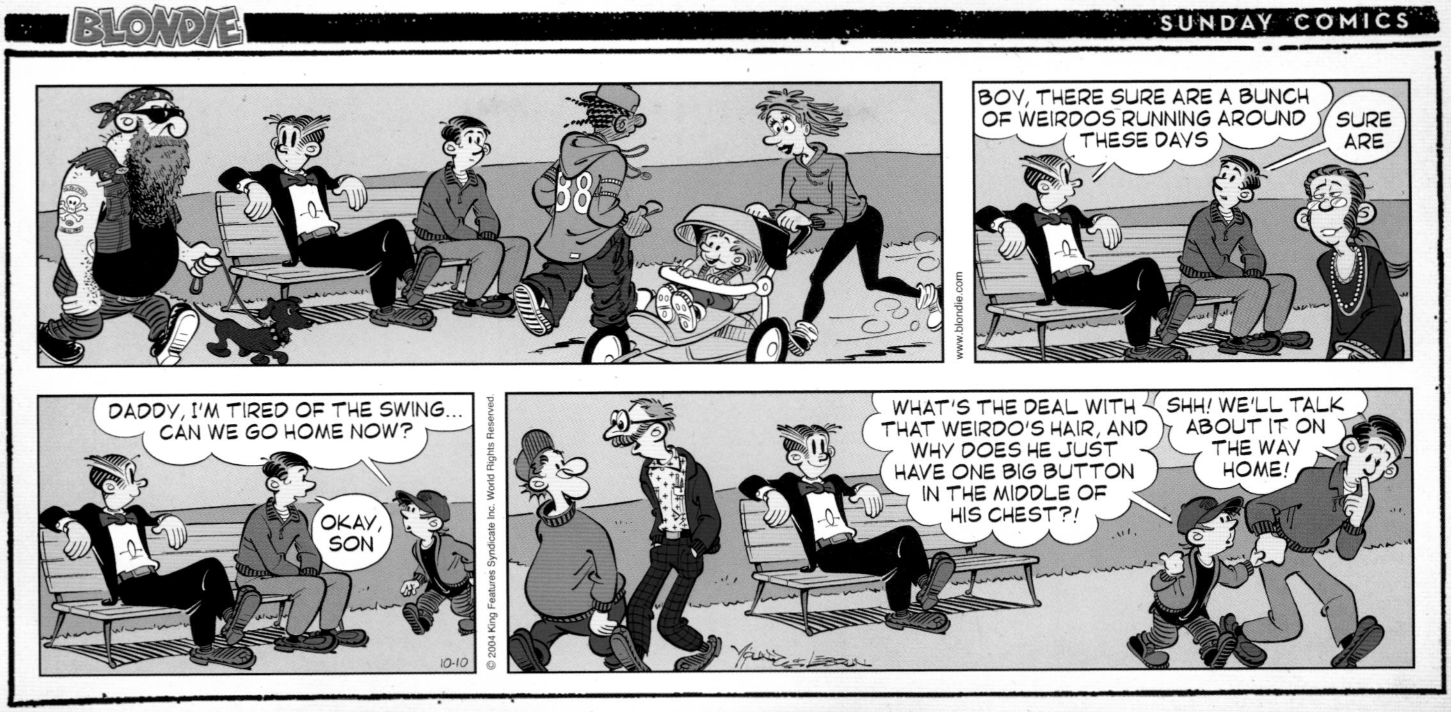
BLONDIE
SUNDAY COMICS
www.blondie.com
BOY, THERE SURE ARE A BUNCH OF WEIRDOS RUNNING AROUND THESE DAYS
SURE ARE
DADDY, I'M TIRED OF THE SWING... CAN WE GO HOME NOW?
OKAY, SON
10-10
© 2004 King Features Syndicate Inc. World Rights Reserved.
WHAT'S THE DEAL WITH THAT WEIRDO'S HAIR, AND WHY DOES HE JUST HAVE ONE BIG BUTTON IN THE MIDDLE OF HIS CHEST?!
SHH! WE'LL TALK ABOUT IT ON THE WAY HOME!

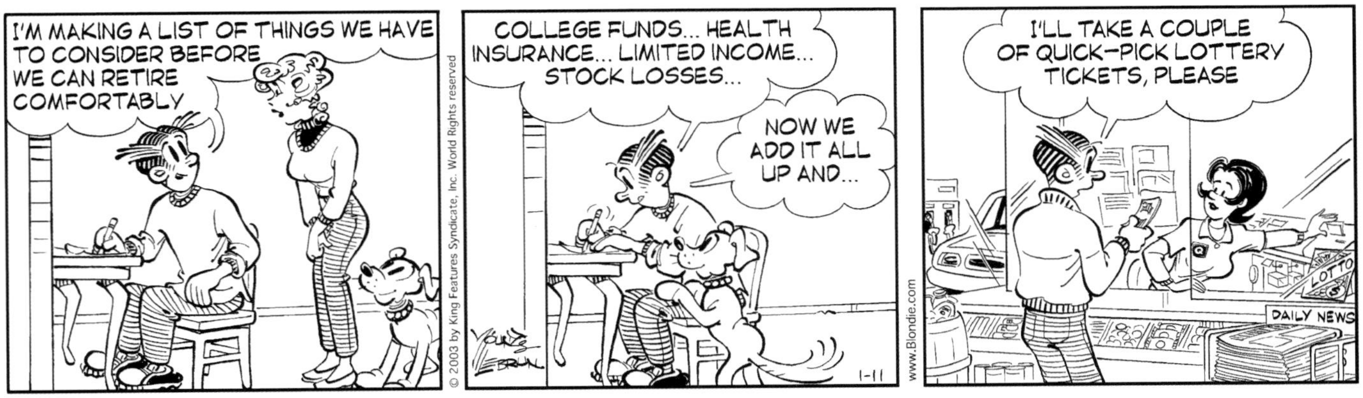
I'M MAKING A LIST OF THINGS WE HAVE TO CONSIDER BEFORE WE CAN RETIRE COMFORTABLY
© 2003 by King Features Syndicate, Inc. World Rights reserved
COLLEGE FUNDS... HEALTH INSURANCE... LIMITED INCOME... STOCK LOSSES...
NOW WE ADD IT ALL UP AND...
1-11
www.Blondie.com
I'LL TAKE A COUPLE OF QUICK-PICK LOTTERY TICKETS, PLEASE
LOTTO
DAILY NEWS

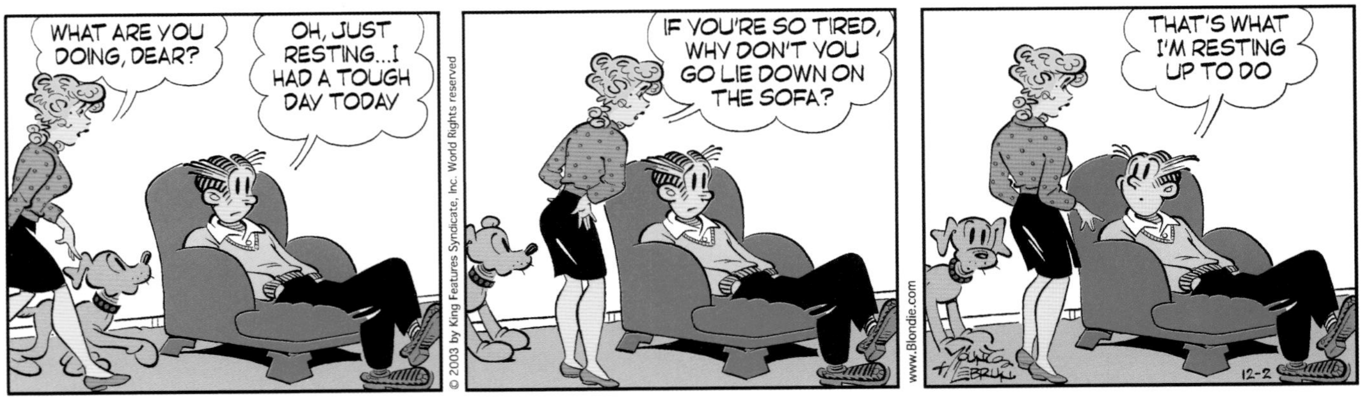
WHAT ARE YOU DOING, DEAR?
OH, JUST RESTING...I HAD A TOUGH DAY TODAY
© 2003 by King Features Syndicate, Inc. World Rights reserved
IF YOU'RE SO TIRED, WHY DON'T YOU GO LIE DOWN ON THE SOFA?
www.Blondie.com
THAT'S WHAT I'M RESTING UP TO DO
12-2

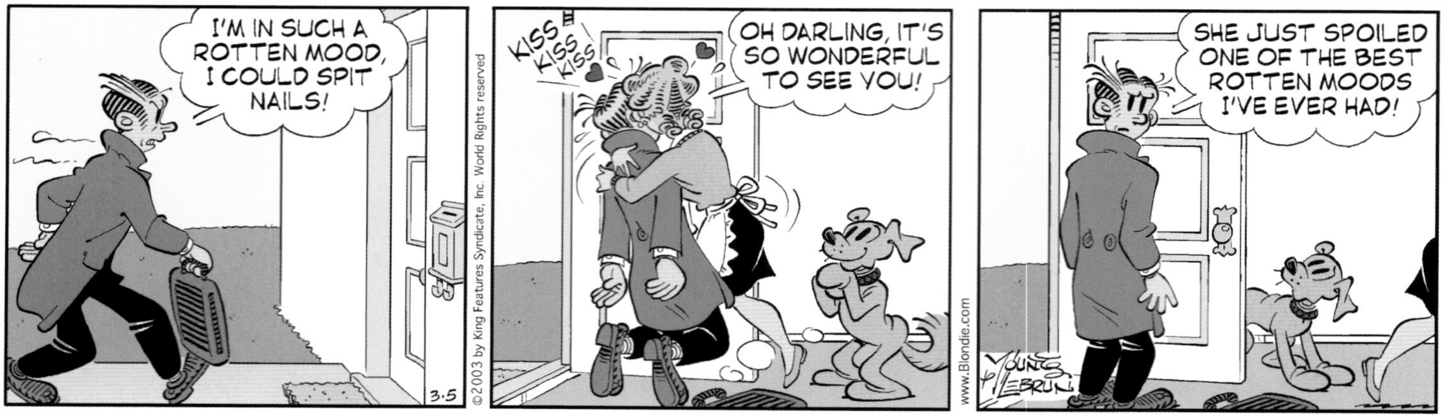
I'M IN SUCH A ROTTEN MOOD, I COULD SPIT NAILS!
3·5
© 2003 by King Features Syndicate, Inc. World Rights reserved
KISS KISS KISS
OH DARLING, IT'S SO WONDERFUL TO SEE YOU!
www.Blondie.com
SHE JUST SPOILED ONE OF THE BEST ROTTEN MOODS I'VE EVER HAD!
YOUNG LEBRUN

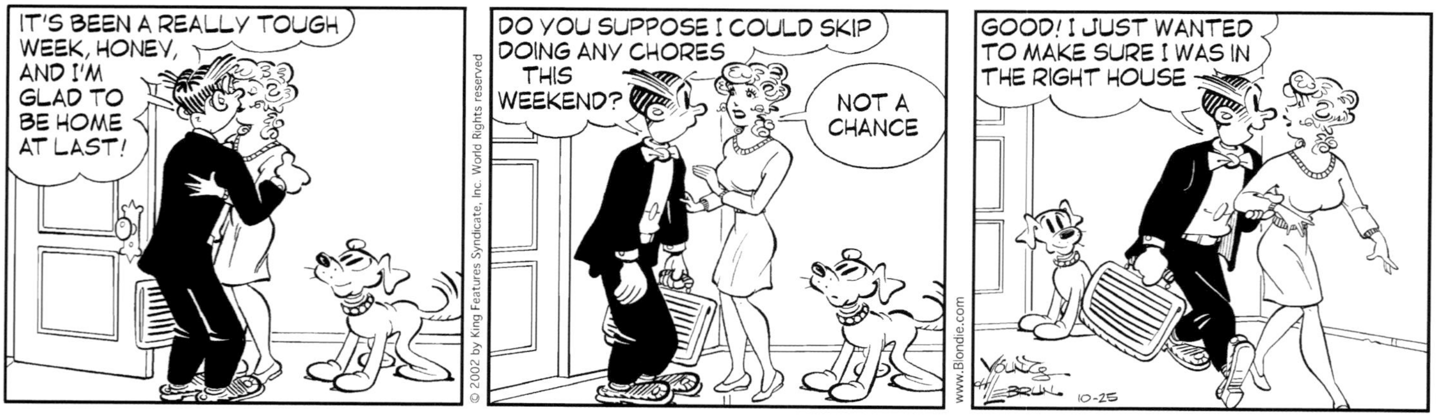
IT'S BEEN A REALLY TOUGH WEEK, HONEY, AND I'M GLAD TO BE HOME AT LAST!
© 2002 by King Features Syndicate, Inc. World Rights reserved
DO YOU SUPPOSE I COULD SKIP DOING ANY CHORES THIS WEEKEND?
NOT A CHANCE
www.Blondie.com
GOOD! I JUST WANTED TO MAKE SURE I WAS IN THE RIGHT HOUSE
YOUNG LEBRUN
10-25

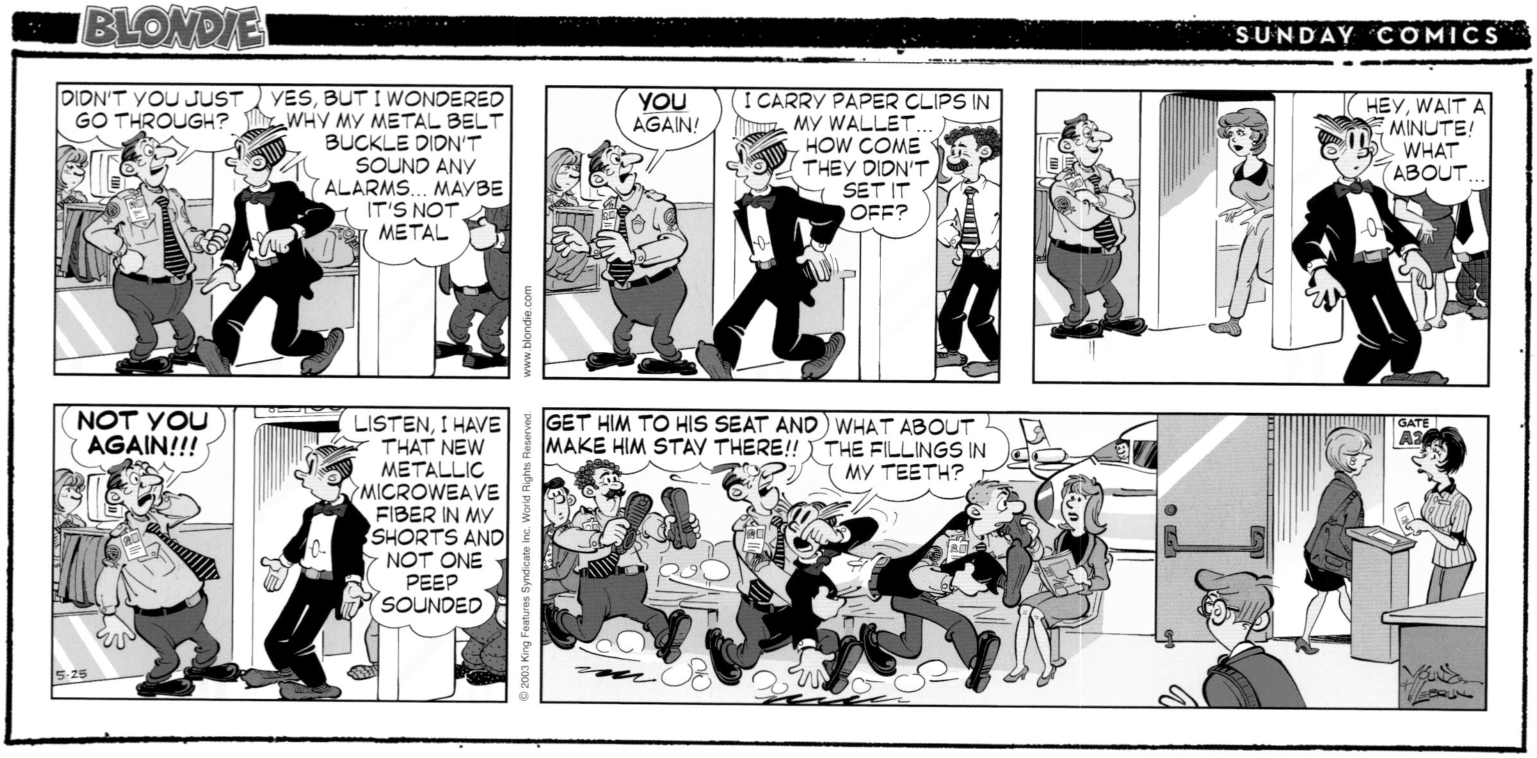
BLONDIE
SUNDAY COMICS
DIDN'T YOU JUST GO THROUGH?
YES, BUT I WONDERED WHY MY METAL BELT BUCKLE DIDN'T SOUND ANY ALARMS... MAYBE IT'S NOT METAL
www.blondie.com
YOU AGAIN!
I CARRY PAPER CLIPS IN MY WALLET... HOW COME THEY DIDN'T SET IT OFF?
HEY, WAIT A MINUTE! WHAT ABOUT...
NOT YOU AGAIN!!!
LISTEN, I HAVE THAT NEW METALLIC MICROWEAVE FIBER IN MY SHORTS AND NOT ONE PEEP SOUNDED
5-25
© 2003 King Features Syndicate Inc. World Rights Reserved.
GET HIM TO HIS SEAT AND MAKE HIM STAY THERE!!
WHAT ABOUT THE FILLINGS IN MY TEETH?
GATE
YOUNG LEBRUN

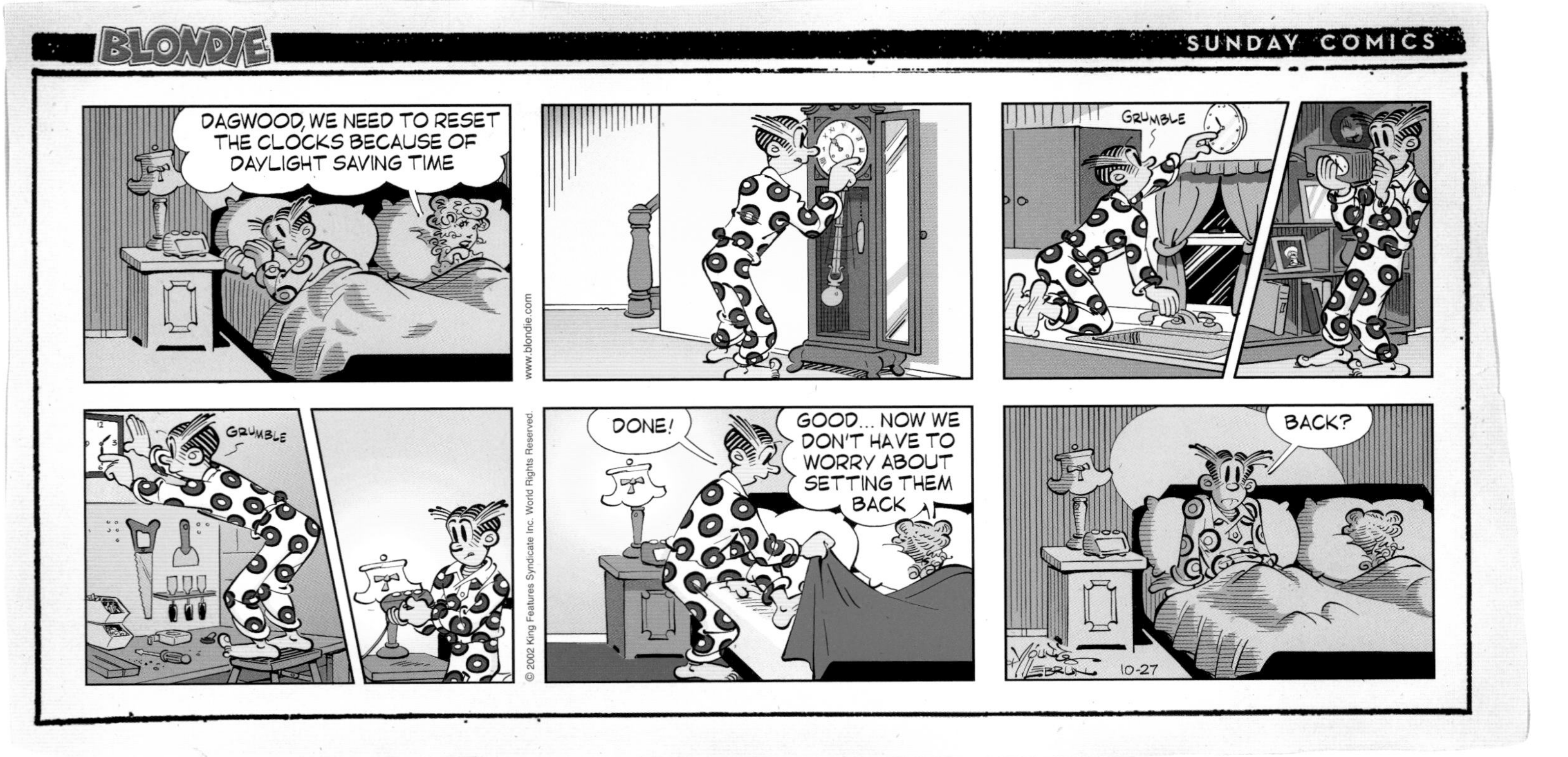
BLONDIE
SUNDAY COMICS
DAGWOOD, WE NEED TO RESET THE CLOCKS BECAUSE OF DAYLIGHT SAVING TIME
www.blondie.com
GRUMBLE
GRUMBLE
© 2002 King Features Syndicate Inc. World Rights Reserved.
DONE!
GOOD... NOW WE DON'T HAVE TO WORRY ABOUT SETTING THEM BACK
BACK?
YOUNG LEBRUN 10-27

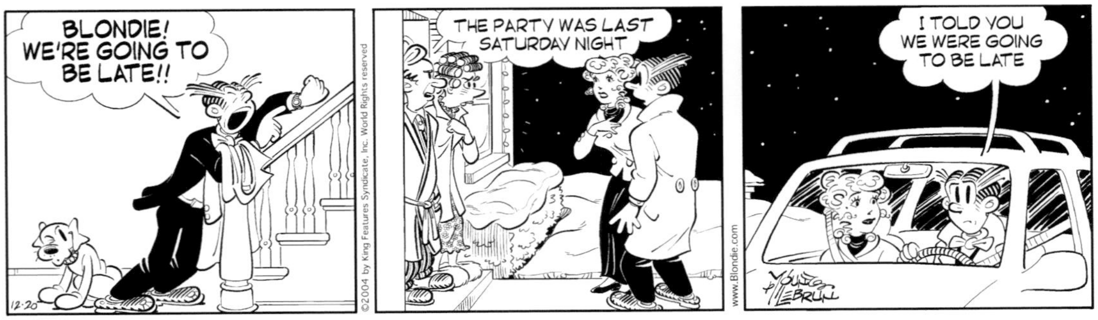
BLONDIE! WE'RE GOING TO BE LATE!!
12-20
©2004 by King Features Syndicate, Inc. World Rights reserved
THE PARTY WAS LAST SATURDAY NIGHT
I TOLD YOU WE WERE GOING TO BE LATE
www.Blondie.com
YOUNG LEBRUN

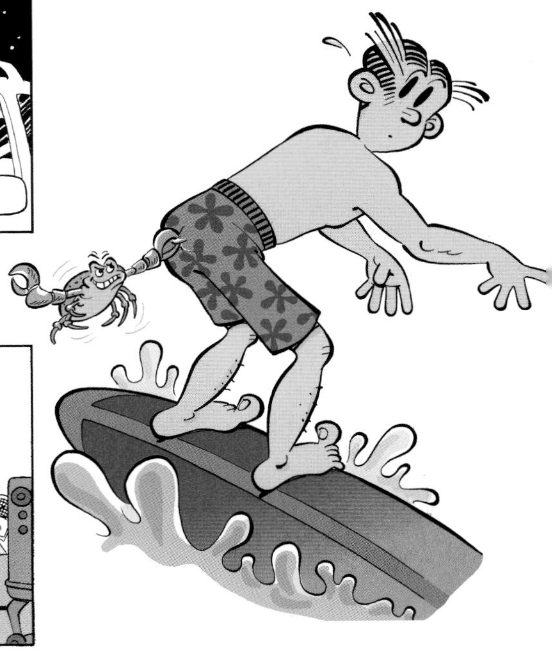

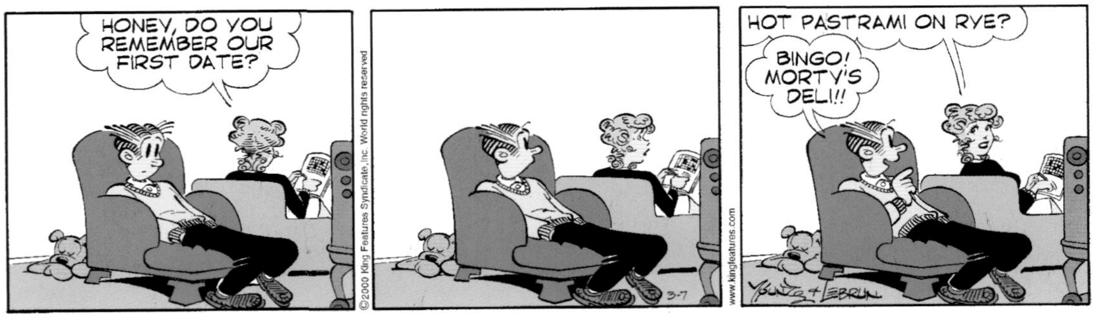
HONEY, DO YOU REMEMBER OUR FIRST DATE?
©2000 King Features Syndicate, Inc. World rights reserved
3-7
www.kingfeatures.com
HOT PASTRAMI ON RYE?
BINGO! MORTY'S DEL!!!
YOUNG LEBRUN

ALEXANDER

The eldest Bumstead child was born on April 15, 1934, after a pregnancy so uneventful, it nearly qualified as immaculate. Nicknamed "Baby Dumpling," the little boy was the son the Bumsteads always wanted—adorable, outgoing, and quick with a quip. Luckily, he didn't grow up quickly—his childhood spanned the 1930s to the 70s. After nagging his parents a lot, he eventually lost the embarrassing appellation. For any child, being publicly known as Baby Dumpling would be kind of like having everyone in the world see your first bathtub pics. His full given name, Alexander, was chosen in honor of Alex Raymond, an early assistant to Chic Young, and the brother of Jim Raymond, who became Chic and Dean's longtime collaborator.

Now Alexander has finally graduated to teenager-hood, a condition that's much more difficult to outgrow. He will likely remain there for as long as there is comic tension to be mined from the relationship between teenagers and their parents—which is to say, forever.

As a teenager, Alexander is nothing if not normal. He goes to school, plays football and basketball, fights with his sister, slacks off, and above all, remains firm in the conviction that his parents—especially his father—are endless sources of affection, amusement, and cash. (Not necessarily in that order.) But while Dagwood's bumbling nature has not escaped his son's notice—how could it?—he has a lot more in common with his dad than just unruly hair.

In fact, in many ways, Alexander is a junior Dagwood—albeit with hipper clothing and musical taste. Their shared DNA is most obvious in the kitchen, where Alexander's appetite and sandwich-making skills may soon grow to rival his dad's. Well, almost. Only the truly advanced of character can stomach the sardines. Still, watching his son slap together a few (dozen) slices of cold cuts and cheese, smother them with assorted condiments, and stack it all between a hunk (loaf) of bread may be one of Dagwood's proudest moments.

And when he's not busy practicing with his band, denting the car, or asking for cash, Alexander does manage to absorb some lessons in the fatherly

HEY DAD, WHICH TIE SHOULD I WEAR TO A FANCY RESTAURANT, STRIPES OR PLAID?
PLAID
© 2001 King Features Syndicate, Inc. World rights reserved.
ARE YOU SURE?
POSITIVE
4·13
www.blondie.com
STRIPES IT IS

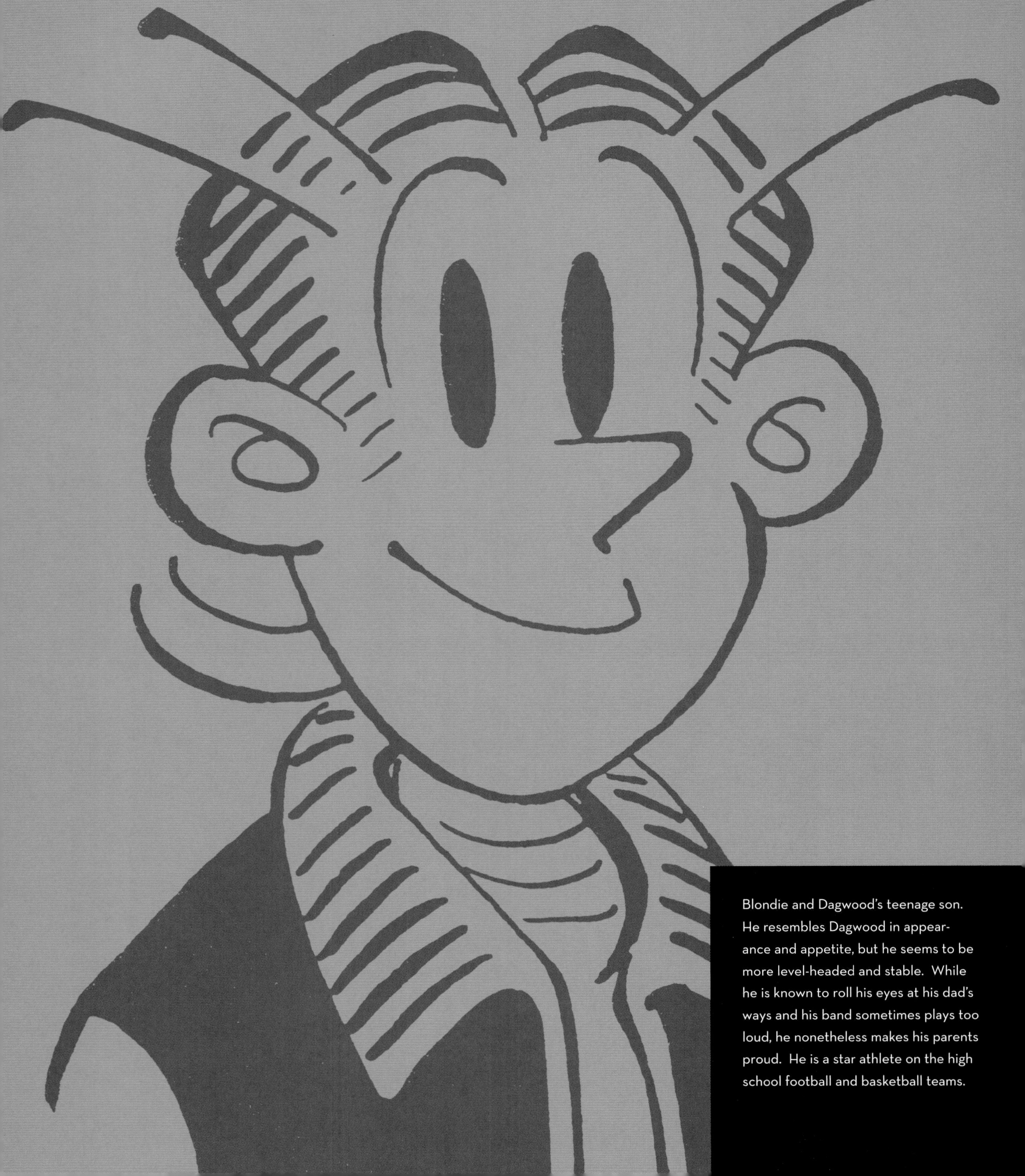

Blondie and Dagwood's teenage son. He resembles Dagwood in appearance and appetite, but he seems to be more level-headed and stable. While he is known to roll his eyes at his dad's ways and his band sometimes plays too loud, he nonetheless makes his parents proud. He is a star athlete on the high school football and basketball teams.

Alexander is a junior Dagwood—albeit with hipper clothing and musical taste.

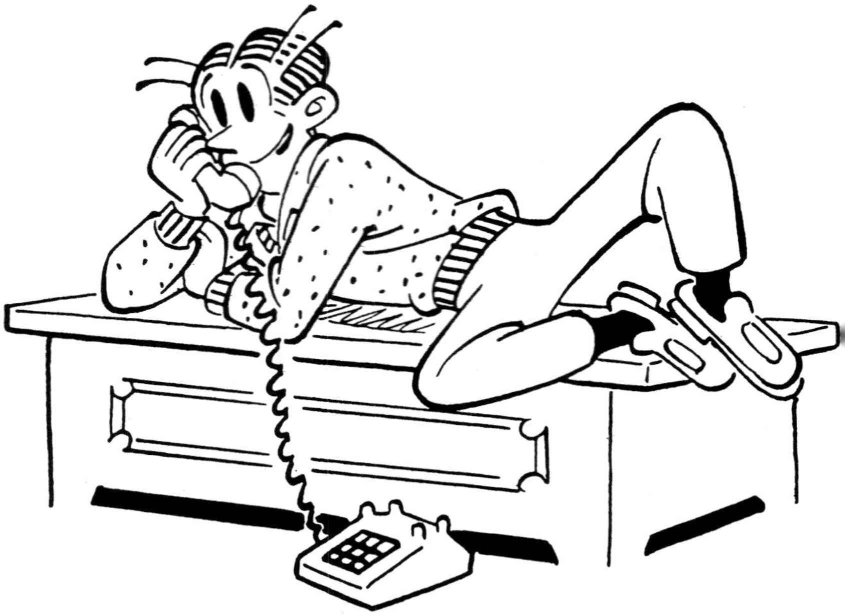

arts: snacking, napping, and leisure studies (avoiding chores, TV-watching). Occasionally, he even notices that there is something to be learned from the old man—a realization it takes the rest of us most of adulthood to achieve. Maybe, after all these years, Alexander has really become wiser, sharper, and more mature . . . nah. He is still his father's son.

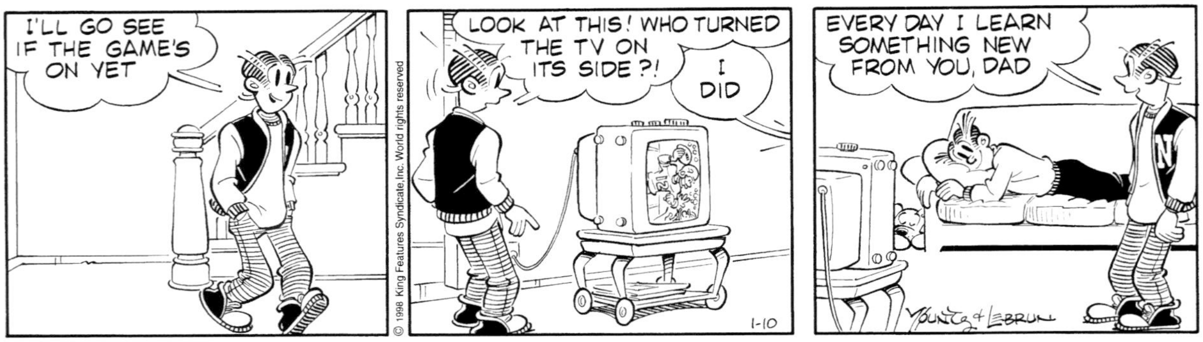

I'LL GO SEE IF THE GAME'S ON YET
LOOK AT THIS! WHO TURNED THE TV ON ITS SIDE?!
I DID
EVERY DAY I LEARN SOMETHING NEW FROM YOU, DAD
© 1998 King Features Syndicate,Inc. World rights reserved
1-10

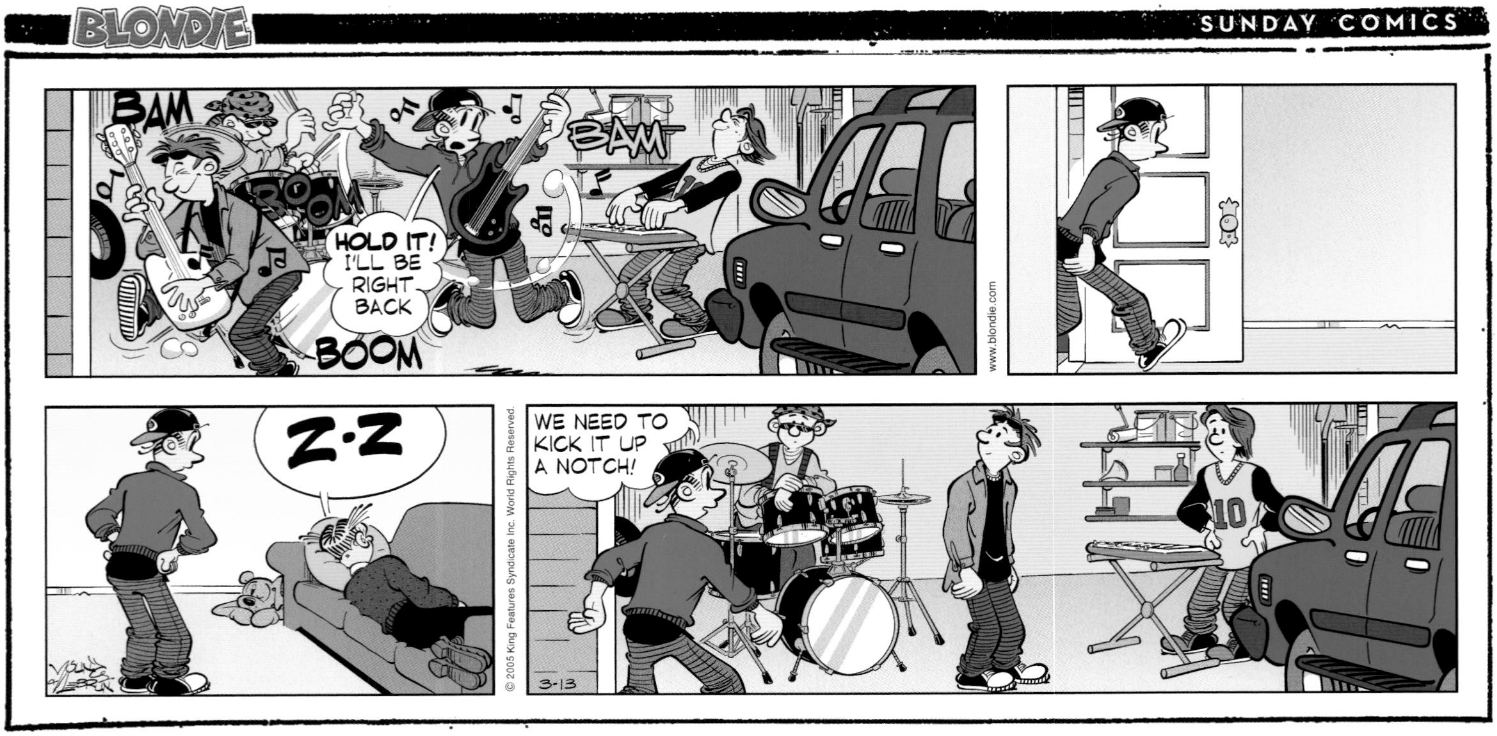

BLONDIE
SUNDAY COMICS
BAM
BOOM
BAM
HOLD IT! I'LL BE RIGHT BACK
BOOM
www.blondie.com
Z-Z
© 2005 King Features Syndicate Inc. World Rights Reserved.
WE NEED TO KICK IT UP A NOTCH!
3-13

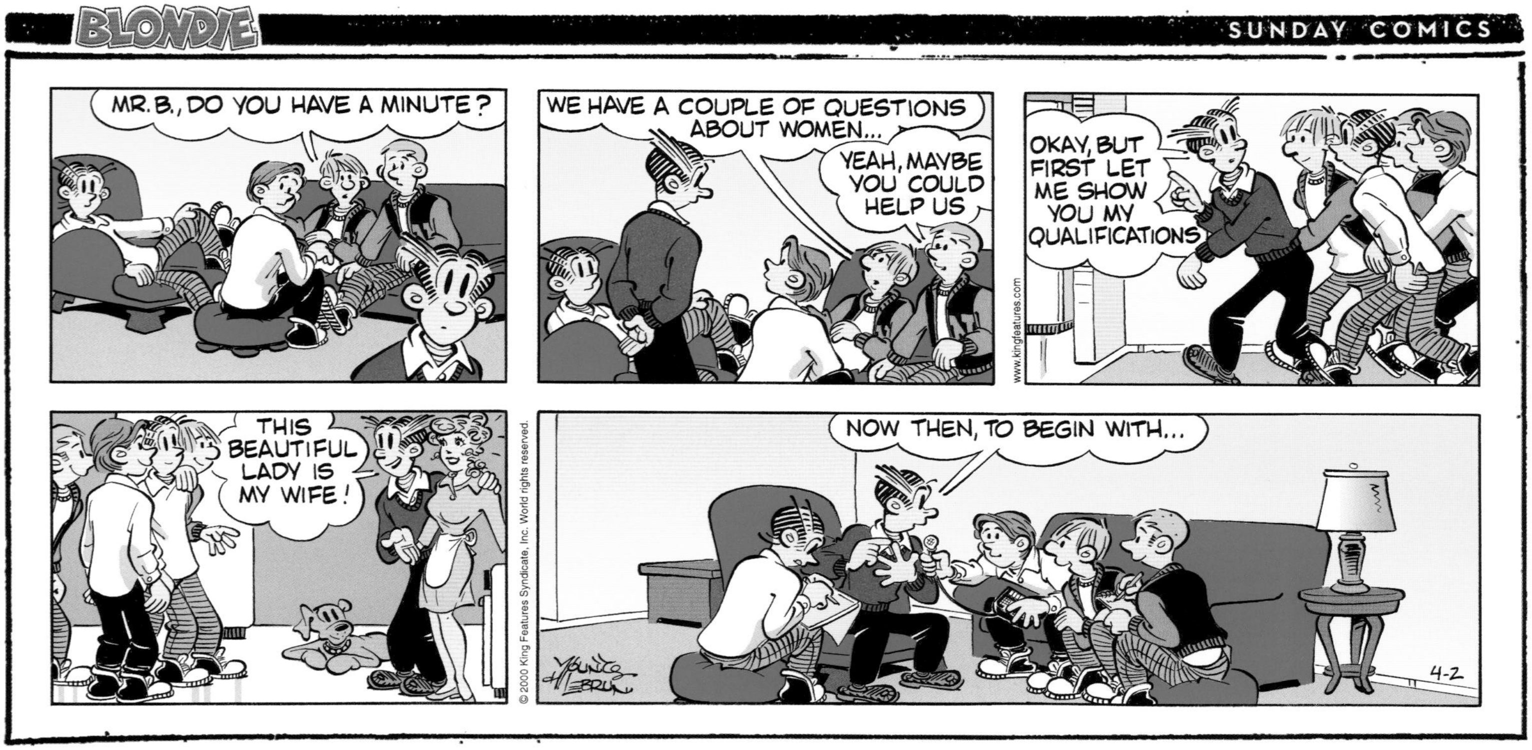
BLONDIE
SUNDAY COMICS
MR. B., DO YOU HAVE A MINUTE?
WE HAVE A COUPLE OF QUESTIONS ABOUT WOMEN...
YEAH, MAYBE YOU COULD HELP US
OKAY, BUT FIRST LET ME SHOW YOU MY QUALIFICATIONS
www.kingfeatures.com
THIS BEAUTIFUL LADY IS MY WIFE!
© 2000 King Features Syndicate, Inc. World rights reserved.
NOW THEN, TO BEGIN WITH...
4-2

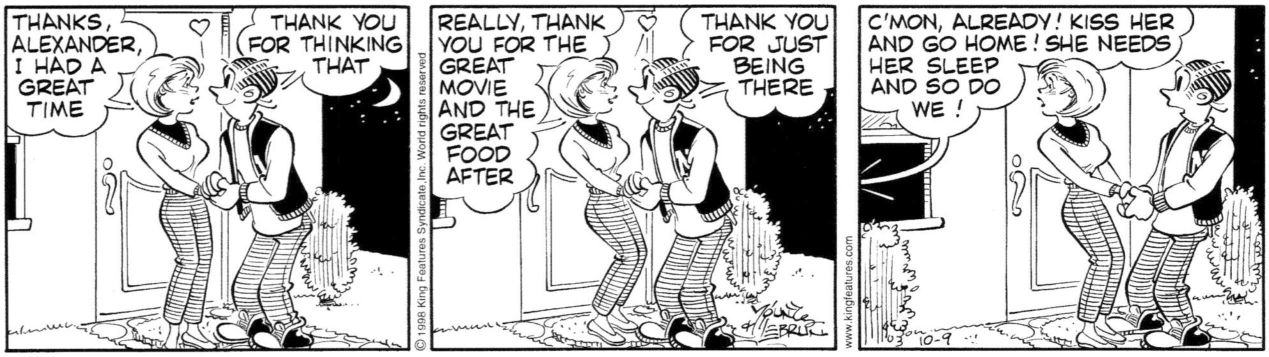
THANKS, ALEXANDER, I HAD A GREAT TIME
THANK YOU FOR THINKING THAT
© 1998 King Features Syndicate, Inc. World rights reserved
REALLY, THANK YOU FOR THE GREAT MOVIE AND THE GREAT FOOD AFTER
THANK YOU FOR JUST BEING THERE
www.kingfeatures.com
C'MON, ALREADY! KISS HER AND GO HOME! SHE NEEDS HER SLEEP AND SO DO WE!
10-9

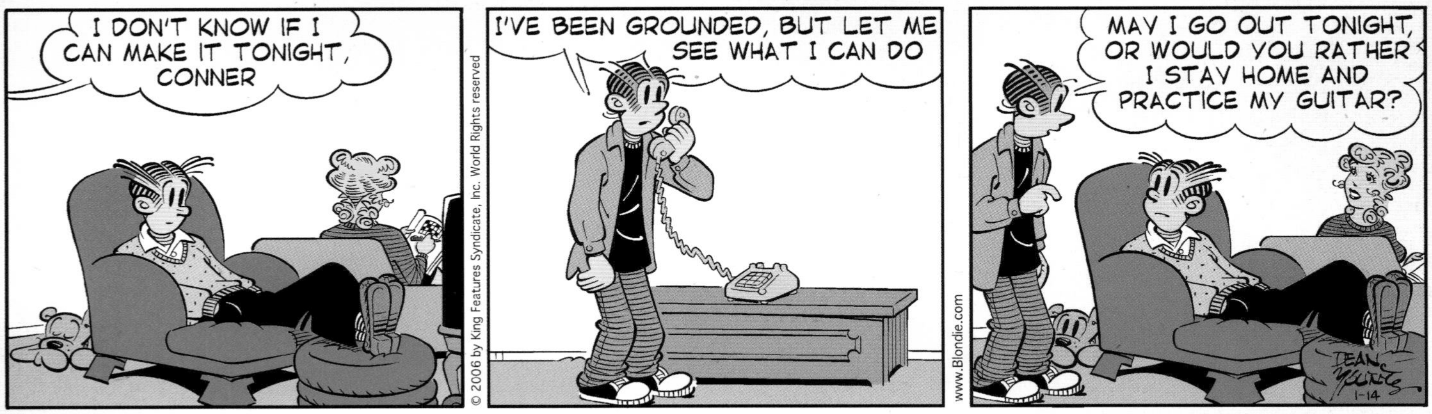
I DON'T KNOW IF I CAN MAKE IT TONIGHT, CONNER
© 2006 by King Features Syndicate, Inc. World Rights reserved
I'VE BEEN GROUNDED, BUT LET ME SEE WHAT I CAN DO
www.Blondie.com
MAY I GO OUT TONIGHT, OR WOULD YOU RATHER I STAY HOME AND PRACTICE MY GUITAR?
1-14

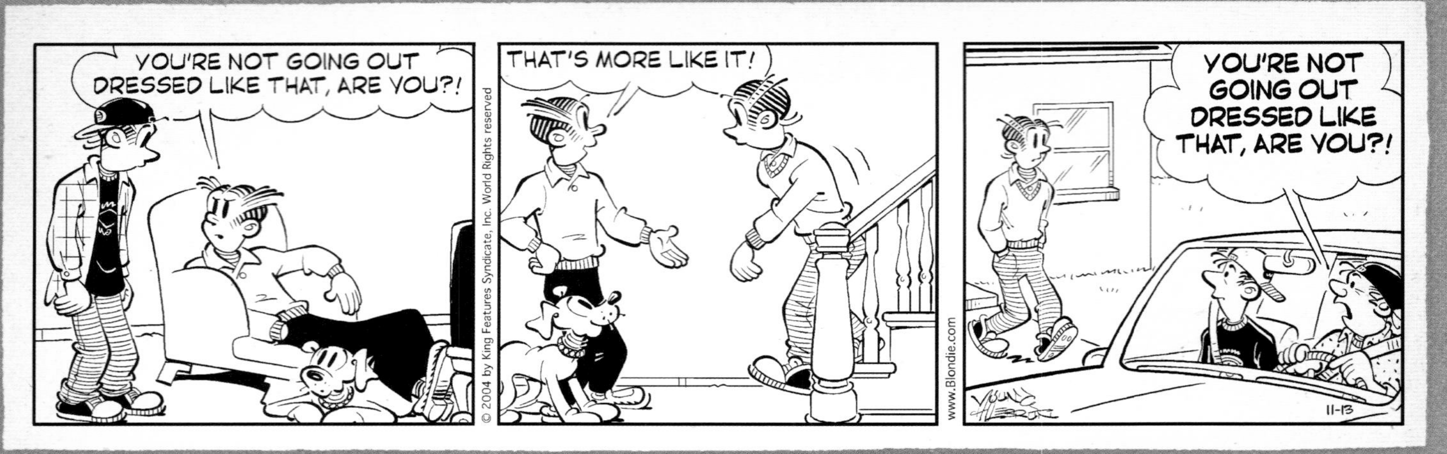
YOU'RE NOT GOING OUT DRESSED LIKE THAT, ARE YOU?!
THAT'S MORE LIKE IT!
YOU'RE NOT GOING OUT DRESSED LIKE THAT, ARE YOU?!
© 2004 by King Features Syndicate, Inc. World Rights reserved
www.Blondie.com
11-13

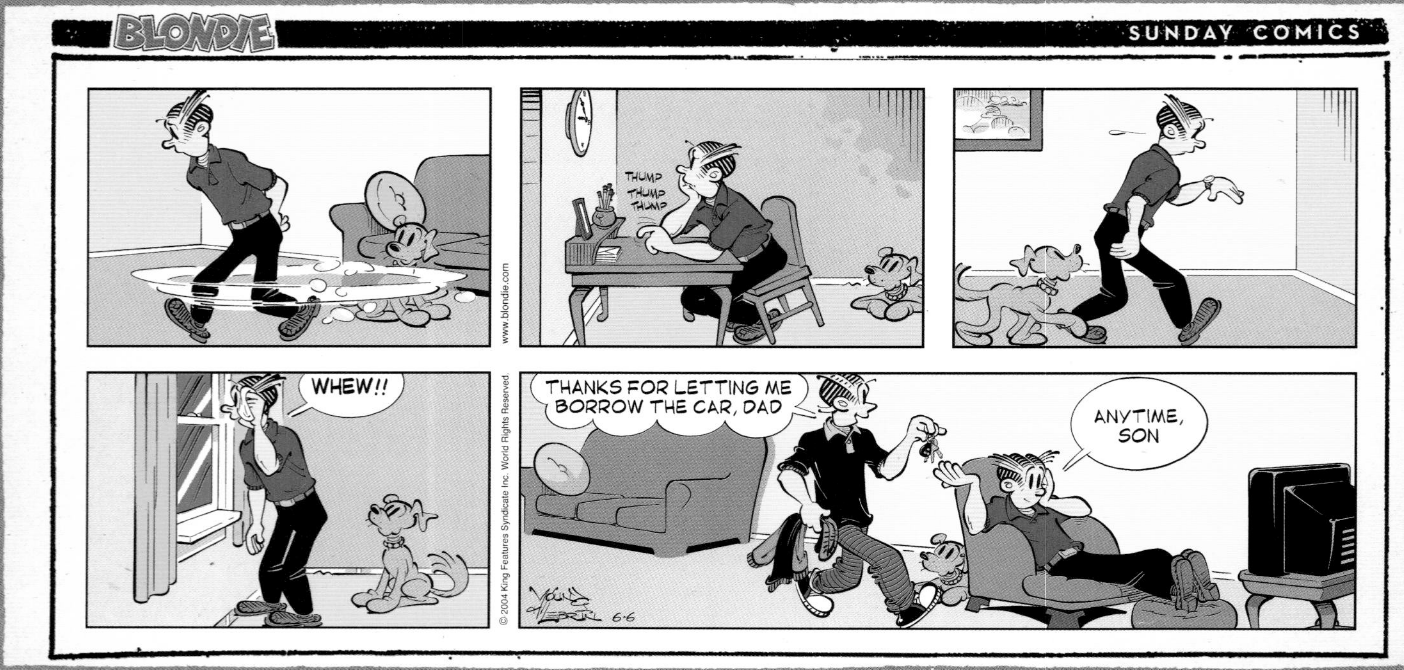
BLONDIE
SUNDAY COMICS
THUMP
THUMP
THUMP
www.blondie.com
WHEW!!
THANKS FOR LETTING ME BORROW THE CAR, DAD
ANYTIME, SON
© 2004 King Features Syndicate Inc. World Rights Reserved.
6-6

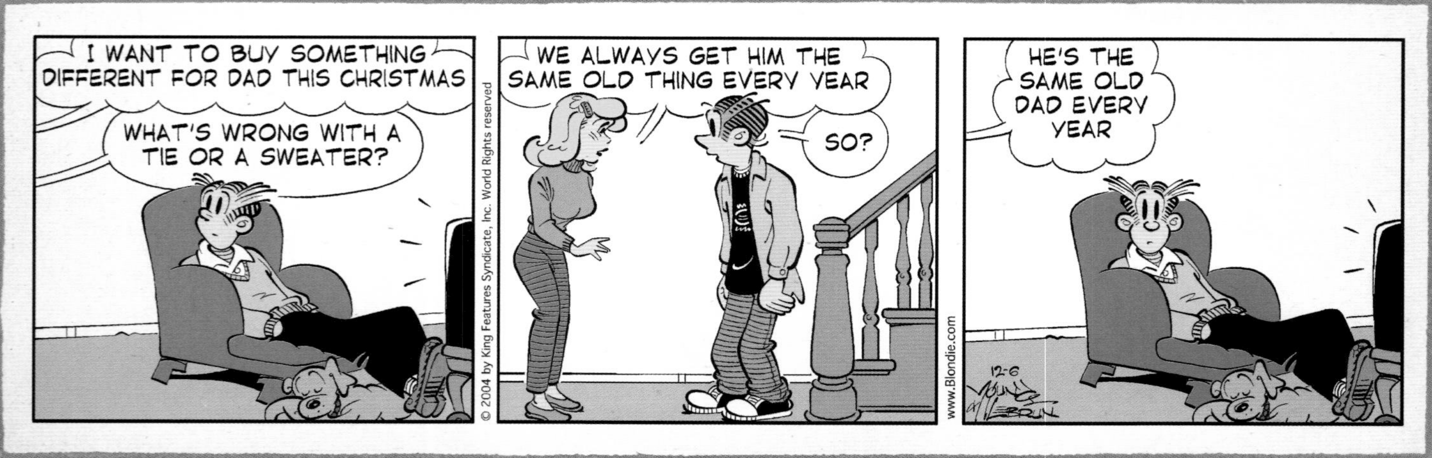
I WANT TO BUY SOMETHING DIFFERENT FOR DAD THIS CHRISTMAS
WHAT'S WRONG WITH A TIE OR A SWEATER?
WE ALWAYS GET HIM THE SAME OLD THING EVERY YEAR
SO?
HE'S THE SAME OLD DAD EVERY YEAR
© 2004 by King Features Syndicate, Inc. World Rights reserved
www.Blondie.com
12-6

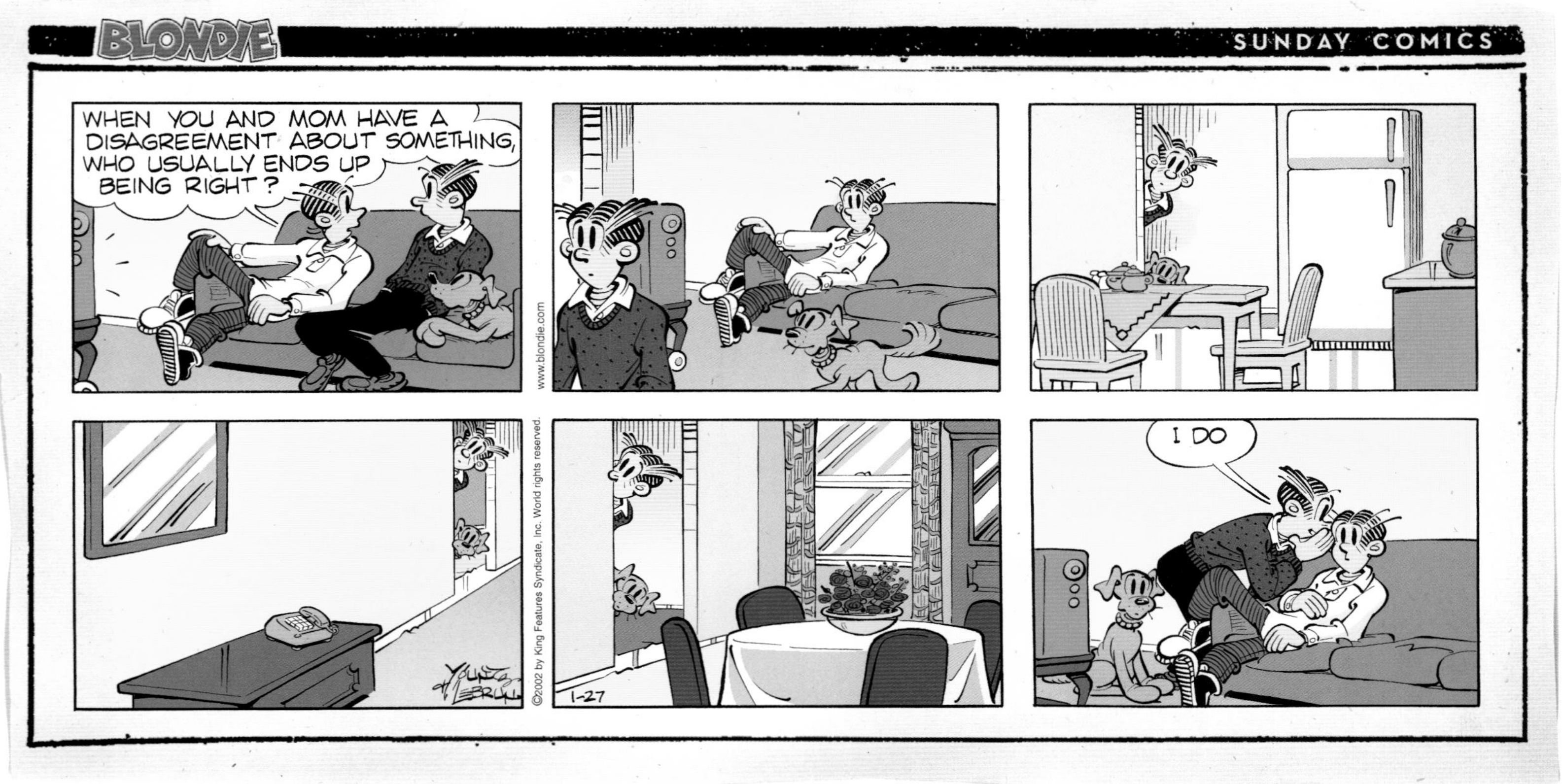
BLONDIE
SUNDAY COMICS
WHEN YOU AND MOM HAVE A DISAGREEMENT ABOUT SOMETHING, WHO USUALLY ENDS UP BEING RIGHT?
I DO
www.blondie.com
©2002 by King Features Syndicate, Inc. World rights reserved.
1-27

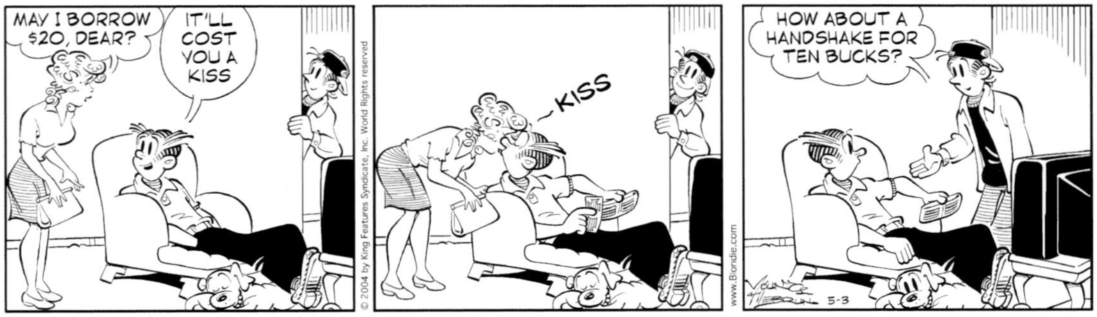
MAY I BORROW $20, DEAR?
IT'LL COST YOU A KISS
KISS
HOW ABOUT A HANDSHAKE FOR TEN BUCKS?
© 2004 by King Features Syndicate, Inc. World Rights reserved
www.Blondie.com
5-3

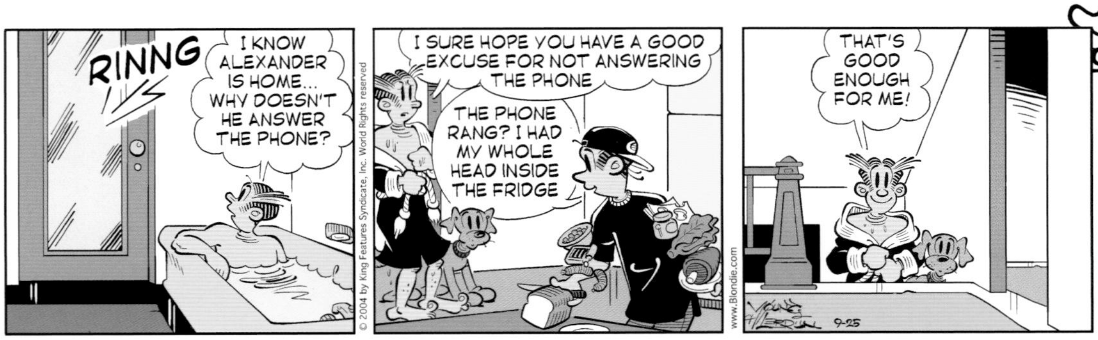
RINNG
I KNOW ALEXANDER IS HOME... WHY DOESN'T HE ANSWER THE PHONE?
I SURE HOPE YOU HAVE A GOOD EXCUSE FOR NOT ANSWERING THE PHONE
THE PHONE RANG? I HAD MY WHOLE HEAD INSIDE THE FRIDGE
THAT'S GOOD ENOUGH FOR ME!
© 2004 by King Features Syndicate, Inc. World Rights reserved
www.Blondie.com
9-25

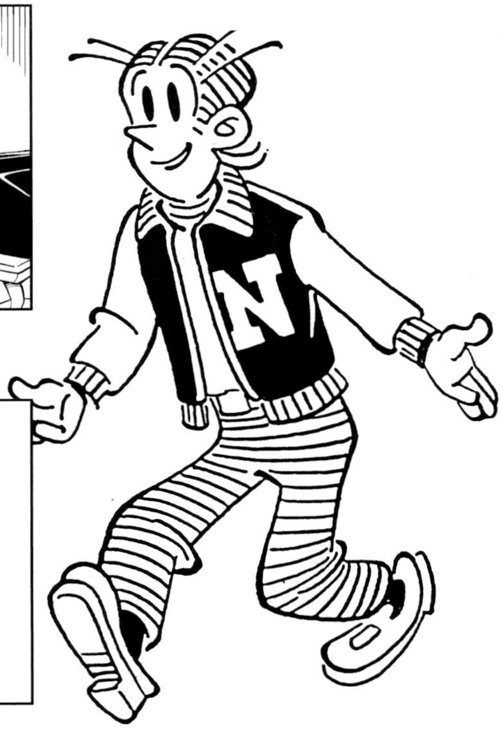

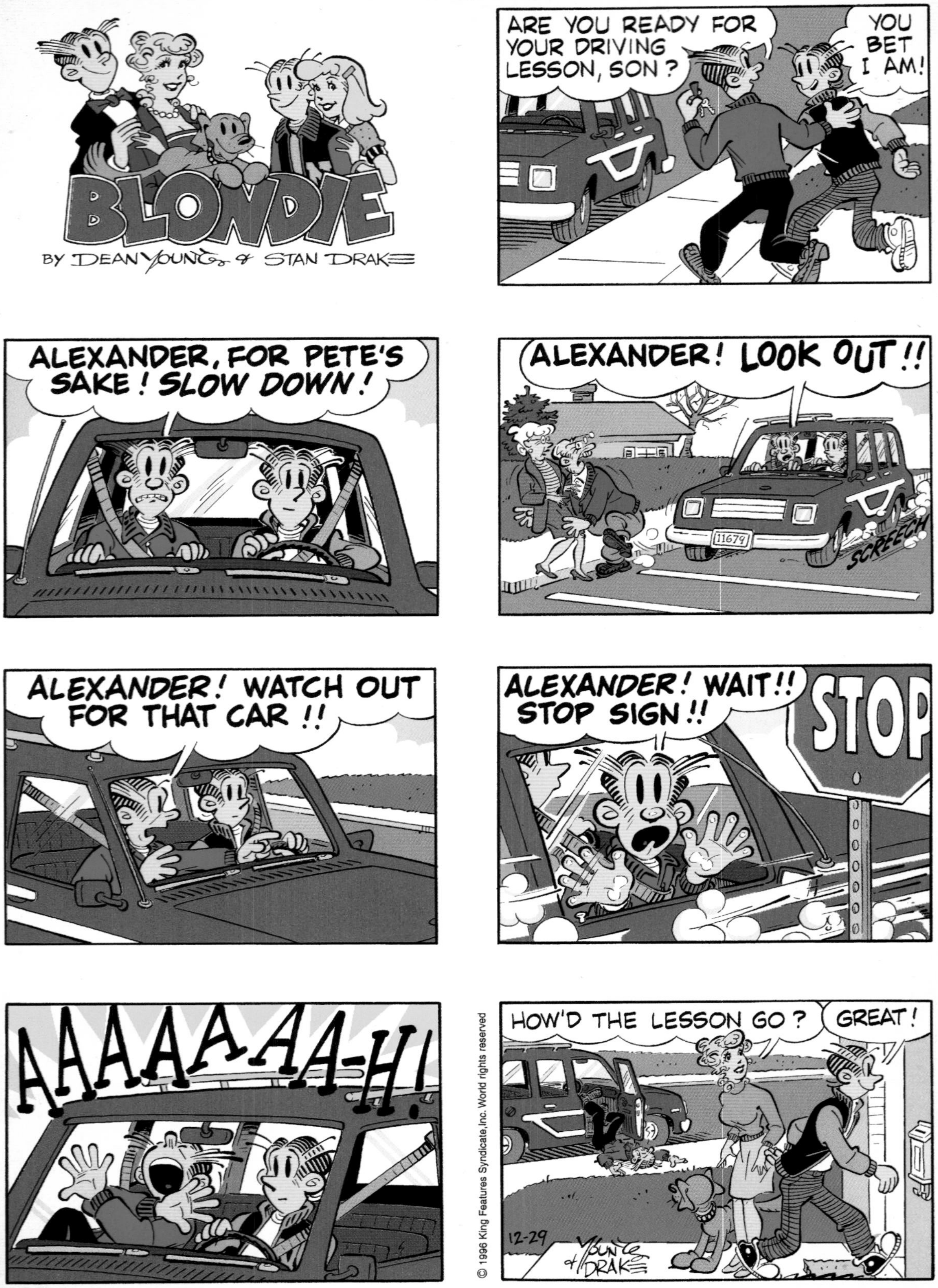
BLONDIE
BY DEAN YOUNG & STAN DRAKE
ARE YOU READY FOR YOUR DRIVING LESSON, SON?
YOU BET I AM!
ALEXANDER, FOR PETE'S SAKE! SLOW DOWN!
ALEXANDER! LOOK OUT!!
11679
SCREECH
ALEXANDER! WATCH OUT FOR THAT CAR!!
ALEXANDER! WAIT!! STOP SIGN!!
STOP
AAAAAAA-H!
HOW'D THE LESSON GO?
GREAT!
12-29
YOUNG & DRAKE

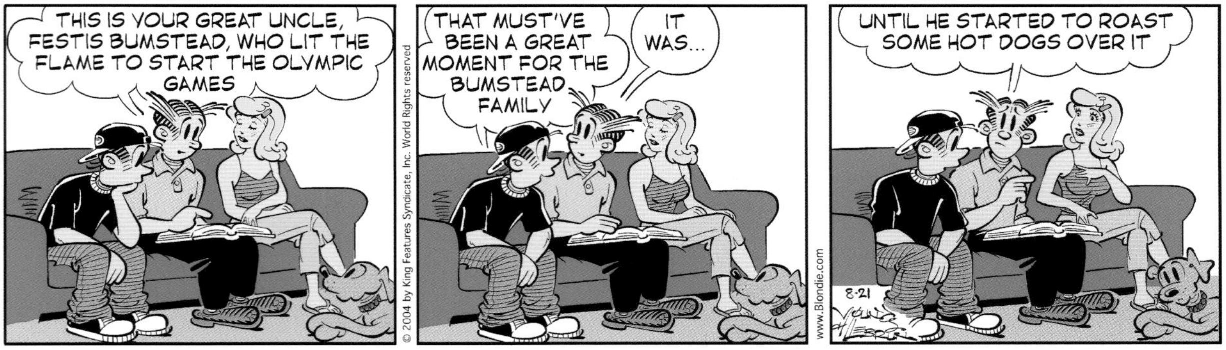
THIS IS YOUR GREAT UNCLE, FESTIS BUMSTEAD, WHO LIT THE FLAME TO START THE OLYMPIC GAMES
THAT MUST'VE BEEN A GREAT MOMENT FOR THE BUMSTEAD FAMILY
IT WAS...
UNTIL HE STARTED TO ROAST SOME HOT DOGS OVER IT
© 2004 by King Features Syndicate, Inc. World Rights reserved
www.Blondie.com
8-21

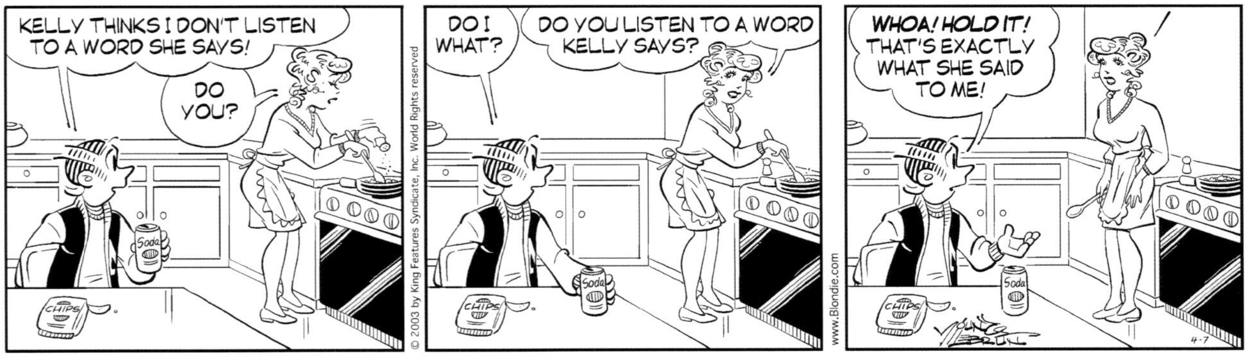
KELLY THINKS I DON'T LISTEN TO A WORD SHE SAYS!
DO YOU?
DO I WHAT?
DO YOU LISTEN TO A WORD KELLY SAYS?
WHOA! HOLD IT! THAT'S EXACTLY WHAT SHE SAID TO ME!
© 2003 by King Features Syndicate, Inc. World Rights reserved
www.Blondie.com
4-7

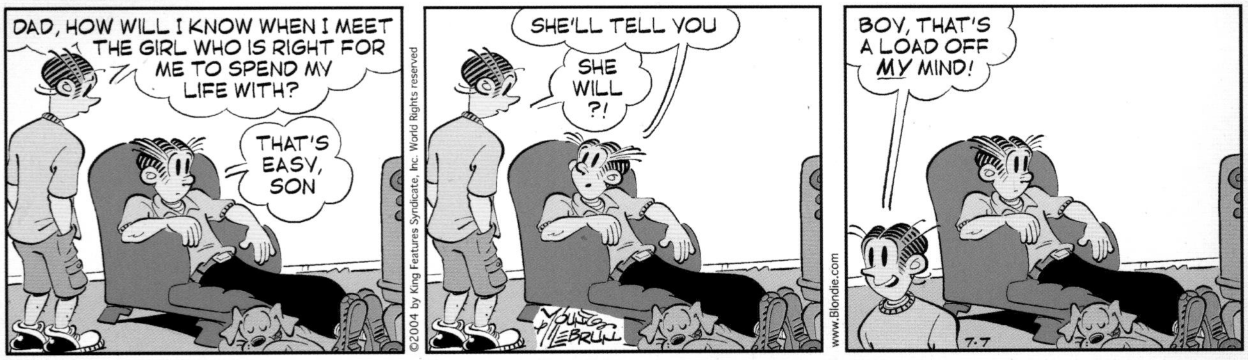
DAD, HOW WILL I KNOW WHEN I MEET THE GIRL WHO IS RIGHT FOR ME TO SPEND MY LIFE WITH?
THAT'S EASY, SON
SHE'LL TELL YOU
SHE WILL ?!
BOY, THAT'S A LOAD OFF MY MIND!
©2004 by King Features Syndicate, Inc. World Rights reserved
www.Blondie.com
7-7

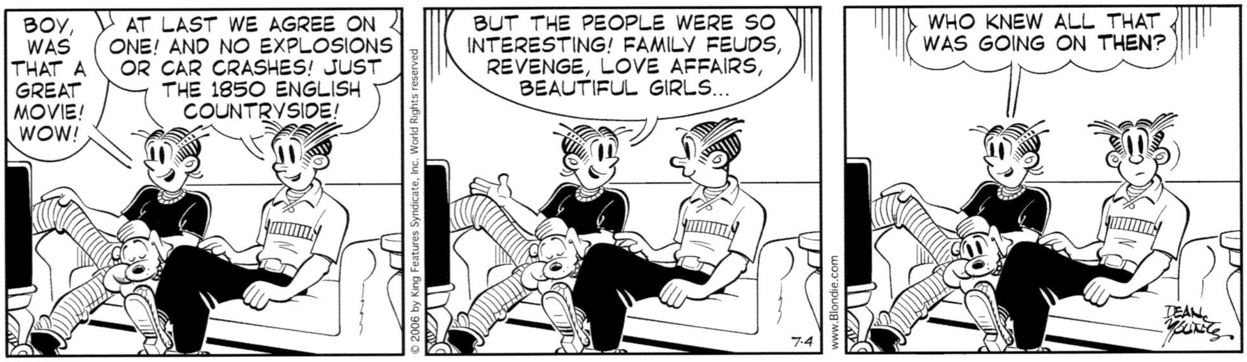
BOY, WAS THAT A GREAT MOVIE! WOW!
AT LAST WE AGREE ON ONE! AND NO EXPLOSIONS OR CAR CRASHES! JUST THE 1850 ENGLISH COUNTRYSIDE!
BUT THE PEOPLE WERE SO INTERESTING! FAMILY FEUDS, REVENGE, LOVE AFFAIRS, BEAUTIFUL GIRLS...
WHO KNEW ALL THAT WAS GOING ON THEN?
© 2006 by King Features Syndicate, Inc. World Rights reserved
www.Blondie.com
7-4

COOKIE

Like her mother, Cookie is levelheaded, cheerful, and good-looking. Now a spunky teenager, the Bumstead daughter was born on April 11, 1941. More than 430,000 people entered a nationwide contest to come up with her name. The winner was Beatrice Barken, a Cleveland housewife, who received one hundred dollars and lifelong bragging rights.

With her flippy blonde hair and belly-baring tops, Cookie looks like every post–Britney Spears adolescent girl, but she's no lightweight. A straight "A" student and a member of the varsity cheerleading squad, Cookie is every bit the pretty, well-liked Big (but small) Woman on Campus; she even has a blog to prove it.

Unlike her sloppy brother Alexander, Cookie is always perfectly coiffed, her room always neat and clean, her manners always impeccable. It's a winning combination that she often uses to sweet-talk her unsuspecting daddy, whose wallet may not survive his children's teenage years intact. (Especially since, even by today's long-adolescence standards, these kids have been acting like teenagers for a long, long, long time.)

Still, the only time Cookie really gives her parents cause to complain is . . . every night, when the endless parade of inappropriate dates commences. Her suitors have included a tattooed punk, a joker without a watch, a geek, and just about every boy next door. (One guy, a star athlete, did meet with Dad's approval, which no doubt meant that Cookie couldn't care less about him.) Given Cookie's popularity since birth, it's no surprise that she's got such a wide appeal, but her father probably wouldn't mind if his daughter were just a smidge less attractive to the boys she goes out with. While Dagwood waits up, paces, or tags along on his daughter's dates, Blondie is more secure. She is confident that sooner or later her daughter will make the right choice—just as she did.

So will Cookie eventually find love with someone like her father?

"I hope not," said Dean Young, a father of three daughters. As a cartoonist, though, he has a hunch it would make for some potently funny chemistry.

I HAVE A DATE WITH COOKIE
WAIT ONE SECOND, PLEASE
WOW, COOKIE! I DIDN'T KNOW YOUR FAMILY WAS WEALTHY ENOUGH TO HAVE A CHAUFFEUR!

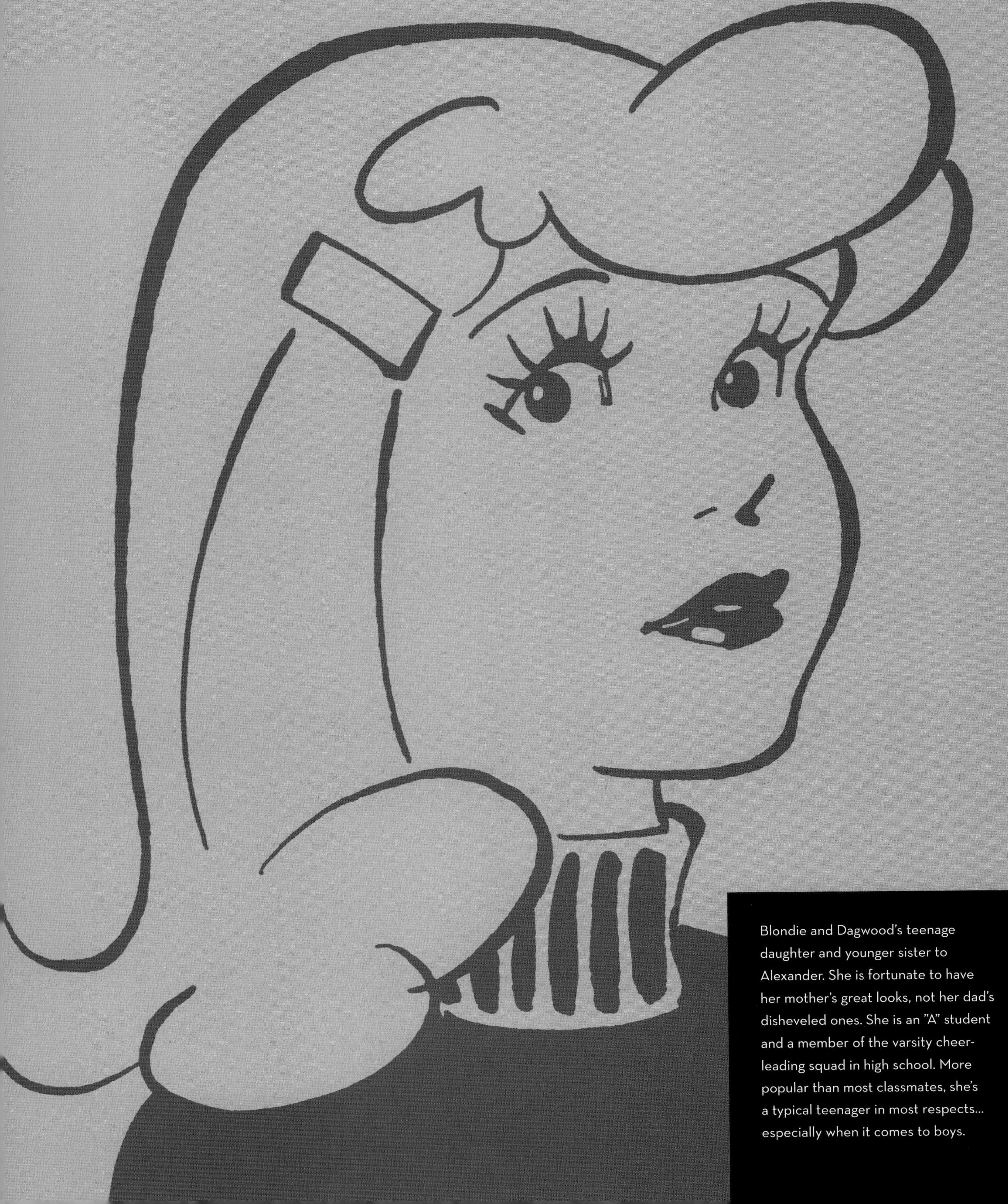

Blondie and Dagwood's teenage daughter and younger sister to Alexander. She is fortunate to have her mother's great looks, not her dad's disheveled ones. She is an "A" student and a member of the varsity cheer-leading squad in high school. More popular than most classmates, she's a typical teenager in most respects… especially when it comes to boys.

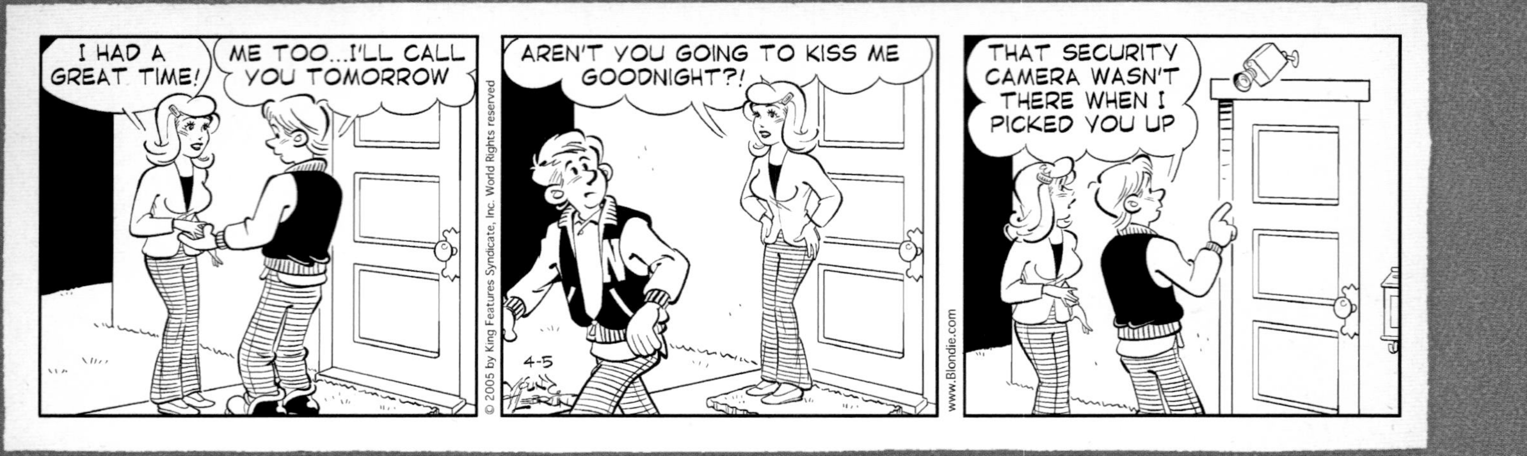
I HAD A GREAT TIME!
ME TOO...I'LL CALL YOU TOMORROW
© 2005 by King Features Syndicate, Inc. World Rights reserved
AREN'T YOU GOING TO KISS ME GOODNIGHT?!
4-5
THAT SECURITY CAMERA WASN'T THERE WHEN I PICKED YOU UP
www.Blondie.com

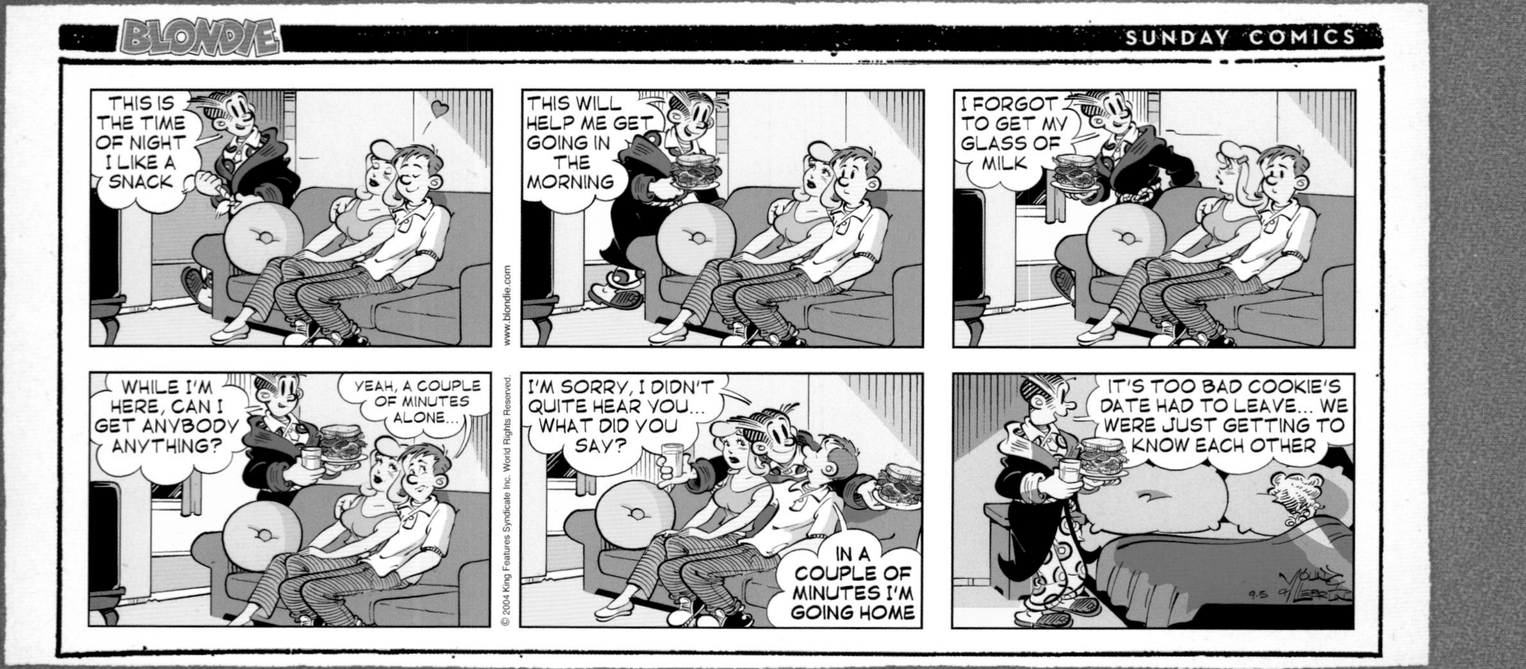
BLONDIE
SUNDAY COMICS
THIS IS THE TIME OF NIGHT I LIKE A SNACK
www.blondie.com
THIS WILL HELP ME GET GOING IN THE MORNING
I FORGOT TO GET MY GLASS OF MILK
WHILE I'M HERE, CAN I GET ANYBODY ANYTHING?
YEAH, A COUPLE OF MINUTES ALONE...
© 2004 King Features Syndicate Inc. World Rights Reserved.
I'M SORRY, I DIDN'T QUITE HEAR YOU... WHAT DID YOU SAY?
IN A COUPLE OF MINUTES I'M GOING HOME
IT'S TOO BAD COOKIE'S DATE HAD TO LEAVE... WE WERE JUST GETTING TO KNOW EACH OTHER
9-5

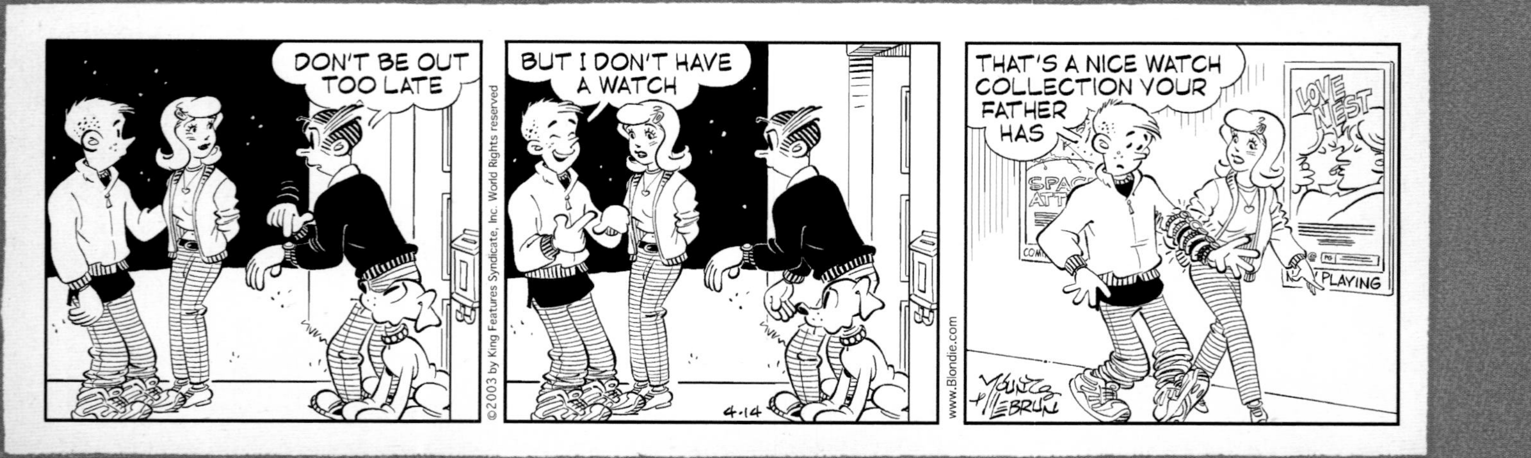
DON'T BE OUT TOO LATE
© 2003 by King Features Syndicate, Inc. World Rights reserved
BUT I DON'T HAVE A WATCH
4-14
www.Blondie.com
THAT'S A NICE WATCH COLLECTION YOUR FATHER HAS
LOVE NEST
PLAYING

I WISH YOU COULD'VE STAYED OUT A LITTLE LONGER TONIGHT
ME, TOO...
BUT MY DAD'S GOTTA GET TO BED!
Z-Z
© 2006 by King Features Syndicate, Inc. World Rights reserved
www.Blondie.com

JUSTIN AND I HAD A BIG FIGHT AND BROKE UP! I WANT YOU TO CALL HIM AND TELL HIM I APOLOGIZE
WHY DON'T YOU CALL HIM AND APOLOGIZE YOURSELF ?
HEY, C'MON, I HAVE SOME PRIDE!
© 1999 King Features Syndicate, Inc. World rights reserved
www.kingfeatures.com

THIS IS MY FATHER, THE GREATEST DADDY ANYONE EVER HAD!
HE'S A TOP EXECUTIVE, AND MAKES THE BEST SANDWICHES IN THE UNIVERSE!
AND I'LL BET ONE OF MY CHRISTMAS PRESENTS IS GOING TO BE A RAISE IN ALLOWANCE
I'D SAY THAT'S A PRETTY SAFE BET
© 1995 King Features Syndicate, Inc. World rights reserved.

WHAT ARE YOU DOING, HONEY?
BLOGGING MY PERSONAL LIFE ON-LINE
DADDY! PLEASE! DON'T LOOK! THIS IS PRIVATE!!
© 2006 by King Features Syndicate, Inc. World Rights reserved
www.Blondie.com

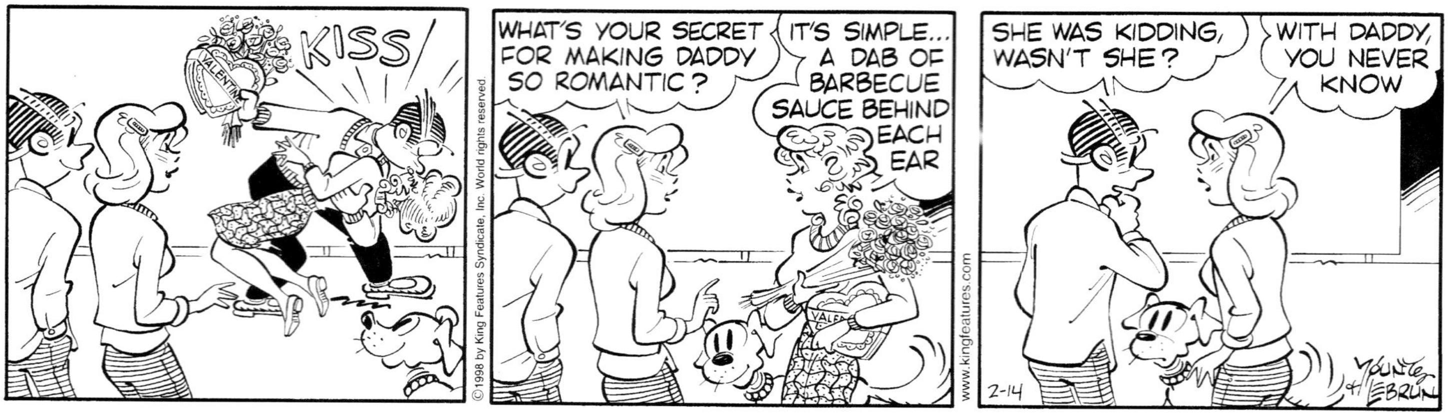

KISS
WHAT'S YOUR SECRET FOR MAKING DADDY SO ROMANTIC?
IT'S SIMPLE... A DAB OF BARBECUE SAUCE BEHIND EACH EAR
SHE WAS KIDDING, WASN'T SHE?
WITH DADDY, YOU NEVER KNOW
© 1998 by King Features Syndicate, Inc. World rights reserved.
www.kingfeatures.com
2-14

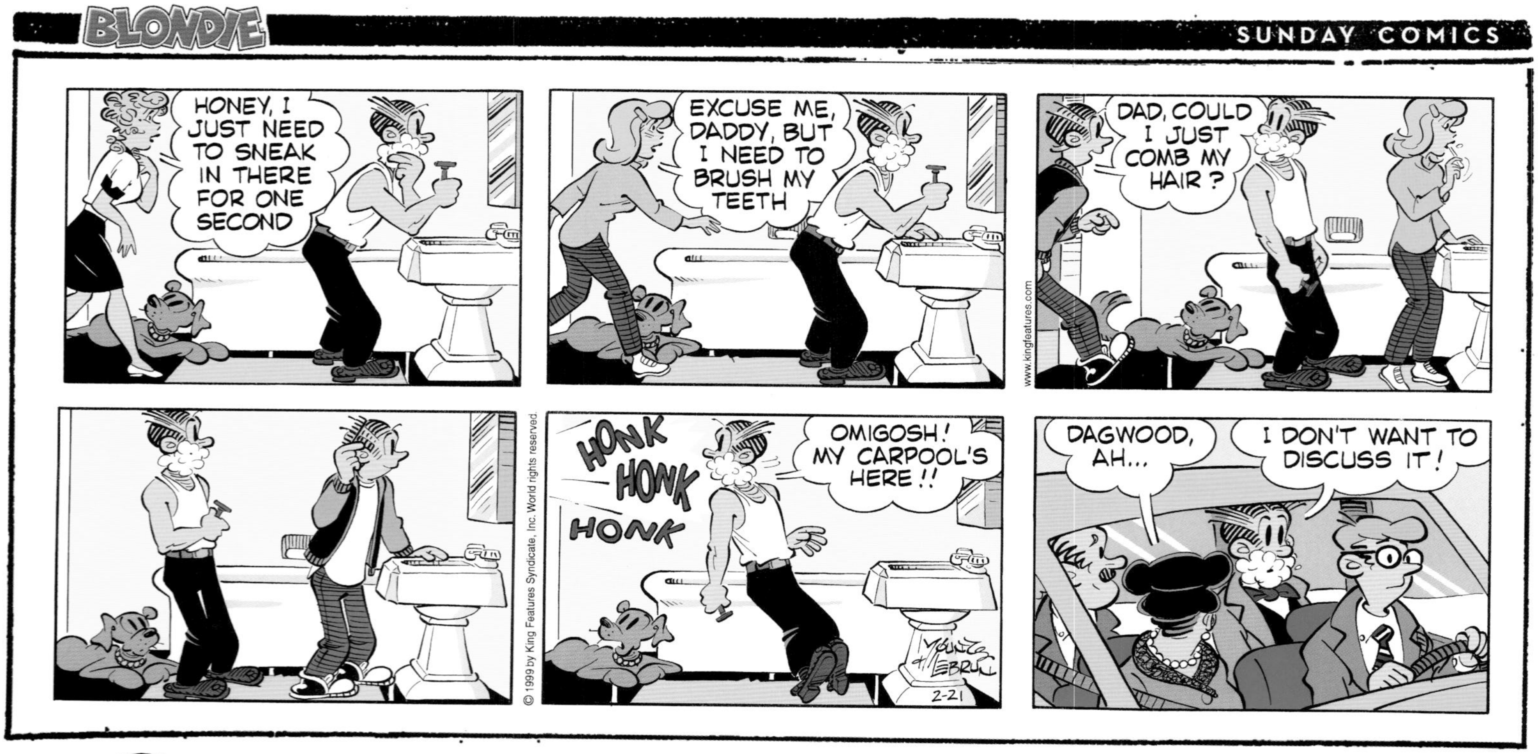

BLONDIE
SUNDAY COMICS
HONEY, I JUST NEED TO SNEAK IN THERE FOR ONE SECOND
EXCUSE ME, DADDY, BUT I NEED TO BRUSH MY TEETH
DAD, COULD I JUST COMB MY HAIR?
www.kingfeatures.com
© 1999 by King Features Syndicate, Inc. World rights reserved.
HONK HONK HONK
OMIGOSH! MY CARPOOL'S HERE!!
2-21
DAGWOOD, AH...
I DON'T WANT TO DISCUSS IT!

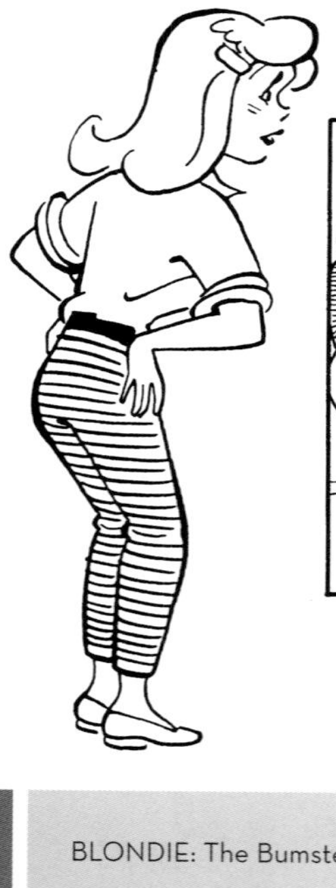

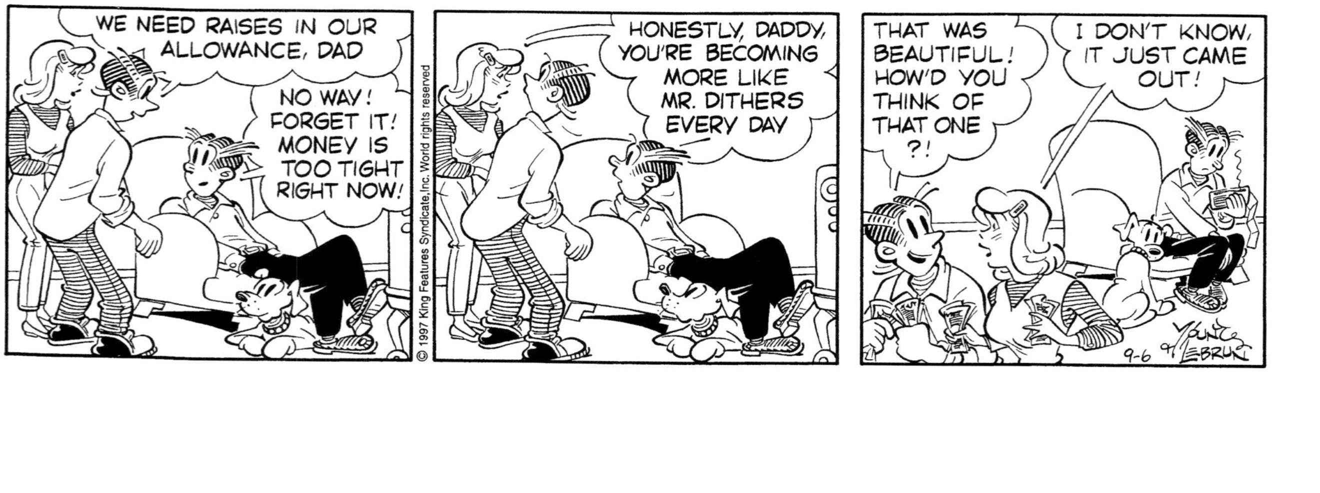

WE NEED RAISES IN OUR ALLOWANCE, DAD
NO WAY! FORGET IT! MONEY IS TOO TIGHT RIGHT NOW!
© 1997 King Features Syndicate, Inc. World rights reserved
HONESTLY, DADDY, YOU'RE BECOMING MORE LIKE MR. DITHERS EVERY DAY
THAT WAS BEAUTIFUL! HOW'D YOU THINK OF THAT ONE ?!
I DON'T KNOW, IT JUST CAME OUT!
9-6

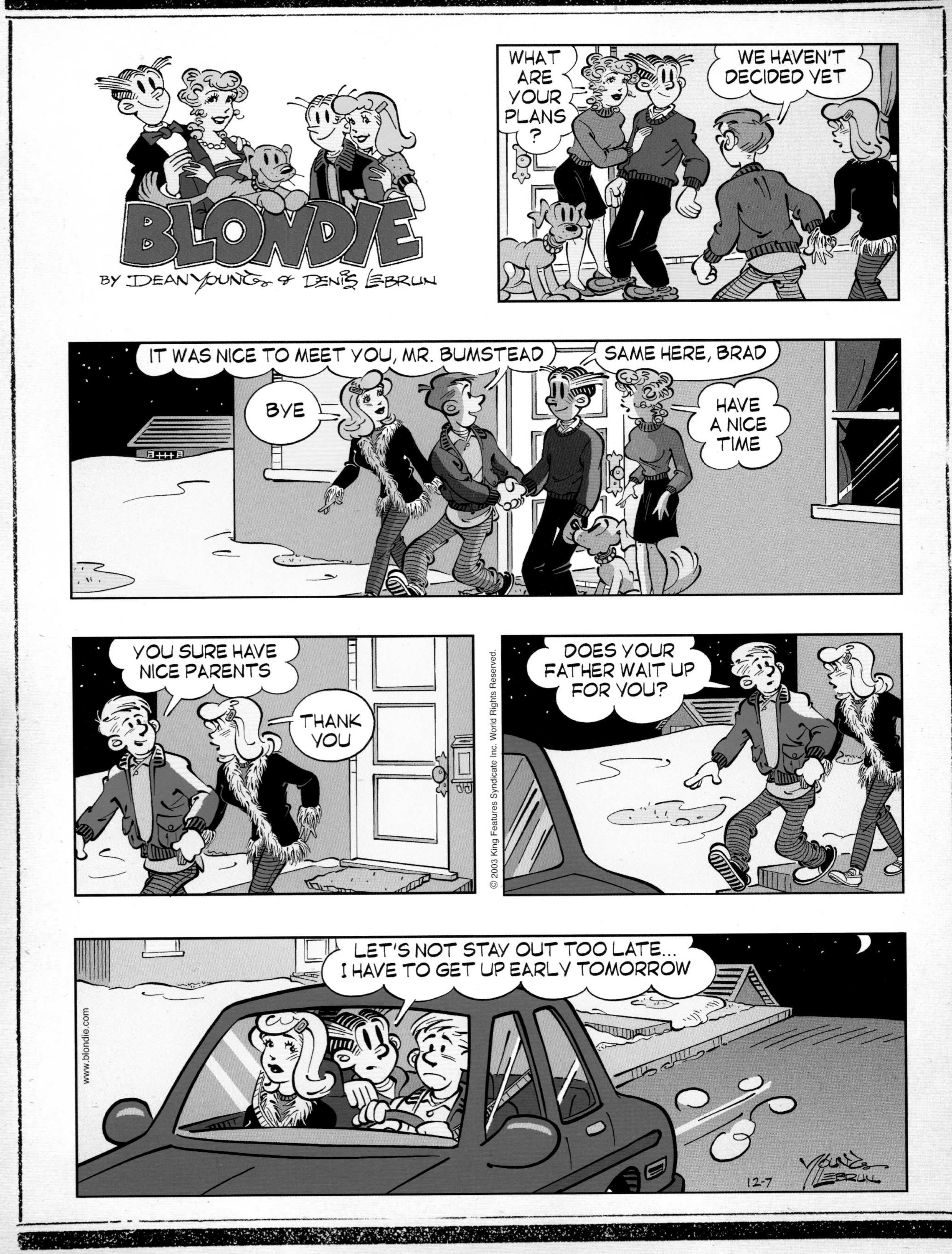
BLONDIE
BY DEAN YOUNG & DENIS LEBRUN
WHAT ARE YOUR PLANS?
WE HAVEN'T DECIDED YET
IT WAS NICE TO MEET YOU, MR. BUMSTEAD
SAME HERE, BRAD
BYE
HAVE A NICE TIME
YOU SURE HAVE NICE PARENTS
THANK YOU
© 2003 King Features Syndicate Inc. World Rights Reserved.
DOES YOUR FATHER WAIT UP FOR YOU?
LET'S NOT STAY OUT TOO LATE... I HAVE TO GET UP EARLY TOMORROW
www.blondie.com
YOUNG LEBRUN
12-7

DAISY

A mutt, "Heinz 57 variety"—that's what Dean Young calls Daisy, the Bumsteads' loyal dog. Rescued from a pound in the early days of the strip, Daisy, with her bright collar, saucer eyes, and oddly blue-gray fur (she would have to be a mutt with that coloring), has remained a comedic mainstay for nearly three-quarters of a century—or almost 525 dog years. Woof!

The family dog even had a family of her own—she gave birth to a litter of five pups shortly after baby Cookie arrived in the pages of Blondie. Named after a famous Depression-era set of Canadian quintuplets, the Dionne quints, the five pups were a lot of fun. But they were also a handful—not to mention a mouthful to feed—and when newspaper comics shrunk, Dean Young and then-artist Jim Raymond found that configuring six animals in one panel was too much of a zoo. In the 1970s, Daisy's offspring were phased out, adopted by the Bumsteads' neighbors.

Daisy, though, is a constant presence, as a much-loved pet should be. She often appears at the foot of Blondie or Dagwood's chair, or sprawled in front of the couch, or searching for scraps in the kitchen. In fact, her affinity for two of her owner's most beloved hobbies—sleeping and eating—and her predilection for getting into trouble (watch out, neighborhood kitties!) has made her not only Dagwood's best friend but also his canine alter ego.

This four-legged fur ball can sometimes have more sense than the man of the house. In between her many naps and snacks, Daisy can often be found in the last panel of the strip, reacting to Dagwood's boundless foibles with a floppy-eared, quizzical look or a deadpan expression. Her doggy double-takes and I-can't-believe-he's-at-it-again pose (paws over her eyes, with just enough room for peeking) have made her one famously animated mutt.

In fact, as a shrewd witness to what goes on in the Bumstead household, Daisy has become a stand-in for *Blondie's* numerous faithful fans, many of whom may also be covering their eyes and thinking I-can't-believe-he's-at-it-again. Luckily, Daisy never spoils the gag. Though she does sometimes chew the scenery.

IT SAYS PRESIDENT BUSH IS PUTTING TOGETHER HIS NEW BUDGET PROPOSAL FOR IRAQ
IT SAYS HE'S EXPECTING A LOT OF BIPARTISAN HAGGLING AND THAT PASSAGE WILL BE PROBLEMATIC WITHOUT MASSIVE REVISIONS
I WISH DOGS COULD READ, SO YOU DIDN'T HAVE TO EXPLAIN EVERYTHING TO THEM
© 2006 by King Features Syndicate, Inc. World Rights reserved
2-20
www.Blondie.com

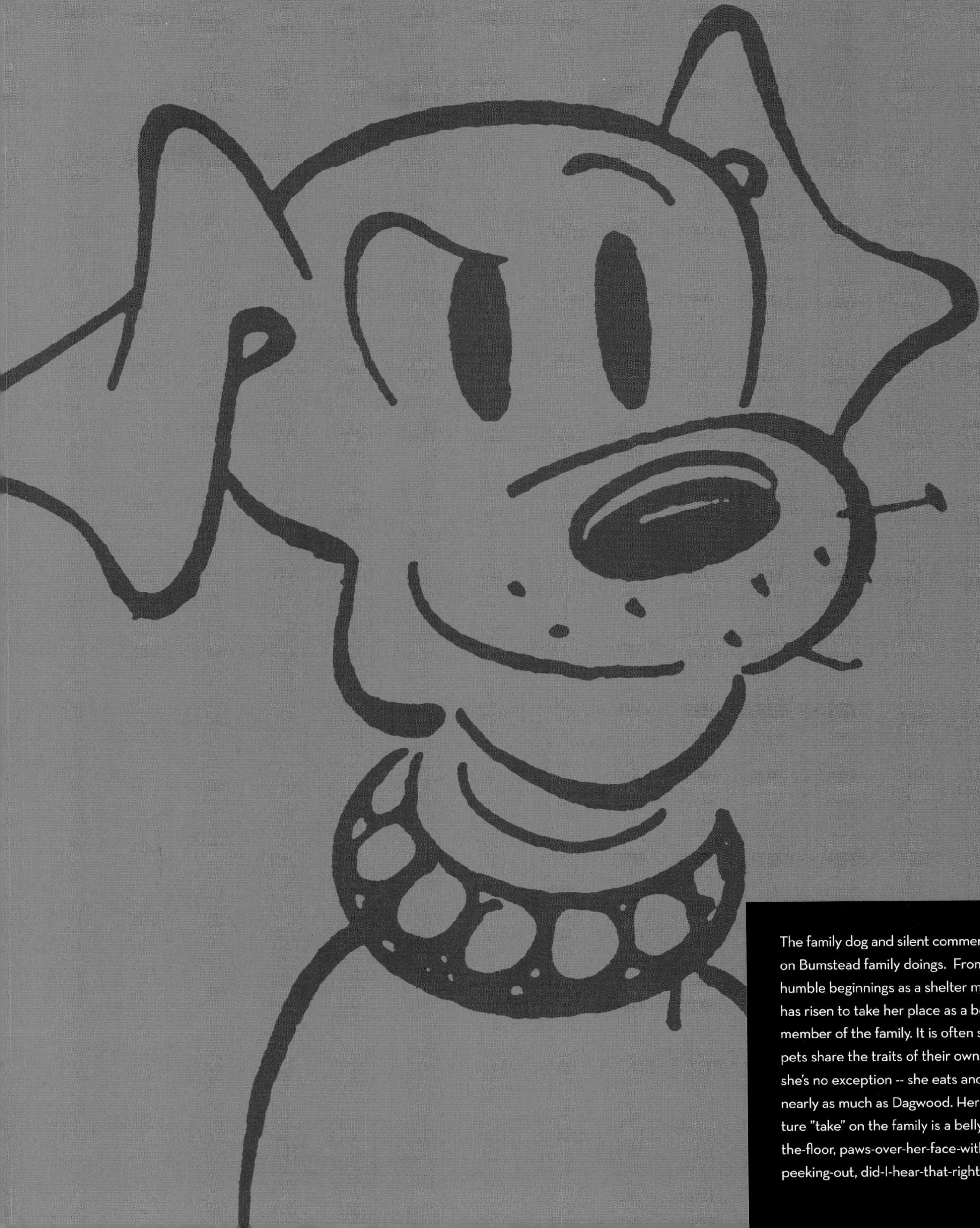

The family dog and silent commentator on Bumstead family doings. From humble beginnings as a shelter mutt, she has risen to take her place as a beloved member of the family. It is often said that pets share the traits of their owners and she's no exception -- she eats and sleeps nearly as much as Dagwood. Her signature "take" on the family is a belly-to-the-floor, paws-over-her-face-with-eyes-peeking-out, did-I-hear-that-right pose.

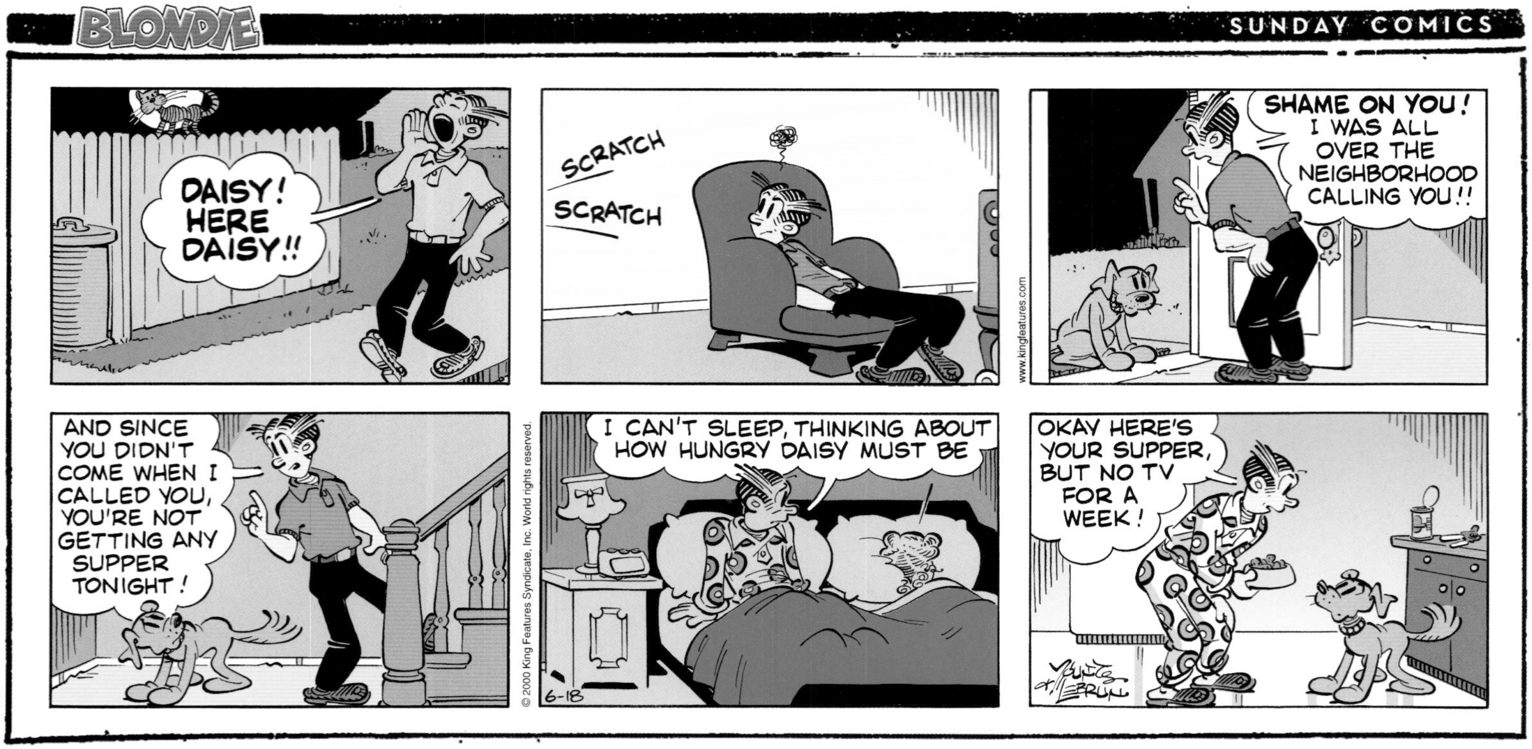

BLONDIE
SUNDAY COMICS
DAISY! HERE DAISY!!
SCRATCH
SCRATCH
SHAME ON YOU! I WAS ALL OVER THE NEIGHBORHOOD CALLING YOU!!
www.kingfeatures.com
AND SINCE YOU DIDN'T COME WHEN I CALLED YOU, YOU'RE NOT GETTING ANY SUPPER TONIGHT!
© 2000 King Features Syndicate, Inc. World rights reserved.
6-18
I CAN'T SLEEP, THINKING ABOUT HOW HUNGRY DAISY MUST BE
OKAY HERE'S YOUR SUPPER, BUT NO TV FOR A WEEK!
YOUNG & LEBRUN

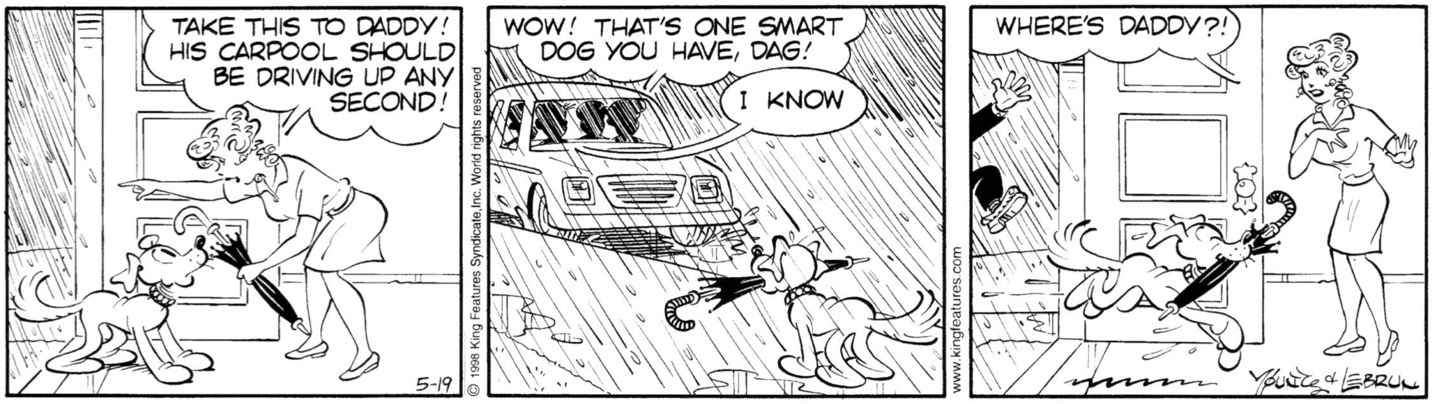

TAKE THIS TO DADDY! HIS CARPOOL SHOULD BE DRIVING UP ANY SECOND!
5-19
© 1998 King Features Syndicate, Inc. World rights reserved
WOW! THAT'S ONE SMART DOG YOU HAVE, DAG!
I KNOW
www.kingfeatures.com
WHERE'S DADDY?!
YOUNG & LEBRUN

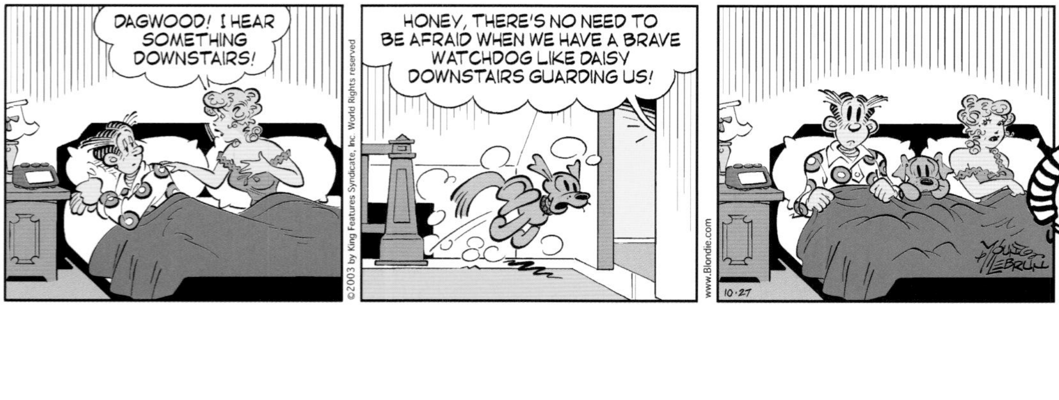

DAGWOOD! I HEAR SOMETHING DOWNSTAIRS!
©2003 by King Features Syndicate, Inc. World Rights reserved
HONEY, THERE'S NO NEED TO BE AFRAID WHEN WE HAVE A BRAVE WATCHDOG LIKE DAISY DOWNSTAIRS GUARDING US!
www.Blondie.com
10-27
YOUNG & LEBRUN

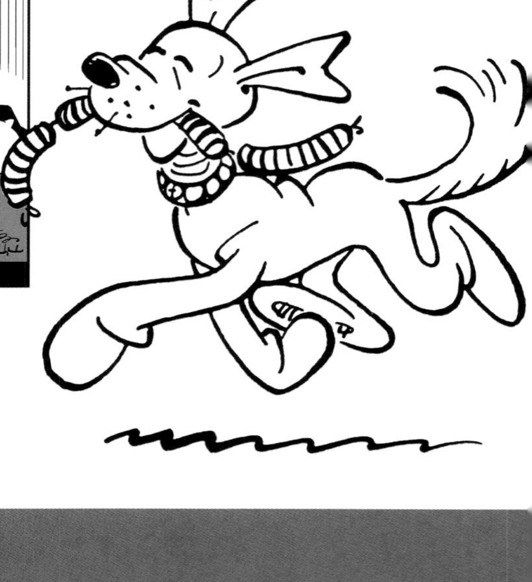

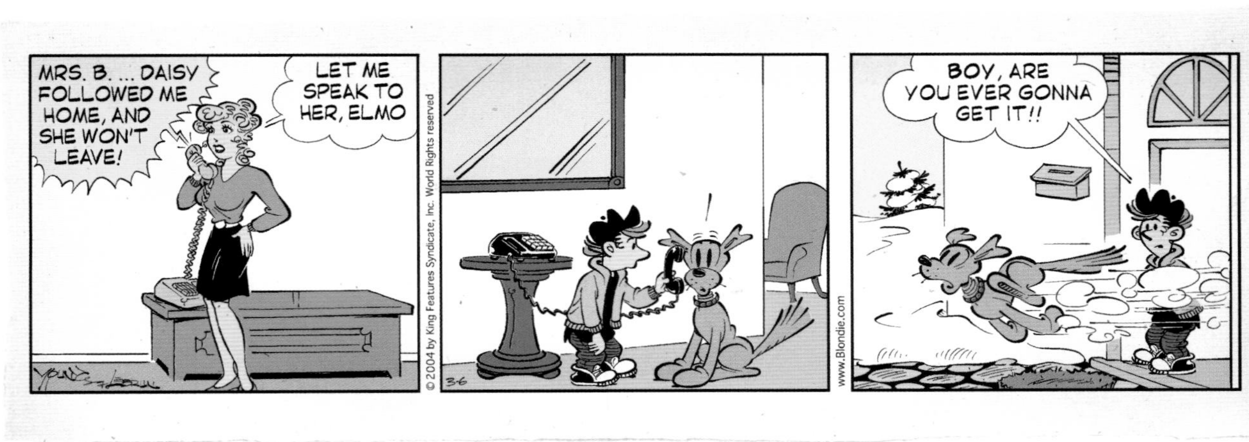
MRS. B. ... DAISY FOLLOWED ME HOME, AND SHE WON'T LEAVE!
LET ME SPEAK TO HER, ELMO
© 2004 by King Features Syndicate, Inc. World Rights reserved
3-6
www.Blondie.com
BOY, ARE YOU EVER GONNA GET IT!!

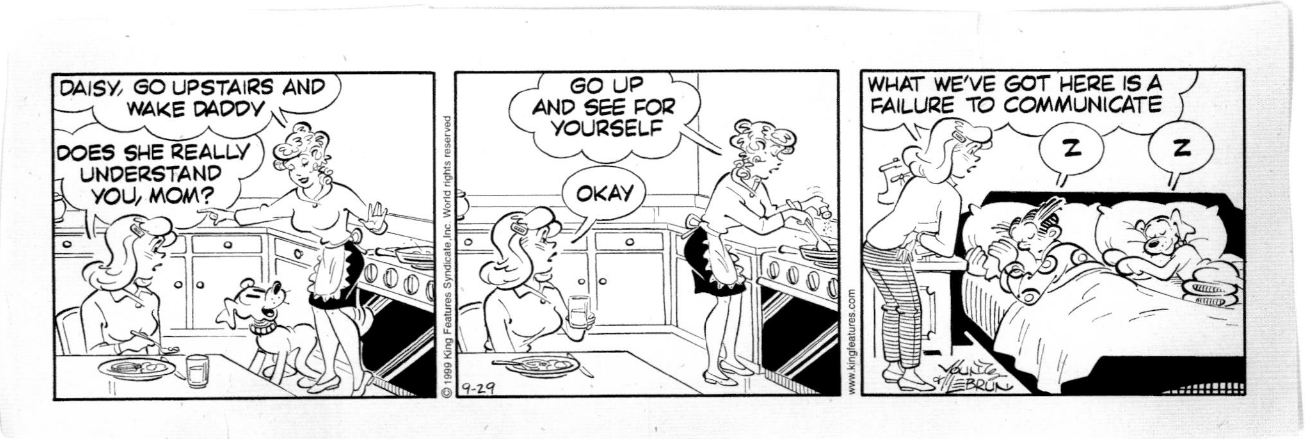
DAISY, GO UPSTAIRS AND WAKE DADDY
DOES SHE REALLY UNDERSTAND YOU, MOM?
© 1999 King Features Syndicate, Inc. World rights reserved
9-29
GO UP AND SEE FOR YOURSELF
OKAY
www.kingfeatures.com
WHAT WE'VE GOT HERE IS A FAILURE TO COMMUNICATE
Z
Z

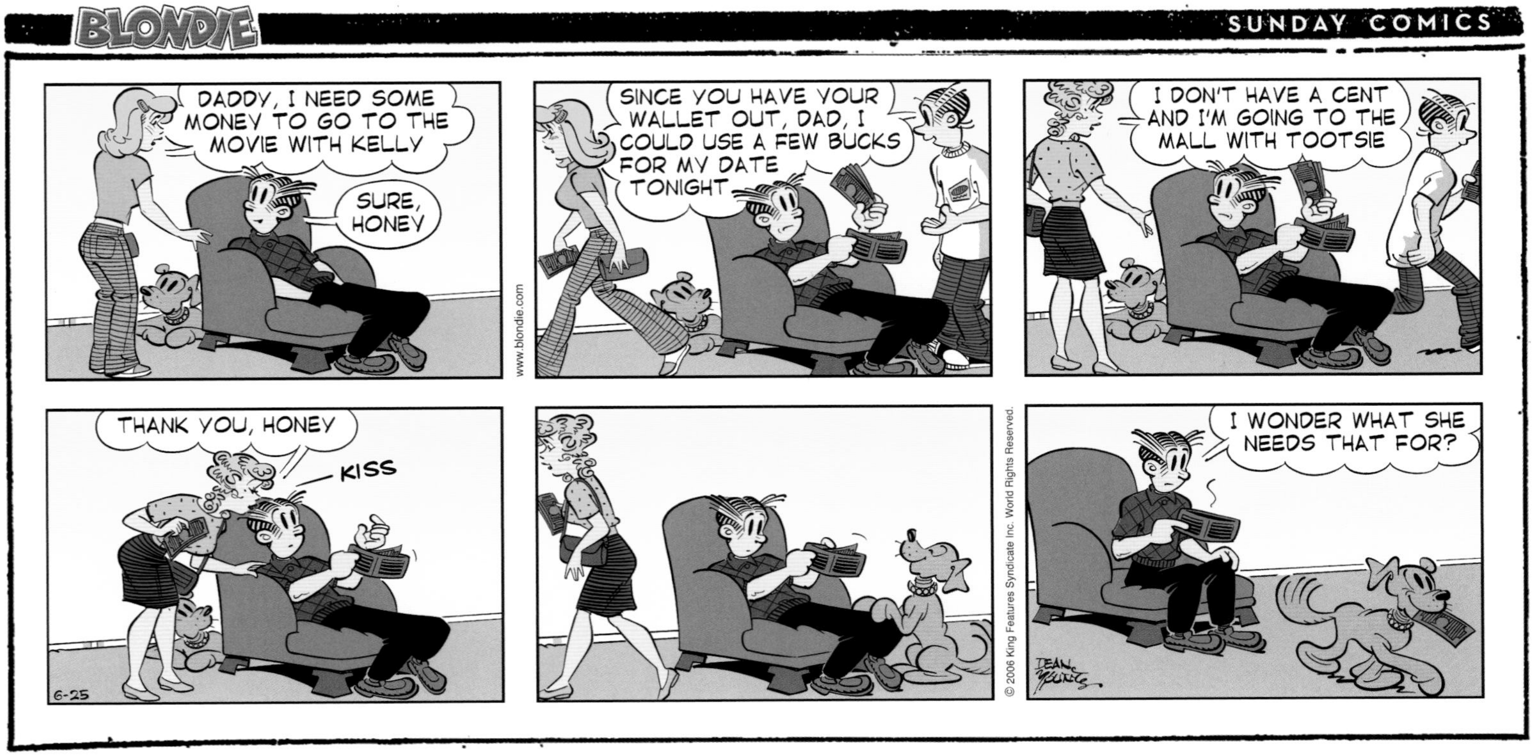
BLONDIE
SUNDAY COMICS
DADDY, I NEED SOME MONEY TO GO TO THE MOVIE WITH KELLY
SURE, HONEY
www.blondie.com
SINCE YOU HAVE YOUR WALLET OUT, DAD, I COULD USE A FEW BUCKS FOR MY DATE TONIGHT
I DON'T HAVE A CENT AND I'M GOING TO THE MALL WITH TOOTSIE
THANK YOU, HONEY
KISS
6-25
© 2006 King Features Syndicate Inc. World Rights Reserved.
I WONDER WHAT SHE NEEDS THAT FOR?

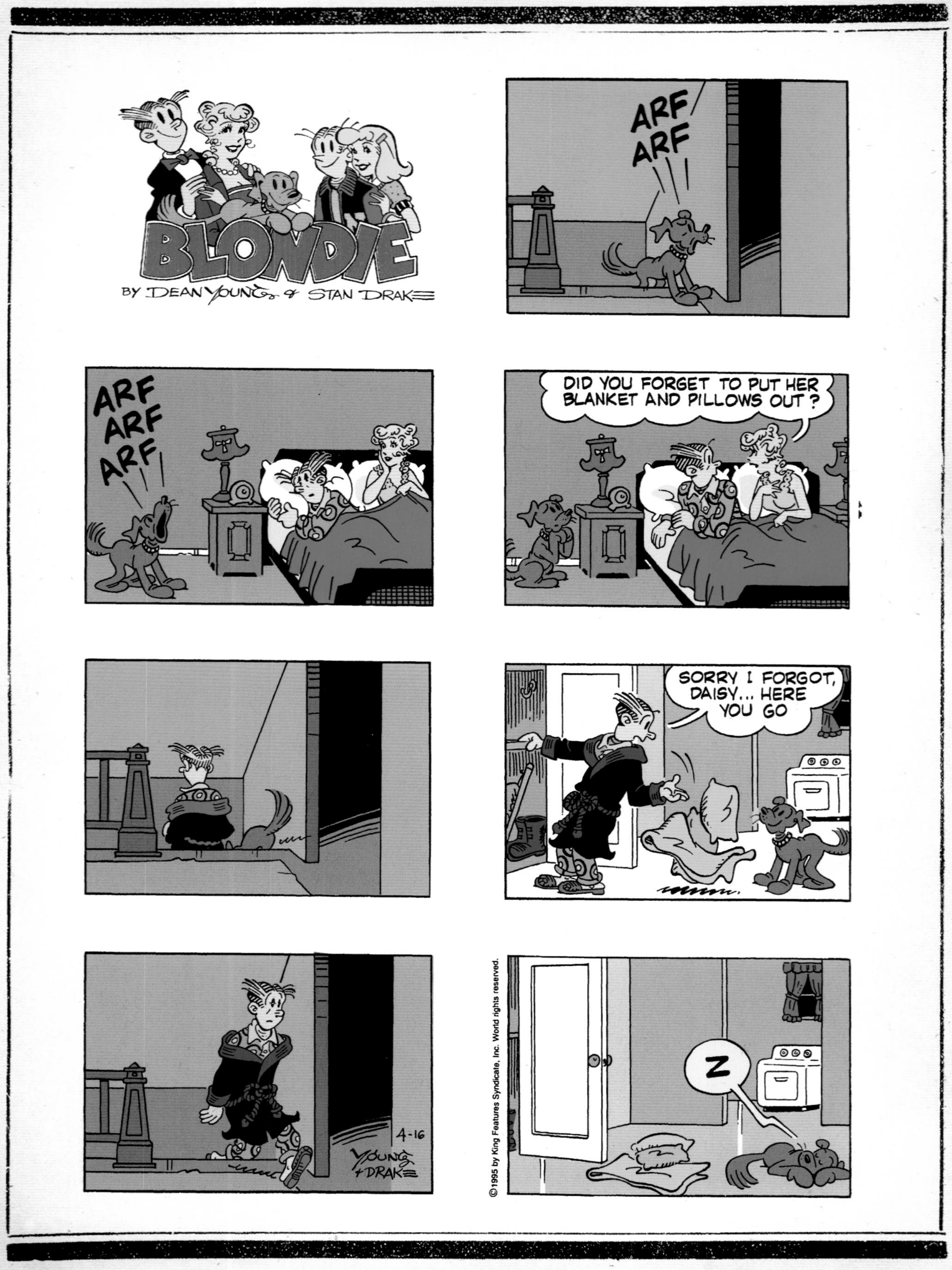
BLONDIE
BY DEAN YOUNG & STAN DRAKE
ARF ARF
ARF ARF ARF
DID YOU FORGET TO PUT HER BLANKET AND PILLOWS OUT?
SORRY I FORGOT, DAISY... HERE YOU GO
4-16
YOUNG & DRAKE
Z

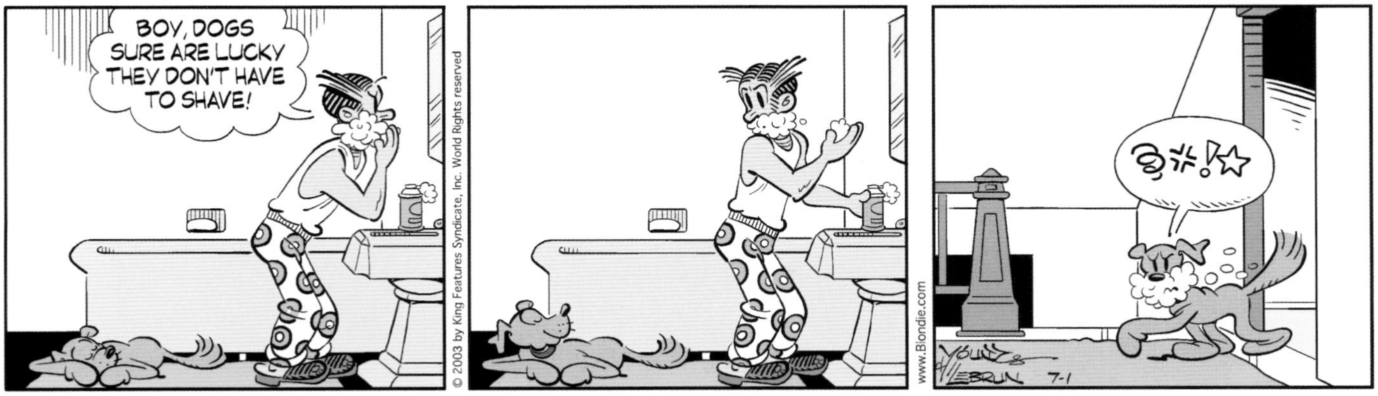
BOY, DOGS SURE ARE LUCKY THEY DON'T HAVE TO SHAVE!
© 2003 by King Features Syndicate, Inc. World Rights reserved
www.Blondie.com
YOUNG & LEBRUN 7-1

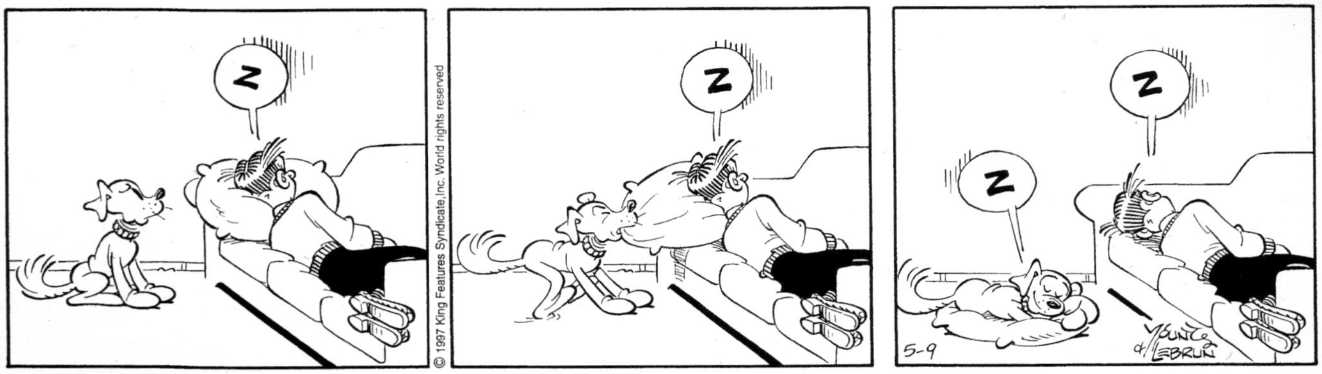
Z
Z
Z
Z
© 1997 King Features Syndicate,Inc. World rights reserved
5-9
YOUNG & LEBRUN

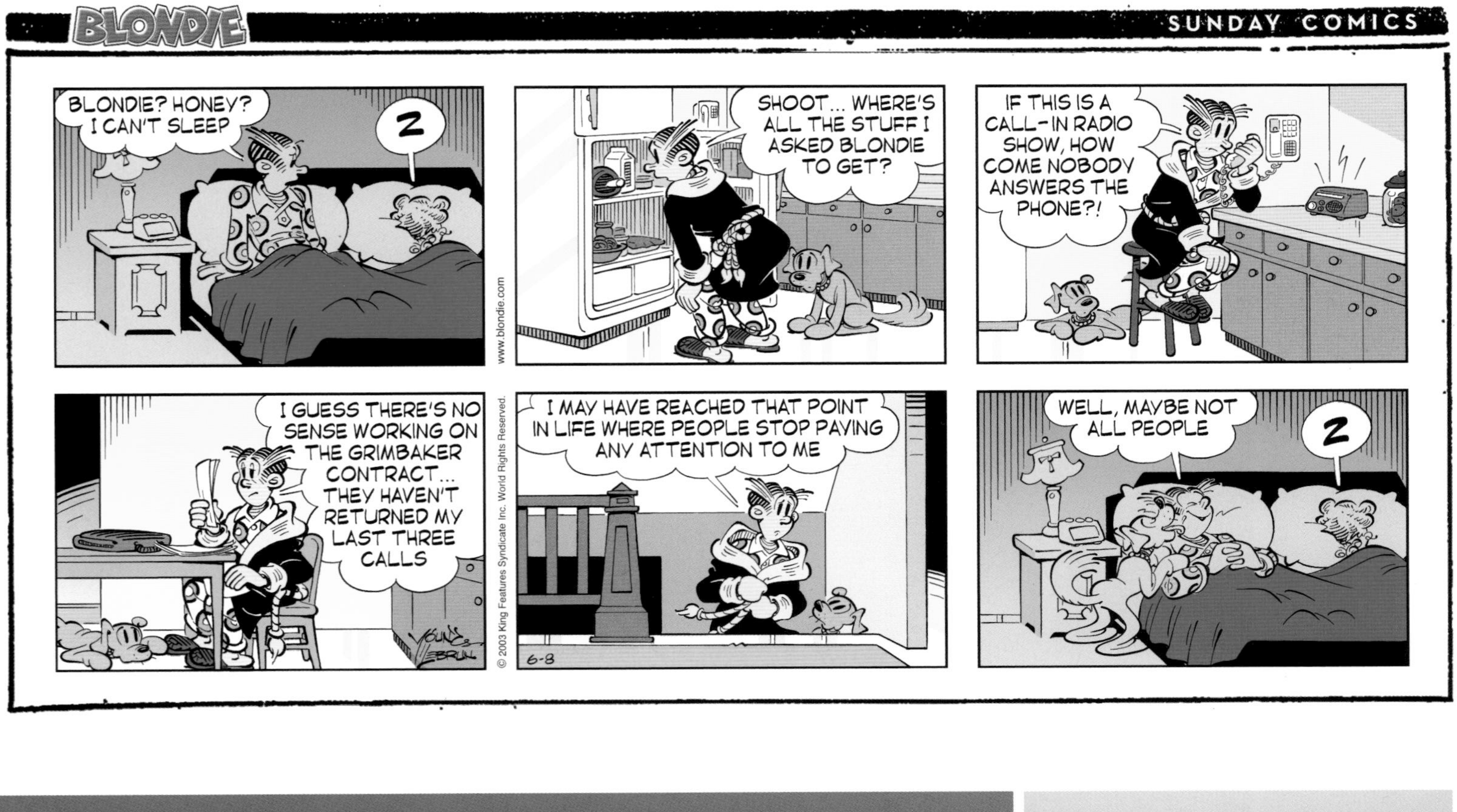
BLONDIE
SUNDAY COMICS
BLONDIE? HONEY? I CAN'T SLEEP
Z
SHOOT... WHERE'S ALL THE STUFF I ASKED BLONDIE TO GET?
IF THIS IS A CALL-IN RADIO SHOW, HOW COME NOBODY ANSWERS THE PHONE?!
www.blondie.com
I GUESS THERE'S NO SENSE WORKING ON THE GRIMBAKER CONTRACT... THEY HAVEN'T RETURNED MY LAST THREE CALLS
YOUNG LEBRUN
© 2003 King Features Syndicate Inc. World Rights Reserved.
I MAY HAVE REACHED THAT POINT IN LIFE WHERE PEOPLE STOP PAYING ANY ATTENTION TO ME
6-8
WELL, MAYBE NOT ALL PEOPLE
Z

MR. DITHERS

In the annals of terrible bosses, there is Genghis Khan—and there is Mr. Julius C. Dithers. A tyrant with a temper to rival a roomful of anger management drop-outs, Dithers, founder of the J. C. Dithers Construction Company (whose clients he poached from his former boss—his father-in-law), has been in business for nearly three-quarters of a century. And he's been fighting with Dagwood for most of them. *Blondie* cast members make only infrequent use of thought balloons, but if Dithers had one, it would look like this:

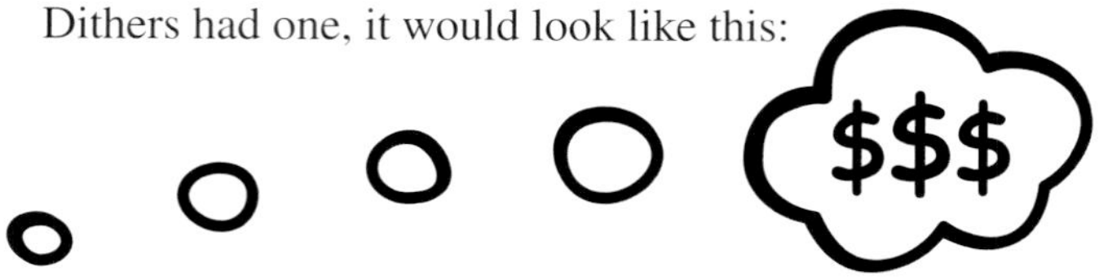
$$$

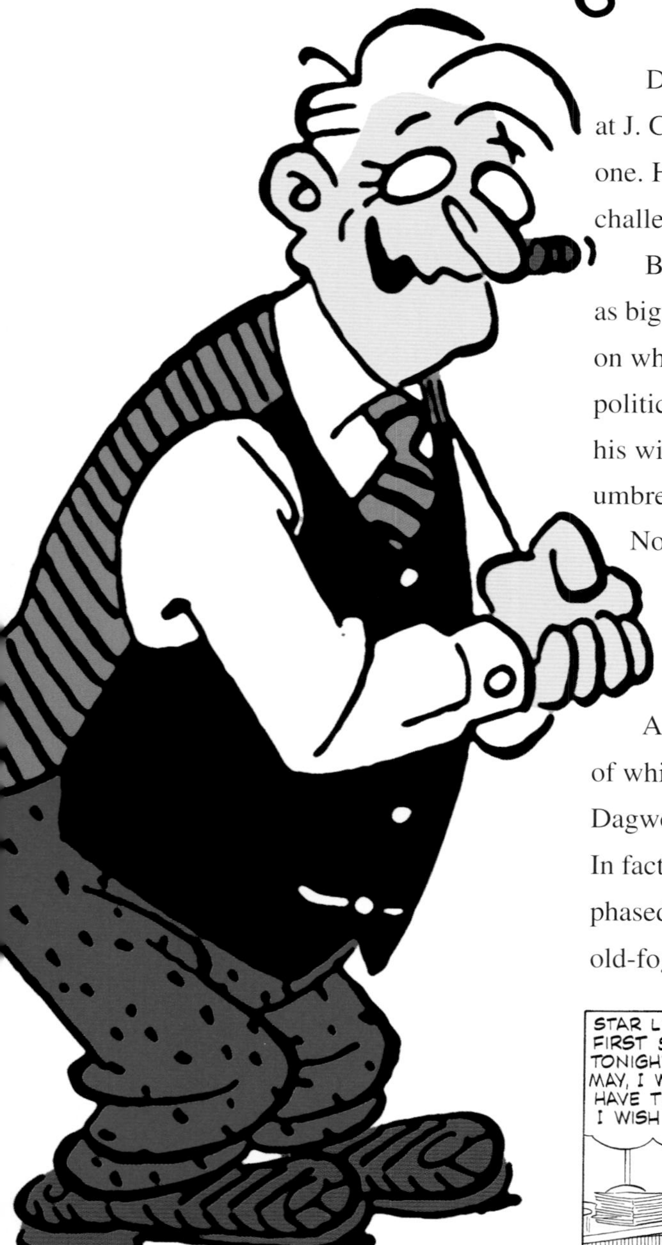

Driven by greed and a Draconian work ethic (there are no "personal days" at J. C. Dithers Co.), Mr. Dithers runs his office like a dictatorship—a cheap one. His stinginess is as legendary as his tantrums, and his insensitivity would challenge even the most politically correct professional.

But he's not all bad. As Dithers would be the first to tell you, he's got a heart as big as all outdoors. He did outfit his office with Kleenex, for the many occasions on which he makes his employees cry, so he's not totally devoid of empathy (or political correctness). And at home he's as meek as a mouse—largely thanks to his wife, Cora Dithers. In the early days of the strip, she wielded her large, pointy umbrella the way a lion tamer would a whip, using it to keep her husband in line. Nowadays she's fond of the verbal approach, chastising and cutting with a quick turn of phrase. And when Dithers can't retaliate on the home front, he takes it out on his employees. In the office, at least, he's master of his domain.

A short, stout, mustachioed gentleman with a generous gut and a shock of white hair, Dithers bears a suspicious resemblance to J. Bolling Bumstead, Dagwood's father. Both are angry industrialists who think little of their charges. In fact, Dithers appeared in the strip at about the same time that J. Bolling was phased out, which is no coincidence. "As a comic character, the irascible, rich, old-fogy patriarch is almost unparalleled," says Dean Young.

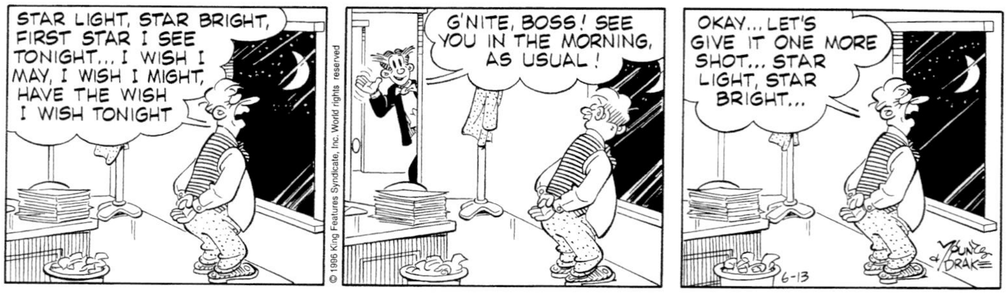
STAR LIGHT, STAR BRIGHT, FIRST STAR I SEE TONIGHT... I WISH I MAY, I WISH I MIGHT, HAVE THE WISH I WISH TONIGHT
G'NITE, BOSS! SEE YOU IN THE MORNING, AS USUAL!
OKAY... LET'S GIVE IT ONE MORE SHOT... STAR LIGHT, STAR BRIGHT...
6-13
YOUNG & DRAKE

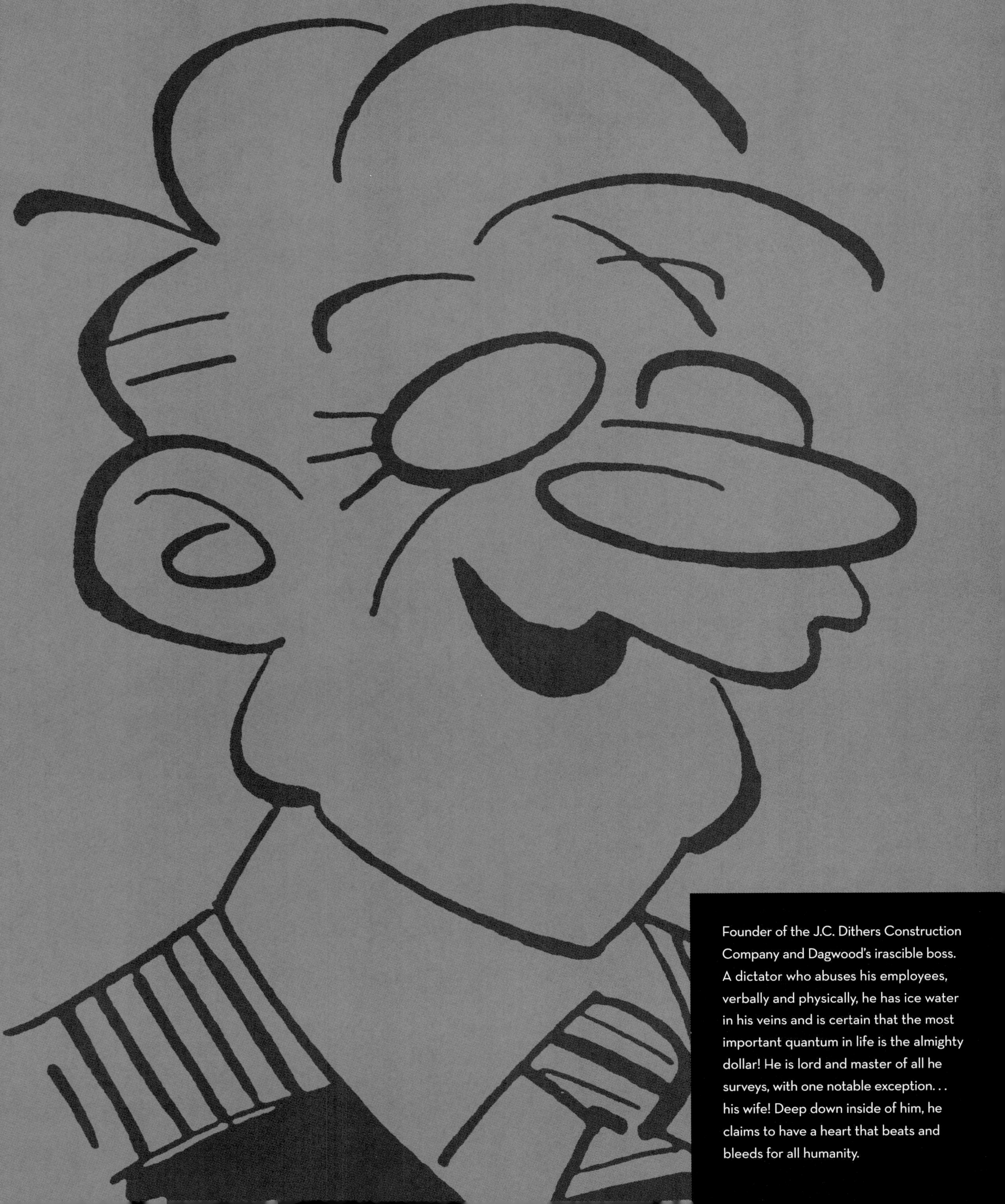

Founder of the J.C. Dithers Construction Company and Dagwood's irascible boss. A dictator who abuses his employees, verbally and physically, he has ice water in his veins and is certain that the most important quantum in life is the almighty dollar! He is lord and master of all he surveys, with one notable exception. . . his wife! Deep down inside of him, he claims to have a heart that beats and bleeds for all humanity.

"I think my dad realized that the father was really funny, and he wanted that character back in the strip, so he morphed him into Dithers," Young recalled. And for a cartoonist, embodying the boss from hell is oddly gratifying.

Mr. Dithers would definitely make the Hall of Fame for bad bosses.

"I live for that vitriol, because it goes to the comedic level where everything is heightened to the nth degree," Young said ruefully. "Dithers makes that job easy because he's already up there."

The comedy in this case is not exaggerated. Everyone has had a terrible boss—an inflexible micromanager whose greatest joy comes from saying no—a demanding autocrat with a weakness for pinching pennies, a superior who acts it. Mr. Dithers would definitely make the Hall of Fame for bad bosses. When it comes to mismanagement, humor is universal and a character like Dithers is recognizable the world over. Take that, Mr. Khan!

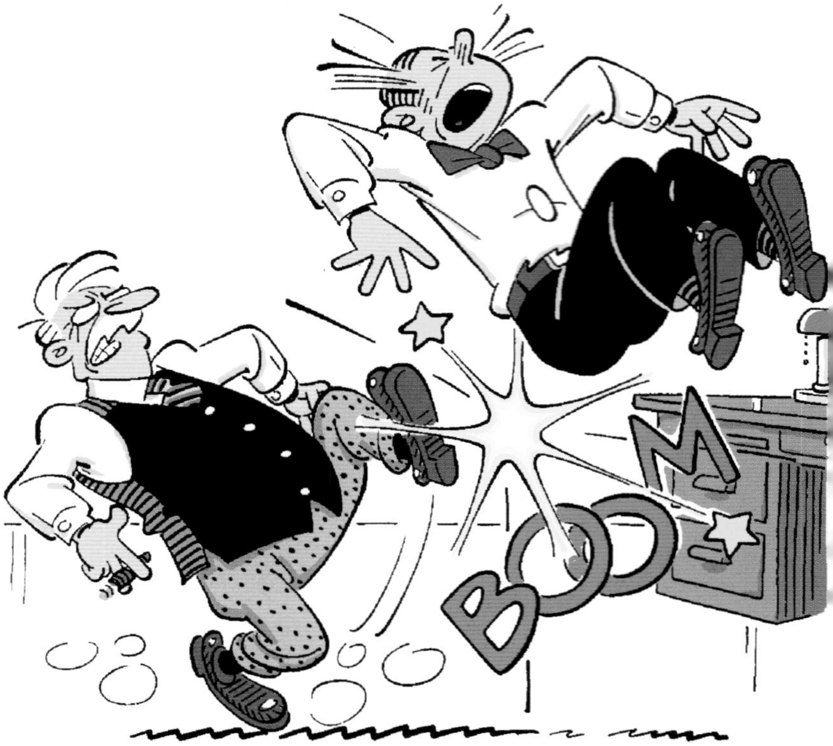
BOOM

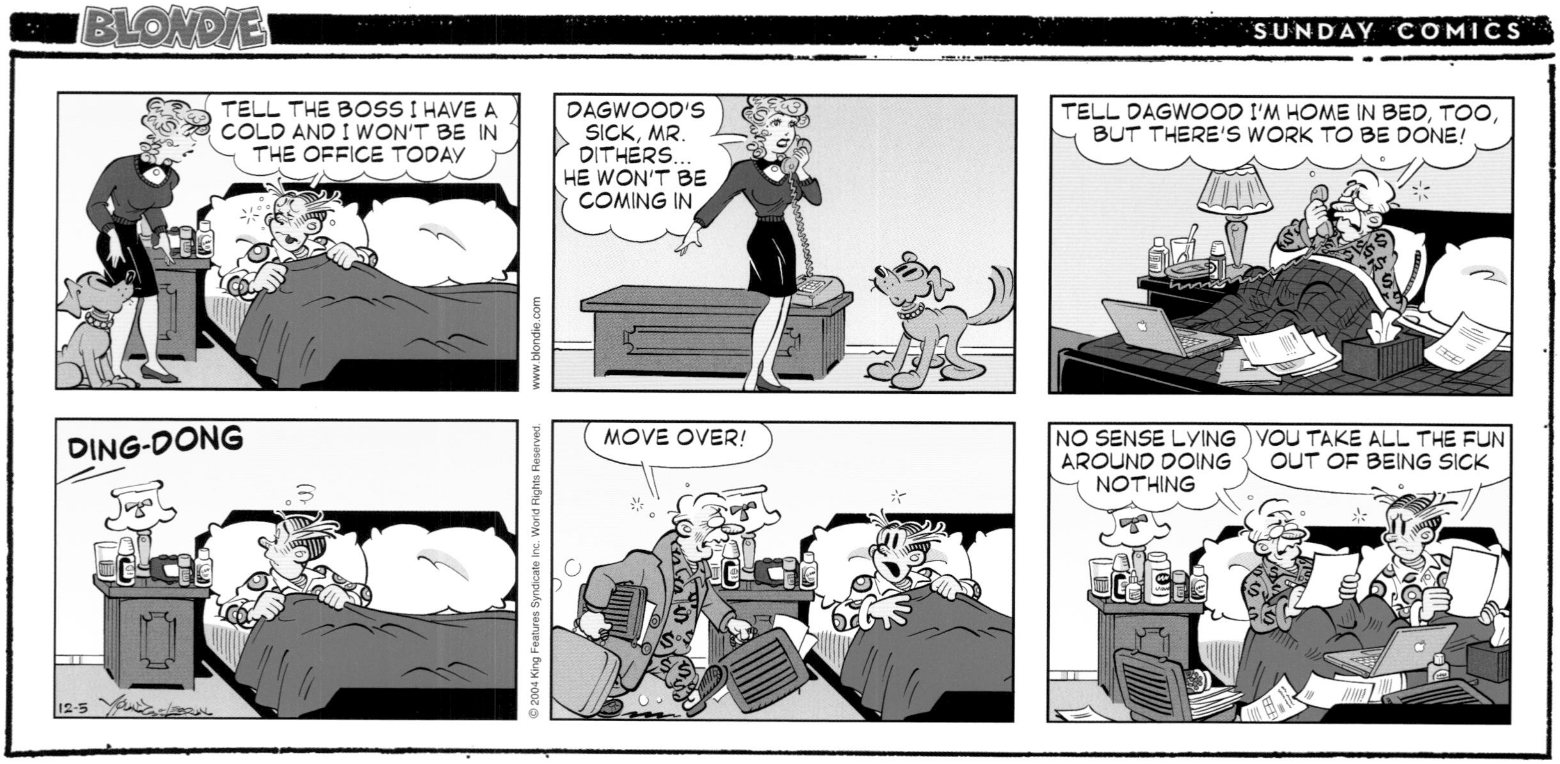
BLONDIE
SUNDAY COMICS
TELL THE BOSS I HAVE A COLD AND I WON'T BE IN THE OFFICE TODAY
DAGWOOD'S SICK, MR. DITHERS... HE WON'T BE COMING IN
TELL DAGWOOD I'M HOME IN BED, TOO, BUT THERE'S WORK TO BE DONE!
DING-DONG
MOVE OVER!
NO SENSE LYING AROUND DOING NOTHING
YOU TAKE ALL THE FUN OUT OF BEING SICK
12-5
www.blondie.com
© 2004 King Features Syndicate Inc. World Rights Reserved.

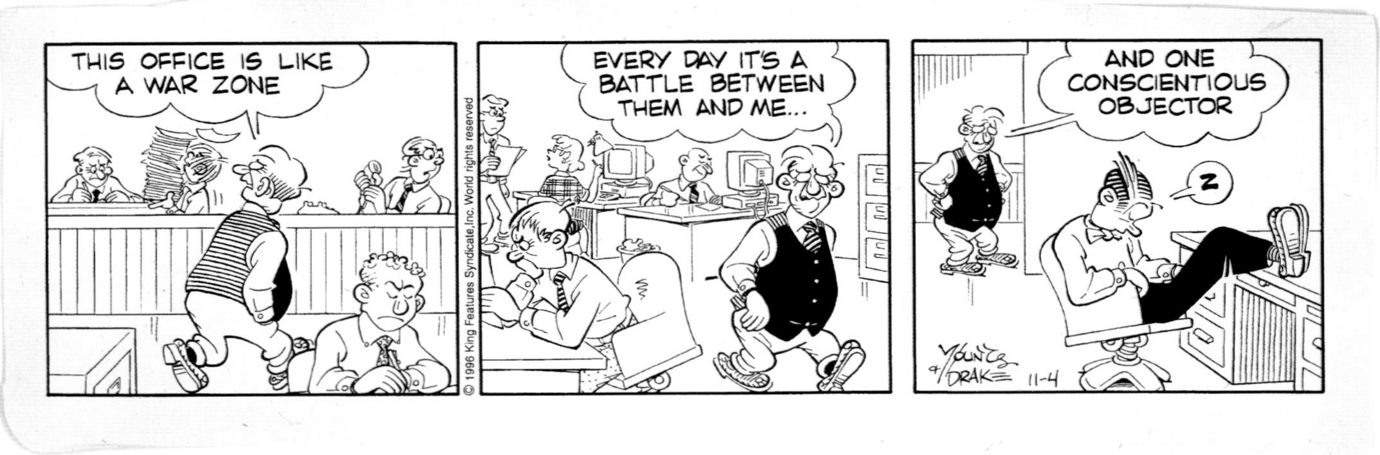
THIS OFFICE IS LIKE A WAR ZONE
© 1996 King Features Syndicate,Inc. World rights reserved
EVERY DAY IT'S A BATTLE BETWEEN THEM AND ME...
AND ONE CONSCIENTIOUS OBJECTOR
Z
11-4

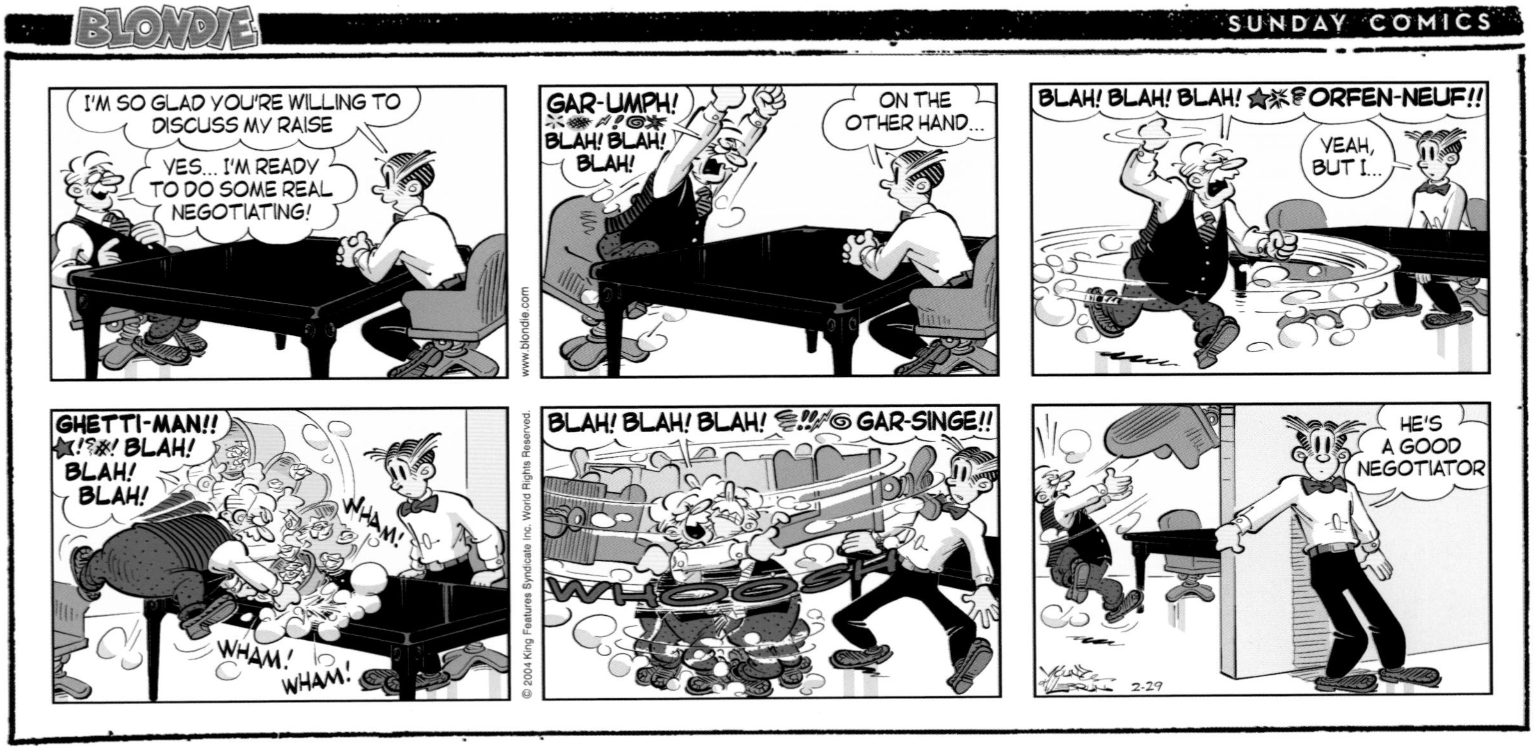
BLONDIE
SUNDAY COMICS
I'M SO GLAD YOU'RE WILLING TO DISCUSS MY RAISE
YES... I'M READY TO DO SOME REAL NEGOTIATING!
www.blondie.com
GAR-UMPH! BLAH! BLAH! BLAH!
ON THE OTHER HAND...
BLAH! BLAH! BLAH! ORFEN-NEUF!!
YEAH, BUT I...
GHETTI-MAN!! BLAH! BLAH! BLAH!
WHAM!
WHAM!
WHAM!
© 2004 King Features Syndicate Inc. World Rights Reserved.
BLAH! BLAH! BLAH! GAR-SINGE!!
WHOOSH
HE'S A GOOD NEGOTIATOR
2-29

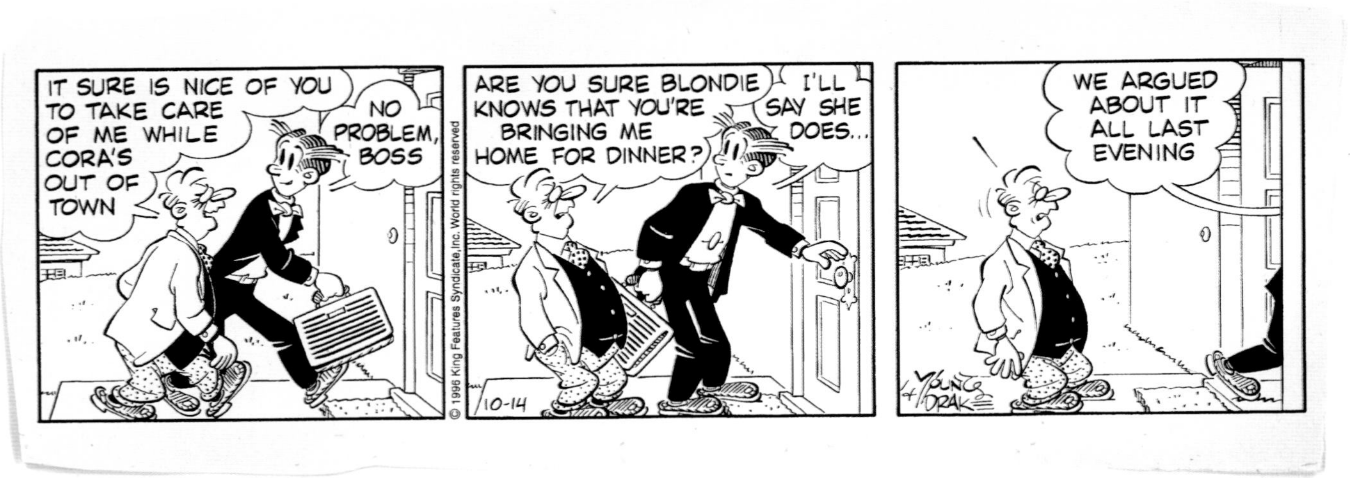
IT SURE IS NICE OF YOU TO TAKE CARE OF ME WHILE CORA'S OUT OF TOWN
NO PROBLEM, BOSS
© 1996 King Features Syndicate,Inc. World rights reserved
ARE YOU SURE BLONDIE KNOWS THAT YOU'RE BRINGING ME HOME FOR DINNER?
I'LL SAY SHE DOES...
10-14
WE ARGUED ABOUT IT ALL LAST EVENING

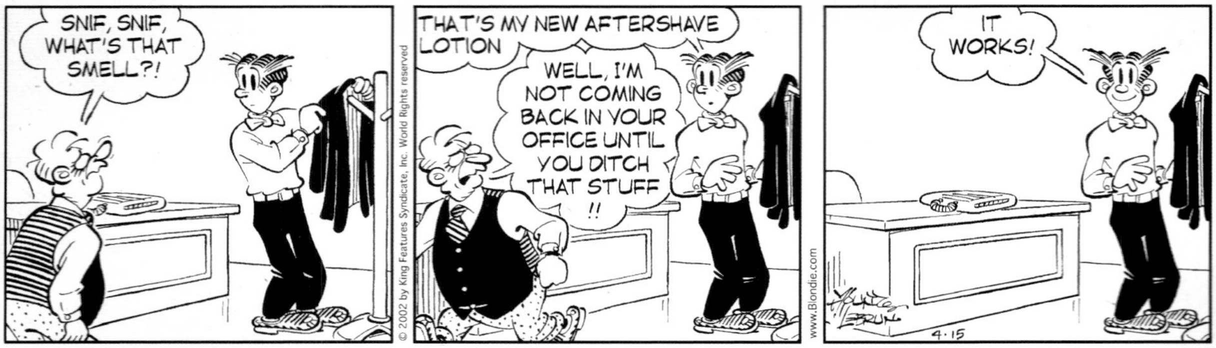
SNIF, SNIF, WHAT'S THAT SMELL?!
© 2002 by King Features Syndicate, Inc. World Rights reserved
THAT'S MY NEW AFTERSHAVE LOTION
WELL, I'M NOT COMING BACK IN YOUR OFFICE UNTIL YOU DITCH THAT STUFF!!
www.Blondie.com
IT WORKS!
4·15

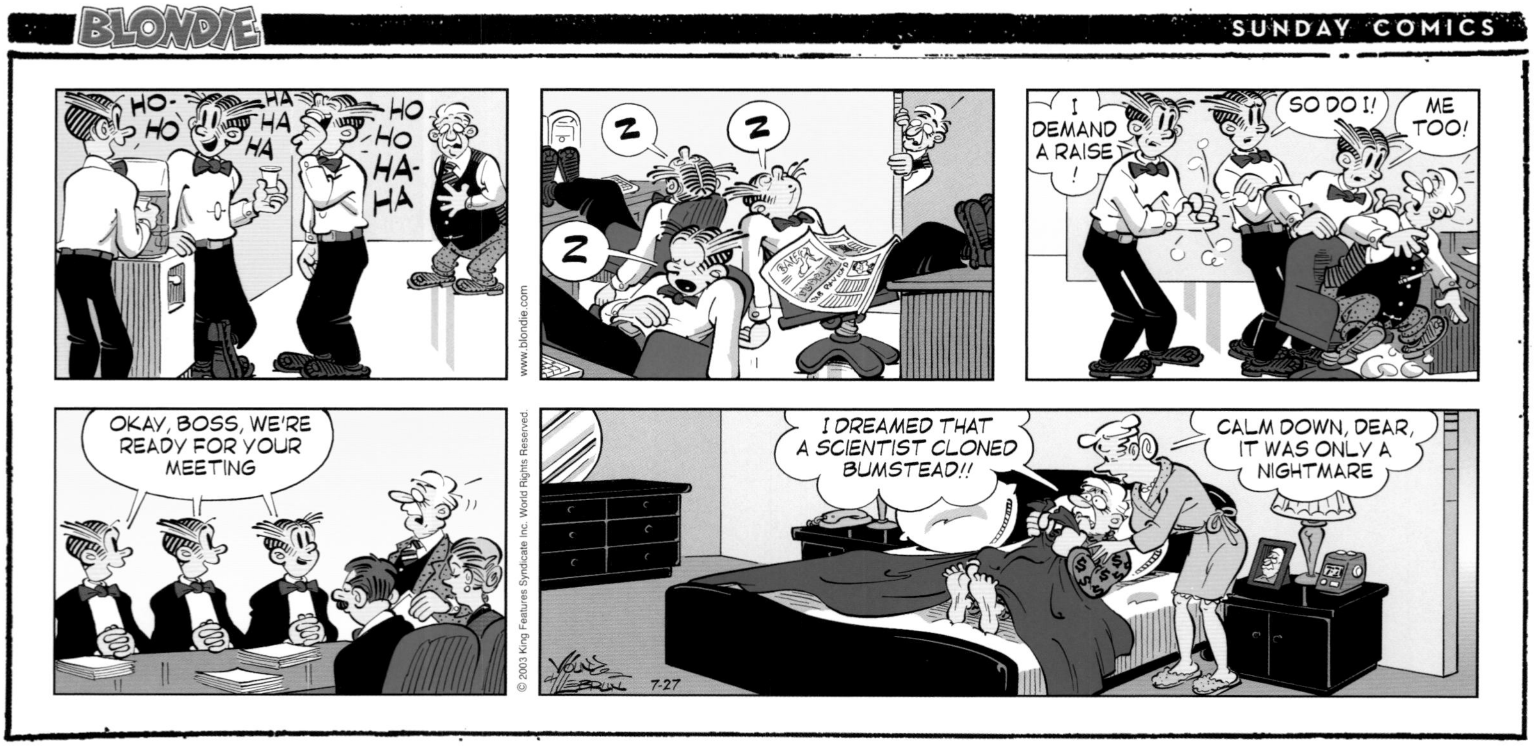
BLONDIE
SUNDAY COMICS
HO-HO
HA HA HA
HO HO HA-HA
www.blondie.com
Z
Z
Z
I DEMAND A RAISE!
SO DO I!
ME TOO!
OKAY, BOSS, WE'RE READY FOR YOUR MEETING
© 2003 King Features Syndicate Inc. World Rights Reserved.
7-27
I DREAMED THAT A SCIENTIST CLONED BUMSTEAD!!
CALM DOWN, DEAR, IT WAS ONLY A NIGHTMARE

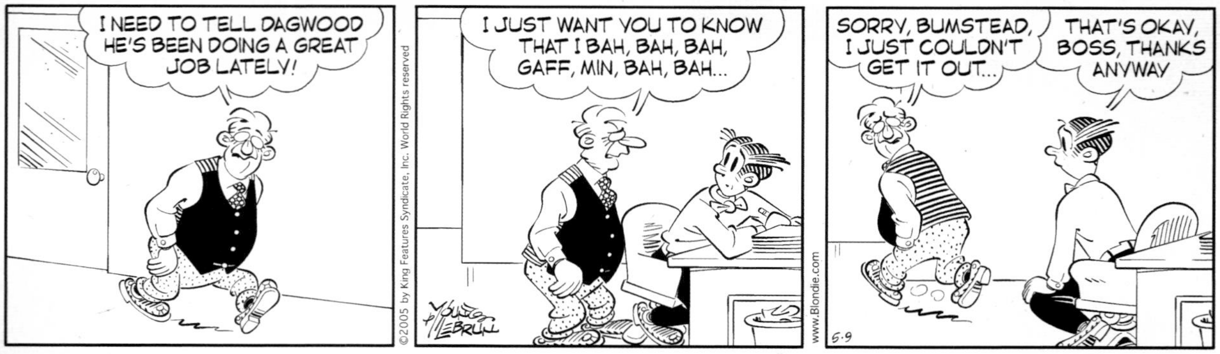
I NEED TO TELL DAGWOOD HE'S BEEN DOING A GREAT JOB LATELY!
©2005 by King Features Syndicate, Inc. World Rights reserved
I JUST WANT YOU TO KNOW THAT I BAH, BAH, BAH, GAFF, MIN, BAH, BAH...
www.Blondie.com
5·9
SORRY, BUMSTEAD, I JUST COULDN'T GET IT OUT...
THAT'S OKAY, BOSS, THANKS ANYWAY

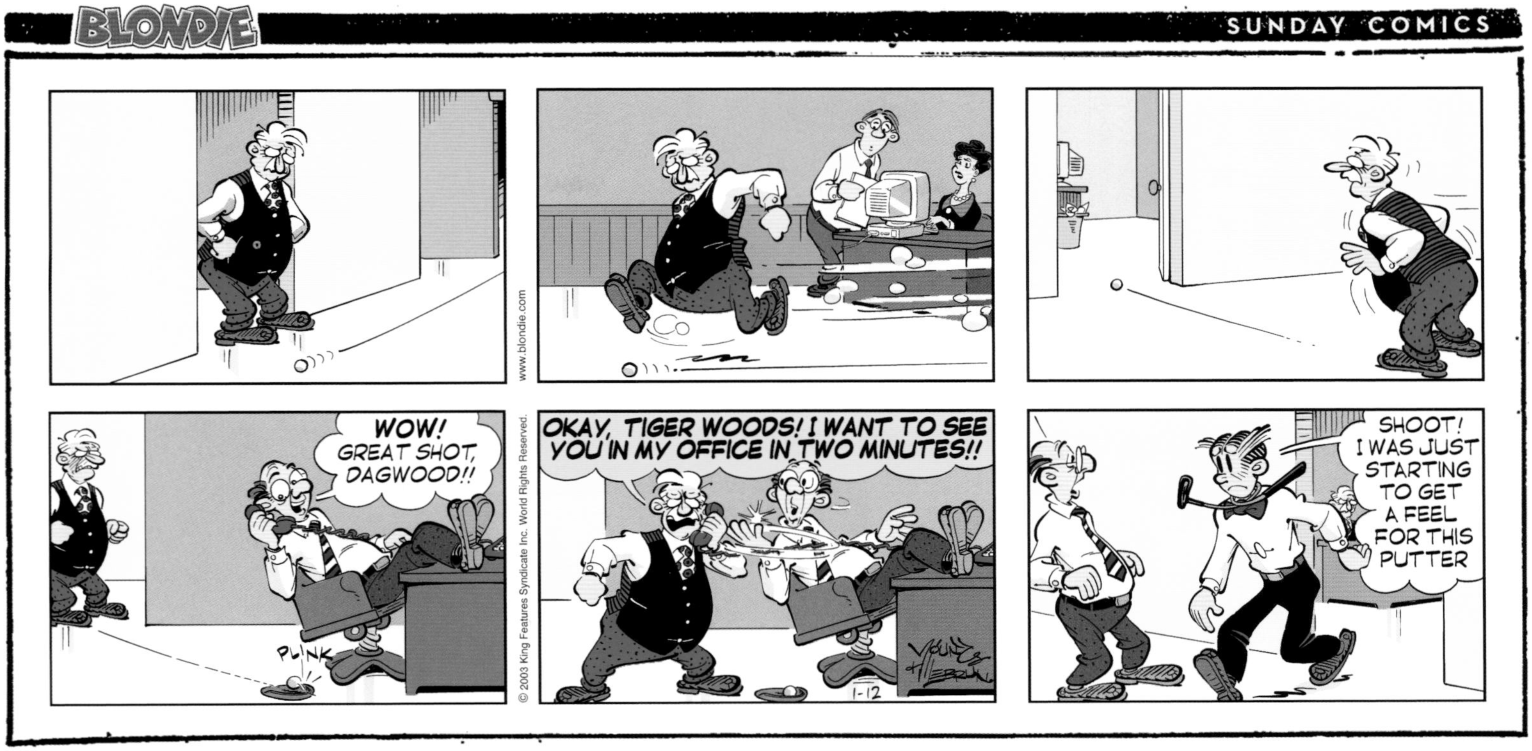
BLONDIE
SUNDAY COMICS
WOW! GREAT SHOT, DAGWOOD!!
PLINK
OKAY, TIGER WOODS! I WANT TO SEE YOU IN MY OFFICE IN TWO MINUTES!!
SHOOT! I WAS JUST STARTING TO GET A FEEL FOR THIS PUTTER
www.blondie.com
© 2003 King Features Syndicate Inc. World Rights Reserved.
1-12

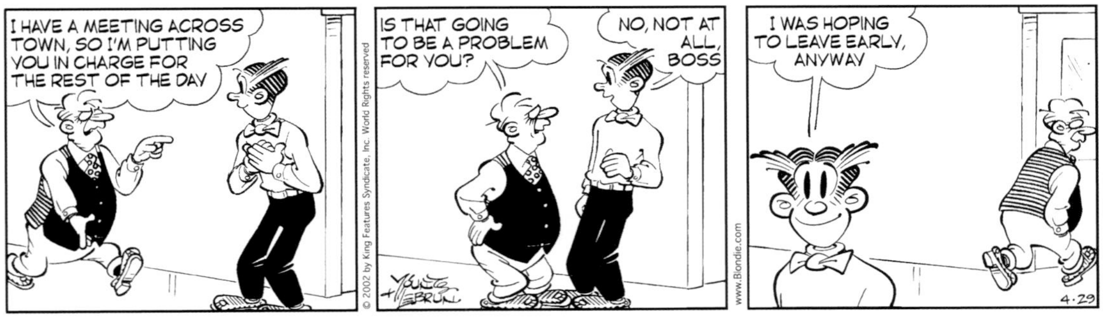
I HAVE A MEETING ACROSS TOWN, SO I'M PUTTING YOU IN CHARGE FOR THE REST OF THE DAY
IS THAT GOING TO BE A PROBLEM FOR YOU?
NO, NOT AT ALL, BOSS
I WAS HOPING TO LEAVE EARLY, ANYWAY
© 2002 by King Features Syndicate, Inc. World Rights reserved
www.Blondie.com
4-29

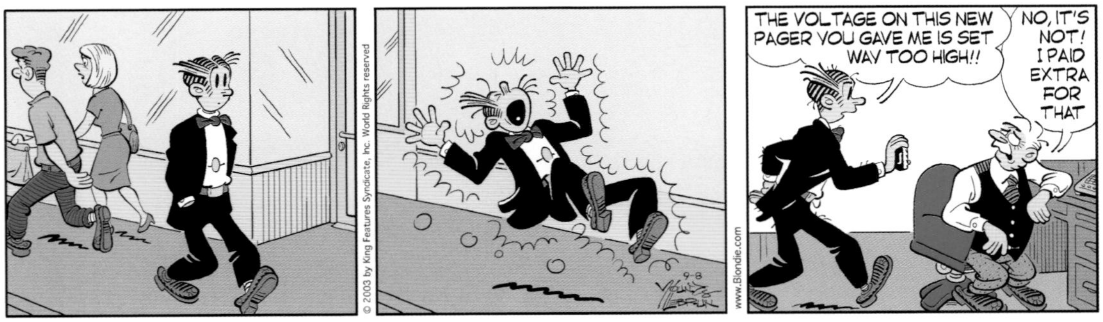
THE VOLTAGE ON THIS NEW PAGER YOU GAVE ME IS SET WAY TOO HIGH!!
NO, IT'S NOT! I PAID EXTRA FOR THAT
© 2003 by King Features Syndicate, Inc. World Rights reserved
www.Blondie.com

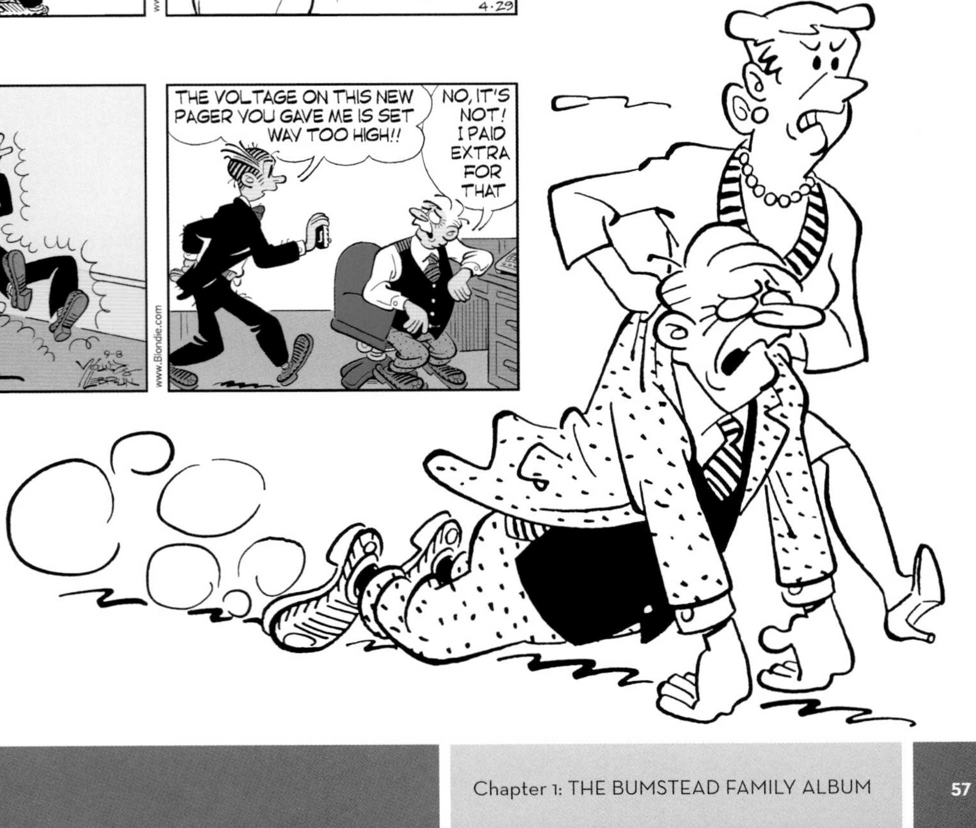

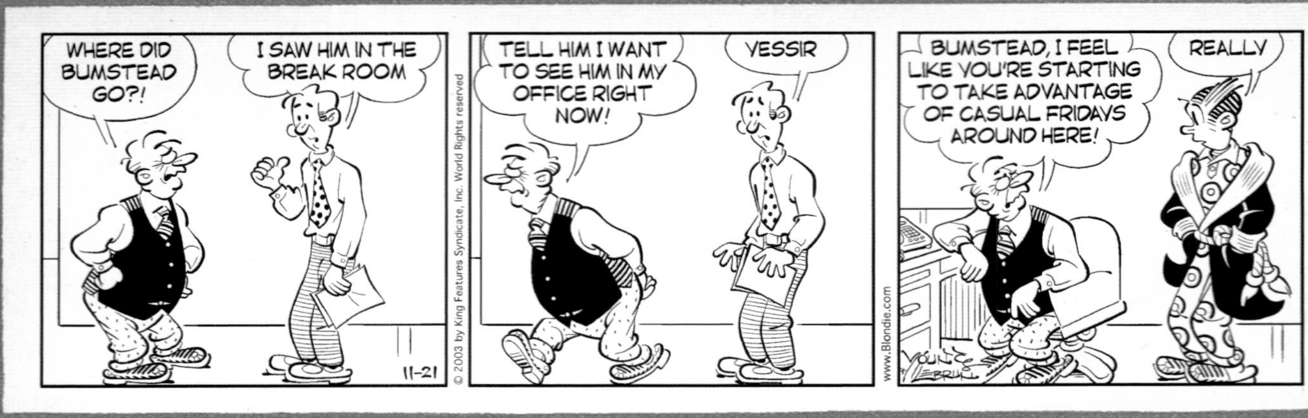
WHERE DID BUMSTEAD GO?!
I SAW HIM IN THE BREAK ROOM
TELL HIM I WANT TO SEE HIM IN MY OFFICE RIGHT NOW!
YESSIR
BUMSTEAD, I FEEL LIKE YOU'RE STARTING TO TAKE ADVANTAGE OF CASUAL FRIDAYS AROUND HERE!
REALLY
11-21
© 2003 by King Features Syndicate, Inc. World Rights reserved
www.Blondie.com

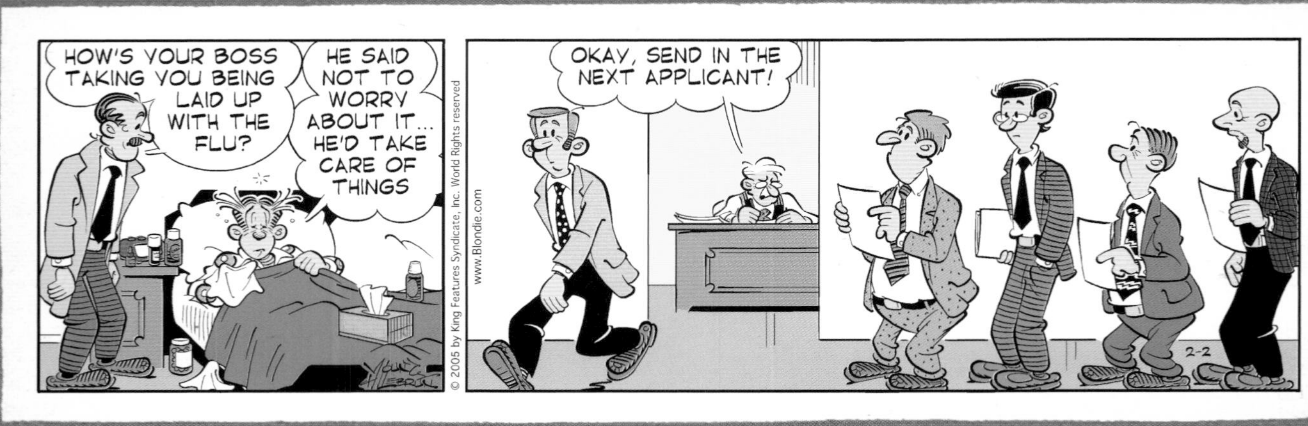
HOW'S YOUR BOSS TAKING YOU BEING LAID UP WITH THE FLU?
HE SAID NOT TO WORRY ABOUT IT... HE'D TAKE CARE OF THINGS
OKAY, SEND IN THE NEXT APPLICANT!
2-2
© 2005 by King Features Syndicate, Inc. World Rights reserved
www.Blondie.com

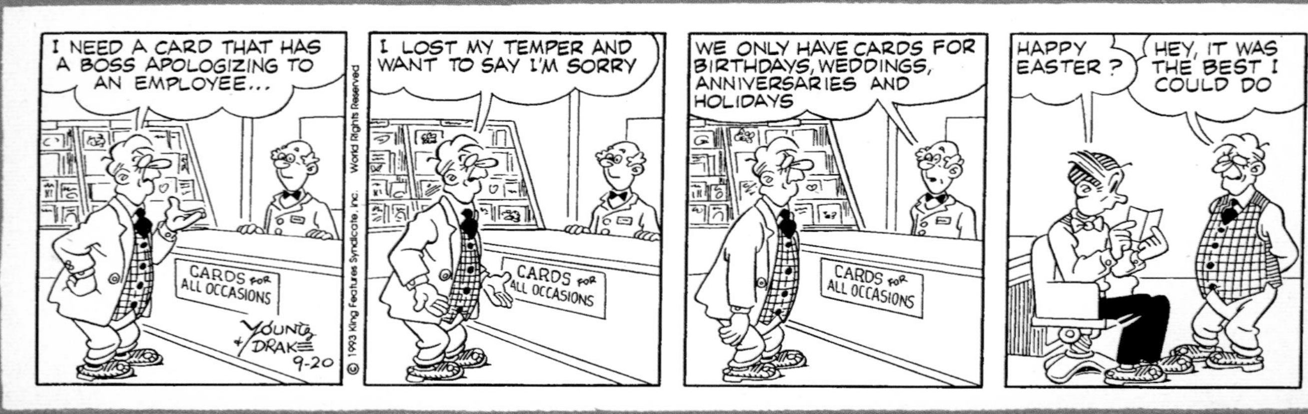
I NEED A CARD THAT HAS A BOSS APOLOGIZING TO AN EMPLOYEE...
CARDS FOR ALL OCCASIONS
YOUNG DRAKE
9-20
© 1993 King Features Syndicate, Inc. World Rights Reserved
I LOST MY TEMPER AND WANT TO SAY I'M SORRY
CARDS FOR ALL OCCASIONS
WE ONLY HAVE CARDS FOR BIRTHDAYS, WEDDINGS, ANNIVERSARIES AND HOLIDAYS
CARDS FOR ALL OCCASIONS
HAPPY EASTER ?
HEY, IT WAS THE BEST I COULD DO

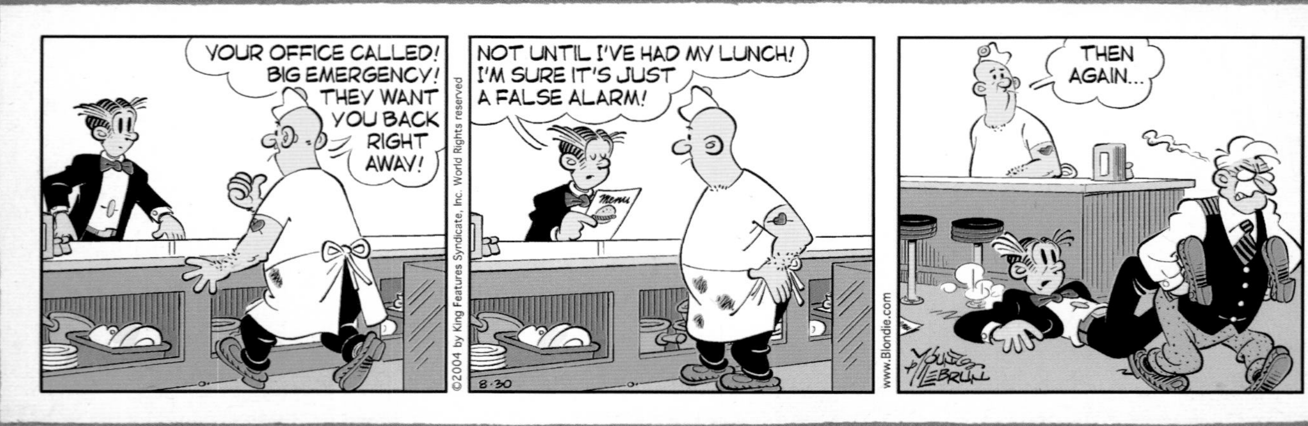
YOUR OFFICE CALLED! BIG EMERGENCY! THEY WANT YOU BACK RIGHT AWAY!
©2004 by King Features Syndicate, Inc. World Rights reserved
NOT UNTIL I'VE HAD MY LUNCH! I'M SURE IT'S JUST A FALSE ALARM!
MENU
8-30
THEN AGAIN...
www.Blondie.com

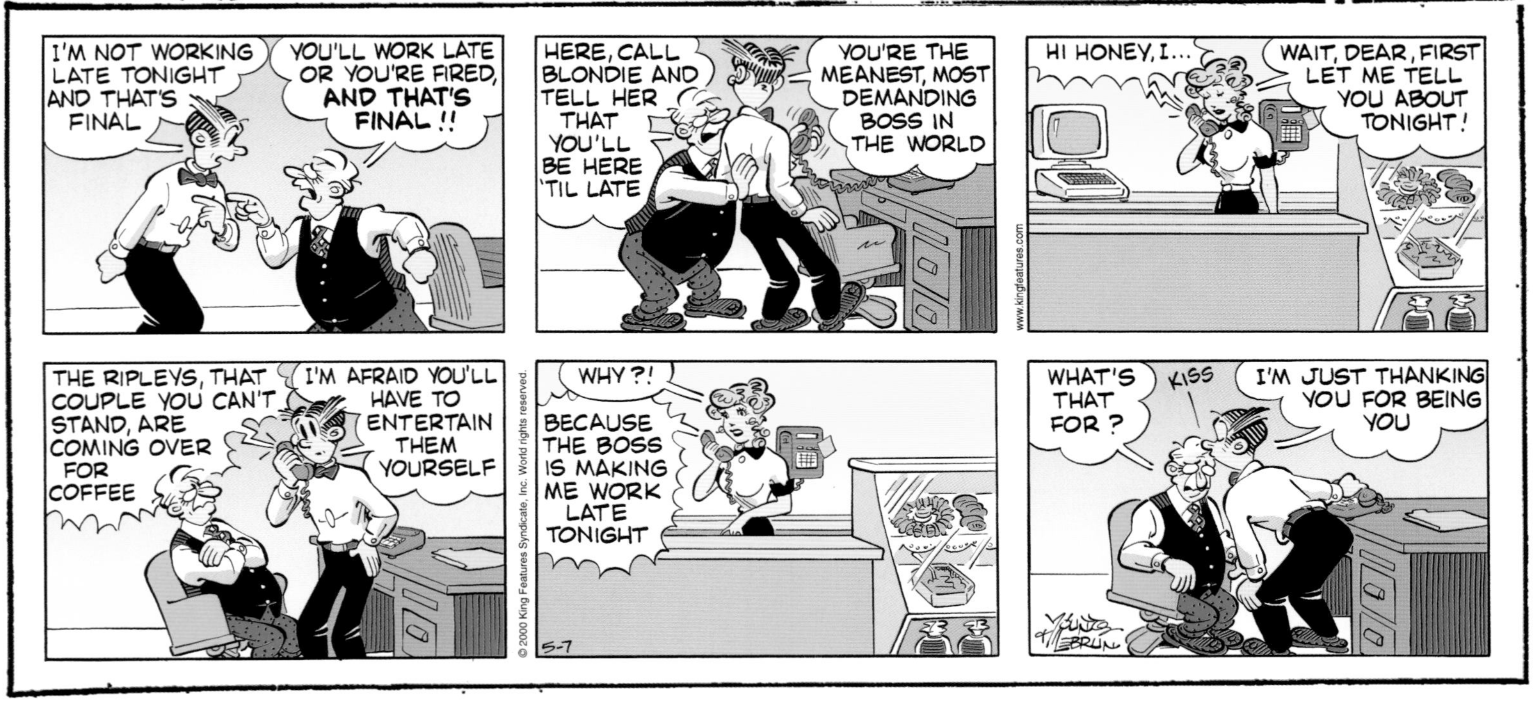
I'M NOT WORKING LATE TONIGHT AND THAT'S FINAL
YOU'LL WORK LATE OR YOU'RE FIRED, AND THAT'S FINAL!!
HERE, CALL BLONDIE AND TELL HER THAT YOU'LL BE HERE 'TIL LATE
YOU'RE THE MEANEST, MOST DEMANDING BOSS IN THE WORLD
HI HONEY, I...
WAIT, DEAR, FIRST LET ME TELL YOU ABOUT TONIGHT!
www.kingfeatures.com
THE RIPLEYS, THAT COUPLE YOU CAN'T STAND, ARE COMING OVER FOR COFFEE
I'M AFRAID YOU'LL HAVE TO ENTERTAIN THEM YOURSELF
© 2000 King Features Syndicate, Inc. World rights reserved.
WHY?!
BECAUSE THE BOSS IS MAKING ME WORK LATE TONIGHT
5-7
WHAT'S THAT FOR?
KISS
I'M JUST THANKING YOU FOR BEING YOU
YOUNG BRUN

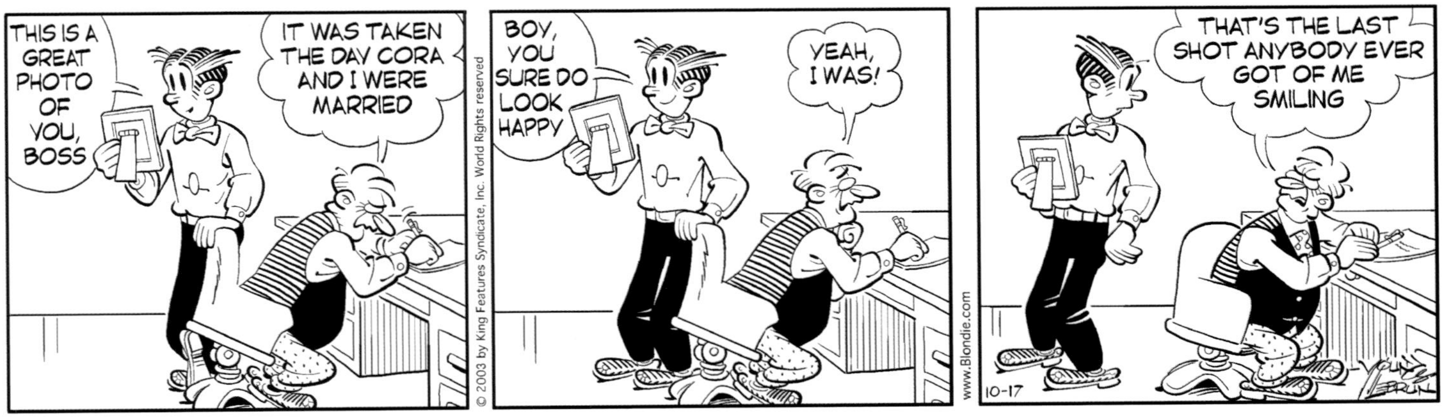
THIS IS A GREAT PHOTO OF YOU, BOSS
IT WAS TAKEN THE DAY CORA AND I WERE MARRIED
© 2003 by King Features Syndicate, Inc. World Rights reserved
BOY, YOU SURE DO LOOK HAPPY
YEAH, I WAS!
www.Blondie.com
10-17
THAT'S THE LAST SHOT ANYBODY EVER GOT OF ME SMILING
YOUNG BRUN

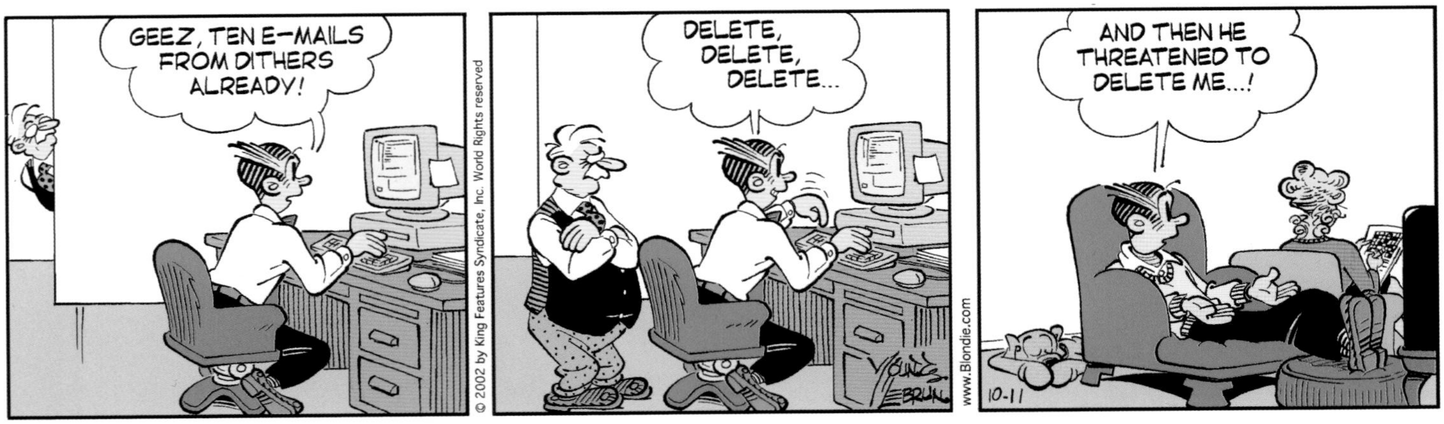
GEEZ, TEN E-MAILS FROM DITHERS ALREADY!
© 2002 by King Features Syndicate, Inc. World Rights reserved
DELETE, DELETE, DELETE...
YOUNG BRUN
www.Blondie.com
10-11
AND THEN HE THREATENED TO DELETE ME...!

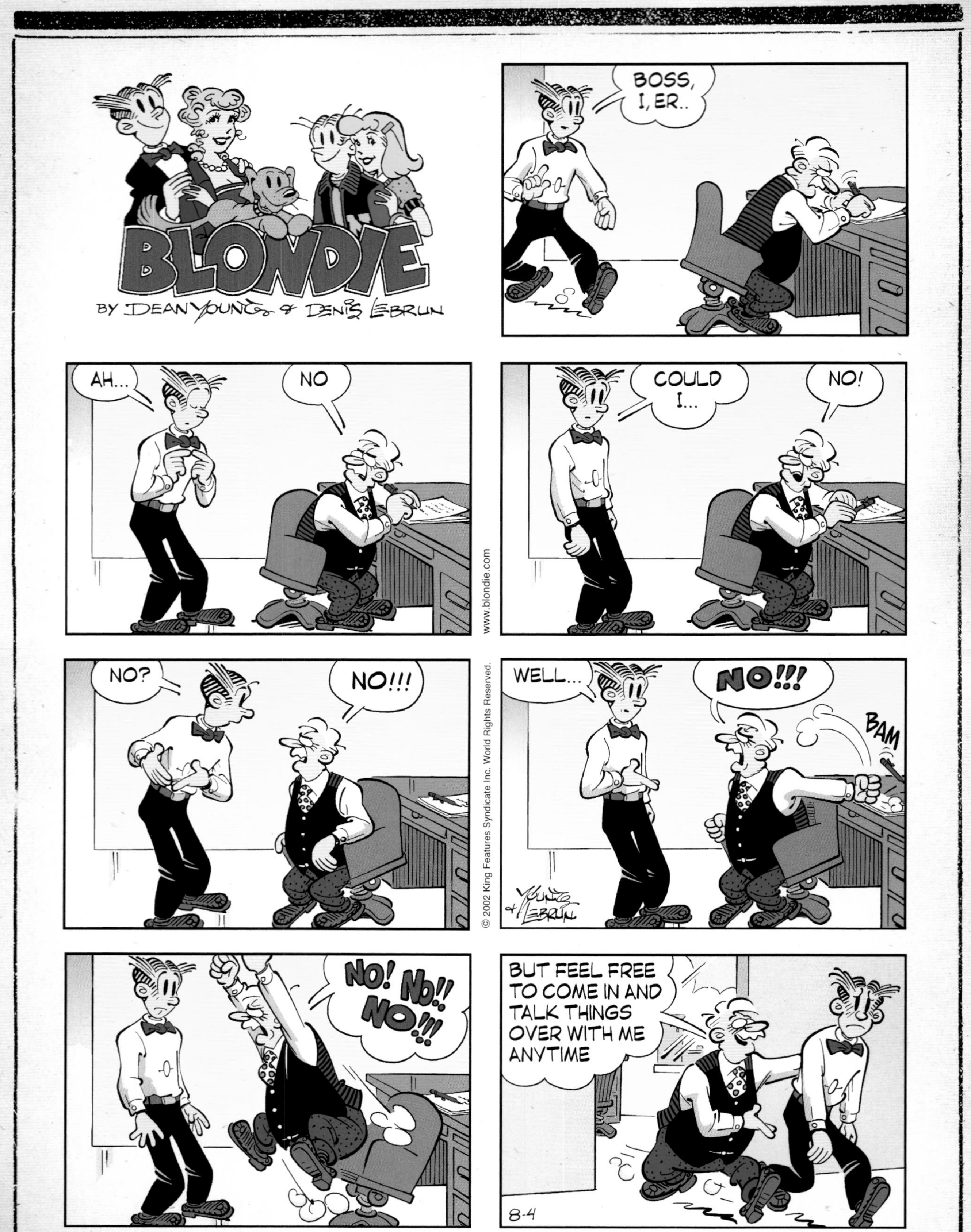
BLONDIE
BY DEAN YOUNG & DENIS LEBRUN
BOSS, I, ER..
AH...
NO
COULD I...
NO!
NO?
NO!!!
WELL...
NO!!!
BAM
YOUNG & LEBRUN
© 2002 King Features Syndicate Inc. World Rights Reserved. www.blondie.com
NO! NO!! NO!!!
BUT FEEL FREE TO COME IN AND TALK THINGS OVER WITH ME ANYTIME
8-4

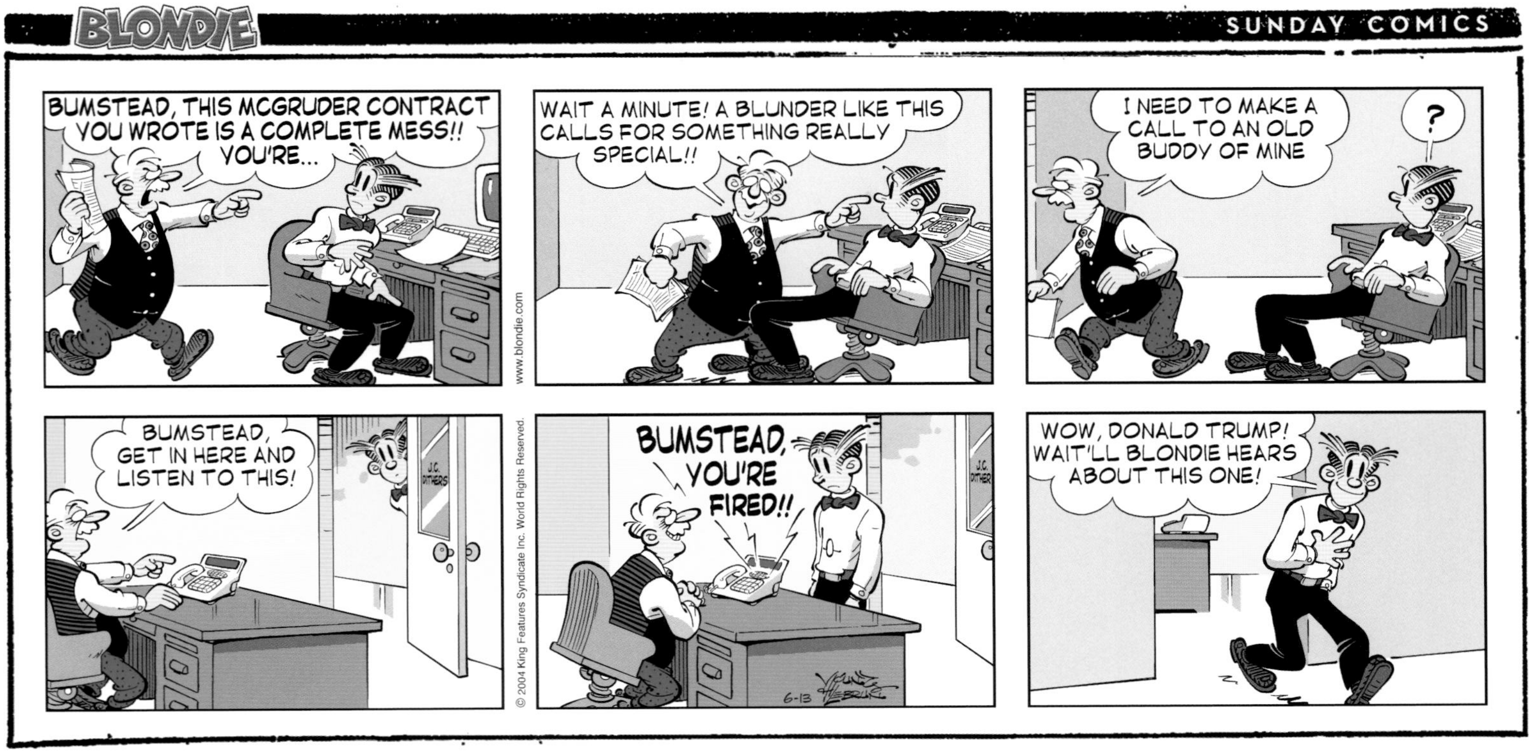
BLONDIE
SUNDAY COMICS
BUMSTEAD, THIS MCGRUDER CONTRACT YOU WROTE IS A COMPLETE MESS!! YOU'RE...
WAIT A MINUTE! A BLUNDER LIKE THIS CALLS FOR SOMETHING REALLY SPECIAL!!
I NEED TO MAKE A CALL TO AN OLD BUDDY OF MINE
?
BUMSTEAD, GET IN HERE AND LISTEN TO THIS!
J.C. DITHERS
BUMSTEAD, YOU'RE FIRED!!
WOW, DONALD TRUMP! WAIT'LL BLONDIE HEARS ABOUT THIS ONE!
www.blondie.com
© 2004 King Features Syndicate Inc. World Rights Reserved.
6-13

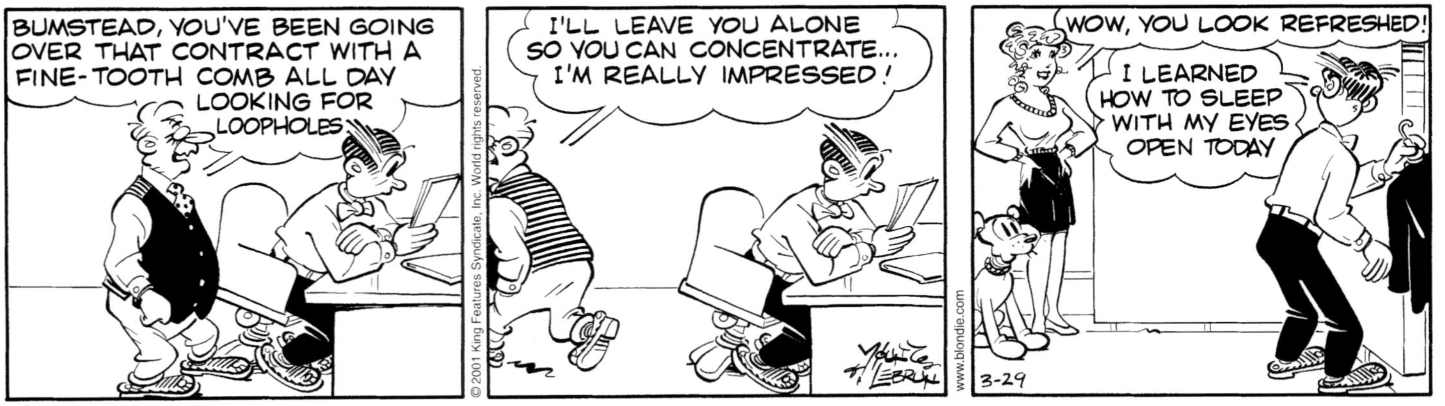
BUMSTEAD, YOU'VE BEEN GOING OVER THAT CONTRACT WITH A FINE-TOOTH COMB ALL DAY LOOKING FOR LOOPHOLES
I'LL LEAVE YOU ALONE SO YOU CAN CONCENTRATE... I'M REALLY IMPRESSED!
WOW, YOU LOOK REFRESHED!
I LEARNED HOW TO SLEEP WITH MY EYES OPEN TODAY
© 2001 King Features Syndicate, Inc. World rights reserved.
www.blondie.com
3-29

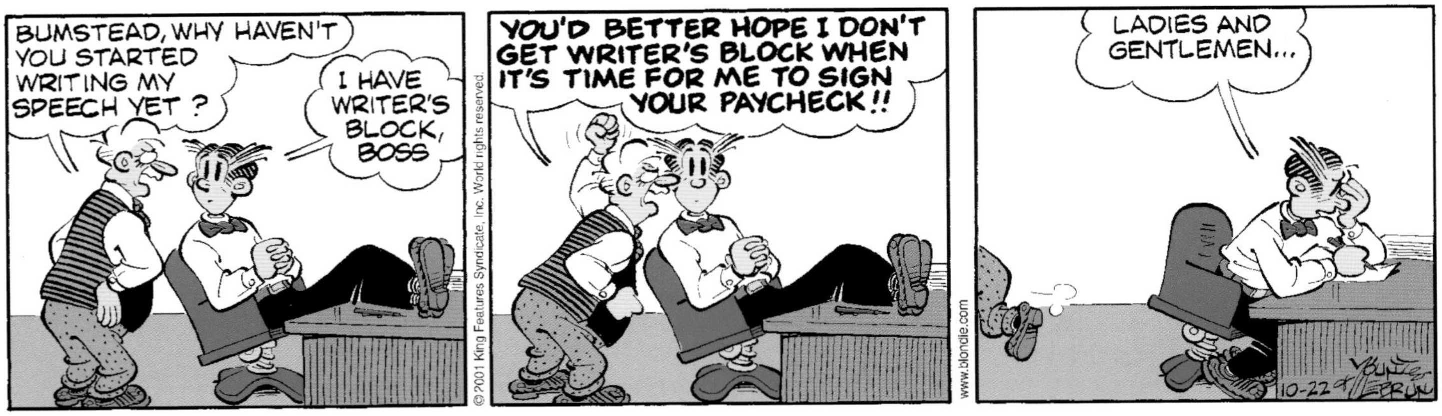
BUMSTEAD, WHY HAVEN'T YOU STARTED WRITING MY SPEECH YET ?
I HAVE WRITER'S BLOCK, BOSS
YOU'D BETTER HOPE I DON'T GET WRITER'S BLOCK WHEN IT'S TIME FOR ME TO SIGN YOUR PAYCHECK!!
LADIES AND GENTLEMEN...
© 2001 King Features Syndicate, Inc. World rights reserved.
www.blondie.com
10-22

I DON'T SEE WHY EXECUTIVES HAVE TO STEAL MONEY FROM THEIR COMPANIES!
WHY CAN'T THEY EARN MONEY THE OLD-FASHIONED WAY?
YOU MEAN BY BEING CHEAP?
EXACTLY!
© 2004 by King Features Syndicate, Inc. World Rights reserved
8-17
www.Blondie.com

CORA AND I HAD A BIG FIGHT LAST NIGHT, BUT EVERYTHING TURNED OUT ALL RIGHT
DID YOU KISS AND MAKE UP ?
ACTUALLY, WE JUST SHOOK HANDS
© 2004 by King Features Syndicate, Inc. World Rights reserved
9-29
www.Blondie.com

WHAT'S UP WITH THE PHONE, BOSS?
MY WIFE'S ON THE PHONE AND SHE'S BAWLING ME OUT
EVERY FIVE MINUTES I OPEN THE DRAWER AND TELL HER TO CALM DOWN
I'M SORRY I ASKED
FOR CRYING OUT LOUD, CALM DOWN!
© 2003 by King Features Syndicate, Inc. World Rights reserved
www.Blondie.com
7-29

BOSS, I THINK I'D LIKE TO TAKE A LITTLE SABBATICAL
FROM WHAT, BUMSTEAD?
BOY, I'D GIVE ANYTHING TO THINK UP A REALLY GOOD COMEBACK FOR THAT!
© 2003 by King Features Syndicate, Inc. World Rights reserved
www.Blondie.com
3-26

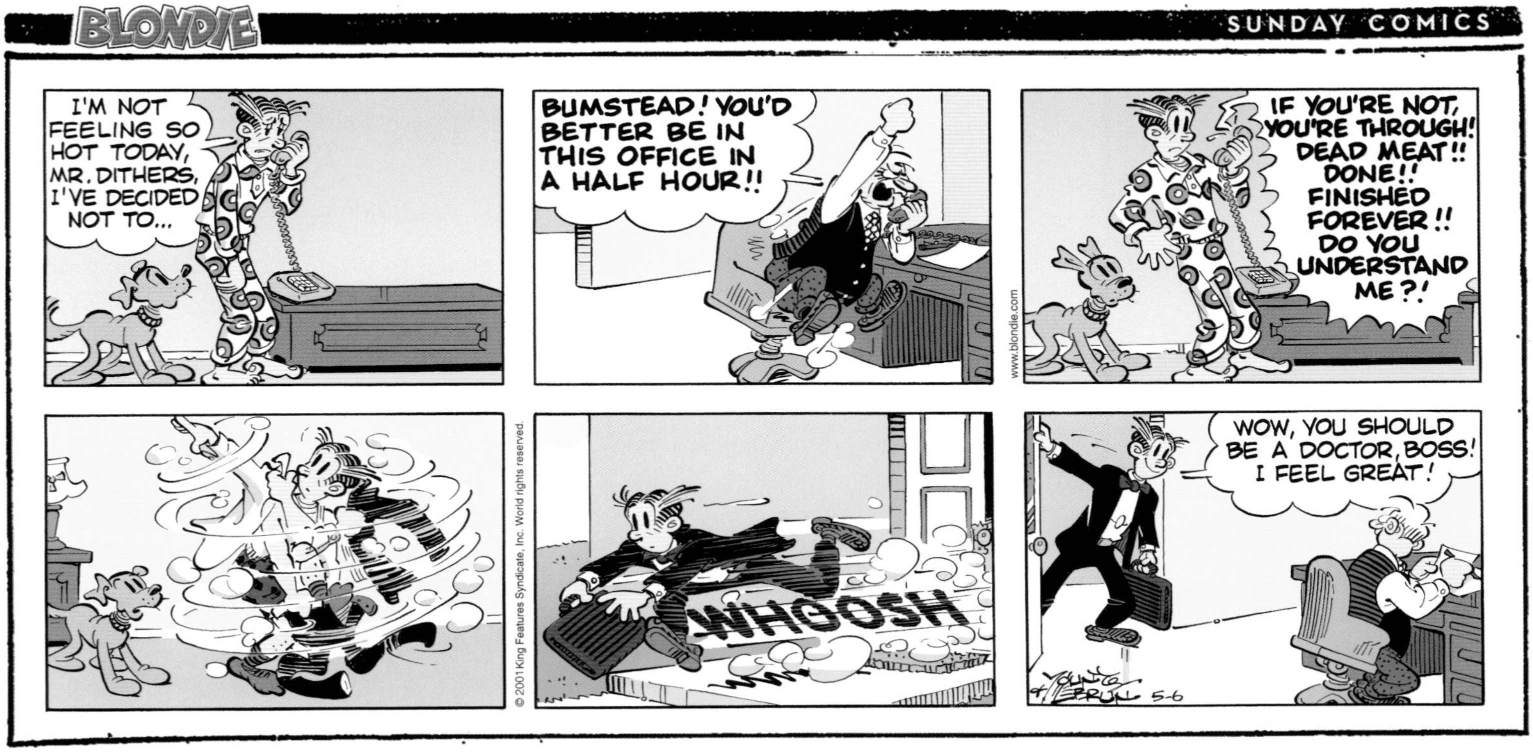
BLONDIE
SUNDAY COMICS
I'M NOT FEELING SO HOT TODAY, MR. DITHERS, I'VE DECIDED NOT TO...
BUMSTEAD! YOU'D BETTER BE IN THIS OFFICE IN A HALF HOUR!!
IF YOU'RE NOT, YOU'RE THROUGH! DEAD MEAT!! DONE!! FINISHED FOREVER!! DO YOU UNDERSTAND ME?!
www.blondie.com
© 2001 King Features Syndicate, Inc. World rights reserved.
WHOOSH
WOW, YOU SHOULD BE A DOCTOR, BOSS! I FEEL GREAT!
5-6

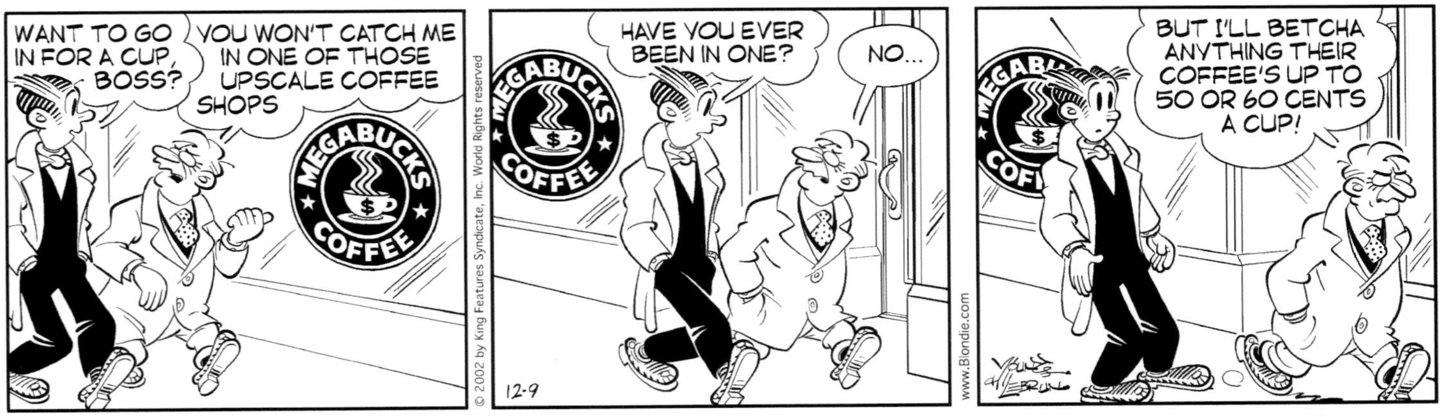
WANT TO GO IN FOR A CUP, BOSS?
YOU WON'T CATCH ME IN ONE OF THOSE UPSCALE COFFEE SHOPS
MEGABUCKS COFFEE
© 2002 by King Features Syndicate, Inc. World Rights reserved
12-9
HAVE YOU EVER BEEN IN ONE?
NO...
www.Blondie.com
BUT I'LL BETCHA ANYTHING THEIR COFFEE'S UP TO 50 OR 60 CENTS A CUP!

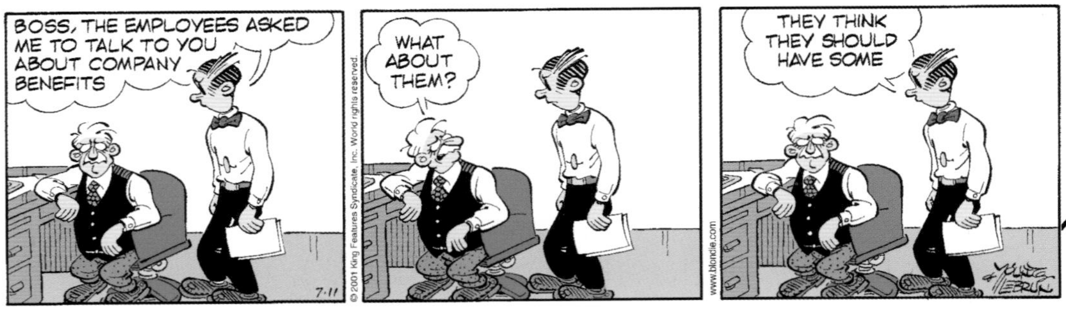
BOSS, THE EMPLOYEES ASKED ME TO TALK TO YOU ABOUT COMPANY BENEFITS
7-11
© 2001 King Features Syndicate, Inc. World rights reserved.
WHAT ABOUT THEM?
www.blondie.com
THEY THINK THEY SHOULD HAVE SOME

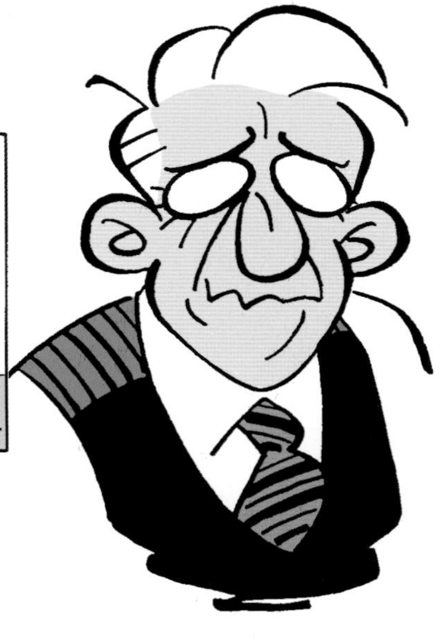

THE WOODLEYS

Every great hero—or heroine—deserves a sidekick, and Blondie and Dagwood Bumstead are lucky that they've each found theirs—Tootsie and Herb Woodley. From the moment they moved in next door in the spring of 1933, the Woodleys and the Bumsteads have been great friends and neighbors. They work together (in Blondie and Tootsie's case), play together (in Dagwood and Herb's case), and create mischief together (in everyone's case). Down to the family pets (the Woodleys have a cat), these two couples are following a parallel suburban path.

Best pals and business partners, Blondie and Tootsie even look alike—or at least, they both have bodies that most women would kill for. And they outfit them well. Brunette Tootsie and blonde, uh, Blondie spend a lot of time together over coffee at the kitchen table, where they dish about the many misdeeds of their well-meaning guys. In 1991 the ladies went into business together at Blondie's Catering Shop. Their success is emblematic of their friendship—they're fair, generous, and savvy. And if managing those lay-about men—and catering to their appetites—gave them a (well-shaped) leg up on the competition, these girlfriends are not likely to admit it.

As a duo, Herb and Dagwood are "double trouble," said Dean Young. Though Herb has a bit more money—and a bit less hair—than his buddy, he is in many respects Dagwood's equal.

"When they're together," says Young, "it's almost as if there are two Dagwoods out there."

Look out world! Whether they're golfing, bowling, car-pooling, playing poker, fishing, fighting over borrowed tools, or just generally hanging out, these guys cannot help but foul up. Herb is loyal, but not stupid—he knows that Dagwood can sometimes lead him astray (and vice versa). Their relationship is a series of misadventures—but at least they've still got those knockout wives to look after them.

In fact, the Woodleys and the Bumsteads sort of look after each other. Over the years they've established the kind of routines—backyard barbeques, dinner parties, and weekend outings—that everlasting friendships are made of.

IS THIS THE WOODLEY RESIDENCE? I HAVE ONE SUPER DELUXE PIZZA WITH EVERYTHING ON IT
© 2002 by King Features Syndicate, Inc. World Rights reserved
NO, BUT C'MON, I'LL SHOW YOU WHERE IT IS
www.Blondie.com
SINCE WHEN DID THEY START DELIVERING DINNER GUESTS WITH THEIR PIZZA?
3-18

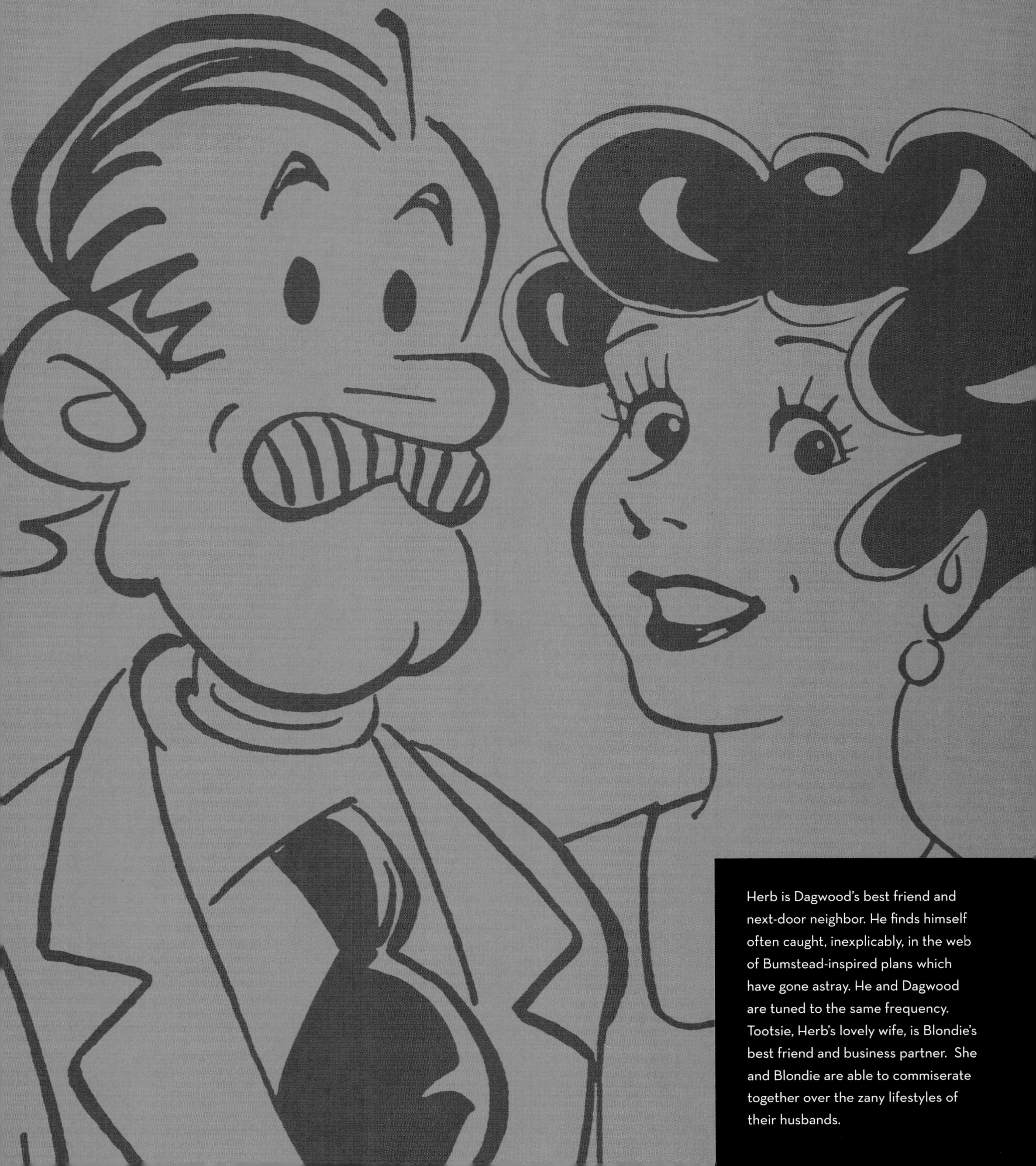

Herb is Dagwood's best friend and next-door neighbor. He finds himself often caught, inexplicably, in the web of Bumstead-inspired plans which have gone astray. He and Dagwood are tuned to the same frequency. Tootsie, Herb's lovely wife, is Blondie's best friend and business partner. She and Blondie are able to commiserate together over the zany lifestyles of their husbands.

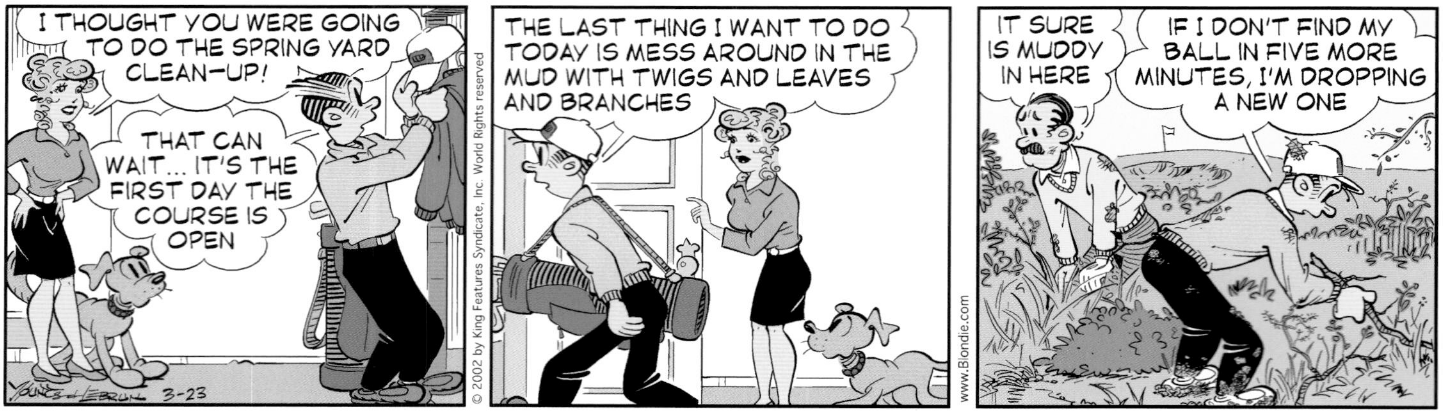
I THOUGHT YOU WERE GOING TO DO THE SPRING YARD CLEAN-UP!
THAT CAN WAIT... IT'S THE FIRST DAY THE COURSE IS OPEN
3-23
© 2002 by King Features Syndicate, Inc. World Rights reserved
THE LAST THING I WANT TO DO TODAY IS MESS AROUND IN THE MUD WITH TWIGS AND LEAVES AND BRANCHES
www.Blondie.com
IT SURE IS MUDDY IN HERE
IF I DON'T FIND MY BALL IN FIVE MORE MINUTES, I'M DROPPING A NEW ONE

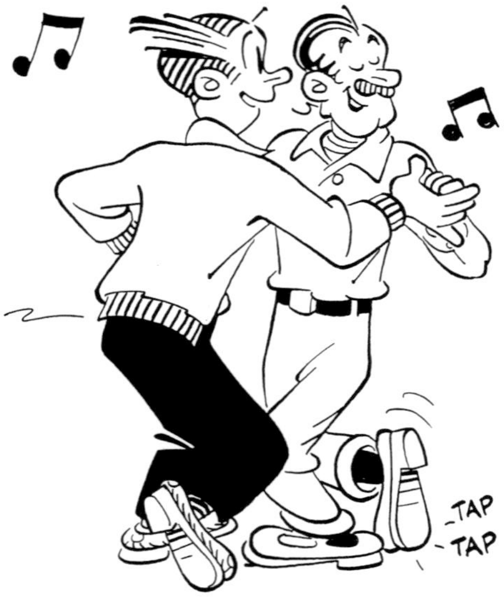
TAP
TAP

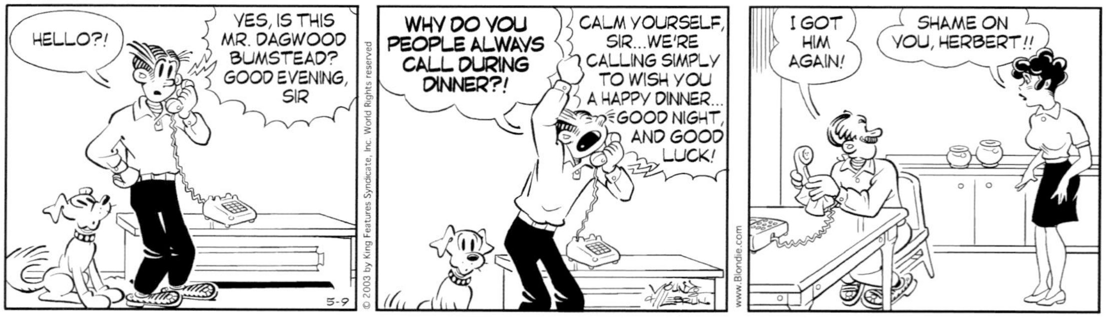
HELLO?!
YES, IS THIS MR. DAGWOOD BUMSTEAD? GOOD EVENING, SIR
5-9
© 2003 by King Features Syndicate, Inc. World Rights reserved
WHY DO YOU PEOPLE ALWAYS CALL DURING DINNER?!
CALM YOURSELF, SIR...WE'RE CALLING SIMPLY TO WISH YOU A HAPPY DINNER... GOOD NIGHT, AND GOOD LUCK!
www.Blondie.com
I GOT HIM AGAIN!
SHAME ON YOU, HERBERT!!

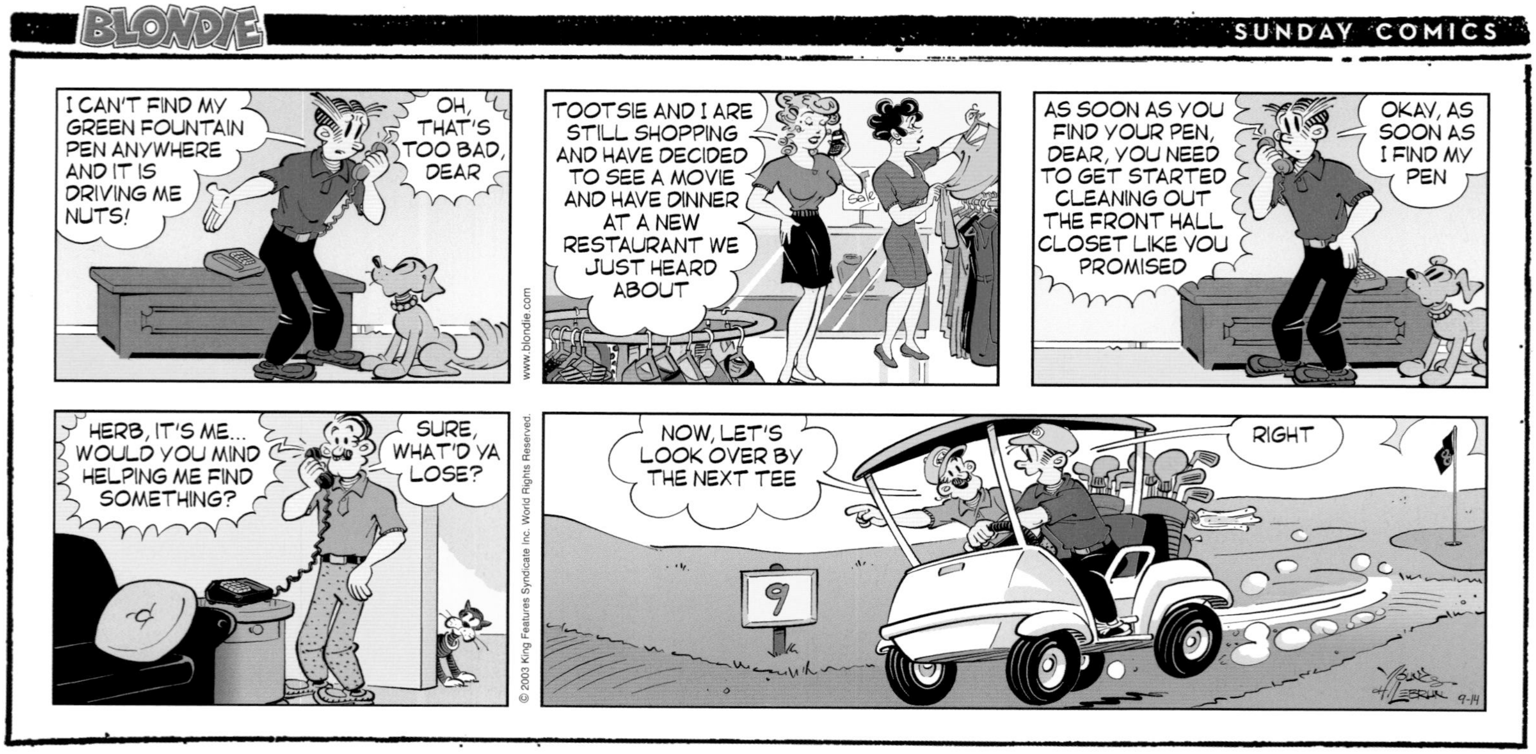
BLONDIE
SUNDAY COMICS
I CAN'T FIND MY GREEN FOUNTAIN PEN ANYWHERE AND IT IS DRIVING ME NUTS!
OH, THAT'S TOO BAD, DEAR
www.blondie.com
TOOTSIE AND I ARE STILL SHOPPING AND HAVE DECIDED TO SEE A MOVIE AND HAVE DINNER AT A NEW RESTAURANT WE JUST HEARD ABOUT
AS SOON AS YOU FIND YOUR PEN, DEAR, YOU NEED TO GET STARTED CLEANING OUT THE FRONT HALL CLOSET LIKE YOU PROMISED
OKAY, AS SOON AS I FIND MY PEN
HERB, IT'S ME... WOULD YOU MIND HELPING ME FIND SOMETHING?
SURE, WHAT'D YA LOSE?
© 2003 King Features Syndicate Inc. World Rights Reserved.
NOW, LET'S LOOK OVER BY THE NEXT TEE
RIGHT
9
9-14

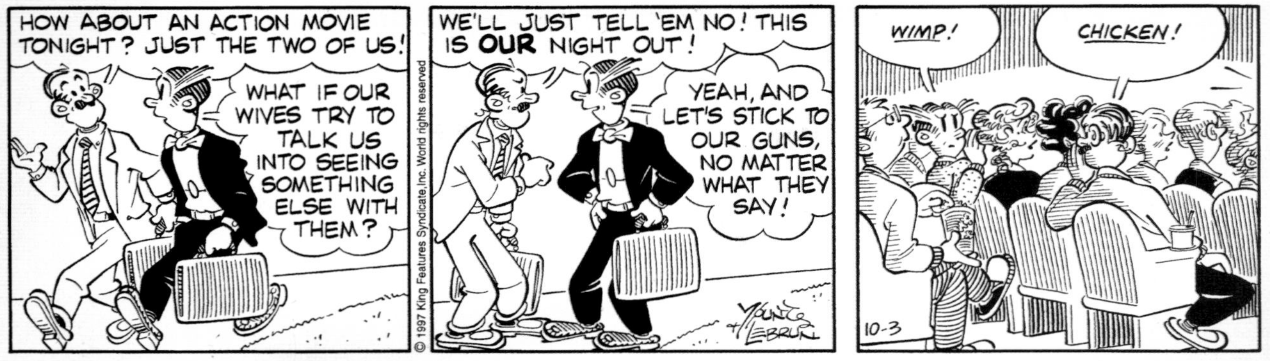
HOW ABOUT AN ACTION MOVIE TONIGHT? JUST THE TWO OF US!
WHAT IF OUR WIVES TRY TO TALK US INTO SEEING SOMETHING ELSE WITH THEM?
WE'LL JUST TELL 'EM NO! THIS IS OUR NIGHT OUT!
YEAH, AND LET'S STICK TO OUR GUNS, NO MATTER WHAT THEY SAY!
WIMP!
CHICKEN!
© 1997 King Features Syndicate, Inc. World rights reserved
10-3

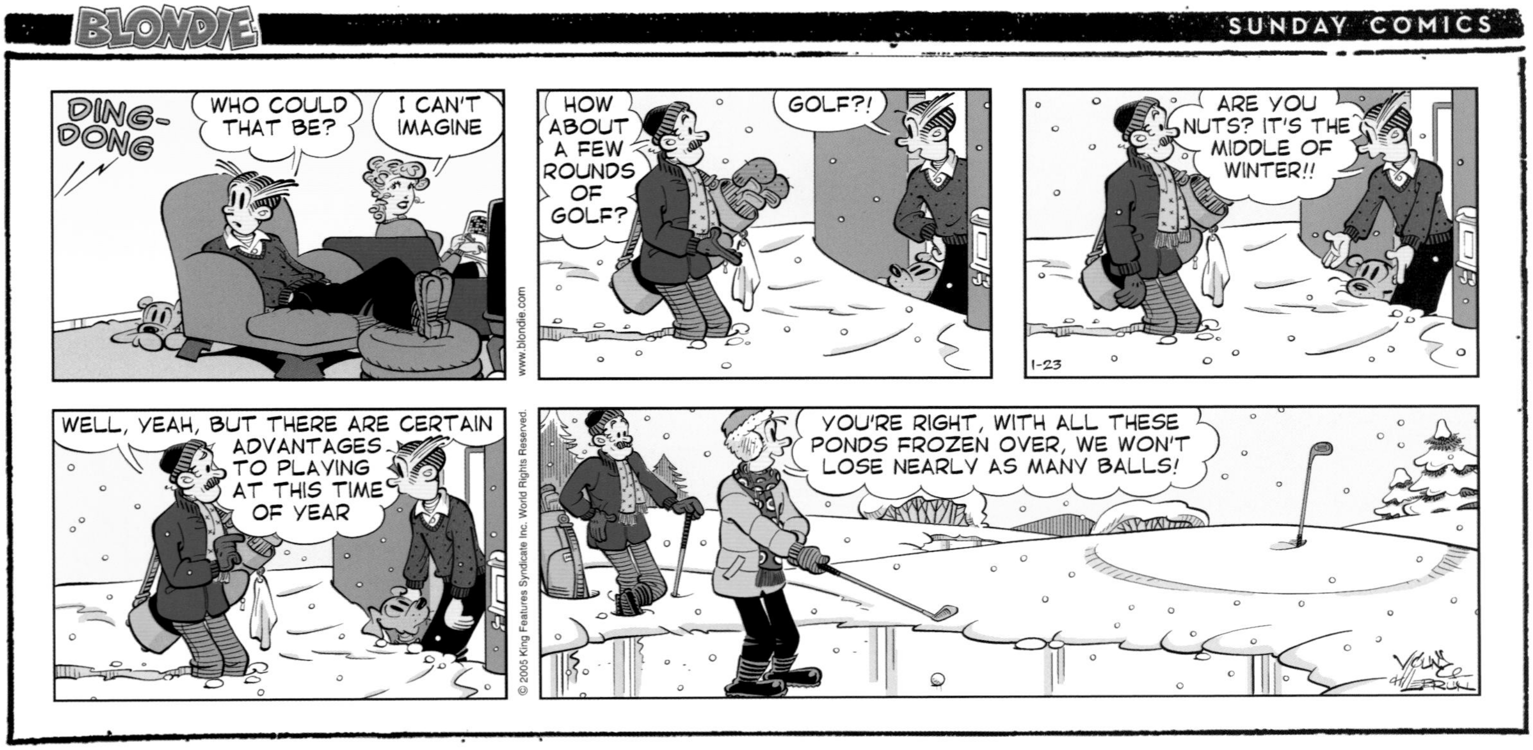
BLONDIE
SUNDAY COMICS
DING-DONG
WHO COULD THAT BE?
I CAN'T IMAGINE
HOW ABOUT A FEW ROUNDS OF GOLF?
GOLF?!
ARE YOU NUTS? IT'S THE MIDDLE OF WINTER!!
1-23
www.blondie.com
WELL, YEAH, BUT THERE ARE CERTAIN ADVANTAGES TO PLAYING AT THIS TIME OF YEAR
YOU'RE RIGHT, WITH ALL THESE PONDS FROZEN OVER, WE WON'T LOSE NEARLY AS MANY BALLS!
© 2005 King Features Syndicate Inc. World Rights Reserved.

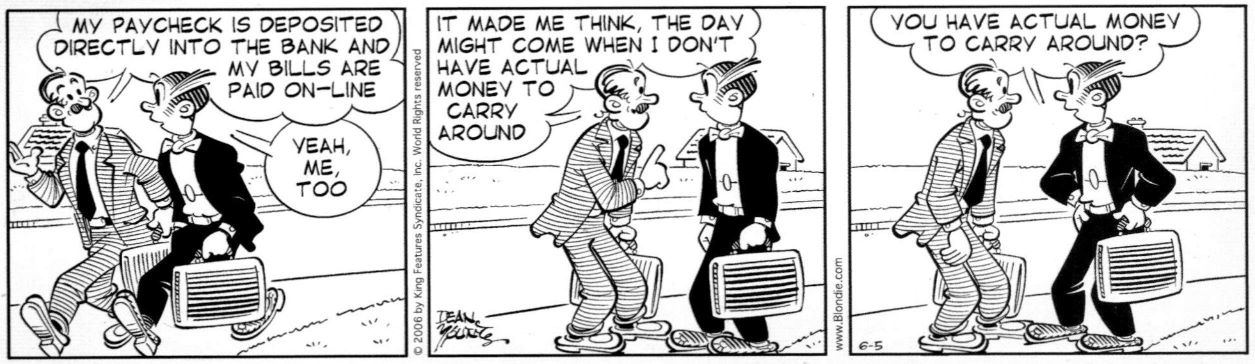
MY PAYCHECK IS DEPOSITED DIRECTLY INTO THE BANK AND MY BILLS ARE PAID ON-LINE
YEAH, ME, TOO
IT MADE ME THINK, THE DAY MIGHT COME WHEN I DON'T HAVE ACTUAL MONEY TO CARRY AROUND
YOU HAVE ACTUAL MONEY TO CARRY AROUND?
© 2006 by King Features Syndicate, Inc. World Rights reserved
www.Blondie.com
6-5

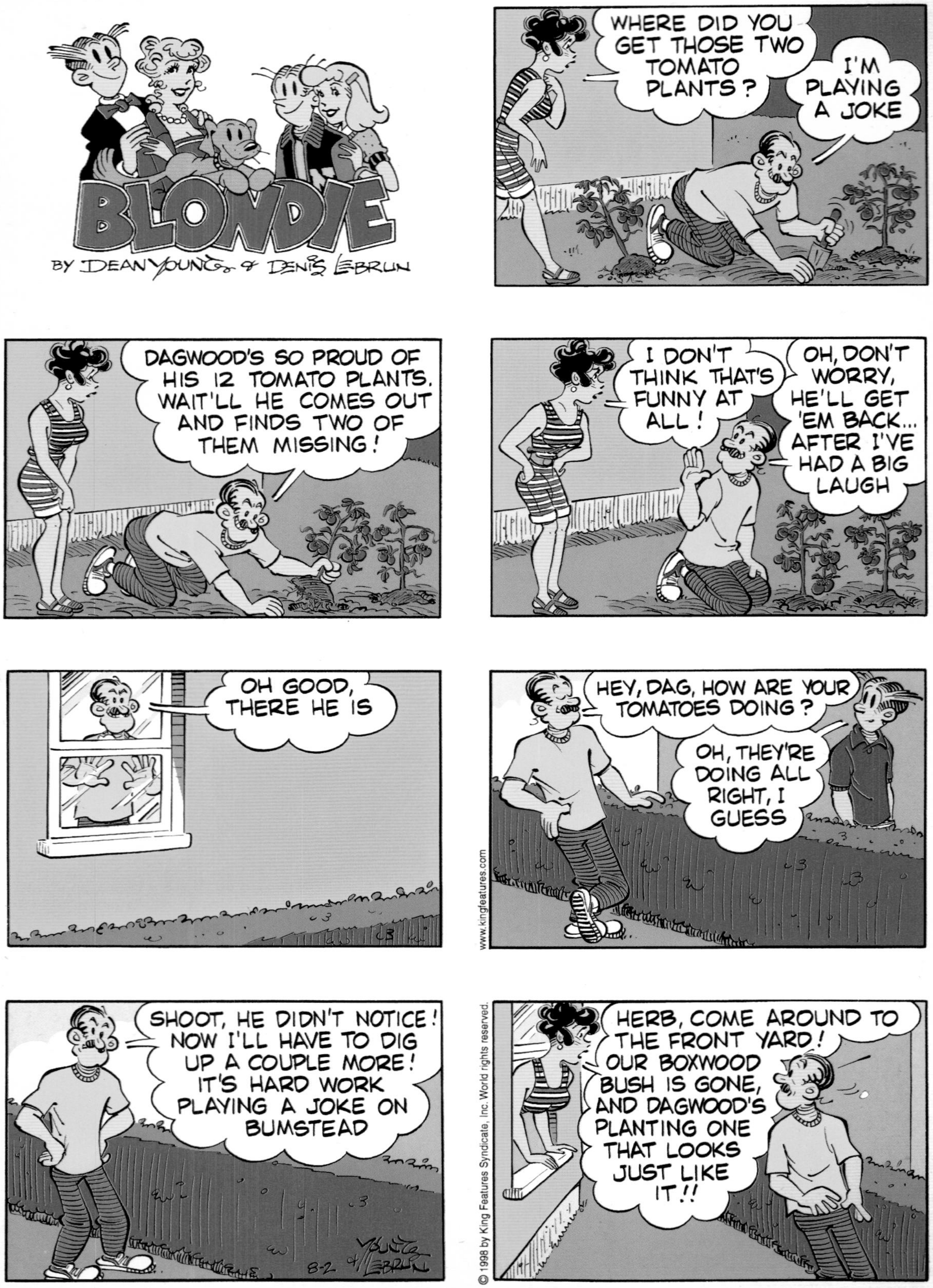
BLONDIE
BY DEAN YOUNG & DENIS LEBRUN
WHERE DID YOU GET THOSE TWO TOMATO PLANTS ?
I'M PLAYING A JOKE
DAGWOOD'S SO PROUD OF HIS 12 TOMATO PLANTS. WAIT'LL HE COMES OUT AND FINDS TWO OF THEM MISSING!
I DON'T THINK THAT'S FUNNY AT ALL!
OH, DON'T WORRY, HE'LL GET 'EM BACK... AFTER I'VE HAD A BIG LAUGH
OH GOOD, THERE HE IS
HEY, DAG, HOW ARE YOUR TOMATOES DOING ?
OH, THEY'RE DOING ALL RIGHT, I GUESS
www.kingfeatures.com
SHOOT, HE DIDN'T NOTICE! NOW I'LL HAVE TO DIG UP A COUPLE MORE! IT'S HARD WORK PLAYING A JOKE ON BUMSTEAD
© 1998 by King Features Syndicate, Inc. World rights reserved.
HERB, COME AROUND TO THE FRONT YARD! OUR BOXWOOD BUSH IS GONE, AND DAGWOOD'S PLANTING ONE THAT LOOKS JUST LIKE IT!!
8-2

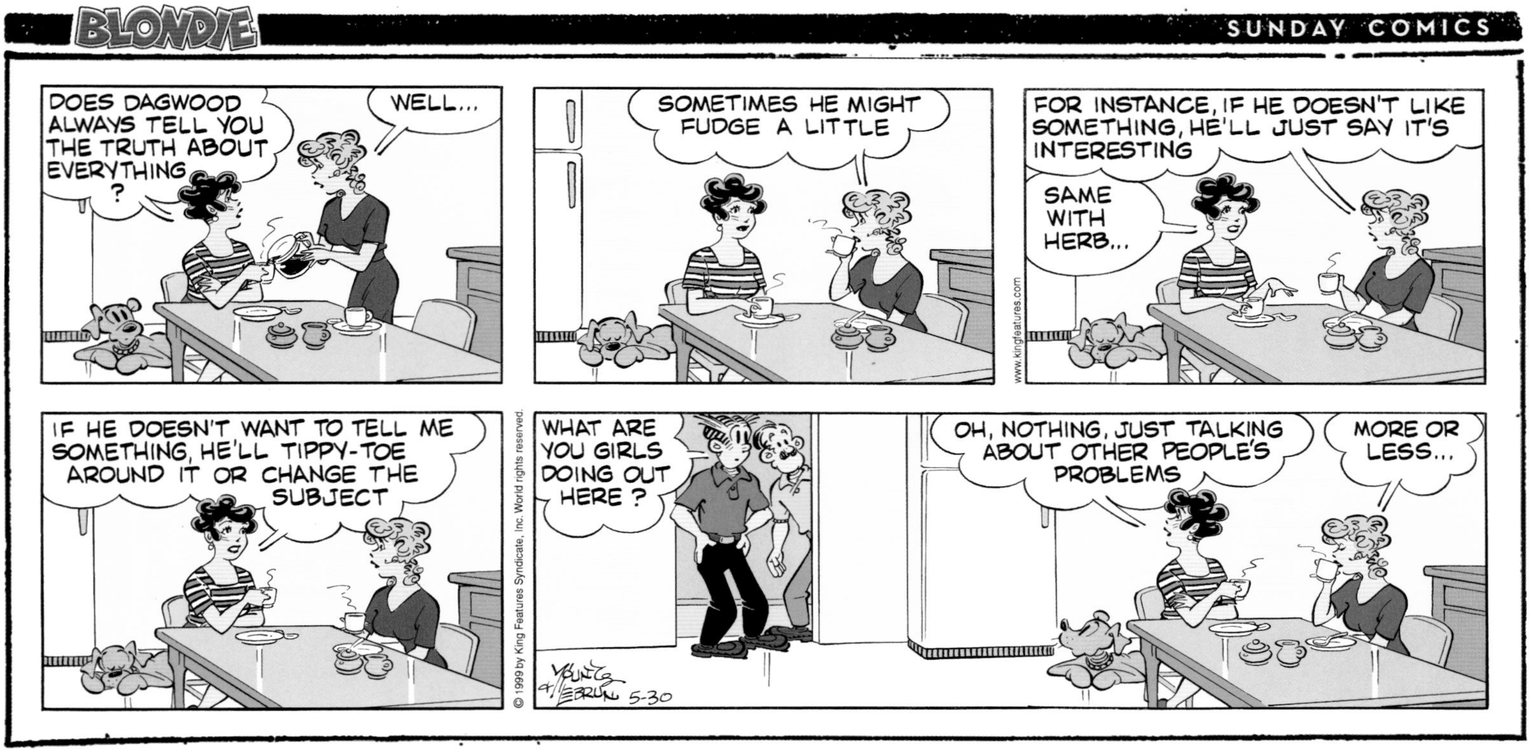
BLONDIE
SUNDAY COMICS
DOES DAGWOOD ALWAYS TELL YOU THE TRUTH ABOUT EVERYTHING ?
WELL...
SOMETIMES HE MIGHT FUDGE A LITTLE
FOR INSTANCE, IF HE DOESN'T LIKE SOMETHING, HE'LL JUST SAY IT'S INTERESTING
SAME WITH HERB...
www.kingfeatures.com
IF HE DOESN'T WANT TO TELL ME SOMETHING, HE'LL TIPPY-TOE AROUND IT OR CHANGE THE SUBJECT
© 1999 by King Features Syndicate, Inc. World rights reserved.
WHAT ARE YOU GIRLS DOING OUT HERE ?
OH, NOTHING, JUST TALKING ABOUT OTHER PEOPLE'S PROBLEMS
MORE OR LESS...
5-30

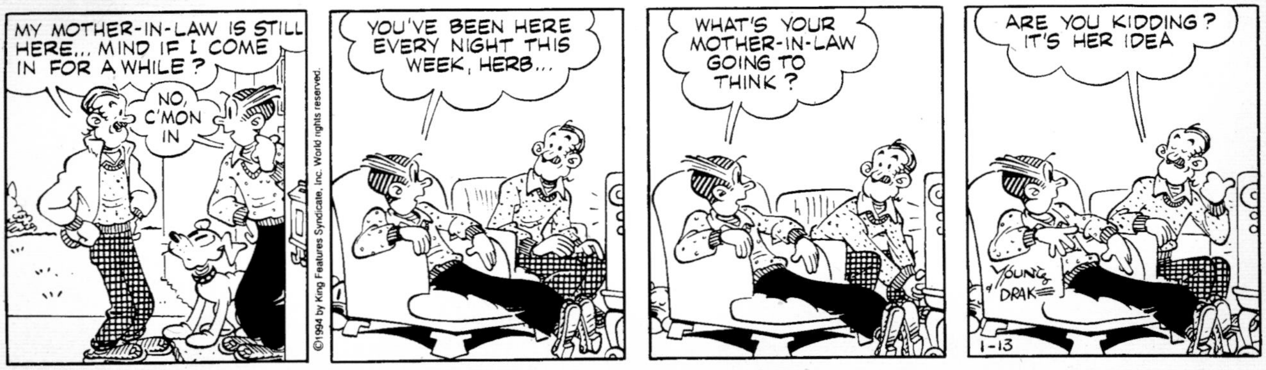
MY MOTHER-IN-LAW IS STILL HERE... MIND IF I COME IN FOR A WHILE ?
NO, C'MON IN
© 1994 by King Features Syndicate, Inc. World rights reserved.
YOU'VE BEEN HERE EVERY NIGHT THIS WEEK, HERB...
WHAT'S YOUR MOTHER-IN-LAW GOING TO THINK ?
ARE YOU KIDDING ? IT'S HER IDEA
1-13

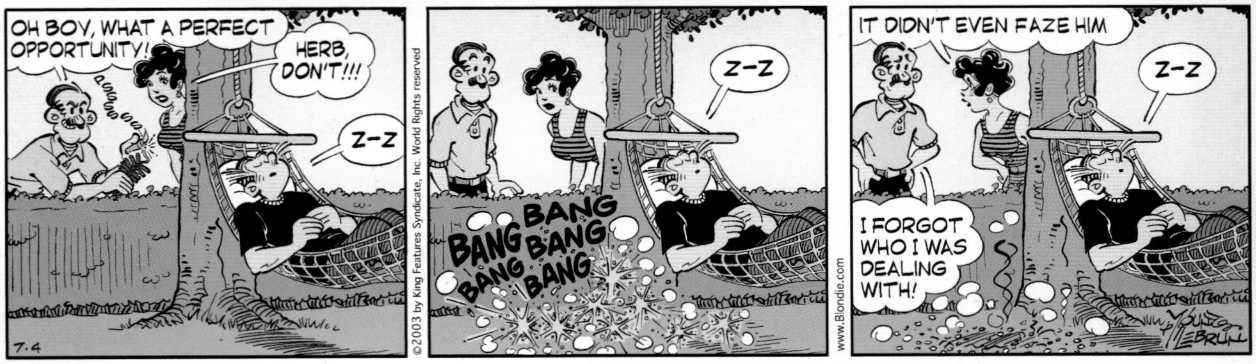
OH BOY, WHAT A PERFECT OPPORTUNITY!
HERB, DON'T!!!
Z-Z
7-4
©2003 by King Features Syndicate, Inc. World Rights reserved
Z-Z
BANG BANG BANG BANG BANG BANG
www.Blondie.com
IT DIDN'T EVEN FAZE HIM
Z-Z
I FORGOT WHO I WAS DEALING WITH!

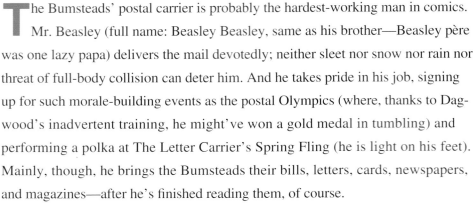

MR. BEASLEY

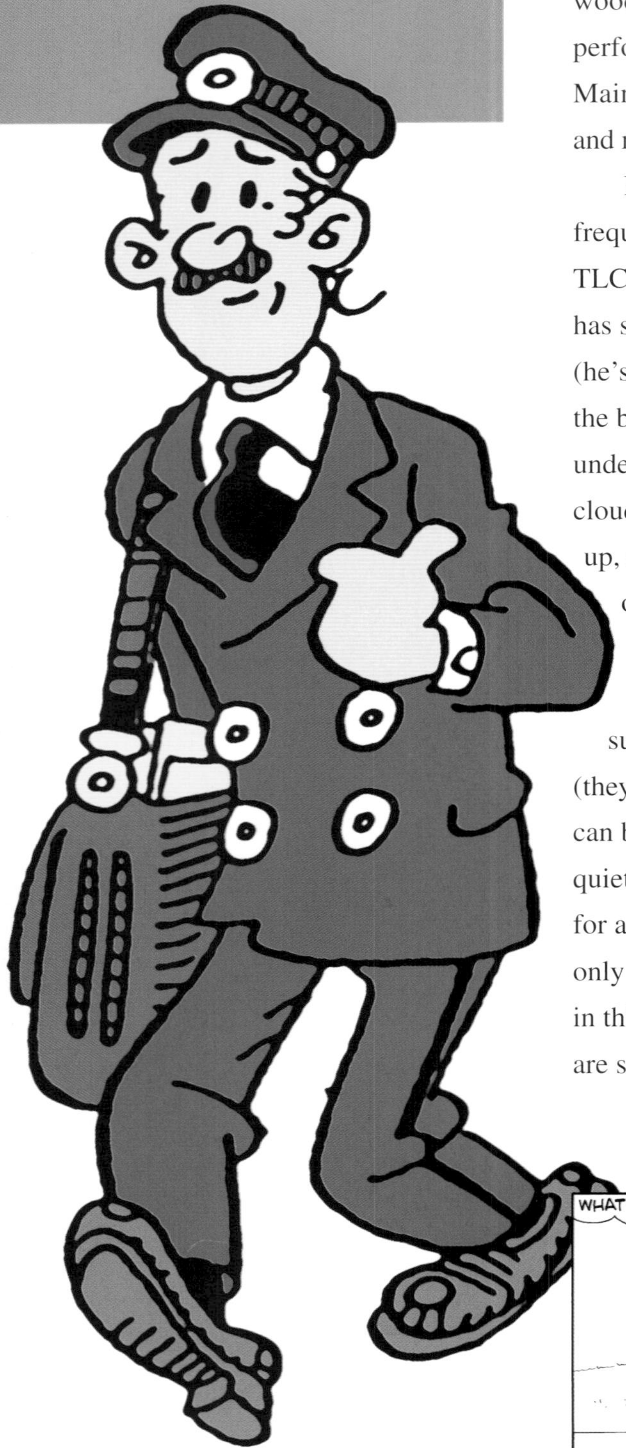

The Bumsteads' postal carrier is probably the hardest-working man in comics. Mr. Beasley (full name: Beasley Beasley, same as his brother—Beasley père was one lazy papa) delivers the mail devotedly; neither sleet nor snow nor rain nor threat of full-body collision can deter him. And he takes pride in his job, signing up for such morale-building events as the postal Olympics (where, thanks to Dagwood's inadvertent training, he might've won a gold medal in tumbling) and performing a polka at The Letter Carrier's Spring Fling (he is light on his feet). Mainly, though, he brings the Bumsteads their bills, letters, cards, newspapers, and magazines—after he's finished reading them, of course.

But even someone as dedicated as Beasley needs to rest, which he does frequently—on the Bumsteads' couch. And why not? Blondie treats him to some TLC. Though if anyone had cause to "go postal," it would be Mr. Beasley, who has suffered nearly every indignity known to his profession, from yapping pets (he's been bitten by dogs, cats, and even a parrot—incidentally the only one of the bunch to apologize), to angry customers, to kids throwing snowballs, to the undeniable terrible certainty that sooner or later . . . wham! Down he'll go, in a cloud of arms and legs and hair, letters and packages, airmail flying, only to get up, dust himself off, retrieve his mail, and start all over again as Dagwood rushes off, ready to do the same.

From 1936 when he first meandered slowly—sometimes very slowly—down his route, Beasley has served to slyly reference both our deepest suspicions about the men and women that come into contact with our mail (they must read the postcards, right?) and our best wishes for them—that they can be a part of our family. His bond with the Bumsteads is reminiscent of a quieter period in American life, when we had the time to invite the postman in for a cup of coffee, a slice of pie, and a chat. Now figures like Mr. Beasley may only be able to survive in the pages of the comics, but it's nice to know that even in this era of electronic missives and digital communiqués, some things are still as constant as the mail.

WHAT'VE YOU GOT FOR ME TODAY?
NO MAIL, BUT HERE'S A NICE STICK OF GUM FOR YOU!
IF I DON'T BRING HIM SOMETHING, HE POUTS

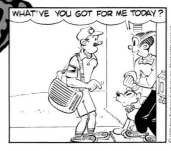

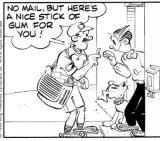

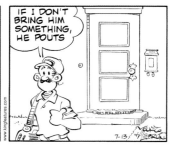

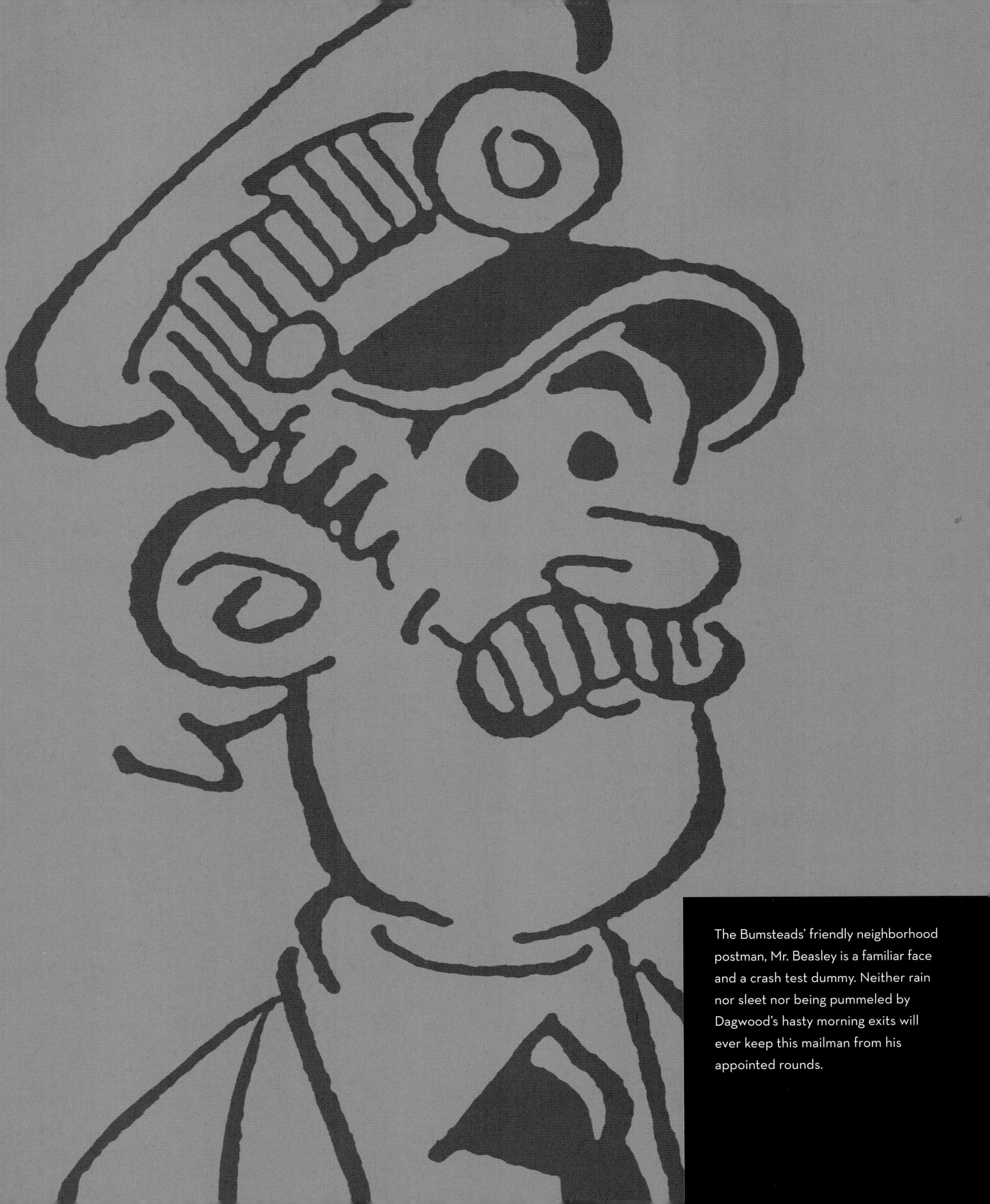

The Bumsteads' friendly neighborhood postman, Mr. Beasley is a familiar face and a crash test dummy. Neither rain nor sleet nor being pummeled by Dagwood's hasty morning exits will ever keep this mailman from his appointed rounds.

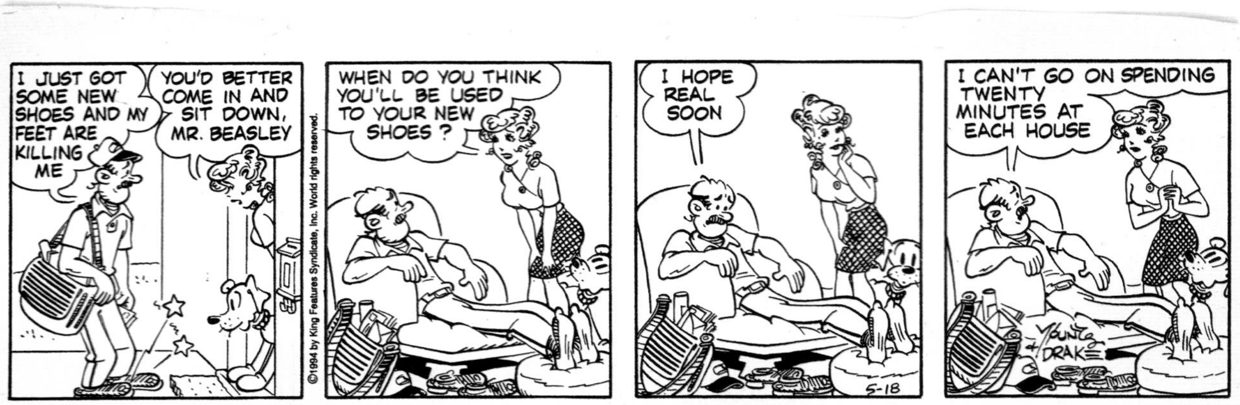
I JUST GOT SOME NEW SHOES AND MY FEET ARE KILLING ME
YOU'D BETTER COME IN AND SIT DOWN, MR. BEASLEY
©1994 by King Features Syndicate, Inc. World rights reserved.
WHEN DO YOU THINK YOU'LL BE USED TO YOUR NEW SHOES ?
I HOPE REAL SOON
5-18
I CAN'T GO ON SPENDING TWENTY MINUTES AT EACH HOUSE
YOUNG DRAKE

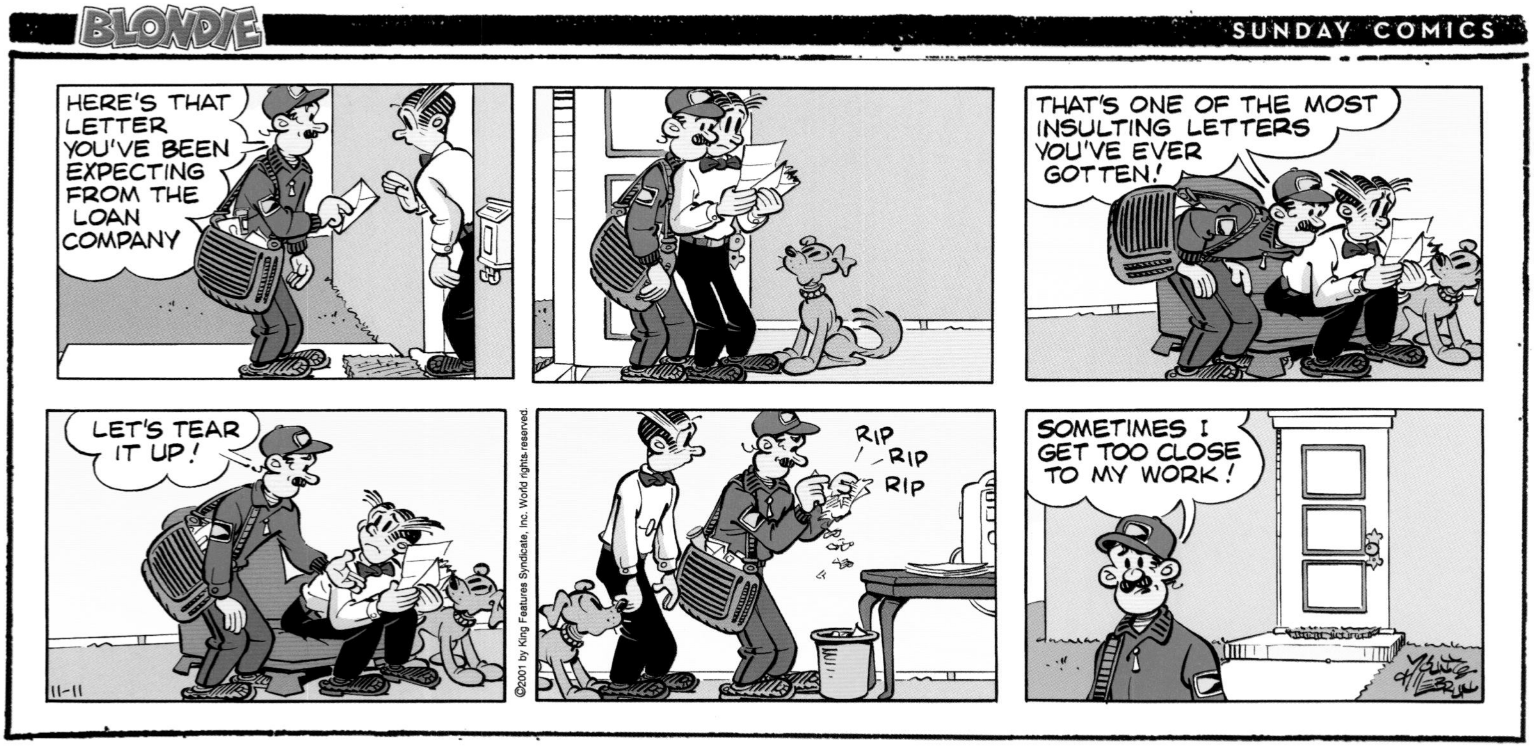
BLONDIE
SUNDAY COMICS
HERE'S THAT LETTER YOU'VE BEEN EXPECTING FROM THE LOAN COMPANY
THAT'S ONE OF THE MOST INSULTING LETTERS YOU'VE EVER GOTTEN!
LET'S TEAR IT UP!
11-11
©2001 by King Features Syndicate, Inc. World rights reserved.
RIP RIP RIP
SOMETIMES I GET TOO CLOSE TO MY WORK!

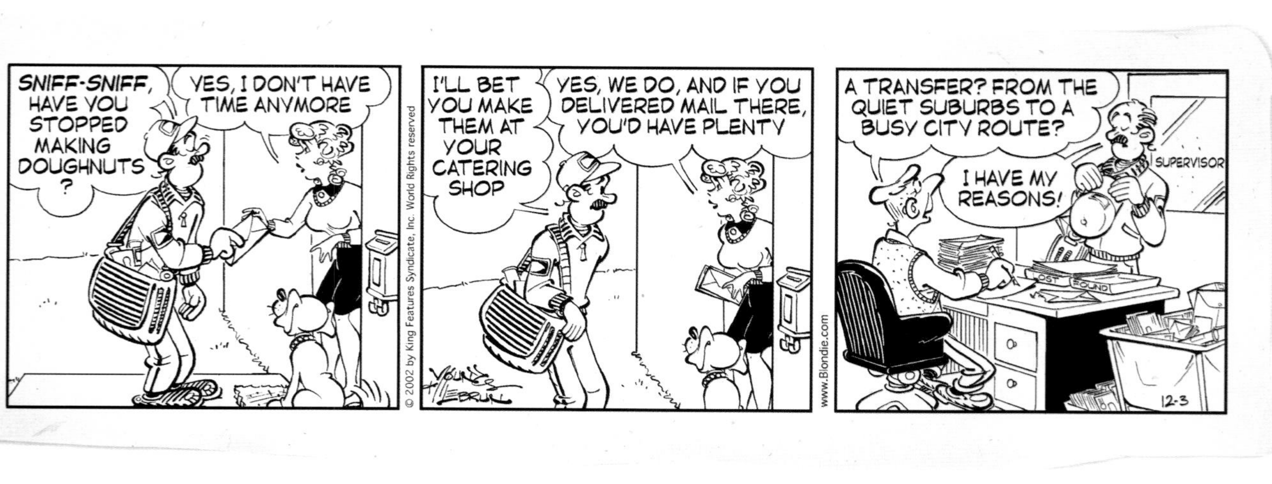
SNIFF-SNIFF, HAVE YOU STOPPED MAKING DOUGHNUTS ?
YES, I DON'T HAVE TIME ANYMORE
© 2002 by King Features Syndicate, Inc. World Rights reserved
I'LL BET YOU MAKE THEM AT YOUR CATERING SHOP
YES, WE DO, AND IF YOU DELIVERED MAIL THERE, YOU'D HAVE PLENTY
www.Blondie.com
A TRANSFER? FROM THE QUIET SUBURBS TO A BUSY CITY ROUTE?
I HAVE MY REASONS!
SUPERVISOR
LOST FOUND
12-3

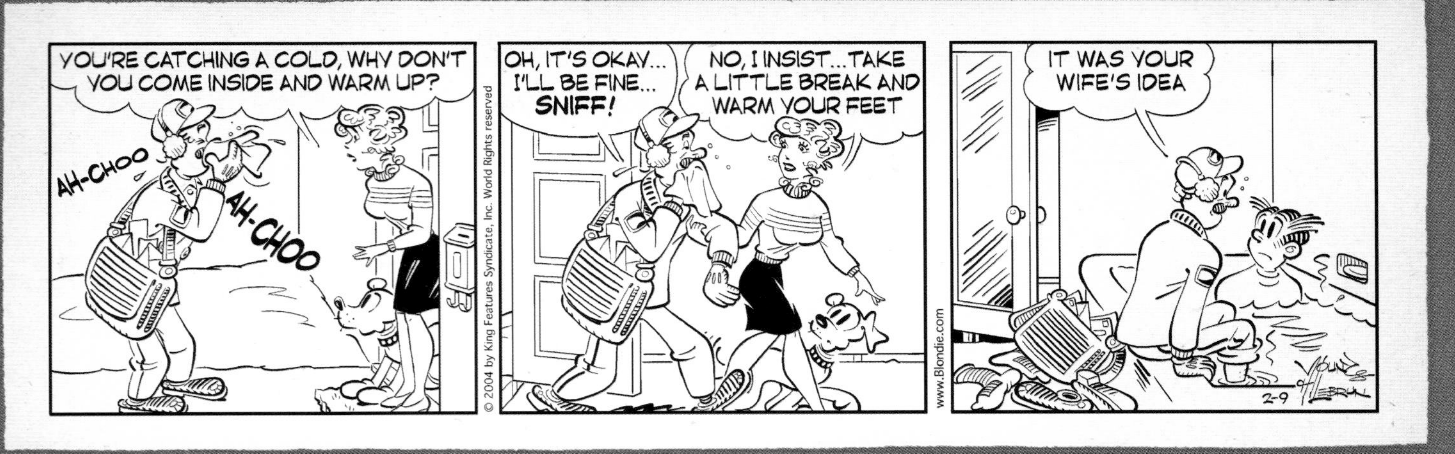
YOU'RE CATCHING A COLD, WHY DON'T YOU COME INSIDE AND WARM UP?
AH-CHOO
AH-CHOO
© 2004 by King Features Syndicate, Inc. World Rights reserved
OH, IT'S OKAY... I'LL BE FINE... SNIFF!
NO, I INSIST...TAKE A LITTLE BREAK AND WARM YOUR FEET
www.Blondie.com
IT WAS YOUR WIFE'S IDEA
2-9

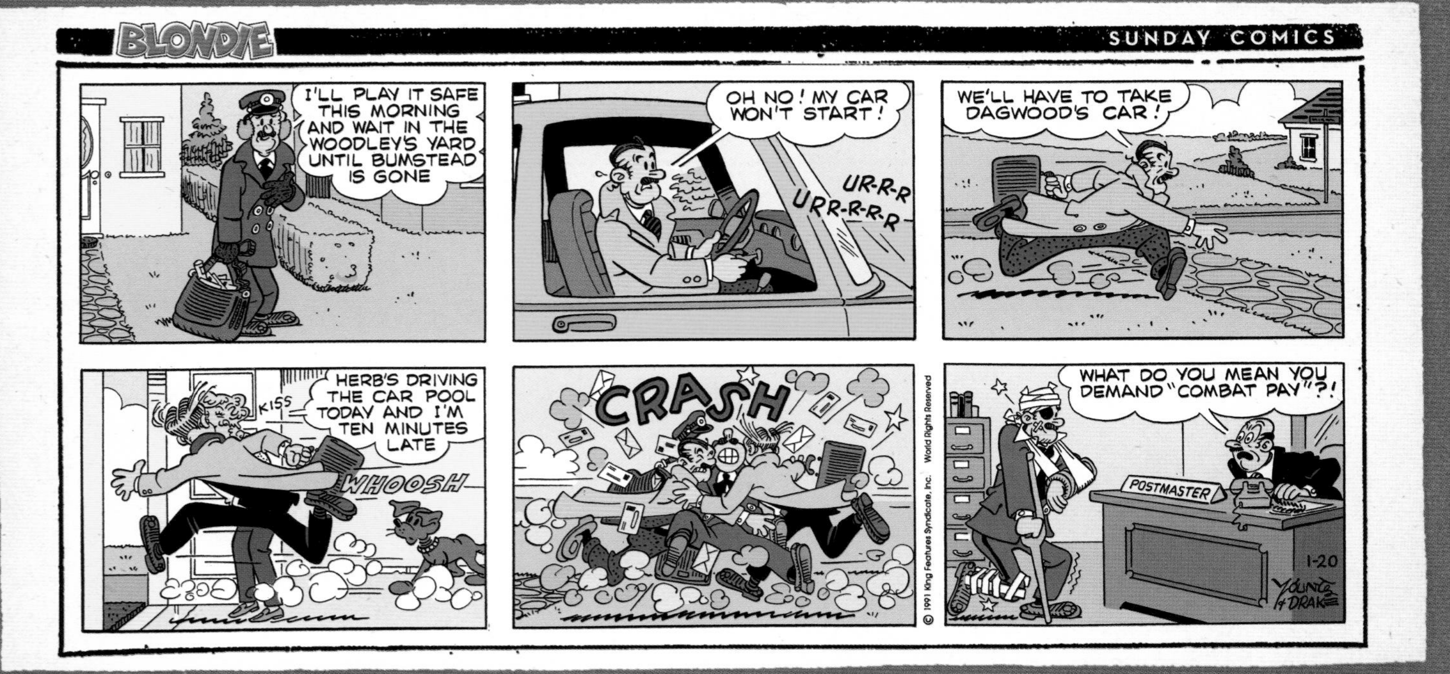
BLONDIE
SUNDAY COMICS
I'LL PLAY IT SAFE THIS MORNING AND WAIT IN THE WOODLEY'S YARD UNTIL BUMSTEAD IS GONE
OH NO! MY CAR WON'T START!
UR-R-R
URR-R-R-R
WE'LL HAVE TO TAKE DAGWOOD'S CAR!
KISS
HERB'S DRIVING THE CAR POOL TODAY AND I'M TEN MINUTES LATE
WHOOSH
CRASH
© 1991 King Features Syndicate, Inc. World Rights Reserved
WHAT DO YOU MEAN YOU DEMAND "COMBAT PAY"?!
POSTMASTER
1-20

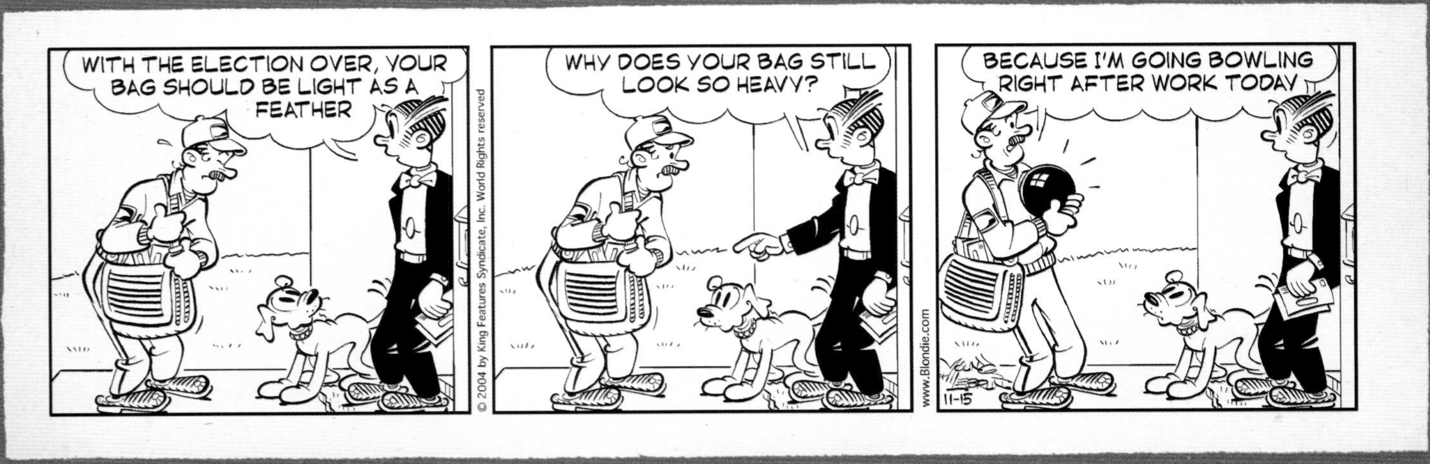
WITH THE ELECTION OVER, YOUR BAG SHOULD BE LIGHT AS A FEATHER
© 2004 by King Features Syndicate, Inc. World Rights reserved
WHY DOES YOUR BAG STILL LOOK SO HEAVY?
www.Blondie.com
BECAUSE I'M GOING BOWLING RIGHT AFTER WORK TODAY
11-15

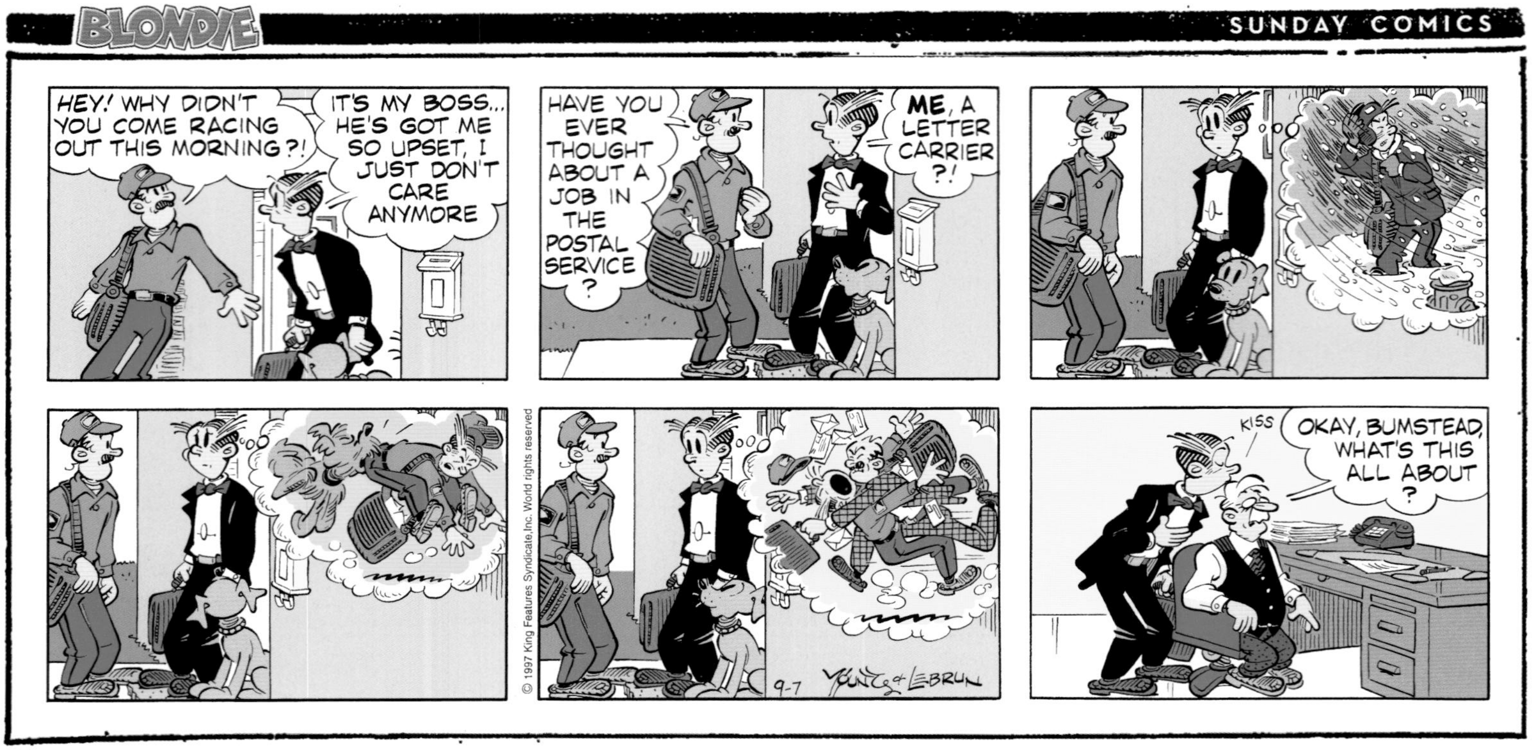
BLONDIE
SUNDAY COMICS
HEY! WHY DIDN'T YOU COME RACING OUT THIS MORNING?!
IT'S MY BOSS... HE'S GOT ME SO UPSET, I JUST DON'T CARE ANYMORE
HAVE YOU EVER THOUGHT ABOUT A JOB IN THE POSTAL SERVICE?
ME, A LETTER CARRIER?!
© 1997 King Features Syndicate, Inc. World rights reserved
9-7
YOUNG & LEBRUN
KISS
OKAY, BUMSTEAD, WHAT'S THIS ALL ABOUT?

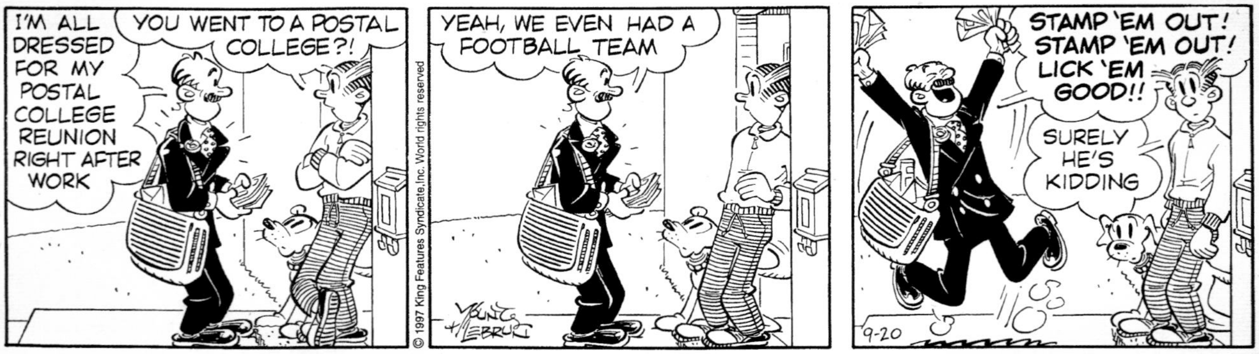
I'M ALL DRESSED FOR MY POSTAL COLLEGE REUNION RIGHT AFTER WORK
YOU WENT TO A POSTAL COLLEGE?!
YOUNG & LEBRUN
© 1997 King Features Syndicate, Inc. World rights reserved
YEAH, WE EVEN HAD A FOOTBALL TEAM
STAMP 'EM OUT! STAMP 'EM OUT! LICK 'EM GOOD!!
SURELY HE'S KIDDING
9-20

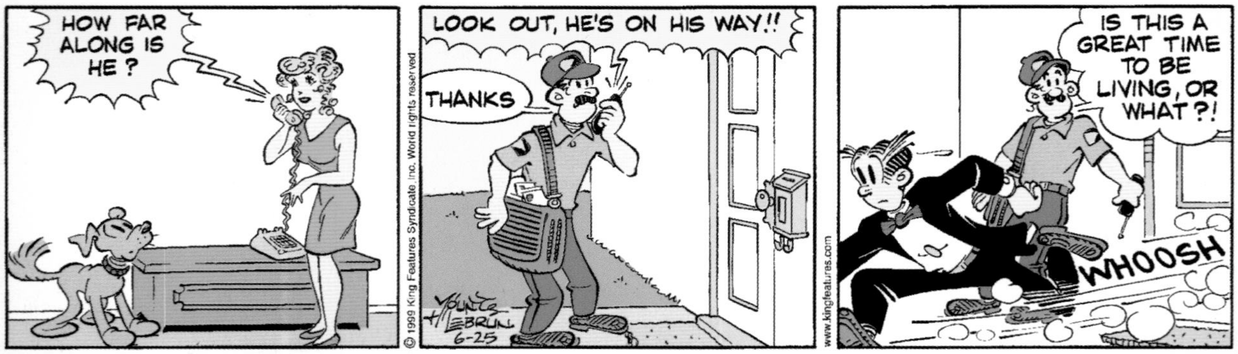
HOW FAR ALONG IS HE?
© 1999 King Features Syndicate, Inc. World rights reserved
LOOK OUT, HE'S ON HIS WAY!!
THANKS
YOUNG & LEBRUN 6-25
www.kingfeatures.com
IS THIS A GREAT TIME TO BE LIVING, OR WHAT?!
WHOOSH

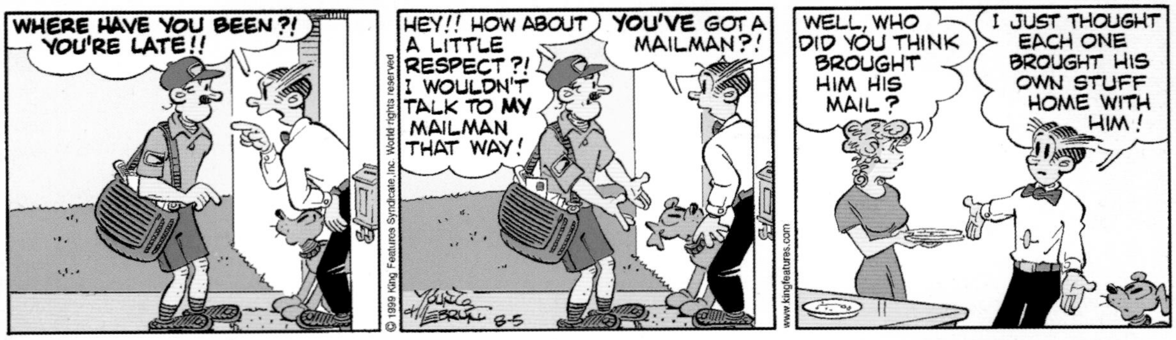
WHERE HAVE YOU BEEN?! YOU'RE LATE!!
HEY!! HOW ABOUT A LITTLE RESPECT?! I WOULDN'T TALK TO MY MAILMAN THAT WAY!
YOU'VE GOT A MAILMAN?!
WELL, WHO DID YOU THINK BROUGHT HIM HIS MAIL?
I JUST THOUGHT EACH ONE BROUGHT HIS OWN STUFF HOME WITH HIM!
© 1999 King Features Syndicate, Inc. World rights reserved
www.kingfeatures.com
8-5

“Mr. Beasley is probably the hardest-working man in comics; neither sleet nor snow nor rain nor threat of full-body collision can deter him.”

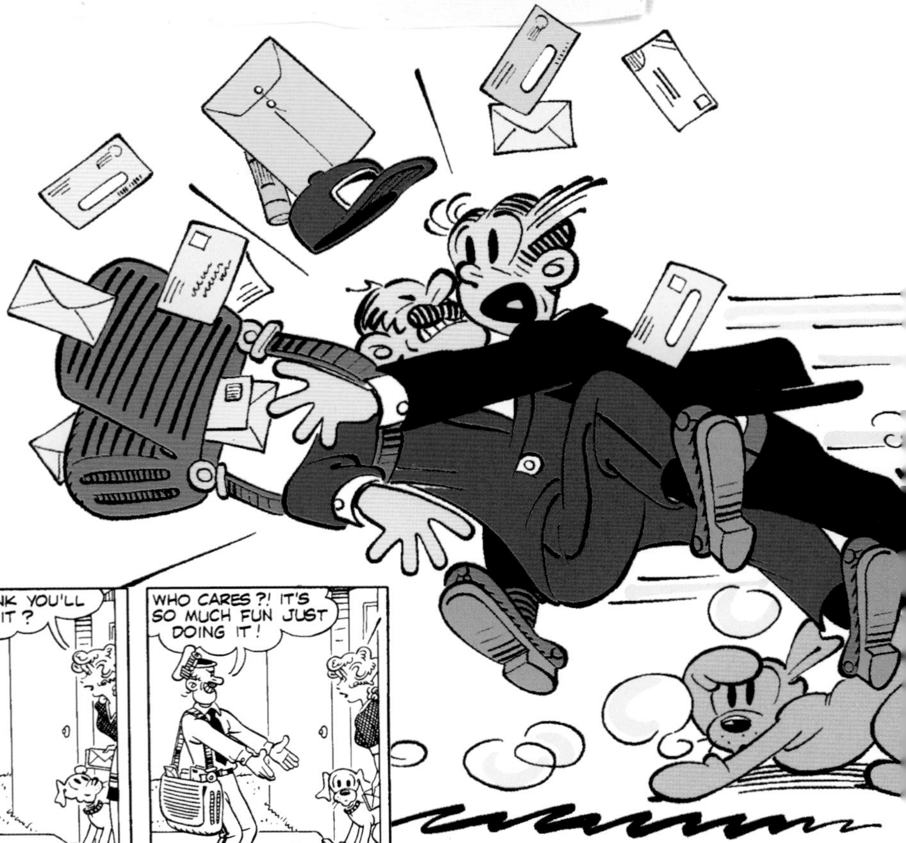

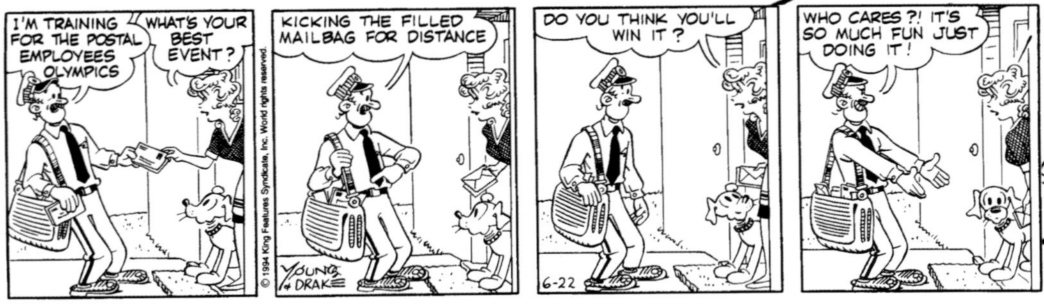
I'M TRAINING FOR THE POSTAL EMPLOYEES OLYMPICS
WHAT'S YOUR BEST EVENT?
KICKING THE FILLED MAILBAG FOR DISTANCE
DO YOU THINK YOU'LL WIN IT?
WHO CARES?! IT'S SO MUCH FUN JUST DOING IT!
© 1994 King Features Syndicate, Inc. World rights reserved
6-22

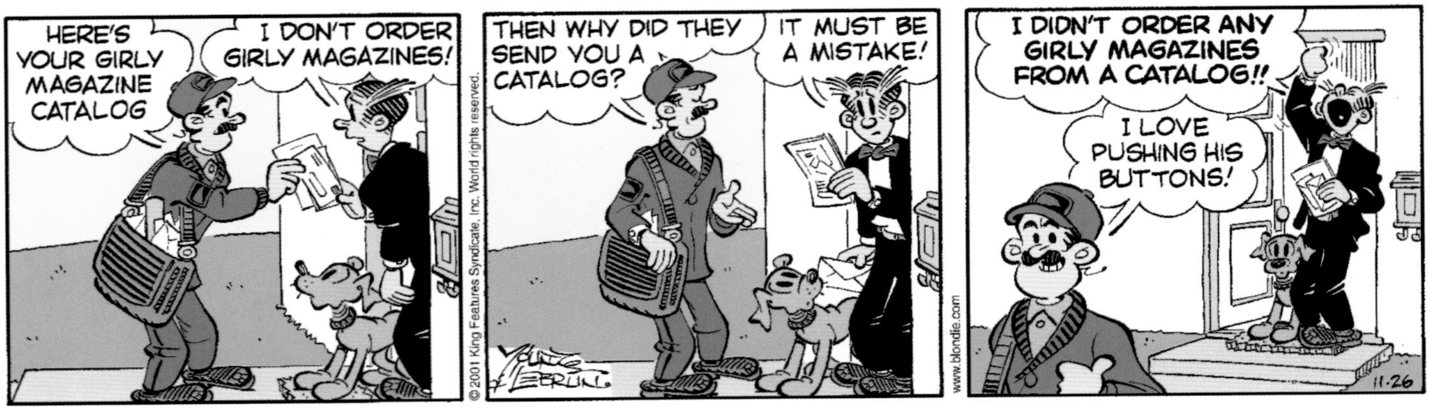
HERE'S YOUR GIRLY MAGAZINE CATALOG
I DON'T ORDER GIRLY MAGAZINES!
THEN WHY DID THEY SEND YOU A CATALOG?
IT MUST BE A MISTAKE!
I DIDN'T ORDER ANY GIRLY MAGAZINES FROM A CATALOG!!
I LOVE PUSHING HIS BUTTONS!
© 2001 King Features Syndicate, Inc. World rights reserved.
www.blondie.com
11-26

ELMO

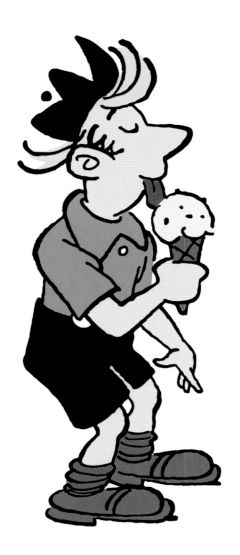

With Alexander and Cookie firmly ensconced in their teenage years—as mature as they're going to get—Chic Young turned to Elmo Tuttle to fulfill the role of the playful, inquisitive child. Perpetually five-year-old Elmo lives across the street from Dagwood and Blondie (and Herb and Tootsie, though he doesn't seem to bother them nearly as much). Clad in an ever-present baseball hat and sporting a wide grin, Elmo's carefree (and oddly parent-free) days are filled with softball games, hockey games, skateboarding, and general childhood fun. His companion—and occasional nemesis—for much of this? Dagwood Bumstead, or as Elmo refers to him, Mr. B.

Mr. B. can fix anything. He's an expert on many vital kindergarten concerns, like snow angels and playground bullies. In the early-morning hours, when Elmo and he wait on the corner for their respective rides (school bus for Elmo, car pool for Mr. B.), he can answer questions about the important things in life: women, money, and bologna. He's also, Elmo has found, easy to manipulate: he's a continual source of golf course employment, despite Elmo's obvious lack of skill—and strength—as a caddy.

But their friendship isn't one-sided; Dagwood needs Elmo to remind him of his role as an authority figure (his own children have long since forgotten that he is one) and to keep him up-to-date. A comic staple and a point of reference for *Blondie's* youngest fans, Elmo is probably the most in touch with today's technology and trends. Like any five-year-old, he has play dates and camera phones. But at heart, he remains a sweet little boy, with boundless enthusiasm and curiosity—especially about food—which is probably why he gets along with Dagwood so well. It's symbiosis at its most basic—and most tasty.

Elmo's carefree days are filled with softball games, hockey games, skateboarding, and general childhood fun.

MR. B., I'M NOT GETTING SUCH GOOD GRADES IN SCHOOL
WELL, DON'T WORRY TOO MUCH...
2-7
© 2005 by King Features Syndicate, Inc. World Rights reserved
I DIDN'T GET SUCH GOOD GRADES EITHER, BUT LOOK AT ME NOW!
www.Blondie.com
WHERE ARE YOU GOING?
HOME TO STUDY!

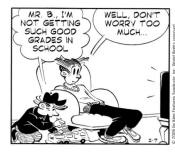

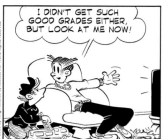

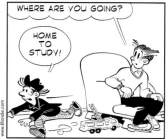

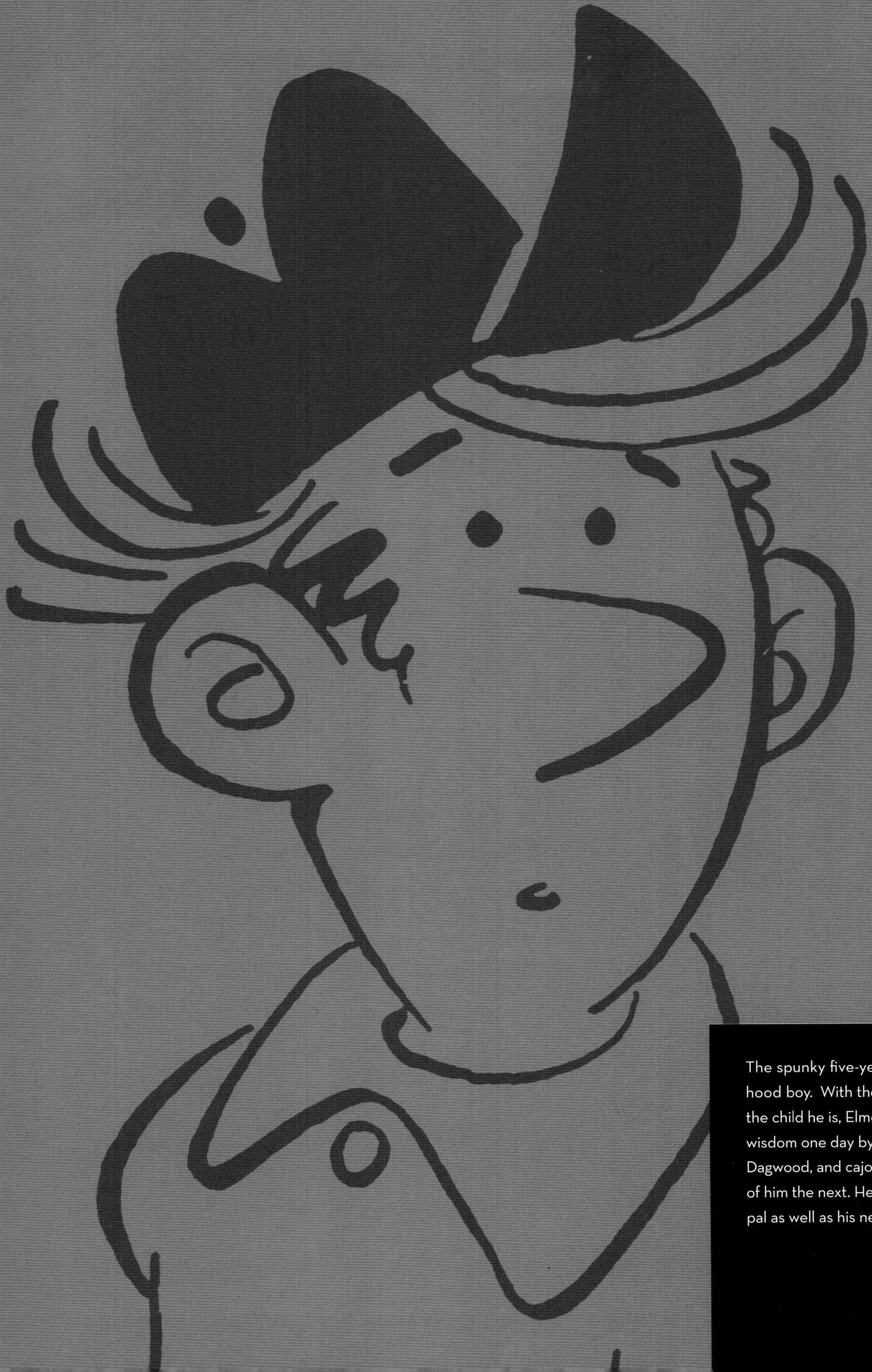

The spunky five-year old neighborhood boy. With the curiosity of the child he is, Elmo can seek adult wisdom one day by questioning Dagwood, and cajole something out of him the next. He is Dagwood's little pal as well as his nemesis.

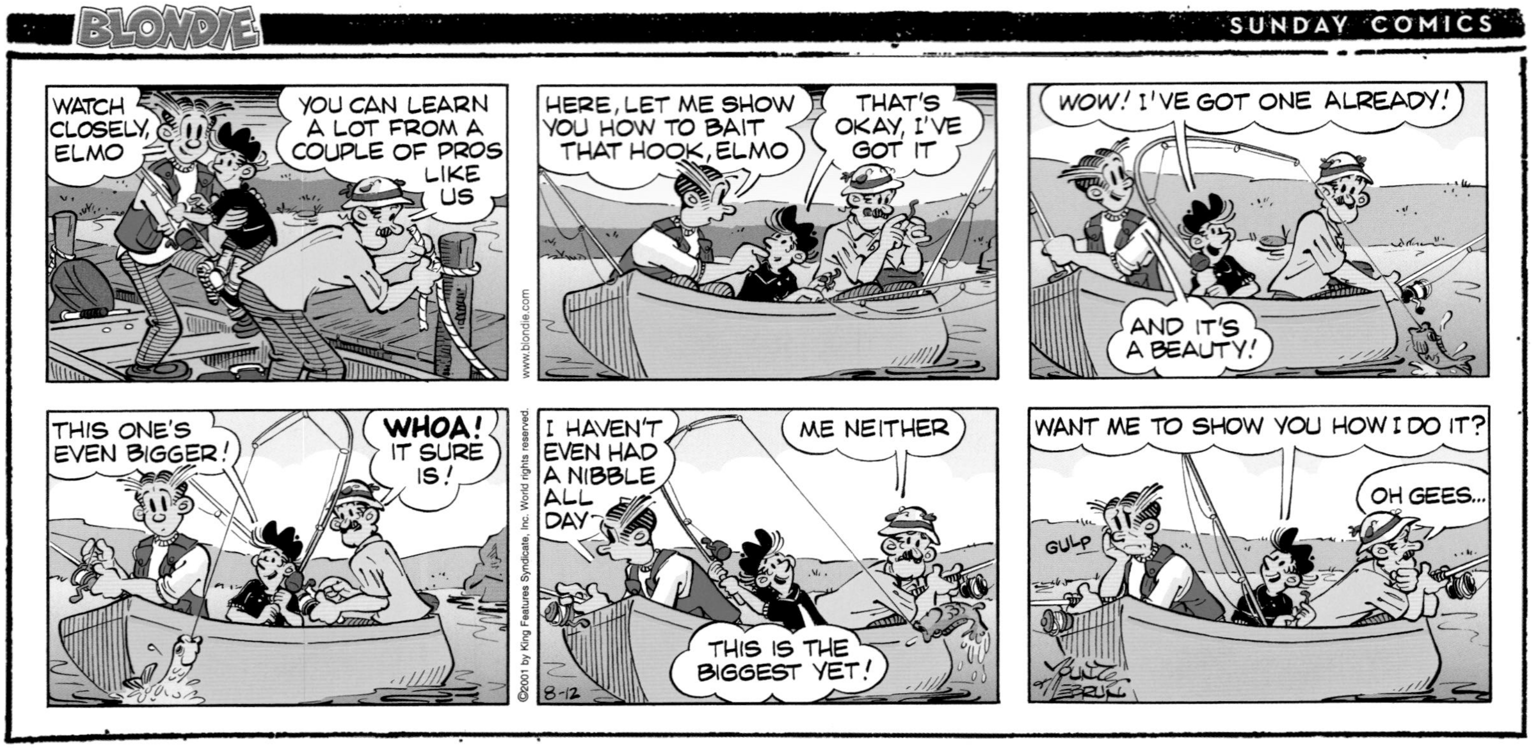
BLONDIE
SUNDAY COMICS
WATCH CLOSELY, ELMO
YOU CAN LEARN A LOT FROM A COUPLE OF PROS LIKE US
HERE, LET ME SHOW YOU HOW TO BAIT THAT HOOK, ELMO
THAT'S OKAY, I'VE GOT IT
WOW! I'VE GOT ONE ALREADY!
AND IT'S A BEAUTY!
THIS ONE'S EVEN BIGGER!
WHOA! IT SURE IS!
I HAVEN'T EVEN HAD A NIBBLE ALL DAY
ME NEITHER
THIS IS THE BIGGEST YET!
WANT ME TO SHOW YOU HOW I DO IT?
OH GEES...
GULP
www.blondie.com
©2001 by King Features Syndicate, Inc. World rights reserved.
8-12

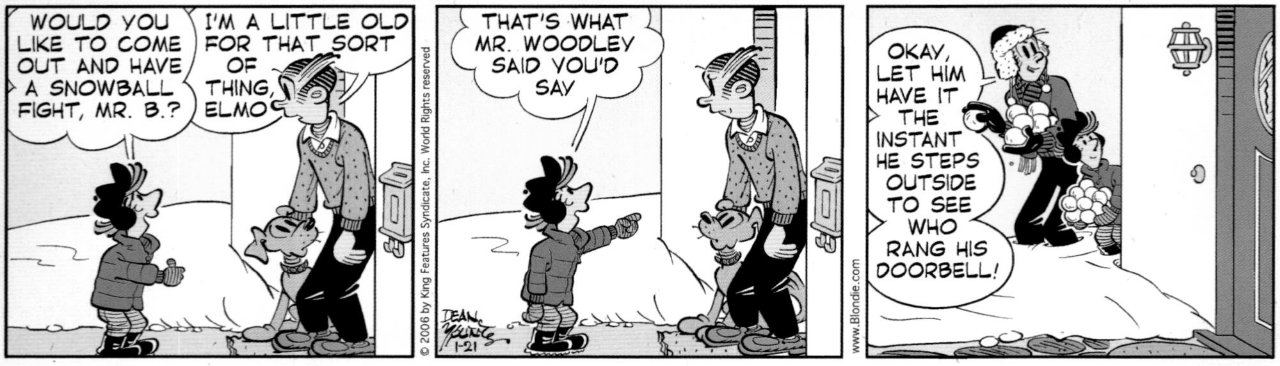
WOULD YOU LIKE TO COME OUT AND HAVE A SNOWBALL FIGHT, MR. B.?
I'M A LITTLE OLD FOR THAT SORT OF THING, ELMO
THAT'S WHAT MR. WOODLEY SAID YOU'D SAY
OKAY, LET HIM HAVE IT THE INSTANT HE STEPS OUTSIDE TO SEE WHO RANG HIS DOORBELL!
© 2006 by King Features Syndicate, Inc. World Rights reserved
1-21
www.Blondie.com

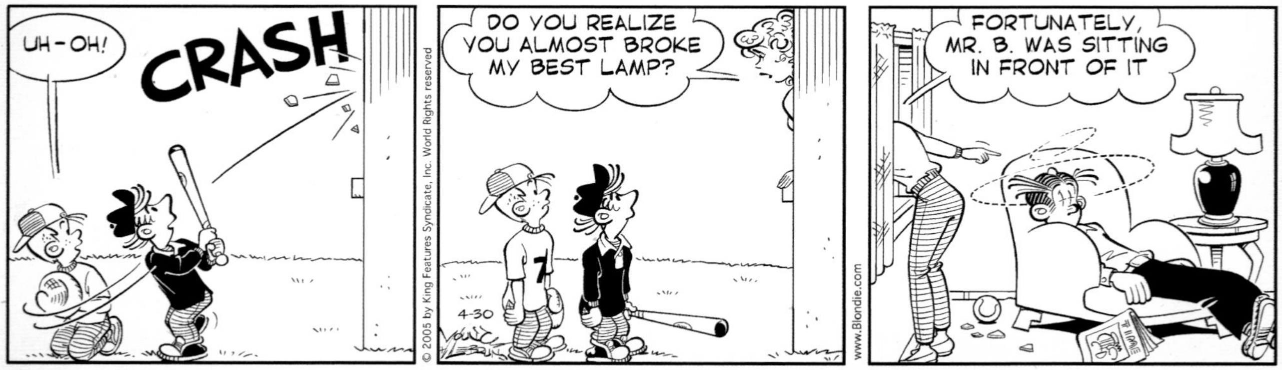
UH-OH!
CRASH
DO YOU REALIZE YOU ALMOST BROKE MY BEST LAMP?
FORTUNATELY, MR. B. WAS SITTING IN FRONT OF IT
© 2005 by King Features Syndicate, Inc. World Rights reserved
4-30
www.Blondie.com

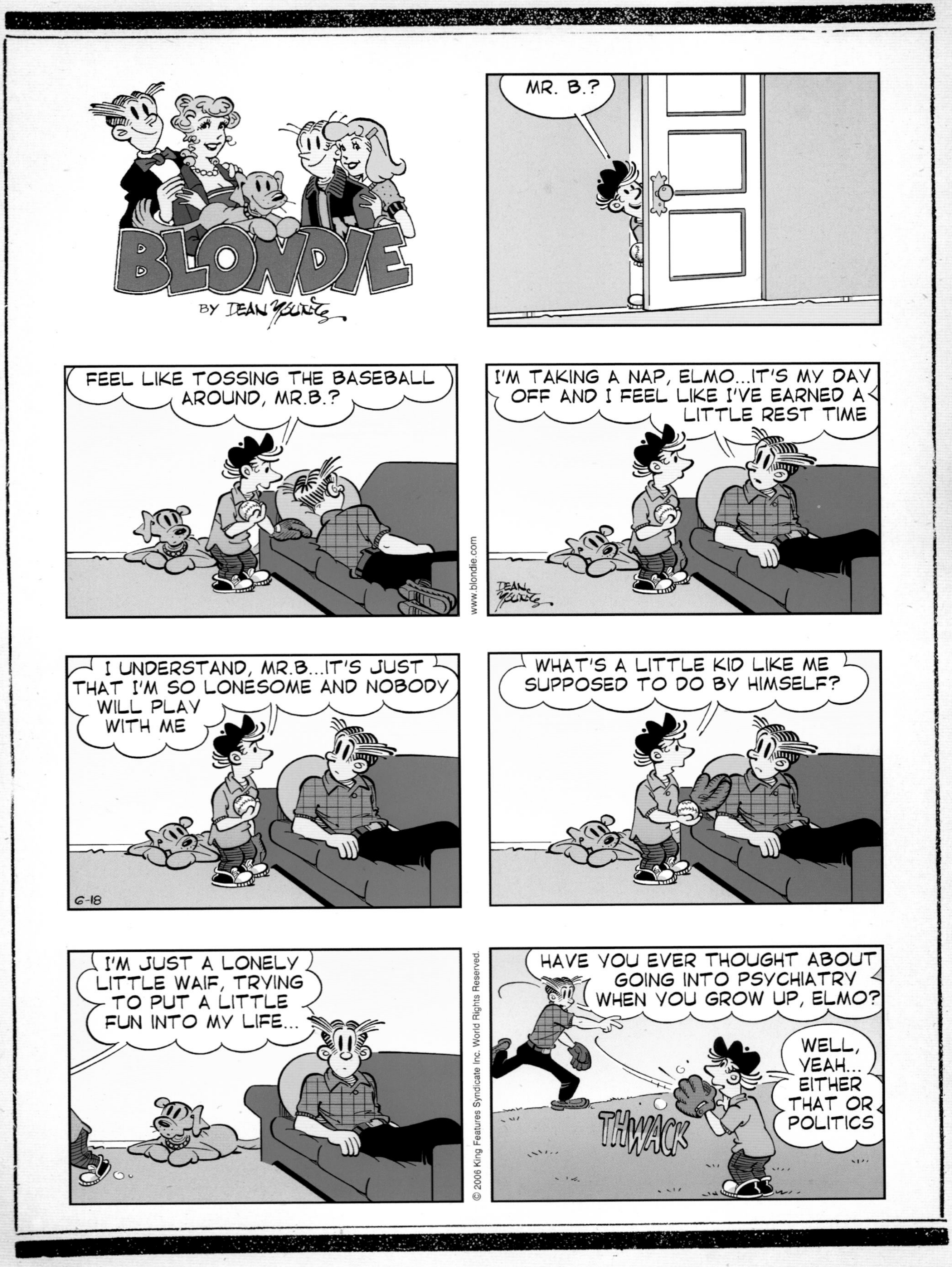
BLONDIE
BY DEAN YOUNG
MR. B.?
FEEL LIKE TOSSING THE BASEBALL AROUND, MR.B.?
I'M TAKING A NAP, ELMO...IT'S MY DAY OFF AND I FEEL LIKE I'VE EARNED A LITTLE REST TIME
I UNDERSTAND, MR.B...IT'S JUST THAT I'M SO LONESOME AND NOBODY WILL PLAY WITH ME
WHAT'S A LITTLE KID LIKE ME SUPPOSED TO DO BY HIMSELF?
I'M JUST A LONELY LITTLE WAIF, TRYING TO PUT A LITTLE FUN INTO MY LIFE...
HAVE YOU EVER THOUGHT ABOUT GOING INTO PSYCHIATRY WHEN YOU GROW UP, ELMO?
WELL, YEAH... EITHER THAT OR POLITICS
THWACK
6-18
www.blondie.com

OH BOY, IT'LL FEEL GOOD TO GET SOME EXERCISE AFTER MY BIG NAP
CAN YOU SHOW ME HOW TO MAKE A SNOW ANGEL, MR. B.?
SURE, ELMO! JUST LIE DOWN AND MOVE YOUR ARMS BACK AND FORTH
SEE?
HONESTLY, THAT MAN CAN'T STAY OFF HIS BACK FOR MORE THAN TWO MINUTES
© 2002 King Features Syndicate, Inc. World rights reserved.
www.blondie.com
2-7

YOU KNOW WHAT WOULD REALLY BE COOL, MR. B.?
WHAT'S THAT, ELMO?
PIZZA-FLAVORED TOOTHPASTE
YOU KNOW WHAT WOULD REALLY BE COOL, HONEY?
© 2005 by King Features Syndicate, Inc. World Rights reserved
www.Blondie.com
3-5

GUESS WHAT I'M WEARING, MR. BUMSTEAD
WHAT'S THAT, ELMO?
REAL DOCTOR'S GLOVES
IS THAT BECAUSE YOU WANT TO BE A DOCTOR WHEN YOU GROW UP?
HECK NO, IT'S SO I DON'T HAVE TO WASH MY HANDS
© 1995 King Features Syndicate, Inc. World rights reserved.
YOUNG & DRAKE
8-29

GO AWAY, ELMO, I NEED A TEN-MINUTE NAP
HOW ABOUT FIVE MINUTES?
HOW ABOUT SEVEN?
LET'S COMPROMISE... MAKE IT SIX
OKAY, THE FIRST MINUTE'S UP... YOU'VE GOT FIVE MORE TO GO!
© 1999 King Features Syndicate Inc. World rights reserved
www.kingfeatures.com

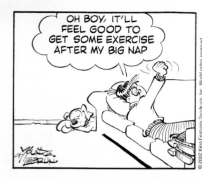

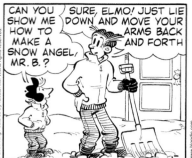

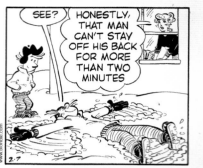

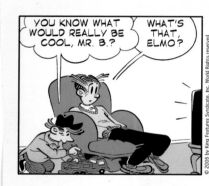

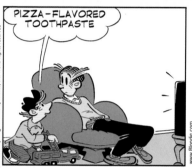

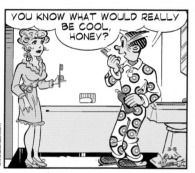

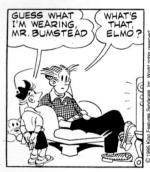

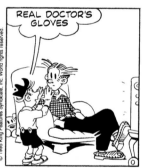

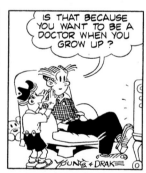

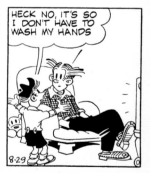

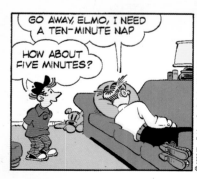

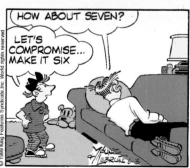

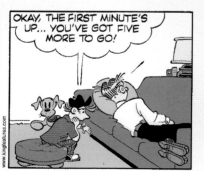

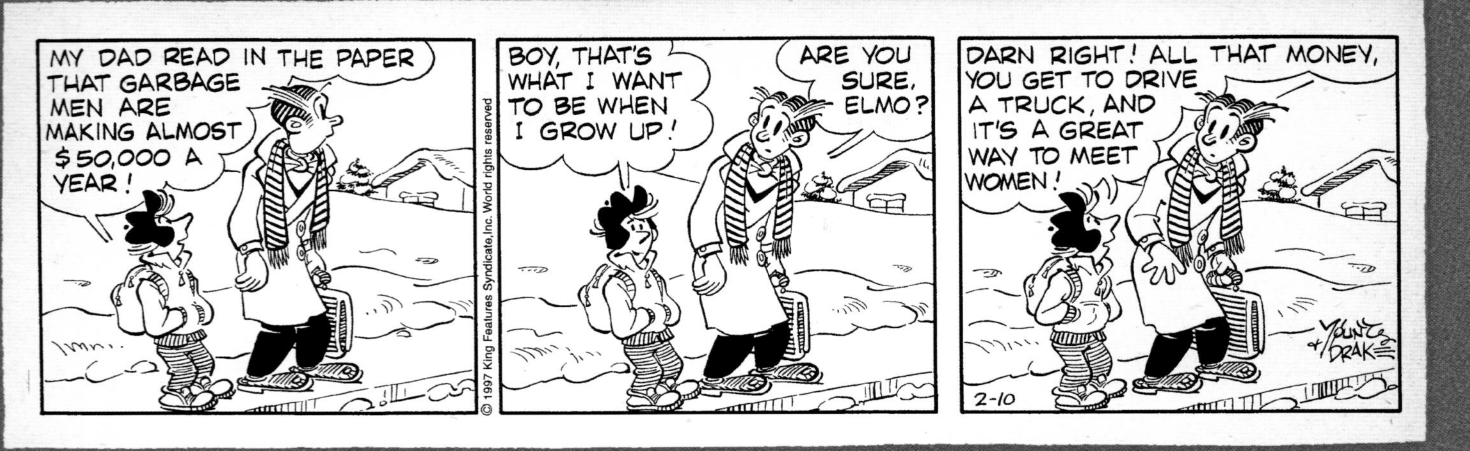
MY DAD READ IN THE PAPER THAT GARBAGE MEN ARE MAKING ALMOST $50,000 A YEAR!
BOY, THAT'S WHAT I WANT TO BE WHEN I GROW UP!
ARE YOU SURE, ELMO?
DARN RIGHT! ALL THAT MONEY, YOU GET TO DRIVE A TRUCK, AND IT'S A GREAT WAY TO MEET WOMEN!
2-10
YOUNG & DRAKE

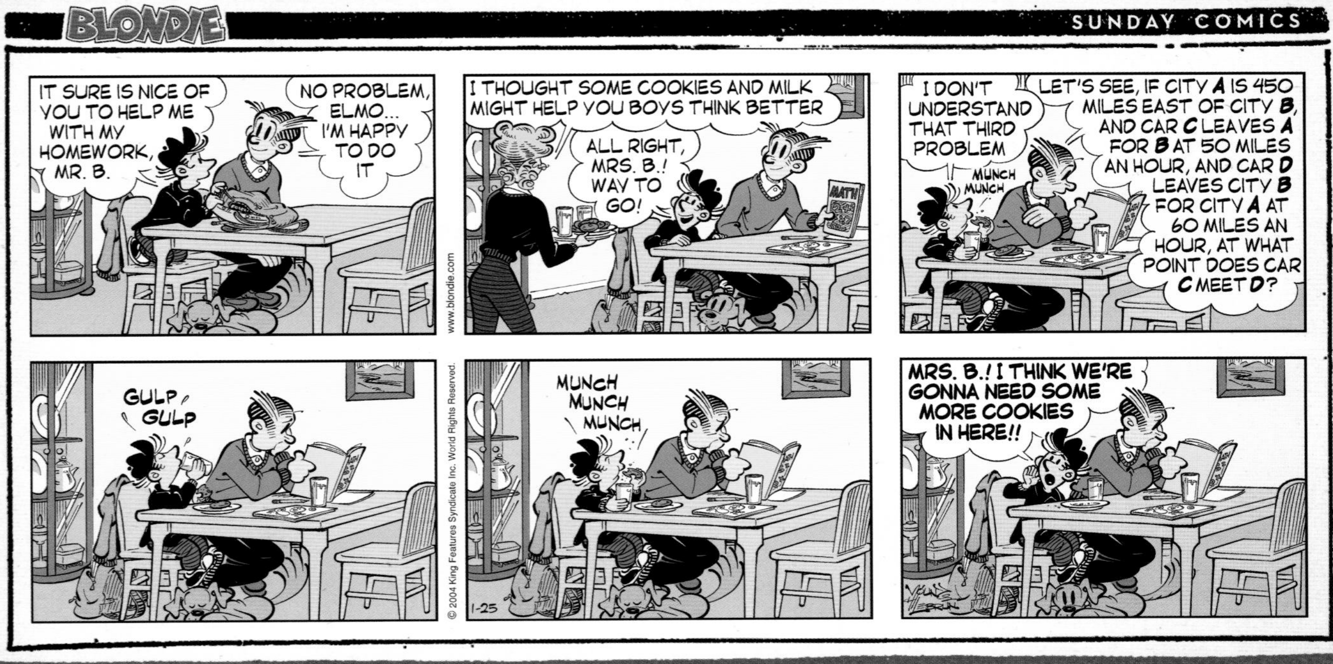
BLONDIE
SUNDAY COMICS
IT SURE IS NICE OF YOU TO HELP ME WITH MY HOMEWORK, MR. B.
NO PROBLEM, ELMO... I'M HAPPY TO DO IT
I THOUGHT SOME COOKIES AND MILK MIGHT HELP YOU BOYS THINK BETTER
ALL RIGHT, MRS. B.! WAY TO GO!
MATH
I DON'T UNDERSTAND THAT THIRD PROBLEM
MUNCH MUNCH
LET'S SEE, IF CITY A IS 450 MILES EAST OF CITY B, AND CAR C LEAVES A FOR B AT 50 MILES AN HOUR, AND CAR D LEAVES CITY B FOR CITY A AT 60 MILES AN HOUR, AT WHAT POINT DOES CAR C MEET D?
GULP GULP
MUNCH MUNCH MUNCH
MRS. B.! I THINK WE'RE GONNA NEED SOME MORE COOKIES IN HERE!!
1-25

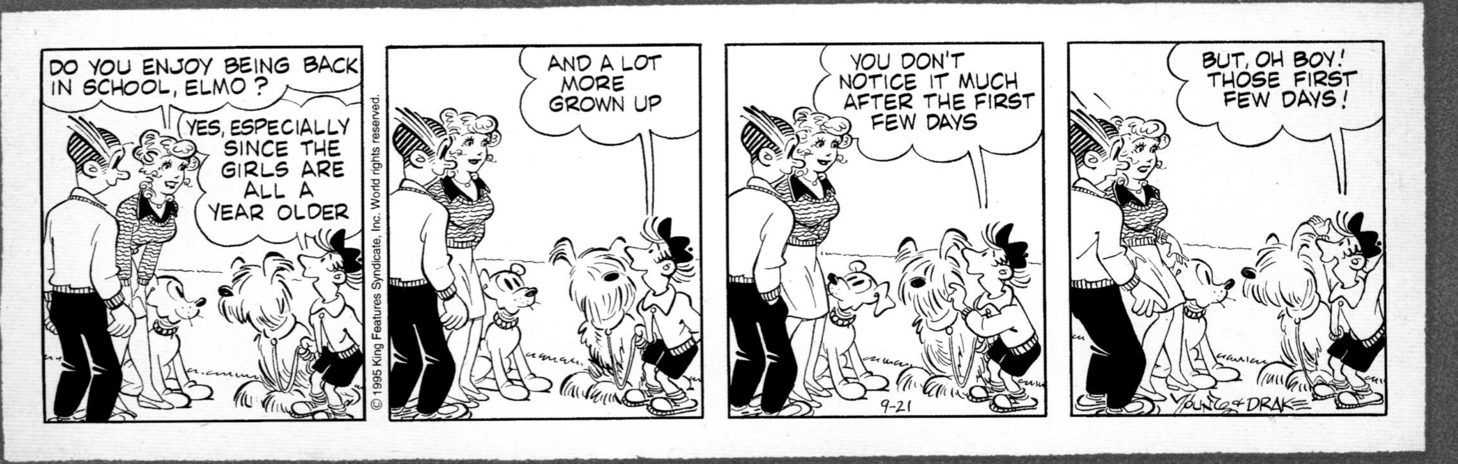
DO YOU ENJOY BEING BACK IN SCHOOL, ELMO?
YES, ESPECIALLY SINCE THE GIRLS ARE ALL A YEAR OLDER
AND A LOT MORE GROWN UP
YOU DON'T NOTICE IT MUCH AFTER THE FIRST FEW DAYS
BUT, OH BOY! THOSE FIRST FEW DAYS!
9-21
YOUNG & DRAKE

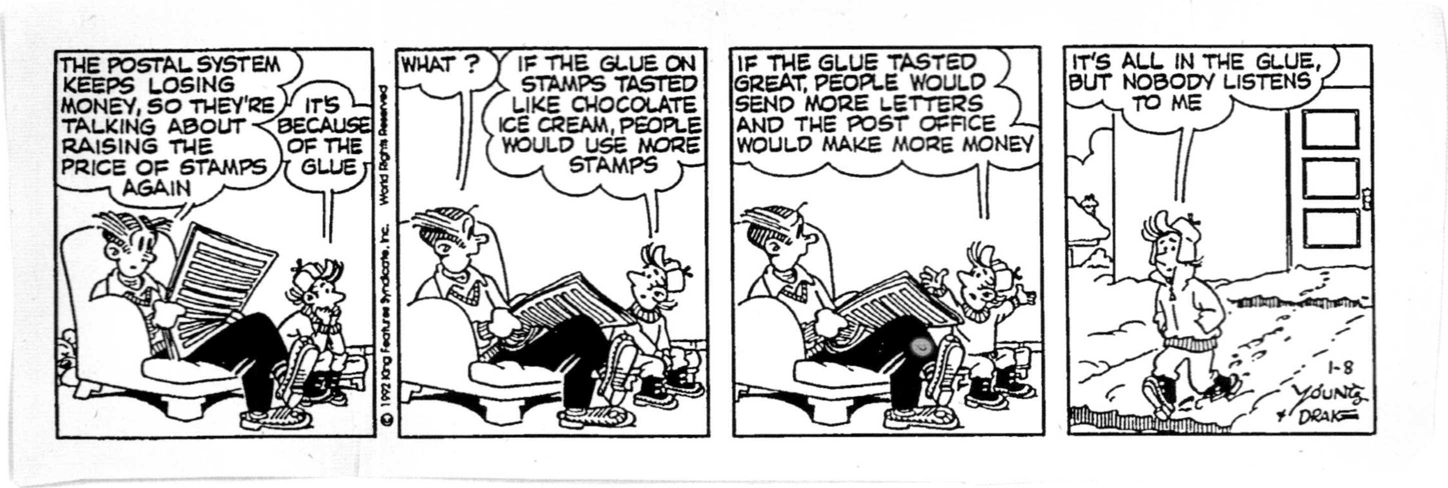
THE POSTAL SYSTEM KEEPS LOSING MONEY, SO THEY'RE TALKING ABOUT RAISING THE PRICE OF STAMPS AGAIN
IT'S BECAUSE OF THE GLUE
© 1992 King Features Syndicate, Inc. World Rights Reserved
WHAT ?
IF THE GLUE ON STAMPS TASTED LIKE CHOCOLATE ICE CREAM, PEOPLE WOULD USE MORE STAMPS
IF THE GLUE TASTED GREAT, PEOPLE WOULD SEND MORE LETTERS AND THE POST OFFICE WOULD MAKE MORE MONEY
IT'S ALL IN THE GLUE, BUT NOBODY LISTENS TO ME
1-8
YOUNG + DRAKE

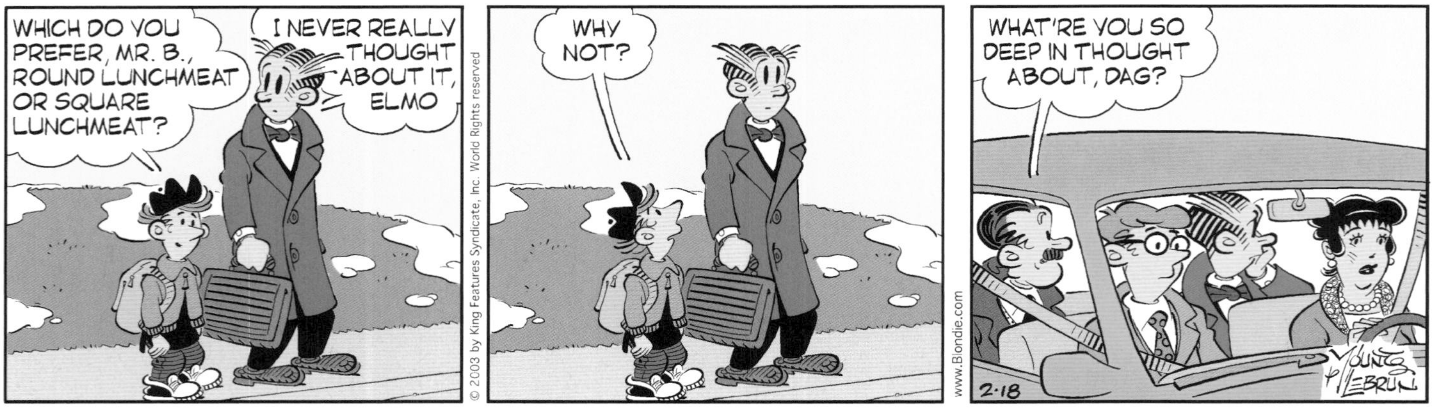
WHICH DO YOU PREFER, MR. B., ROUND LUNCHMEAT OR SQUARE LUNCHMEAT?
I NEVER REALLY THOUGHT ABOUT IT, ELMO
© 2003 by King Features Syndicate, Inc. World Rights reserved
WHY NOT?
www.Blondie.com
WHAT'RE YOU SO DEEP IN THOUGHT ABOUT, DAG?
2·18
YOUNG + LEBRUN

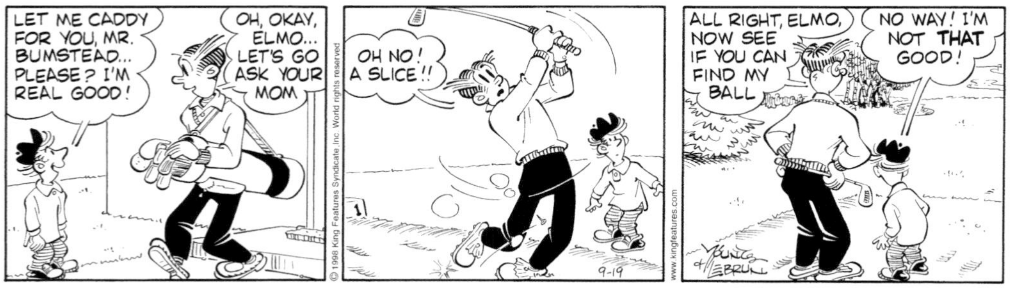
LET ME CADDY FOR YOU, MR. BUMSTEAD... PLEASE? I'M REAL GOOD!
OH, OKAY, ELMO... LET'S GO ASK YOUR MOM
© 1998 King Features Syndicate Inc. World rights reserved
OH NO! A SLICE!!
9-19
www.kingfeatures.com
ALL RIGHT, ELMO, NOW SEE IF YOU CAN FIND MY BALL
NO WAY! I'M NOT THAT GOOD!
YOUNG + LEBRUN

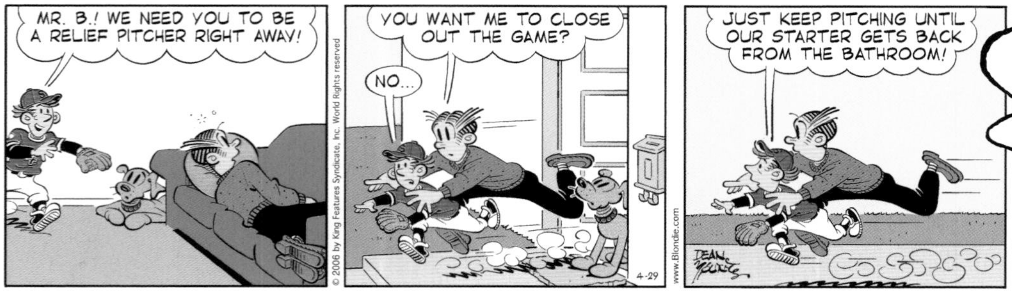
MR. B.! WE NEED YOU TO BE A RELIEF PITCHER RIGHT AWAY!
© 2006 by King Features Syndicate, Inc. World Rights reserved
YOU WANT ME TO CLOSE OUT THE GAME?
NO...
4-29
www.Blondie.com
JUST KEEP PITCHING UNTIL OUR STARTER GETS BACK FROM THE BATHROOM!
DEAN YOUNG

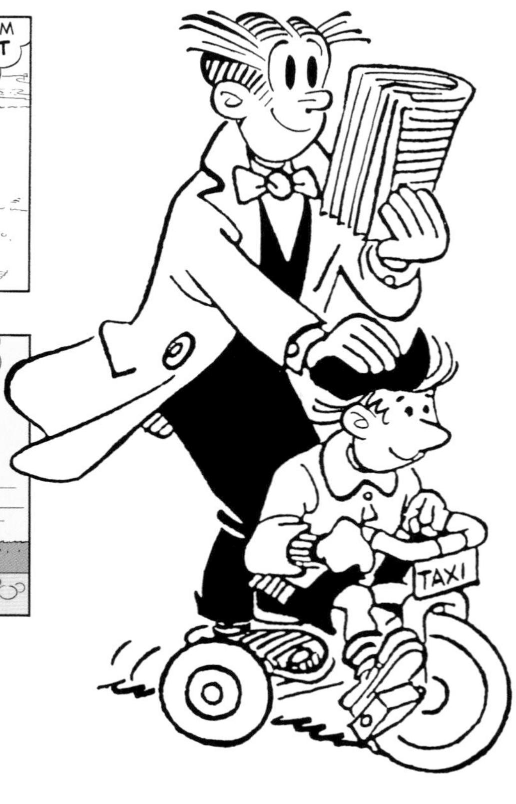
TAXI

CHAPTER 2

GETTING MARRIED

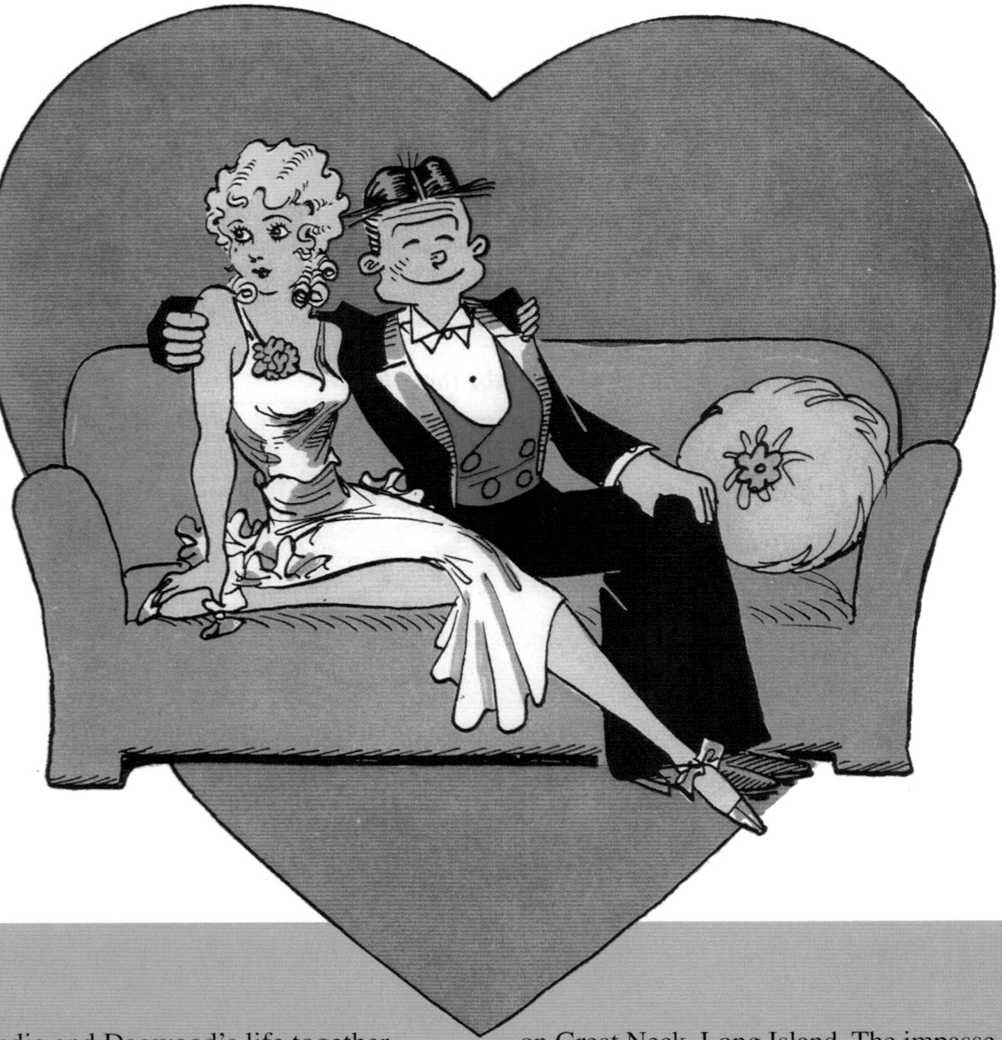

Though Blondie and Dagwood's life together officially began on their wedding date, their relationship started earlier, in the imagination of visionary *Blondie* creator Chic Young.

Chic was already a successful cartoonist, with several well-loved and widely syndicated strips to his credit, when he set out to create *Blondie* in 1930. A Dithers-like dispute with his boss at the newspaper syndicate over—what else?—a raise and ownership of his then most popular strip, *Dumb Dora* (whose titular character was also a flapper), had resulted in a stalemate. In protest, Chic engineered a work stoppage, eventually retreating to his home studio on Great Neck, Long Island. The impasse didn't last long. Within a few weeks, the boss had second thoughts, and Chic got back to work. In the summer of 1930, he drafted what would become the world's most popular comic strip, *Blondie*. With his determination, he became one of the first cartoonists to retain the rights to his own work.

In its earliest incarnation, *Blondie* was about the clash of social classes and backgrounds, contemporary and traditional mores, and of course, men and women. Dagwood was a rich and important, if awkward, man about town; Blondie was a poor—but beautiful—nobody. Their attraction was that of opposites—she was as out of place in his family drawing room as he was in her dancehalls. And in the beginning, their love wasn't exactly exclusive—both had other suitors.

Blondie had a succession of boyfriends, including a studly, barrel-chested mechanic, Gil McDonald. Dagwood, at his parents' behest, became engaged to not one, but two women, but was saved from the clutches of matrimony by, first, an incredible legal loophole and, then, a nick-of-time rescue. Through it all, this unlikely couple kept returning to each other, professing their love and devotion.

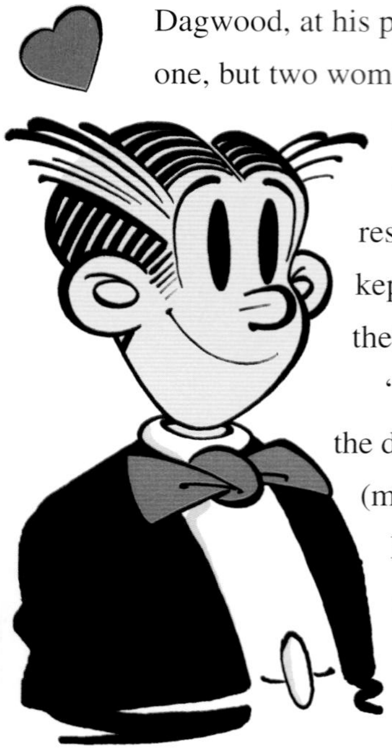

"My precious girl, gladly I'd grovel in the dirt at your feet," Dagwood would say (men were more romantic back then), while Blondie fluttered her eyelashes. Their main obstacle was a big one: the Bumstead family. These pillars of society—especially Mrs. Bumstead, a literal pillar—rejected Blondie, who in their eyes was nothing but a social-climbing money-grubber. Surely she was after his fortune and not him, because, well, just look at him!

> **Dagwood was a rich, if awkward, man about town; Blondie was a poor—but beautiful—nobody.**

But Dagwood remained loyally lovesick. It was Blondie—and no one else—that he wanted. The couple was determined to marry, but the Bumsteads would not have it. So in the winter of 1933, Dagwood embarked upon a historic and life-changing protest—a hunger strike.

Seeing the poor infatuated Dagwood take to his bed in starving dissent galvanized the country. The strike generated news stories, gossip column mentions, and thousands upon thousands of letters and telegrams from readers. One young man in Nebraska even initiated a

When Dagwood first introduced Blondie to his father, their love was an obvious attraction of opposites.

BUT, SON, I'M AWFULLY BUSY -- I'M WORKING OUT THE PLANS FOR THIS NEW MERGER
BUT POP -- I WANT YOU TO MEET BLONDIE WE'RE ENGAGED, YOU KNOW
?
THIS IS BLONDIE DAD-- SHE'S AWFULLY BASHFUL AND SHY ---YOU'LL LOVE HER
OH, TEE-HEE, I ALWAYS FEEL SO BOO-BOOP-A-DOOP WHEN I MEET MY BOY FRIENDS' PAPAS--
BUT I USUALLY LIKE THEM BETTER THAN THE SONS ---- CAN'T I CALL YOU "POP," MR. BUMSTEAD? TEE-HEE
COME, BLONDIE WE MUST GO --- DAD IS AWFULLY BUSY ----- HE'S WORKING OUT THE PLANS FOR HIS NEW MERGER
OH POP -- IF YOU AREN'T THE TERROR! WHAT ARE YOU GOING TO DO WITH YOUR OLD WIFE?
ISN'T SHE CUTE, DAD?
© 1930, King Features Syndicate, Inc., Great Britain rights reserved
CHIC YOUNG

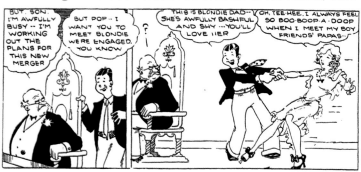

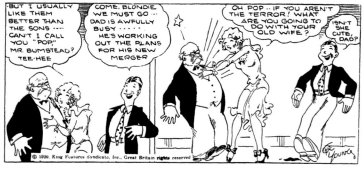

At times Blondie and Dagwood's relationship had a rocky start.

BLONDIE SAID SHE NEVER WANTED TO SEE MY FACE AGAIN --IT WAS ALL MY FAULT FOR BEING SO MEAN --I'LL GO OVER AND APOLOGIZE
© 1931, King Features Syndicate, Inc., Great Britain rights reserved
RING
BLONDIE, OPEN THE DOOR ----- I KNOW YOU'RE IN THERE
NOK
NOK
NOK
HOW DO YOU KNOW ?
CHIC YOUNG
2 6

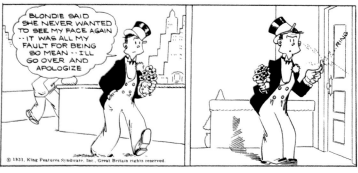

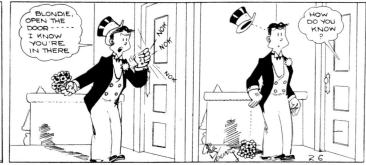

copycat strike, defying his parents and his stomach in the name of love. *Blondie* was more popular than ever.

Meanwhile Dagwood was languishing, delirious and dreaming of his two great loves, Blondie—and food. His mind was filled with thoughts of stuffed turkeys, flying sandwiches, and parading desserts. It was a prophetic moment, a foreshadowing of the man he would become—obsessively in love and obsessively hungry.

Twenty-eight days, seven hours, eight minutes, and twenty-two seconds into the hunger strike, Dagwood's parents relented, and gave him permission to marry his beloved Blondie—with the caveat that he would nonetheless be disinherited if he did so. Dagwood, glad to at least be eating again, accepted. The showdown with his parents not only proved him to be a worthy hero for the strip, it also accomplished the neat trick of doing away with the millionaire storyline, which frugal Chic Young felt was unseemly in light of the growing poverty in the country following the 1929 crash. That many of the movies of the day still dealt with the lifestyles of the rich and fabulous only served to make Dagwood more of a populist hero. And Blondie's commitment—she stood by her man even as he grew leaner in body and billfold—attested to the fact that she was no gold-digger, but a woman deeply in love.

Blondie and Dagwood's marriage in February 1933—before their families, God, and everybody—was one of the great events of the funny pages, where weddings were still a rarity. And it set the happy couple on a journey that has endeared them to millions of readers around the world, from the U.S. to Japan, Iceland to Germany.

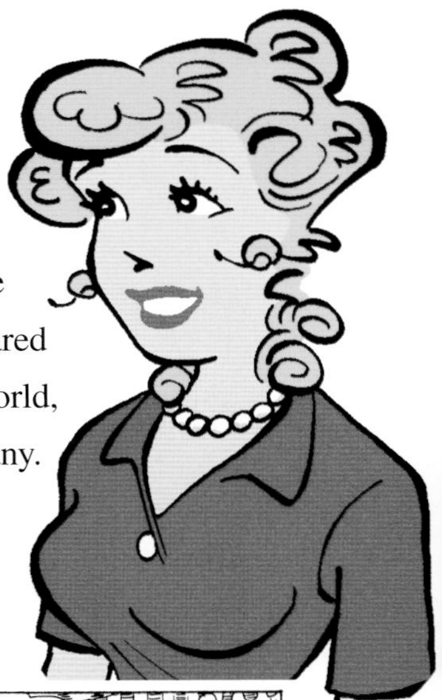

In one fell swoop, Chic Young had set up a storyline based around a

Their love wasn't exactly exclusive and both had other suitors.

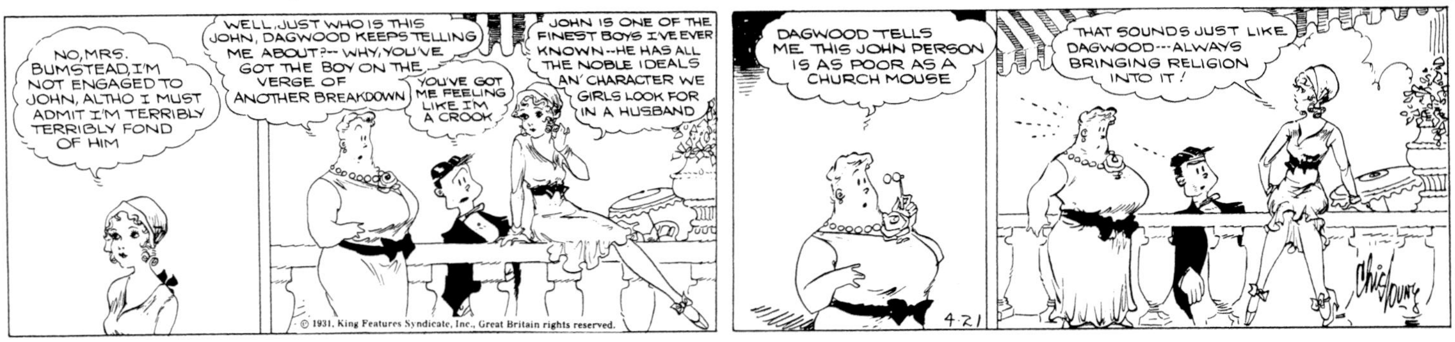
NO, MRS. BUMSTEAD, I'M NOT ENGAGED TO JOHN, ALTHO I MUST ADMIT I'M TERRIBLY TERRIBLY FOND OF HIM
WELL, JUST WHO IS THIS JOHN, DAGWOOD KEEPS TELLING ME ABOUT?-- WHY, YOU'VE GOT THE BOY ON THE VERGE OF ANOTHER BREAKDOWN
YOU'VE GOT ME FEELING LIKE I'M A CROOK
JOHN IS ONE OF THE FINEST BOYS I'VE EVER KNOWN--HE HAS ALL THE NOBLE IDEALS AN' CHARACTER WE GIRLS LOOK FOR IN A HUSBAND
© 1931, King Features Syndicate, Inc., Great Britain rights reserved.
DAGWOOD TELLS ME THIS JOHN PERSON IS AS POOR AS A CHURCH MOUSE
4-21
THAT SOUNDS JUST LIKE DAGWOOD---ALWAYS BRINGING RELIGION INTO IT!
Chic Young

But no one could deny their happiness or doubt their love.

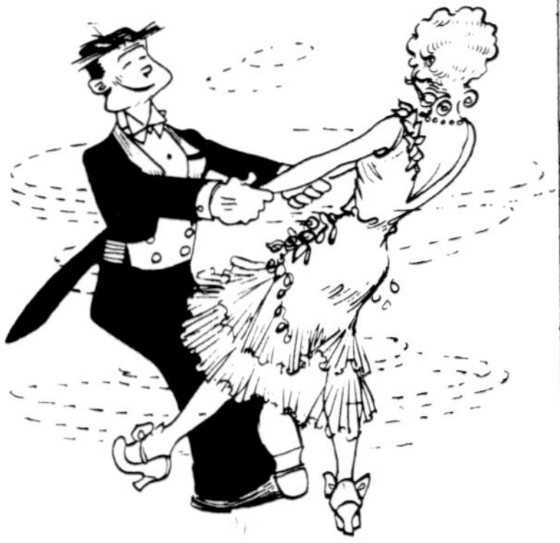

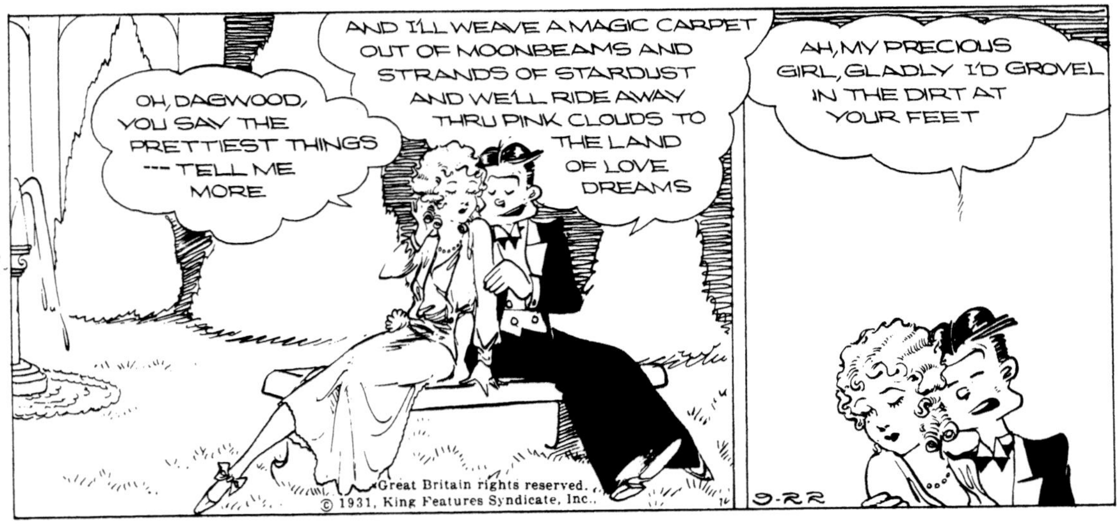
OH, DAGWOOD, YOU SAY THE PRETTIEST THINGS --- TELL ME MORE
AND I'LL WEAVE A MAGIC CARPET OUT OF MOONBEAMS AND STRANDS OF STARDUST AND WE'LL RIDE AWAY THRU PINK CLOUDS TO THE LAND OF LOVE DREAMS
Great Britain rights reserved. © 1931, King Features Syndicate, Inc.
AH, MY PRECIOUS GIRL, GLADLY I'D GROVEL IN THE DIRT AT YOUR FEET
9-22

couple—Dagwood, the slacker loser with an unyielding appetite and a born-and-bred reluctance to work (he had been a millionaire, after all) forced to do so to justify his marriage; and his beautiful, growing-savvier-by-the-minute bride, Blondie. One of her first questions to her new husband post-marriage was, "You'll help with the dishes, won't you?" And this was in 1933! That storyline has created comedy for decades. Dean Young says that the secret is the affection that his father had for his characters, and the affection Blondie and Dagwood have for each other.

"You can equate their love with Romeo and Juliet, with Antony and Cleopatra," he said. "I think that's part of the fiber of the strip—the love they have. I like to show that and the readers like to see it."

"But," he added, "that all happened when Blondie and Dagwood got in the real world and had to hack it like the rest of us. That's when they really fell in love—madly and deeply in love—and the strip soared because of it."

Real love and real life. In the pages of the comics, that turned out to be the perfect union.

Dagwood's parents encouraged a marriage with Irma, a girl more Dagwood's "social equal" and Blondie's roommate.

CAN'T YOU PICTURE US IN THE BLUE MEDITERRANEAN, FLOATING ALONG ON THAT BIG YACHT YOUR PAPA SAID HE'D BUY US FOR A WEDDING PRESENT ?
OH, IRMA, CAN'T YOU SEE THE FOLLY OF ALL THIS --- I DON'T LOVE YOU ? I LOVE MY PRECIOUS BLONDIE
I KNOW MY FOLKS WANT ME TO MARRY YOU AND FORGET BLONDIE BECAUSE SHE'S NOT MY SOCIAL EQUAL, BUT IT CANNOT BE !
FORGET ALL THAT !
I LOVE YOU MORE THAN BLONDIE DOES --- OH, COME ON, PROPOSE TO ME --- LET'S GET THE PLANS FOR THE WEDDING STARTED
I TELL YOU, IRMA, IT'S NO USE, I DON'T LOVE YOU
© 1931, King Features Syndicate, Inc., Great Britain rights reserved.
12-11
Chic Young

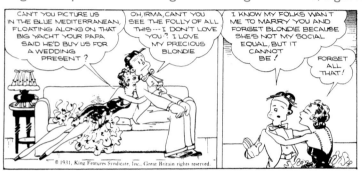

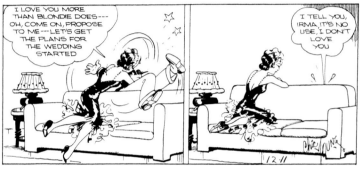

However, Blondie discouraged Dagwood's relationship with Irma in whatever way she could.

DAGWOOD, I WANT YOU TO PHONE IRMA AND INVITE HER TO DINNER
OH, THE FOLLY OF YOUR FORCING IRMA ON ME WHEN YOU KNOW IT'S BLONDIE WHOM I LOVE
DO AS YOUR MOTHER TELLS YOU
BLONDIE, THIS IS DAGWOOD --- I WANT TO SPEAK TO IRMA
HOLD THE LINE
© 1931, King Features Syndicate, Inc., Great Britain rights reserved.
12-7
Chic Young
I'M SORRY, IRMA CAN'T COME TO THE PHONE --- SHE'S IN HER BATHTUB

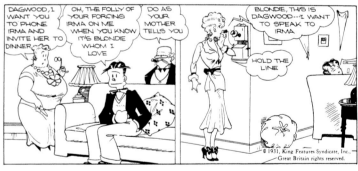

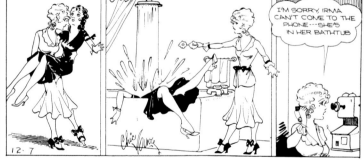

But J. Bolling Bumstead would not be crossed. A marriage to Irma it is!

IT'S UNBEARABLE AROUND OUR HOUSE, THE WAY THEY'RE HOUNDING ME --- AND THE THINGS THEY SAY ABOUT YOU -- I CAN'T STAND IT MUCH LONGER
DAGWOOD --- I DON'T WANT YOU TO GET IN TROUBLE ON MY ACCOUNT --- MAYBE YOUR FOLKS ARE RIGHT --- IT WOULD BE BEST TO FORGET ME
FORGET BLONDIE ? -- NEVER ! AND WHAT'S MORE, MY FOLKS AREN'T GOING TO FORCE A LOVELESS MARRIAGE ON ME FOR SOCIAL REASONS --- I'LL PUT MY FOOT DOWN --- I'M NO NINNY
DAGWOOD, IT'S A SHAME THE WAY YOU'VE BEEN TREATING IRMA -- SHE FEELS TERRIBLE
YOUNG MAN, YOU MIGHT AS WELL FORGET BLONDIE -- WE INSIST YOU MARRY IRMA
AND WHAT IF I TELL YOU I REFUSE ?
© 1931, King Features Syndicate, Inc., Great Britain rights reserved.
12-21
I'LL STOP YOUR ALLOWANCE -- DISINHERIT YOU AND KICK YOU OUT IN THE COLD --- J. BOLLING BUMSTEAD WILL NOT BE CROSSED
Chic Young

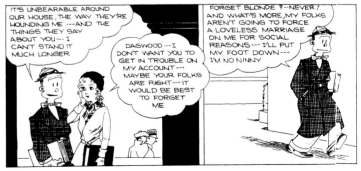

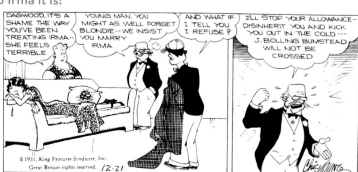

And so Dagwood and Irma were married.

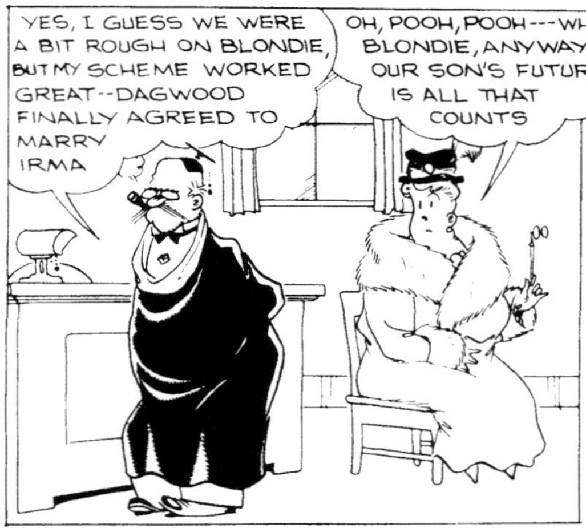

YES, I GUESS WE WERE A BIT ROUGH ON BLONDIE, BUT MY SCHEME WORKED GREAT--DAGWOOD FINALLY AGREED TO MARRY IRMA
OH, POOH, POOH---WHO'S BLONDIE, ANYWAY--? OUR SON'S FUTURE IS ALL THAT COUNTS

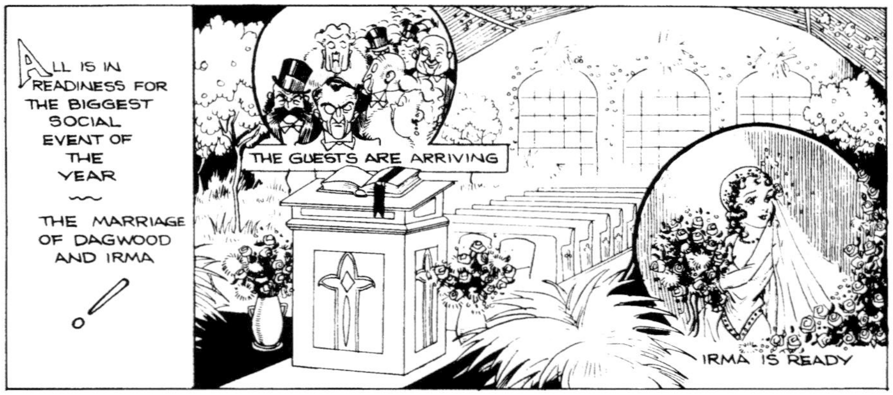

ALL IS IN READINESS FOR THE BIGGEST SOCIAL EVENT OF THE YEAR ~~ THE MARRIAGE OF DAGWOOD AND IRMA !
THE GUESTS ARE ARRIVING
IRMA IS READY

Dagwood and Blondie say their parting words.

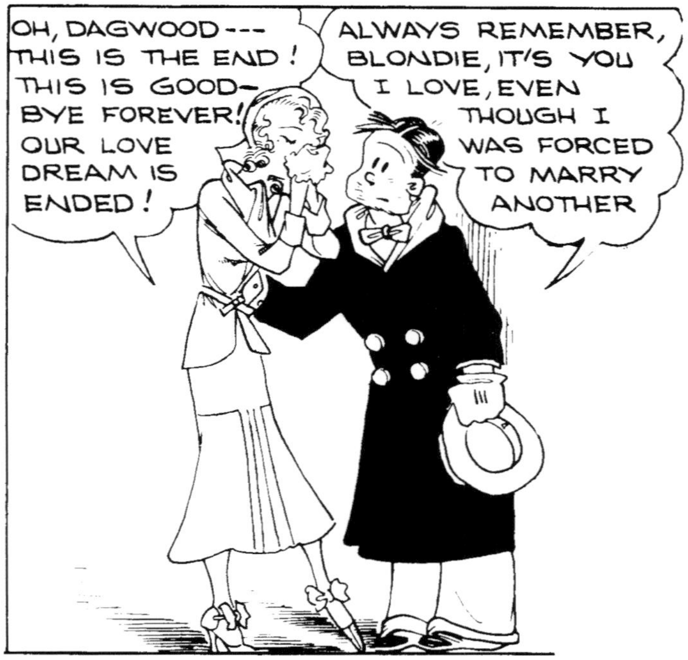

OH, DAGWOOD--- THIS IS THE END! THIS IS GOOD-BYE FOREVER! OUR LOVE DREAM IS ENDED!
ALWAYS REMEMBER, BLONDIE, IT'S YOU I LOVE, EVEN THOUGH I WAS FORCED TO MARRY ANOTHER

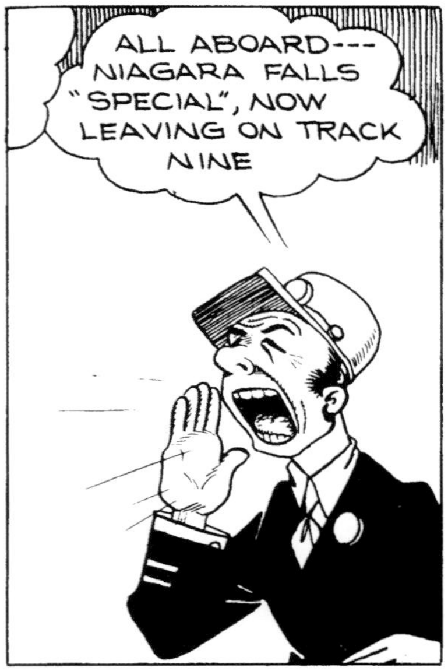

ALL ABOARD--- NIAGARA FALLS "SPECIAL", NOW LEAVING ON TRACK NINE

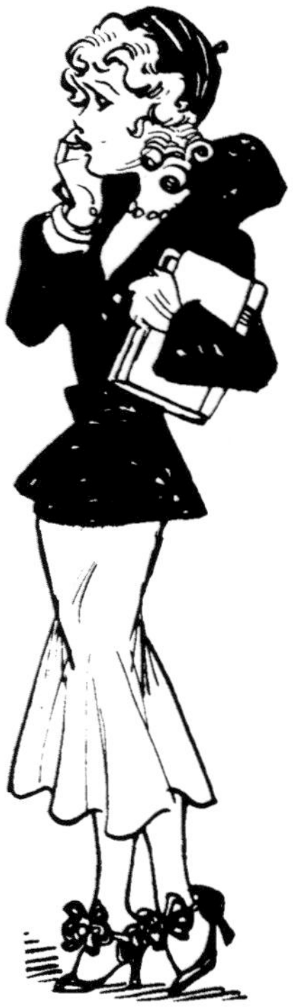

At the last minute, it's discovered that Dagwood's marriage to Irma was not legal.

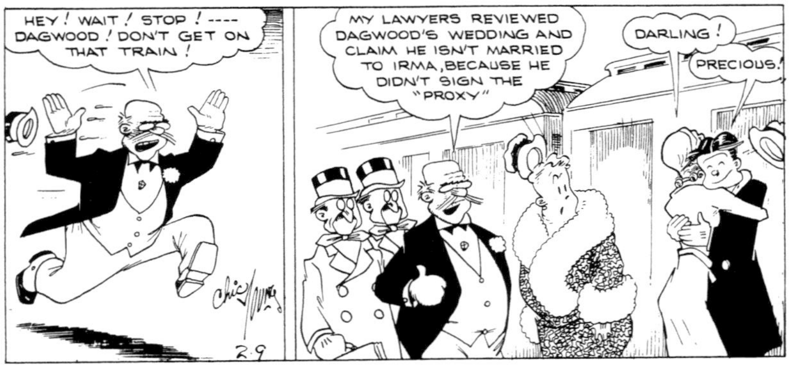

HEY! WAIT! STOP! ---- DAGWOOD! DON'T GET ON THAT TRAIN!
MY LAWYERS REVIEWED DAGWOOD'S WEDDING AND CLAIM HE ISN'T MARRIED TO IRMA, BECAUSE HE DIDN'T SIGN THE "PROXY"
DARLING!
PRECIOUS!

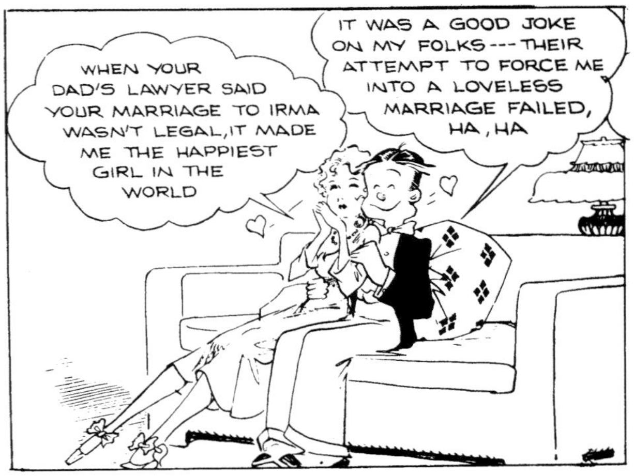

WHEN YOUR DAD'S LAWYER SAID YOUR MARRIAGE TO IRMA WASN'T LEGAL, IT MADE ME THE HAPPIEST GIRL IN THE WORLD
IT WAS A GOOD JOKE ON MY FOLKS---THEIR ATTEMPT TO FORCE ME INTO A LOVELESS MARRIAGE FAILED, HA, HA

The drama continues on the high seas as Mrs. Bumstead and Lady Whistlestop conspire to have Dagwood marry Alicia Whistlestop.

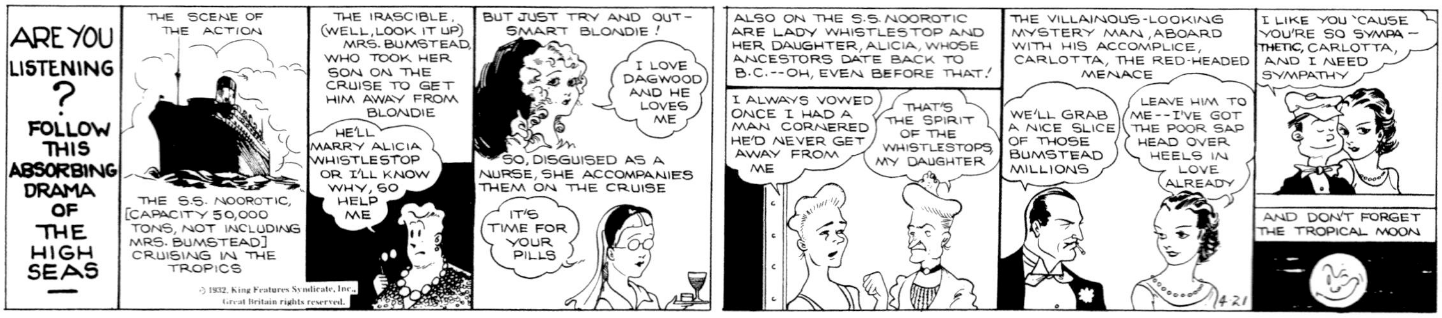
ARE YOU LISTENING ? FOLLOW THIS ABSORBING DRAMA OF THE HIGH SEAS —
THE SCENE OF THE ACTION
THE S.S. NOOROTIC, [CAPACITY 50,000 TONS, NOT INCLUDING MRS. BUMSTEAD] CRUISING IN THE TROPICS
© 1932, King Features Syndicate, Inc., Great Britain rights reserved.
THE IRASCIBLE, (WELL, LOOK IT UP) MRS. BUMSTEAD, WHO TOOK HER SON ON THE CRUISE TO GET HIM AWAY FROM BLONDIE
HE'LL MARRY ALICIA WHISTLESTOP OR I'LL KNOW WHY, SO HELP ME
BUT JUST TRY AND OUT-SMART BLONDIE !
I LOVE DAGWOOD AND HE LOVES ME
SO, DISGUISED AS A NURSE, SHE ACCOMPANIES THEM ON THE CRUISE
IT'S TIME FOR YOUR PILLS
ALSO ON THE S.S. NOOROTIC ARE LADY WHISTLESTOP AND HER DAUGHTER, ALICIA, WHOSE ANCESTORS DATE BACK TO B.C.--OH, EVEN BEFORE THAT!
I ALWAYS VOWED ONCE I HAD A MAN CORNERED HE'D NEVER GET AWAY FROM ME
THAT'S THE SPIRIT OF THE WHISTLESTOPS, MY DAUGHTER
THE VILLAINOUS-LOOKING MYSTERY MAN, ABOARD WITH HIS ACCOMPLICE, CARLOTTA, THE RED-HEADED MENACE
WE'LL GRAB A NICE SLICE OF THOSE BUMSTEAD MILLIONS
LEAVE HIM TO ME--I'VE GOT THE POOR SAP HEAD OVER HEELS IN LOVE ALREADY
4-21
I LIKE YOU 'CAUSE YOU'RE SO SYMPA-THETIC, CARLOTTA, AND I NEED SYMPATHY
AND DON'T FORGET THE TROPICAL MOON

Discouraged, Blondie becomes engaged to Gil.

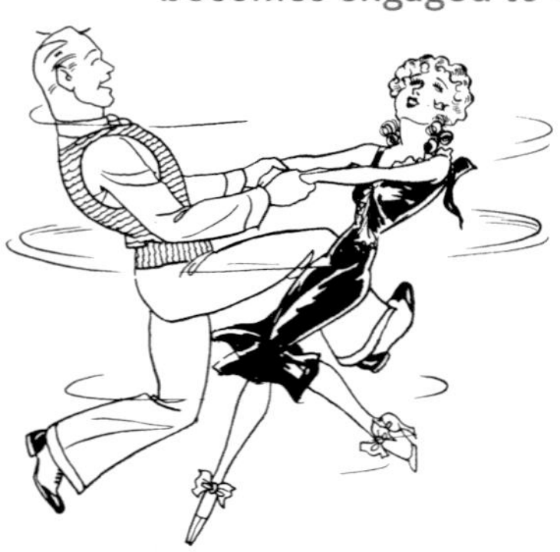

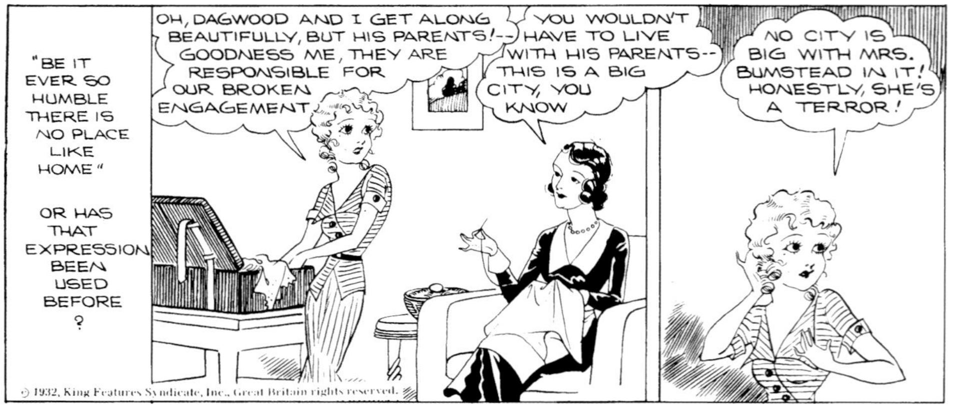
"BE IT EVER SO HUMBLE THERE IS NO PLACE LIKE HOME"
OR HAS THAT EXPRESSION BEEN USED BEFORE ?
OH, DAGWOOD AND I GET ALONG BEAUTIFULLY, BUT HIS PARENTS!-- GOODNESS ME, THEY ARE RESPONSIBLE FOR OUR BROKEN ENGAGEMENT
YOU WOULDN'T HAVE TO LIVE WITH HIS PARENTS-- THIS IS A BIG CITY, YOU KNOW
NO CITY IS BIG WITH MRS. BUMSTEAD IN IT! HONESTLY, SHE'S A TERROR!
© 1932, King Features Syndicate, Inc., Great Britain rights reserved.

Dagwood's mother says he can marry Blondie, but Dagwood finds out Blondie is engaged to Gil. And you thought TV soap operas were complicated!

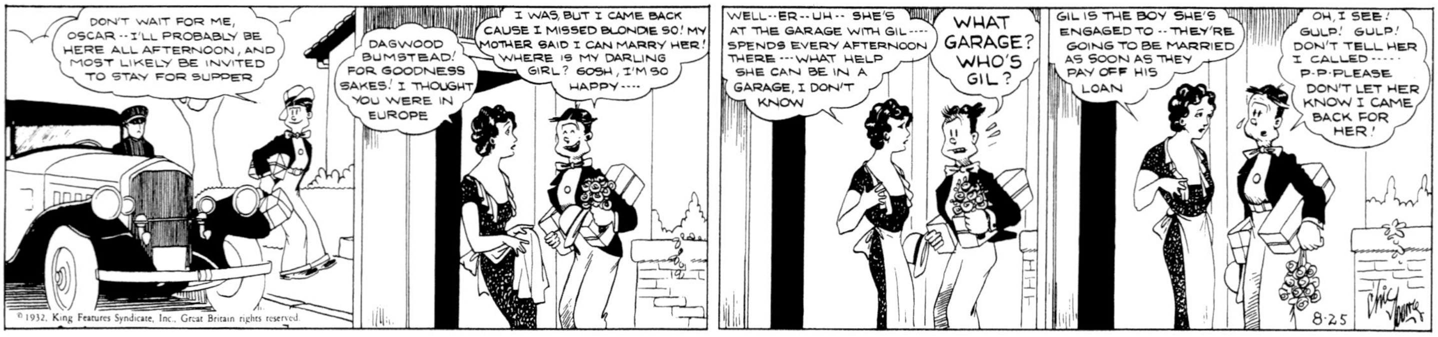
DON'T WAIT FOR ME, OSCAR--I'LL PROBABLY BE HERE ALL AFTERNOON, AND MOST LIKELY BE INVITED TO STAY FOR SUPPER
© 1932, King Features Syndicate, Inc., Great Britain rights reserved
DAGWOOD BUMSTEAD! FOR GOODNESS SAKES! I THOUGHT YOU WERE IN EUROPE
I WAS, BUT I CAME BACK CAUSE I MISSED BLONDIE SO! MY MOTHER SAID I CAN MARRY HER! WHERE IS MY DARLING GIRL? GOSH, I'M SO HAPPY----
WELL--ER--UH-- SHE'S AT THE GARAGE WITH GIL---- SPENDS EVERY AFTERNOON THERE---WHAT HELP SHE CAN BE IN A GARAGE, I DON'T KNOW
WHAT GARAGE? WHO'S GIL?
GIL IS THE BOY SHE'S ENGAGED TO--THEY'RE GOING TO BE MARRIED AS SOON AS THEY PAY OFF HIS LOAN
OH, I SEE! GULP! GULP! DON'T TELL HER I CALLED---- P-P-PLEASE DON'T LET HER KNOW I CAME BACK FOR HER!
8-25

Showing his true love for Blondie, Dagwood agrees to marry Elaine so that Blondie can marry Gil. But guess who stops the wedding because Gil is underage?

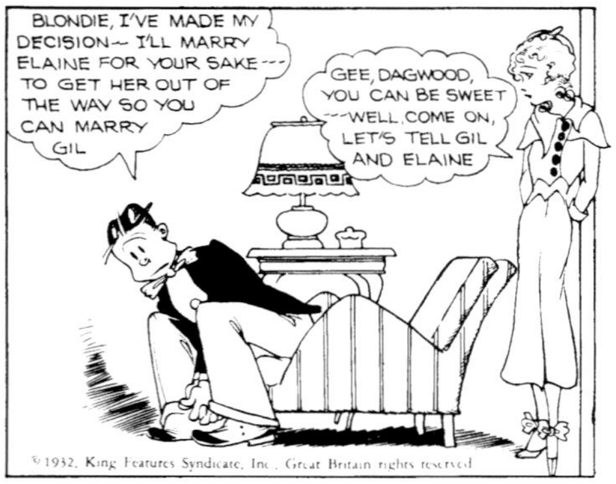
BLONDIE, I'VE MADE MY DECISION-- I'LL MARRY ELAINE FOR YOUR SAKE--- TO GET HER OUT OF THE WAY SO YOU CAN MARRY GIL
GEE, DAGWOOD, YOU CAN BE SWEET ---WELL, COME ON, LET'S TELL GIL AND ELAINE
© 1932, King Features Syndicate, Inc., Great Britain rights reserved.

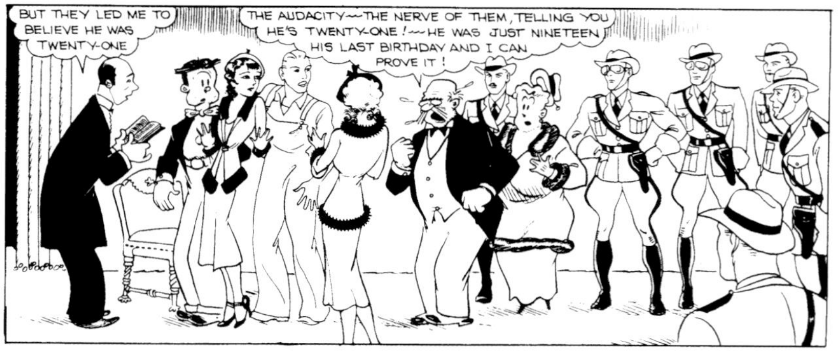
BUT THEY LED ME TO BELIEVE HE WAS TWENTY-ONE
THE AUDACITY--THE NERVE OF THEM, TELLING YOU HE'S TWENTY-ONE!--HE WAS JUST NINETEEN HIS LAST BIRTHDAY AND I CAN PROVE IT !

When Gil and Elaine marry and Dagwood rushes to propose to Blondie....

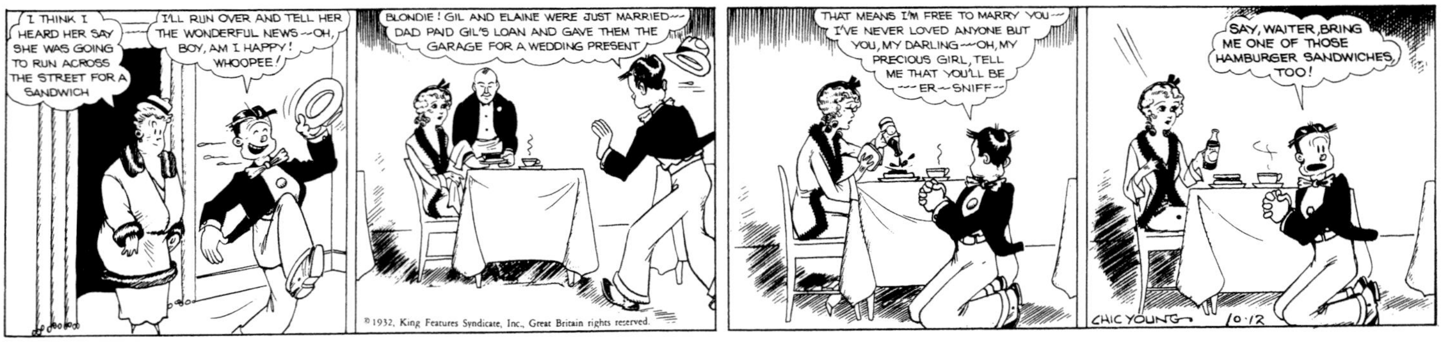

I THINK I HEARD HER SAY SHE WAS GOING TO RUN ACROSS THE STREET FOR A SANDWICH
I'LL RUN OVER AND TELL HER THE WONDERFUL NEWS --OH, BOY, AM I HAPPY! WHOOPEE!
BLONDIE! GIL AND ELAINE WERE JUST MARRIED--- DAD PAID GIL'S LOAN AND GAVE THEM THE GARAGE FOR A WEDDING PRESENT
© 1932, King Features Syndicate, Inc., Great Britain rights reserved.
THAT MEANS I'M FREE TO MARRY YOU--- I'VE NEVER LOVED ANYONE BUT YOU, MY DARLING--OH, MY PRECIOUS GIRL, TELL ME THAT YOU'LL BE ---ER--SNIFF--
SAY, WAITER, BRING ME ONE OF THOSE HAMBURGER SANDWICHES, TOO!
CHIC YOUNG 10-12

True love overcomes all obstacles.

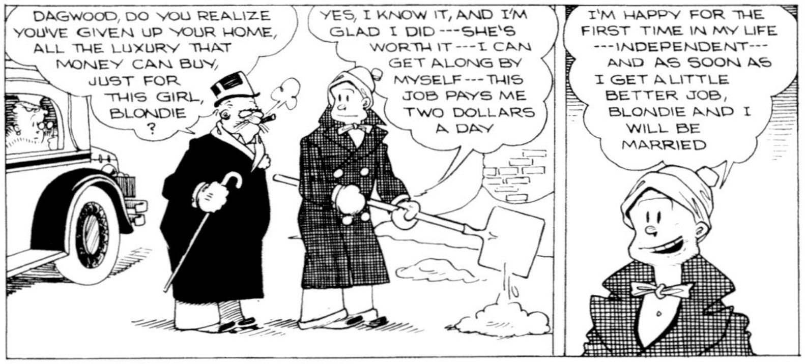

DAGWOOD, DO YOU REALIZE YOU'VE GIVEN UP YOUR HOME, ALL THE LUXURY THAT MONEY CAN BUY, JUST FOR THIS GIRL, BLONDIE?
YES, I KNOW IT, AND I'M GLAD I DID ---SHE'S WORTH IT---I CAN GET ALONG BY MYSELF---THIS JOB PAYS ME TWO DOLLARS A DAY
I'M HAPPY FOR THE FIRST TIME IN MY LIFE ---INDEPENDENT--- AND AS SOON AS I GET A LITTLE BETTER JOB, BLONDIE AND I WILL BE MARRIED

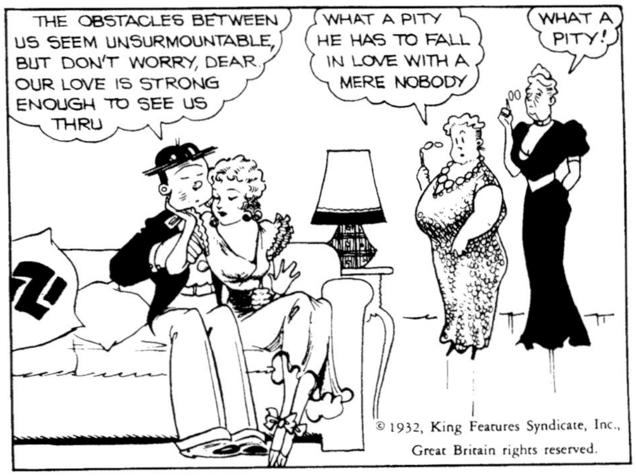

THE OBSTACLES BETWEEN US SEEM UNSURMOUNTABLE, BUT DON'T WORRY, DEAR OUR LOVE IS STRONG ENOUGH TO SEE US THRU
WHAT A PITY HE HAS TO FALL IN LOVE WITH A MERE NOBODY
WHAT A PITY!
© 1932, King Features Syndicate, Inc., Great Britain rights reserved.

Dagwood falls ill, and his parents still insist that he marry ABB (Anyone But Blondie).

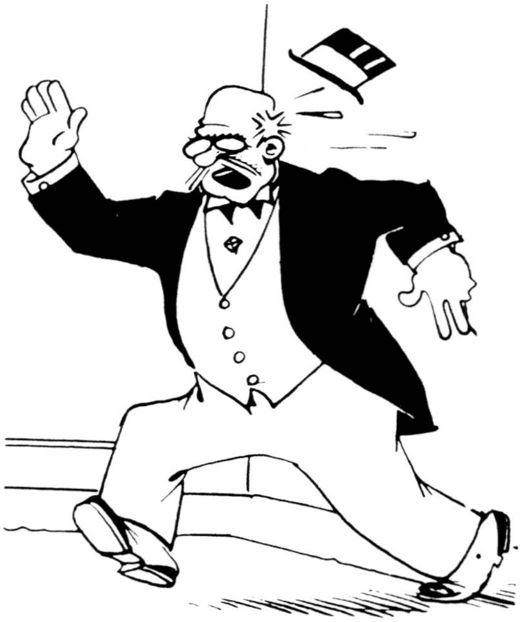

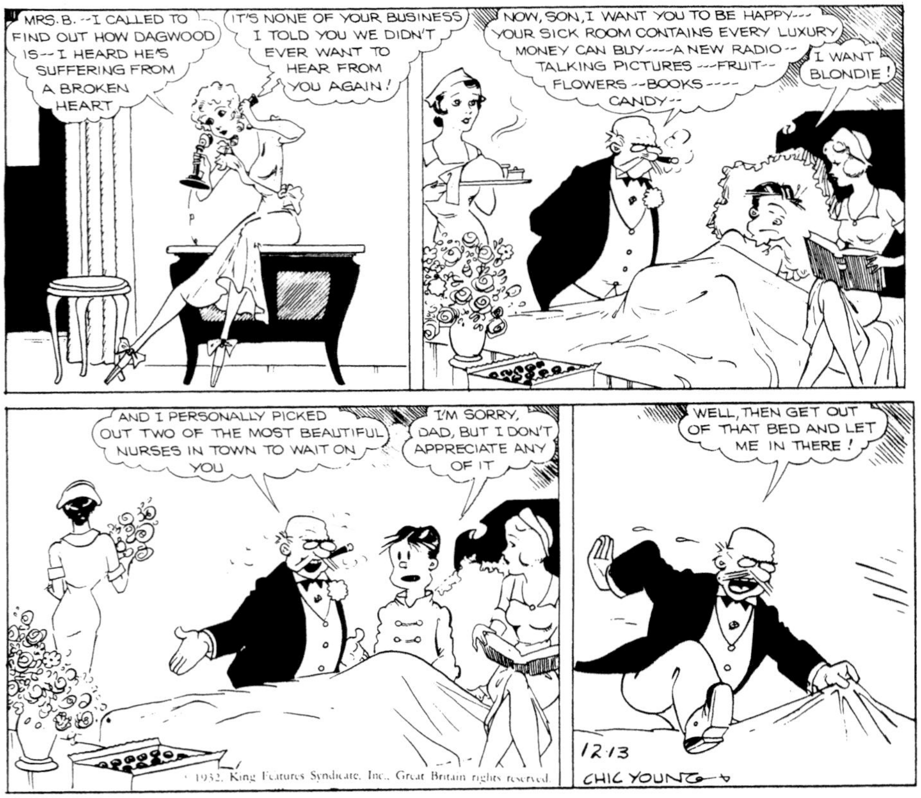

MRS. B.--I CALLED TO FIND OUT HOW DAGWOOD IS--I HEARD HE'S SUFFERING FROM A BROKEN HEART
IT'S NONE OF YOUR BUSINESS I TOLD YOU WE DIDN'T EVER WANT TO HEAR FROM YOU AGAIN!
NOW, SON, I WANT YOU TO BE HAPPY--- YOUR SICK ROOM CONTAINS EVERY LUXURY MONEY CAN BUY----A NEW RADIO-- TALKING PICTURES ---FRUIT-- FLOWERS--BOOKS---- CANDY--
I WANT BLONDIE!
AND I PERSONALLY PICKED OUT TWO OF THE MOST BEAUTIFUL NURSES IN TOWN TO WAIT ON YOU
I'M SORRY, DAD, BUT I DON'T APPRECIATE ANY OF IT
© 1932, King Features Syndicate, Inc., Great Britain rights reserved.
WELL, THEN GET OUT OF THAT BED AND LET ME IN THERE!
12-13
CHIC YOUNG

Blondie is pushed away once more and she is determined to start a new life, "like all girls disappointed in love."

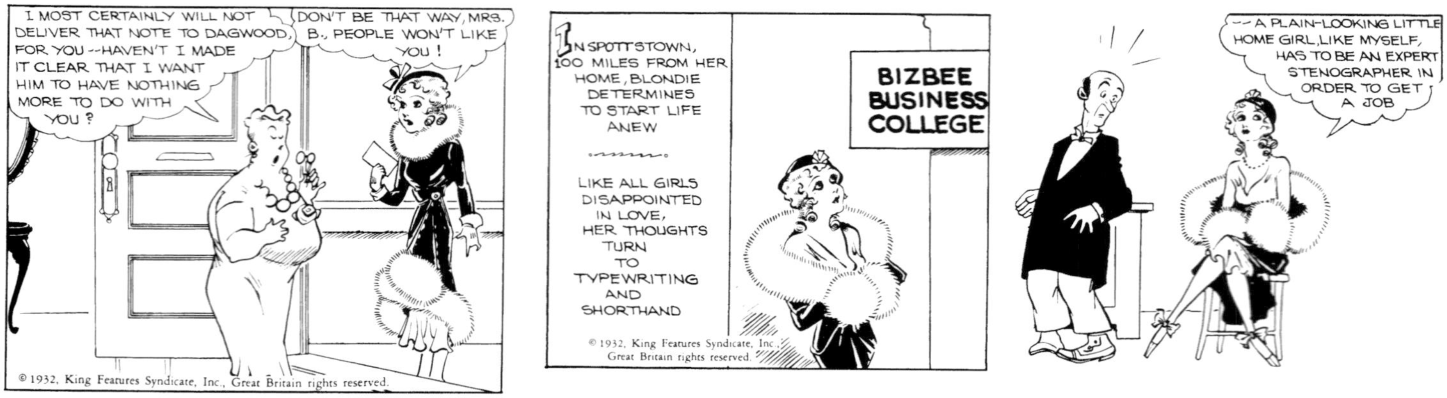
I MOST CERTAINLY WILL NOT DELIVER THAT NOTE TO DAGWOOD, FOR YOU--HAVEN'T I MADE IT CLEAR THAT I WANT HIM TO HAVE NOTHING MORE TO DO WITH YOU?
DON'T BE THAT WAY, MRS. B., PEOPLE WON'T LIKE YOU!
© 1932, King Features Syndicate, Inc., Great Britain rights reserved.
IN SPOTTSTOWN, 100 MILES FROM HER HOME, BLONDIE DETERMINES TO START LIFE ANEW
LIKE ALL GIRLS DISAPPOINTED IN LOVE, HER THOUGHTS TURN TO TYPEWRITING AND SHORTHAND
© 1932, King Features Syndicate, Inc., Great Britain rights reserved.
BIZBEE BUSINESS COLLEGE
--A PLAIN-LOOKING LITTLE HOME GIRL, LIKE MYSELF, HAS TO BE AN EXPERT STENOGRAPHER IN ORDER TO GET A JOB

Dagwood decides on drastic action. The famous hunger strike begins!

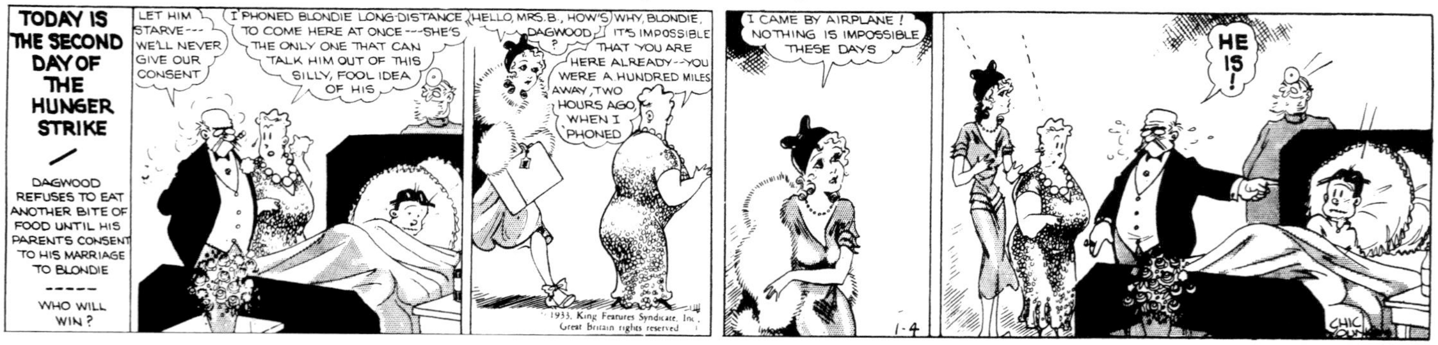
TODAY IS THE SECOND DAY OF THE HUNGER STRIKE
DAGWOOD REFUSES TO EAT ANOTHER BITE OF FOOD UNTIL HIS PARENTS CONSENT TO HIS MARRIAGE TO BLONDIE
WHO WILL WIN?
LET HIM STARVE--- WE'LL NEVER GIVE OUR CONSENT
I PHONED BLONDIE LONG-DISTANCE TO COME HERE AT ONCE---SHE'S THE ONLY ONE THAT CAN TALK HIM OUT OF THIS SILLY, FOOL IDEA OF HIS
HELLO, MRS. B., HOW'S DAGWOOD?
WHY, BLONDIE, IT'S IMPOSSIBLE THAT YOU ARE HERE ALREADY--YOU WERE A HUNDRED MILES AWAY, TWO HOURS AGO, WHEN I PHONED
© 1933, King Features Syndicate, Inc., Great Britain rights reserved
I CAME BY AIRPLANE! NOTHING IS IMPOSSIBLE THESE DAYS
1-4
HE IS!
CHIC YOUNG

The hunger strike goes on . . . and on . . .

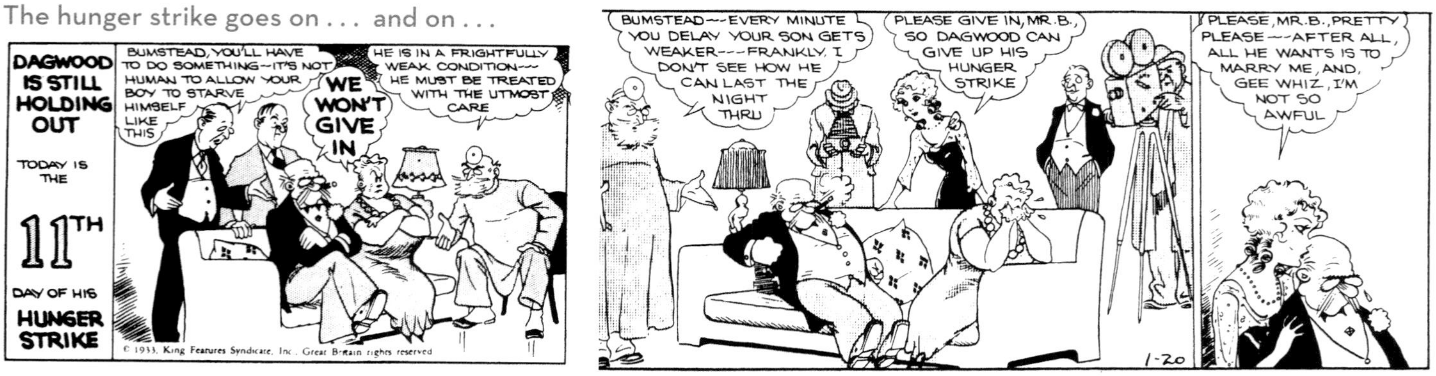
DAGWOOD IS STILL HOLDING OUT
TODAY IS THE 11TH DAY OF HIS HUNGER STRIKE
BUMSTEAD, YOU'LL HAVE TO DO SOMETHING--IT'S NOT HUMAN TO ALLOW YOUR BOY TO STARVE HIMSELF LIKE THIS
WE WON'T GIVE IN
HE IS IN A FRIGHTFULLY WEAK CONDITION--- HE MUST BE TREATED WITH THE UTMOST CARE
© 1933, King Features Syndicate, Inc., Great Britain rights reserved
BUMSTEAD---EVERY MINUTE YOU DELAY YOUR SON GETS WEAKER---FRANKLY, I DON'T SEE HOW HE CAN LAST THE NIGHT THRU
PLEASE GIVE IN, MR. B., SO DAGWOOD CAN GIVE UP HIS HUNGER STRIKE
1-20
PLEASE, MR. B., PRETTY PLEASE---AFTER ALL, ALL HE WANTS IS TO MARRY ME, AND, GEE WHIZ, I'M NOT SO AWFUL

And on . . .

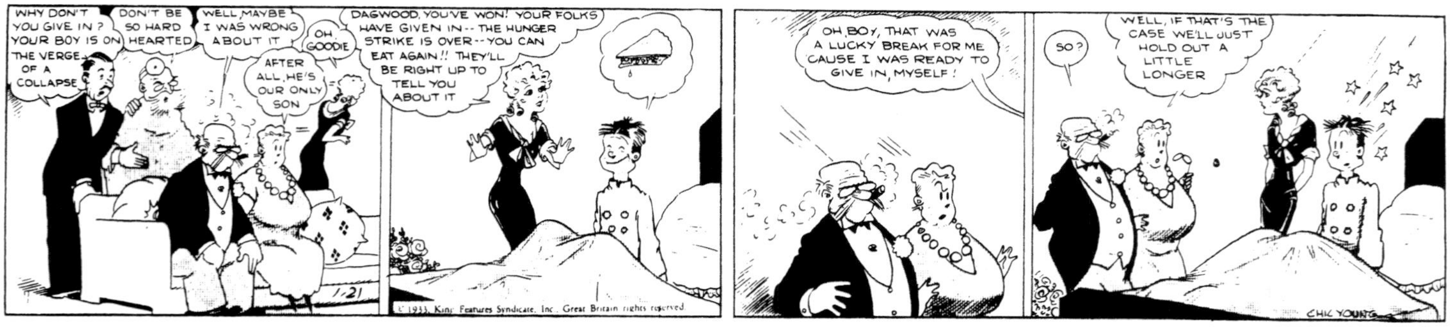
WHY DON'T YOU GIVE IN? YOUR BOY IS ON THE VERGE OF A COLLAPSE
DON'T BE SO HARD HEARTED
WELL, MAYBE I WAS WRONG ABOUT IT
OH, GOODIE
AFTER ALL, HE'S OUR ONLY SON
1-21
DAGWOOD, YOU'VE WON! YOUR FOLKS HAVE GIVEN IN--THE HUNGER STRIKE IS OVER--YOU CAN EAT AGAIN!! THEY'LL BE RIGHT UP TO TELL YOU ABOUT IT
© 1933, King Features Syndicate, Inc., Great Britain rights reserved
OH, BOY, THAT WAS A LUCKY BREAK FOR ME CAUSE I WAS READY TO GIVE IN, MYSELF!
SO?
WELL, IF THAT'S THE CASE WE'LL JUST HOLD OUT A LITTLE LONGER
CHIC YOUNG

All hope for Dagwood is almost gone.

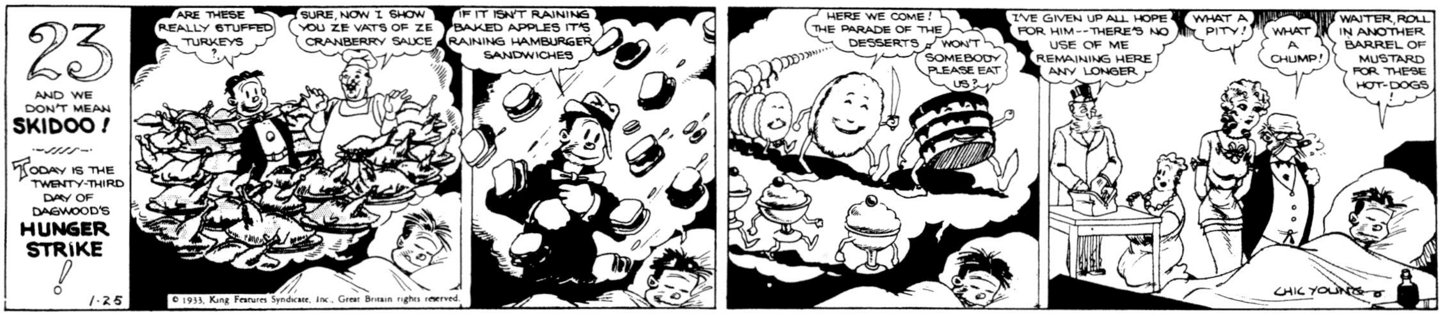
23
AND WE DON'T MEAN SKIDOO!
TODAY IS THE TWENTY-THIRD DAY OF DAGWOOD'S HUNGER STRIKE!
1-25
ARE THESE REALLY STUFFED TURKEYS?
SURE, NOW I SHOW YOU ZE VATS OF ZE CRANBERRY SAUCE
IF IT ISN'T RAINING BAKED APPLES IT'S RAINING HAMBURGER SANDWICHES
© 1933, King Features Syndicate, Inc., Great Britain rights reserved.
HERE WE COME! THE PARADE OF THE DESSERTS
WON'T SOMEBODY PLEASE EAT US?
I'VE GIVEN UP ALL HOPE FOR HIM--THERE'S NO USE OF ME REMAINING HERE ANY LONGER
WHAT A PITY!
WHAT A CHUMP!
WAITER, ROLL IN ANOTHER BARREL OF MUSTARD FOR THESE HOT-DOGS!
CHIC YOUNG

After 28 days, 7 hours, 8 minutes, and 22 seconds, Dagwood's hunger strike is over and the nation rejoices.

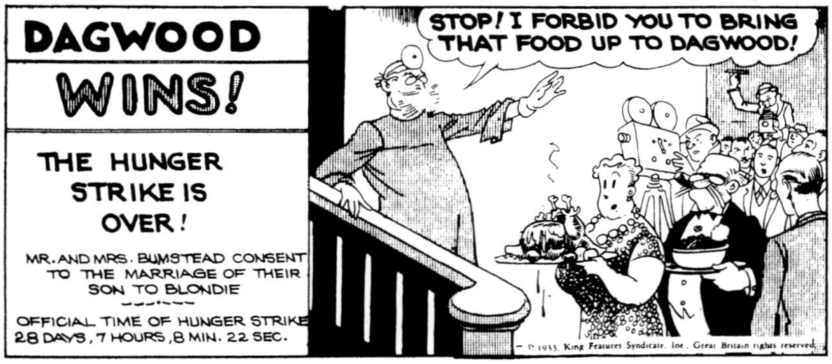
DAGWOOD
WINS!
THE HUNGER STRIKE IS OVER!
MR. AND MRS. BUMSTEAD CONSENT TO THE MARRIAGE OF THEIR SON TO BLONDIE
OFFICIAL TIME OF HUNGER STRIKE 28 DAYS, 7 HOURS, 8 MIN. 22 SEC.
STOP! I FORBID YOU TO BRING THAT FOOD UP TO DAGWOOD!
© 1933, King Features Syndicate, Inc., Great Britain rights reserved.

That's when they really fell in love—madly and deeply in love—and the strip soared because of it.

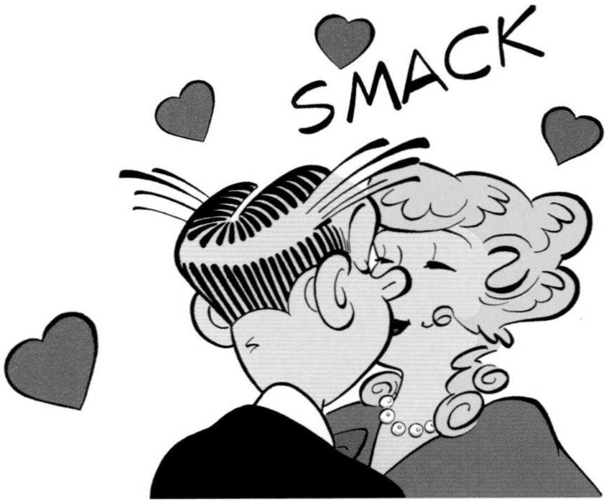
SMACK

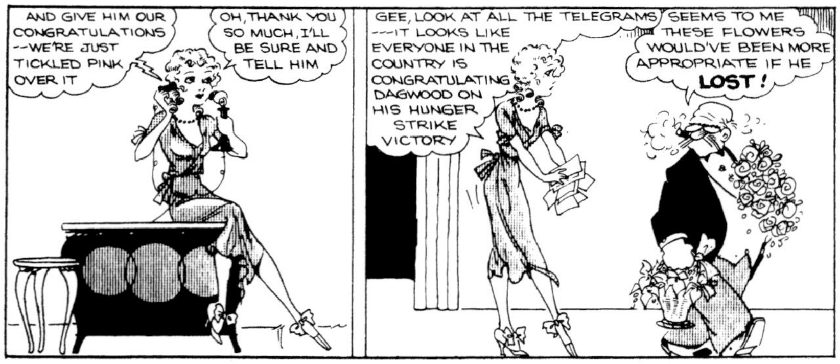
AND GIVE HIM OUR CONGRATULATIONS --WE'RE JUST TICKLED PINK OVER IT
OH, THANK YOU SO MUCH, I'LL BE SURE AND TELL HIM
GEE, LOOK AT ALL THE TELEGRAMS ---IT LOOKS LIKE EVERYONE IN THE COUNTRY IS CONGRATULATING DAGWOOD ON HIS HUNGER STRIKE VICTORY
SEEMS TO ME THESE FLOWERS WOULD'VE BEEN MORE APPROPRIATE IF HE LOST!

Deeply in love and against all obstacles, Dagwood and Blondie marry.

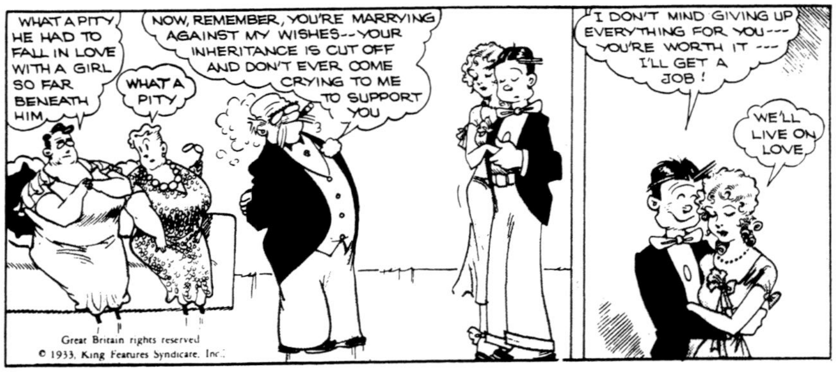
WHAT A PITY HE HAD TO FALL IN LOVE WITH A GIRL SO FAR BENEATH HIM
WHAT A PITY
NOW, REMEMBER, YOU'RE MARRYING AGAINST MY WISHES--YOUR INHERITANCE IS CUT OFF AND DON'T EVER COME CRYING TO ME TO SUPPORT YOU
I DON'T MIND GIVING UP EVERYTHING FOR YOU--- YOU'RE WORTH IT --- I'LL GET A JOB!
WE'LL LIVE ON LOVE
Great Britain rights reserved
© 1933, King Features Syndicate, Inc.

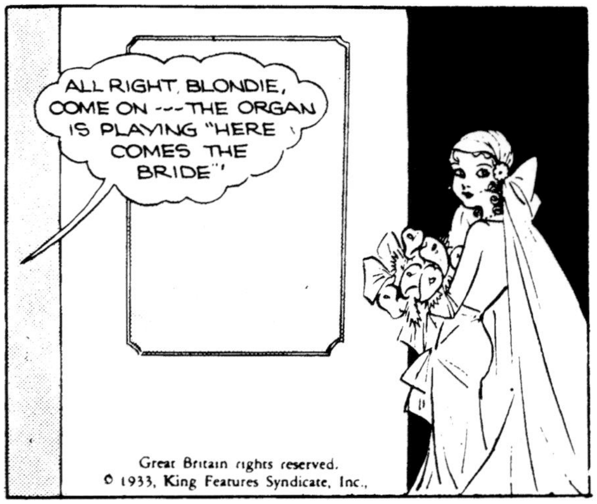
ALL RIGHT, BLONDIE, COME ON ---THE ORGAN IS PLAYING "HERE COMES THE BRIDE"
Great Britain rights reserved.
© 1933, King Features Syndicate, Inc.,

And they began their lives together with the enthusiasm that would carry them through the ups and downs of daily life for decades to come.

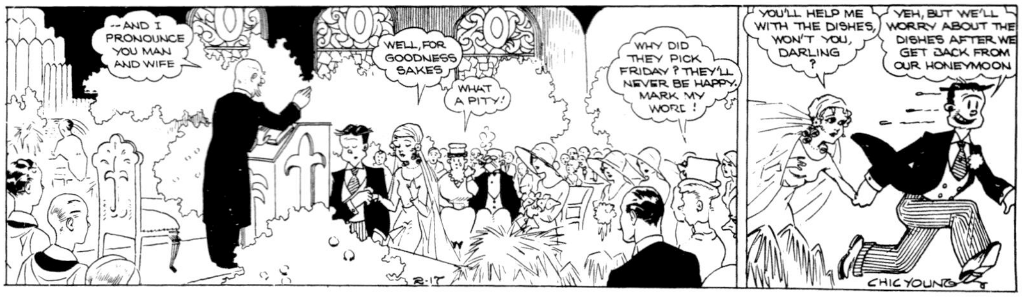

--AND I PRONOUNCE YOU MAN AND WIFE
WELL, FOR GOODNESS SAKES
WHAT A PITY!
WHY DID THEY PICK FRIDAY? THEY'LL NEVER BE HAPPY. MARK MY WORD!
YOU'LL HELP ME WITH THE DISHES, WON'T YOU, DARLING?
YEH, BUT WE'LL WORRY ABOUT THE DISHES AFTER WE GET BACK FROM OUR HONEYMOON
CHIC YOUNG

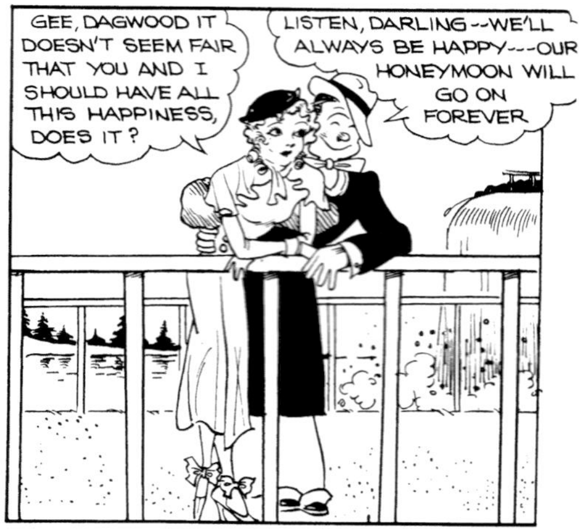

GEE, DAGWOOD IT DOESN'T SEEM FAIR THAT YOU AND I SHOULD HAVE ALL THIS HAPPINESS, DOES IT?
LISTEN, DARLING--WE'LL ALWAYS BE HAPPY---OUR HONEYMOON WILL GO ON FOREVER

Blondie reflects on her 50 years with Dagwood in this rare strip which breaks "the fourth wall" and acknowledges itself as a comic strip.

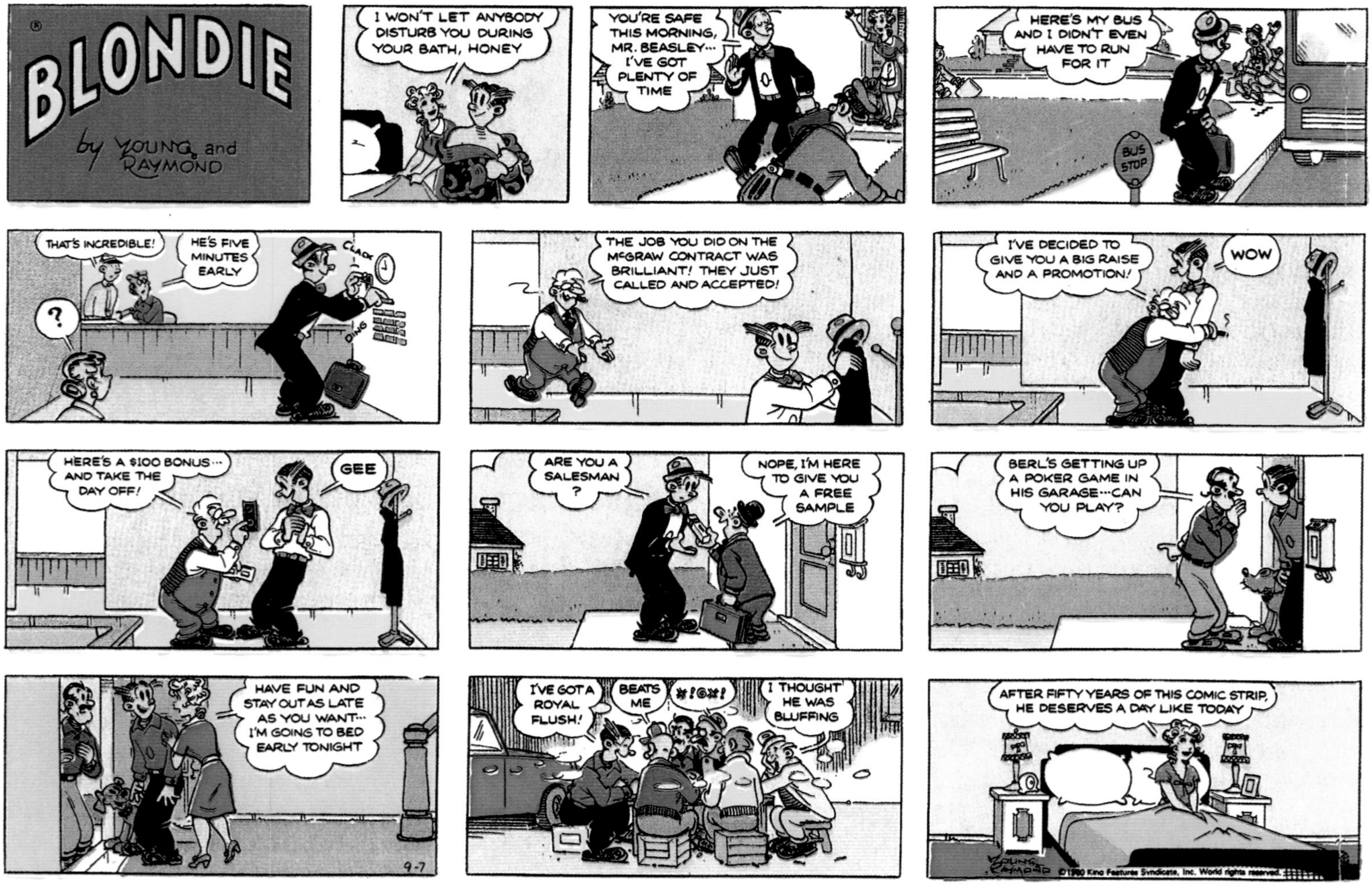

BLONDIE
by YOUNG and RAYMOND
I WON'T LET ANYBODY DISTURB YOU DURING YOUR BATH, HONEY
YOU'RE SAFE THIS MORNING, MR. BEASLEY... I'VE GOT PLENTY OF TIME
HERE'S MY BUS AND I DIDN'T EVEN HAVE TO RUN FOR IT
BUS STOP
THAT'S INCREDIBLE!
HE'S FIVE MINUTES EARLY
?
CLACK
THE JOB YOU DID ON THE McGRAW CONTRACT WAS BRILLIANT! THEY JUST CALLED AND ACCEPTED!
I'VE DECIDED TO GIVE YOU A BIG RAISE AND A PROMOTION!
WOW
HERE'S A $100 BONUS... AND TAKE THE DAY OFF!
GEE
ARE YOU A SALESMAN?
NOPE, I'M HERE TO GIVE YOU A FREE SAMPLE
BERL'S GETTING UP A POKER GAME IN HIS GARAGE...CAN YOU PLAY?
HAVE FUN AND STAY OUT AS LATE AS YOU WANT... I'M GOING TO BED EARLY TONIGHT
9-7
I'VE GOT A ROYAL FLUSH!
BEATS ME
✱!@✱!
I THOUGHT HE WAS BLUFFING
AFTER FIFTY YEARS OF THIS COMIC STRIP, HE DESERVES A DAY LIKE TODAY
YOUNG RAYMOND
©1980 King Features Syndicate, Inc. World rights reserved.

CHAPTER 3

FAMILY LIFE

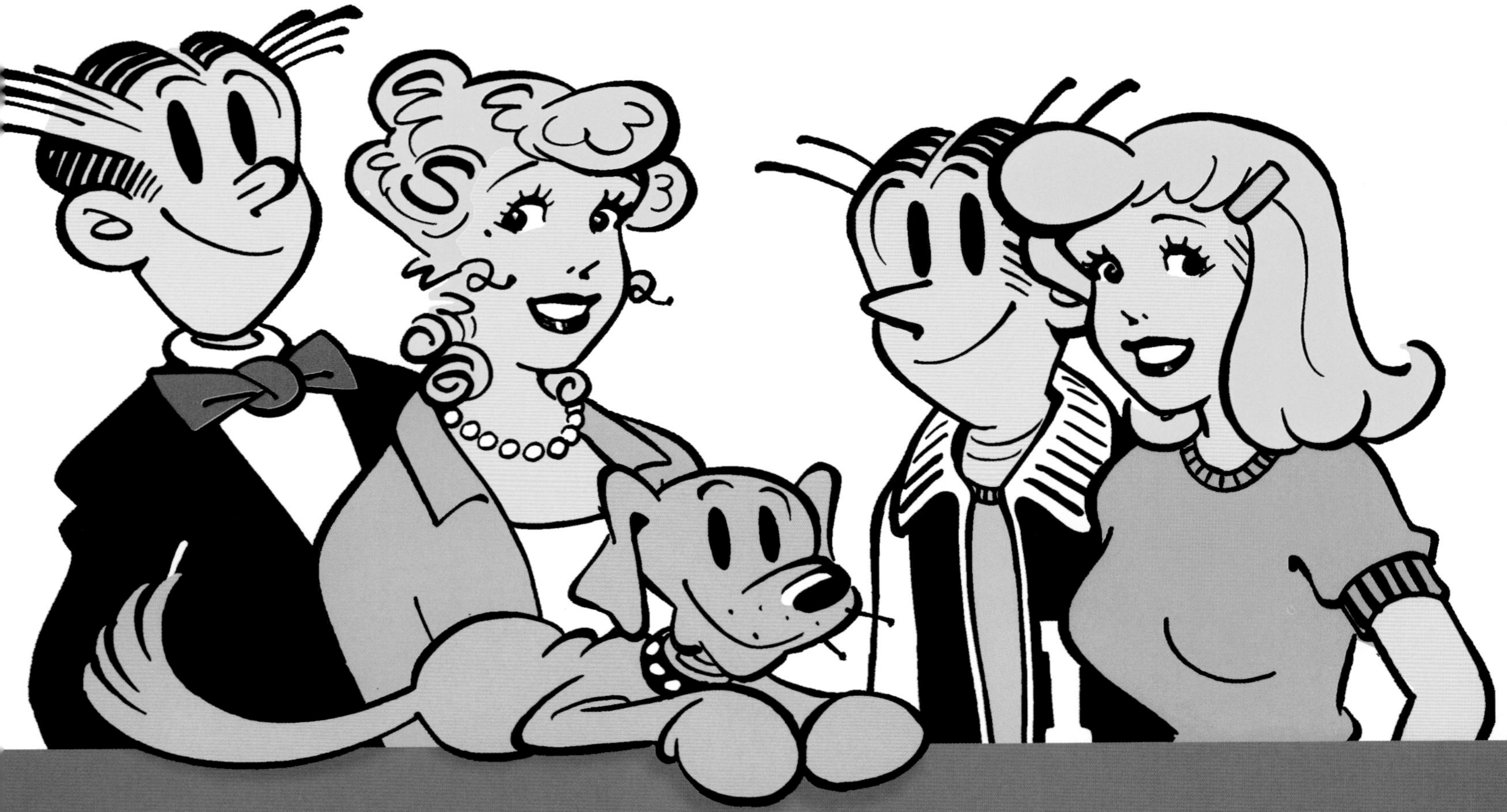

The Bumsteads' life revolves around family. With two teenaged kids, a dog, and two working parents, their home—located, Chic Young felt, in the suburbs of a city like Philadelphia—is a hive of activity. On any given day, with Alexander practicing his drums, Cookie working on her blog, Blondie perfecting recipes for her catering shop, and Dagwood . . . asleep on the couch, they are typically domestic. The relationship between loved ones, one of the universal themes that have kept *Blondie* so relevant for so long, is always prime material for sentiment and humor.

Let's start with the living room, where even the furniture arrangement is comical. Blondie and Dagwood's back-to-side easy chair setup has been the source of a lot of confusion over the years, said Dean Young. Why is it put together that way? The simple answer is graphic convenience. As artist John Marshall can attest, it's a lot easier to fit two people—and a conversation—in one panel when the seating is organized that way.

Of course, the living room doubles as a nap room for Dagwood, who can often be found snoring away on the couch—sknxx-x! It's also the place where the family has many important conversations about their lives, the state of the world, and what's on TV. For Dean, one way to keep the strip up-to-date is to reference real-life events like the Super Bowl or the Oscars. It's another way *Blondie* remains grounded in the everyday realities of people's interests. And, said Dean, "If the reference is timely, it takes the gag up another couple of notches."

Another area that's ripe for joking is the kitchen. Not because of Blondie's cooking—which is, of course, exemplary—but because it's such a locus for misbehavior. Whether Dagwood's fixing—in his own inimitable way—the leaky faucet or scrounging for snacks or planning an after-dinner game just so he can sleep through it, the kitchen is as much a centerpiece for the Bumstead home as it is for any American household. More so, perhaps, because the family dinner hour, once an incontrovertible tradition, now a comparative rarity, still thrives in the pages of *Blondie*. For each family member, there is nothing more important than being home for supper—if only to witness Dagwood's monster appetite in action.

Luckily for them—and us—the Bumsteads are able to poke fun at themselves in any situation.

In fact, aside from the occasional poker game or golf outing with Herb, Dagwood is a homebody, preferring the camaraderie of his family to that of his office-mates or friends. And who can blame him, when he's coming home for a lip-smacking kiss with a woman like Blondie?

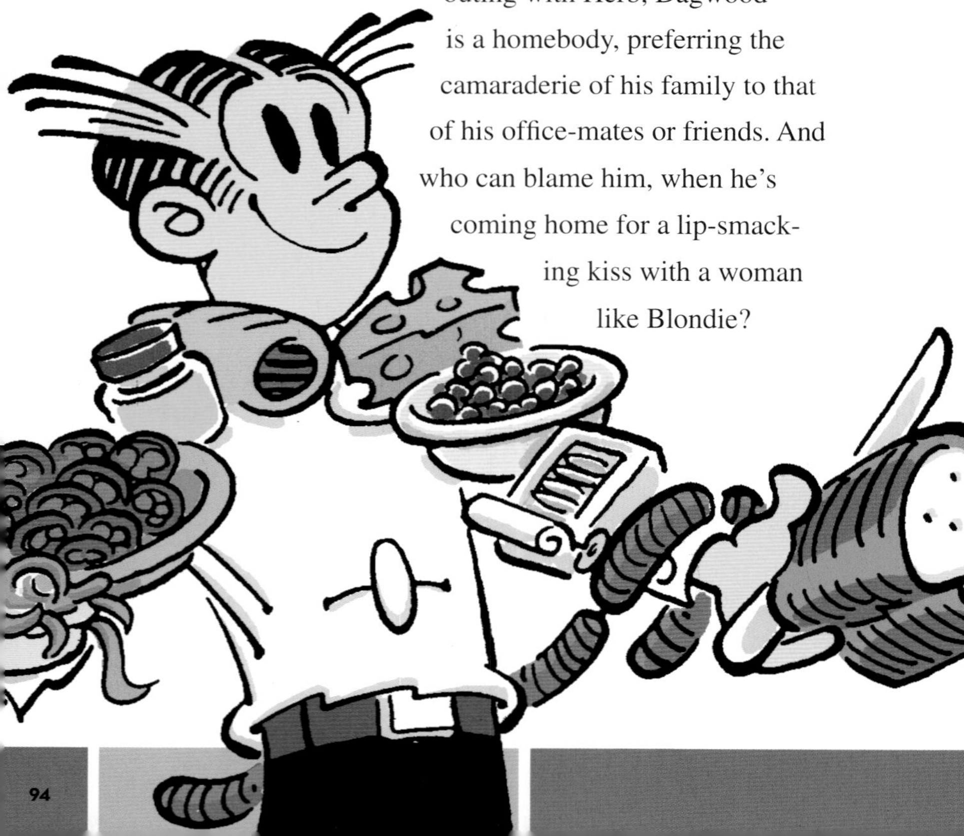

For Dagwood and Blondie, still romantic after all these years, the upstairs bedroom is a sacred space. Not just in the way you're thinking; they have some of their best conversations there. In fact, that intimacy was so important that in the early years of the strip, Chic Young defied convention by depicting the couple in bed together, instead of in two separate beds, á la Lucy and Ricky. These days, with security being what it is, Blondie is less likely to hear a prowler, but Dagwood is still liable to sneak downstairs for a midnight snack. If he runs into Alexander fixing his own, or Cookie coming home from a date, well, that's just another opportunity for family bonding—and joking.

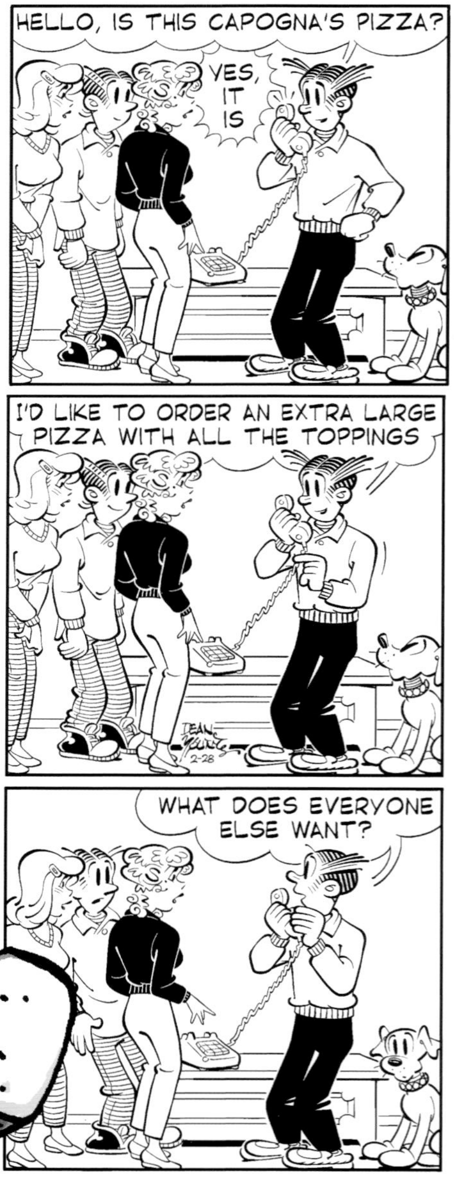
HELLO, IS THIS CAPOGNA'S PIZZA?
YES, IT IS
I'D LIKE TO ORDER AN EXTRA LARGE PIZZA WITH ALL THE TOPPINGS
WHAT DOES EVERYONE ELSE WANT?

But all this togetherness doesn't mean the foursome always gets along. Cookie and Alexander quarrel over computer time, Dagwood grumbles about his wife being perpetually late, and even the usually cheerful Blondie sometimes gets riled about her own limitless list of household tasks or Dagwood eating in bed or Dagwood sneaking food before dinner or Dagwood sleeping late or Dagwood just being Dagwood. After all, the woman isn't a saint, though she's about as close as we can get without Vatican intervention. Luckily for them—and us—the Bumsteads are able to poke fun at themselves in any situation. In this, too, they reflect our experience, because family is nothing if not a collection of shared grudges and in-jokes.

And routines. The complex system that his wife and kids have developed to get Dagwood out of bed each morning is a testament to their affection. And the fact that Dagwood is ready to drop anything to tutor his son in the fine art of sandwich making or to advise his daughter on her love life or to dutifully do the chores Blondie lays out for him each weekend, goes a long way to counteract any of the little foibles and mistakes he foists upon them, day after day after day after day. Throughout it all, the Bumsteads value each other above everything.

"I want to make sure that people realize this family really loves being together," says Dean. "They love each other."

And in the end, of course, that's what makes them such an integral part of our families.

BLONDIE
SUNDAY COMICS
DAGWOOD! YOUR CARPOOL'S GOING TO BE HERE ANY SECOND!!
GREAT! THAT'S JUST WHAT I WANTED TO HEAR!
WHEN I'M ON TIME IN THE MORNING, I'M DULL AND LISTLESS ALL DAY
www.kingfeatures.com
HONK HONK
HONK
BUT WHEN I HAVE TO RACE, I'M AT MY PEAK ALL DAY LONG!
DAGWOOD! YOUR CARPOOL'S LEAVING WITHOUT YOU!!
BEING LATE IS THE BEST WAY FOR ME TO START EACH DAY!
© 1998 by King Features Syndicate, Inc. World rights reserved.
BUT, UNFORTUNATELY, IT ONLY SEEMS TO WORK FOR ME
11-22

WHAT ARE YOU DOING, DEAR?
I'M GOING TO MAKE A SARDINE SANDWICH
© 1994 King Features Syndicate, Inc. World rights reserved.
HI, FELLAS! CROWDED IN THERE?
DON'T WORRY... I'LL HAVE YOU ALL OUT IN A JIFFY
THAT'S THE ONE THING YOUR FATHER'S NEVER OUTGROWN, PLAYING WITH HIS FOOD
6-14

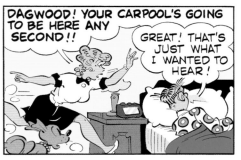

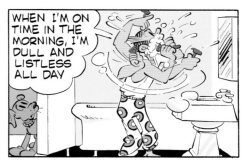

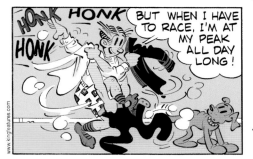

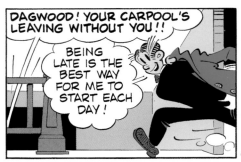

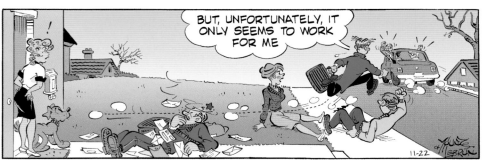

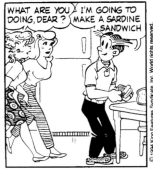

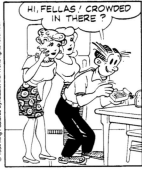

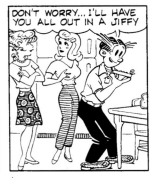

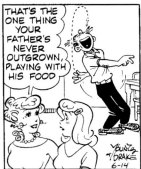

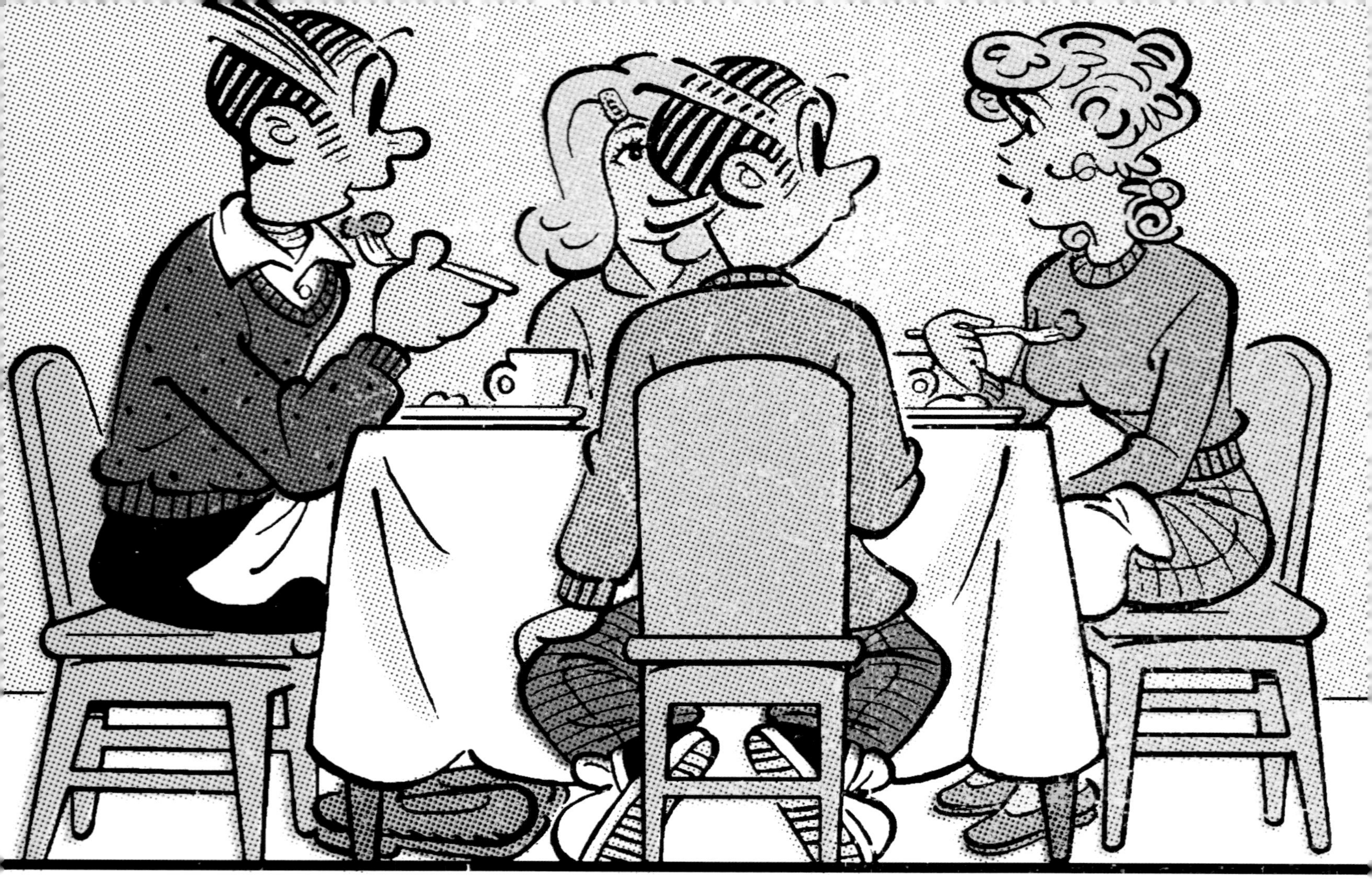

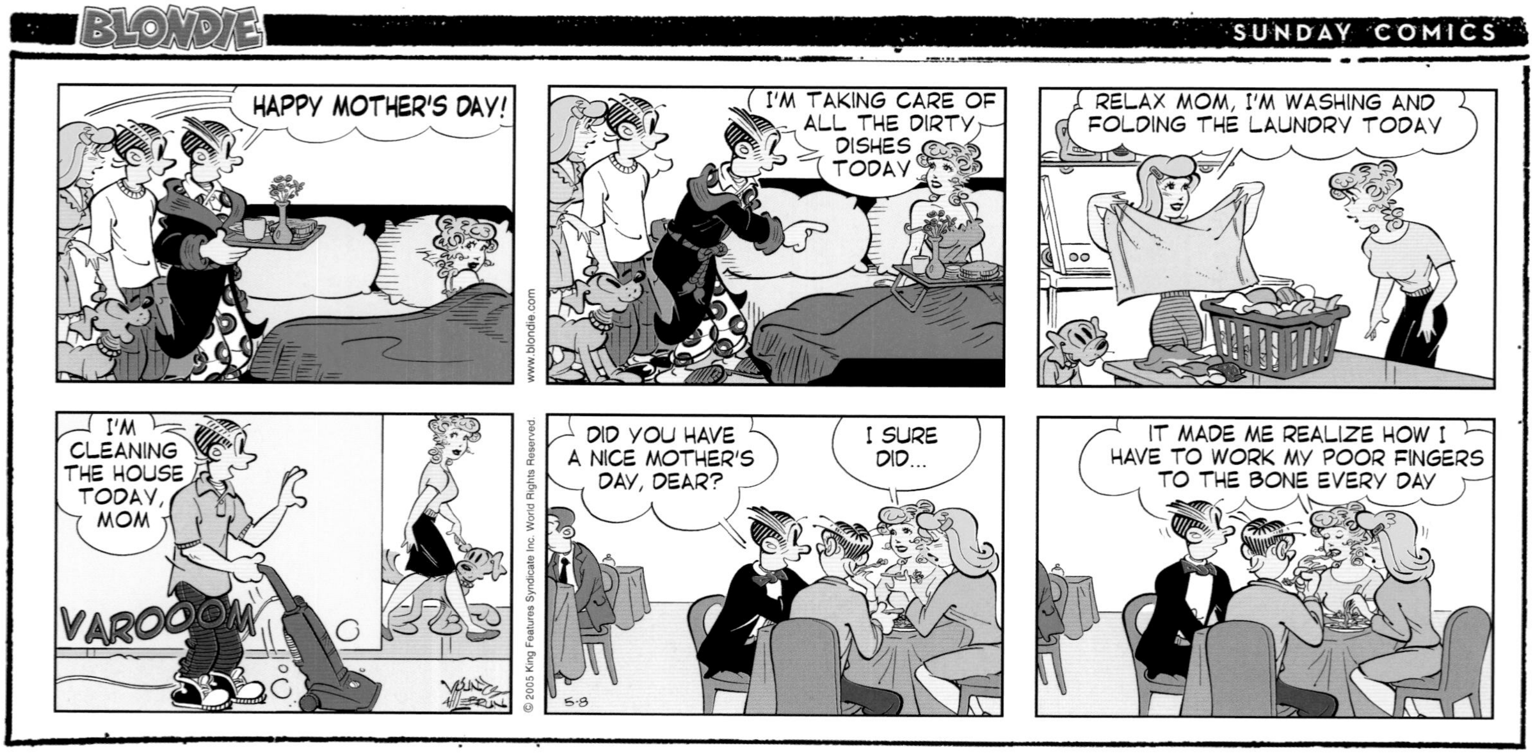
BLONDIE
SUNDAY COMICS
HAPPY MOTHER'S DAY!
I'M TAKING CARE OF ALL THE DIRTY DISHES TODAY
RELAX MOM, I'M WASHING AND FOLDING THE LAUNDRY TODAY
I'M CLEANING THE HOUSE TODAY, MOM
VAROOOM
DID YOU HAVE A NICE MOTHER'S DAY, DEAR?
I SURE DID...
IT MADE ME REALIZE HOW I HAVE TO WORK MY POOR FINGERS TO THE BONE EVERY DAY
www.blondie.com
© 2005 King Features Syndicate Inc. World Rights Reserved.
5-8

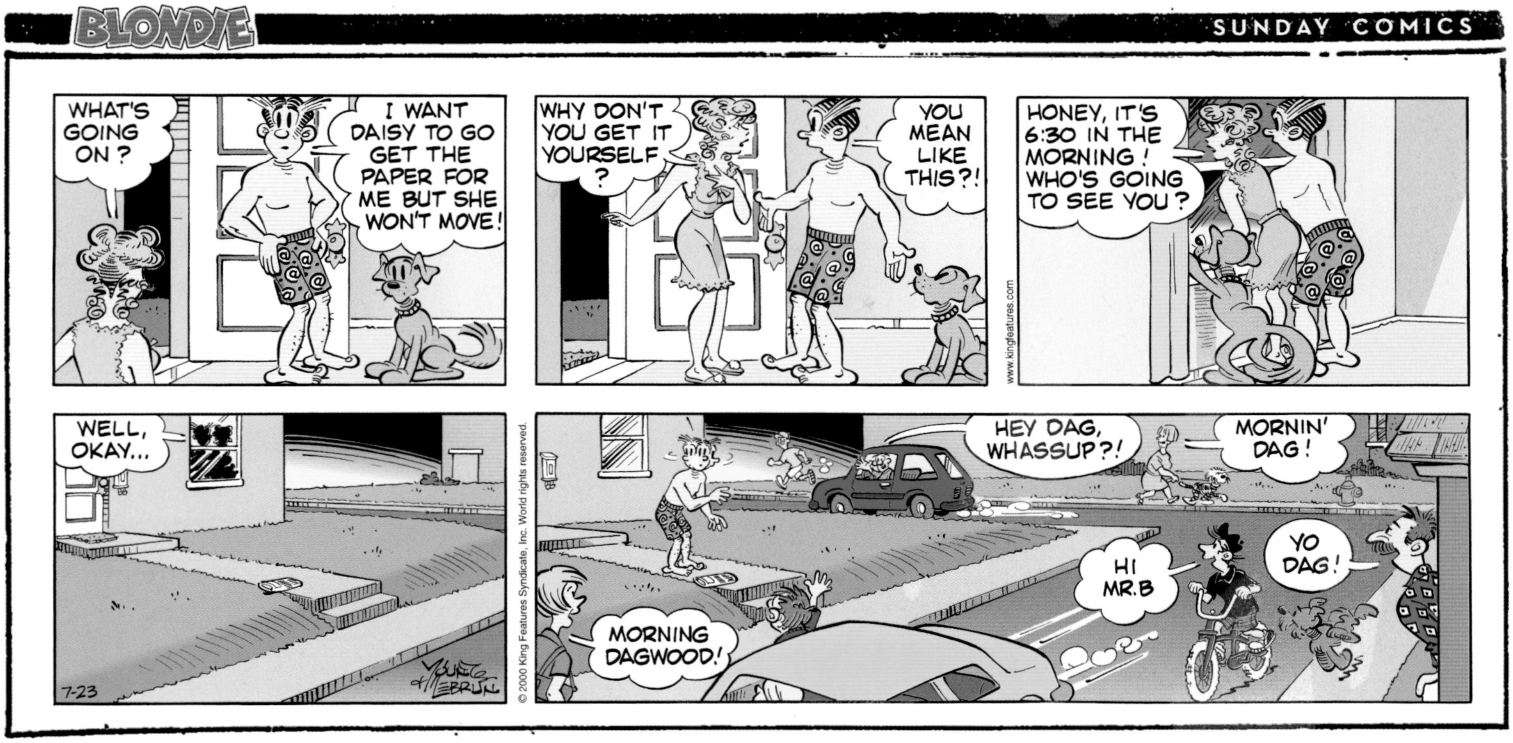
BLONDIE
SUNDAY COMICS
WHAT'S GOING ON?
I WANT DAISY TO GO GET THE PAPER FOR ME BUT SHE WON'T MOVE!
WHY DON'T YOU GET IT YOURSELF?
YOU MEAN LIKE THIS?!
HONEY, IT'S 6:30 IN THE MORNING! WHO'S GOING TO SEE YOU?
www.kingfeatures.com
WELL, OKAY...
7-23
© 2000 King Features Syndicate, Inc. World rights reserved.
HEY DAG, WHASSUP?!
MORNIN' DAG!
HI MR.B
YO DAG!
MORNING DAGWOOD!

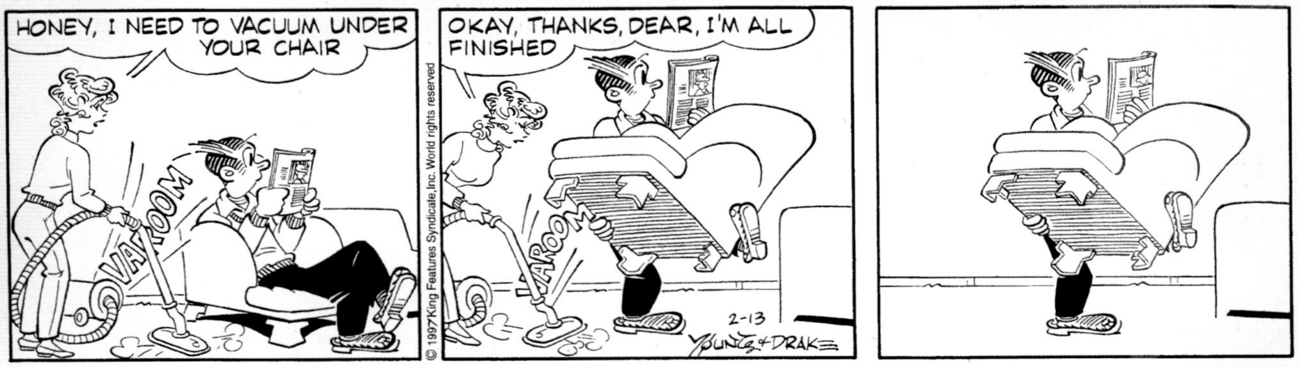
HONEY, I NEED TO VACUUM UNDER YOUR CHAIR
VAROOM
© 1997 King Features Syndicate, Inc. World rights reserved
OKAY, THANKS, DEAR, I'M ALL FINISHED
VAROOM
2-13
YOUNG & DRAKE

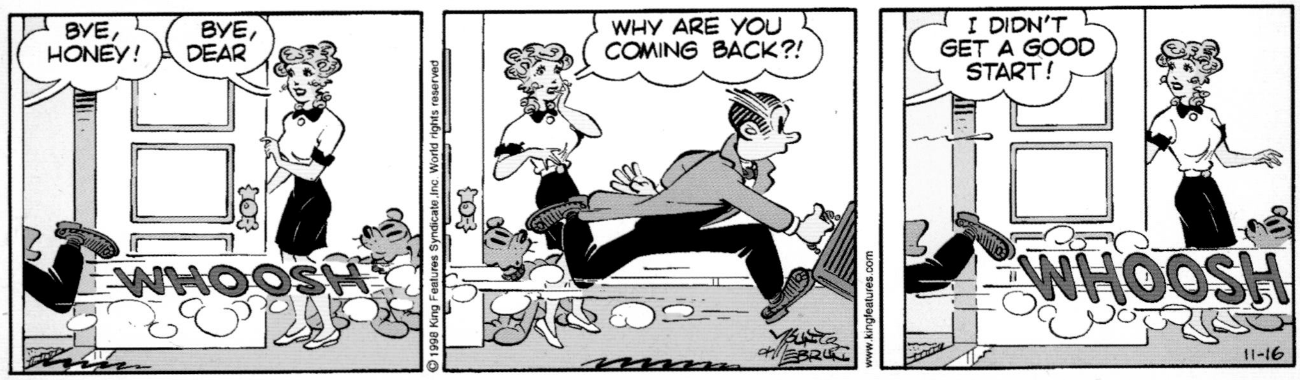
BYE, HONEY!
BYE, DEAR
WHOOSH
© 1998 King Features Syndicate, Inc. World rights reserved
WHY ARE YOU COMING BACK?!
www.kingfeatures.com
I DIDN'T GET A GOOD START!
WHOOSH
11-16

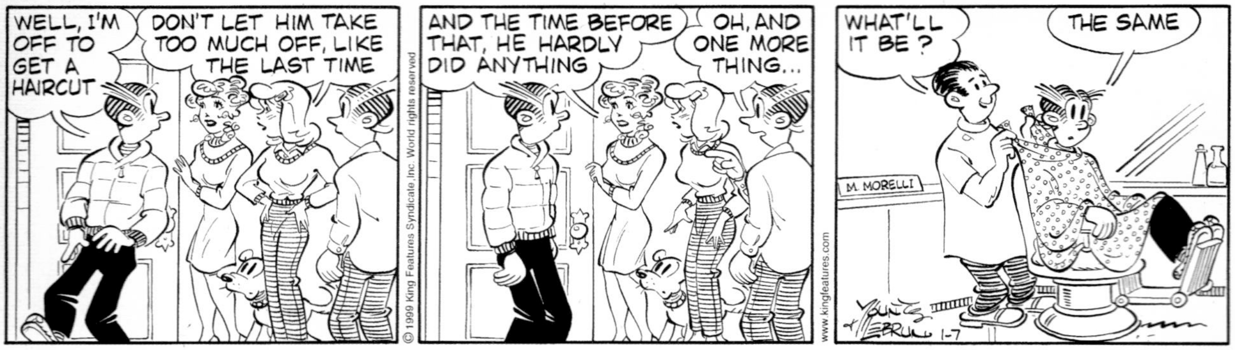
WELL, I'M OFF TO GET A HAIRCUT
DON'T LET HIM TAKE TOO MUCH OFF, LIKE THE LAST TIME
© 1999 King Features Syndicate, Inc. World rights reserved
AND THE TIME BEFORE THAT, HE HARDLY DID ANYTHING
OH, AND ONE MORE THING...
www.kingfeatures.com
WHAT'LL IT BE ?
THE SAME
M. MORELLI
1-7

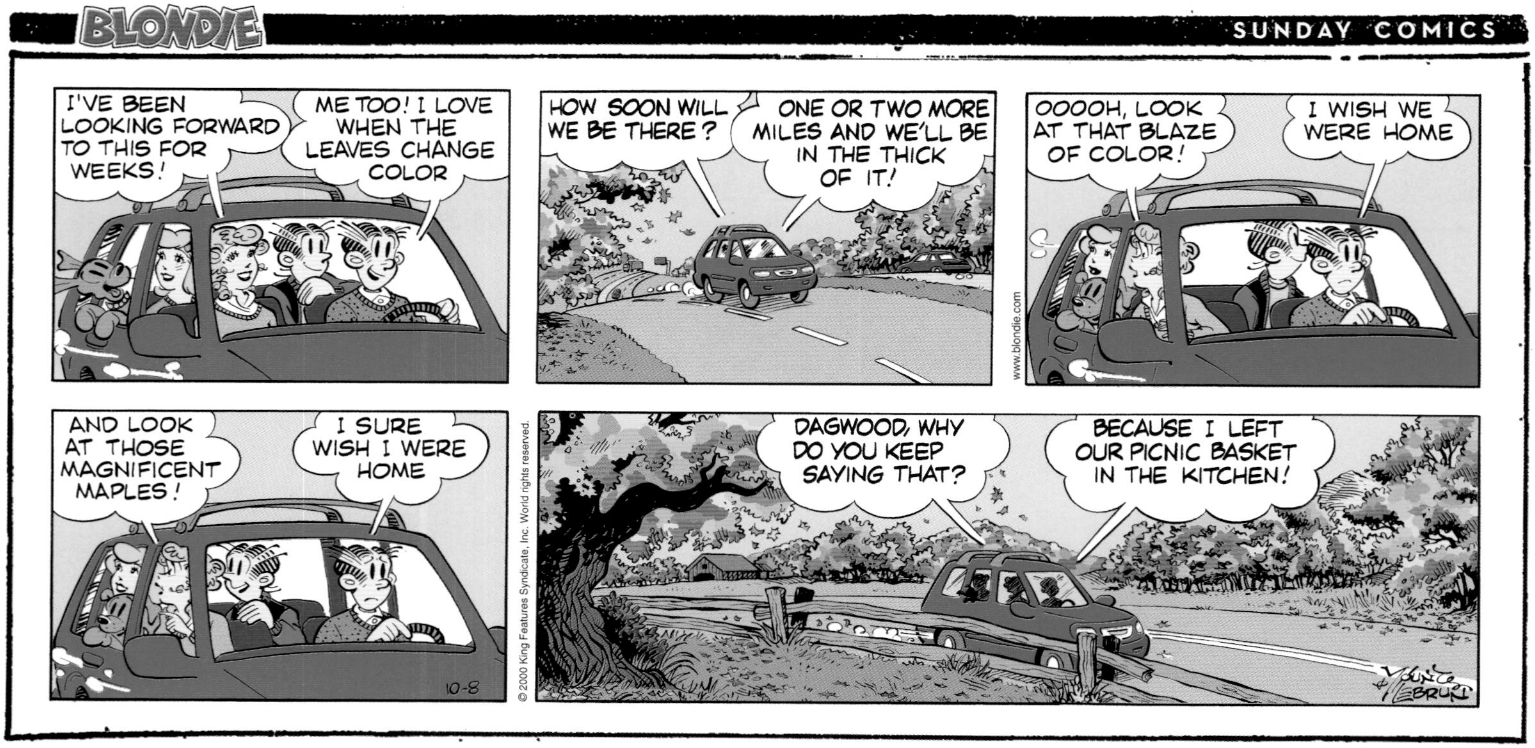
BLONDIE
SUNDAY COMICS
I'VE BEEN LOOKING FORWARD TO THIS FOR WEEKS!
ME TOO! I LOVE WHEN THE LEAVES CHANGE COLOR
HOW SOON WILL WE BE THERE?
ONE OR TWO MORE MILES AND WE'LL BE IN THE THICK OF IT!
OOOOH, LOOK AT THAT BLAZE OF COLOR!
I WISH WE WERE HOME
www.blondie.com
AND LOOK AT THOSE MAGNIFICENT MAPLES!
I SURE WISH I WERE HOME
10-8
© 2000 King Features Syndicate, Inc. World rights reserved.
DAGWOOD, WHY DO YOU KEEP SAYING THAT?
BECAUSE I LEFT OUR PICNIC BASKET IN THE KITCHEN!

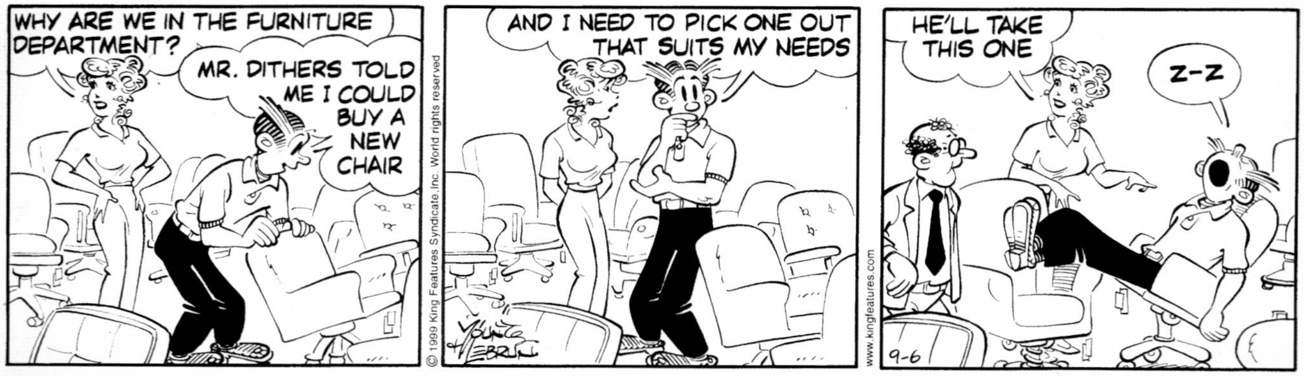
WHY ARE WE IN THE FURNITURE DEPARTMENT?
MR. DITHERS TOLD ME I COULD BUY A NEW CHAIR
© 1999 King Features Syndicate, Inc. World rights reserved
AND I NEED TO PICK ONE OUT THAT SUITS MY NEEDS
www.kingfeatures.com
HE'LL TAKE THIS ONE
Z-Z
9-6

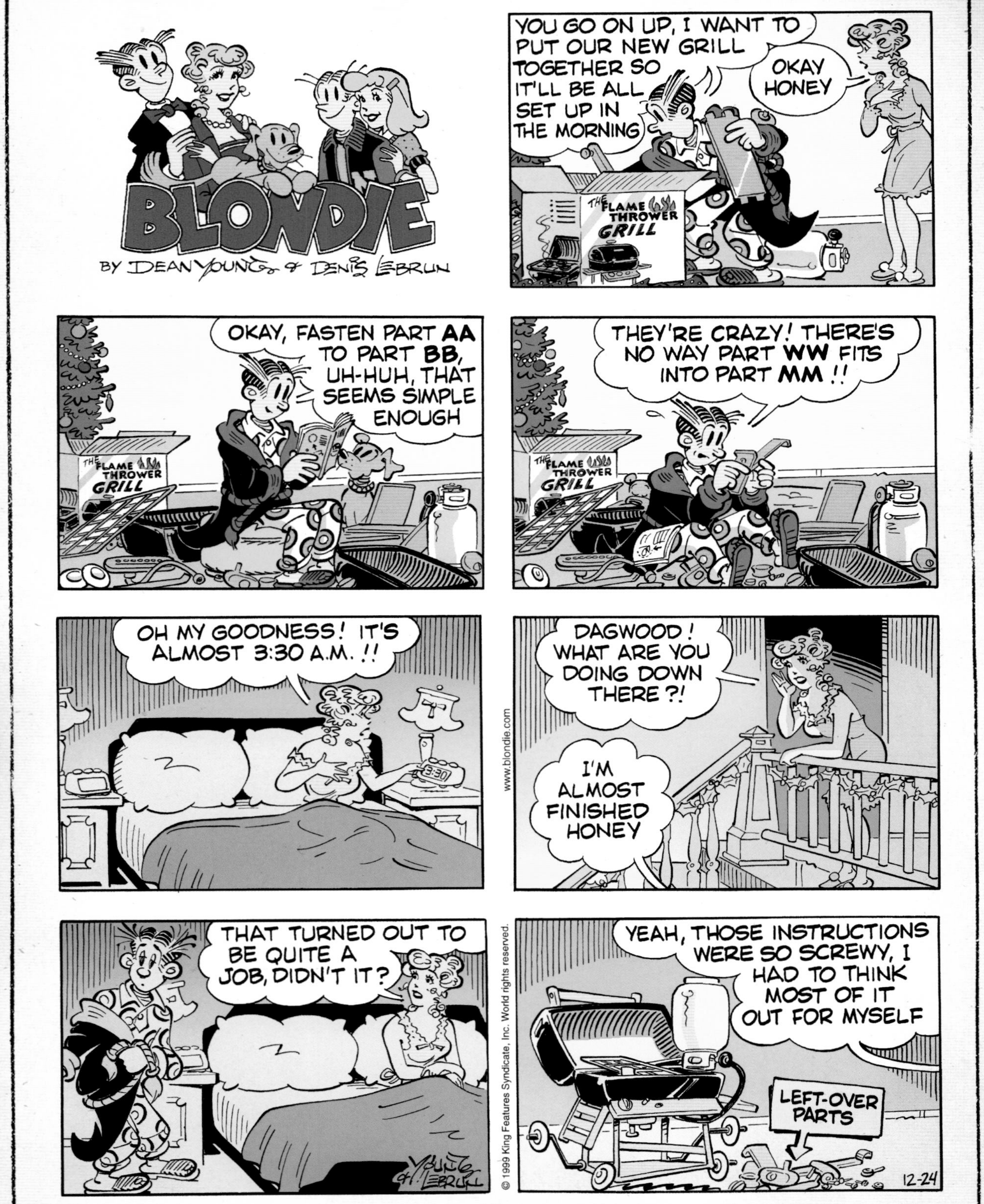
BLONDIE
BY DEAN YOUNG & DENIS LEBRUN
YOU GO ON UP, I WANT TO PUT OUR NEW GRILL TOGETHER SO IT'LL BE ALL SET UP IN THE MORNING
OKAY HONEY
THE FLAME THROWER GRILL
OKAY, FASTEN PART AA TO PART BB, UH-HUH, THAT SEEMS SIMPLE ENOUGH
THEY'RE CRAZY! THERE'S NO WAY PART WW FITS INTO PART MM !!
OH MY GOODNESS! IT'S ALMOST 3:30 A.M. !!
3:30
DAGWOOD! WHAT ARE YOU DOING DOWN THERE ?!
I'M ALMOST FINISHED HONEY
THAT TURNED OUT TO BE QUITE A JOB, DIDN'T IT?
YEAH, THOSE INSTRUCTIONS WERE SO SCREWY, I HAD TO THINK MOST OF IT OUT FOR MYSELF
LEFT-OVER PARTS
YOUNG & LEBRUN
12-24
www.blondie.com
© 1999 King Features Syndicate, Inc. World rights reserved.

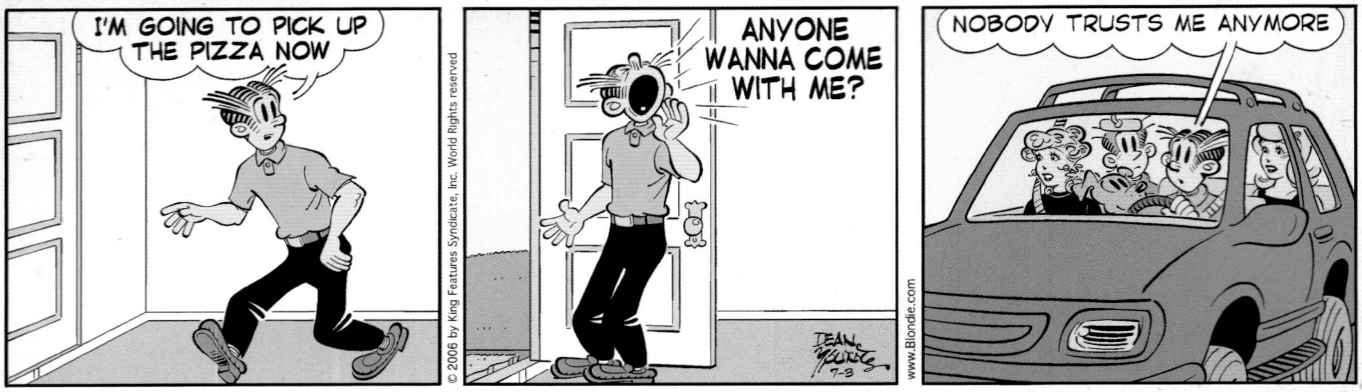
I'M GOING TO PICK UP THE PIZZA NOW
ANYONE WANNA COME WITH ME?
NOBODY TRUSTS ME ANYMORE
© 2006 by King Features Syndicate, Inc. World Rights reserved
DEAN YOUNG 7-3
www.Blondie.com

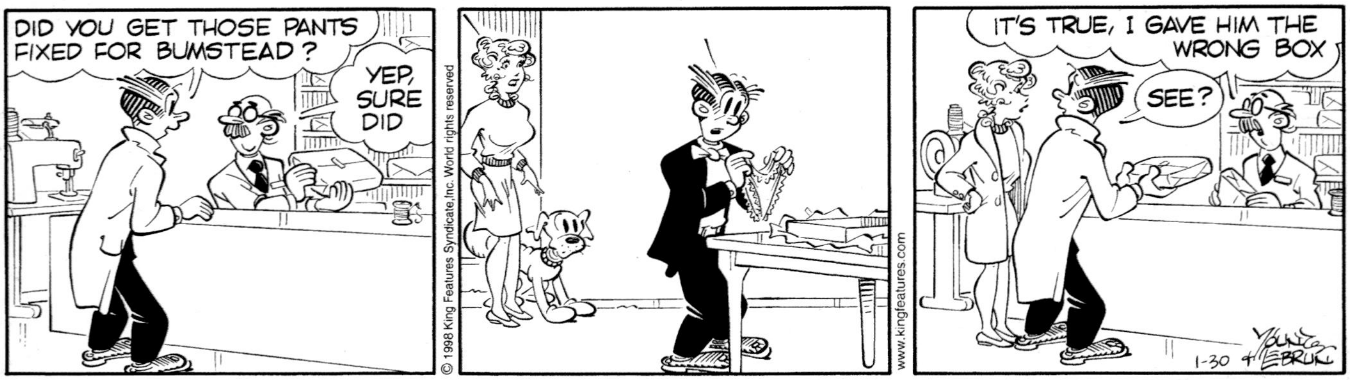
DID YOU GET THOSE PANTS FIXED FOR BUMSTEAD?
YEP, SURE DID
IT'S TRUE, I GAVE HIM THE WRONG BOX
SEE?
© 1998 King Features Syndicate,Inc. World rights reserved
www.kingfeatures.com
1-30 YOUNG & LEBRUN

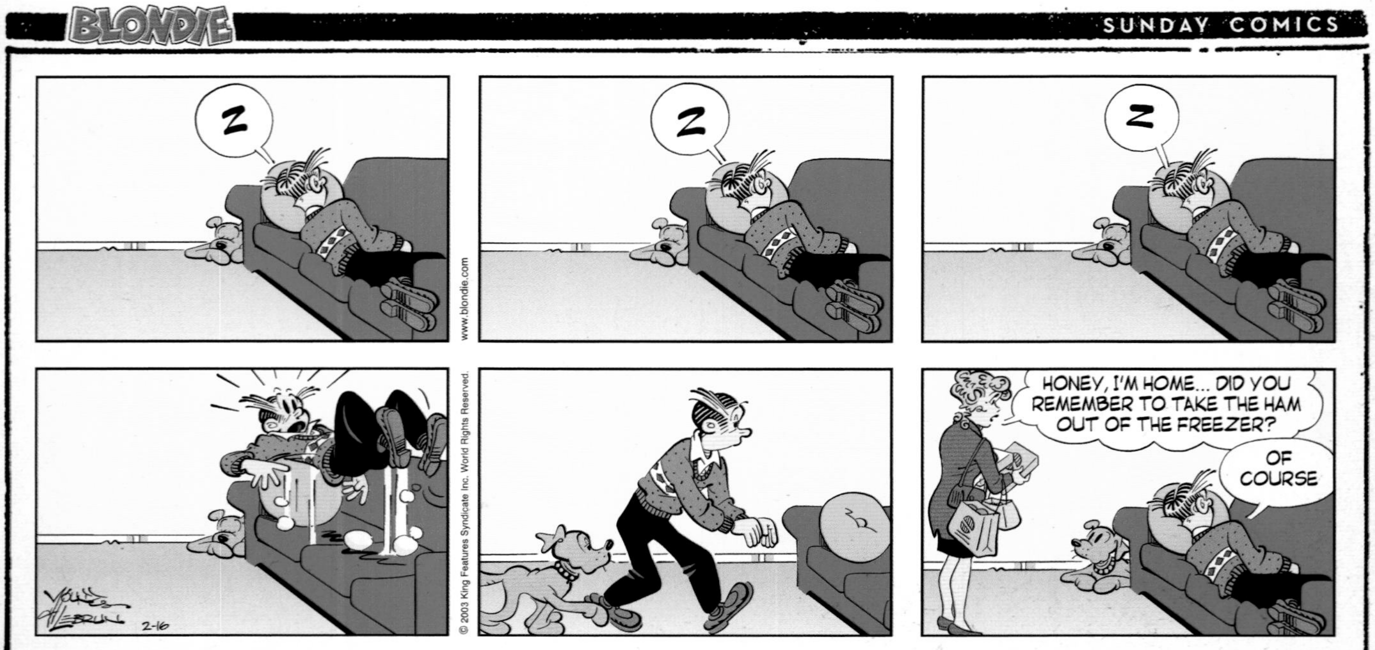
BLONDIE
SUNDAY COMICS
Z
Z
Z
HONEY, I'M HOME... DID YOU REMEMBER TO TAKE THE HAM OUT OF THE FREEZER?
OF COURSE
www.blondie.com
© 2003 King Features Syndicate Inc. World Rights Reserved.
YOUNG & LEBRUN 2-16

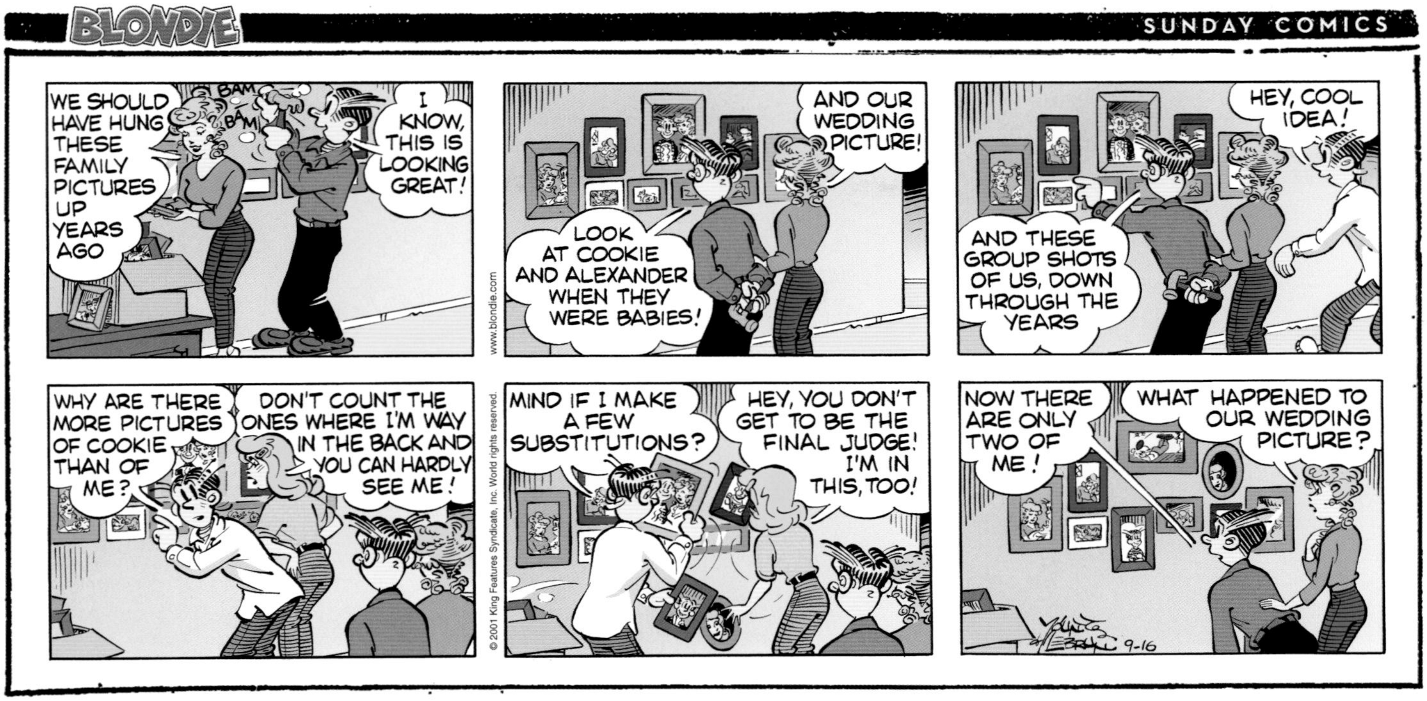
BLONDIE
SUNDAY COMICS
WE SHOULD HAVE HUNG THESE FAMILY PICTURES UP YEARS AGO
BAM BAM
I KNOW, THIS IS LOOKING GREAT!
AND OUR WEDDING PICTURE!
LOOK AT COOKIE AND ALEXANDER WHEN THEY WERE BABIES!
HEY, COOL IDEA!
AND THESE GROUP SHOTS OF US, DOWN THROUGH THE YEARS
WHY ARE THERE MORE PICTURES OF COOKIE THAN OF ME?
DON'T COUNT THE ONES WHERE I'M WAY IN THE BACK AND YOU CAN HARDLY SEE ME!
MIND IF I MAKE A FEW SUBSTITUTIONS?
HEY, YOU DON'T GET TO BE THE FINAL JUDGE! I'M IN THIS, TOO!
NOW THERE ARE ONLY TWO OF ME!
WHAT HAPPENED TO OUR WEDDING PICTURE?
www.blondie.com
© 2001 King Features Syndicate, Inc. World rights reserved.
9-16

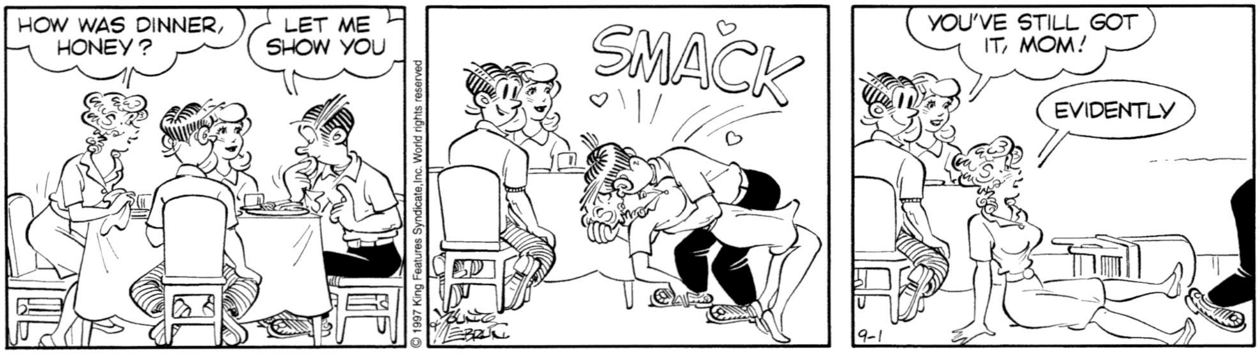
HOW WAS DINNER, HONEY?
LET ME SHOW YOU
SMACK
YOU'VE STILL GOT IT, MOM!
EVIDENTLY
© 1997 King Features Syndicate, Inc. World rights reserved
9-1

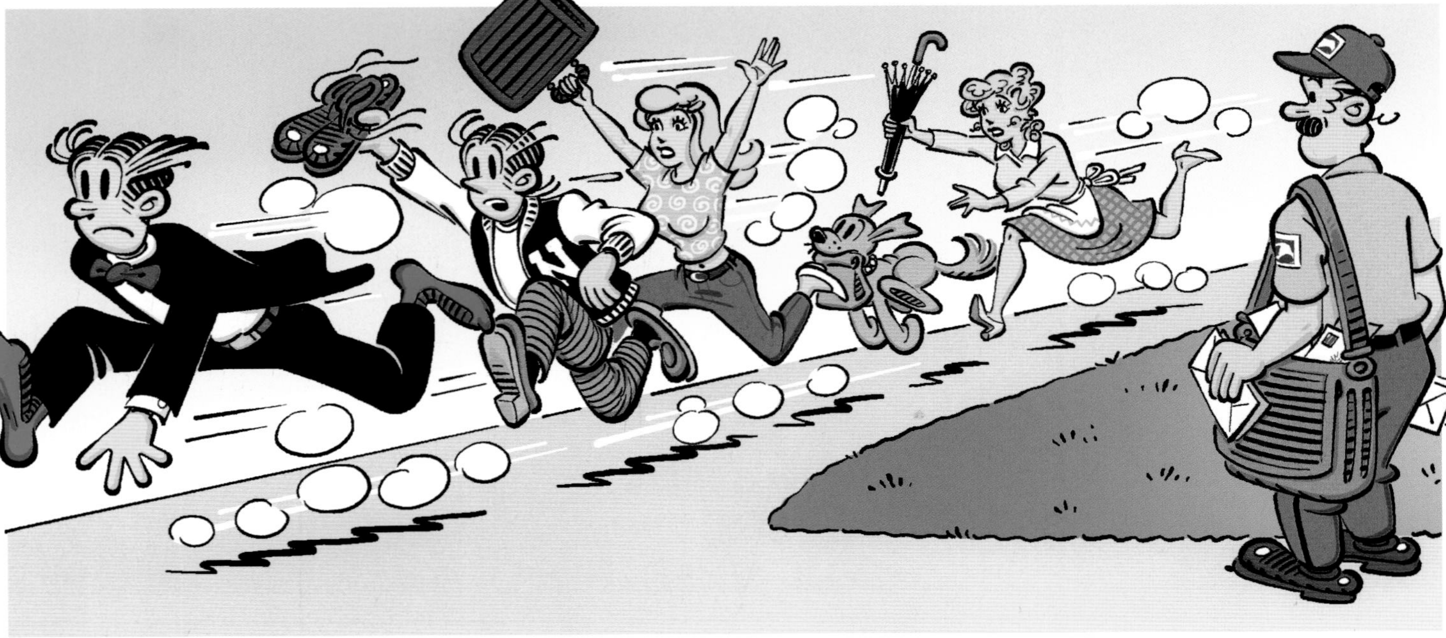

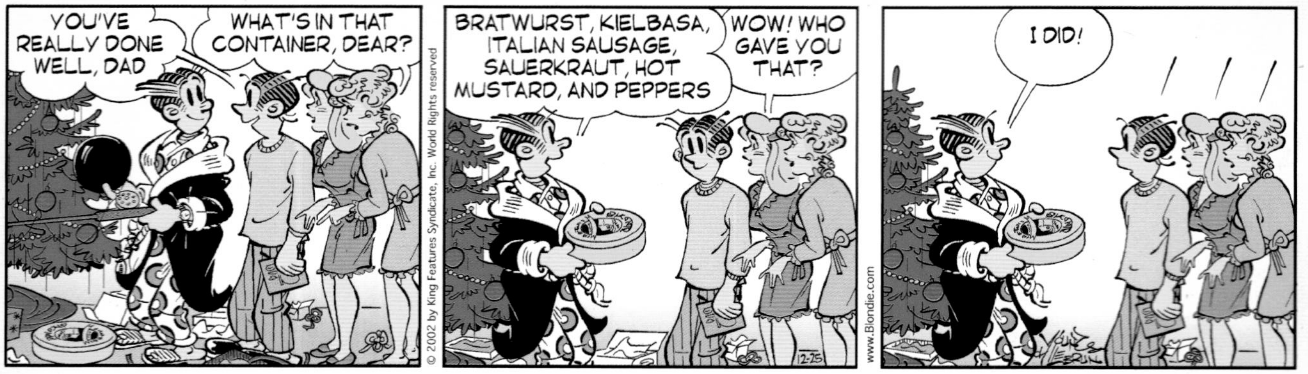
YOU'VE REALLY DONE WELL, DAD
WHAT'S IN THAT CONTAINER, DEAR?
© 2002 by King Features Syndicate, Inc. World Rights reserved
BRATWURST, KIELBASA, ITALIAN SAUSAGE, SAUERKRAUT, HOT MUSTARD, AND PEPPERS
WOW! WHO GAVE YOU THAT?
12-25
www.Blondie.com
I DID!

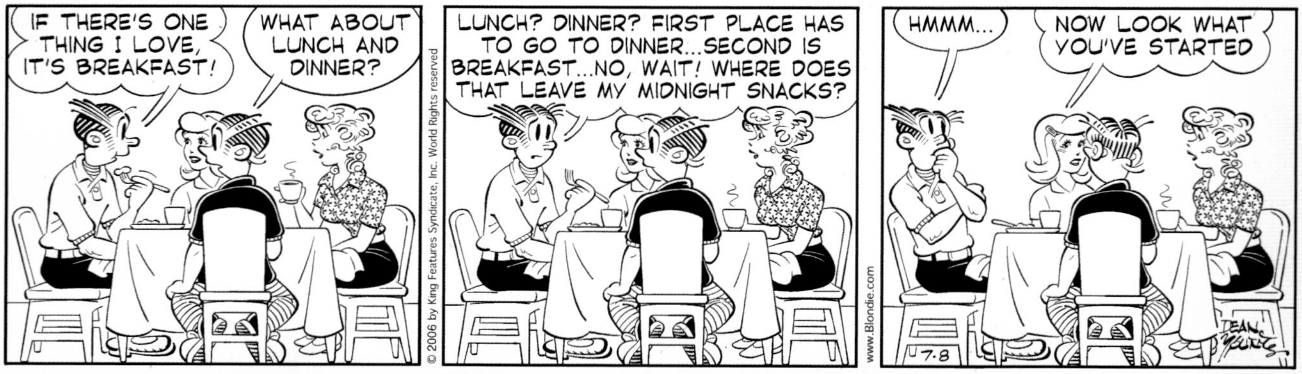
IF THERE'S ONE THING I LOVE, IT'S BREAKFAST!
WHAT ABOUT LUNCH AND DINNER?
© 2006 by King Features Syndicate, Inc. World Rights reserved
LUNCH? DINNER? FIRST PLACE HAS TO GO TO DINNER...SECOND IS BREAKFAST...NO, WAIT! WHERE DOES THAT LEAVE MY MIDNIGHT SNACKS?
www.Blondie.com
HMMM...
NOW LOOK WHAT YOU'VE STARTED
7-8

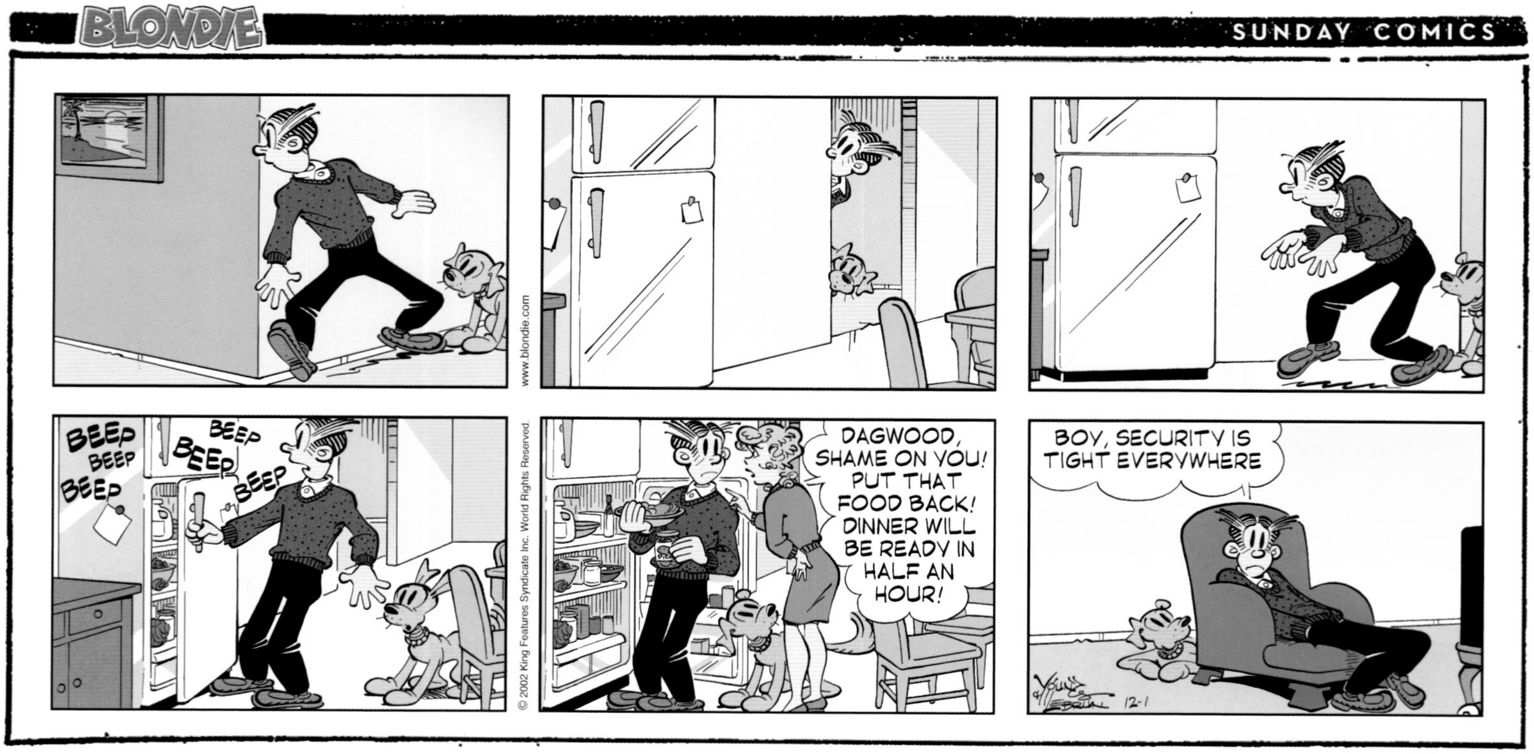
BLONDIE
SUNDAY COMICS
www.blondie.com
BEEP BEEP BEEP BEEP BEEP BEEP
© 2002 King Features Syndicate Inc. World Rights Reserved.
DAGWOOD, SHAME ON YOU! PUT THAT FOOD BACK! DINNER WILL BE READY IN HALF AN HOUR!
BOY, SECURITY IS TIGHT EVERYWHERE
12-1

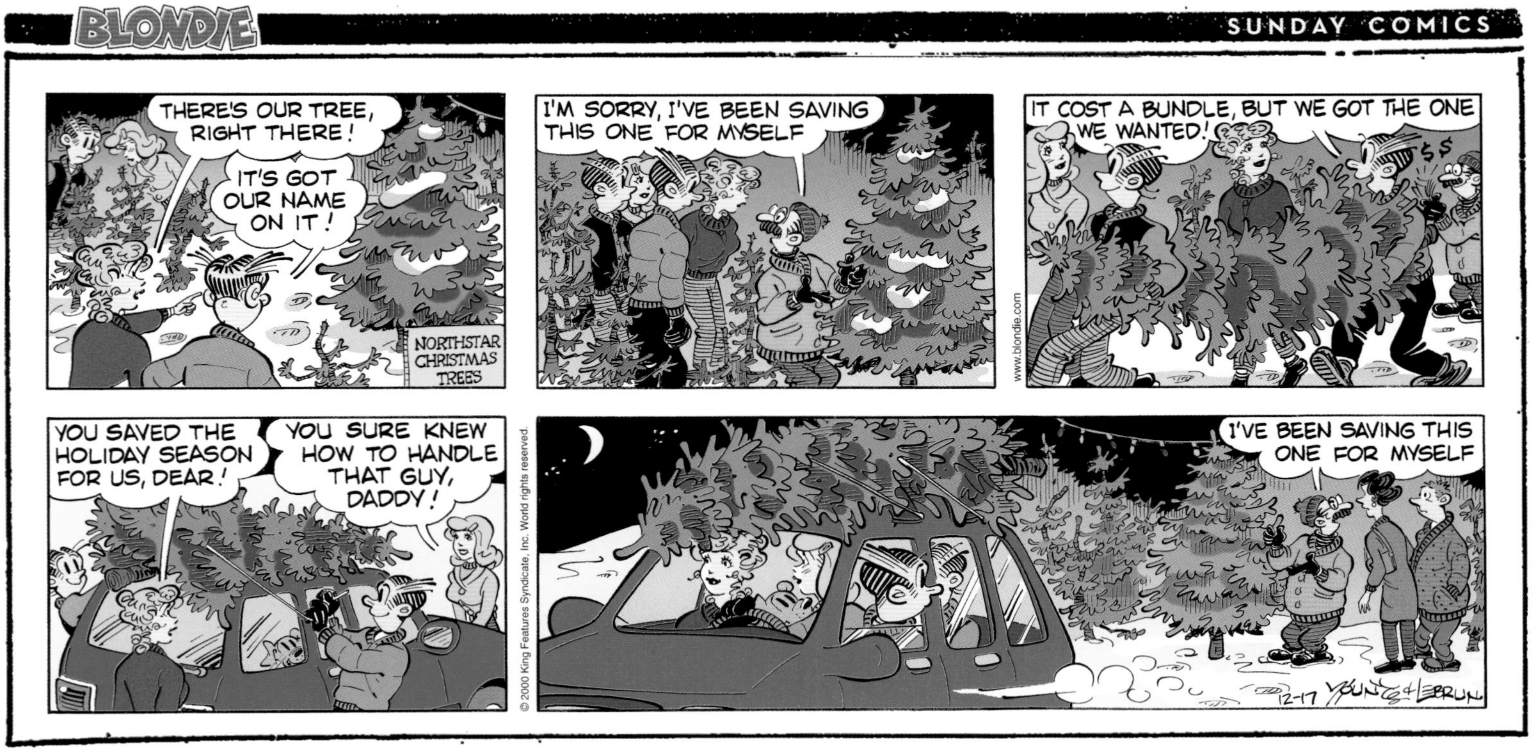
BLONDIE
SUNDAY COMICS
THERE'S OUR TREE, RIGHT THERE!
IT'S GOT OUR NAME ON IT!
NORTHSTAR CHRISTMAS TREES
I'M SORRY, I'VE BEEN SAVING THIS ONE FOR MYSELF
IT COST A BUNDLE, BUT WE GOT THE ONE WE WANTED!
$ $
www.blondie.com
YOU SAVED THE HOLIDAY SEASON FOR US, DEAR!
YOU SURE KNEW HOW TO HANDLE THAT GUY, DADDY!
© 2000 King Features Syndicate, Inc. World rights reserved.
I'VE BEEN SAVING THIS ONE FOR MYSELF
12-17

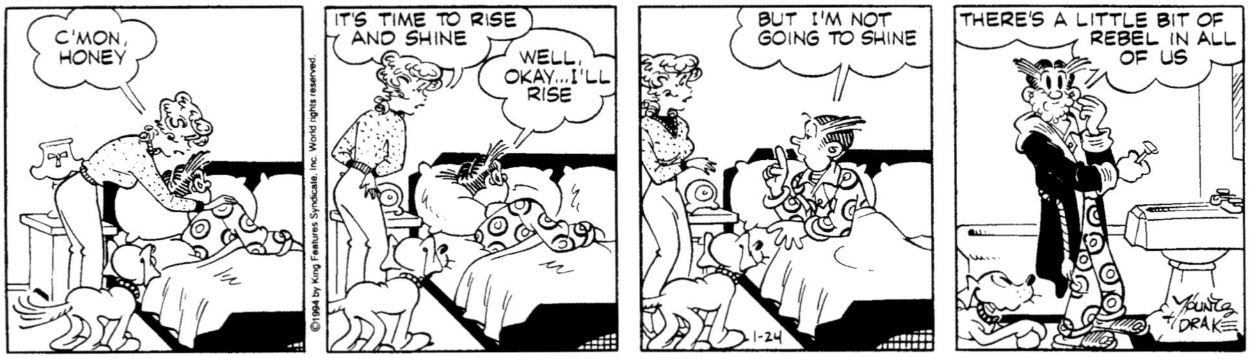
C'MON, HONEY
©1994 by King Features Syndicate, Inc. World rights reserved.
IT'S TIME TO RISE AND SHINE
WELL, OKAY...I'LL RISE
BUT I'M NOT GOING TO SHINE
1-24
THERE'S A LITTLE BIT OF REBEL IN ALL OF US

"I like to think of Blondie and Dagwood as intelligent human beings going through life together sharing and caring for all the things two people in love have to share and care about," says Dean.

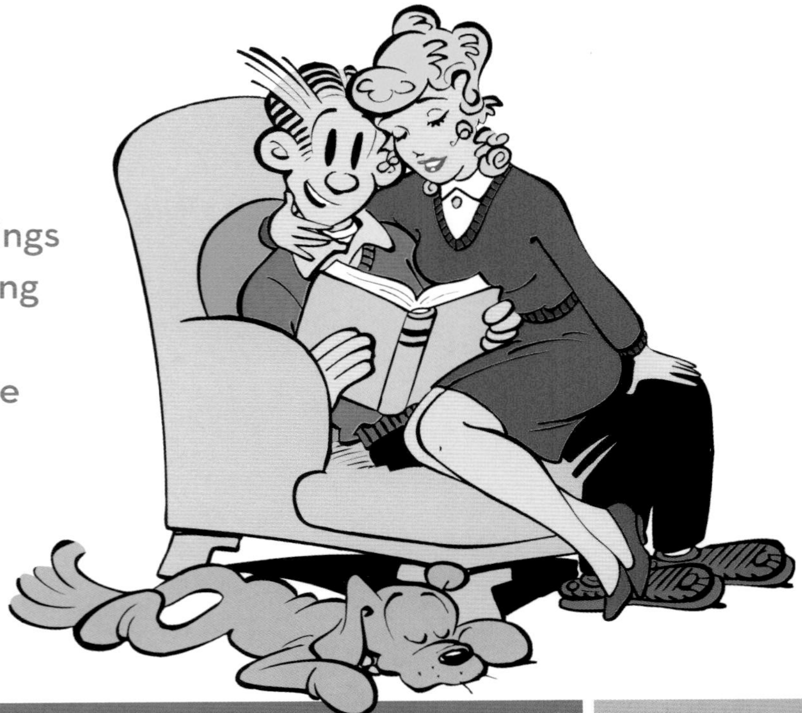

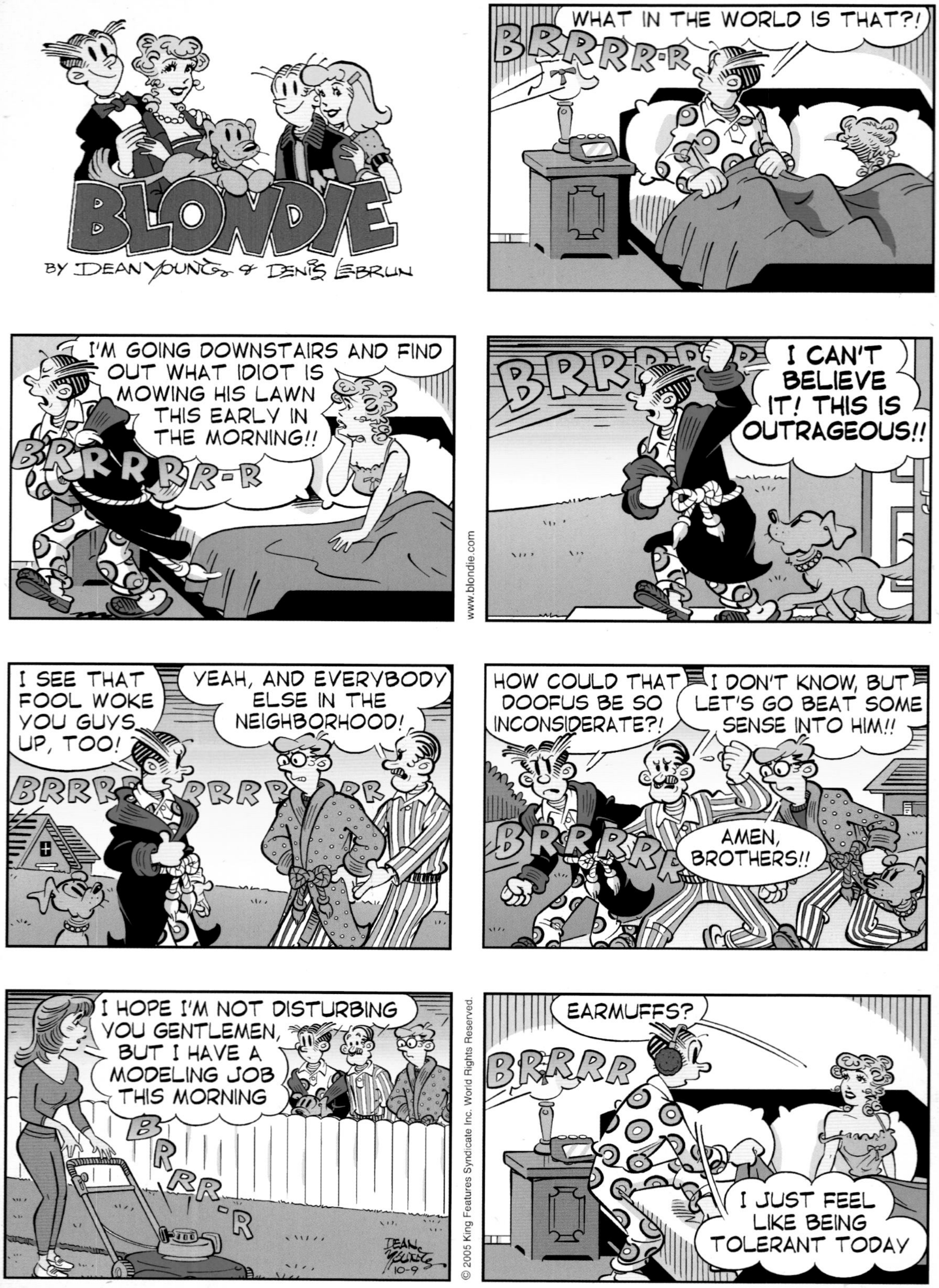
BLONDIE
BY DEAN YOUNG & DENIS LEBRUN
BRRRRR-R
WHAT IN THE WORLD IS THAT?!
I'M GOING DOWNSTAIRS AND FIND OUT WHAT IDIOT IS MOWING HIS LAWN THIS EARLY IN THE MORNING!!
BRRRRRR-R
BRRRRR
I CAN'T BELIEVE IT! THIS IS OUTRAGEOUS!!
I SEE THAT FOOL WOKE YOU GUYS UP, TOO!
YEAH, AND EVERYBODY ELSE IN THE NEIGHBORHOOD!
BRRRRRRRRR
HOW COULD THAT DOOFUS BE SO INCONSIDERATE?!
I DON'T KNOW, BUT LET'S GO BEAT SOME SENSE INTO HIM!!
AMEN, BROTHERS!!
BRRRRRR
I HOPE I'M NOT DISTURBING YOU GENTLEMEN, BUT I HAVE A MODELING JOB THIS MORNING
BRRR-R
DEAN YOUNG 10-9
EARMUFFS?
BRRRR
I JUST FEEL LIKE BEING TOLERANT TODAY
www.blondie.com

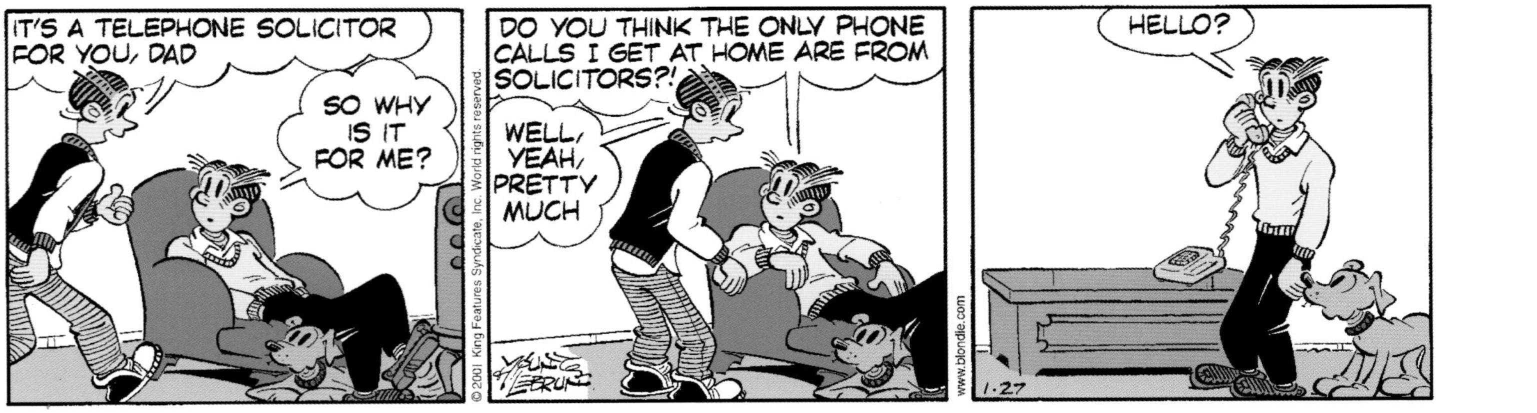
IT'S A TELEPHONE SOLICITOR FOR YOU, DAD
SO WHY IS IT FOR ME?
DO YOU THINK THE ONLY PHONE CALLS I GET AT HOME ARE FROM SOLICITORS?!
WELL, YEAH, PRETTY MUCH
HELLO?
© 2001 King Features Syndicate, Inc. World rights reserved.
www.blondie.com
1·27

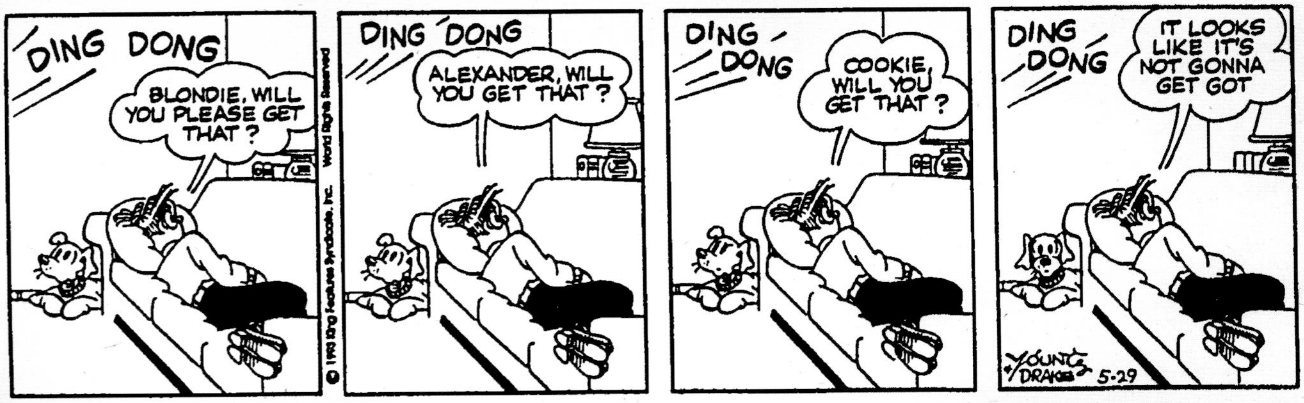
DING DONG
BLONDIE, WILL YOU PLEASE GET THAT?
DING DONG
ALEXANDER, WILL YOU GET THAT?
DING DONG
COOKIE, WILL YOU GET THAT?
DING DONG
IT LOOKS LIKE IT'S NOT GONNA GET GOT
5·29

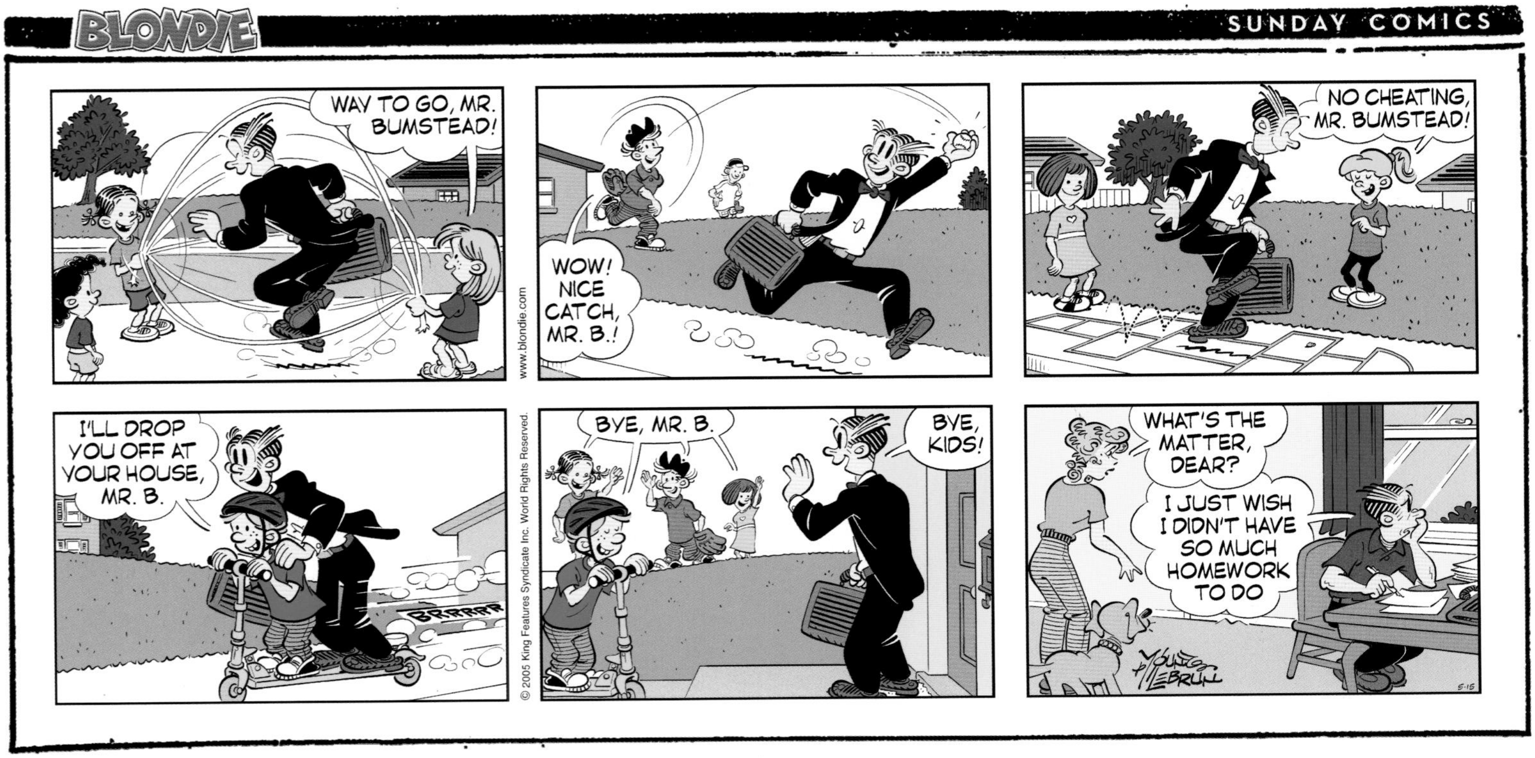
BLONDIE
SUNDAY COMICS
WAY TO GO, MR. BUMSTEAD!
WOW! NICE CATCH, MR. B.!
NO CHEATING, MR. BUMSTEAD!
I'LL DROP YOU OFF AT YOUR HOUSE, MR. B.
BRRRRR
BYE, MR. B.
BYE, KIDS!
WHAT'S THE MATTER, DEAR?
I JUST WISH I DIDN'T HAVE SO MUCH HOMEWORK TO DO
© 2005 King Features Syndicate Inc. World Rights Reserved.
www.blondie.com

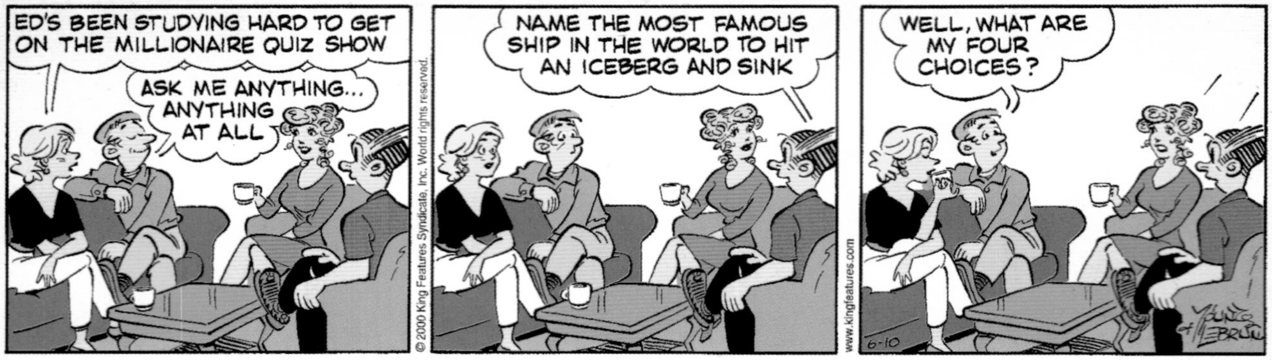
ED'S BEEN STUDYING HARD TO GET ON THE MILLIONAIRE QUIZ SHOW
ASK ME ANYTHING... ANYTHING AT ALL
NAME THE MOST FAMOUS SHIP IN THE WORLD TO HIT AN ICEBERG AND SINK
WELL, WHAT ARE MY FOUR CHOICES?

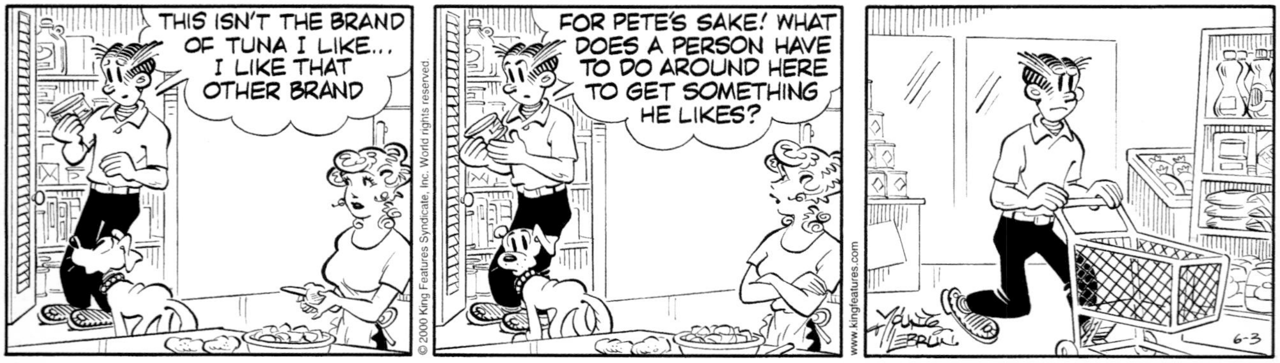
THIS ISN'T THE BRAND OF TUNA I LIKE... I LIKE THAT OTHER BRAND
FOR PETE'S SAKE! WHAT DOES A PERSON HAVE TO DO AROUND HERE TO GET SOMETHING HE LIKES?

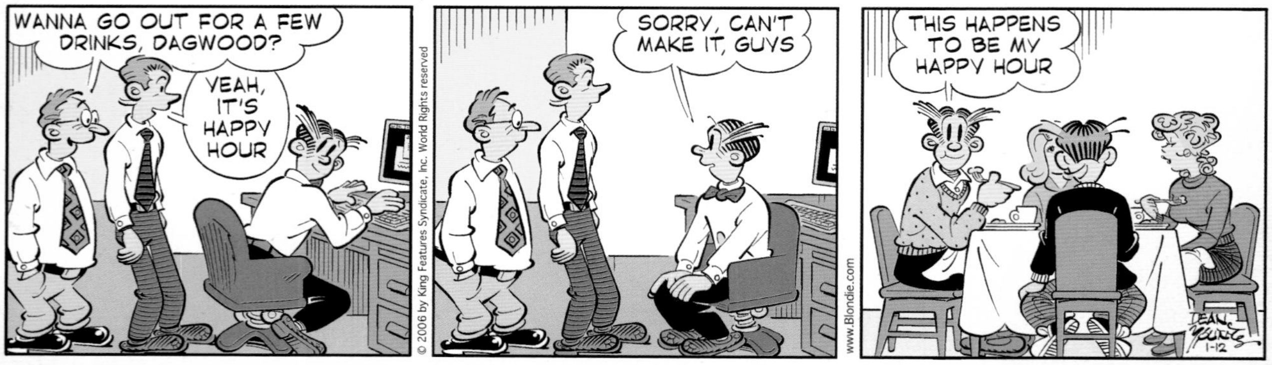
WANNA GO OUT FOR A FEW DRINKS, DAGWOOD?
YEAH, IT'S HAPPY HOUR
SORRY, CAN'T MAKE IT, GUYS
THIS HAPPENS TO BE MY HAPPY HOUR

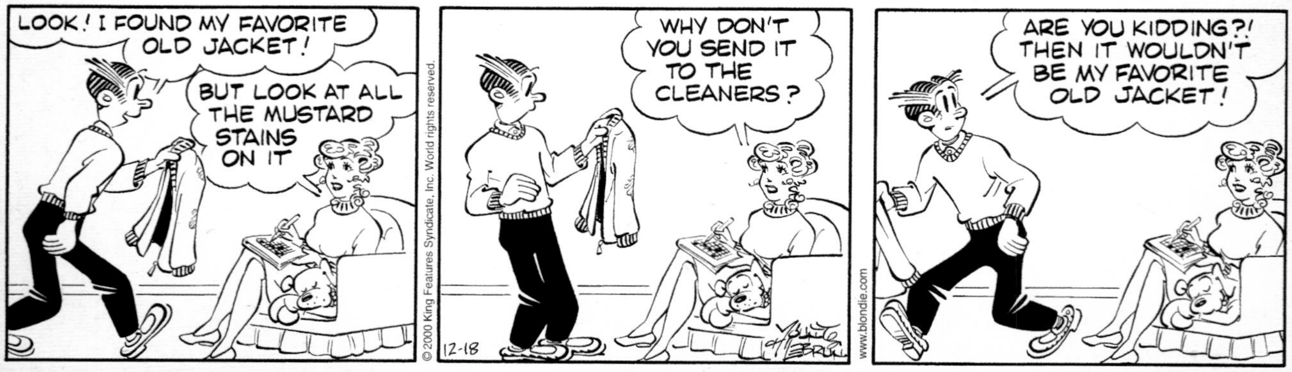
LOOK! I FOUND MY FAVORITE OLD JACKET!
BUT LOOK AT ALL THE MUSTARD STAINS ON IT
WHY DON'T YOU SEND IT TO THE CLEANERS?
ARE YOU KIDDING?! THEN IT WOULDN'T BE MY FAVORITE OLD JACKET!

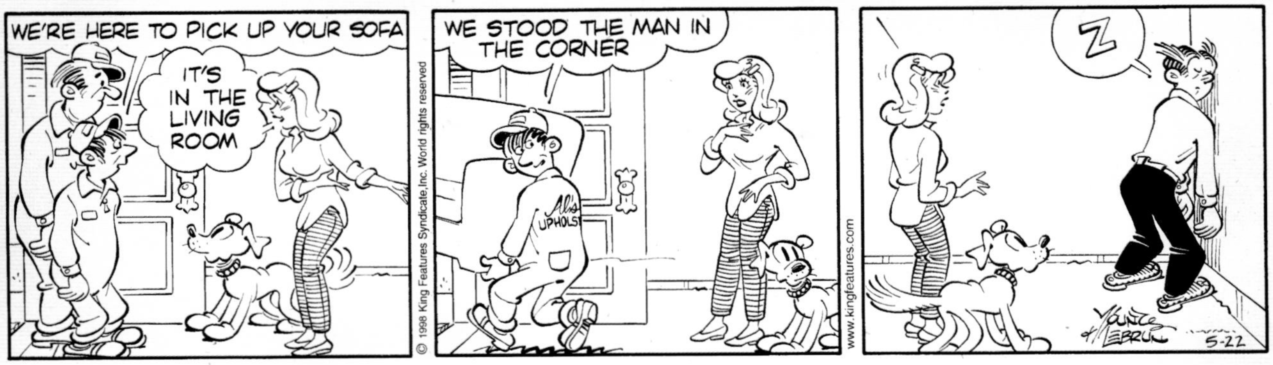
WE'RE HERE TO PICK UP YOUR SOFA
IT'S IN THE LIVING ROOM
WE STOOD THE MAN IN THE CORNER
Z
© 1998 King Features Syndicate, Inc. World rights reserved
www.kingfeatures.com
5-22

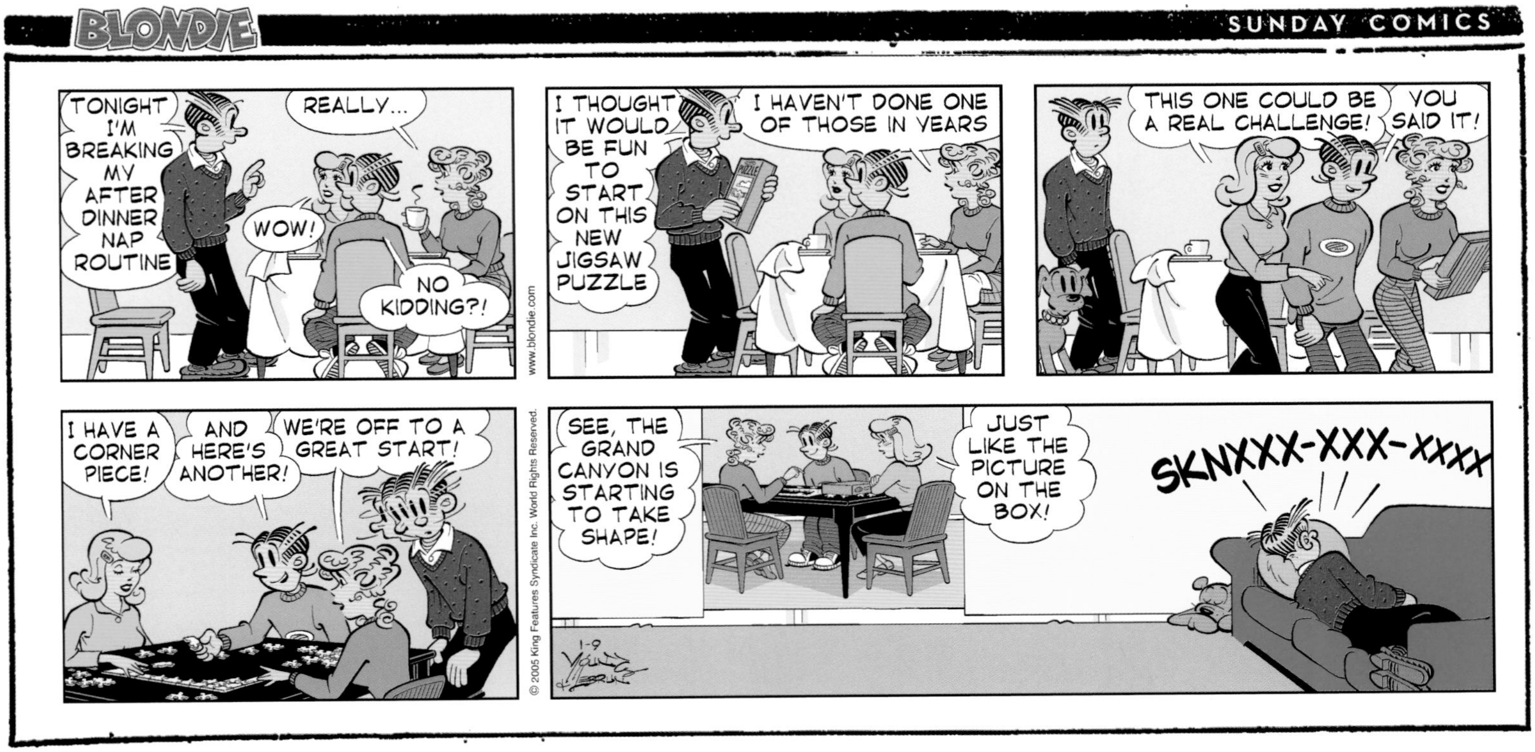
BLONDIE
SUNDAY COMICS
TONIGHT I'M BREAKING MY AFTER DINNER NAP ROUTINE
REALLY...
WOW!
NO KIDDING?!
I THOUGHT IT WOULD BE FUN TO START ON THIS NEW JIGSAW PUZZLE
I HAVEN'T DONE ONE OF THOSE IN YEARS
THIS ONE COULD BE A REAL CHALLENGE!
YOU SAID IT!
I HAVE A CORNER PIECE!
AND HERE'S ANOTHER!
WE'RE OFF TO A GREAT START!
SEE, THE GRAND CANYON IS STARTING TO TAKE SHAPE!
JUST LIKE THE PICTURE ON THE BOX!
SKNXXX-XXX-XXXX
www.blondie.com
© 2005 King Features Syndicate Inc. World Rights Reserved.
1-9

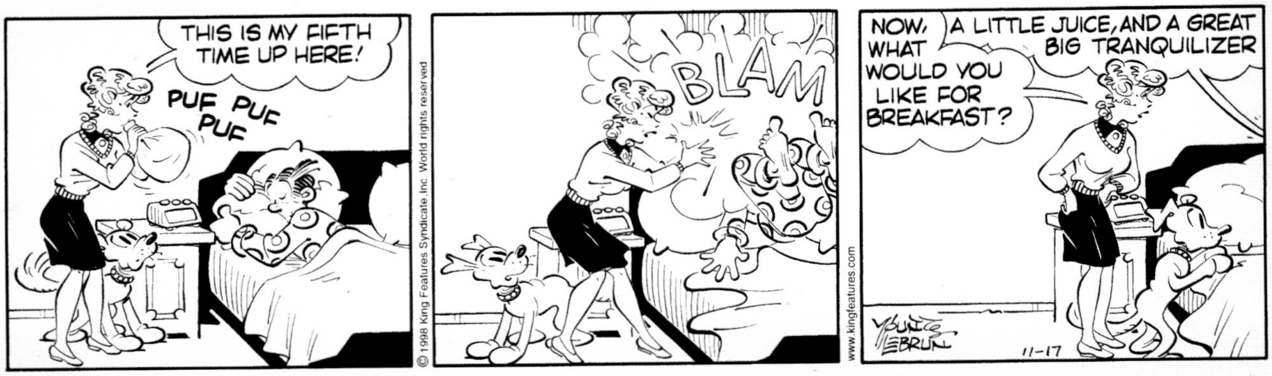
THIS IS MY FIFTH TIME UP HERE!
PUF PUF PUF
BLAM
NOW, WHAT WOULD YOU LIKE FOR BREAKFAST?
A LITTLE JUICE, AND A GREAT BIG TRANQUILIZER
© 1998 King Features Syndicate Inc. World rights reserved
www.kingfeatures.com
11-17

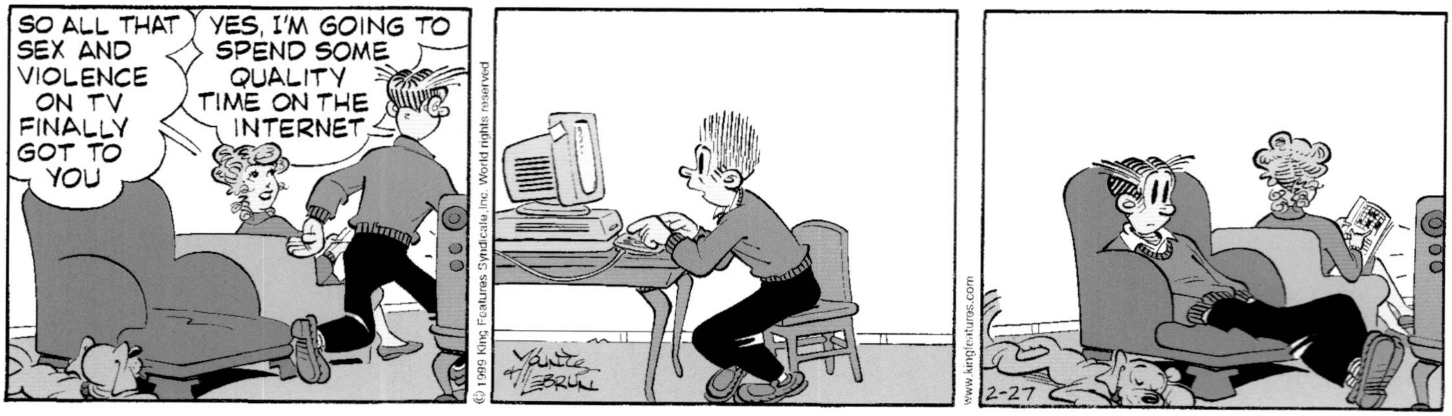
SO ALL THAT SEX AND VIOLENCE ON TV FINALLY GOT TO YOU
YES, I'M GOING TO SPEND SOME QUALITY TIME ON THE INTERNET
© 1999 King Features Syndicate, Inc. World rights reserved.
YOUNG & LEBRUN
www.kingfeatures.com
2-27

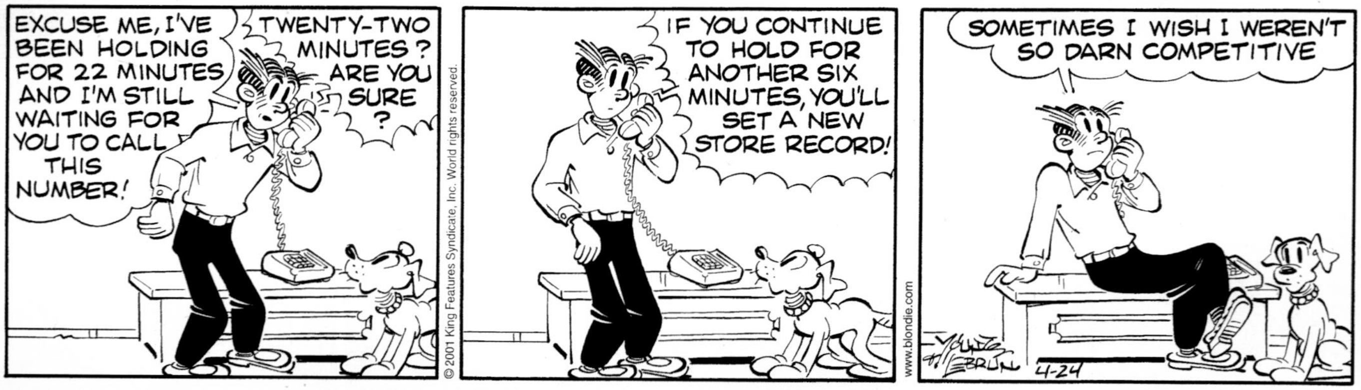
EXCUSE ME, I'VE BEEN HOLDING FOR 22 MINUTES AND I'M STILL WAITING FOR YOU TO CALL THIS NUMBER!
TWENTY-TWO MINUTES? ARE YOU SURE?
© 2001 King Features Syndicate, Inc. World rights reserved.
IF YOU CONTINUE TO HOLD FOR ANOTHER SIX MINUTES, YOU'LL SET A NEW STORE RECORD!
www.blondie.com
SOMETIMES I WISH I WEREN'T SO DARN COMPETITIVE
YOUNG & LEBRUN
4-24

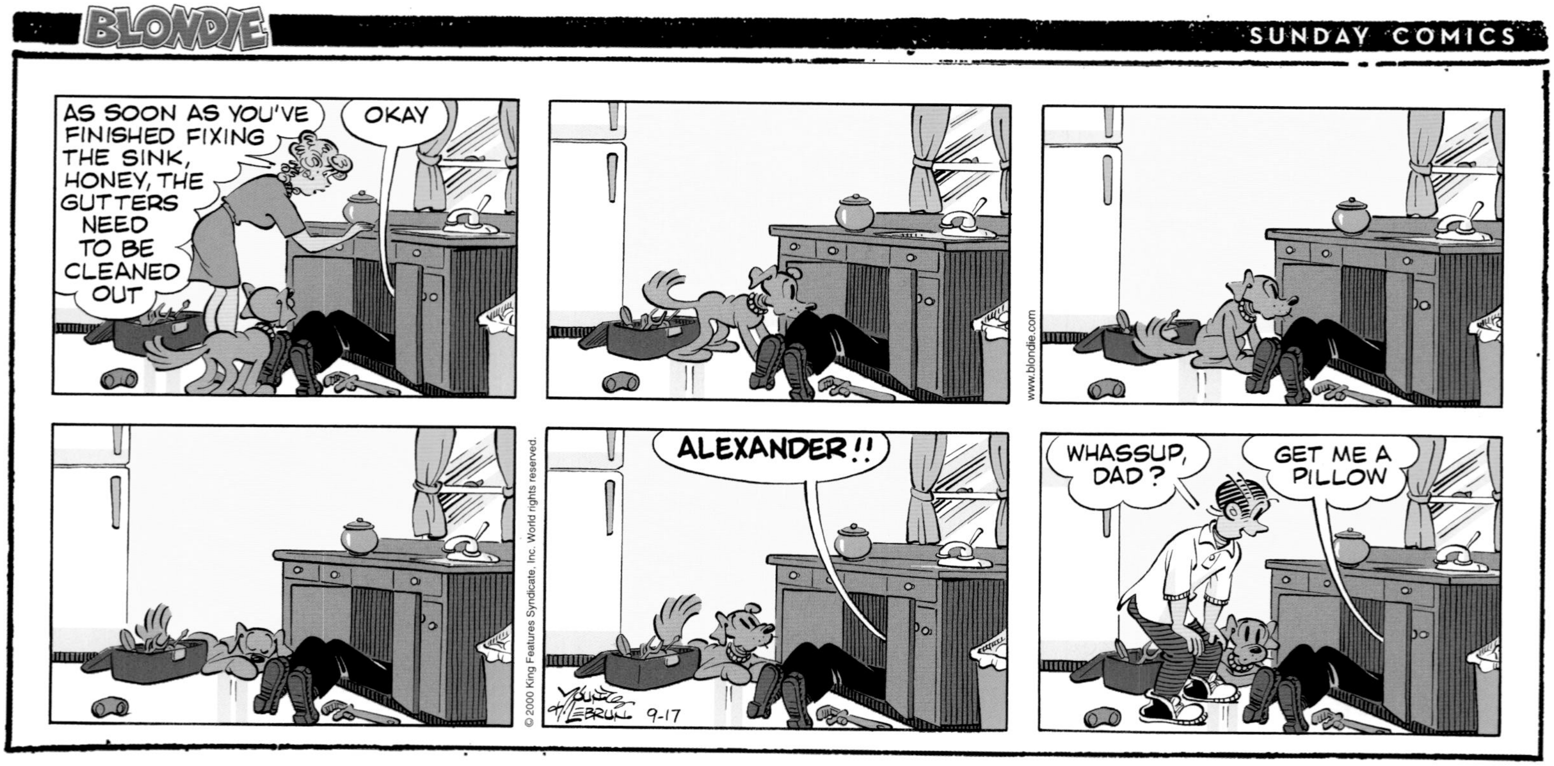
BLONDIE
SUNDAY COMICS
AS SOON AS YOU'VE FINISHED FIXING THE SINK, HONEY, THE GUTTERS NEED TO BE CLEANED OUT
OKAY
www.blondie.com
© 2000 King Features Syndicate, Inc. World rights reserved.
ALEXANDER!!
YOUNG & LEBRUN
9-17
WHASSUP, DAD?
GET ME A PILLOW

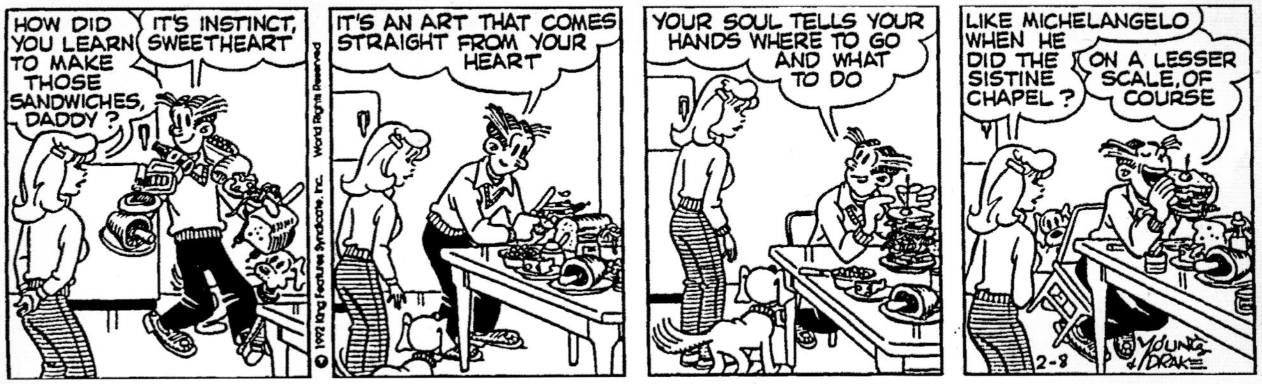
HOW DID YOU LEARN TO MAKE THOSE SANDWICHES, DADDY?
IT'S INSTINCT, SWEETHEART
© 1992 King Features Syndicate, Inc. World Rights Reserved
IT'S AN ART THAT COMES STRAIGHT FROM YOUR HEART
YOUR SOUL TELLS YOUR HANDS WHERE TO GO AND WHAT TO DO
LIKE MICHELANGELO WHEN HE DID THE SISTINE CHAPEL?
ON A LESSER SCALE, OF COURSE
2-8

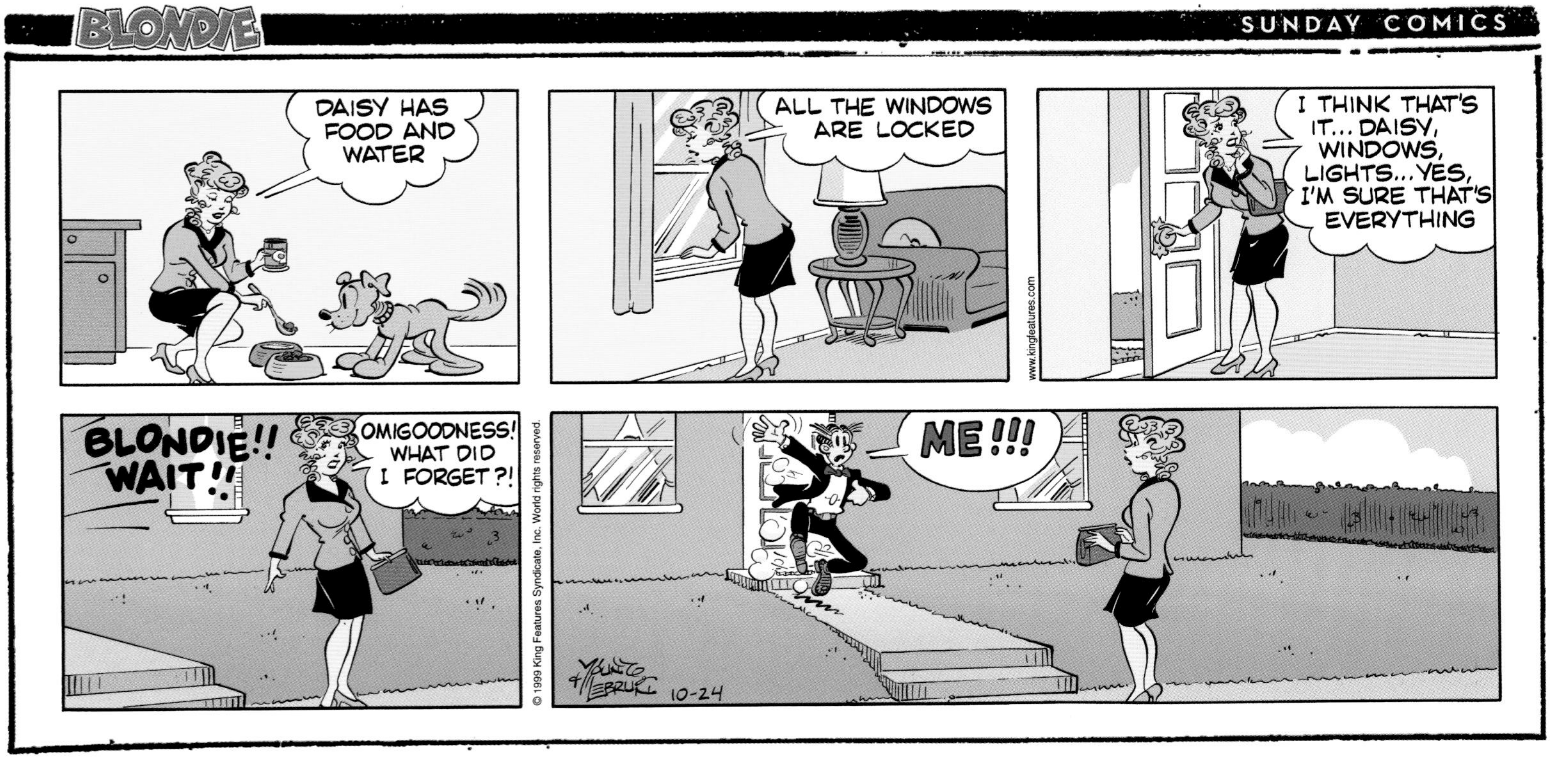
BLONDIE
SUNDAY COMICS
DAISY HAS FOOD AND WATER
ALL THE WINDOWS ARE LOCKED
I THINK THAT'S IT... DAISY, WINDOWS, LIGHTS... YES, I'M SURE THAT'S EVERYTHING
www.kingfeatures.com
BLONDIE!! WAIT!!
OMIGOODNESS! WHAT DID I FORGET?!
© 1999 King Features Syndicate, Inc. World rights reserved.
ME!!!
10-24

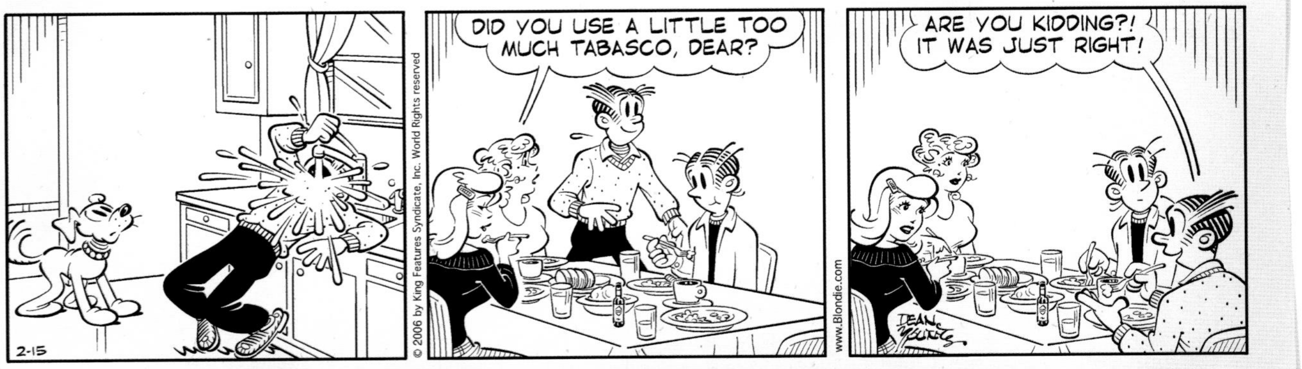
2-15
© 2006 by King Features Syndicate, Inc. World Rights reserved
DID YOU USE A LITTLE TOO MUCH TABASCO, DEAR?
www.Blondie.com
ARE YOU KIDDING?! IT WAS JUST RIGHT!

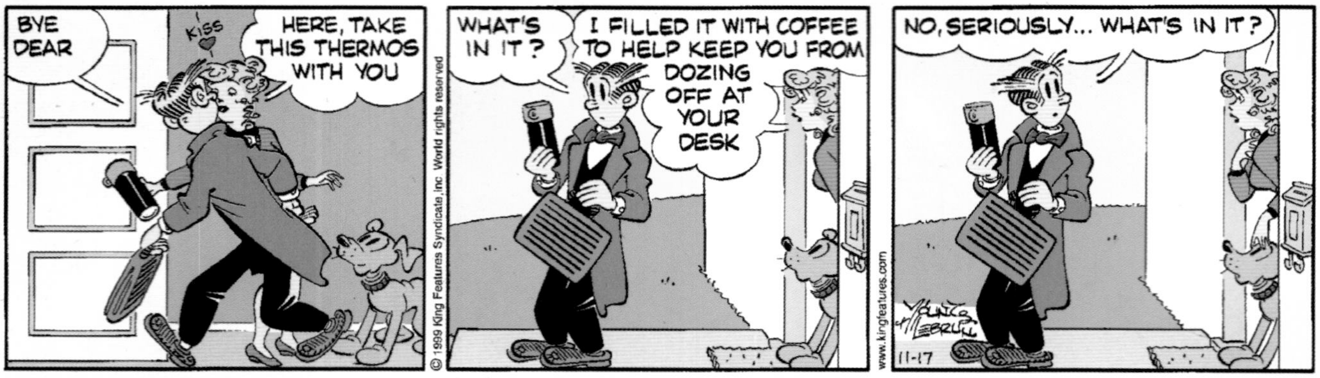
BYE DEAR
KISS
HERE, TAKE THIS THERMOS WITH YOU
WHAT'S IN IT?
I FILLED IT WITH COFFEE TO HELP KEEP YOU FROM DOZING OFF AT YOUR DESK
NO, SERIOUSLY... WHAT'S IN IT?
© 1999 King Features Syndicate, inc. World rights reserved
www.kingfeatures.com
11-17

"I want to make sure that people realize this family really loves being together," says Dean.

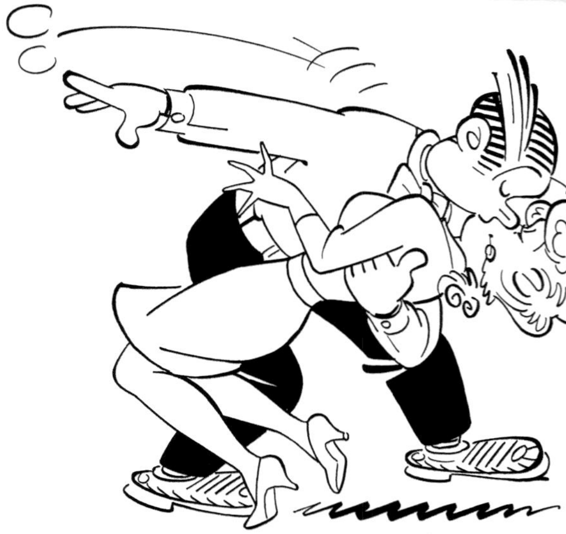

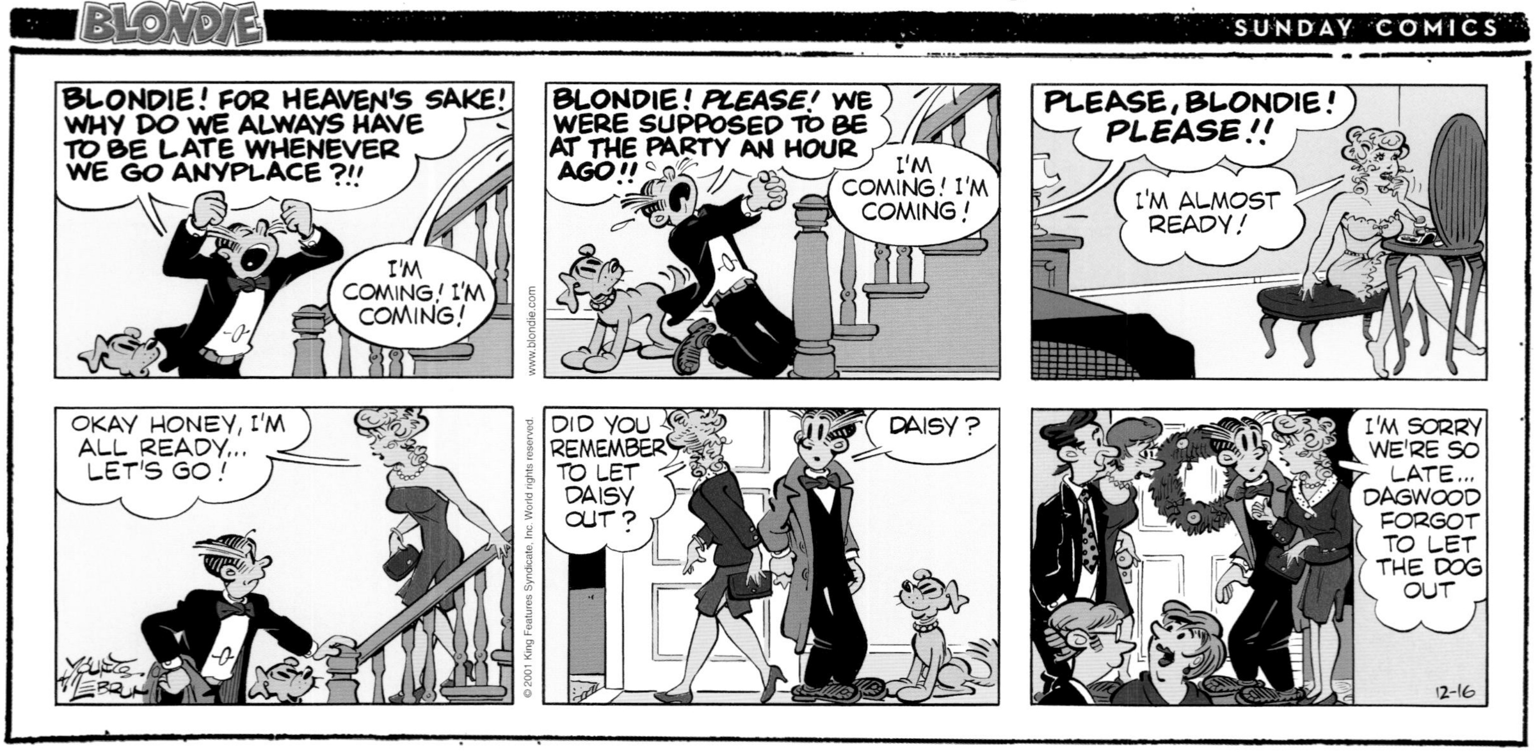
BLONDIE
SUNDAY COMICS
BLONDIE! FOR HEAVEN'S SAKE! WHY DO WE ALWAYS HAVE TO BE LATE WHENEVER WE GO ANYPLACE?!!
I'M COMING! I'M COMING!
BLONDIE! PLEASE! WE WERE SUPPOSED TO BE AT THE PARTY AN HOUR AGO!!
I'M COMING! I'M COMING!
PLEASE, BLONDIE! PLEASE!!
I'M ALMOST READY!
OKAY HONEY, I'M ALL READY... LET'S GO!
DID YOU REMEMBER TO LET DAISY OUT?
DAISY?
I'M SORRY WE'RE SO LATE... DAGWOOD FORGOT TO LET THE DOG OUT
www.blondie.com
© 2001 King Features Syndicate, Inc. World rights reserved.
12-16

CHAPTER 4

DAGWOOD AT WORK

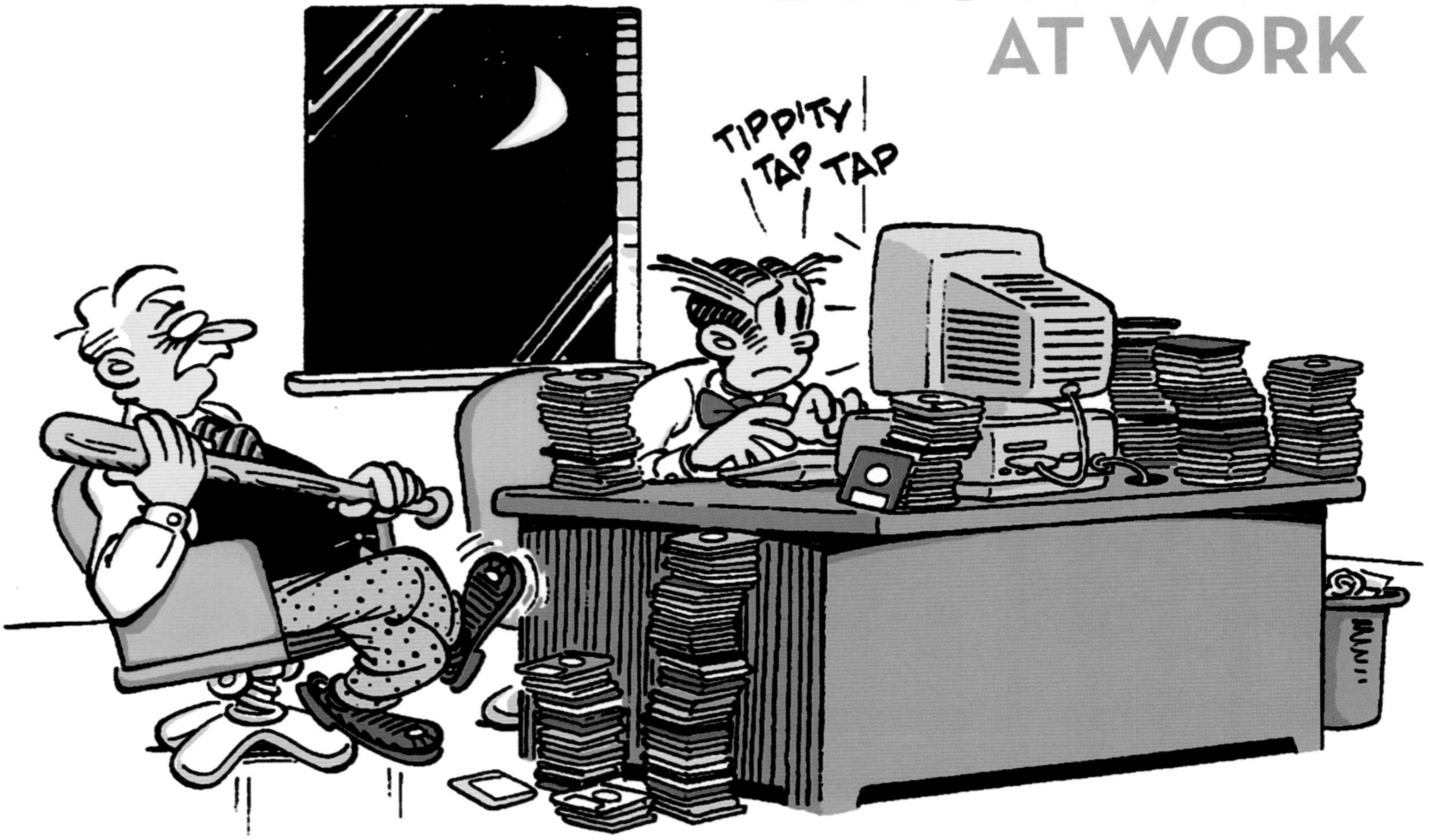
TIPPITY
TAP TAP

As an office manager at the J. C. Dithers Construction Company, Dagwood Bumstead is reliable, responsible, and a hard worker.

Well, he would be, if *Blondie* weren't a comic strip.

Instead, Dagwood is perhaps the world's most laughably substandard employee. Of course, growing up as the son of a millionaire, he didn't really expect to become a workingman. And his aversion to labor is evident day after day at the office, where his job title might as well be "office procrastinator."

Who else would consider, for example, regularly scheduling naps behind his desk? Who else can chronically come in late and leave early? Who would dare to simply delete the boss's e-mails without reading them, or frankly put off projects until someone else comes by to pick up the slack?

Some employee in every office, that's who. By acting out the worst behavior of that universally known goofball, the freeloading colleague, Dagwood is familiar to every manager, supervisor, and corporate honcho in the world—though they probably would've fired him by now.

Dagwood's boss Dithers is somewhat more forgiving—if a despot who's liable to go apoplectic over a misplaced memo, whose very joy in life is berating his employees to the point of hair-curling awe, can be called forgiving. At the very least, he hasn't forced Dagwood out yet, though he has steadfastly refused to grant him a raise. And really, can you blame him?

But Dagwood's slackerdom also makes him identifiable to a big portion of the population—anybody who's ever been an underling. His refusal to kowtow to any standards of industriousness or productivity makes him a hero to the millions of people who dream of putting in as little effort as he does. Who among us hasn't wanted to rest our feet on the desk from time to time, or tell off the boss, or shirk some particularly inane assignment? Acting like the unchecked id of the office worker, Dagwood lives out the secret fantasies of employees the world over. He sticks it to the man and the system, so the rest of us don't have to.

"Every once in a while I have him do something right at the office," says Dean.

Still, though there's a rise in productivity whenever Dagwood goes on vacation, he's not all play and no work. "Every once in a while I have him do something right at the office," says Dean. "He can't just be a total bumbler all the time—you wouldn't respect him."

As part of the ongoing modernization of the strip, Dagwood has become technologically savvy. "He knows

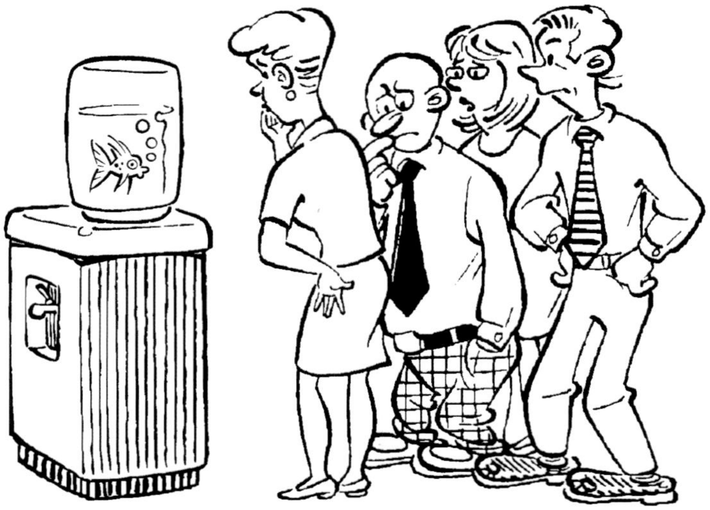

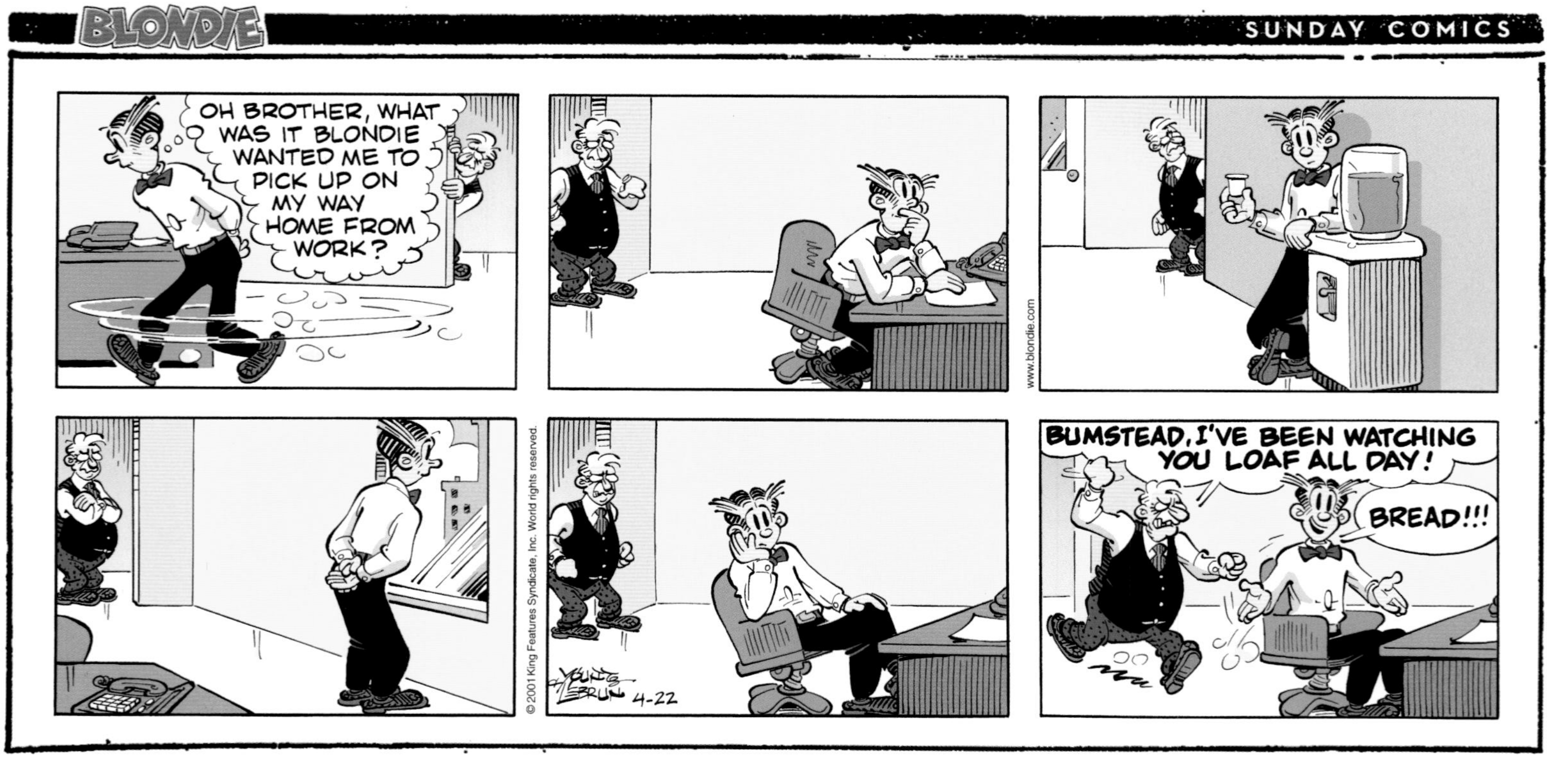
BLONDIE
SUNDAY COMICS
OH BROTHER, WHAT WAS IT BLONDIE WANTED ME TO PICK UP ON MY WAY HOME FROM WORK?
www.blondie.com
© 2001 King Features Syndicate, Inc. World rights reserved.
4-22
BUMSTEAD, I'VE BEEN WATCHING YOU LOAF ALL DAY!
BREAD!!!

THIS IS OUR EARNINGS CHART FOR LAST YEAR!
WHAT CAUSED THAT NICE LITTLE UPSWING, BOSS?
THAT'S WHEN YOU WERE ON VACATION!!
© 2000 King Features Syndicate, Inc. World rights reserved
www.kingfeatures.com

SO, THIS IS BUMSTEAD?!
YEP
SEE?
I'LL BE DARNED
I WONDER WHAT THAT'S ALL ABOUT?
© 2001 King Features Syndicate, Inc. World rights reserved.
www.blondie.com

WHO'LL VOLUNTEER TO MEET WITH ME TONIGHT ?
I WILL, BOSS
THANK YOU DAGWOOD, YOU WERE THE ONLY ONE WILLING TO MEET WITH ME
MEET?!!
I THOUGHT HE SAID EAT!
© 1999 King Features Syndicate, Inc. World rights reserved
www.kingfeatures.com

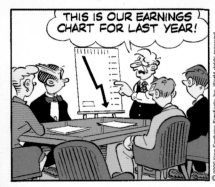

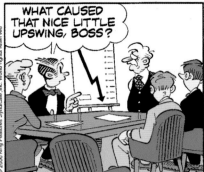

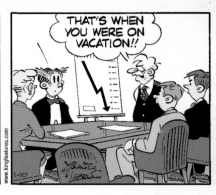

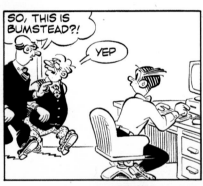

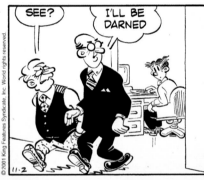

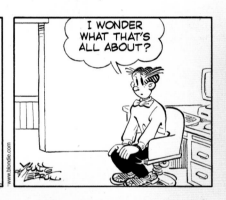

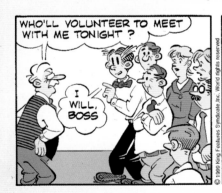

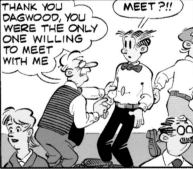

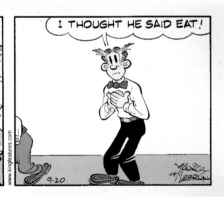

how to use a computer," notes Dean. "His password might be pastrami, but still and all, he's in today's world."

He has to be, because in today's world, even millionaires' sons have to make money. Employment has always been a central concern of *Blondie*, not only because of all the absurdities inherent in professional life, but because, especially these days, no one can afford not to work. It's a subject people the world over can relate to, whether they spend their days in a corporate behemoth or a mom 'n' pop shop. So Dagwood does up his bowtie and marches into the revolving doors of his office skyscraper each and every weekday. Of course, if he had his Dithers—uh, druthers—he'd revolve right back out again. But then, so would the rest of us.

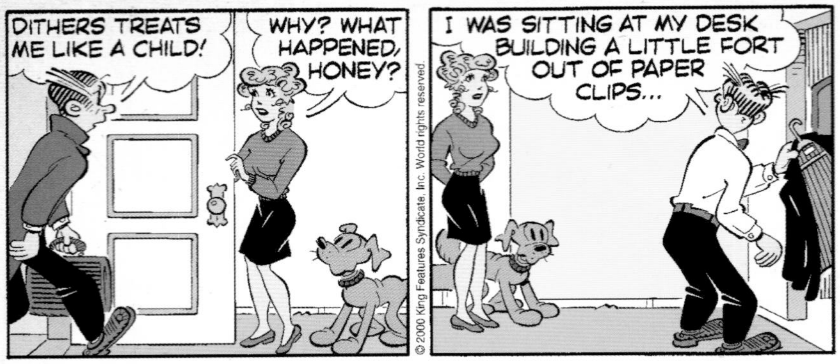
DITHERS TREATS ME LIKE A CHILD!
WHY? WHAT HAPPENED, HONEY?
I WAS SITTING AT MY DESK BUILDING A LITTLE FORT OUT OF PAPER CLIPS...
AND HE SNEAKED UP FROM BEHIND AND SHOT ME WITH A RUBBER BAND!
© 2000 King Features Syndicate, Inc. World rights reserved.
www.kingfeatures.com
YOUNG & LEBRUN 2-7

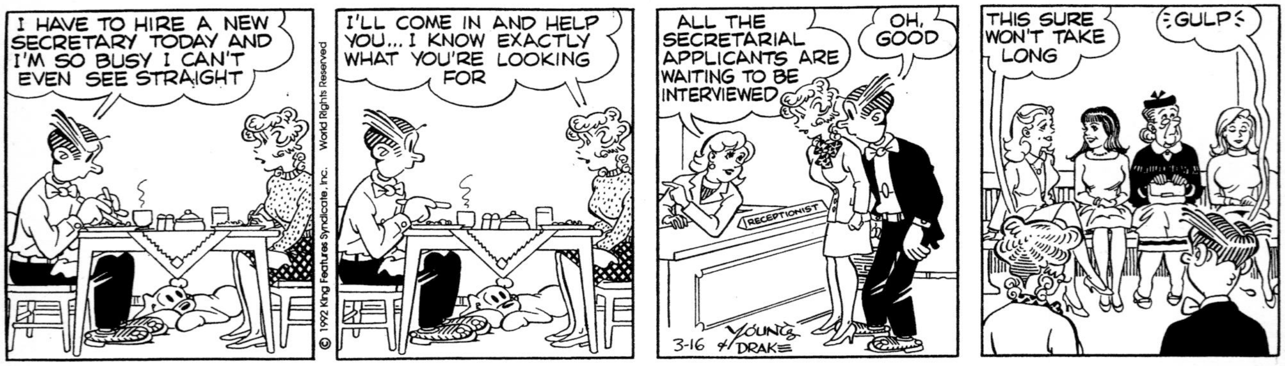
I HAVE TO HIRE A NEW SECRETARY TODAY AND I'M SO BUSY I CAN'T EVEN SEE STRAIGHT
I'LL COME IN AND HELP YOU... I KNOW EXACTLY WHAT YOU'RE LOOKING FOR
ALL THE SECRETARIAL APPLICANTS ARE WAITING TO BE INTERVIEWED
OH, GOOD
RECEPTIONIST
THIS SURE WON'T TAKE LONG
GULP
© 1992 King Features Syndicate, Inc. World Rights Reserved
3-16 YOUNG & DRAKE

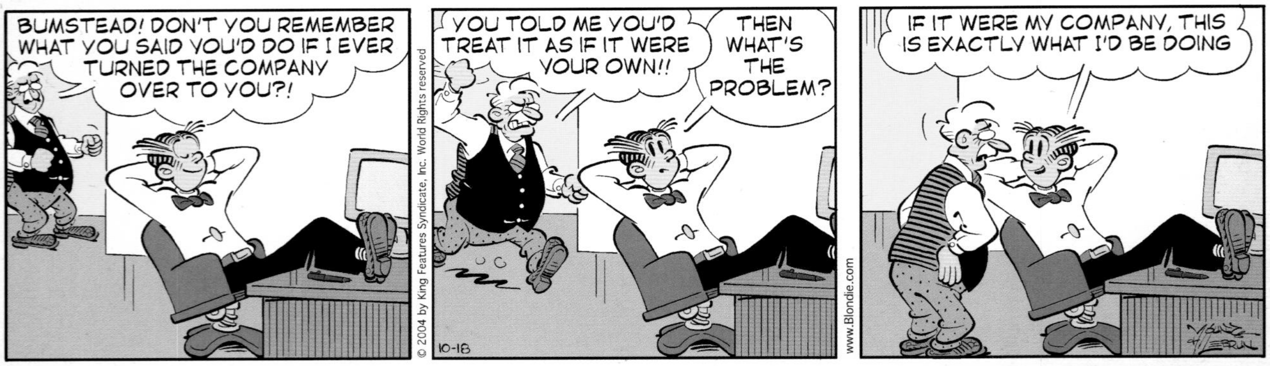
BUMSTEAD! DON'T YOU REMEMBER WHAT YOU SAID YOU'D DO IF I EVER TURNED THE COMPANY OVER TO YOU?!
YOU TOLD ME YOU'D TREAT IT AS IF IT WERE YOUR OWN!!
THEN WHAT'S THE PROBLEM?
IF IT WERE MY COMPANY, THIS IS EXACTLY WHAT I'D BE DOING
© 2004 by King Features Syndicate, Inc. World Rights reserved
10-18
www.Blondie.com

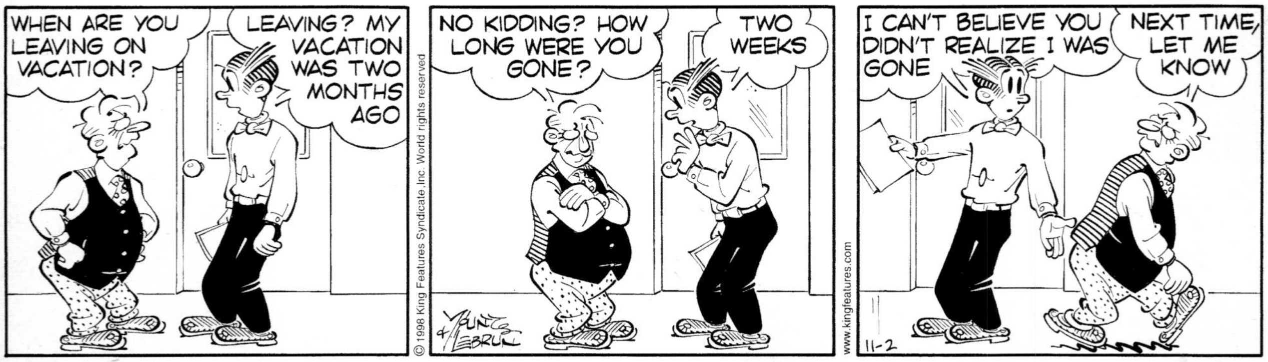
WHEN ARE YOU LEAVING ON VACATION?
LEAVING? MY VACATION WAS TWO MONTHS AGO
NO KIDDING? HOW LONG WERE YOU GONE?
TWO WEEKS
I CAN'T BELIEVE YOU DIDN'T REALIZE I WAS GONE
NEXT TIME, LET ME KNOW
© 1998 King Features Syndicate, Inc. World rights reserved
YOUNG & LEBRUN
www.kingfeatures.com
11-2

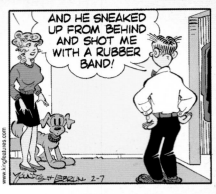

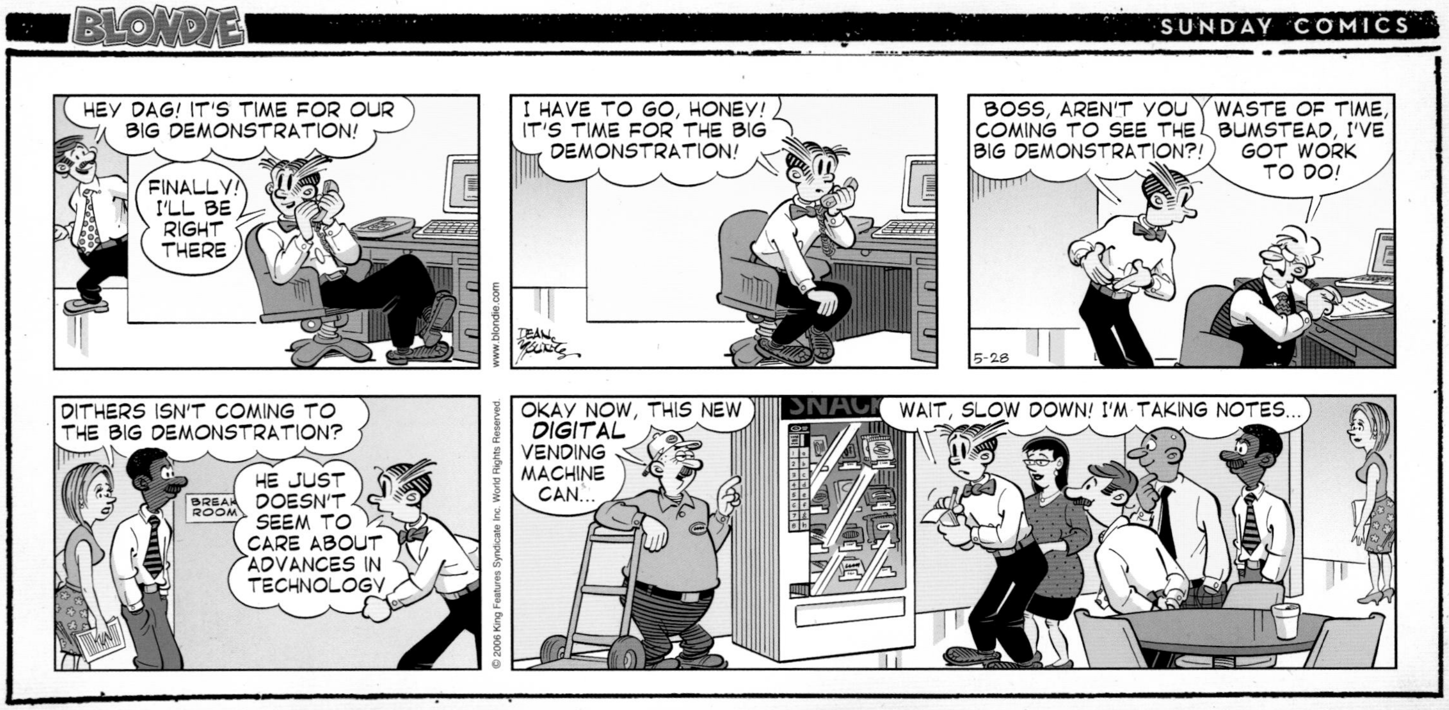
BLONDIE
SUNDAY COMICS
HEY DAG! IT'S TIME FOR OUR BIG DEMONSTRATION!
FINALLY! I'LL BE RIGHT THERE
I HAVE TO GO, HONEY! IT'S TIME FOR THE BIG DEMONSTRATION!
BOSS, AREN'T YOU COMING TO SEE THE BIG DEMONSTRATION?!
WASTE OF TIME, BUMSTEAD, I'VE GOT WORK TO DO!
DITHERS ISN'T COMING TO THE BIG DEMONSTRATION?
BREAK ROOM
HE JUST DOESN'T SEEM TO CARE ABOUT ADVANCES IN TECHNOLOGY
OKAY NOW, THIS NEW DIGITAL VENDING MACHINE CAN...
SNACK
WAIT, SLOW DOWN! I'M TAKING NOTES...
www.blondie.com
5-28
© 2006 King Features Syndicate Inc. World Rights Reserved.

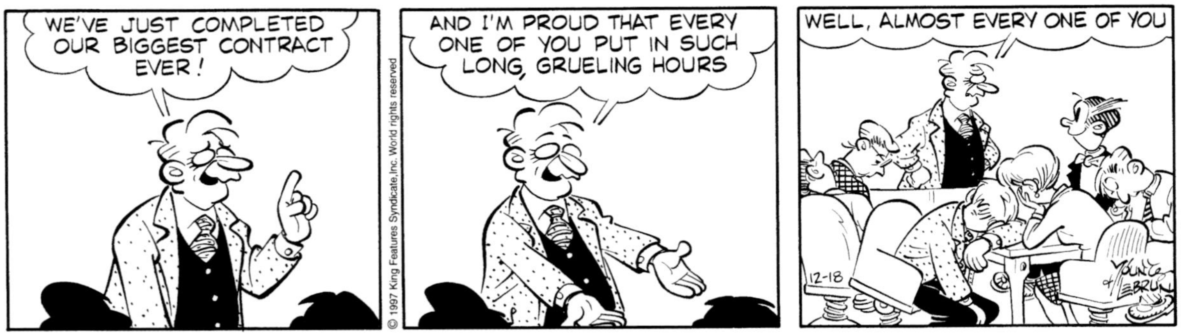
WE'VE JUST COMPLETED OUR BIGGEST CONTRACT EVER!
AND I'M PROUD THAT EVERY ONE OF YOU PUT IN SUCH LONG, GRUELING HOURS
WELL, ALMOST EVERY ONE OF YOU
12-18
© 1997 King Features Syndicate,Inc. World rights reserved

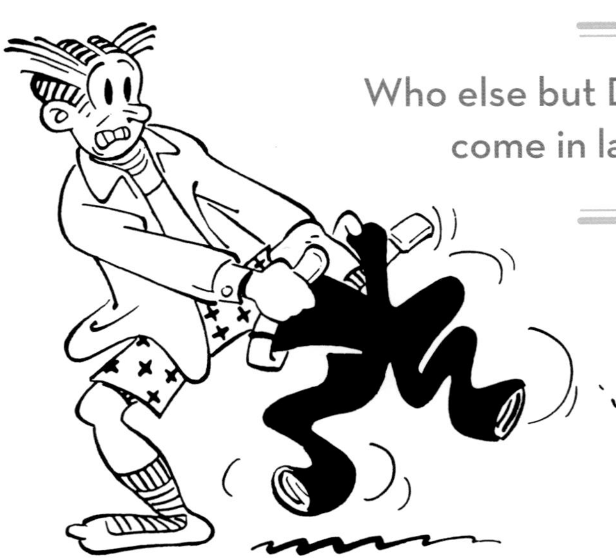

Who else but Dagwood can chronically come in late and leave early?

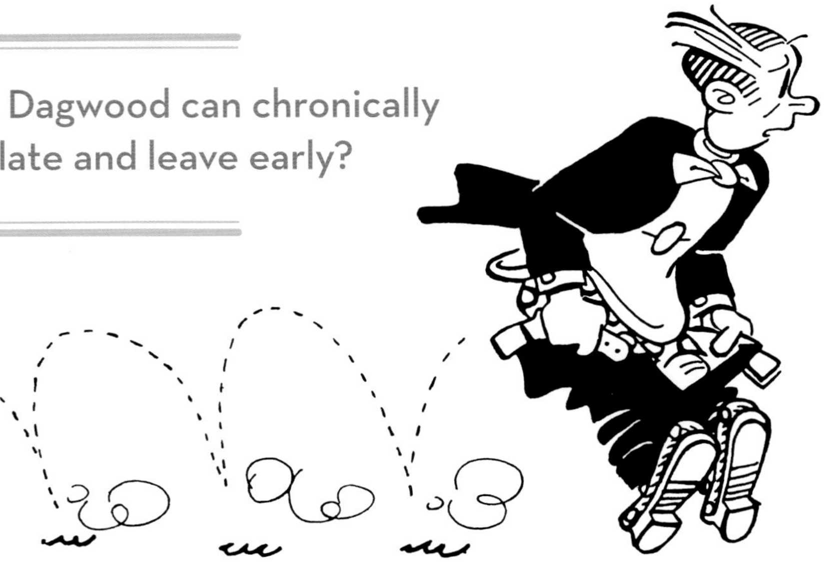

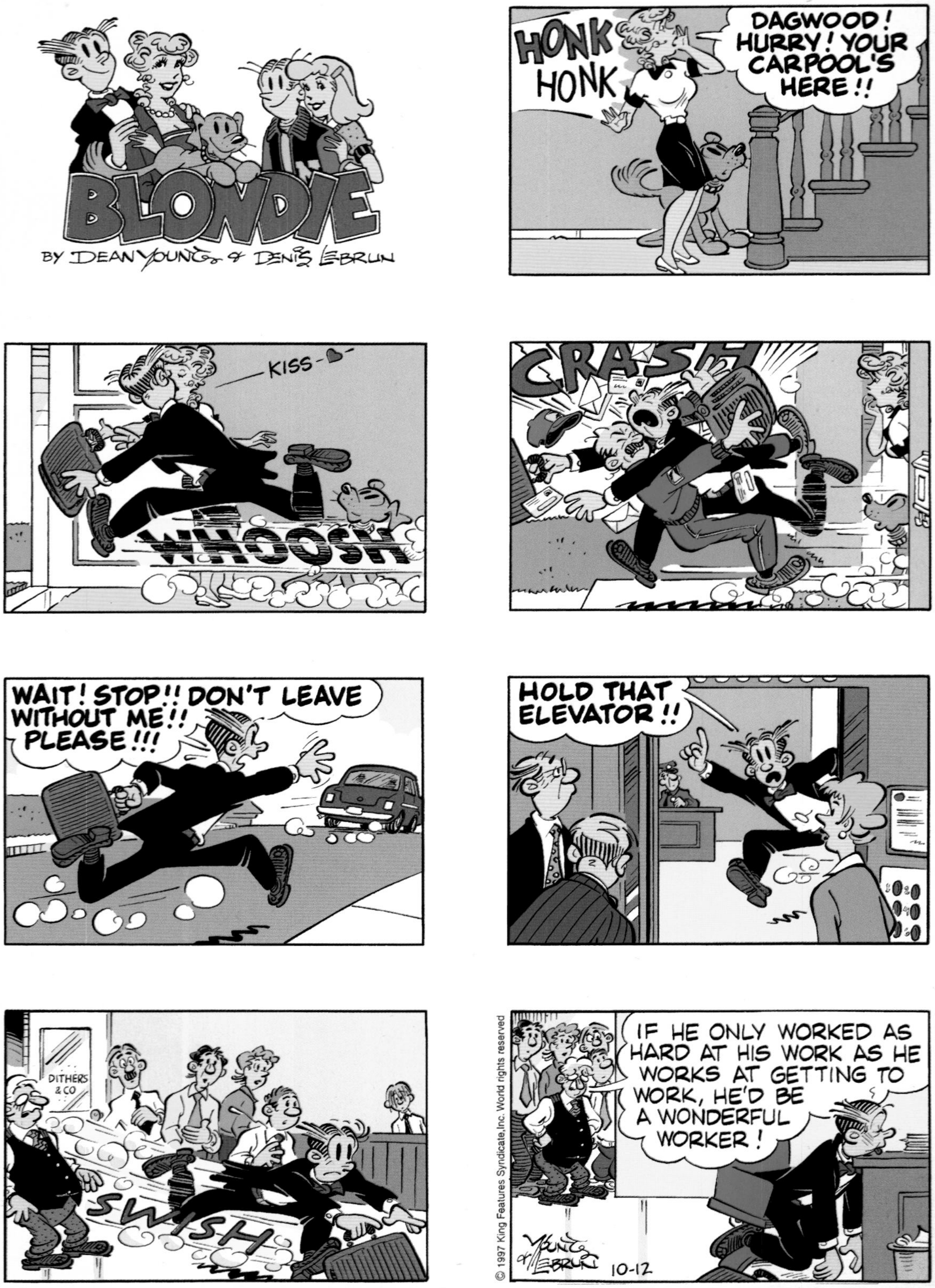
BLONDIE
BY DEAN YOUNG & DENIS LEBRUN
HONK HONK
DAGWOOD! HURRY! YOUR CARPOOL'S HERE!!
KISS
WHOOSH
CRASH
WAIT! STOP!! DON'T LEAVE WITHOUT ME!! PLEASE!!!
HOLD THAT ELEVATOR!!
DITHERS & CO
SWISH
IF HE ONLY WORKED AS HARD AT HIS WORK AS HE WORKS AT GETTING TO WORK, HE'D BE A WONDERFUL WORKER!
© 1997 King Features Syndicate,Inc. World rights reserved
YOUNG & LEBRUN
10-12

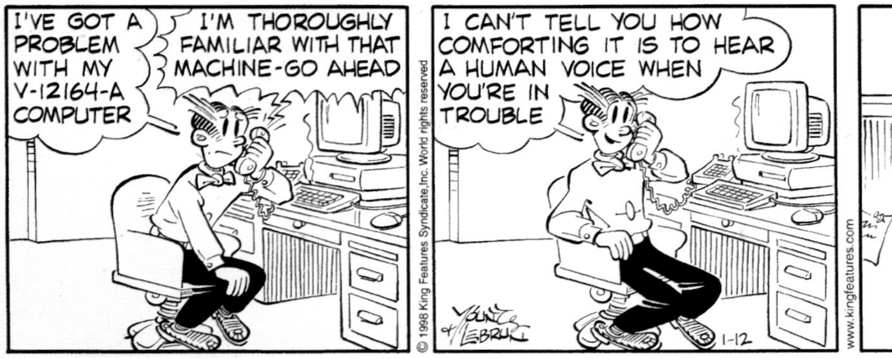
I'VE GOT A PROBLEM WITH MY V-12164-A COMPUTER
I'M THOROUGHLY FAMILIAR WITH THAT MACHINE-GO AHEAD
I CAN'T TELL YOU HOW COMFORTING IT IS TO HEAR A HUMAN VOICE WHEN YOU'RE IN TROUBLE
THAT'S WHAT WE'RE HERE FOR
© 1998 King Features Syndicate, Inc. World rights reserved
www.kingfeatures.com
1-12

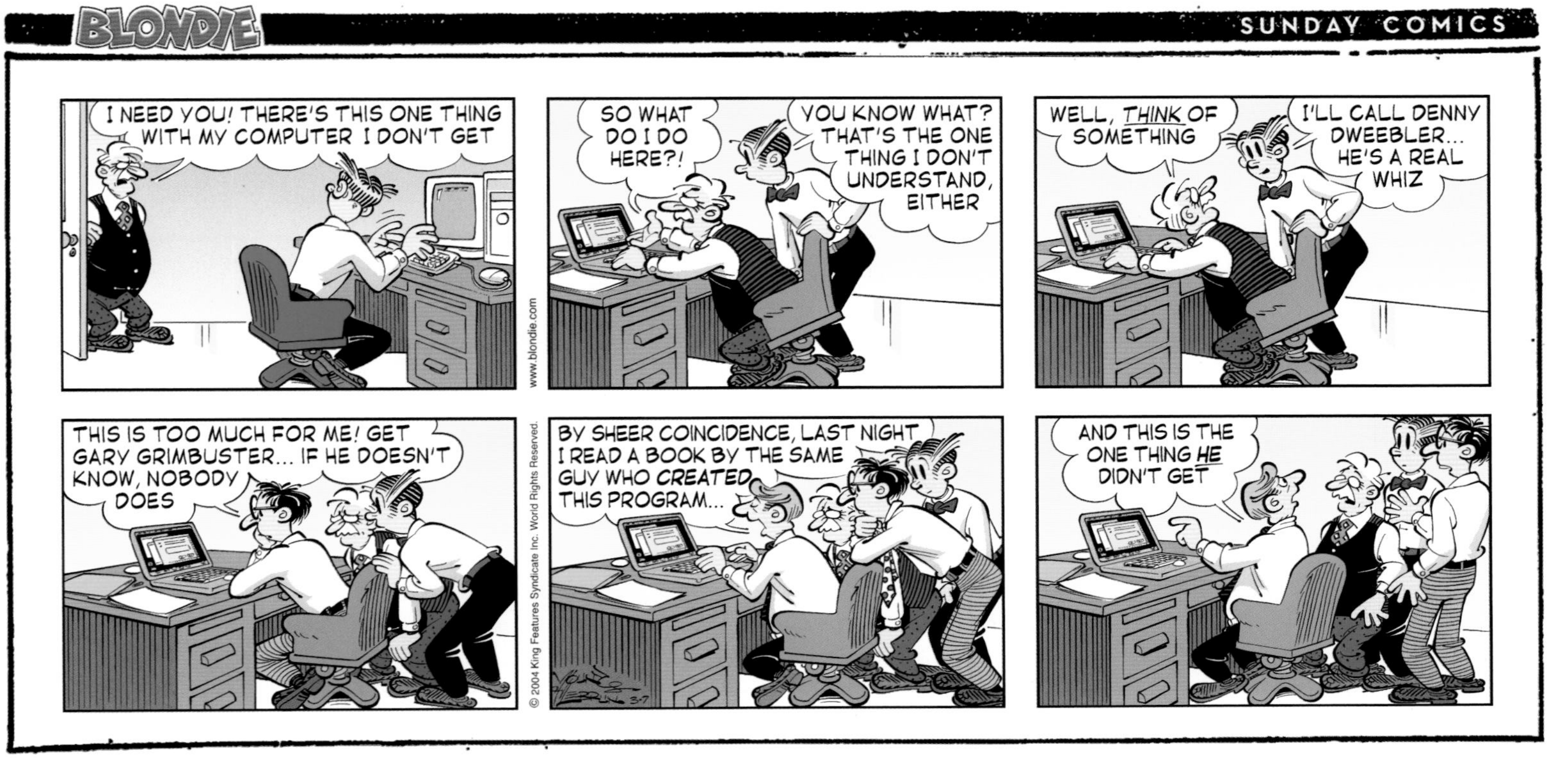
BLONDIE
SUNDAY COMICS
I NEED YOU! THERE'S THIS ONE THING WITH MY COMPUTER I DON'T GET
SO WHAT DO I DO HERE?!
YOU KNOW WHAT? THAT'S THE ONE THING I DON'T UNDERSTAND, EITHER
WELL, THINK OF SOMETHING
I'LL CALL DENNY DWEEBLER... HE'S A REAL WHIZ
THIS IS TOO MUCH FOR ME! GET GARY GRIMBUSTER... IF HE DOESN'T KNOW, NOBODY DOES
BY SHEER COINCIDENCE, LAST NIGHT I READ A BOOK BY THE SAME GUY WHO CREATED THIS PROGRAM...
AND THIS IS THE ONE THING HE DIDN'T GET
www.blondie.com
© 2004 King Features Syndicate Inc. World Rights Reserved.

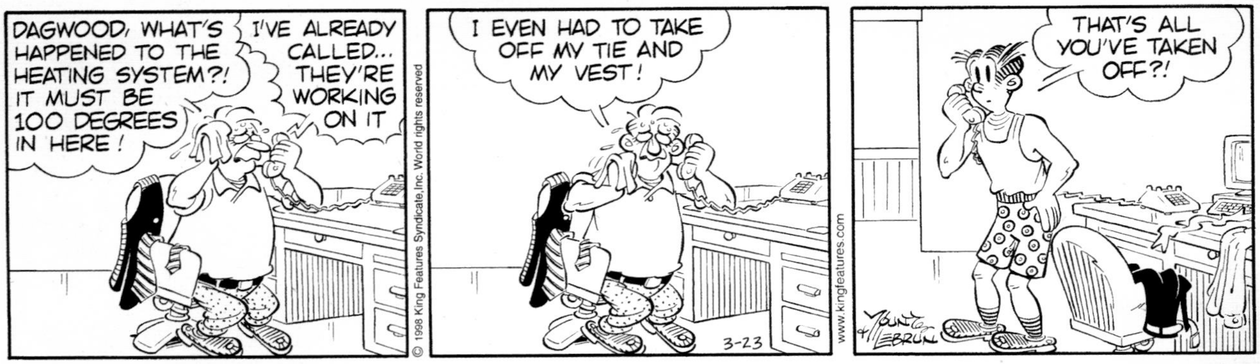
DAGWOOD, WHAT'S HAPPENED TO THE HEATING SYSTEM?! IT MUST BE 100 DEGREES IN HERE!
I'VE ALREADY CALLED... THEY'RE WORKING ON IT
I EVEN HAD TO TAKE OFF MY TIE AND MY VEST!
THAT'S ALL YOU'VE TAKEN OFF?!
© 1998 King Features Syndicate, Inc. World rights reserved
www.kingfeatures.com
3-23

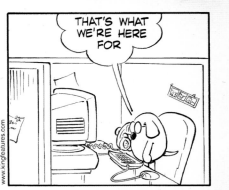

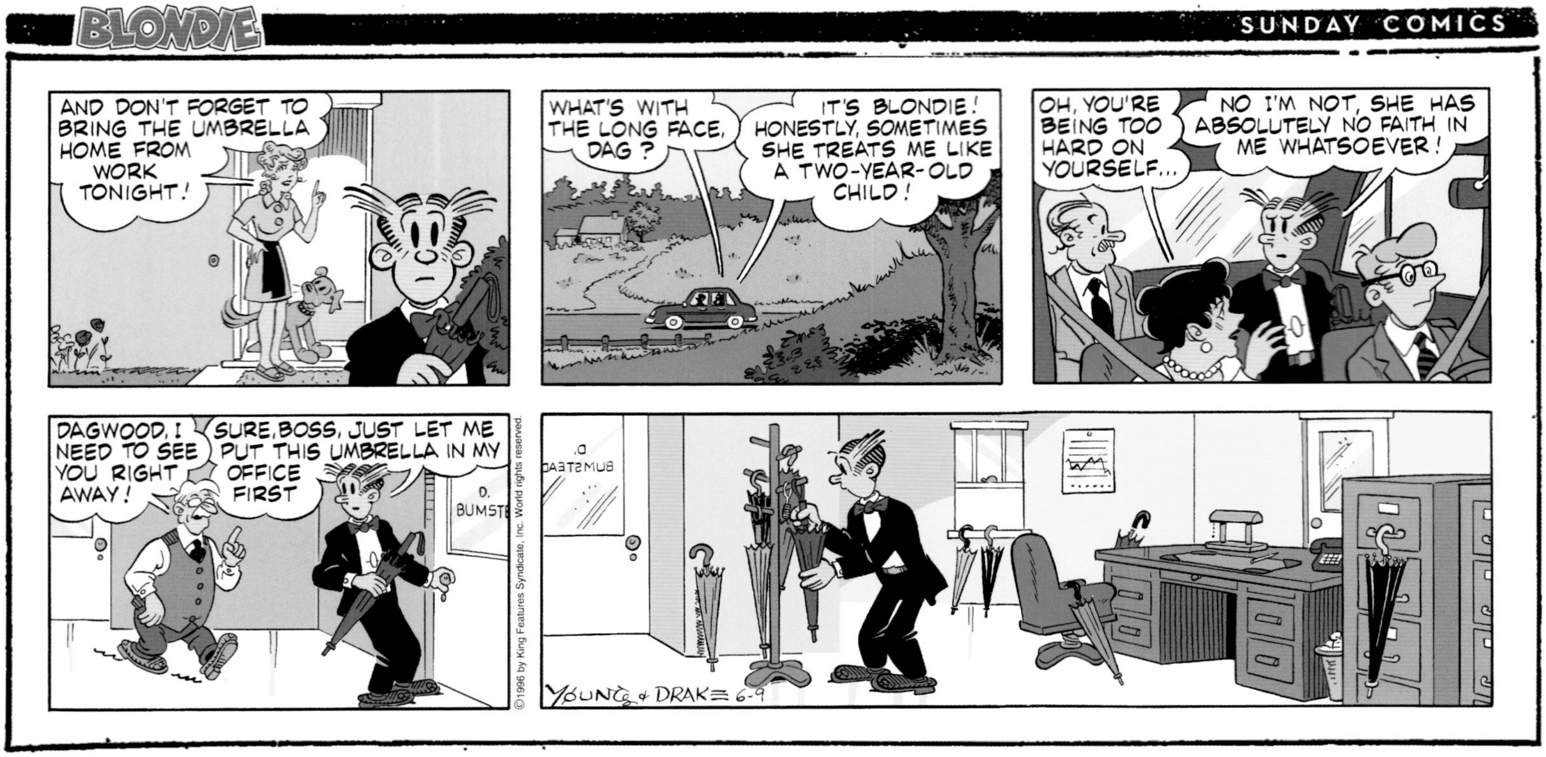
BLONDIE
SUNDAY COMICS
AND DON'T FORGET TO BRING THE UMBRELLA HOME FROM WORK TONIGHT!
WHAT'S WITH THE LONG FACE, DAG ?
IT'S BLONDIE! HONESTLY, SOMETIMES SHE TREATS ME LIKE A TWO-YEAR-OLD CHILD!
OH, YOU'RE BEING TOO HARD ON YOURSELF...
NO I'M NOT, SHE HAS ABSOLUTELY NO FAITH IN ME WHATSOEVER!
DAGWOOD, I NEED TO SEE YOU RIGHT AWAY!
SURE, BOSS, JUST LET ME PUT THIS UMBRELLA IN MY OFFICE FIRST
D. BUMSTEAD
© 1996 by King Features Syndicate, Inc. World rights reserved.
YOUNG & DRAKE 6-9

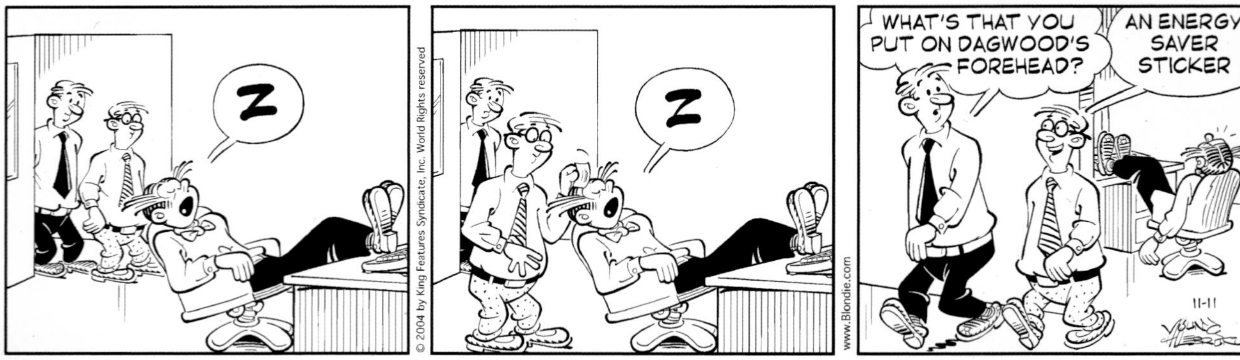
Z
Z
© 2004 by King Features Syndicate, Inc. World Rights reserved
WHAT'S THAT YOU PUT ON DAGWOOD'S FOREHEAD?
AN ENERGY SAVER STICKER
www.Blondie.com
11-11

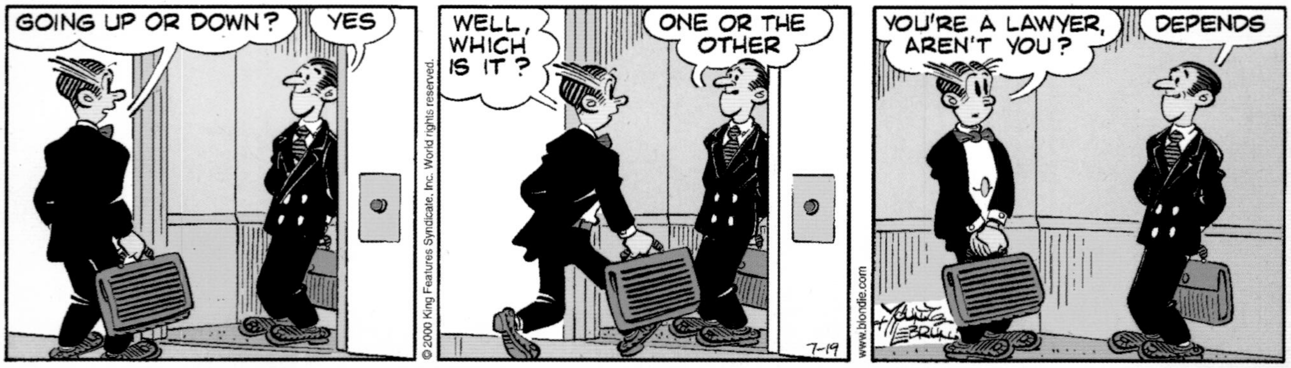
GOING UP OR DOWN?
YES
WELL, WHICH IS IT?
ONE OR THE OTHER
© 2000 King Features Syndicate, Inc. World rights reserved.
7-19
YOU'RE A LAWYER, AREN'T YOU?
DEPENDS
www.blondie.com

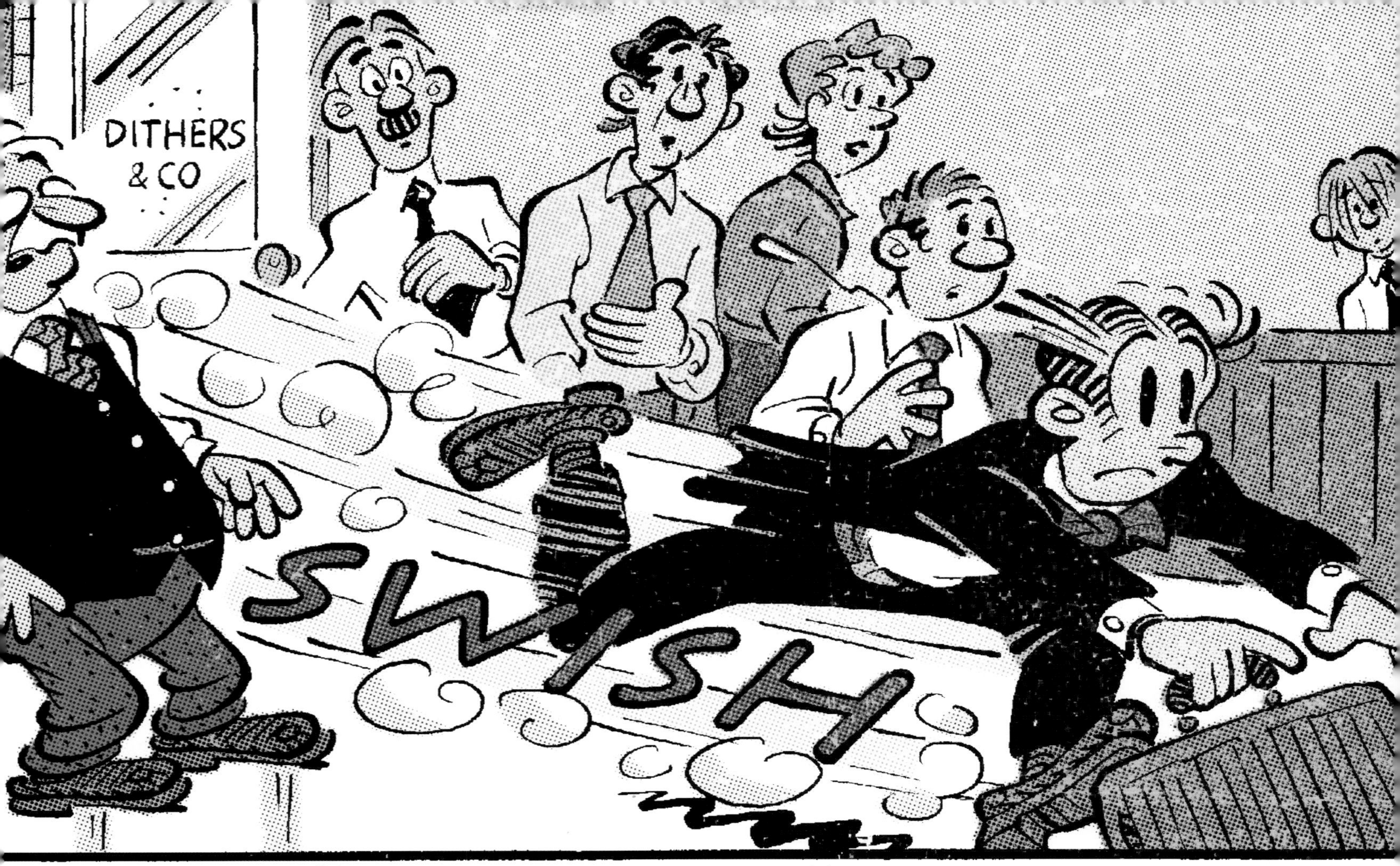
DITHERS & CO
SWISH

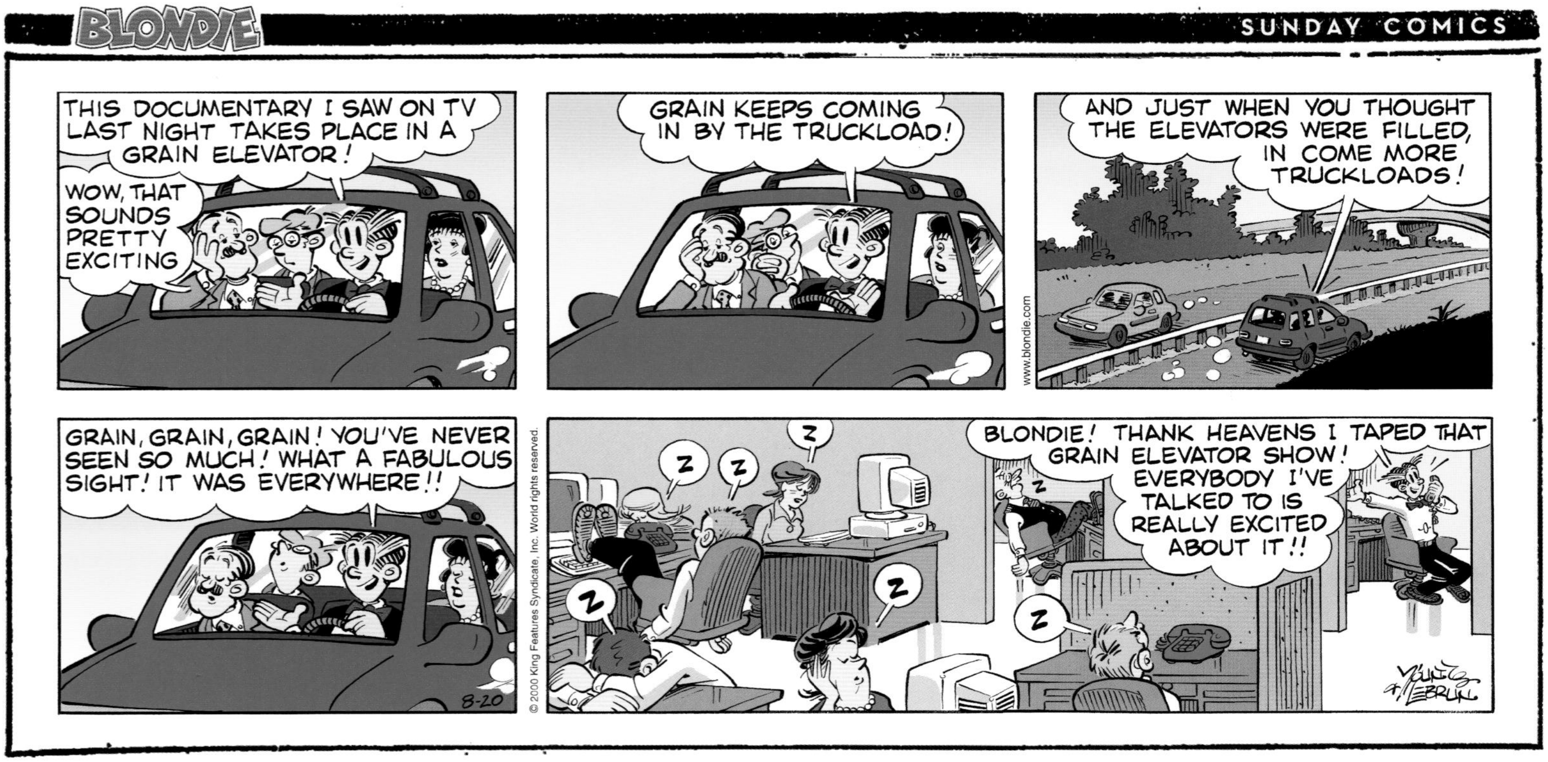
BLONDIE
SUNDAY COMICS
THIS DOCUMENTARY I SAW ON TV LAST NIGHT TAKES PLACE IN A GRAIN ELEVATOR!
WOW, THAT SOUNDS PRETTY EXCITING
GRAIN KEEPS COMING IN BY THE TRUCKLOAD!
AND JUST WHEN YOU THOUGHT THE ELEVATORS WERE FILLED, IN COME MORE TRUCKLOADS!
www.blondie.com
GRAIN, GRAIN, GRAIN! YOU'VE NEVER SEEN SO MUCH! WHAT A FABULOUS SIGHT! IT WAS EVERYWHERE!!
8-20
© 2000 King Features Syndicate, Inc. World rights reserved.
Z
Z
Z
Z
Z
Z
Z
BLONDIE! THANK HEAVENS I TAPED THAT GRAIN ELEVATOR SHOW! EVERYBODY I'VE TALKED TO IS REALLY EXCITED ABOUT IT!!
YOUNG & LEBRUN

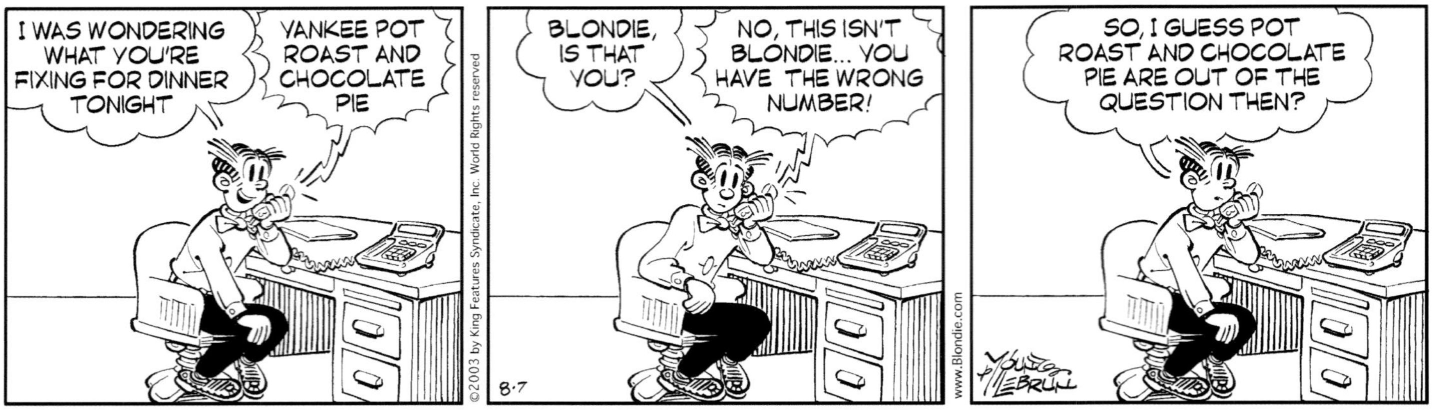
I WAS WONDERING WHAT YOU'RE FIXING FOR DINNER TONIGHT
YANKEE POT ROAST AND CHOCOLATE PIE
©2003 by King Features Syndicate, Inc. World Rights reserved
8-7
BLONDIE, IS THAT YOU?
NO, THIS ISN'T BLONDIE... YOU HAVE THE WRONG NUMBER!
www.Blondie.com
SO, I GUESS POT ROAST AND CHOCOLATE PIE ARE OUT OF THE QUESTION THEN?

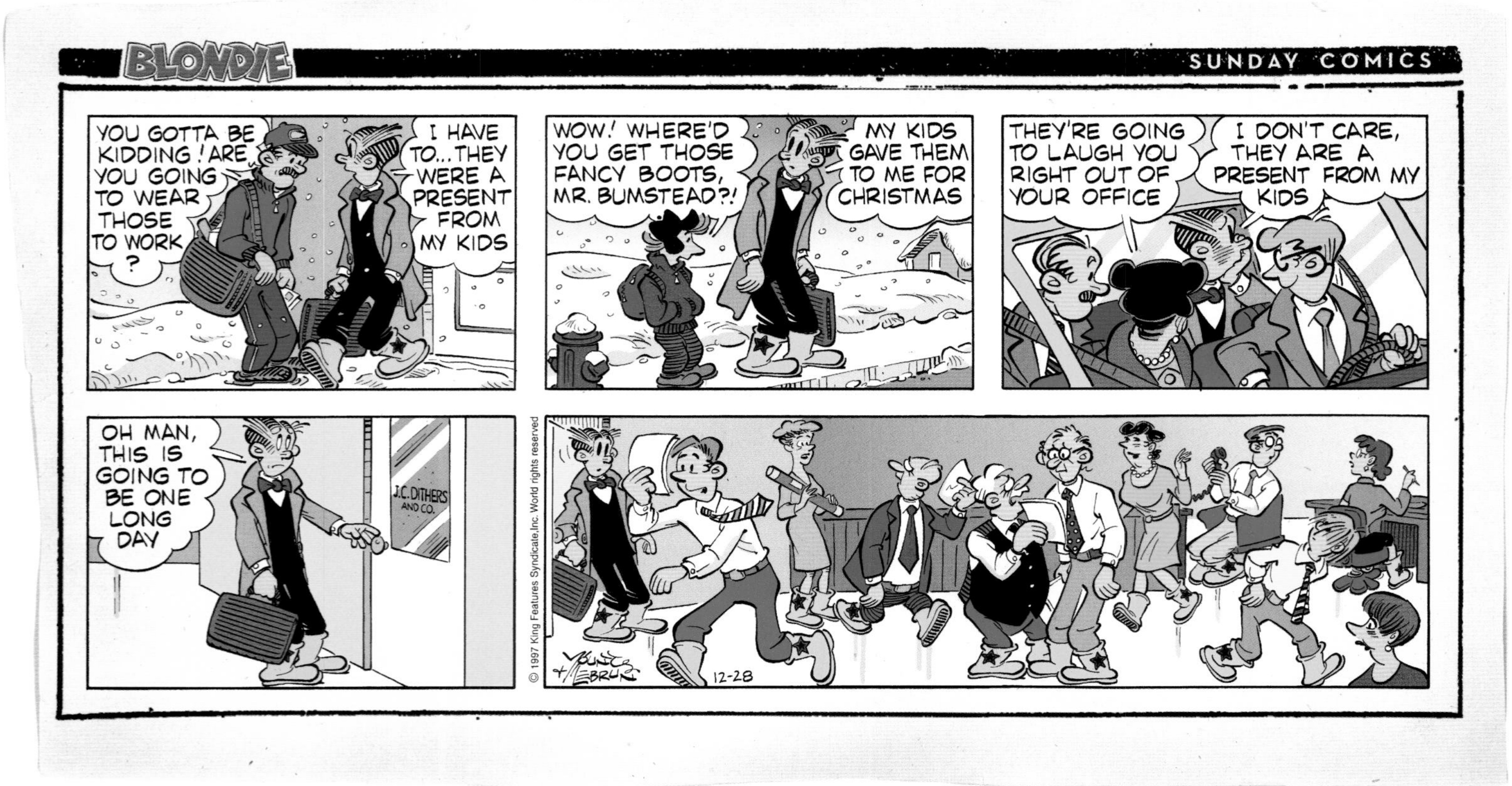
BLONDIE
SUNDAY COMICS
YOU GOTTA BE KIDDING! ARE YOU GOING TO WEAR THOSE TO WORK?
I HAVE TO... THEY WERE A PRESENT FROM MY KIDS
WOW! WHERE'D YOU GET THOSE FANCY BOOTS, MR. BUMSTEAD?!
MY KIDS GAVE THEM TO ME FOR CHRISTMAS
THEY'RE GOING TO LAUGH YOU RIGHT OUT OF YOUR OFFICE
I DON'T CARE, THEY ARE A PRESENT FROM MY KIDS
OH MAN, THIS IS GOING TO BE ONE LONG DAY
J.C. DITHERS AND CO.
© 1997 King Features Syndicate, Inc. World rights reserved
12-28

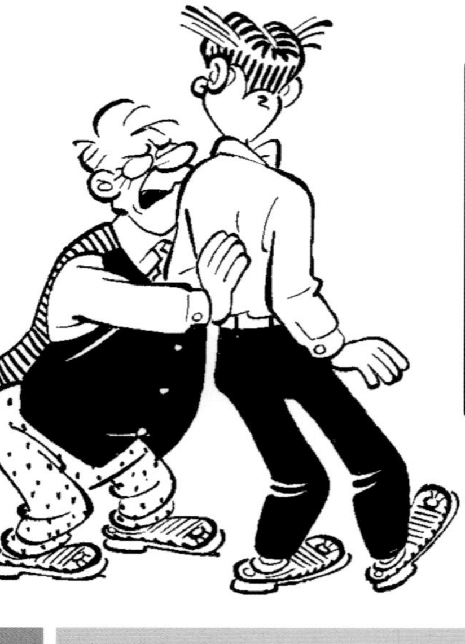

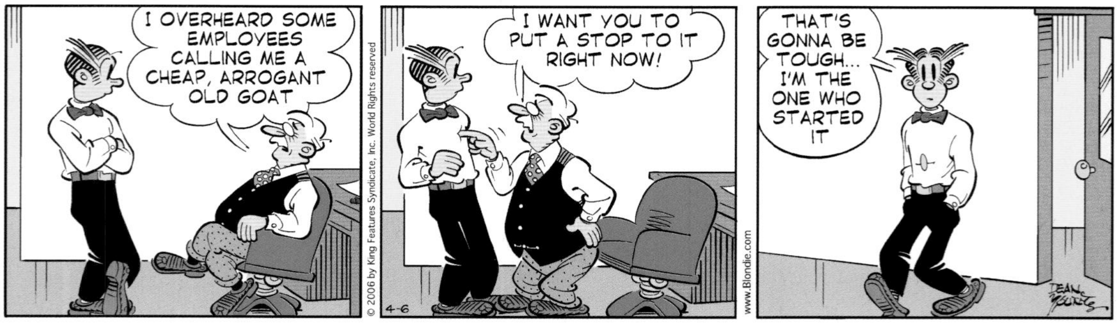
I OVERHEARD SOME EMPLOYEES CALLING ME A CHEAP, ARROGANT OLD GOAT
© 2006 by King Features Syndicate, Inc. World Rights reserved
4-6
I WANT YOU TO PUT A STOP TO IT RIGHT NOW!
www.Blondie.com
THAT'S GONNA BE TOUGH... I'M THE ONE WHO STARTED IT

COMPUTER ASSISTANCE, YOUR NAME, PLEASE?
THIS IS DAGWOOD BUMSTEAD
© 2005 by King Features Syndicate, Inc. World Rights reserved
OH NO! I WAS STUCK WITH YOU LAST TIME!
www.Blondie.com
YOU TAKE HIM THIS TIME, SYLVIA
NO SIR, NOT THIS KID! I HAD HIM TWO CALLS AGO
GIVE HIM TO ED, HE'S NEW HERE!
1-24

THE HUDLEY CORPORATION JUST APPROVED MY CONTRACT!
EXCELLENT!!
© 2000 King Features Syndicate, Inc. World rights reserved
I RAISED THE STAKES ON THE McGRUDER DEAL AND THEY BOUGHT IT!
WONDERFUL!!
www.kingfeatures.com
I JUST MADE 27 OUT OF 35!!
6-19

AH, MR. DITHERS, AH...
WHAT IS IT?! BUT MAKE IT QUICK, I'M REALLY BUSY!!
© 1997 King Features Syndicate, Inc. World rights reserved
RAISE?
NO!
WELL, ANYWAY, IT WAS QUICK
8-25

AND THAT CONCLUDES MY PRESENTATION
ZZZZZZZZZZZZZZZ
3-20
www.Blondie.com
© 2006 by King Features Syndicate, Inc. World Rights reserved
DID THEY LIKE OUR PROPOSAL?
WELL, I DIDN'T HEAR ANY OBJECTIONS

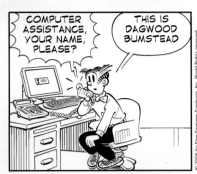

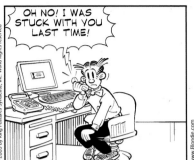

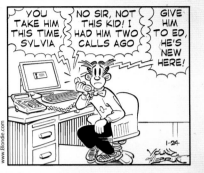

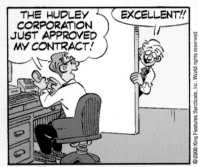

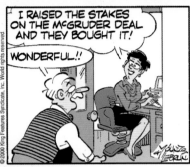

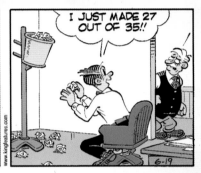

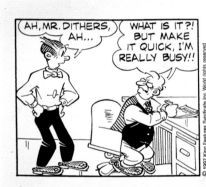

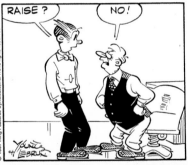

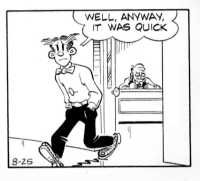

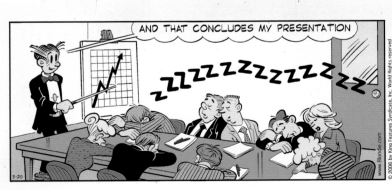

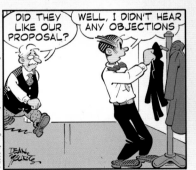

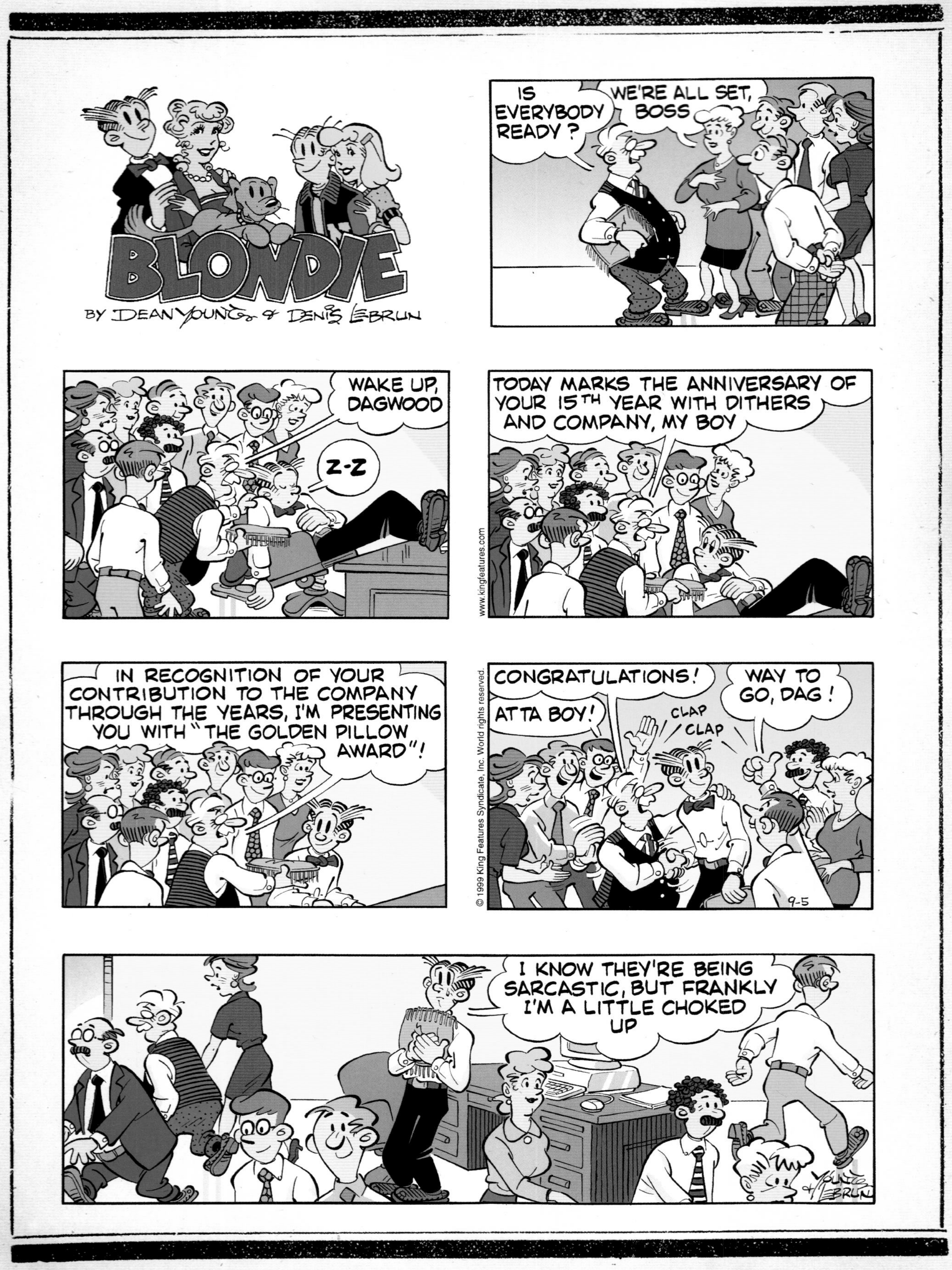
BLONDIE
BY DEAN YOUNG & DENIS LEBRUN
IS EVERYBODY READY ?
WE'RE ALL SET, BOSS
WAKE UP, DAGWOOD
Z-Z
TODAY MARKS THE ANNIVERSARY OF YOUR 15TH YEAR WITH DITHERS AND COMPANY, MY BOY
IN RECOGNITION OF YOUR CONTRIBUTION TO THE COMPANY THROUGH THE YEARS, I'M PRESENTING YOU WITH "THE GOLDEN PILLOW AWARD"!
CONGRATULATIONS!
ATTA BOY!
CLAP
CLAP
WAY TO GO, DAG !
9-5
I KNOW THEY'RE BEING SARCASTIC, BUT FRANKLY I'M A LITTLE CHOKED UP
YOUNG & LEBRUN

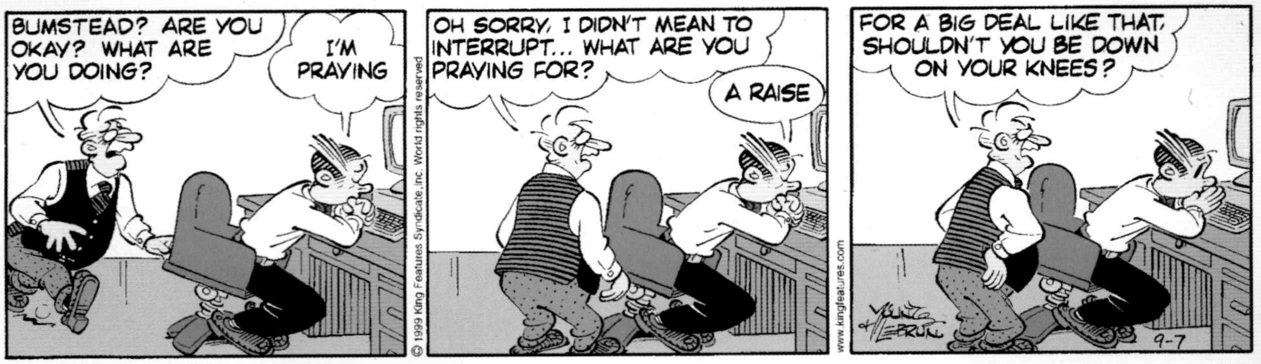
BUMSTEAD? ARE YOU OKAY? WHAT ARE YOU DOING?
I'M PRAYING
© 1999 King Features Syndicate, Inc. World rights reserved
OH SORRY, I DIDN'T MEAN TO INTERRUPT... WHAT ARE YOU PRAYING FOR?
A RAISE
www.kingfeatures.com
FOR A BIG DEAL LIKE THAT, SHOULDN'T YOU BE DOWN ON YOUR KNEES?
YOUNG LEBRUN
9-7

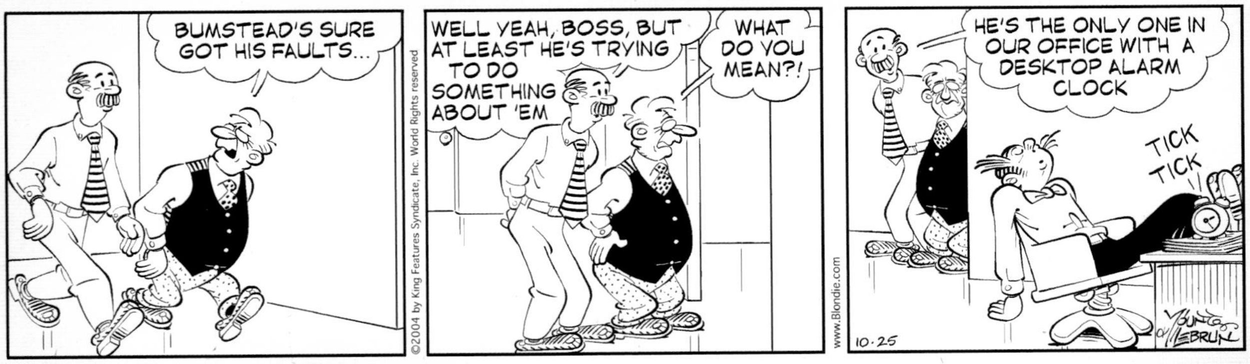
BUMSTEAD'S SURE GOT HIS FAULTS...
©2004 by King Features Syndicate, Inc. World Rights reserved
WELL YEAH, BOSS, BUT AT LEAST HE'S TRYING TO DO SOMETHING ABOUT 'EM
WHAT DO YOU MEAN?!
www.Blondie.com
HE'S THE ONLY ONE IN OUR OFFICE WITH A DESKTOP ALARM CLOCK
TICK
TICK
YOUNG LEBRUN
10·25

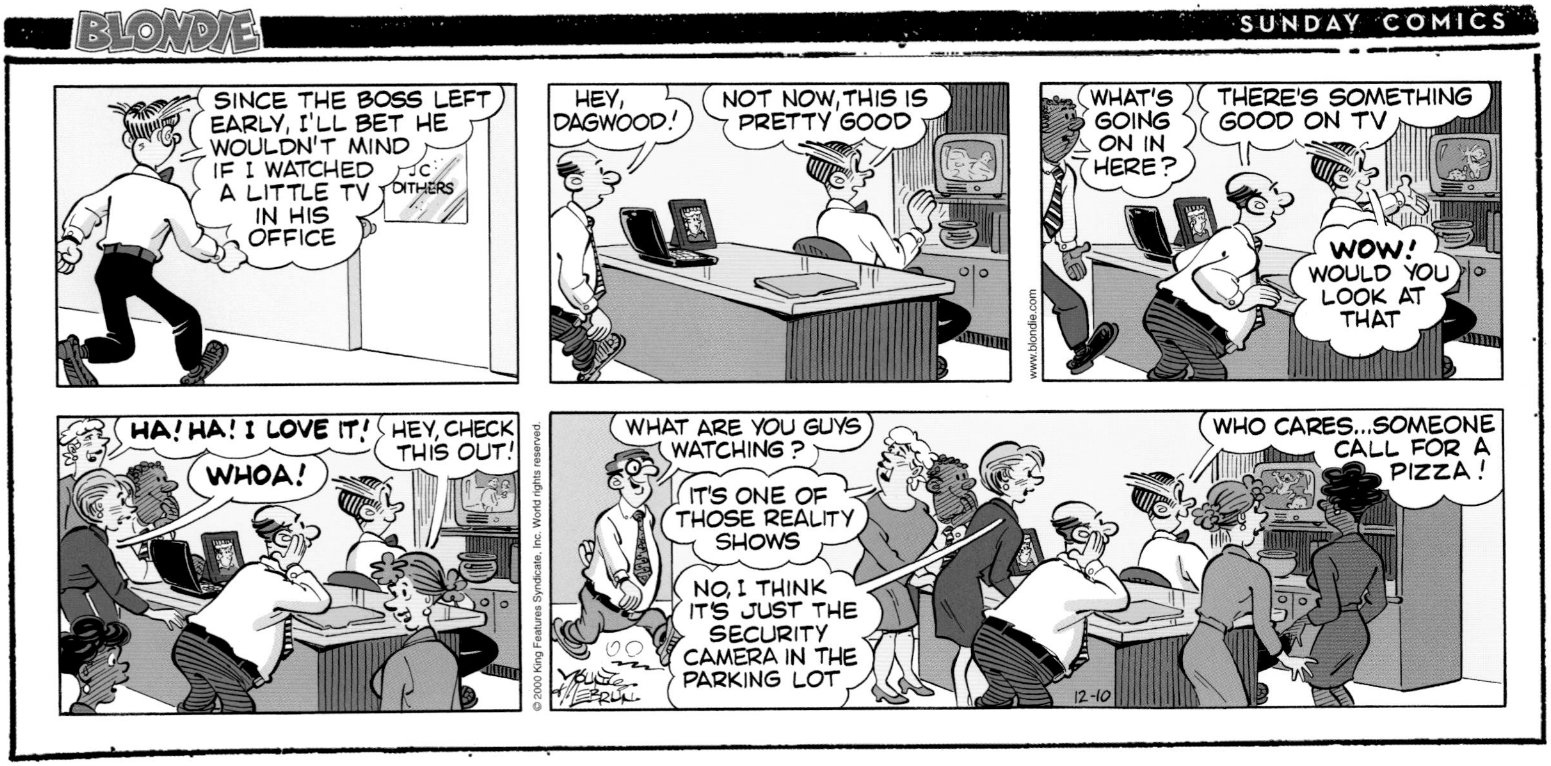
BLONDIE
SUNDAY COMICS
SINCE THE BOSS LEFT EARLY, I'LL BET HE WOULDN'T MIND IF I WATCHED A LITTLE TV IN HIS OFFICE
J.C. DITHERS
HEY, DAGWOOD!
NOT NOW, THIS IS PRETTY GOOD
www.blondie.com
WHAT'S GOING ON IN HERE?
THERE'S SOMETHING GOOD ON TV
WOW! WOULD YOU LOOK AT THAT
HA! HA! I LOVE IT!
WHOA!
HEY, CHECK THIS OUT!
© 2000 King Features Syndicate, Inc. World rights reserved.
WHAT ARE YOU GUYS WATCHING?
IT'S ONE OF THOSE REALITY SHOWS
NO, I THINK IT'S JUST THE SECURITY CAMERA IN THE PARKING LOT
WHO CARES...SOMEONE CALL FOR A PIZZA!
YOUNG LEBRUN
12-10

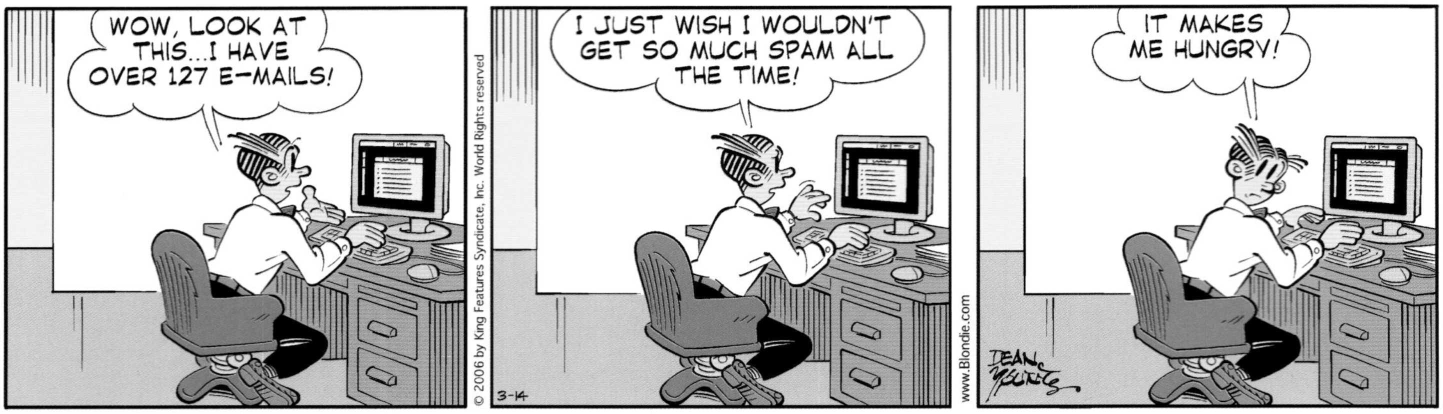
WOW, LOOK AT THIS...I HAVE OVER 127 E-MAILS!
I JUST WISH I WOULDN'T GET SO MUCH SPAM ALL THE TIME!
IT MAKES ME HUNGRY!
© 2006 by King Features Syndicate, Inc. World Rights reserved
3-14
www.Blondie.com
DEAN YOUNG

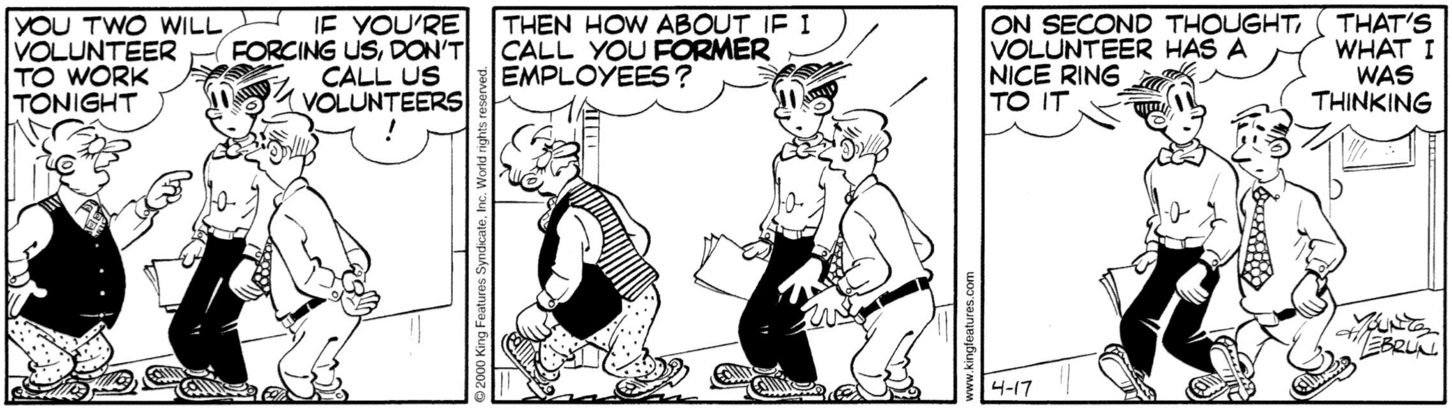
YOU TWO WILL VOLUNTEER TO WORK TONIGHT
IF YOU'RE FORCING US, DON'T CALL US VOLUNTEERS!
THEN HOW ABOUT IF I CALL YOU **FORMER** EMPLOYEES?
ON SECOND THOUGHT, VOLUNTEER HAS A NICE RING TO IT
THAT'S WHAT I WAS THINKING
© 2000 King Features Syndicate, Inc. World rights reserved.
www.kingfeatures.com
4-17
YOUNG LEBRUN

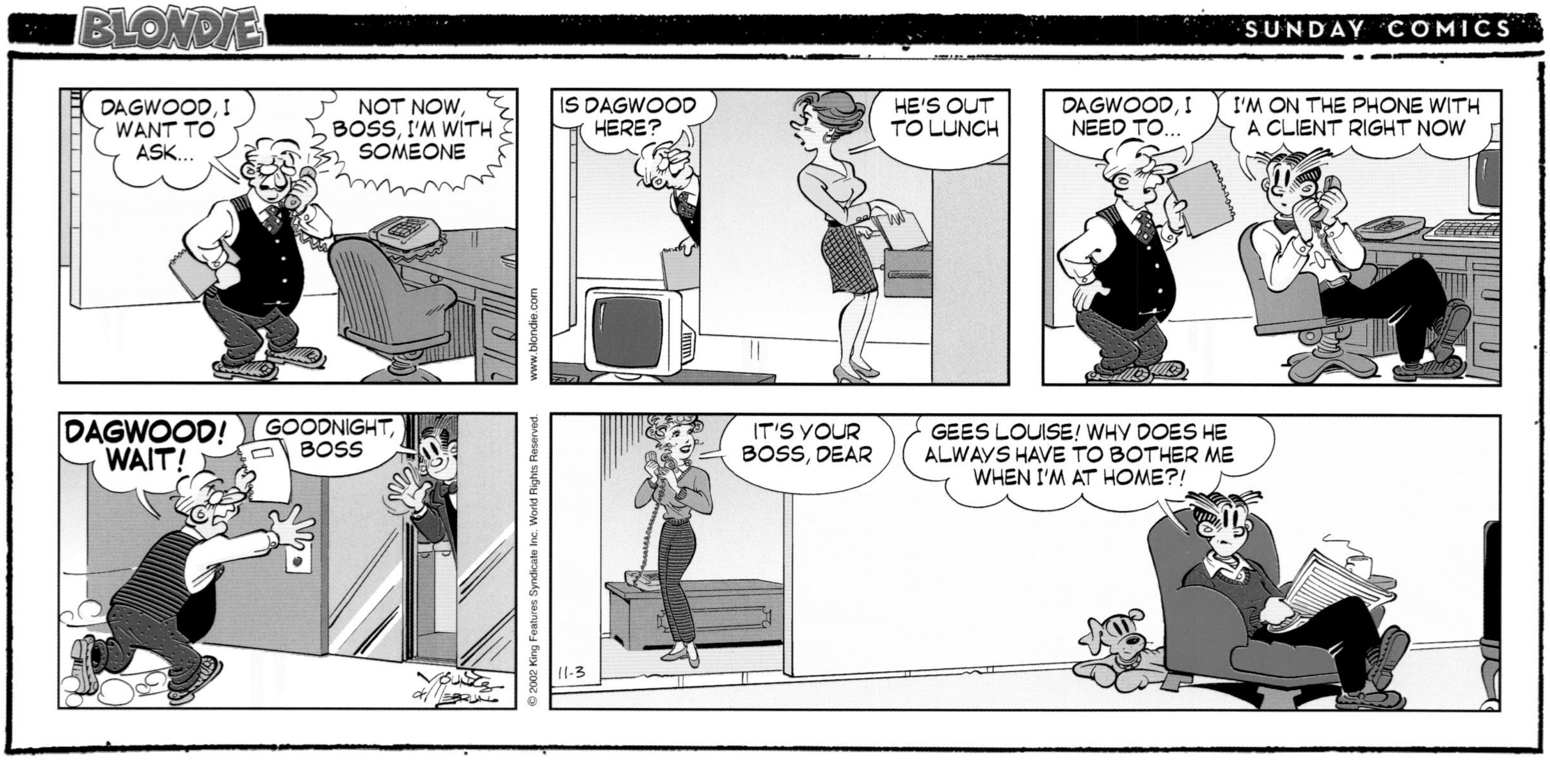
BLONDIE
SUNDAY COMICS
DAGWOOD, I WANT TO ASK...
NOT NOW, BOSS, I'M WITH SOMEONE
IS DAGWOOD HERE?
HE'S OUT TO LUNCH
DAGWOOD, I NEED TO...
I'M ON THE PHONE WITH A CLIENT RIGHT NOW
www.blondie.com
DAGWOOD! WAIT!
GOODNIGHT, BOSS
© 2002 King Features Syndicate Inc. World Rights Reserved.
11-3
IT'S YOUR BOSS, DEAR
GEES LOUISE! WHY DOES HE ALWAYS HAVE TO BOTHER ME WHEN I'M AT HOME?!

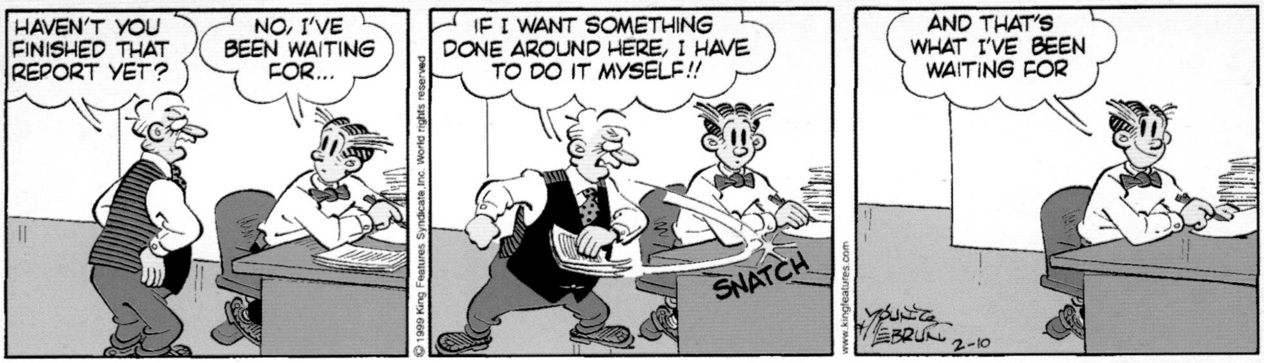
HAVEN'T YOU FINISHED THAT REPORT YET?
NO, I'VE BEEN WAITING FOR...
© 1999 King Features Syndicate, Inc. World rights reserved
IF I WANT SOMETHING DONE AROUND HERE, I HAVE TO DO IT MYSELF!!
SNATCH
www.kingfeatures.com
AND THAT'S WHAT I'VE BEEN WAITING FOR
2-10

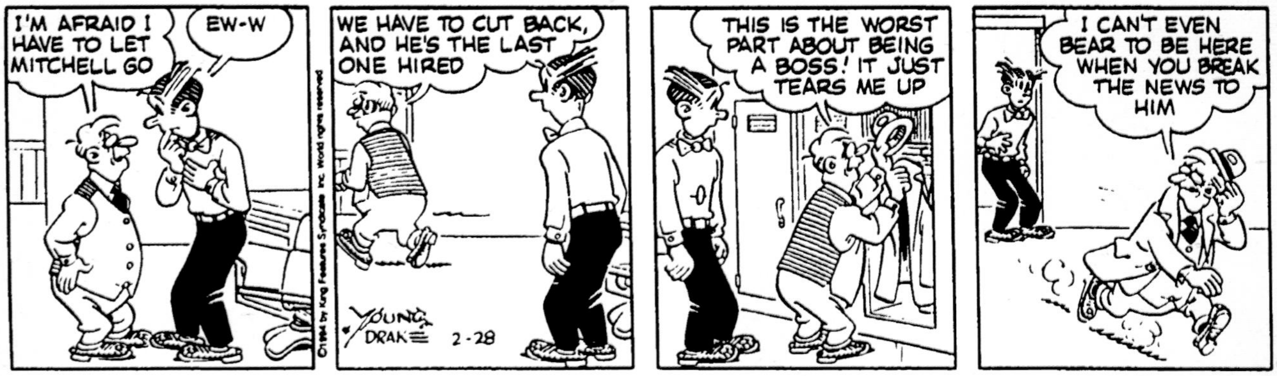
I'M AFRAID I HAVE TO LET MITCHELL GO
EW-W
WE HAVE TO CUT BACK, AND HE'S THE LAST ONE HIRED
YOUNG DRAKE 2-28
THIS IS THE WORST PART ABOUT BEING A BOSS! IT JUST TEARS ME UP
I CAN'T EVEN BEAR TO BE HERE WHEN YOU BREAK THE NEWS TO HIM

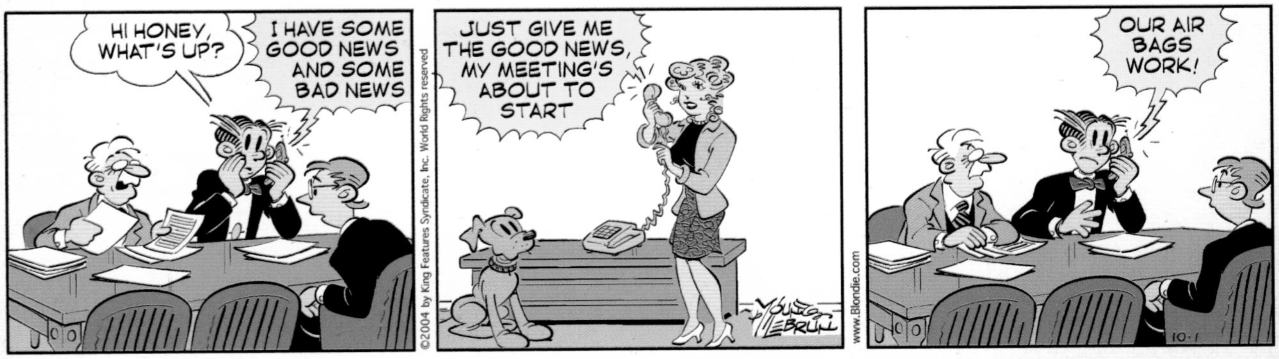
HI HONEY, WHAT'S UP?
I HAVE SOME GOOD NEWS AND SOME BAD NEWS
©2004 by King Features Syndicate, Inc. World Rights reserved
JUST GIVE ME THE GOOD NEWS, MY MEETING'S ABOUT TO START
www.Blondie.com
OUR AIR BAGS WORK!
10-1

Dagwood's job title might as well be office procrastinator.

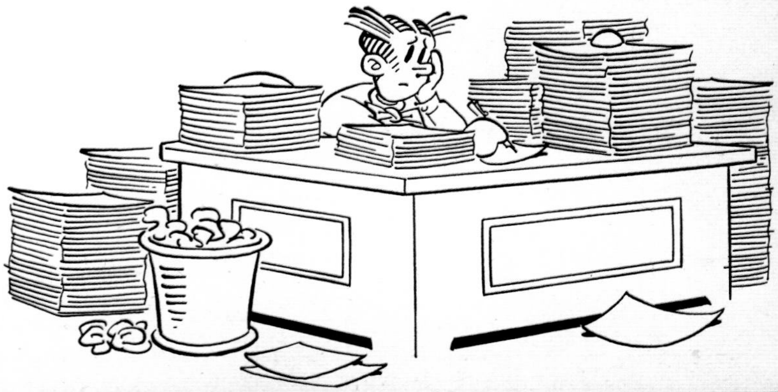

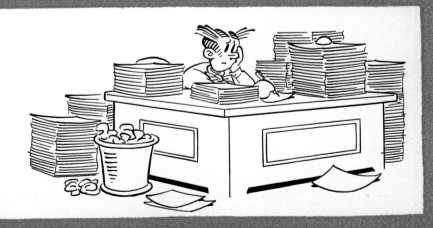

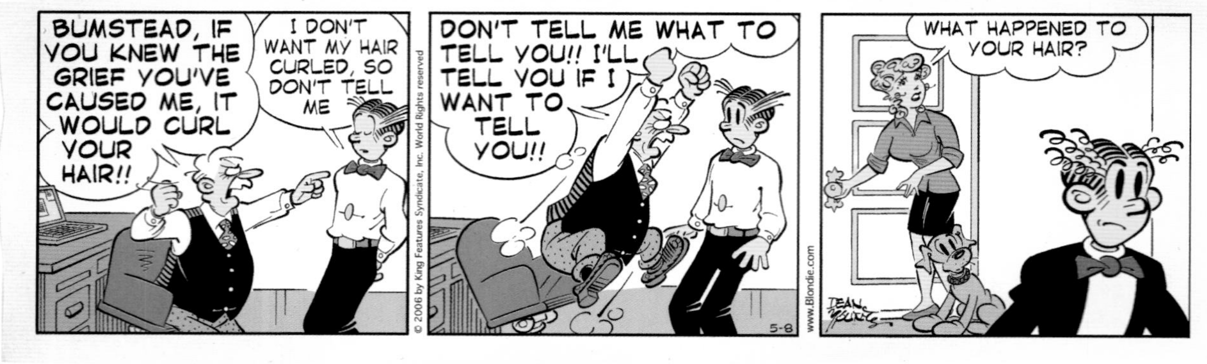
BUMSTEAD, IF YOU KNEW THE GRIEF YOU'VE CAUSED ME, IT WOULD CURL YOUR HAIR!!
I DON'T WANT MY HAIR CURLED, SO DON'T TELL ME
© 2006 by King Features Syndicate, Inc. World Rights reserved
DON'T TELL ME WHAT TO TELL YOU!! I'LL TELL YOU IF I WANT TO TELL YOU!!
5-8
www.Blondie.com
WHAT HAPPENED TO YOUR HAIR?

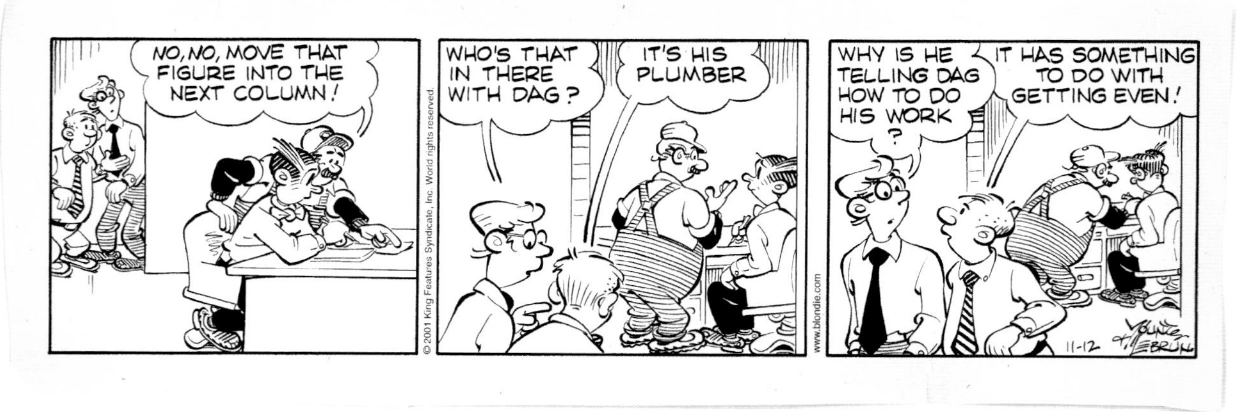
NO, NO, MOVE THAT FIGURE INTO THE NEXT COLUMN!
© 2001 King Features Syndicate, Inc. World rights reserved.
WHO'S THAT IN THERE WITH DAG?
IT'S HIS PLUMBER
www.blondie.com
WHY IS HE TELLING DAG HOW TO DO HIS WORK?
IT HAS SOMETHING TO DO WITH GETTING EVEN!
11-12

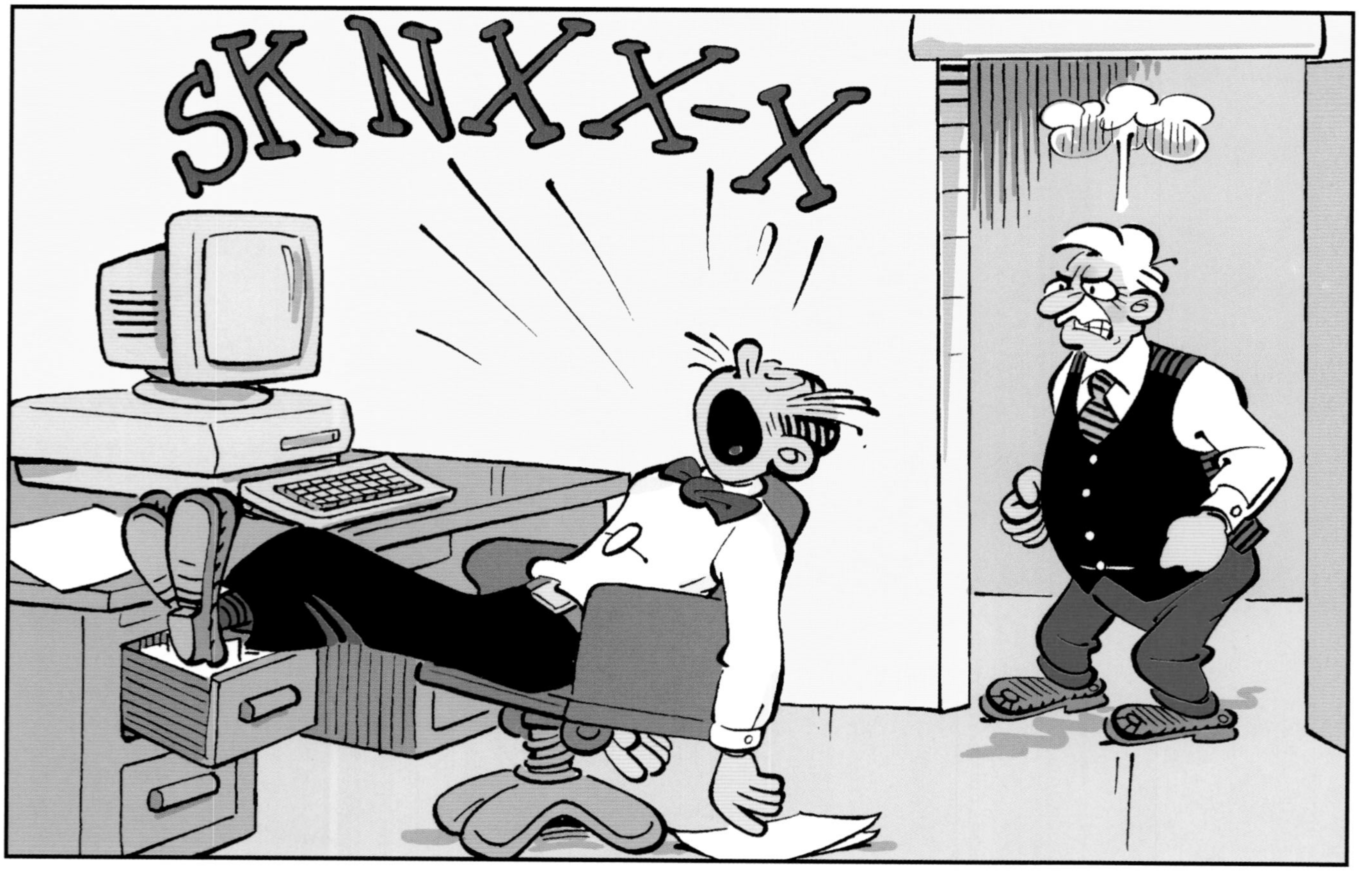
SKNXX-X

CHAPTER 5

BLONDIE GOES TO WORK

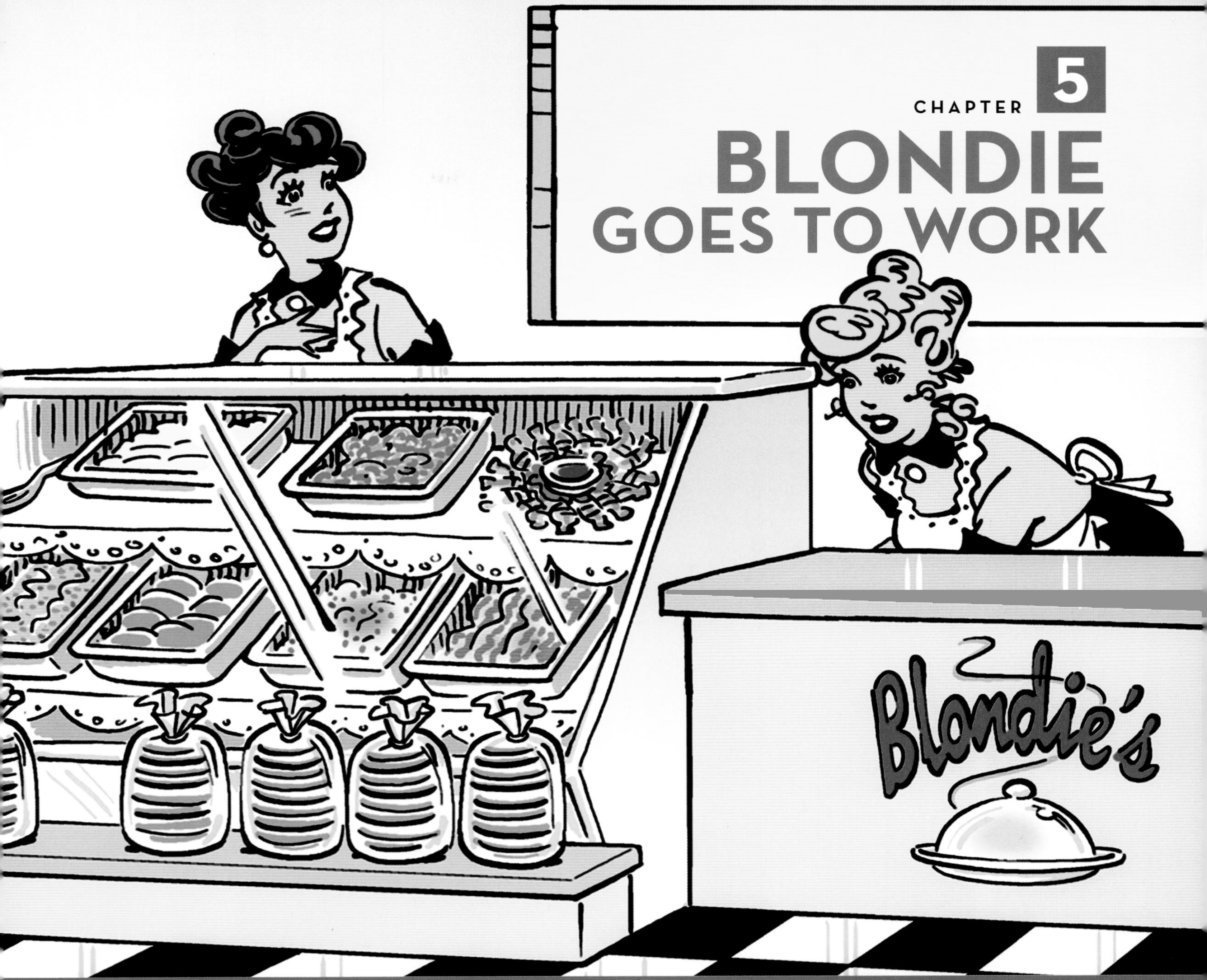
Blondie's

Blondie, on the other hand, loves to work. And her decision to do so proved to be one of the most cataclysmic changes in the history of the comic strip.

For the majority of her life, Blondie, like most of the women of her generation, was a homemaker. Content to run the household—a sizable task, especially when you're married to a guy like Dagwood—she cooked, cleaned, ironed, and raised two children. But as more and more of her compatriots moved into the workforce—changing American life profoundly as they did so—Dean Young began to feel that maybe it was time for Blondie, often called the most famous housewife in America, to join them. In 1991, after months of overtures and hinting, she finally did so, opening Blondie's Catering Shop with her best friend and neighbor, Tootsie Woodley.

The decision was not an easy one.

"I thought about it for a couple of years before I did it," Dean Young said. "I thought about it and thought about it. I was a little apprehensive. All this time I'd been cruising, going along fine, and this was such a departure from the course we'd been on all these years, like going into uncharted waters."

After all, Blondie had happily worked at home for decades and the strip had prospered. Why change it now?

But, Dean said, "I didn't want the strip to be an anachronism. And I saw that more and more women kept going into the workplace. [His own wife, Charlotte, had been a teacher for sixteen years.] I wanted Blondie to be a contemporary woman, to be part of that movement. I thought, *You can't hold this back. It's time to go.*"

Dagwood was harder to convince.

"He was just used to the tried and true," Dean said. "For sixty years he was used to having Blondie be a devoted wife and a wonderful mother, and all of a sudden she wants to break the mold and do something different? It's like whoa, it's going to change the setup of our household, and he didn't realize it was going to be for the better. He sure did like the status quo. His thinking was *Why would you mess with a good thing?*"

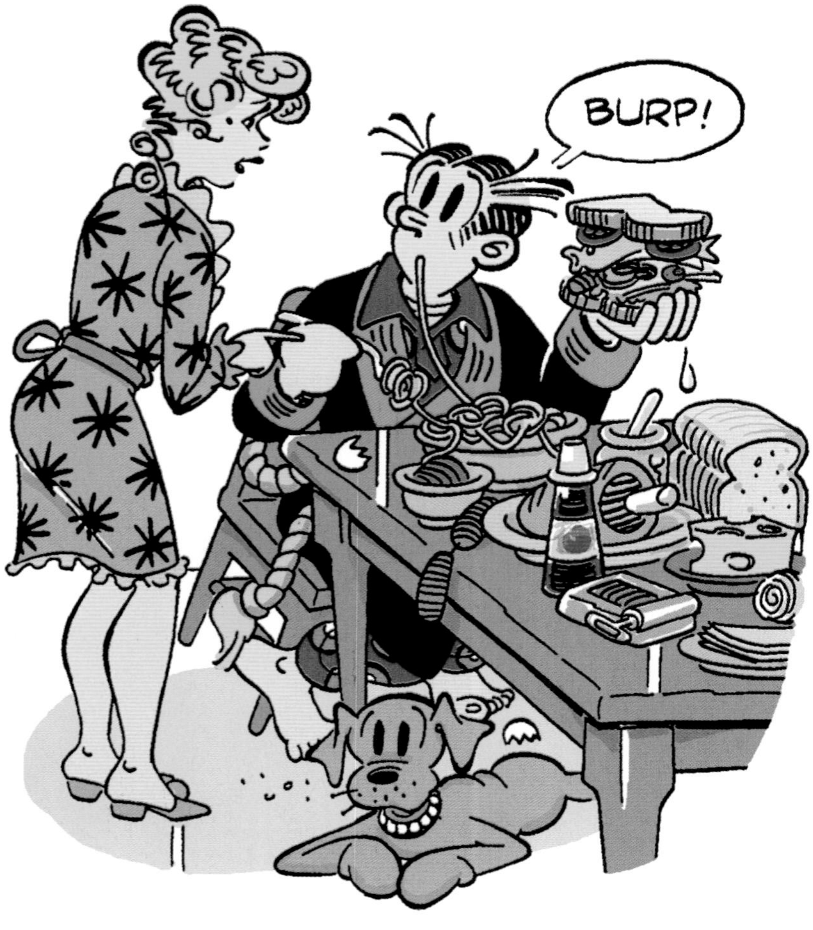
BURP!

Astute readers will note a certain similarity between author and character here. It's far from the only one, but the flesh-and-blood guy is a bit more sophisticated. And he has better hair.

Eventually, though, Dagwood came around—especially when he learned about all the new food he would get to taste-test. Actually, Dean considered several possible careers for Blondie before settling on the catering business. At first, her negotiation skills suggested a very different option: politics.

Blondie has great street smarts, good common sense, she's fast on her feet— and she is a very attractive lady.

"I thought she could run for mayor of her city, or even be a congresswoman or senator," he recalled. "She's got great street smarts, good common sense, she's fast on her feet—she can handle anything—and she's a very attractive lady. That's a good combination for a politician. Anybody she ran against would be in real trouble. How could you not vote for Blondie?"

Luckily for the politicians of the world, though, he decided to go with something closer to home, and on Labor Day 1991, Blondie's Catering opened—in the Bumstead house.

The move sent ripples throughout the nation. An icon of American womanhood, of the "traditional" family archetype, was following in the footsteps of millions of women before her and paving the way for millions since. Articles appeared in hundreds of publications; *Blondie* even made the cover of *Working Mother* magazine. Jay Leno joked about it on his show, and Peter Jennings named Blondie (and Dean) his "person of the week" on *ABC News.* Blondie Bumstead's going to work signaled once and for all that women could be—and were—

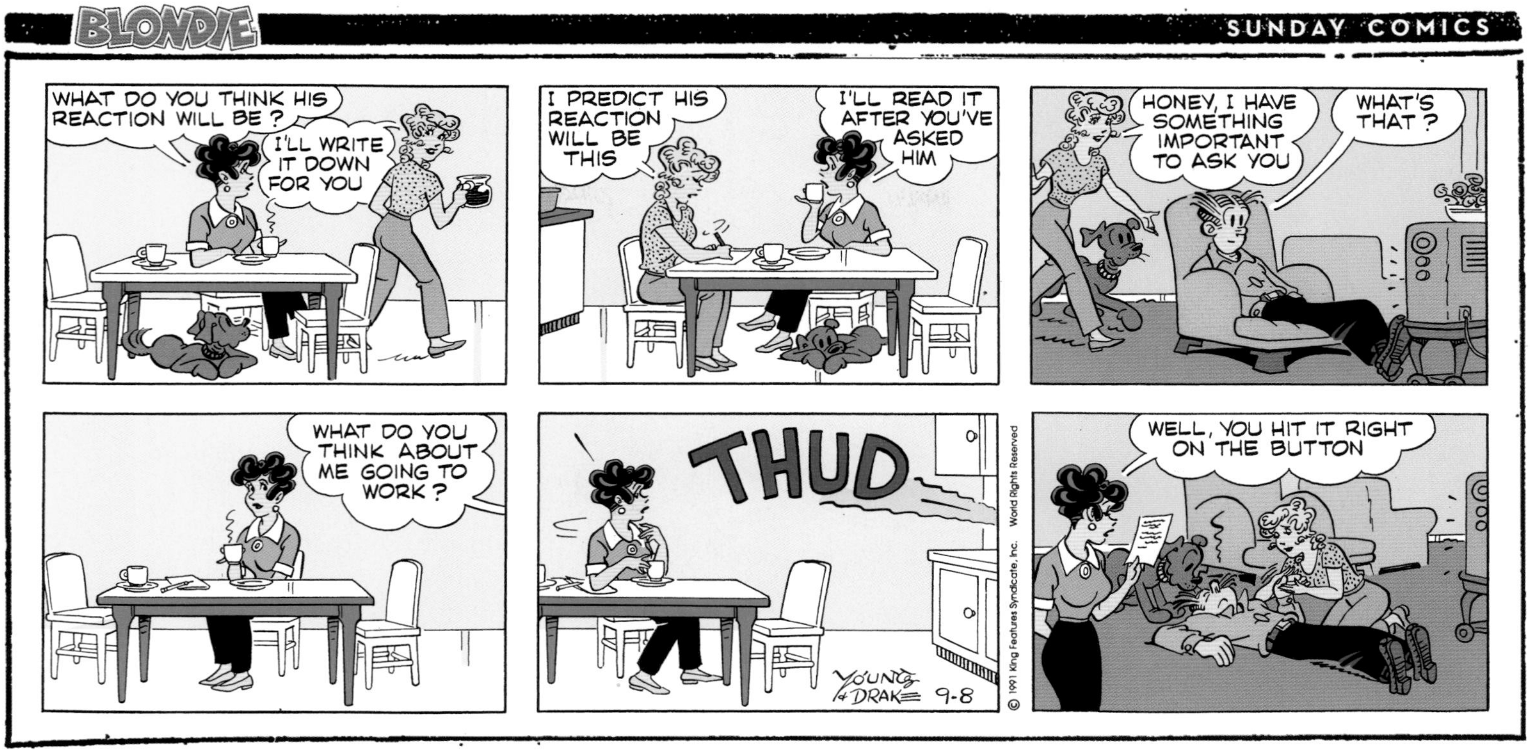
BLONDIE
SUNDAY COMICS
WHAT DO YOU THINK HIS REACTION WILL BE ?
I'LL WRITE IT DOWN FOR YOU
I PREDICT HIS REACTION WILL BE THIS
I'LL READ IT AFTER YOU'VE ASKED HIM
HONEY, I HAVE SOMETHING IMPORTANT TO ASK YOU
WHAT'S THAT ?
WHAT DO YOU THINK ABOUT ME GOING TO WORK ?
THUD
YOUNG & DRAKE 9-8
© 1991 King Features Syndicate, Inc. World Rights Reserved
WELL, YOU HIT IT RIGHT ON THE BUTTON

professionals, wives, and mothers all at the same time. The level of support for the change was astounding. Thousands of letters poured in from readers, men and women all essentially saying the same thing: "You go, girl!"

"It was huge," Dean recalled. "I was really surprised. But after all these years of Blondie being a housewife, and then boom, she goes out and gets a job, that was pretty earth-shattering. Maybe I waited a little too long, but still, for *Blondie* it *was* groundbreaking."

And in the pages of the newspaper, the catering shop was an immediate success. Within a year, Blondie and Tootsie were considering expansion, and in 1995 they moved their endeavor out of the house and into a storefront. Dagwood, as usual, was hesitant about the shift, but he got over it.

"He had to change some of his ideas," Dean said. "But I think there were a lot of men and husbands at the time having to reacquaint themselves with the new way of life. So he wasn't alone."

For perhaps the first time in his long life, Dagwood didn't fall prey to a change in circumstance—he embraced it.

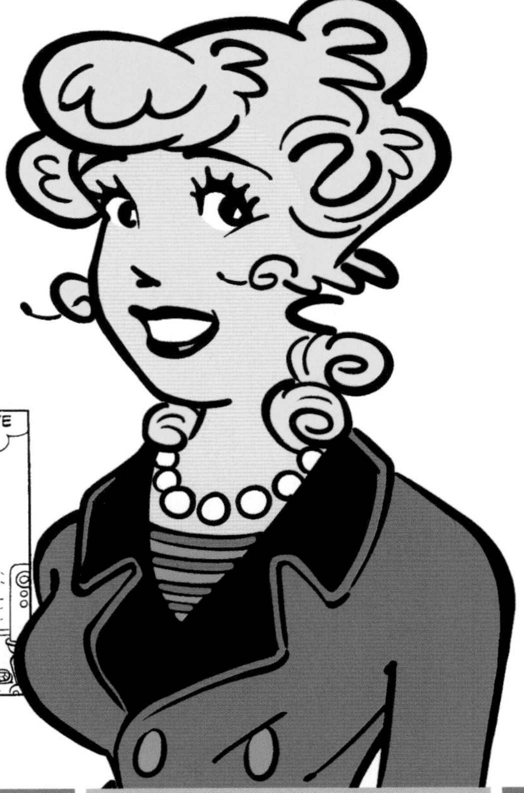

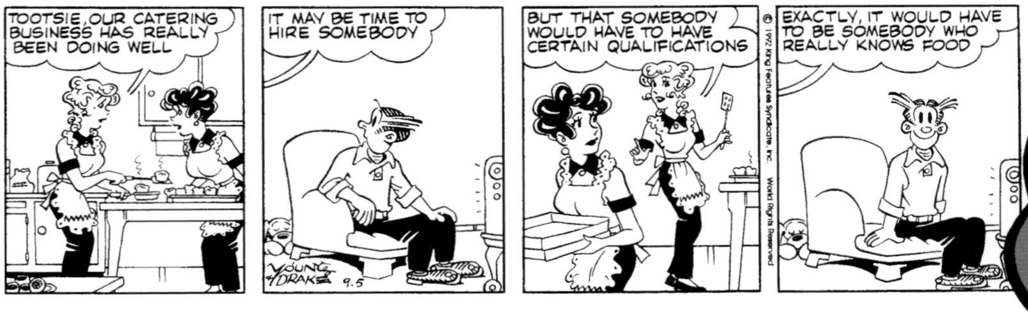
TOOTSIE, OUR CATERING BUSINESS HAS REALLY BEEN DOING WELL
IT MAY BE TIME TO HIRE SOMEBODY
YOUNG & DRAKE 9-5
BUT THAT SOMEBODY WOULD HAVE TO HAVE CERTAIN QUALIFICATIONS
© 1992 King Features Syndicate, Inc. World Rights Reserved
EXACTLY, IT WOULD HAVE TO BE SOMEBODY WHO REALLY KNOWS FOOD

Now he is his wife's number-one fan, customer, and helper, always ready to don an apron—or a napkin—to aid in her pursuit of the perfect meal.

Blondie, too, has gained something—not just admiration from a new set of fans, but a new sense of self. "I think there's a degree of respect and credibility that she gained by going out into the workforce," Dean said. "She's a gal who can do her own thing."

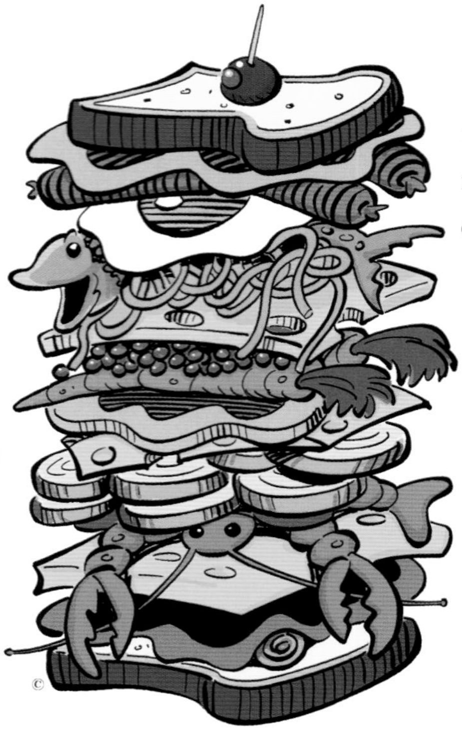

It was quite a transformation, from flighty flapper to professional workingwoman, gold-digger to small-business owner. But the transition from home to work was one that this unflappable lady took in stride. Though the details might be a little different, yet again, Blondie's growth paralleled that of her audience.

"I'm really happy with the choice she made," Dean said. "I'm happy, the Bumsteads are happy, and most importantly, so are the readers."

Blondie's Catering Shop Opening Soon

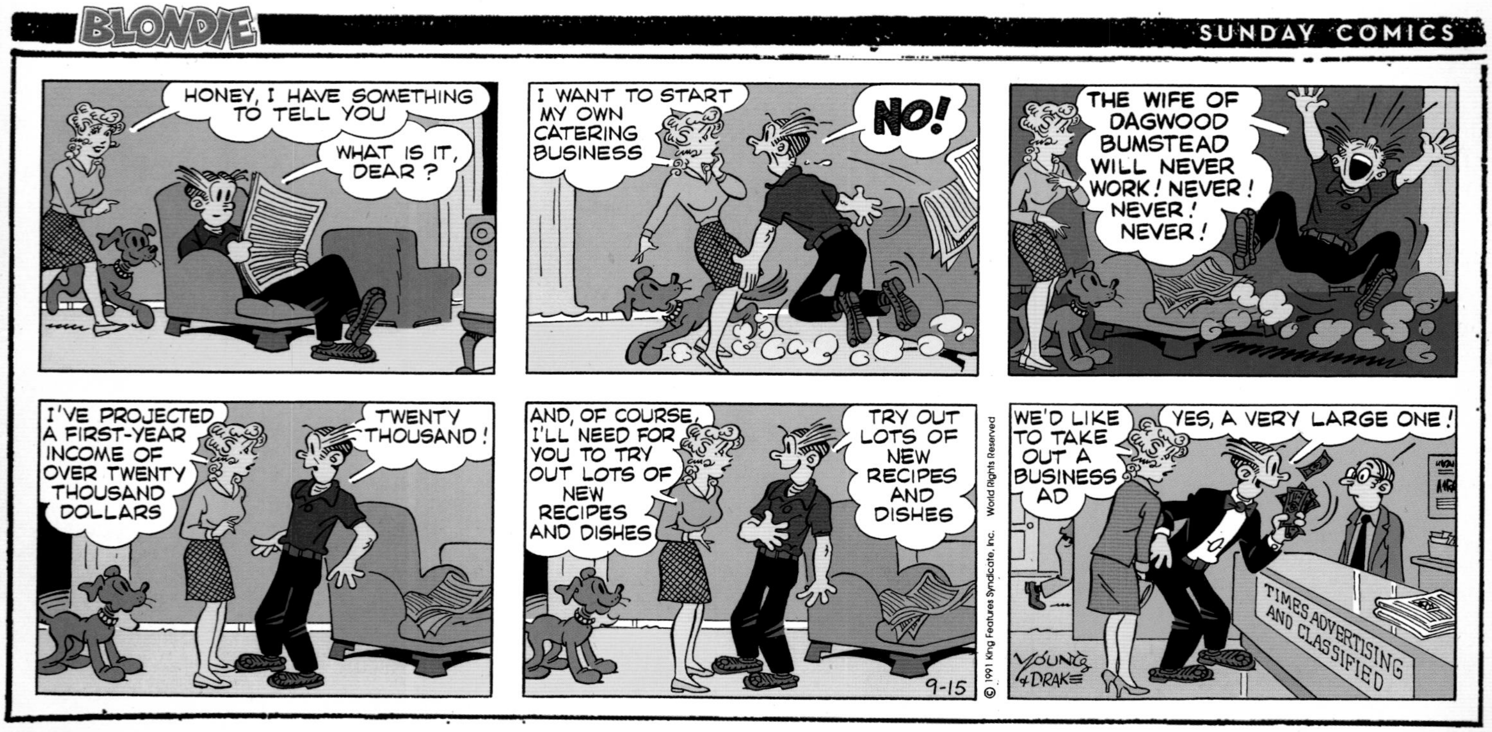
BLONDIE
SUNDAY COMICS
HONEY, I HAVE SOMETHING TO TELL YOU
WHAT IS IT, DEAR ?
I WANT TO START MY OWN CATERING BUSINESS
NO!
THE WIFE OF DAGWOOD BUMSTEAD WILL NEVER WORK! NEVER! NEVER! NEVER!
I'VE PROJECTED A FIRST-YEAR INCOME OF OVER TWENTY THOUSAND DOLLARS
TWENTY THOUSAND!
AND, OF COURSE, I'LL NEED FOR YOU TO TRY OUT LOTS OF NEW RECIPES AND DISHES
TRY OUT LOTS OF NEW RECIPES AND DISHES
9-15
© 1991 King Features Syndicate, Inc. World Rights Reserved
WE'D LIKE TO TAKE OUT A BUSINESS AD
YES, A VERY LARGE ONE!
TIMES ADVERTISING AND CLASSIFIED
YOUNG & DRAKE

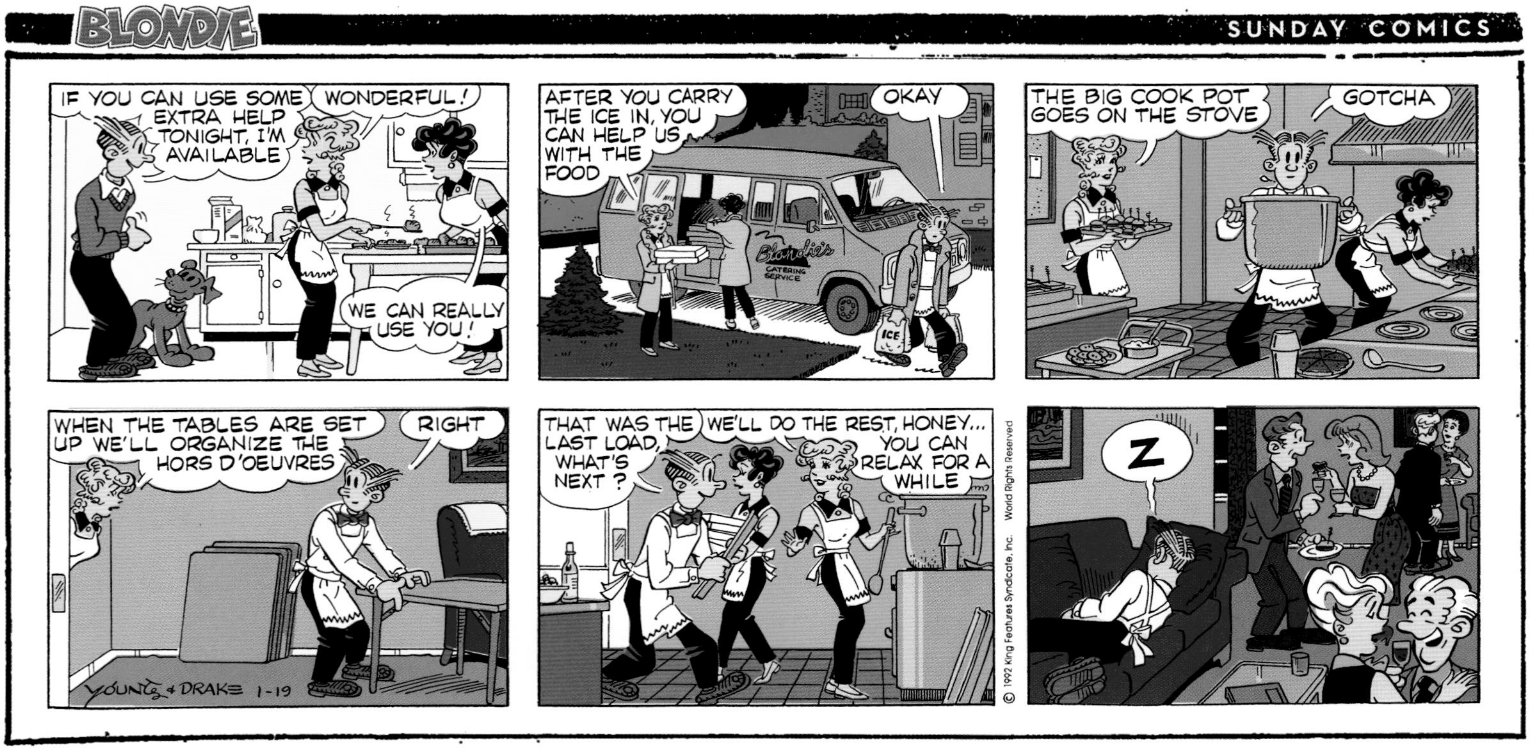
BLONDIE
SUNDAY COMICS
IF YOU CAN USE SOME EXTRA HELP TONIGHT, I'M AVAILABLE
WONDERFUL!
WE CAN REALLY USE YOU!
AFTER YOU CARRY THE ICE IN, YOU CAN HELP US WITH THE FOOD
OKAY
Blondie's CATERING SERVICE
ICE
THE BIG COOK POT GOES ON THE STOVE
GOTCHA
WHEN THE TABLES ARE SET UP WE'LL ORGANIZE THE HORS D'OEUVRES
RIGHT
YOUNG & DRAKE 1-19
THAT WAS THE LAST LOAD, WHAT'S NEXT?
WE'LL DO THE REST, HONEY... YOU CAN RELAX FOR A WHILE
© 1992 King Features Syndicate, Inc. World Rights Reserved
Z

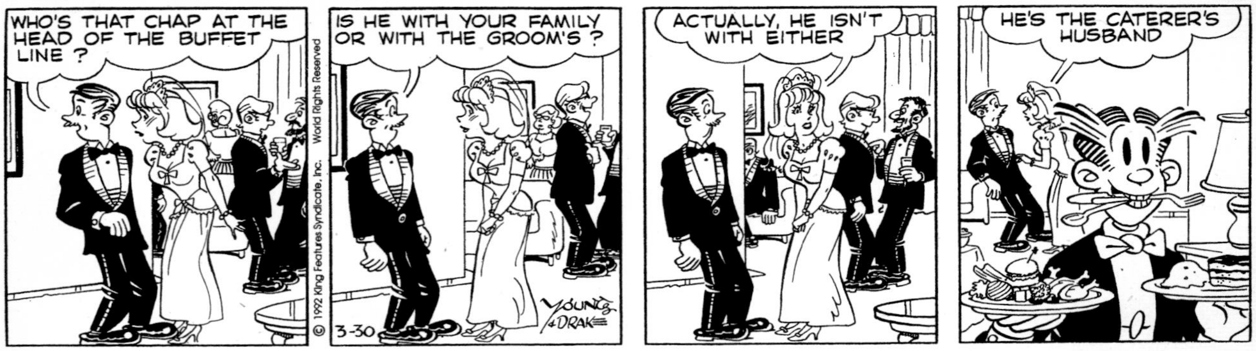
WHO'S THAT CHAP AT THE HEAD OF THE BUFFET LINE?
© 1992 King Features Syndicate, Inc. World Rights Reserved
IS HE WITH YOUR FAMILY OR WITH THE GROOM'S?
3-30
YOUNG & DRAKE
ACTUALLY, HE ISN'T WITH EITHER
HE'S THE CATERER'S HUSBAND

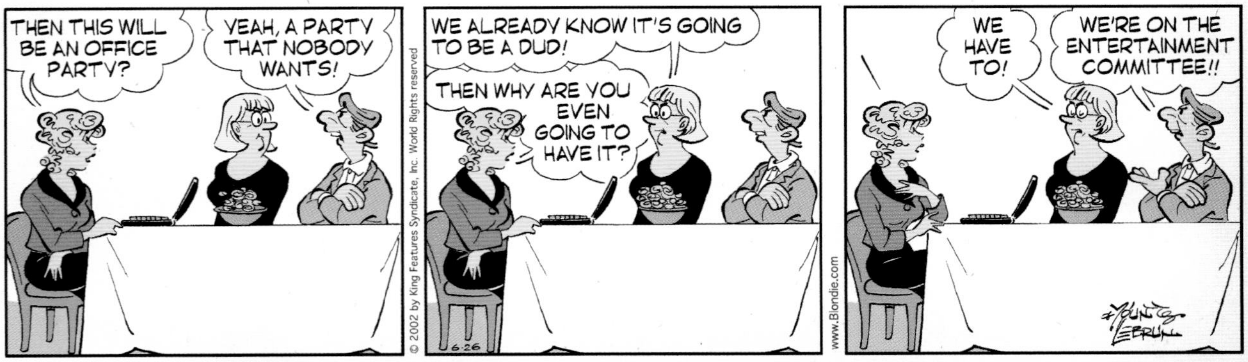
THEN THIS WILL BE AN OFFICE PARTY?
YEAH, A PARTY THAT NOBODY WANTS!
© 2002 by King Features Syndicate, Inc. World Rights reserved
WE ALREADY KNOW IT'S GOING TO BE A DUD!
THEN WHY ARE YOU EVEN GOING TO HAVE IT?
6-26
www.Blondie.com
WE HAVE TO!
WE'RE ON THE ENTERTAINMENT COMMITTEE!!

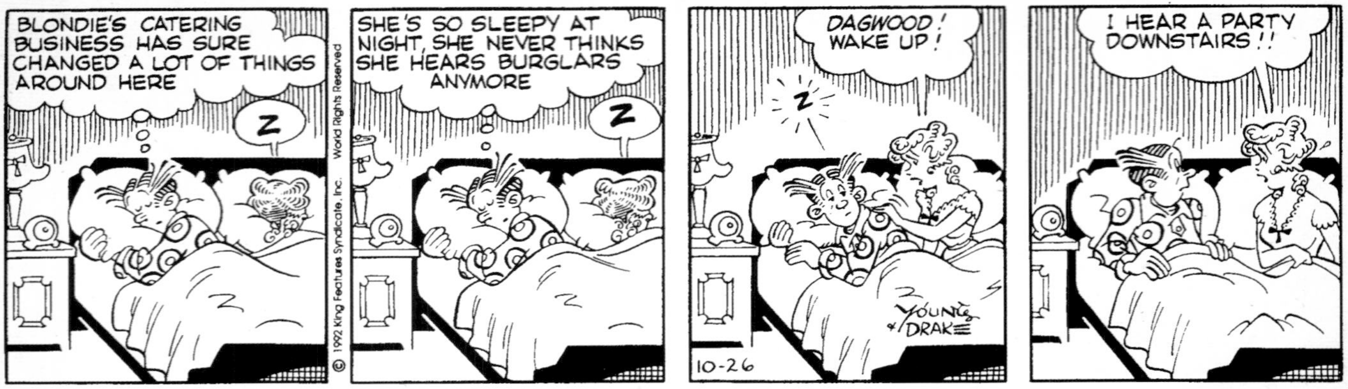
BLONDIE'S CATERING BUSINESS HAS SURE CHANGED A LOT OF THINGS AROUND HERE
Z
SHE'S SO SLEEPY AT NIGHT, SHE NEVER THINKS SHE HEARS BURGLARS ANYMORE
Z
© 1992 King Features Syndicate, Inc. World Rights Reserved
DAGWOOD! WAKE UP!
Z
YOUNG & DRAKE
10-26
I HEAR A PARTY DOWNSTAIRS!!

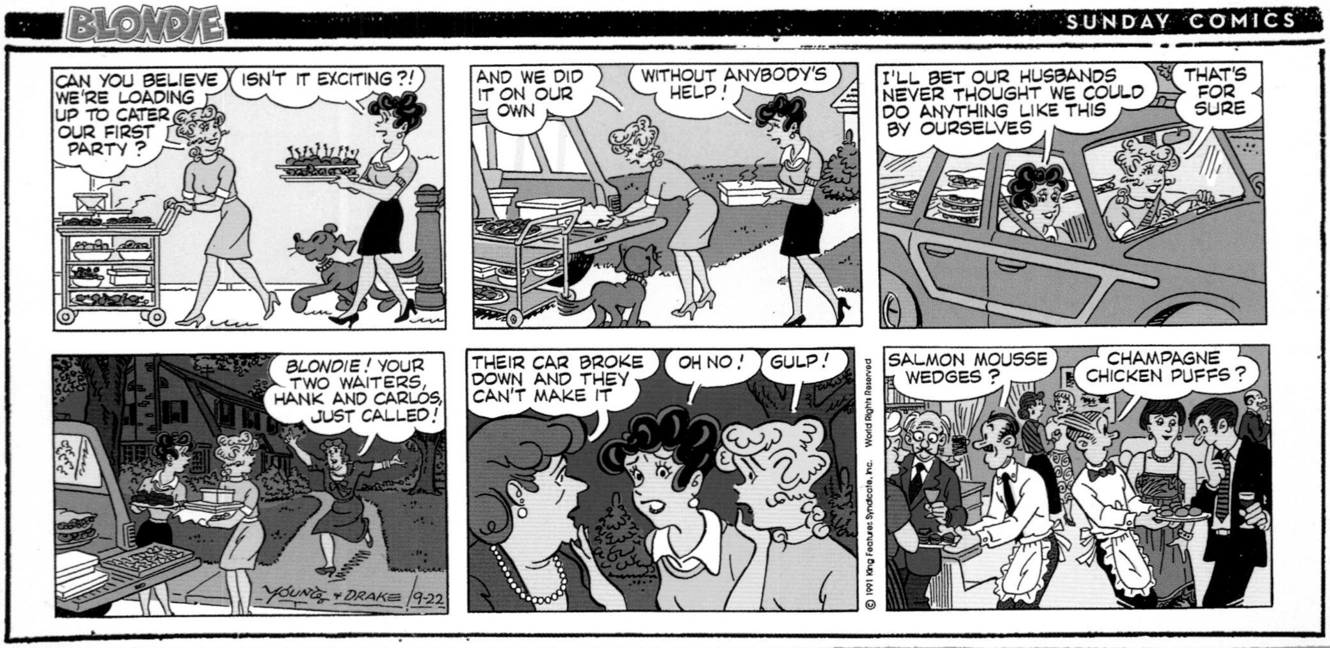
BLONDIE
SUNDAY COMICS
CAN YOU BELIEVE WE'RE LOADING UP TO CATER OUR FIRST PARTY?
ISN'T IT EXCITING?!
AND WE DID IT ON OUR OWN
WITHOUT ANYBODY'S HELP!
I'LL BET OUR HUSBANDS NEVER THOUGHT WE COULD DO ANYTHING LIKE THIS BY OURSELVES
THAT'S FOR SURE
BLONDIE! YOUR TWO WAITERS, HANK AND CARLOS, JUST CALLED!
YOUNG & DRAKE 9-22
THEIR CAR BROKE DOWN AND THEY CAN'T MAKE IT
OH NO!
GULP!
© 1991 King Features Syndicate, Inc. World Rights Reserved
SALMON MOUSSE WEDGES?
CHAMPAGNE CHICKEN PUFFS?

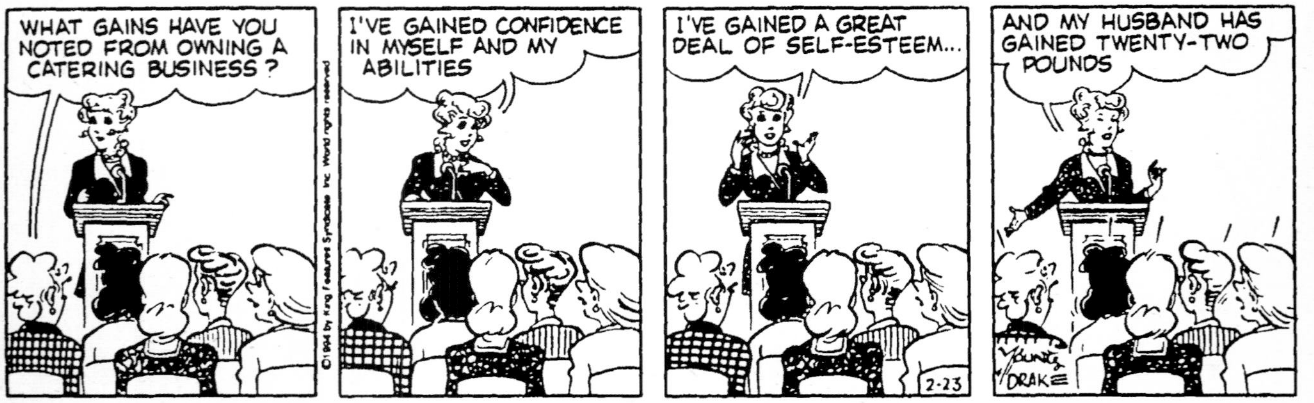
WHAT GAINS HAVE YOU NOTED FROM OWNING A CATERING BUSINESS?
© 1994 by King Features Syndicate Inc. World rights reserved
I'VE GAINED CONFIDENCE IN MYSELF AND MY ABILITIES
I'VE GAINED A GREAT DEAL OF SELF-ESTEEM...
2-23
AND MY HUSBAND HAS GAINED TWENTY-TWO POUNDS
YOUNG & DRAKE

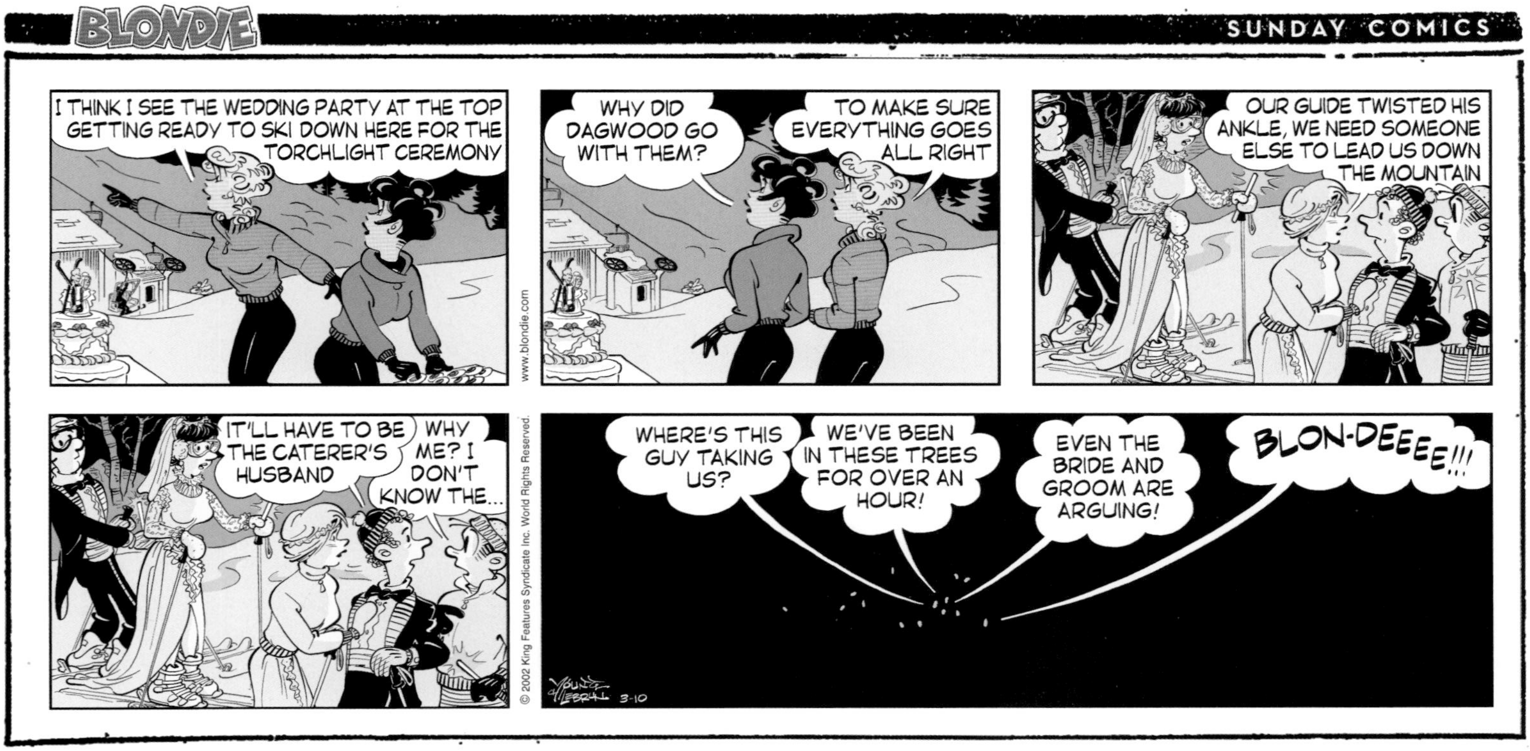
BLONDIE
SUNDAY COMICS
I THINK I SEE THE WEDDING PARTY AT THE TOP GETTING READY TO SKI DOWN HERE FOR THE TORCHLIGHT CEREMONY
WHY DID DAGWOOD GO WITH THEM?
TO MAKE SURE EVERYTHING GOES ALL RIGHT
OUR GUIDE TWISTED HIS ANKLE, WE NEED SOMEONE ELSE TO LEAD US DOWN THE MOUNTAIN
IT'LL HAVE TO BE THE CATERER'S HUSBAND
WHY ME? I DON'T KNOW THE...
WHERE'S THIS GUY TAKING US?
WE'VE BEEN IN THESE TREES FOR OVER AN HOUR!
EVEN THE BRIDE AND GROOM ARE ARGUING!
BLON-DEEEEE!!!
www.blondie.com
© 2002 King Features Syndicate Inc. World Rights Reserved.
3-10

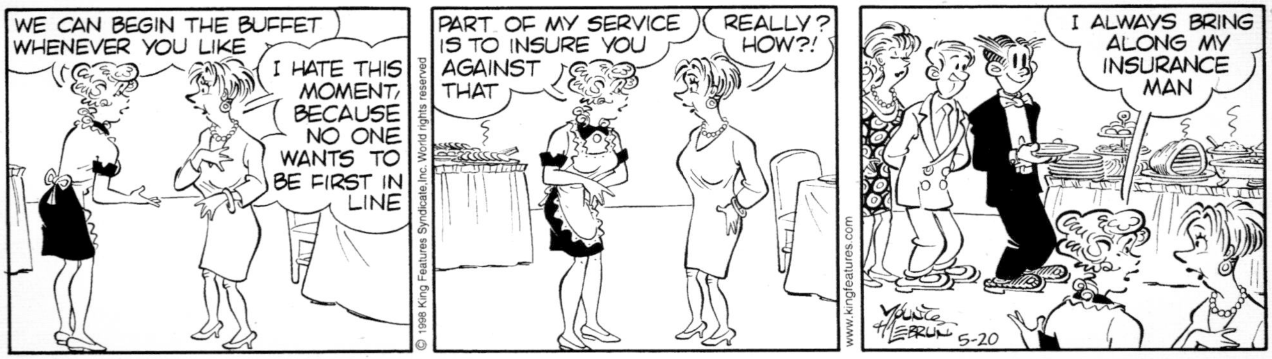
WE CAN BEGIN THE BUFFET WHENEVER YOU LIKE
I HATE THIS MOMENT, BECAUSE NO ONE WANTS TO BE FIRST IN LINE
PART OF MY SERVICE IS TO INSURE YOU AGAINST THAT
REALLY? HOW?!
I ALWAYS BRING ALONG MY INSURANCE MAN
© 1998 King Features Syndicate, Inc. World rights reserved
www.kingfeatures.com
5-20

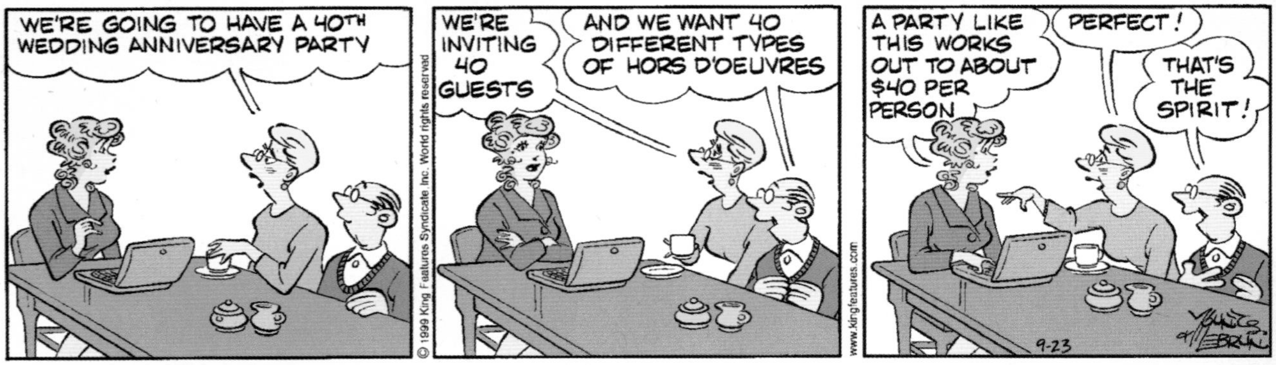
WE'RE GOING TO HAVE A 40TH WEDDING ANNIVERSARY PARTY
WE'RE INVITING 40 GUESTS
AND WE WANT 40 DIFFERENT TYPES OF HORS D'OEUVRES
A PARTY LIKE THIS WORKS OUT TO ABOUT $40 PER PERSON
PERFECT!
THAT'S THE SPIRIT!
© 1999 King Features Syndicate Inc. World rights reserved
www.kingfeatures.com
9-23

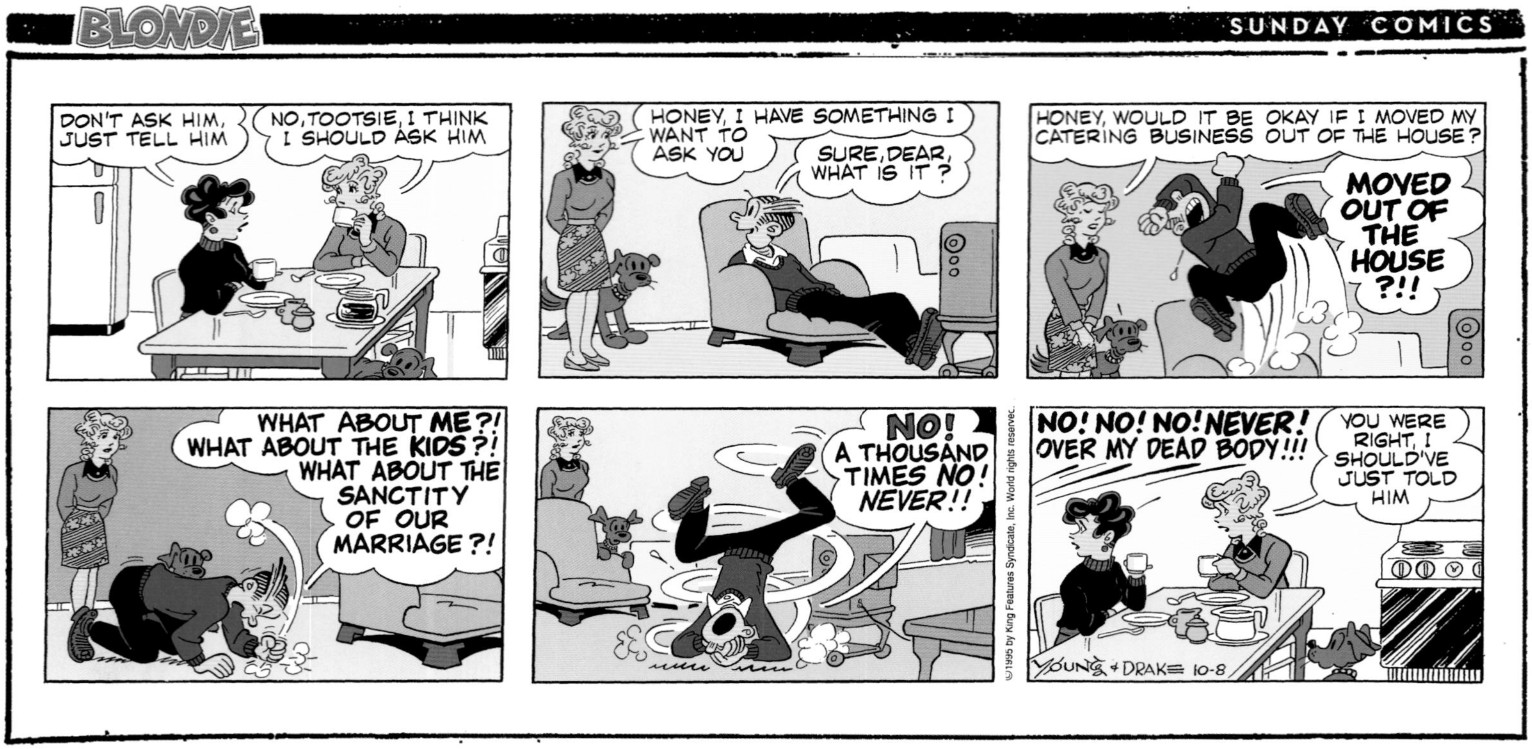
BLONDIE
SUNDAY COMICS
DON'T ASK HIM, JUST TELL HIM
NO, TOOTSIE, I THINK I SHOULD ASK HIM
HONEY, I HAVE SOMETHING I WANT TO ASK YOU
SURE, DEAR, WHAT IS IT ?
HONEY, WOULD IT BE OKAY IF I MOVED MY CATERING BUSINESS OUT OF THE HOUSE ?
MOVED OUT OF THE HOUSE ?!!
WHAT ABOUT ME ?! WHAT ABOUT THE KIDS ?! WHAT ABOUT THE SANCTITY OF OUR MARRIAGE ?!
NO! A THOUSAND TIMES NO! NEVER!!
NO! NO! NO! NEVER! OVER MY DEAD BODY!!!
YOU WERE RIGHT, I SHOULD'VE JUST TOLD HIM
© 1995 by King Features Syndicate, Inc. World rights reserved.
YOUNG & DRAKE 10-8

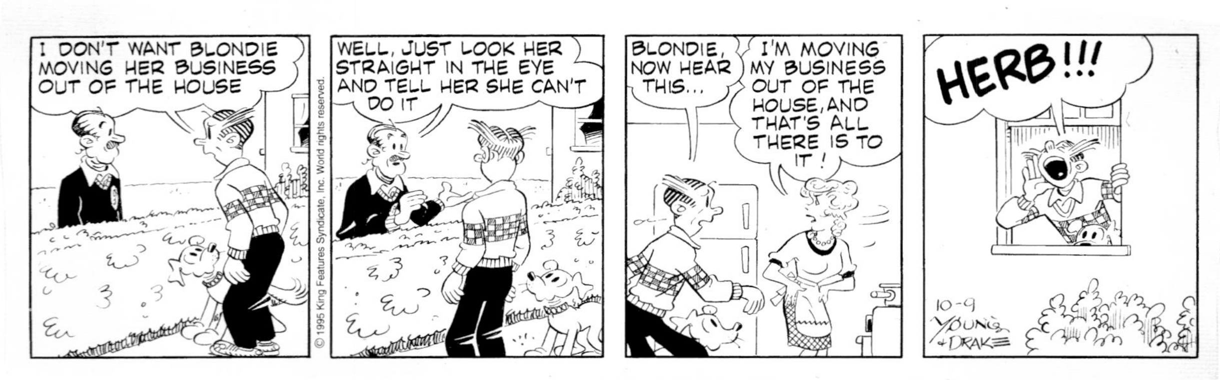
I DON'T WANT BLONDIE MOVING HER BUSINESS OUT OF THE HOUSE
WELL, JUST LOOK HER STRAIGHT IN THE EYE AND TELL HER SHE CAN'T DO IT
© 1995 King Features Syndicate, Inc. World rights reserved.
BLONDIE, NOW HEAR THIS...
I'M MOVING MY BUSINESS OUT OF THE HOUSE, AND THAT'S ALL THERE IS TO IT !
HERB!!!
10-9 YOUNG & DRAKE

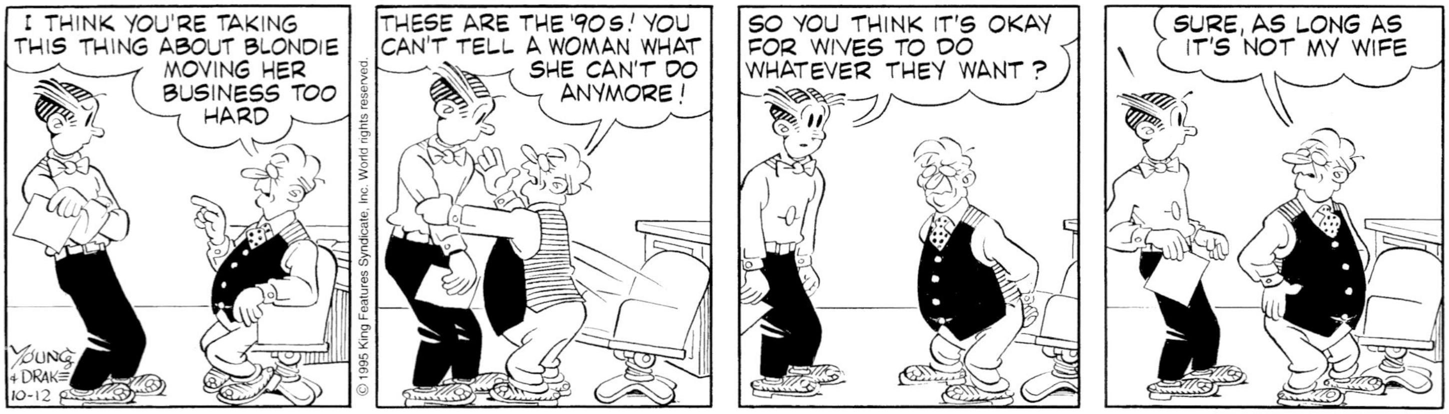
I THINK YOU'RE TAKING THIS THING ABOUT BLONDIE MOVING HER BUSINESS TOO HARD
YOUNG & DRAKE 10-12
© 1995 King Features Syndicate, Inc. World rights reserved.
THESE ARE THE '90S! YOU CAN'T TELL A WOMAN WHAT SHE CAN'T DO ANYMORE!
SO YOU THINK IT'S OKAY FOR WIVES TO DO WHATEVER THEY WANT ?
SURE, AS LONG AS IT'S NOT MY WIFE

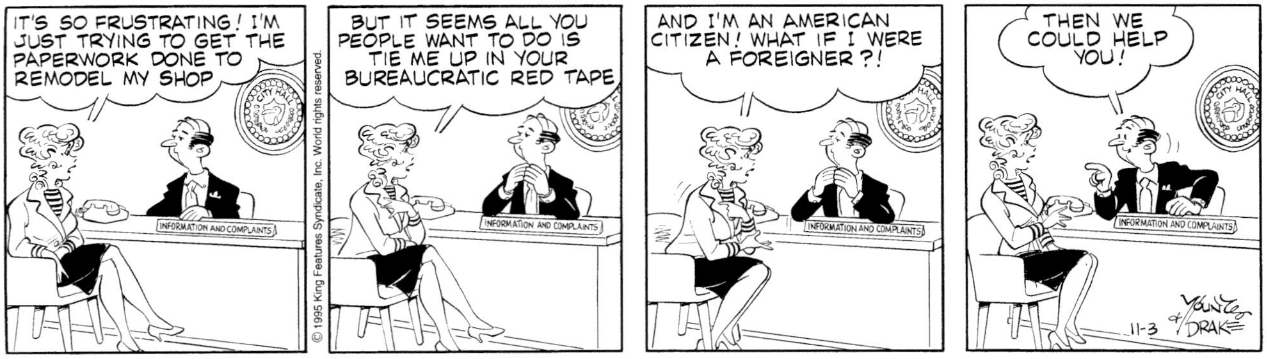
IT'S SO FRUSTRATING! I'M JUST TRYING TO GET THE PAPERWORK DONE TO REMODEL MY SHOP
BUT IT SEEMS ALL YOU PEOPLE WANT TO DO IS TIE ME UP IN YOUR BUREAUCRATIC RED TAPE
AND I'M AN AMERICAN CITIZEN! WHAT IF I WERE A FOREIGNER?!
THEN WE COULD HELP YOU!
INFORMATION AND COMPLAINTS
11-3
YOUNG & DRAKE
© 1995 King Features Syndicate, Inc. World rights reserved.

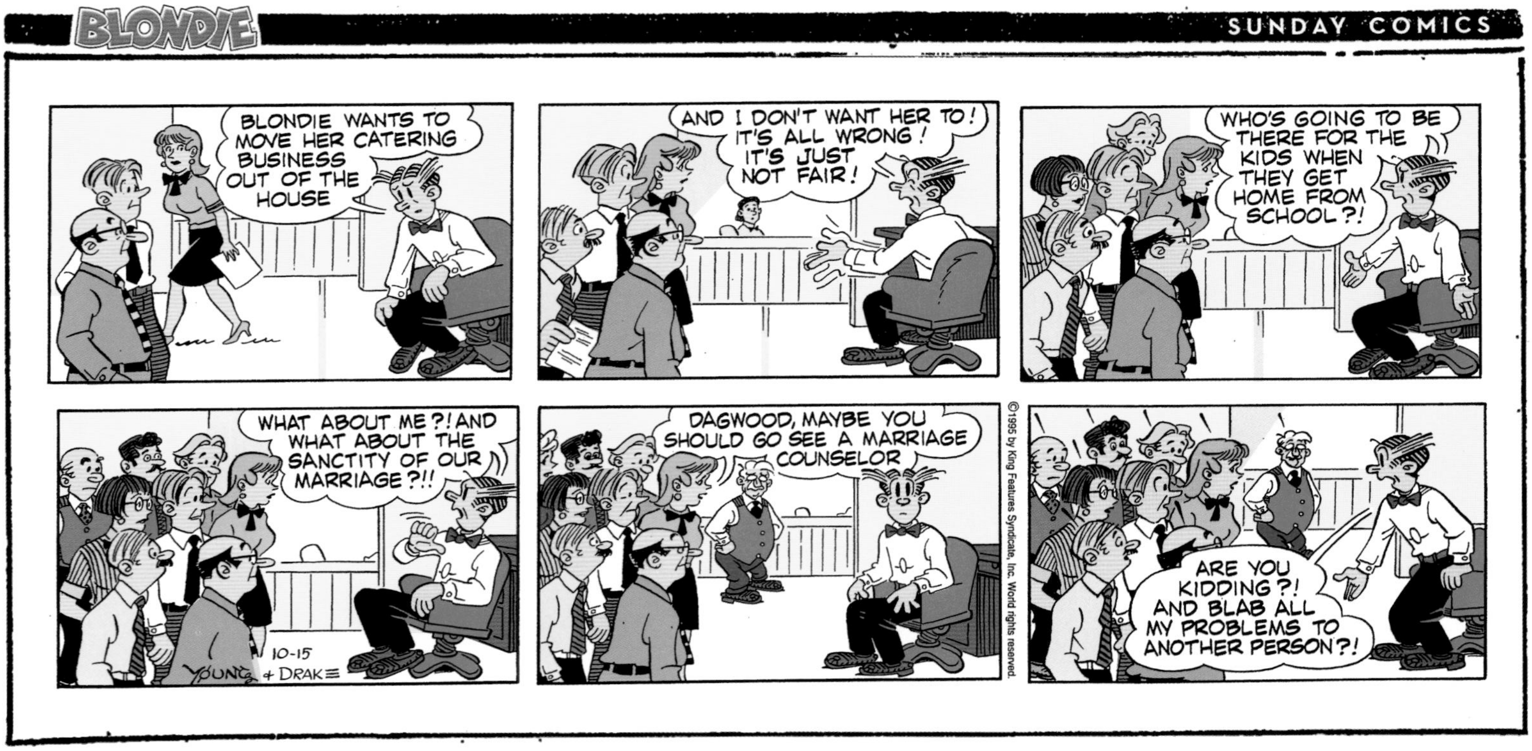
BLONDIE
SUNDAY COMICS
BLONDIE WANTS TO MOVE HER CATERING BUSINESS OUT OF THE HOUSE
AND I DON'T WANT HER TO! IT'S ALL WRONG! IT'S JUST NOT FAIR!
WHO'S GOING TO BE THERE FOR THE KIDS WHEN THEY GET HOME FROM SCHOOL?!
WHAT ABOUT ME?! AND WHAT ABOUT THE SANCTITY OF OUR MARRIAGE?!!
10-15
YOUNG & DRAKE
DAGWOOD, MAYBE YOU SHOULD GO SEE A MARRIAGE COUNSELOR
ARE YOU KIDDING?! AND BLAB ALL MY PROBLEMS TO ANOTHER PERSON?!
© 1995 by King Features Syndicate, Inc. World rights reserved.

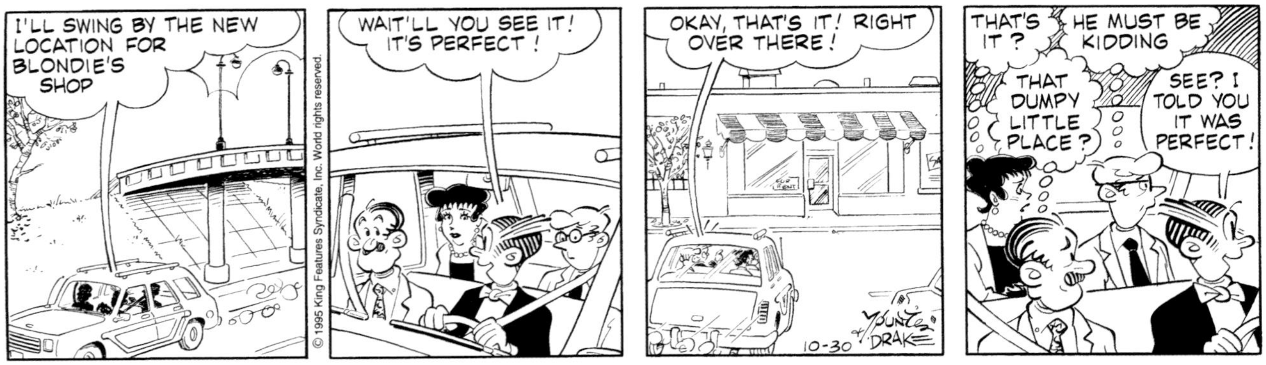
I'LL SWING BY THE NEW LOCATION FOR BLONDIE'S SHOP
WAIT'LL YOU SEE IT! IT'S PERFECT!
OKAY, THAT'S IT! RIGHT OVER THERE!
10-30
YOUNG & DRAKE
THAT'S IT?
HE MUST BE KIDDING
THAT DUMPY LITTLE PLACE?
SEE? I TOLD YOU IT WAS PERFECT!
© 1995 King Features Syndicate, Inc. World rights reserved.

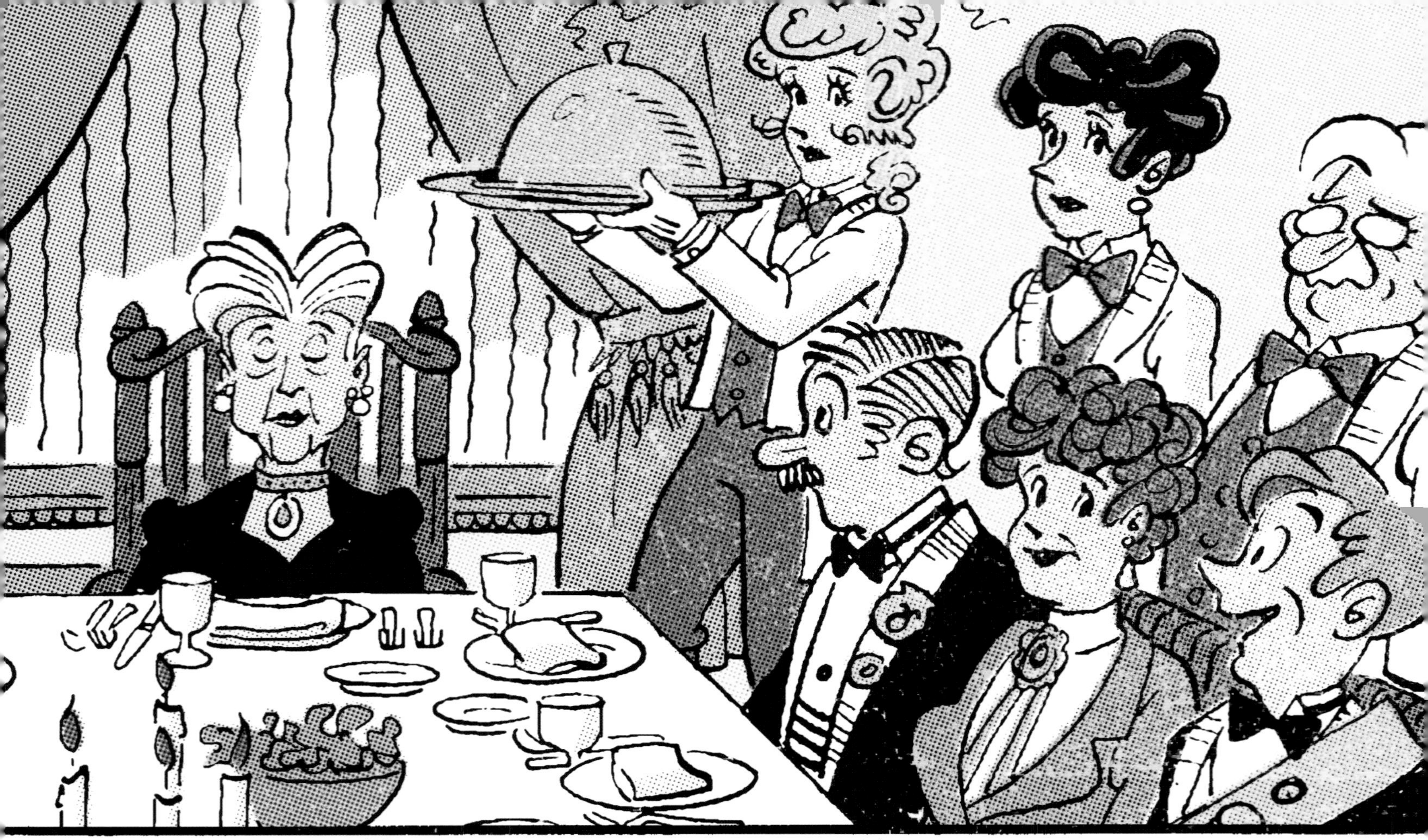

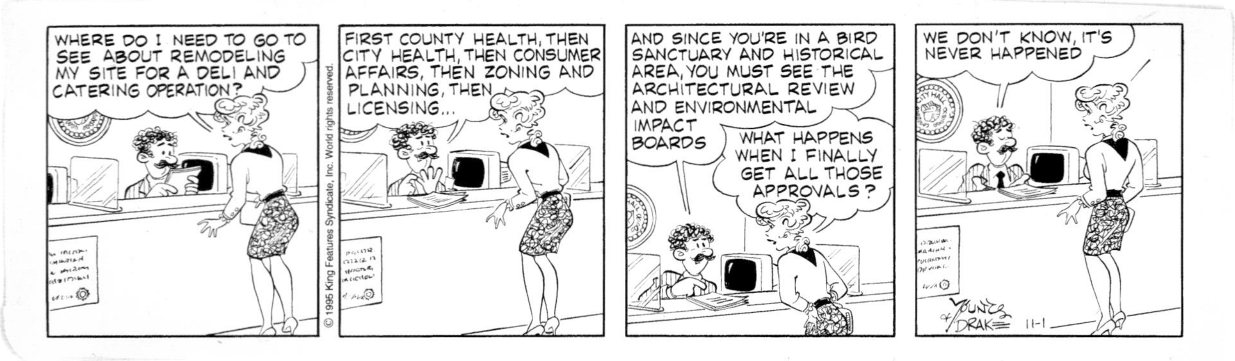

WHERE DO I NEED TO GO TO SEE ABOUT REMODELING MY SITE FOR A DELI AND CATERING OPERATION?
© 1995 King Features Syndicate, Inc. World rights reserved.
FIRST COUNTY HEALTH, THEN CITY HEALTH, THEN CONSUMER AFFAIRS, THEN ZONING AND PLANNING, THEN LICENSING...
AND SINCE YOU'RE IN A BIRD SANCTUARY AND HISTORICAL AREA, YOU MUST SEE THE ARCHITECTURAL REVIEW AND ENVIRONMENTAL IMPACT BOARDS
WHAT HAPPENS WHEN I FINALLY GET ALL THOSE APPROVALS?
WE DON'T KNOW, IT'S NEVER HAPPENED

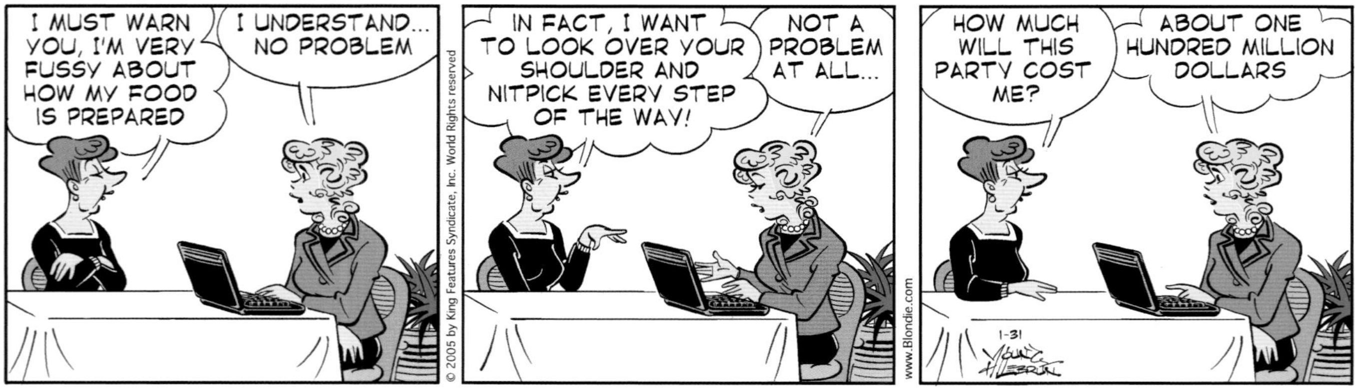

I MUST WARN YOU, I'M VERY FUSSY ABOUT HOW MY FOOD IS PREPARED
I UNDERSTAND... NO PROBLEM
© 2005 by King Features Syndicate, Inc. World Rights reserved
IN FACT, I WANT TO LOOK OVER YOUR SHOULDER AND NITPICK EVERY STEP OF THE WAY!
NOT A PROBLEM AT ALL...
www.Blondie.com
HOW MUCH WILL THIS PARTY COST ME?
ABOUT ONE HUNDRED MILLION DOLLARS
1-31

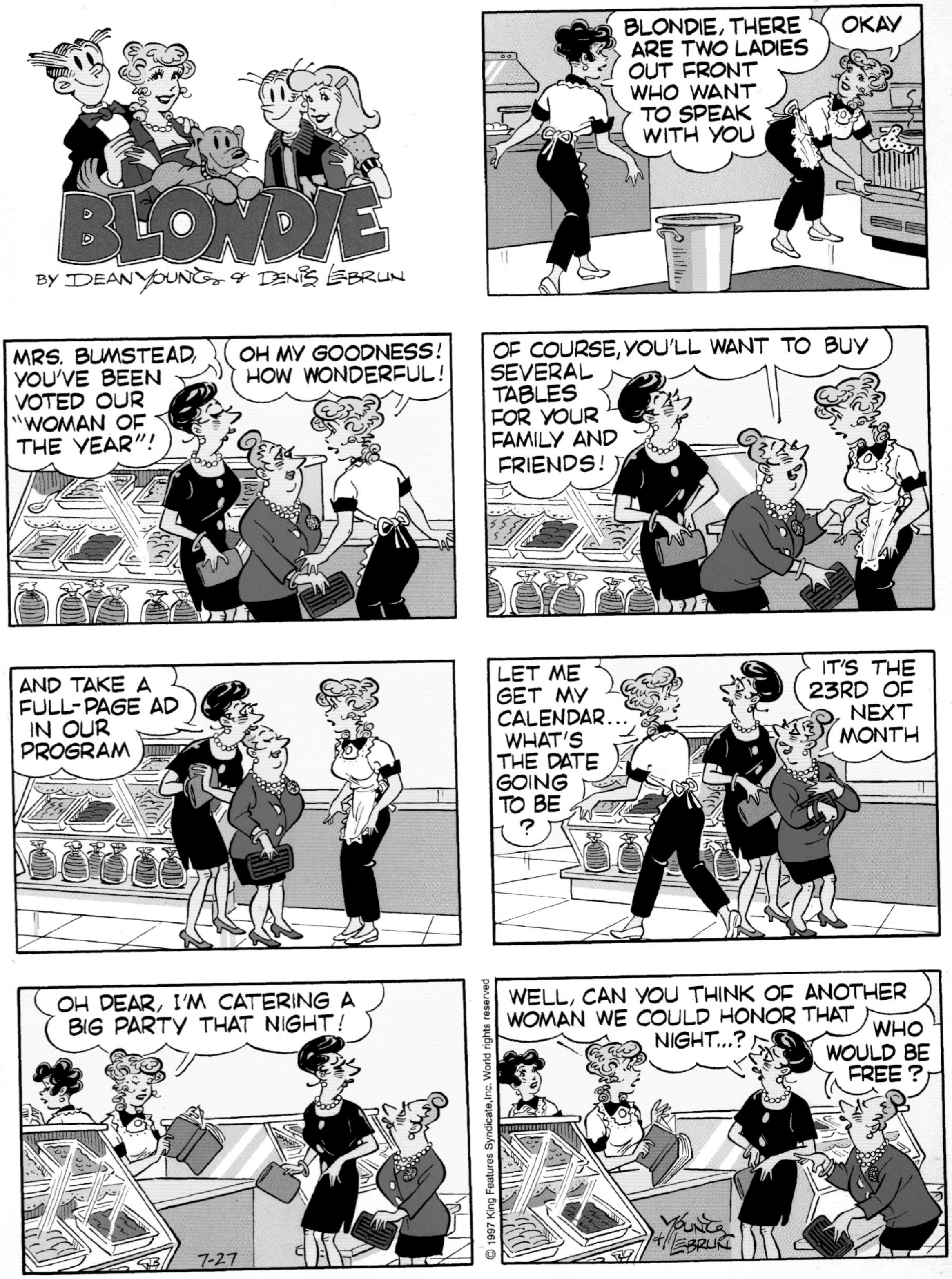
BLONDIE
BY DEAN YOUNG & DENIS LEBRUN
BLONDIE, THERE ARE TWO LADIES OUT FRONT WHO WANT TO SPEAK WITH YOU
OKAY
MRS. BUMSTEAD, YOU'VE BEEN VOTED OUR "WOMAN OF THE YEAR"!
OH MY GOODNESS! HOW WONDERFUL!
OF COURSE, YOU'LL WANT TO BUY SEVERAL TABLES FOR YOUR FAMILY AND FRIENDS!
AND TAKE A FULL-PAGE AD IN OUR PROGRAM
LET ME GET MY CALENDAR... WHAT'S THE DATE GOING TO BE ?
IT'S THE 23RD OF NEXT MONTH
OH DEAR, I'M CATERING A BIG PARTY THAT NIGHT!
7-27
WELL, CAN YOU THINK OF ANOTHER WOMAN WE COULD HONOR THAT NIGHT...?
WHO WOULD BE FREE ?
YOUNG & LEBRUN

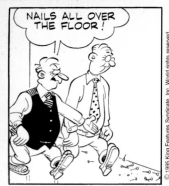

NAILS ALL OVER THE FLOOR!
TRAILS OF SAWDUST!
© 1995 King Features Syndicate, Inc. World rights reserved.
11-28
LUMBER STACKED EVERYWHERE!
D. BUMSTEAD
I SURE WILL BE GLAD WHEN BUMSTEAD GETS THROUGH REMODELING HIS WIFE'S SHOP AFTER WORK EVERY DAY!

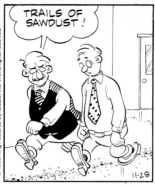

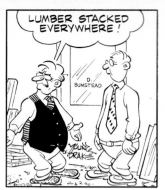

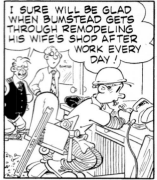

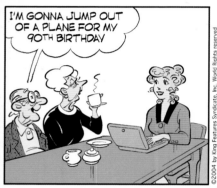

I'M GONNA JUMP OUT OF A PLANE FOR MY 90TH BIRTHDAY
©2004 by King Features Syndicate, Inc. World Rights reserved
11-22
THEY'RE GIVING ME A BIRTHDAY PARTY WHEN I LAND...
www.Blondie.com
EITHER THAT OR A FAREWELL PARTY, DEPENDING UPON HOW HE LANDS!

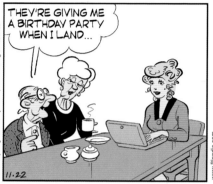

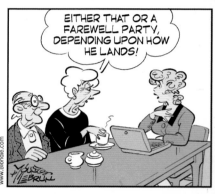

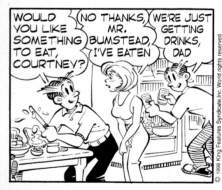

WOULD YOU LIKE SOMETHING TO EAT, COURTNEY?
NO THANKS, MR. BUMSTEAD, I'VE EATEN
WE'RE JUST GETTING DRINKS, DAD
© 1998 King Features Syndicate, Inc. World rights reserved
I KNEW YOUR MOM WAS A CATERER, BUT I DIDN'T KNOW YOUR DAD WAS, TOO
7-18
www.kingfeatures.com
WELL, I GUESS HE IS... BUT HE'S ONLY GOT ONE CUSTOMER

Dagwood is his wife's number-one fan, customer, and helper, always ready to don an apron — or a napkin — to aid in her pursuit of the perfect meal.

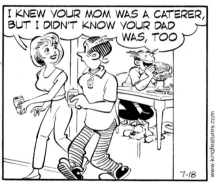

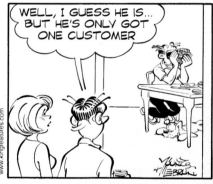

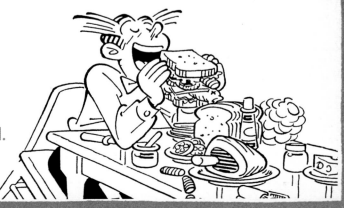

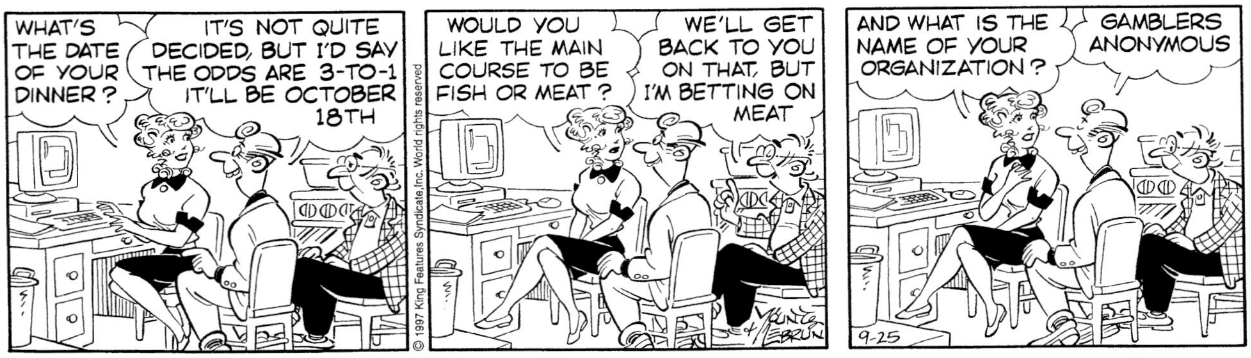
WHAT'S THE DATE OF YOUR DINNER?
IT'S NOT QUITE DECIDED, BUT I'D SAY THE ODDS ARE 3-TO-1 IT'LL BE OCTOBER 18TH
© 1997 King Features Syndicate, Inc. World rights reserved
WOULD YOU LIKE THE MAIN COURSE TO BE FISH OR MEAT?
WE'LL GET BACK TO YOU ON THAT, BUT I'M BETTING ON MEAT
AND WHAT IS THE NAME OF YOUR ORGANIZATION?
GAMBLERS ANONYMOUS
9-25

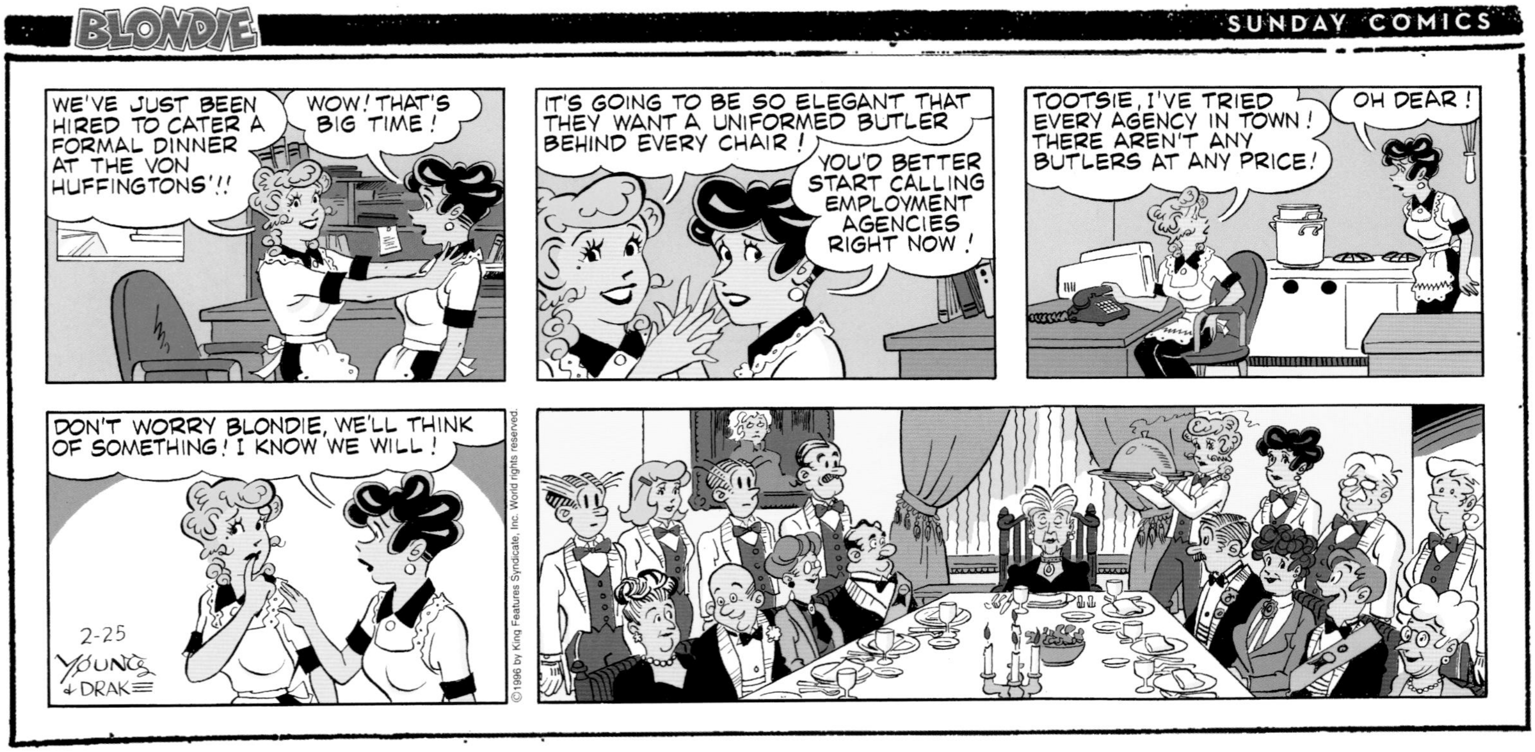
BLONDIE
SUNDAY COMICS
WE'VE JUST BEEN HIRED TO CATER A FORMAL DINNER AT THE VON HUFFINGTONS'!!
WOW! THAT'S BIG TIME!
IT'S GOING TO BE SO ELEGANT THAT THEY WANT A UNIFORMED BUTLER BEHIND EVERY CHAIR!
YOU'D BETTER START CALLING EMPLOYMENT AGENCIES RIGHT NOW!
TOOTSIE, I'VE TRIED EVERY AGENCY IN TOWN! THERE AREN'T ANY BUTLERS AT ANY PRICE!
OH DEAR!
DON'T WORRY BLONDIE, WE'LL THINK OF SOMETHING! I KNOW WE WILL!
2-25
YOUNG & DRAKE
© 1996 by King Features Syndicate, Inc. World rights reserved.

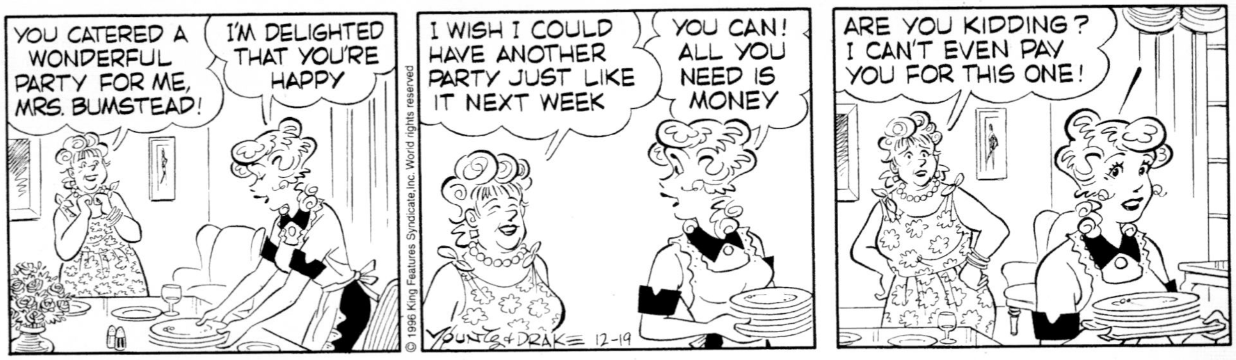
YOU CATERED A WONDERFUL PARTY FOR ME, MRS. BUMSTEAD!
I'M DELIGHTED THAT YOU'RE HAPPY
© 1996 King Features Syndicate, Inc. World rights reserved
I WISH I COULD HAVE ANOTHER PARTY JUST LIKE IT NEXT WEEK
YOU CAN! ALL YOU NEED IS MONEY
YOUNG & DRAKE 12-19
ARE YOU KIDDING? I CAN'T EVEN PAY YOU FOR THIS ONE!

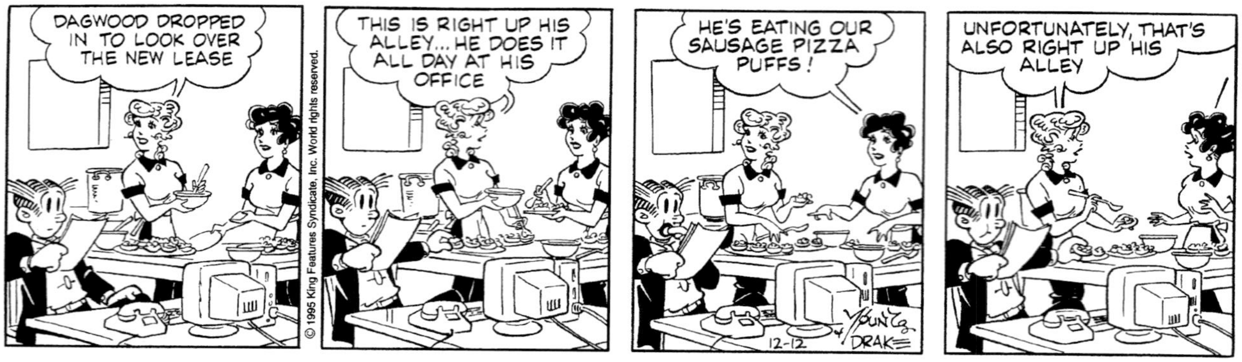

DAGWOOD DROPPED IN TO LOOK OVER THE NEW LEASE
© 1995 King Features Syndicate, Inc. World rights reserved.
THIS IS RIGHT UP HIS ALLEY... HE DOES IT ALL DAY AT HIS OFFICE
HE'S EATING OUR SAUSAGE PIZZA PUFFS!
12-12
YOUNG & DRAKE
UNFORTUNATELY, THAT'S ALSO RIGHT UP HIS ALLEY

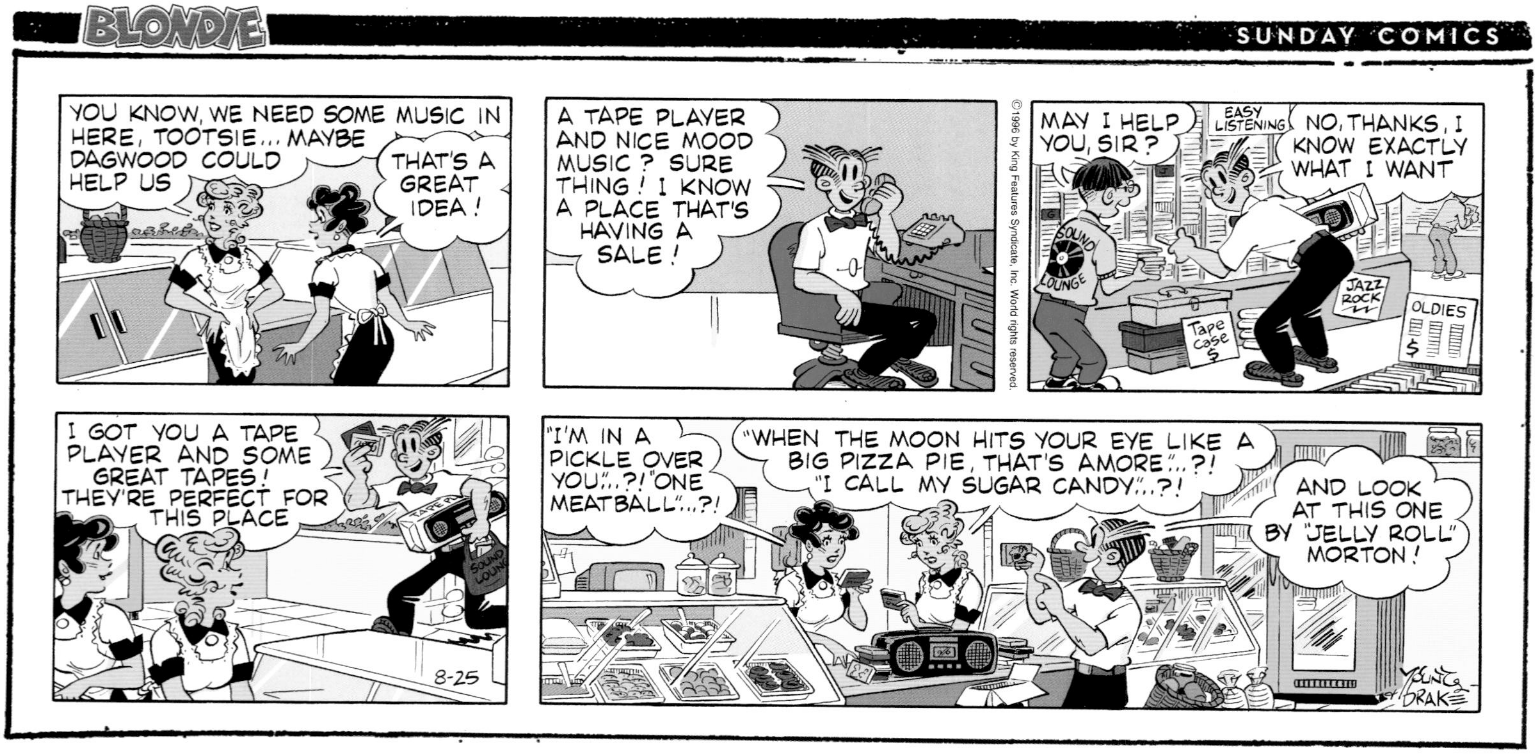

BLONDIE
SUNDAY COMICS
YOU KNOW, WE NEED SOME MUSIC IN HERE, TOOTSIE... MAYBE DAGWOOD COULD HELP US
THAT'S A GREAT IDEA!
A TAPE PLAYER AND NICE MOOD MUSIC? SURE THING! I KNOW A PLACE THAT'S HAVING A SALE!
© 1996 by King Features Syndicate, Inc. World rights reserved.
MAY I HELP YOU, SIR?
EASY LISTENING
NO, THANKS, I KNOW EXACTLY WHAT I WANT
SOUND LOUNGE
JAZZ ROCK
Tape case $
OLDIES $
I GOT YOU A TAPE PLAYER AND SOME GREAT TAPES! THEY'RE PERFECT FOR THIS PLACE
8-25
"I'M IN A PICKLE OVER YOU"..?!"ONE MEATBALL"..?!
"WHEN THE MOON HITS YOUR EYE LIKE A BIG PIZZA PIE, THAT'S AMORE"..?! "I CALL MY SUGAR CANDY"..?!
AND LOOK AT THIS ONE BY "JELLY ROLL" MORTON!
YOUNG & DRAKE

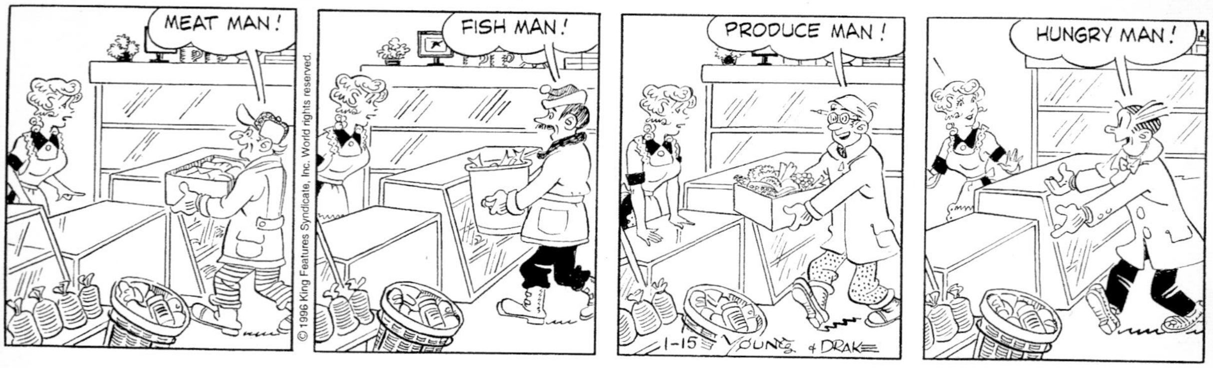

MEAT MAN!
© 1996 King Features Syndicate, Inc. World rights reserved.
FISH MAN!
PRODUCE MAN!
1-15 YOUNG & DRAKE
HUNGRY MAN!

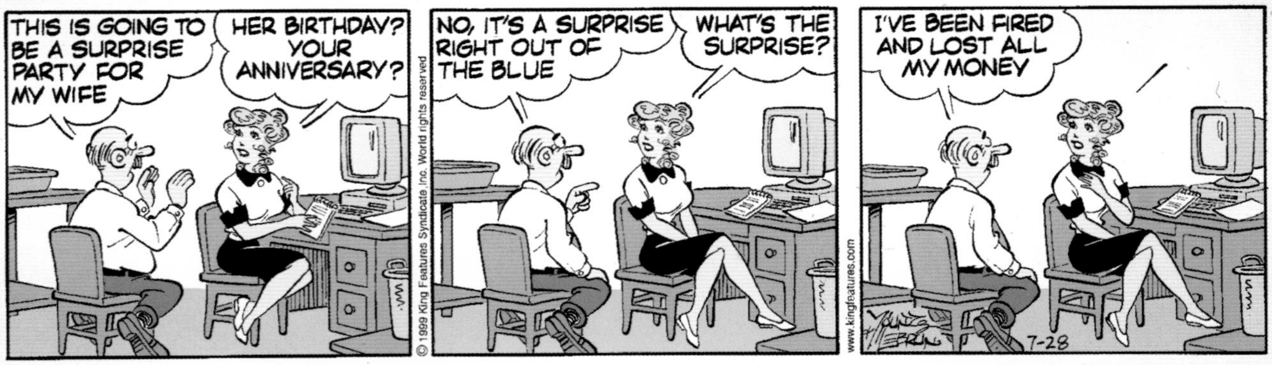
THIS IS GOING TO BE A SURPRISE PARTY FOR MY WIFE
HER BIRTHDAY? YOUR ANNIVERSARY?
NO, IT'S A SURPRISE RIGHT OUT OF THE BLUE
WHAT'S THE SURPRISE?
I'VE BEEN FIRED AND LOST ALL MY MONEY
© 1999 King Features Syndicate, Inc. World rights reserved
www.kingfeatures.com
7-28

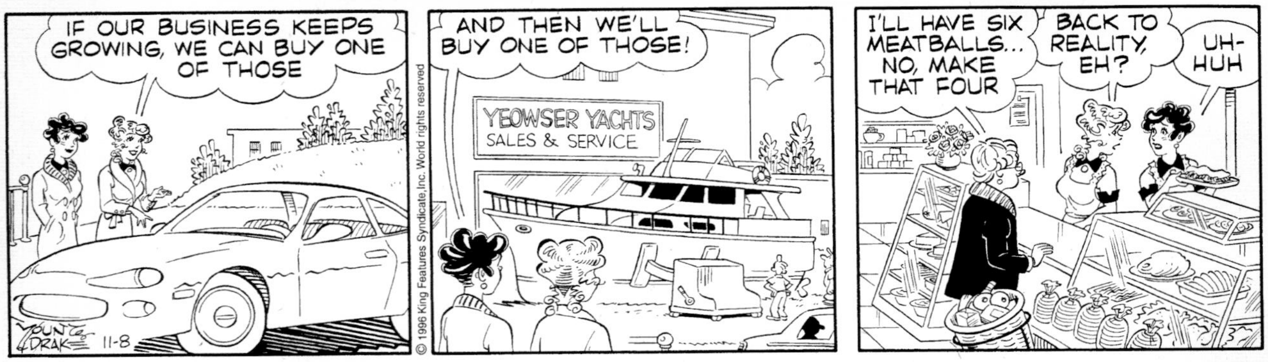
IF OUR BUSINESS KEEPS GROWING, WE CAN BUY ONE OF THOSE
11-8
AND THEN WE'LL BUY ONE OF THOSE!
YEOWSER YACHTS
SALES & SERVICE
© 1996 King Features Syndicate, Inc. World rights reserved
I'LL HAVE SIX MEATBALLS... NO, MAKE THAT FOUR
BACK TO REALITY, EH?
UH-HUH

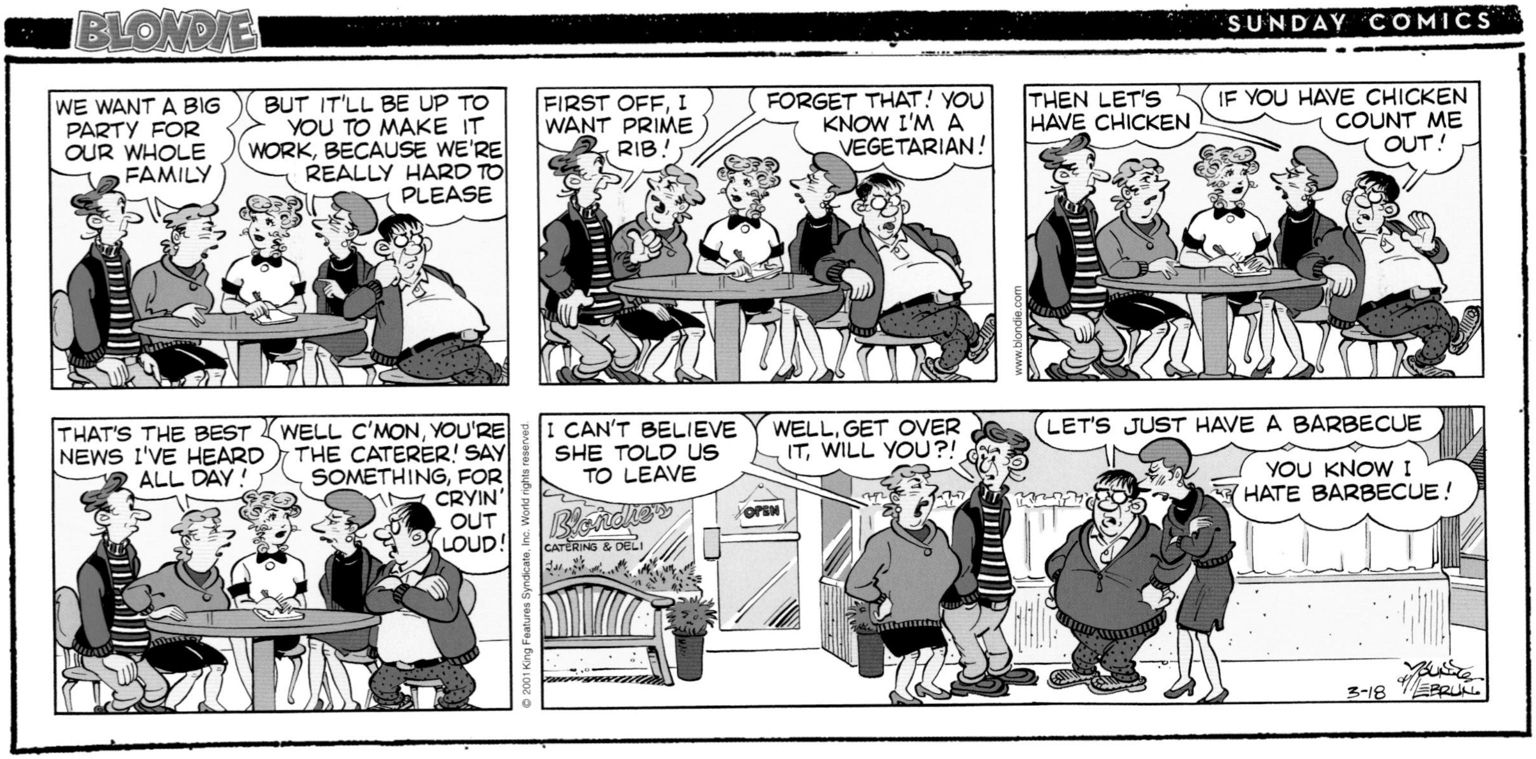
BLONDIE
SUNDAY COMICS
WE WANT A BIG PARTY FOR OUR WHOLE FAMILY
BUT IT'LL BE UP TO YOU TO MAKE IT WORK, BECAUSE WE'RE REALLY HARD TO PLEASE
FIRST OFF, I WANT PRIME RIB!
FORGET THAT! YOU KNOW I'M A VEGETARIAN!
THEN LET'S HAVE CHICKEN
IF YOU HAVE CHICKEN COUNT ME OUT!
www.blondie.com
THAT'S THE BEST NEWS I'VE HEARD ALL DAY!
WELL C'MON, YOU'RE THE CATERER! SAY SOMETHING, FOR CRYIN' OUT LOUD!
© 2001 King Features Syndicate, Inc. World rights reserved.
I CAN'T BELIEVE SHE TOLD US TO LEAVE
WELL, GET OVER IT, WILL YOU?!
LET'S JUST HAVE A BARBECUE
YOU KNOW I HATE BARBECUE!
Blondie's
CATERING & DELI
OPEN
3-18

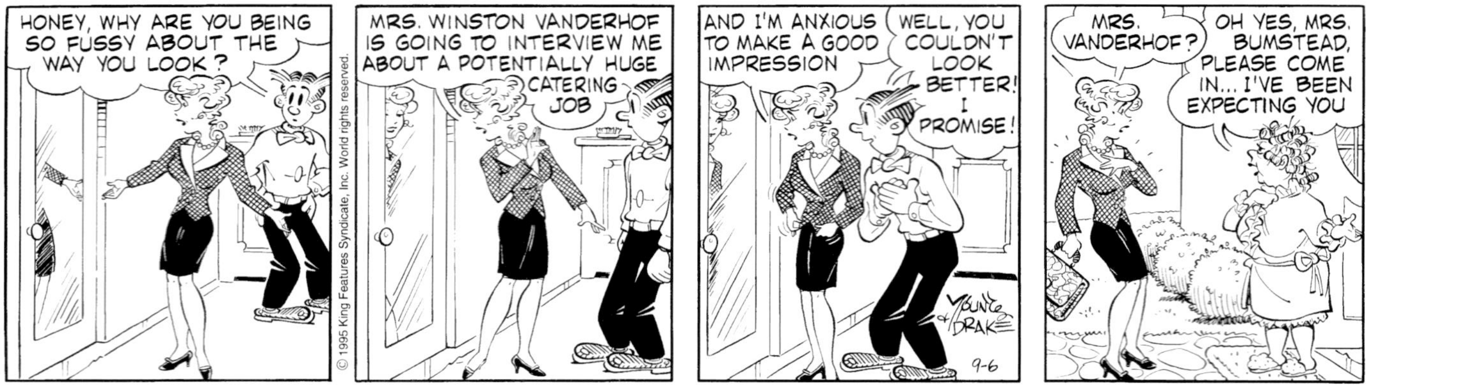
HONEY, WHY ARE YOU BEING SO FUSSY ABOUT THE WAY YOU LOOK?
© 1995 King Features Syndicate, Inc. World rights reserved.
MRS. WINSTON VANDERHOF IS GOING TO INTERVIEW ME ABOUT A POTENTIALLY HUGE CATERING JOB
AND I'M ANXIOUS TO MAKE A GOOD IMPRESSION
WELL, YOU COULDN'T LOOK BETTER! I PROMISE!
YOUNG & DRAKE
9-6
MRS. VANDERHOF?
OH YES, MRS. BUMSTEAD, PLEASE COME IN... I'VE BEEN EXPECTING YOU

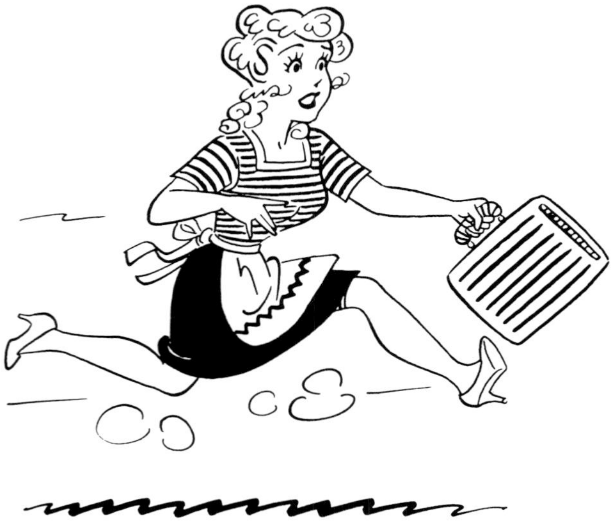

The transition from home to work was one that this unflappable lady took in stride.

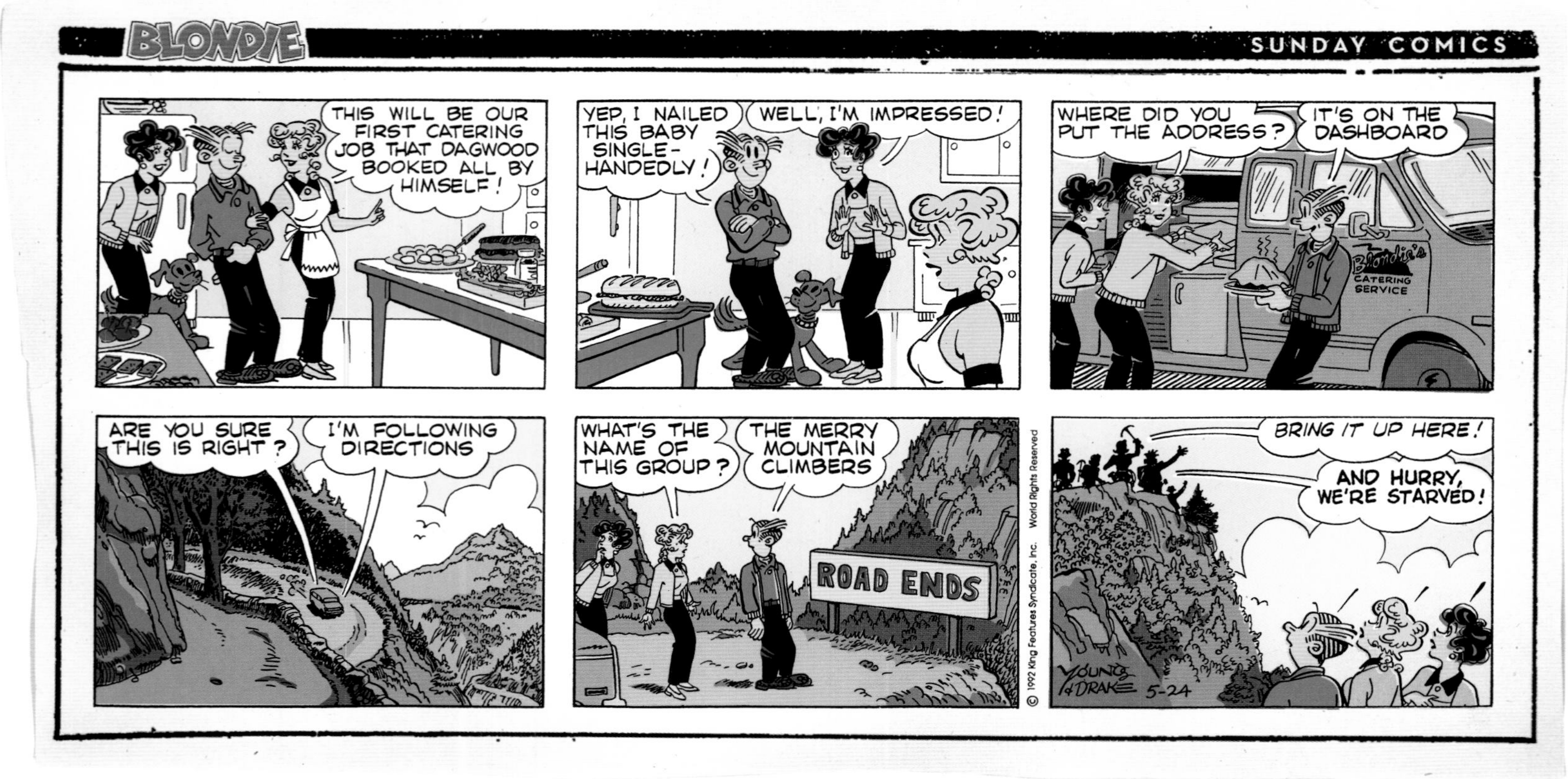
BLONDIE
SUNDAY COMICS
THIS WILL BE OUR FIRST CATERING JOB THAT DAGWOOD BOOKED ALL BY HIMSELF!
YEP, I NAILED THIS BABY SINGLE-HANDEDLY!
WELL, I'M IMPRESSED!
WHERE DID YOU PUT THE ADDRESS?
IT'S ON THE DASHBOARD
Blondie's CATERING SERVICE
ARE YOU SURE THIS IS RIGHT?
I'M FOLLOWING DIRECTIONS
WHAT'S THE NAME OF THIS GROUP?
THE MERRY MOUNTAIN CLIMBERS
ROAD ENDS
© 1992 King Features Syndicate, Inc. World Rights Reserved
BRING IT UP HERE!
AND HURRY, WE'RE STARVED!
YOUNG & DRAKE
5-24

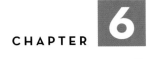

Here is a selection of Dean's favorite strips that deal with everyday situations

CHAPTER 6

FAVORITE STRIPS

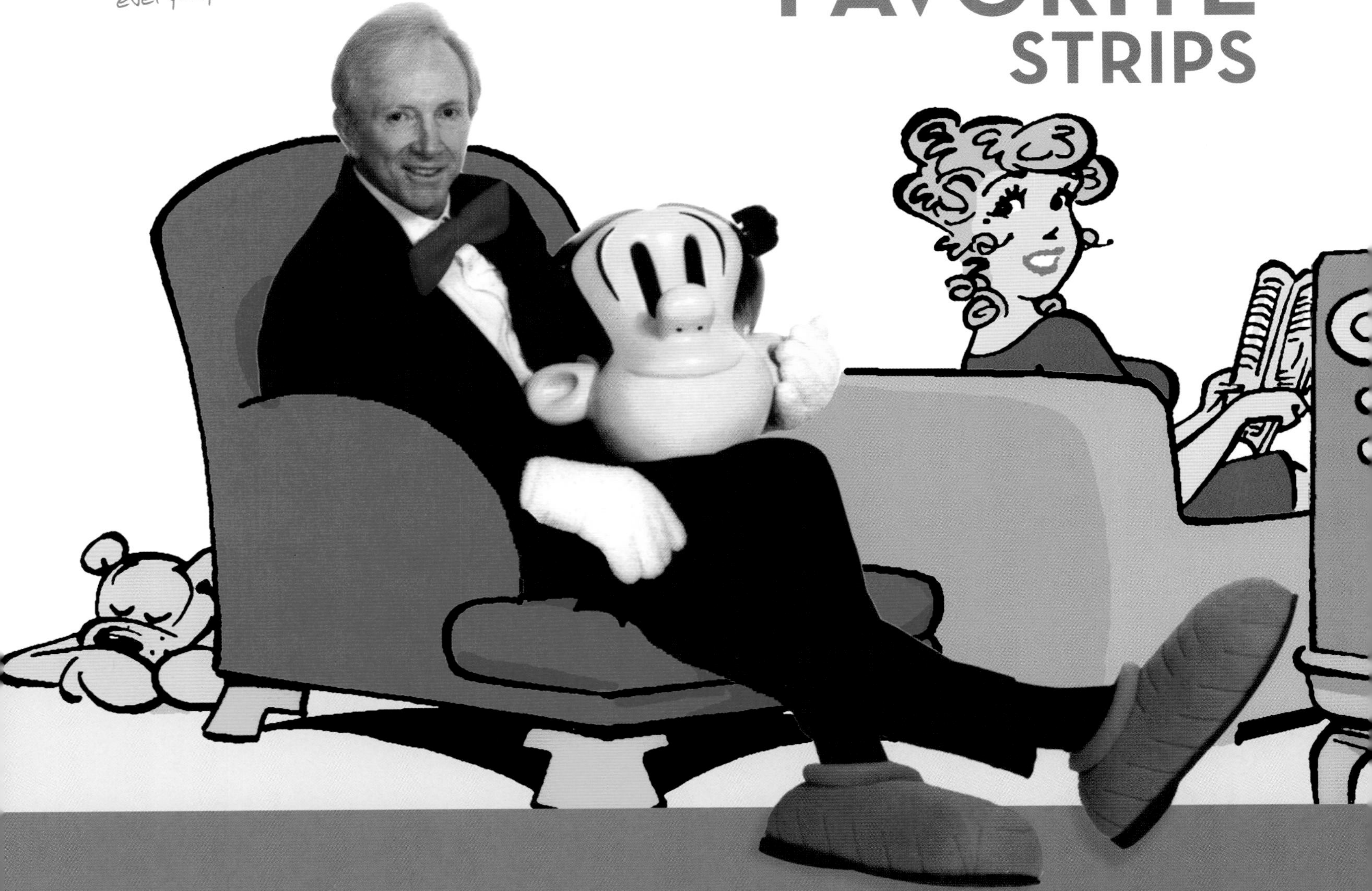

The themes that have been constant in the history of *Blondie*—eating, sleeping, making a living, and raising children—are the focus of most of its thousands of strips and the source of countless jokes, gags, and one-liners. But as the characters and the comic strip have grown, so too have the situations they find themselves in, from the daily car pool to the catering shop.

Each new scenario has presented an opportunity to create new characters—like carpoolers Dwitzel Tweezer and Claudia, the no-nonsense attorney; and the endless parade of kooky clients that come knocking on Blondie's door at the catering shop—and explore a new twist on the Bumstead brand of humor.

"I want to do new stuff that people can relate to, so I keep updating the comic strip," says Dean Young. "I think it's important in the world today that we are current in our thinking."

Of course, some stalwart setups and backdrops have remained comical since the early days. The lunch counter, for example, where the special always seems to come with a side of too-honest-for-its-own-good service. Good plumbers will always be hard to come by and expensive to work with. And while traveling salesmen are an extinct breed these days, telephone solicitors are as prevalent as ever (though they are harder to kick out the door). And Dagwood and his family still interact with a variety of service personnel and professionals, from supermarket managers to pet store employees to dentists and doctors—none of whom know what they're in for when a Bumstead walks in the door.

> **"The themes that have been constant in the history of *Blondie*—eating, sleeping, making a living, and raising children—are the focus of most of its thousands of strips and the source of countless jokes, gags, and one-liners."**

Finding the humor in these everyday situations is as much a *Blondie* trademark as Dagwood's screwy hair. Here is a selection of Dean's favorite strips that deal with the problems that everyone encounters. Hopefully, next time you find yourself stuck with something similar, you'll be more likely to laugh it off.

ROUGH TIME SHAVING THIS MORNING?
I JUST COULDN'T GET MYSELF TOGETHER
FOR SAFETY'S SAKE, YOU SHOULD SWITCH TO AN ELECTRIC RAZOR
THAT'S WHAT I'M USING NOW

HONK
HONK
HONK

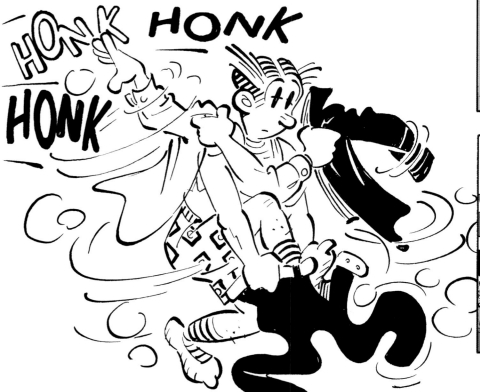

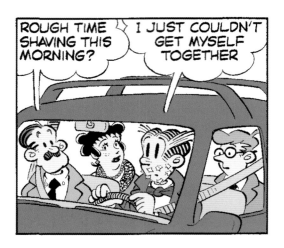

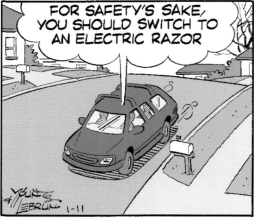

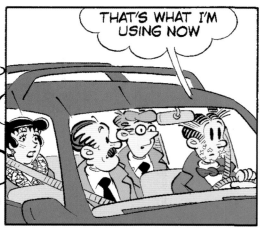

IT'S A PRESENT TO YOU FROM YOUR CARPOOL
I WONDER WHAT IT COULD BE?
OPEN IT UP AND LET'S SEE
I THINK THEY'RE TRYING TO TELL YOU SOMETHING

WELL, YOU WERE ON TIME FOR ONCE... WAY TO GO!
THANKS, I--- WAIT! GO BACK! I FORGOT MY BRIEFCASE!
I KNEW IT WAS TOO GOOD TO BE TRUE
OH, WE'VE ONLY LOST TWO MINUTES
CAN YOU BELIEVE IT? I FORGOT TO EAT MY CEREAL, TOO

BLONDIE'S AFRAID I'M GOING TO FORGET OUR ANNIVERSARY THIS WEEK
WHAT MAKES YOU THINK THAT?
OH, JUST A HUNCH
THREE MORE DAYS!

ALL ABOARD!
ALL HANDS PREPARE TO SHOVE OFF
ALL ASHORE WHO'S GOING ASHORE!
I HATE IT WHEN HE WATCHES THOSE DUMB LATE-NIGHT SEA MOVIES

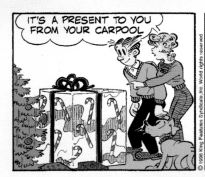

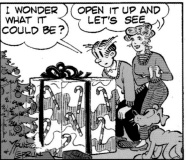

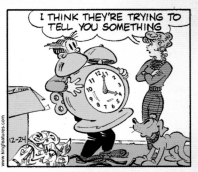

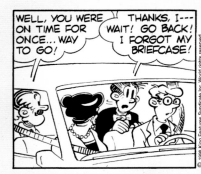

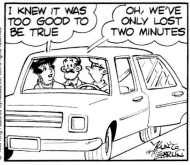

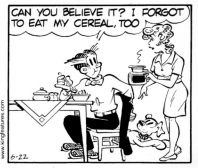

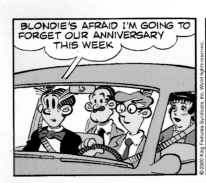

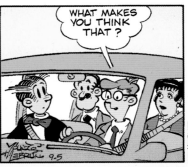

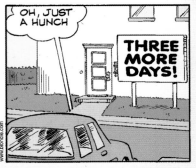

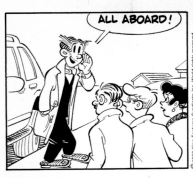

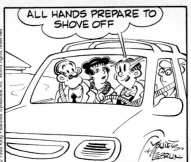

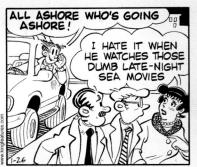

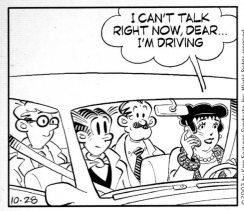

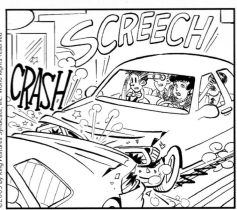

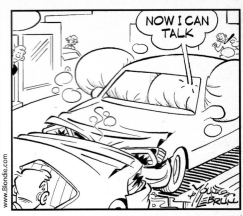

I CAN'T TALK RIGHT NOW, DEAR... I'M DRIVING
10-28
©2003 by King Features Syndicate, Inc. World Rights reserved
SCREECH
CRASH
www.Blondie.com
NOW I CAN TALK
YOUNG & LEBRUN

BLONDIE
SUNDAY COMICS
IS YOUR ARM OKAY, DAGWOOD?
IT'S FINE... THANKS FOR ASKING
www.blondie.com
CAN I GIVE YOU A HAND CARRYING THOSE FILES, DAG?
SURE, THANKS
1-21
NEED ANY HELP WITH ANYTHING, DAGWOOD?
NO THANKS, I GUESS I'M DOING ALL RIGHT
BUMSTEAD, WHY DON'T YOU JUST LEAVE EARLY AND GIVE YOUR ARM A REST?
THANKS, BOSS...I APPRECIATE IT
© 2007 King Features Syndicate Inc. World Rights Reserved.
YOUNG & MARSHALL
ANOTHER GREAT STRIKE, DAGWOOD! YOU'RE REALLY BURNING UP THE WOOD!
I KNOW! I PAMPERED MY ARM ALL DAY SO I'D BE AT THE TOP OF MY GAME TONIGHT

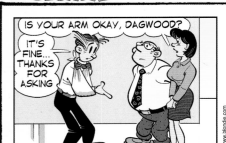

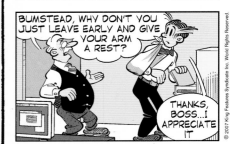

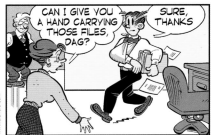

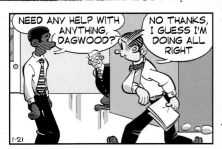

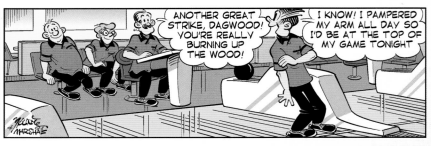

"No wonder Dagwood was inducted into the Detroit Bowling Hall of Fame on November 5, 2000."

I'M CERTAINLY NOT COMPLAINING...
© 2002 by King Features Syndicate, Inc. World Rights reserved
AND I'M NOT A WHINER...
YOUNG & LEBRUN
www.Blondie.com
8-21
BUT WOULD YOU MIND TAKING THAT SIGN OUT OF THE REAR WINDOW?!
BABY ON BOARD

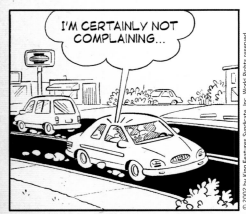

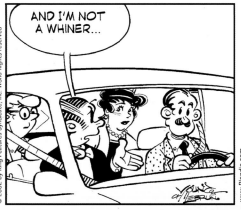

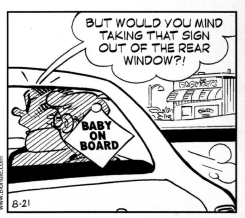

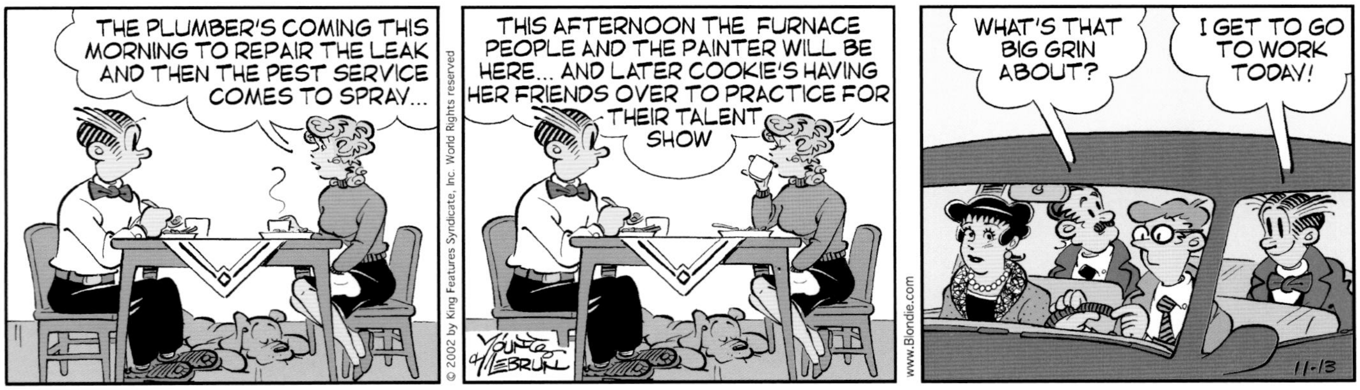
THE PLUMBER'S COMING THIS MORNING TO REPAIR THE LEAK AND THEN THE PEST SERVICE COMES TO SPRAY...
© 2002 by King Features Syndicate, Inc. World Rights reserved
THIS AFTERNOON THE FURNACE PEOPLE AND THE PAINTER WILL BE HERE... AND LATER COOKIE'S HAVING HER FRIENDS OVER TO PRACTICE FOR THEIR TALENT SHOW
www.Blondie.com
WHAT'S THAT BIG GRIN ABOUT?
I GET TO GO TO WORK TODAY!
11-13

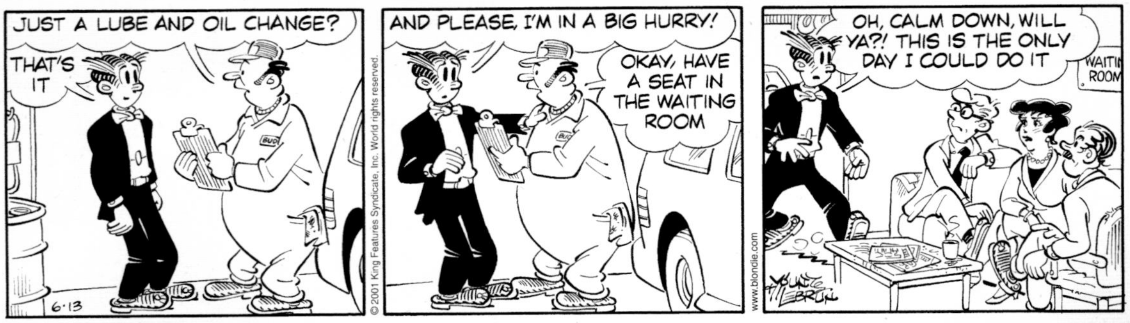
JUST A LUBE AND OIL CHANGE?
THAT'S IT
6-13
© 2001 King Features Syndicate, Inc. World rights reserved.
AND PLEASE, I'M IN A BIG HURRY!
OKAY, HAVE A SEAT IN THE WAITING ROOM
www.blondie.com
OH, CALM DOWN, WILL YA?! THIS IS THE ONLY DAY I COULD DO IT
WAITIN ROOM

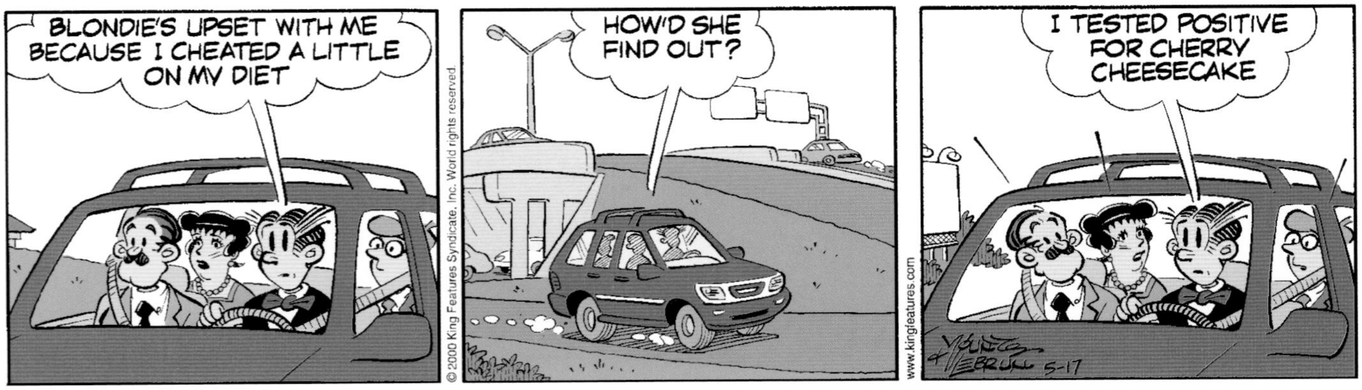
BLONDIE'S UPSET WITH ME BECAUSE I CHEATED A LITTLE ON MY DIET
© 2000 King Features Syndicate, Inc. World rights reserved.
HOW'D SHE FIND OUT?
www.kingfeatures.com
I TESTED POSITIVE FOR CHERRY CHEESECAKE
5-17

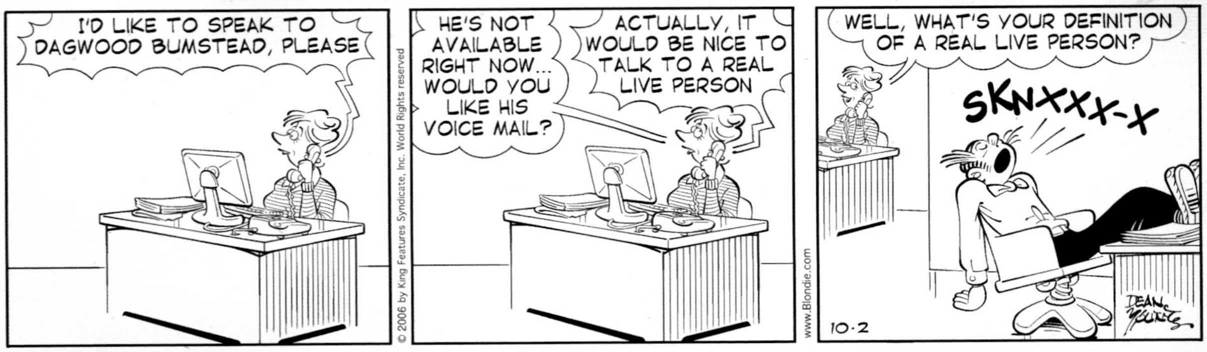
I'D LIKE TO SPEAK TO DAGWOOD BUMSTEAD, PLEASE
© 2006 by King Features Syndicate, Inc. World Rights reserved
HE'S NOT AVAILABLE RIGHT NOW... WOULD YOU LIKE HIS VOICE MAIL?
ACTUALLY, IT WOULD BE NICE TO TALK TO A REAL LIVE PERSON
www.Blondie.com
WELL, WHAT'S YOUR DEFINITION OF A REAL LIVE PERSON?
SKNXXX-X
10-2

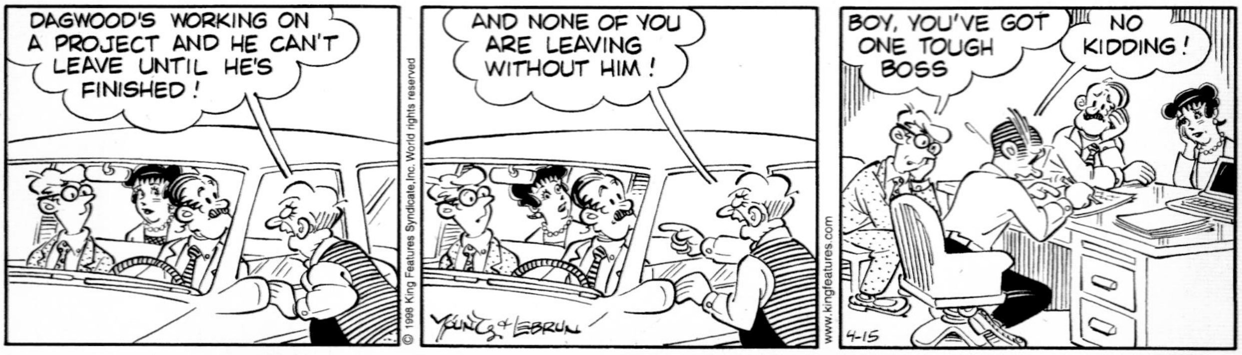
DAGWOOD'S WORKING ON A PROJECT AND HE CAN'T LEAVE UNTIL HE'S FINISHED!
AND NONE OF YOU ARE LEAVING WITHOUT HIM!
BOY, YOU'VE GOT ONE TOUGH BOSS
NO KIDDING!
© 1998 King Features Syndicate, Inc. World rights reserved
YOUNG & LEBRUN
www.kingfeatures.com
4-15

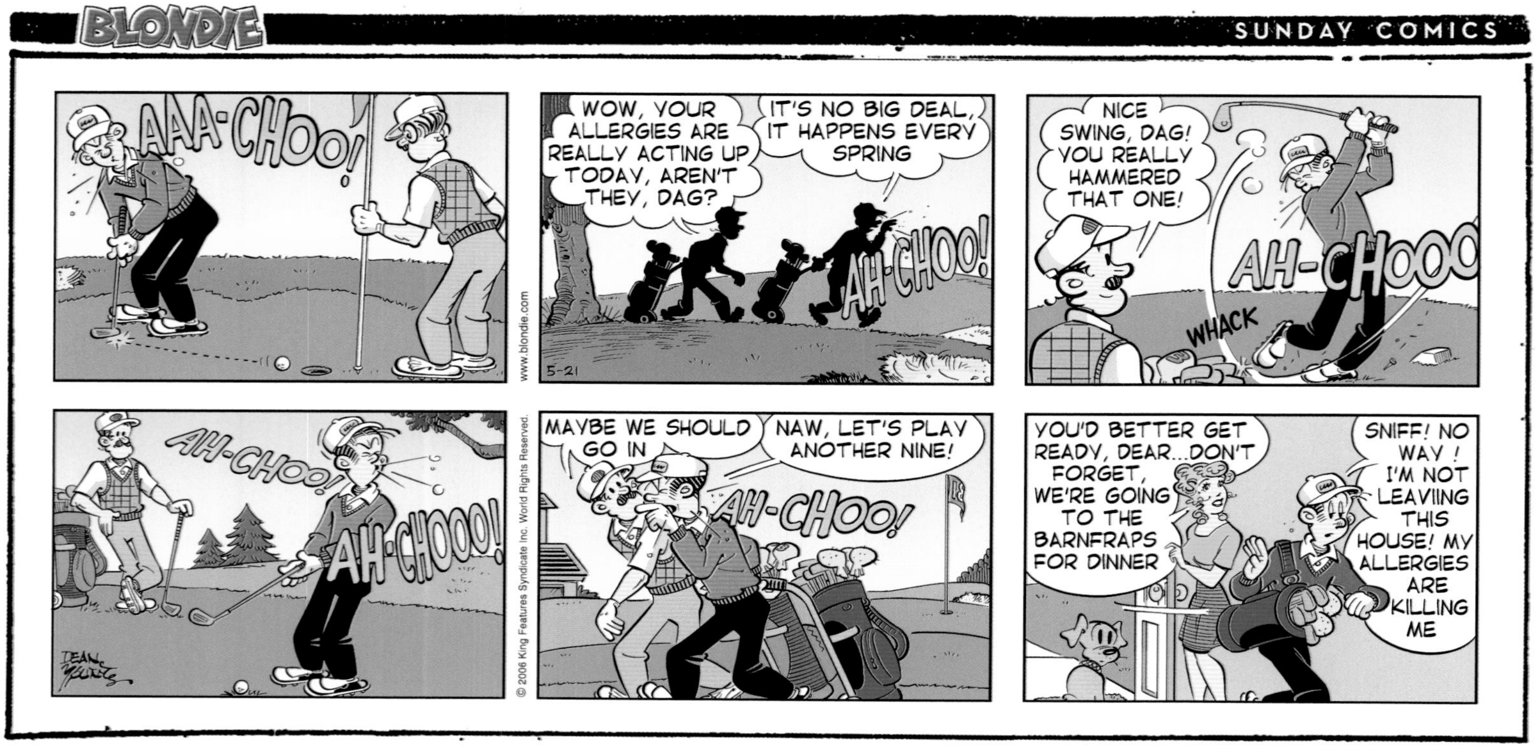
BLONDIE
SUNDAY COMICS
AAA-CHOO!
WOW, YOUR ALLERGIES ARE REALLY ACTING UP TODAY, AREN'T THEY, DAG?
IT'S NO BIG DEAL, IT HAPPENS EVERY SPRING
AH-CHOO!
NICE SWING, DAG! YOU REALLY HAMMERED THAT ONE!
AH-CHOOO
WHACK
AH-CHOO!
AH-CHOOO!
MAYBE WE SHOULD GO IN
NAW, LET'S PLAY ANOTHER NINE!
AH-CHOO!
YOU'D BETTER GET READY, DEAR...DON'T FORGET, WE'RE GOING TO THE BARNFRAPS FOR DINNER
SNIFF! NO WAY! I'M NOT LEAVIING THIS HOUSE! MY ALLERGIES ARE KILLING ME
DEAN YOUNG
www.blondie.com
5-21
© 2006 King Features Syndicate Inc. World Rights Reserved.

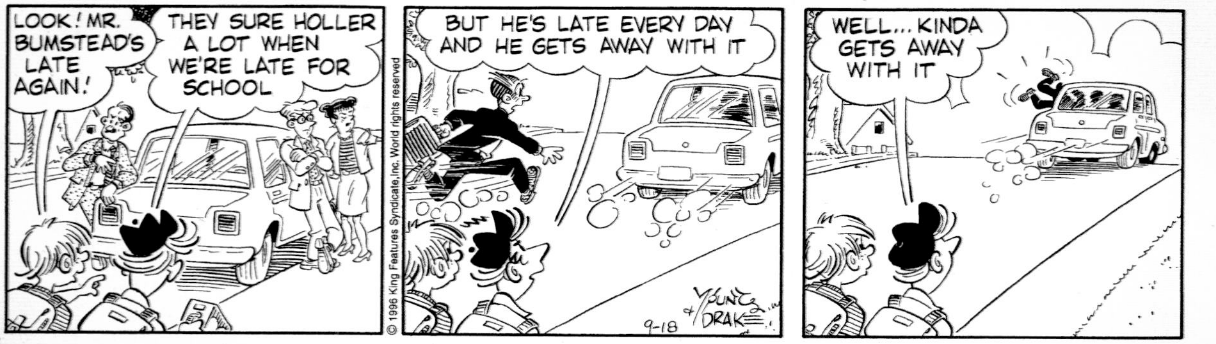
LOOK! MR. BUMSTEAD'S LATE AGAIN!
THEY SURE HOLLER A LOT WHEN WE'RE LATE FOR SCHOOL
BUT HE'S LATE EVERY DAY AND HE GETS AWAY WITH IT
WELL...KINDA GETS AWAY WITH IT
© 1996 King Features Syndicate, Inc. World rights reserved
9-18
YOUNG & DRAKE

"This strip was such a big hit! Readers loved it!"

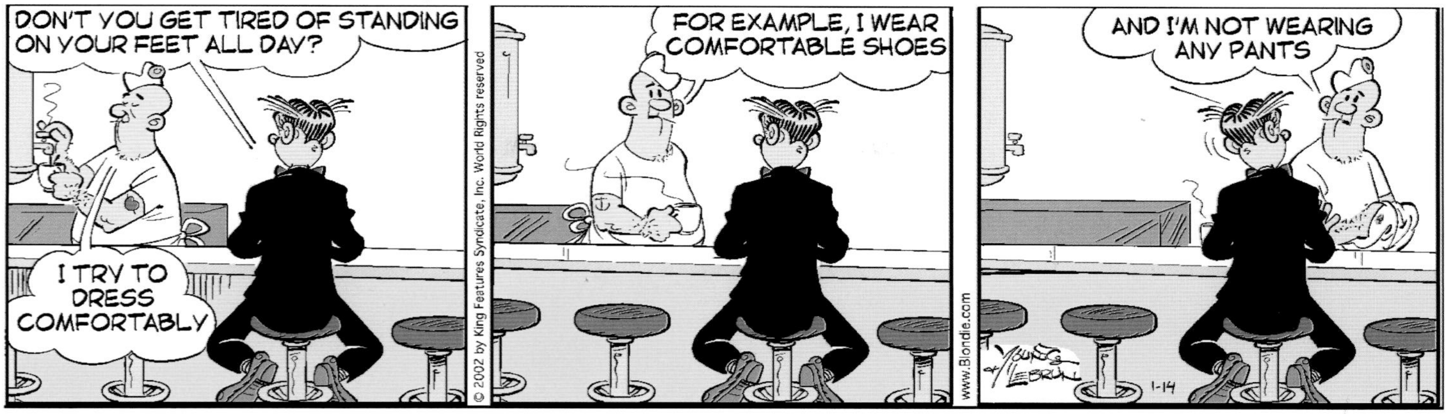

DON'T YOU GET TIRED OF STANDING ON YOUR FEET ALL DAY?
I TRY TO DRESS COMFORTABLY
© 2002 by King Features Syndicate, Inc. World Rights reserved
FOR EXAMPLE, I WEAR COMFORTABLE SHOES
www.Blondie.com
AND I'M NOT WEARING ANY PANTS
1-14

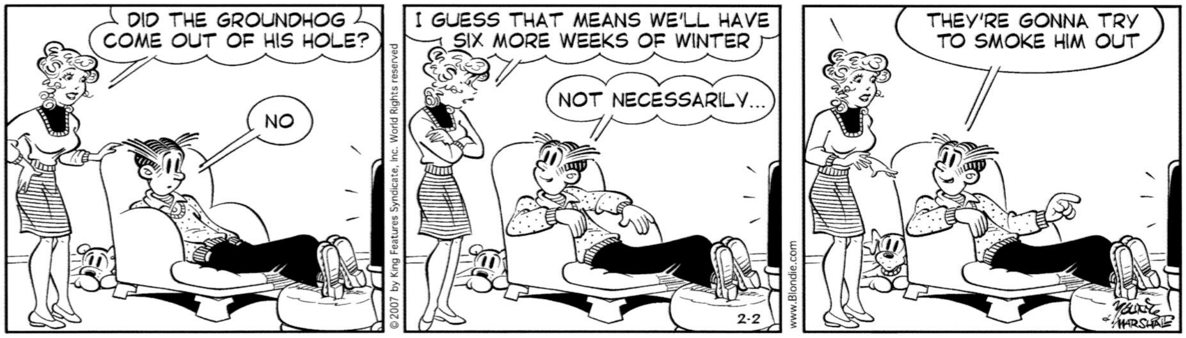

DID THE GROUNDHOG COME OUT OF HIS HOLE?
NO
© 2007 by King Features Syndicate, Inc. World Rights reserved
I GUESS THAT MEANS WE'LL HAVE SIX MORE WEEKS OF WINTER
NOT NECESSARILY...
2-2
www.Blondie.com
THEY'RE GONNA TRY TO SMOKE HIM OUT

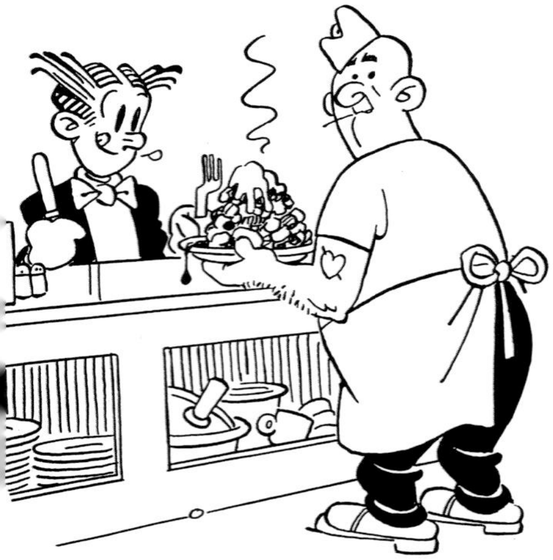

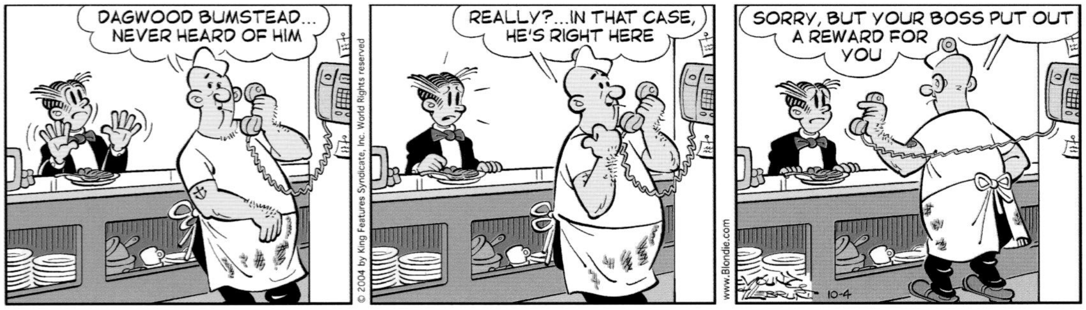

DAGWOOD BUMSTEAD... NEVER HEARD OF HIM
© 2004 by King Features Syndicate, Inc. World Rights reserved
REALLY?...IN THAT CASE, HE'S RIGHT HERE
www.Blondie.com
SORRY, BUT YOUR BOSS PUT OUT A REWARD FOR YOU
10-4

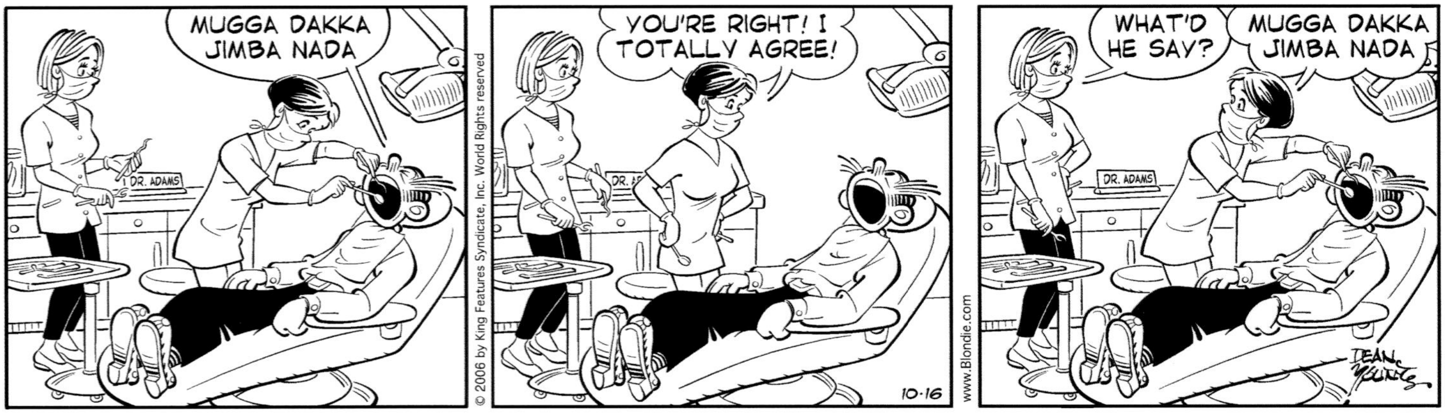

MUGGA DAKKA JIMBA NADA
DR. ADAMS
© 2006 by King Features Syndicate, Inc. World Rights reserved
YOU'RE RIGHT! I TOTALLY AGREE!
10-16
www.Blondie.com
WHAT'D HE SAY?
MUGGA DAKKA JIMBA NADA
DR. ADAMS

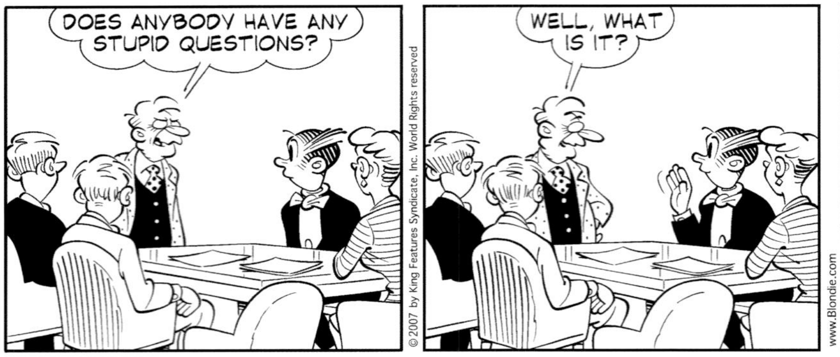
DOES ANYBODY HAVE ANY STUPID QUESTIONS?
WELL, WHAT IS IT?
HOW MANY STUPID QUESTIONS ARE WE ALLOWED TO ASK?
© 2007 by King Features Syndicate, Inc. World Rights reserved
www.Blondie.com
1-22

"It was a great honor for the United States Postal Service to select BLONDIE for one of its stamps." ☆

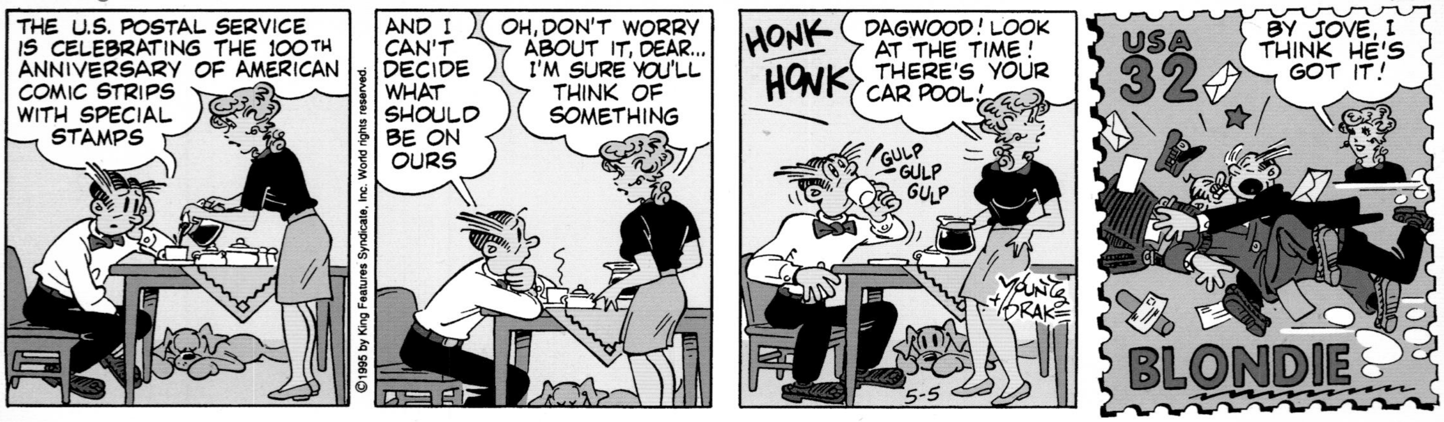
THE U.S. POSTAL SERVICE IS CELEBRATING THE 100TH ANNIVERSARY OF AMERICAN COMIC STRIPS WITH SPECIAL STAMPS
AND I CAN'T DECIDE WHAT SHOULD BE ON OURS
OH, DON'T WORRY ABOUT IT, DEAR... I'M SURE YOU'LL THINK OF SOMETHING
©1995 by King Features Syndicate, Inc. World rights reserved.
HONK
HONK
DAGWOOD! LOOK AT THE TIME! THERE'S YOUR CAR POOL!
GULP
GULP
GULP
5-5
USA
32
BY JOVE, I THINK HE'S GOT IT!
BLONDIE

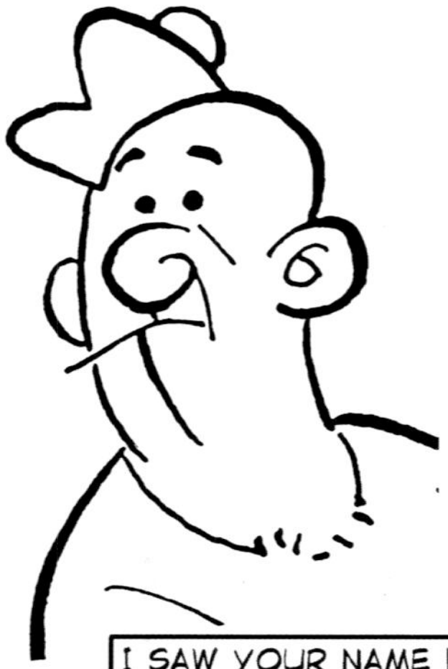

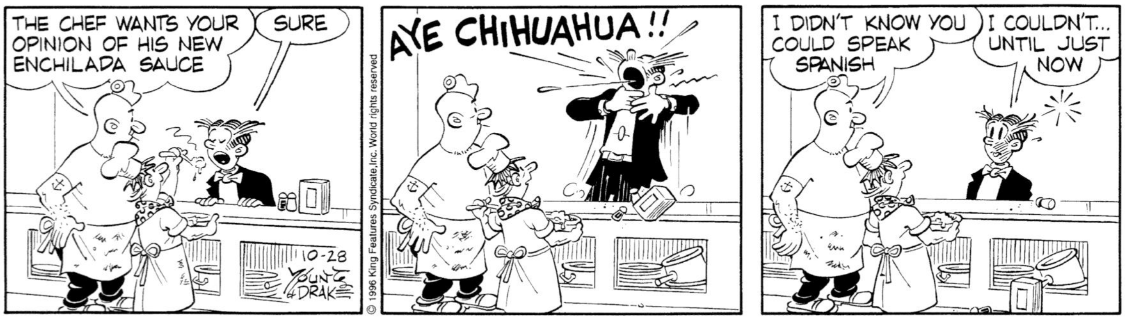
THE CHEF WANTS YOUR OPINION OF HIS NEW ENCHILADA SAUCE
SURE
10-28
© 1996 King Features Syndicate,Inc. World rights reserved
AYE CHIHUAHUA!!
I DIDN'T KNOW YOU COULD SPEAK SPANISH
I COULDN'T... UNTIL JUST NOW

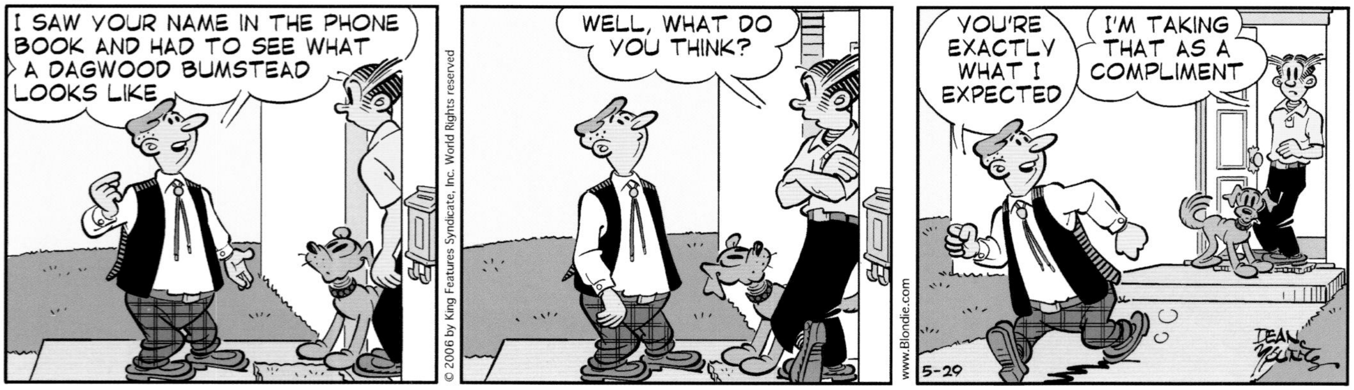
I SAW YOUR NAME IN THE PHONE BOOK AND HAD TO SEE WHAT A DAGWOOD BUMSTEAD LOOKS LIKE
© 2006 by King Features Syndicate, Inc. World Rights reserved
WELL, WHAT DO YOU THINK?
www.Blondie.com
5-29
YOU'RE EXACTLY WHAT I EXPECTED
I'M TAKING THAT AS A COMPLIMENT

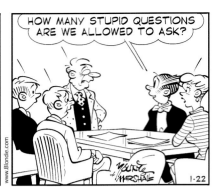

"Dagwood's hair is drawn that way to differentiate him from all the rest of the world. Without those famous cowlicks on his head, Dagwood just wouldn't be Dagwood."

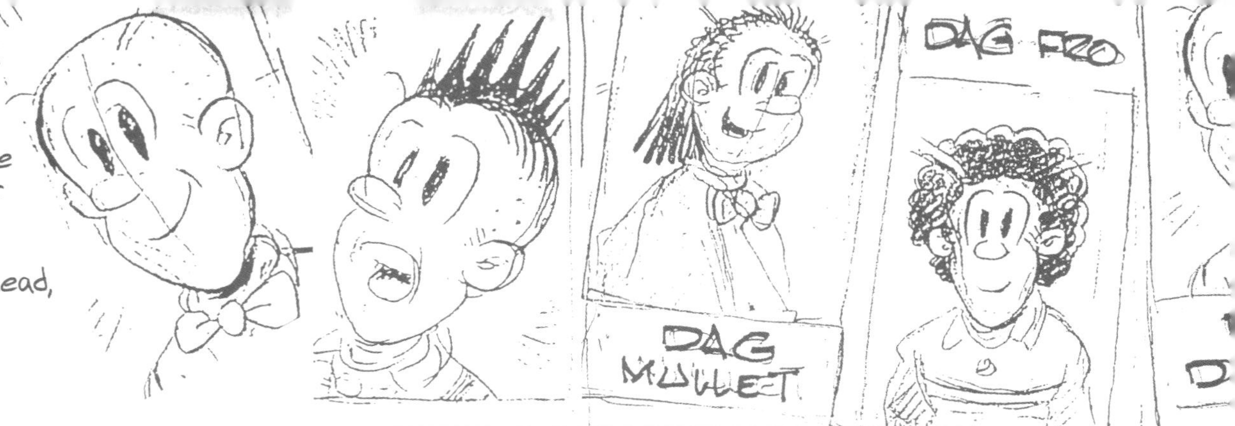

DAG FRO
DAG MULLET

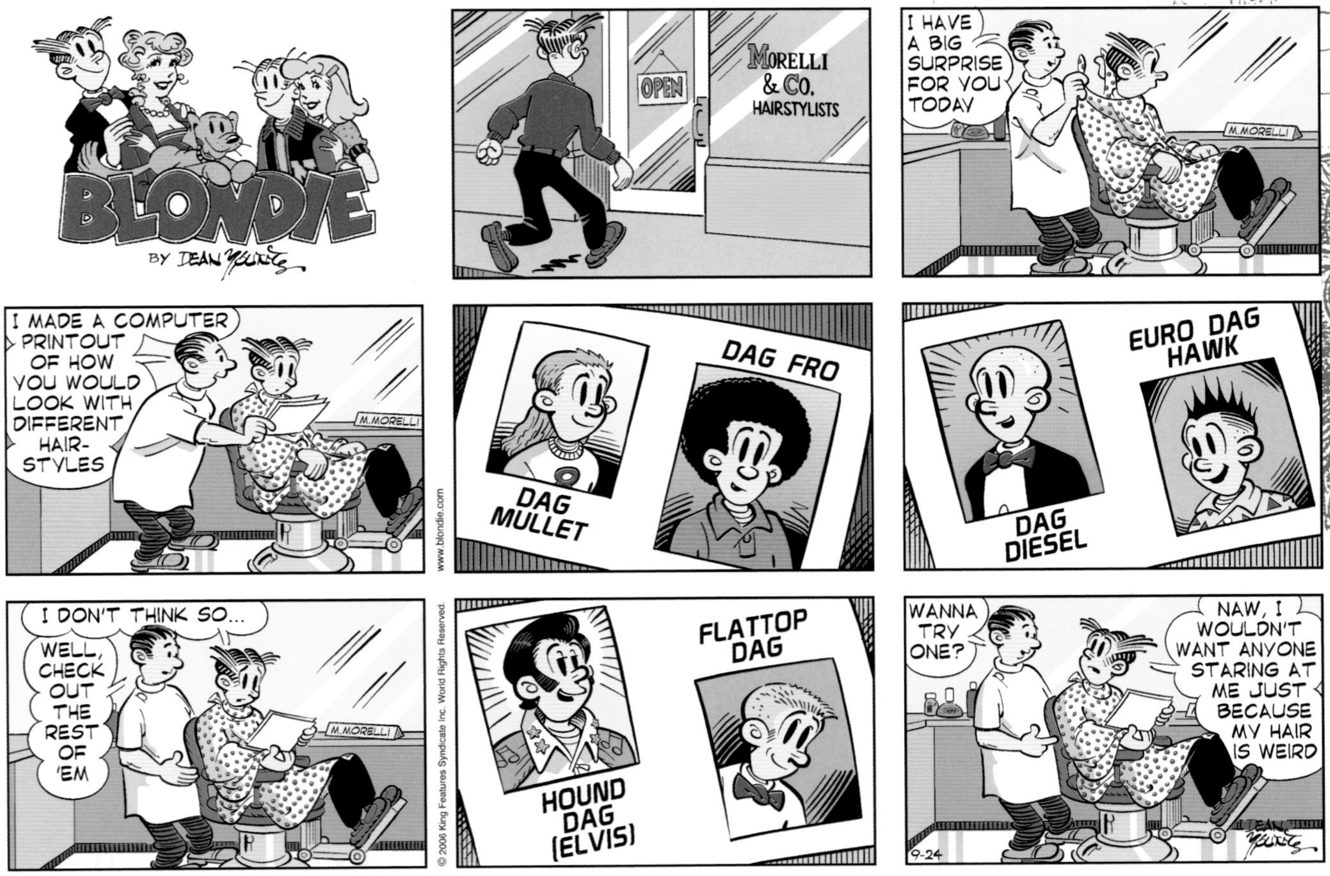

BLONDIE
BY DEAN YOUNG
OPEN
MORELLI & Co. HAIRSTYLISTS
I HAVE A BIG SURPRISE FOR YOU TODAY
M.MORELLI
I MADE A COMPUTER PRINTOUT OF HOW YOU WOULD LOOK WITH DIFFERENT HAIR-STYLES
M.MORELLI
DAG MULLET
DAG FRO
DAG DIESEL
EURO DAG HAWK
www.blondie.com
© 2006 King Features Syndicate Inc. World Rights Reserved.
I DON'T THINK SO...
WELL, CHECK OUT THE REST OF 'EM
M.MORELLI
HOUND DAG (ELVIS)
FLATTOP DAG
WANNA TRY ONE?
NAW, I WOULDN'T WANT ANYONE STARING AT ME JUST BECAUSE MY HAIR IS WEIRD
9-24
DEAN YOUNG

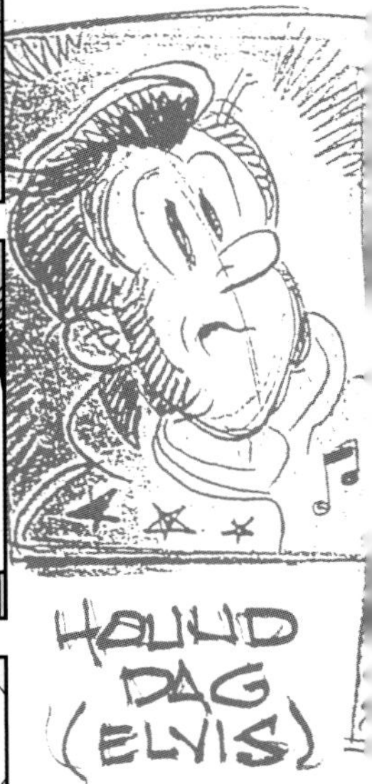

HOUND DAG (ELVIS)

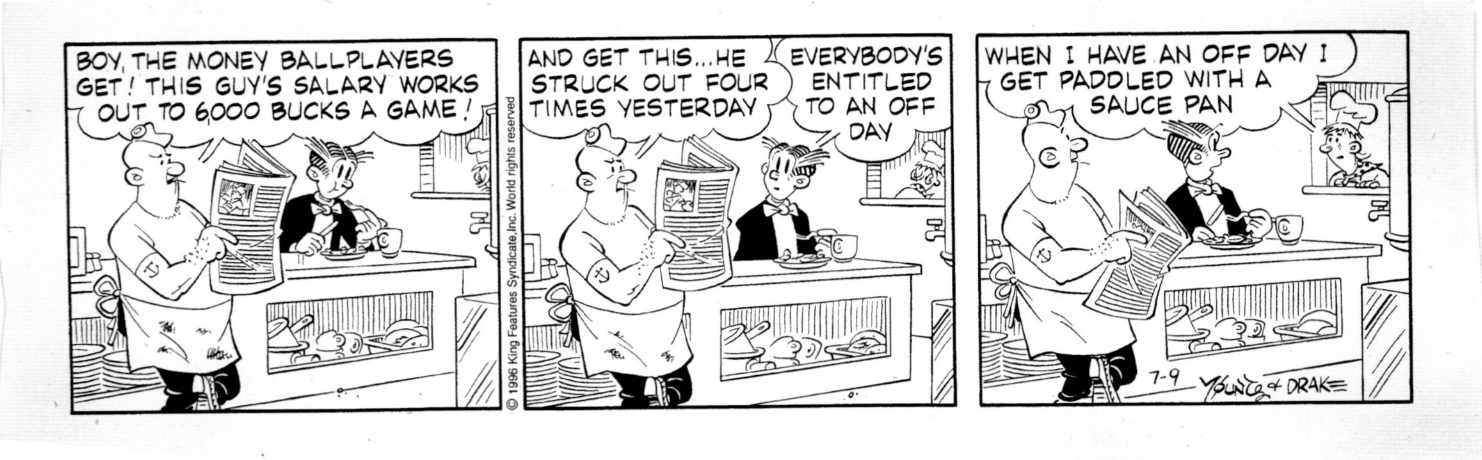

BOY, THE MONEY BALLPLAYERS GET! THIS GUY'S SALARY WORKS OUT TO 6,000 BUCKS A GAME!
© 1996 King Features Syndicate, Inc. World rights reserved
AND GET THIS... HE STRUCK OUT FOUR TIMES YESTERDAY
EVERYBODY'S ENTITLED TO AN OFF DAY
WHEN I HAVE AN OFF DAY I GET PADDLED WITH A SAUCE PAN
7-9
YOUNG & DRAKE

I PROMISED MY WIFE THAT I'D START EATING HEALTHIER FOODS
THEN YOU SHOULD TRY OUR FISH TODAY
© 1998 King Features Syndicate Inc. World rights reserved
NAW, I THINK FISH IS KINDA TASTELESS
IT'S NOT TASTELESS THE WAY WE DO OURS
WE FRY IT IN BACON FAT
1-6
YOUNG LEBRUN

THE COOK WANTS YOUR OPINION OF HIS NEW SAUCE
© 1998 King Features Syndicate Inc. World rights reserved
12-15
BLAAA-A
www.kingfeatures.com
I WANT A SECOND OPINION
YOUNG LEBRUN

THIS IS A WONDERFUL DAY! I WROTE A PERFECT CONTRACT AND I'M GETTING PROMOTED
© 1997 King Features Syndicate, Inc. World rights reserved
THAT'S GREAT! HOW ARE YOU GOING TO CELEBRATE?
WELL, FOR OPENERS, I'M GOING SOMEPLACE ELSE FOR LUNCH
YOUNG LEBRUN
10-21

LOU'S DINER...LOU SPEAKING
© 2006 by King Features Syndicate, Inc. World Rights reserved
YES, WE DELIVER...HANG ON FOR A MINUTE
4-10
www.Blondie.com
DO YOU MIND DROPPING SOMETHING OFF FOR ME ON YOUR WAY BACK TO WORK?
DEAN YOUNG

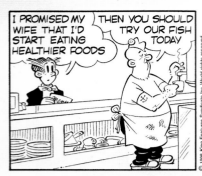

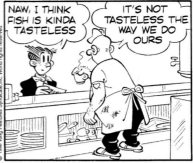

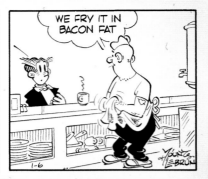

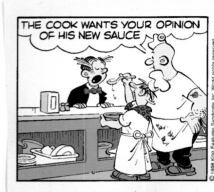

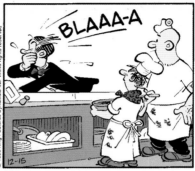

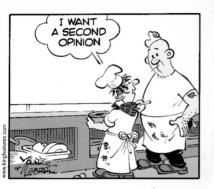

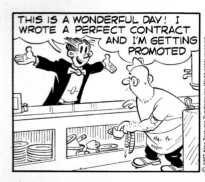

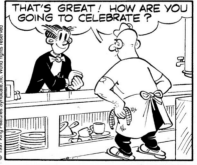

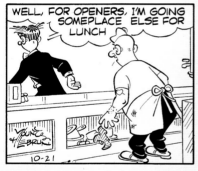

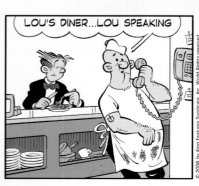

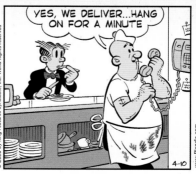

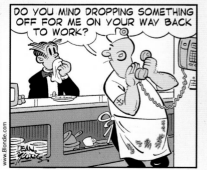

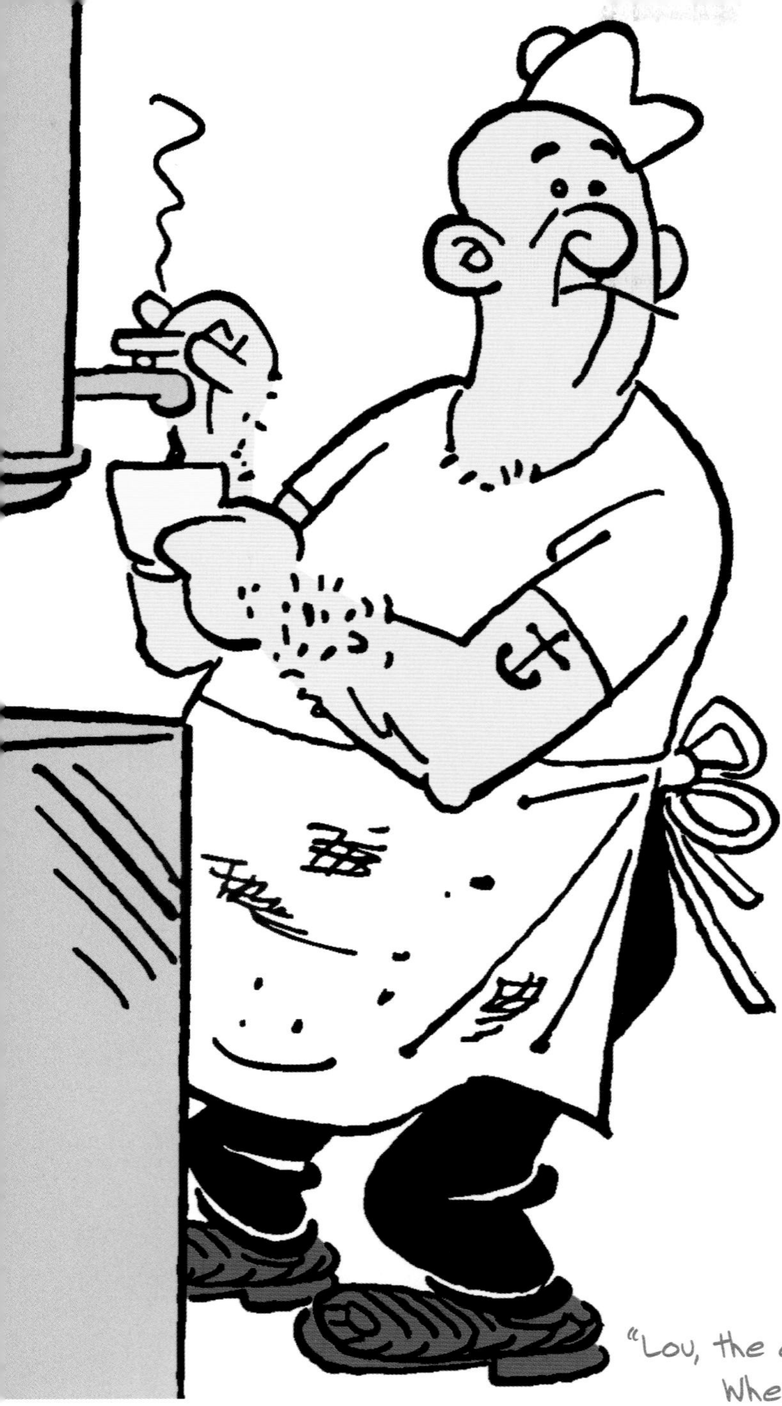

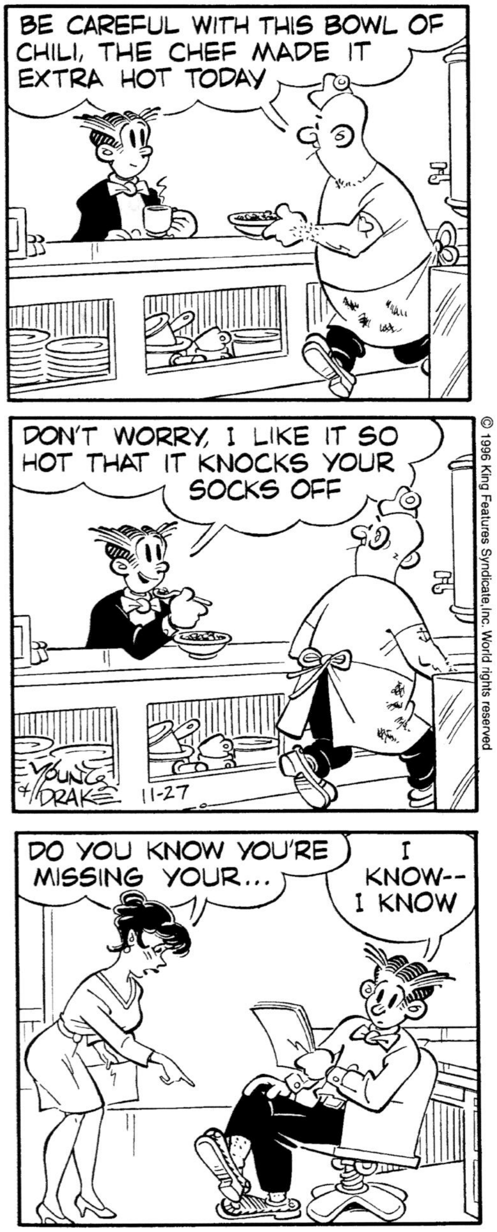

BE CAREFUL WITH THIS BOWL OF CHILI, THE CHEF MADE IT EXTRA HOT TODAY
DON'T WORRY, I LIKE IT SO HOT THAT IT KNOCKS YOUR SOCKS OFF
DO YOU KNOW YOU'RE MISSING YOUR...
I KNOW-- I KNOW

"Lou, the counterman, has been such a joy for me. When I'm desperate for a gag, he's my go-to guy!"

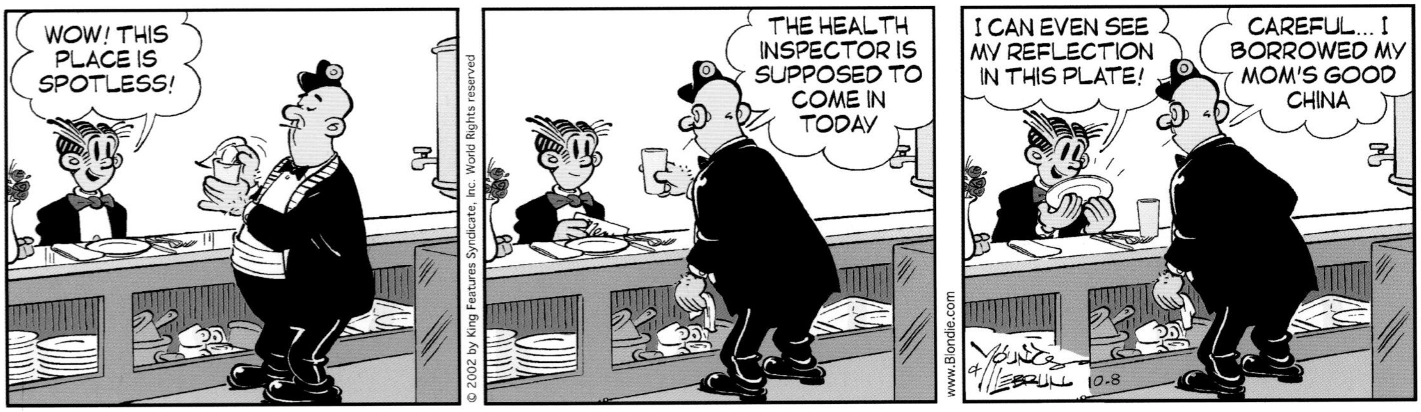

WOW! THIS PLACE IS SPOTLESS!
THE HEALTH INSPECTOR IS SUPPOSED TO COME IN TODAY
I CAN EVEN SEE MY REFLECTION IN THIS PLATE!
CAREFUL... I BORROWED MY MOM'S GOOD CHINA

HUH, I'VE NEVER USED THIS SELF-SERVE CHECKOUT BEFORE!
SELF-SERV
CHECKOU
© 2003 by King Features Syndicate, Inc. World Rights reserved
THIS IS EASY...JUST SCAN THE HAMMER AND SWIPE THE CREDIT CARD
BEEP
www.Blondie.com
LOOK, SOME GUY JUST PAID $553 FOR A HAMMER!
HE MUST'VE BEEN BUYING IT FOR THE PENTAGON

SINCE HURRICANE KATRINA, OUR INSURANCE COMPANY DOESN'T COVER THESE ITEMS ANYMORE
LONG INSURANCE COMPANY
© 2006 by King Features Syndicate, Inc. World Rights reserved
WELL, TELL ME WHAT YOU DO COVER
LONG INSURANCE COMPANY
www.Blondie.com
OUR TRACKS
LONG INSURANCE COMPANY

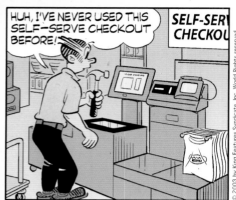

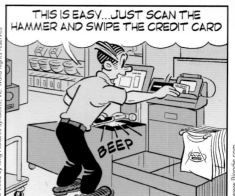

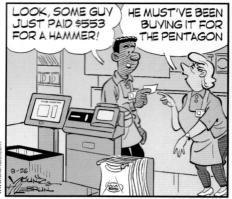

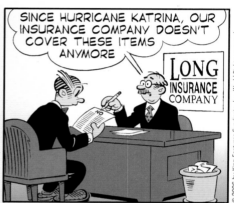

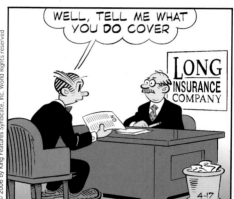

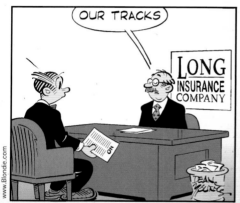

"I love doing new and current stuff because it keeps the strip fresh and up to date."

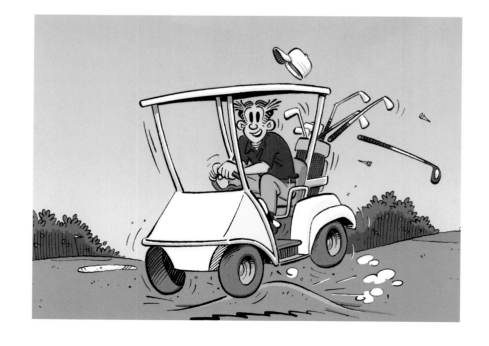

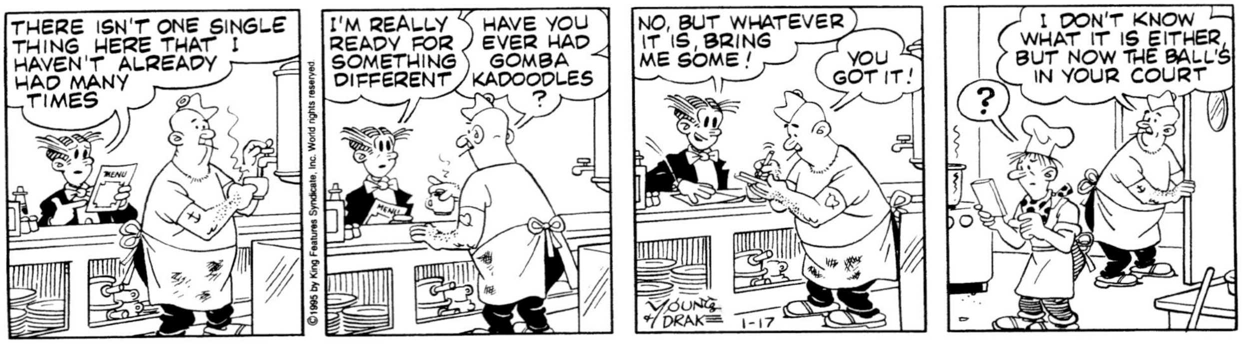
THERE ISN'T ONE SINGLE THING HERE THAT I HAVEN'T ALREADY HAD MANY TIMES
MENU
© 1995 by King Features Syndicate, Inc. World rights reserved
I'M REALLY READY FOR SOMETHING DIFFERENT
HAVE YOU EVER HAD GOMBA KADOODLES?
MENU
NO, BUT WHATEVER IT IS, BRING ME SOME!
YOU GOT IT!
YOUNG & DRAKE 1-17
?
I DON'T KNOW WHAT IT IS EITHER, BUT NOW THE BALL'S IN YOUR COURT

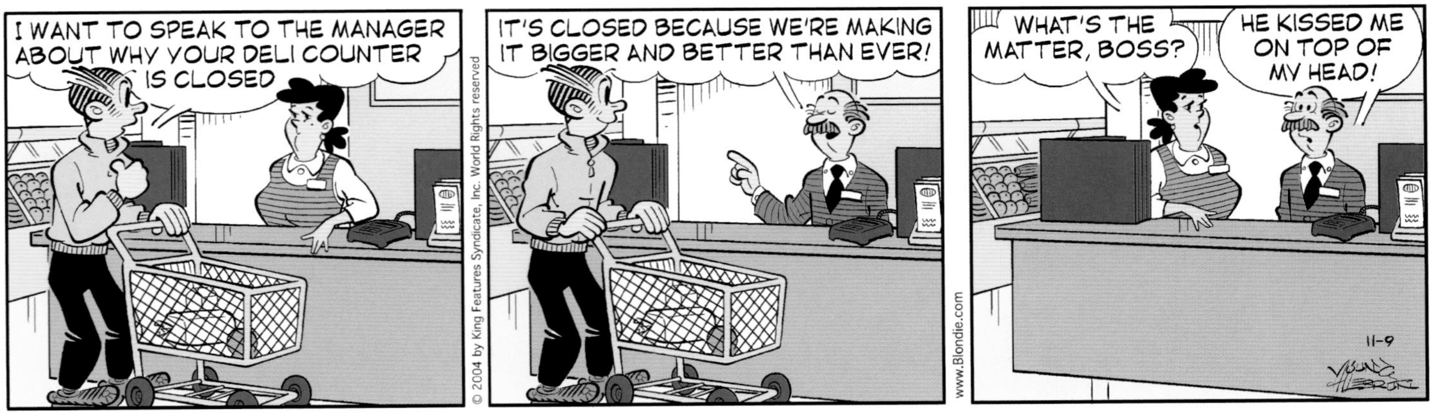
I WANT TO SPEAK TO THE MANAGER ABOUT WHY YOUR DELI COUNTER IS CLOSED
© 2004 by King Features Syndicate, Inc. World Rights reserved
IT'S CLOSED BECAUSE WE'RE MAKING IT BIGGER AND BETTER THAN EVER!
www.Blondie.com
WHAT'S THE MATTER, BOSS?
HE KISSED ME ON TOP OF MY HEAD!
11-9

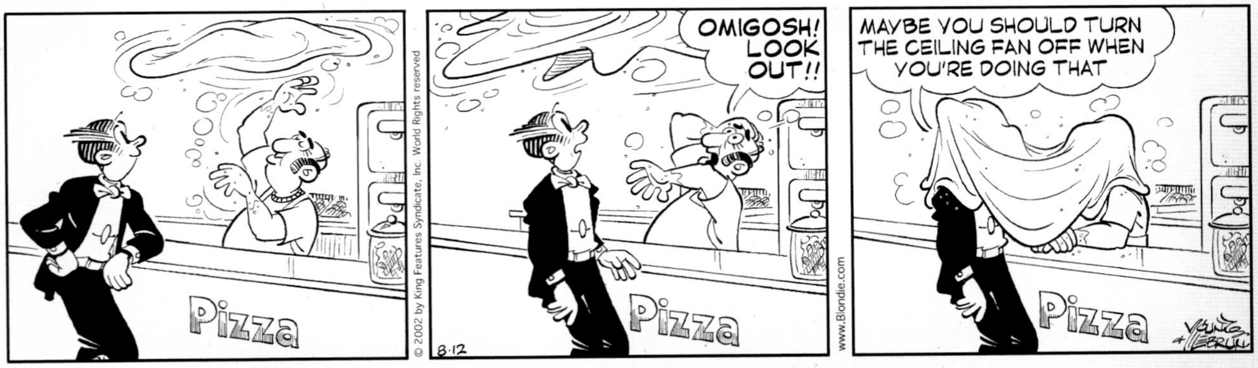
Pizza
© 2002 by King Features Syndicate, Inc. World Rights reserved
8-12
OMIGOSH! LOOK OUT!!
Pizza
www.Blondie.com
MAYBE YOU SHOULD TURN THE CEILING FAN OFF WHEN YOU'RE DOING THAT
Pizza

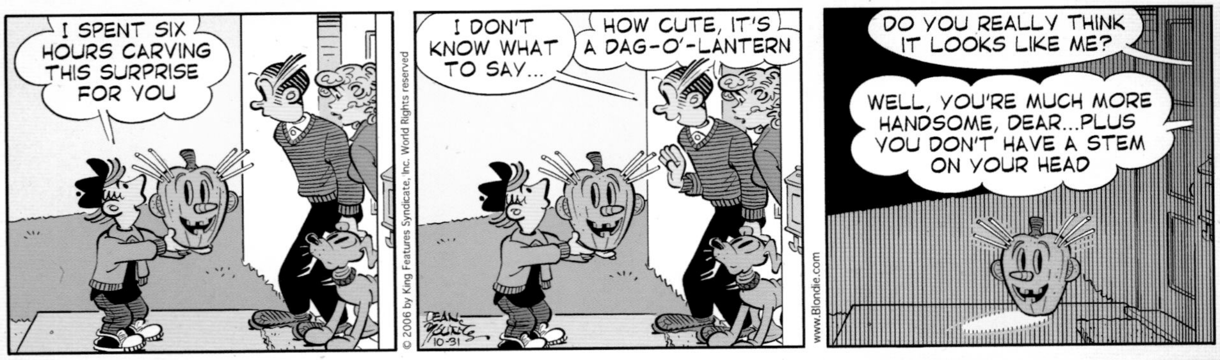
I SPENT SIX HOURS CARVING THIS SURPRISE FOR YOU
© 2006 by King Features Syndicate, Inc. World Rights reserved
I DON'T KNOW WHAT TO SAY...
HOW CUTE, IT'S A DAG-O'-LANTERN
10-31
www.Blondie.com
DO YOU REALLY THINK IT LOOKS LIKE ME?
WELL, YOU'RE MUCH MORE HANDSOME, DEAR...PLUS YOU DON'T HAVE A STEM ON YOUR HEAD

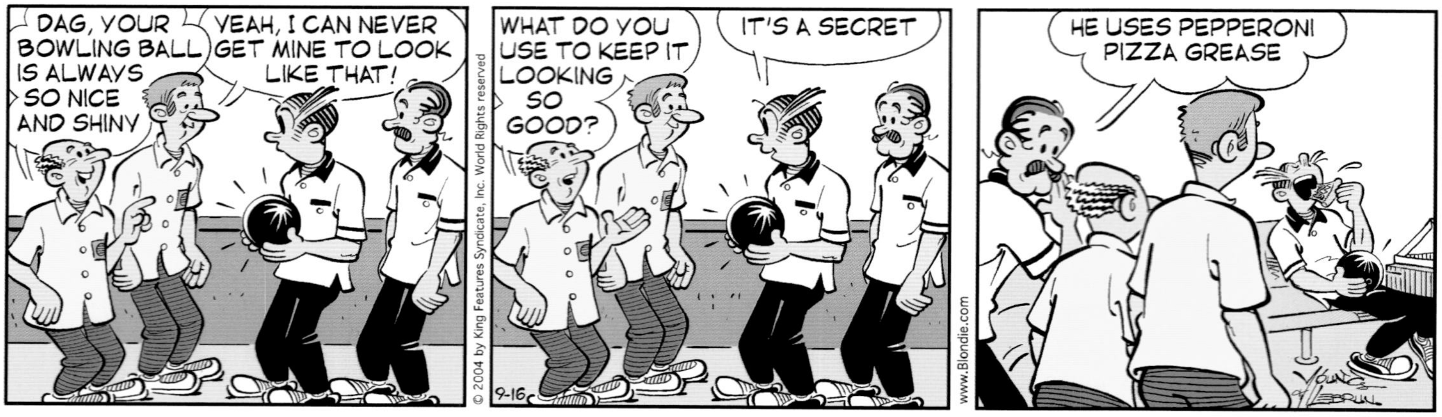
DAG, YOUR BOWLING BALL IS ALWAYS SO NICE AND SHINY
YEAH, I CAN NEVER GET MINE TO LOOK LIKE THAT!
© 2004 by King Features Syndicate, Inc. World Rights reserved
WHAT DO YOU USE TO KEEP IT LOOKING SO GOOD?
IT'S A SECRET
9-16
www.Blondie.com
HE USES PEPPERONI PIZZA GREASE

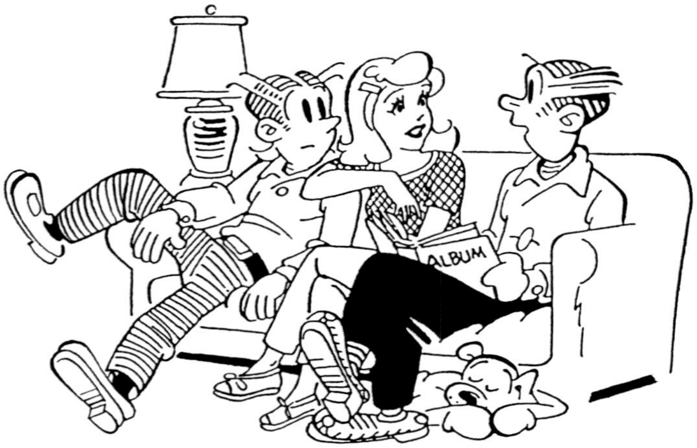
ALBUM

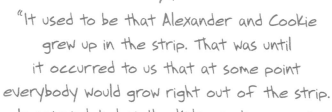

"It used to be that Alexander and Cookie grew up in the strip. That was until it occurred to us that at some point everybody would grow right out of the strip. In my mind today, the kids are teenagers, and Blondie and Dagwood are in their thirties."

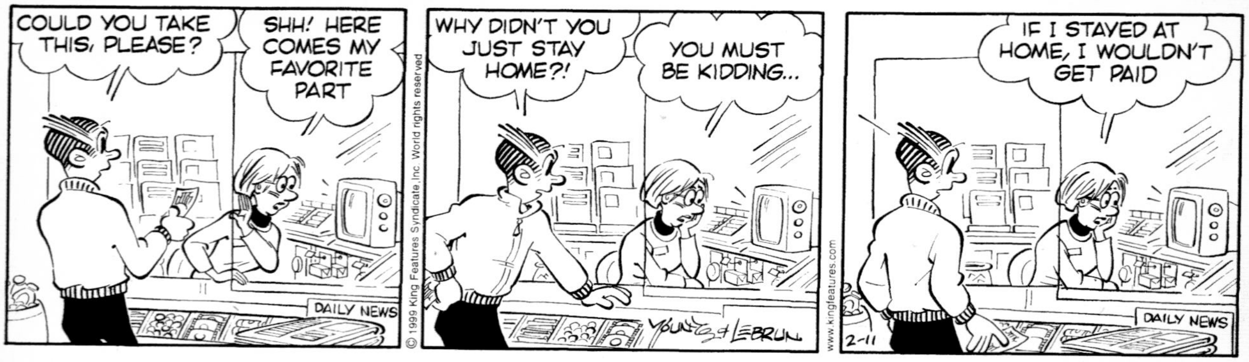
COULD YOU TAKE THIS, PLEASE?
SHH! HERE COMES MY FAVORITE PART
DAILY NEWS
© 1999 King Features Syndicate, Inc. World rights reserved
WHY DIDN'T YOU JUST STAY HOME?!
YOU MUST BE KIDDING...
www.kingfeatures.com
IF I STAYED AT HOME, I WOULDN'T GET PAID
2-11
DAILY NEWS

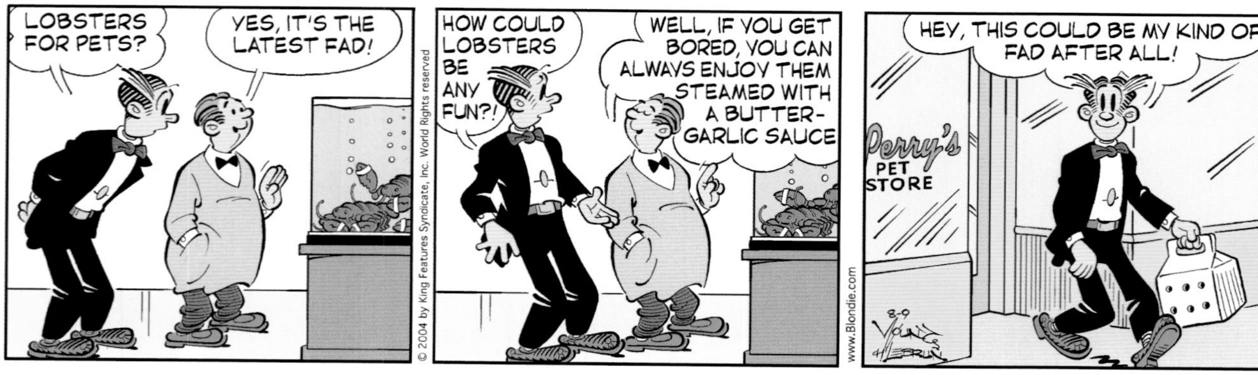
LOBSTERS FOR PETS?
YES, IT'S THE LATEST FAD!
© 2004 by King Features Syndicate, Inc. World Rights reserved
HOW COULD LOBSTERS BE ANY FUN?!
WELL, IF YOU GET BORED, YOU CAN ALWAYS ENJOY THEM STEAMED WITH A BUTTER-GARLIC SAUCE
www.Blondie.com
HEY, THIS COULD BE MY KIND OF FAD AFTER ALL!
Perry's PET STORE
8-9

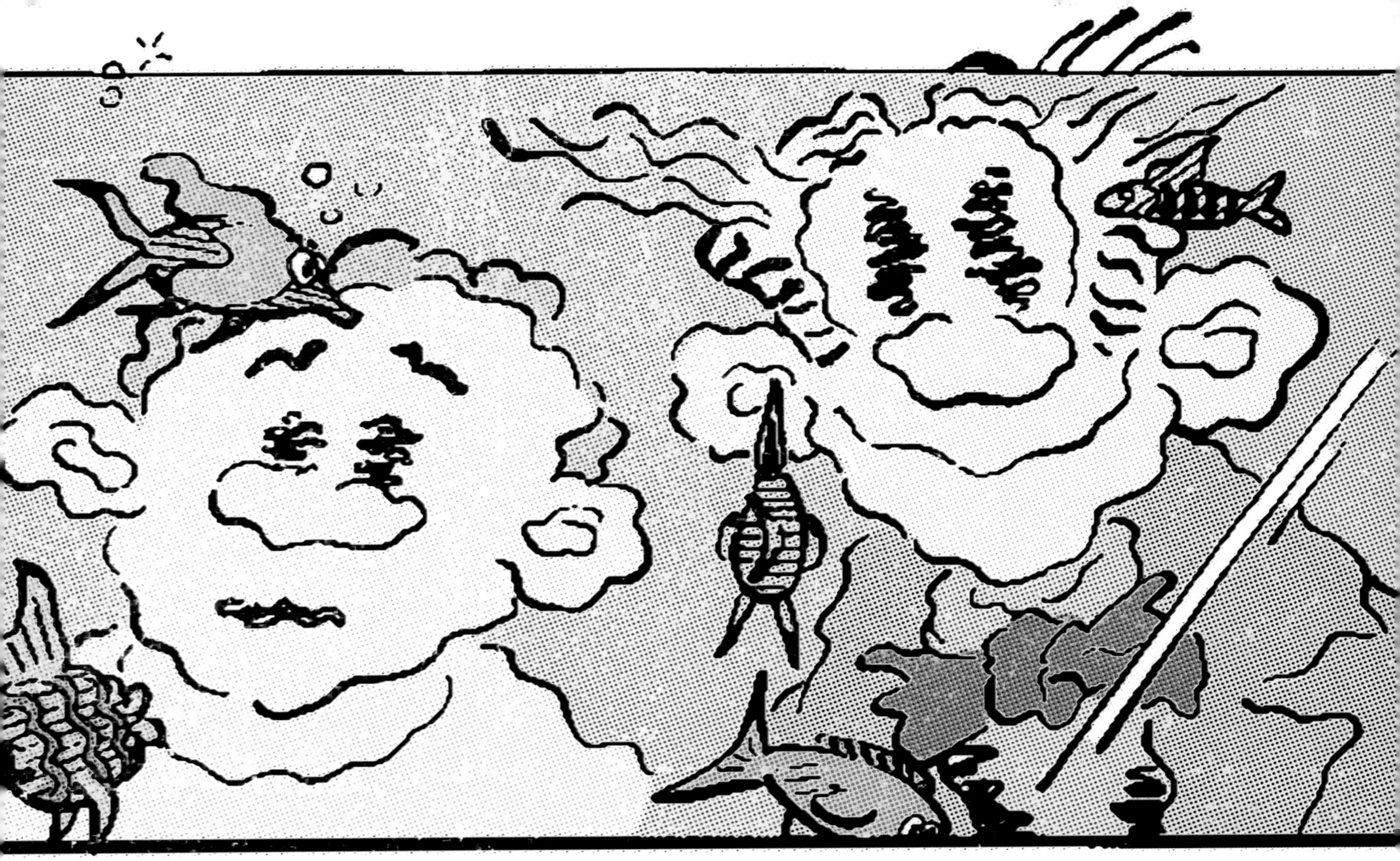

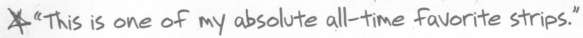

"This is one of my absolute all-time favorite strips."

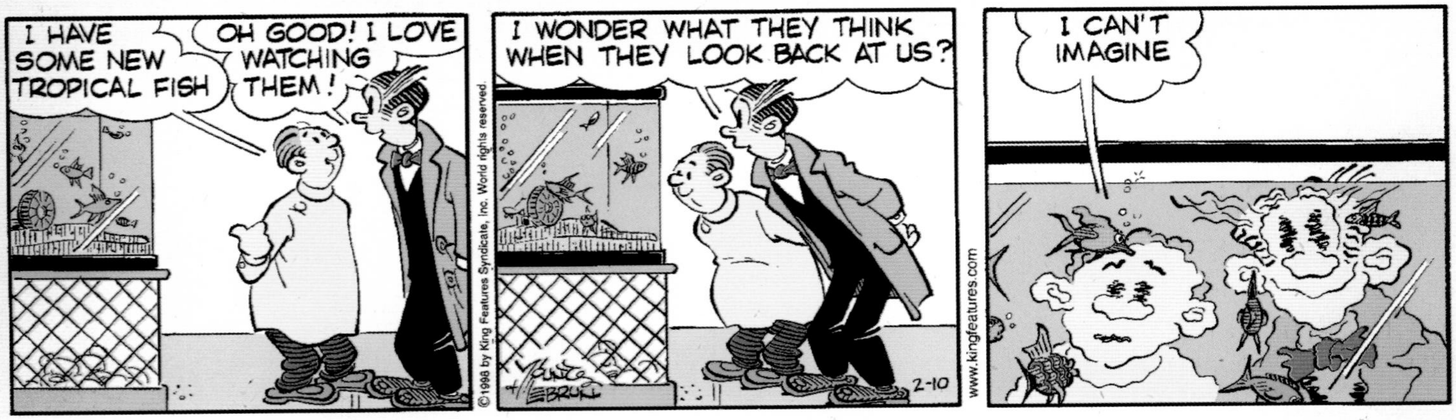
I HAVE SOME NEW TROPICAL FISH
OH GOOD! I LOVE WATCHING THEM!
I WONDER WHAT THEY THINK WHEN THEY LOOK BACK AT US?
I CAN'T IMAGINE
©1998 by King Features Syndicate, Inc. World rights reserved.
2-10
www.kingfeatures.com

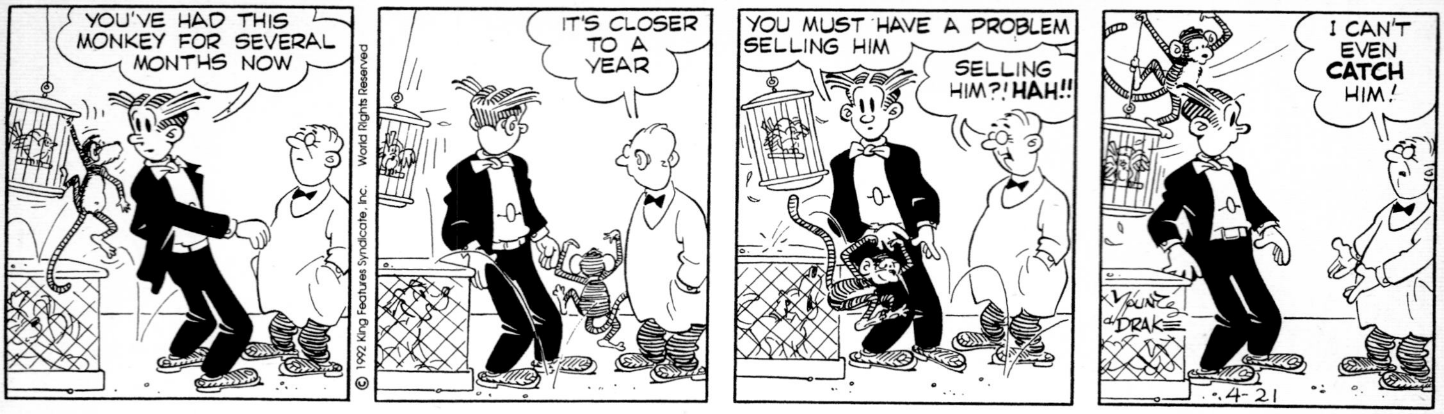
YOU'VE HAD THIS MONKEY FOR SEVERAL MONTHS NOW
IT'S CLOSER TO A YEAR
YOU MUST HAVE A PROBLEM SELLING HIM
SELLING HIM?! HAH!!
I CAN'T EVEN CATCH HIM!
© 1992 King Features Syndicate, Inc. World Rights Reserved
YOUNG & DRAKE
4-21

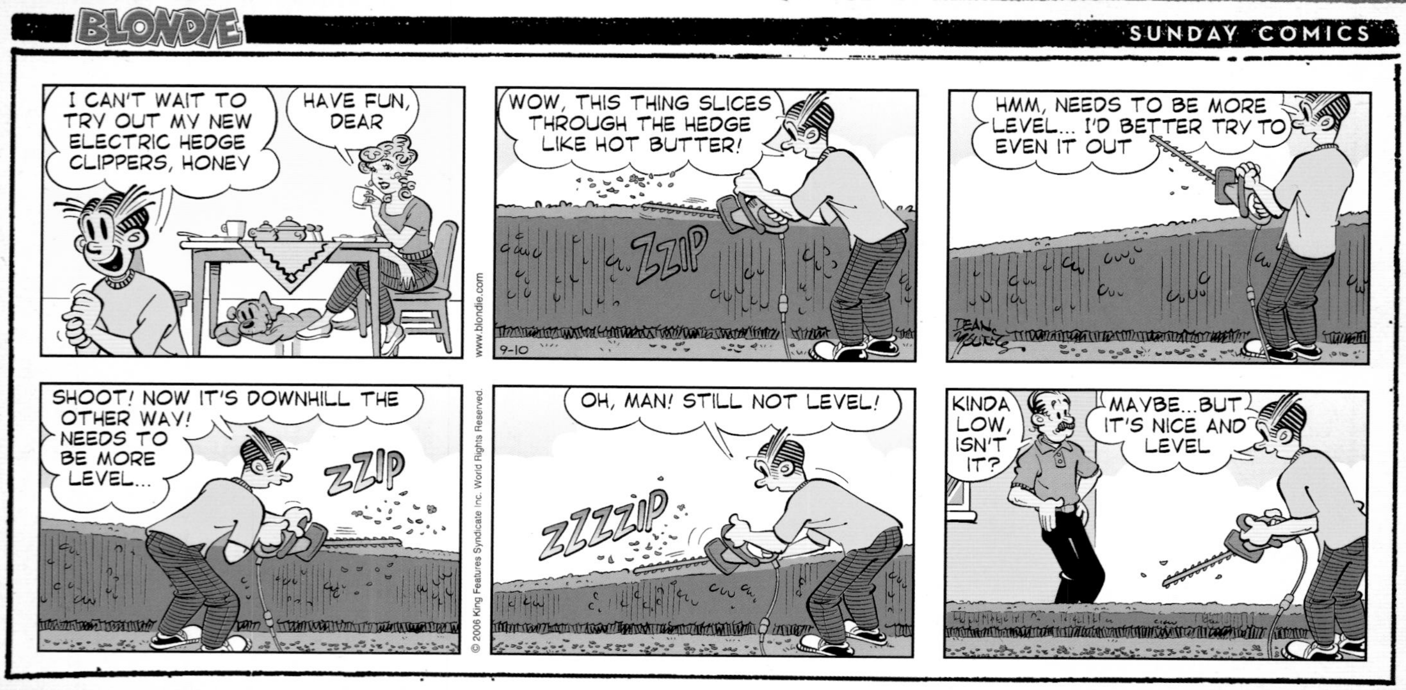
BLONDIE
SUNDAY COMICS
I CAN'T WAIT TO TRY OUT MY NEW ELECTRIC HEDGE CLIPPERS, HONEY
HAVE FUN, DEAR
www.blondie.com
WOW, THIS THING SLICES THROUGH THE HEDGE LIKE HOT BUTTER!
ZZIP
9-10
HMM, NEEDS TO BE MORE LEVEL... I'D BETTER TRY TO EVEN IT OUT
DEAN YOUNG
SHOOT! NOW IT'S DOWNHILL THE OTHER WAY! NEEDS TO BE MORE LEVEL...
ZZIP
© 2006 King Features Syndicate Inc. World Rights Reserved.
OH, MAN! STILL NOT LEVEL!
ZZZZIP
KINDA LOW, ISN'T IT?
MAYBE...BUT IT'S NICE AND LEVEL

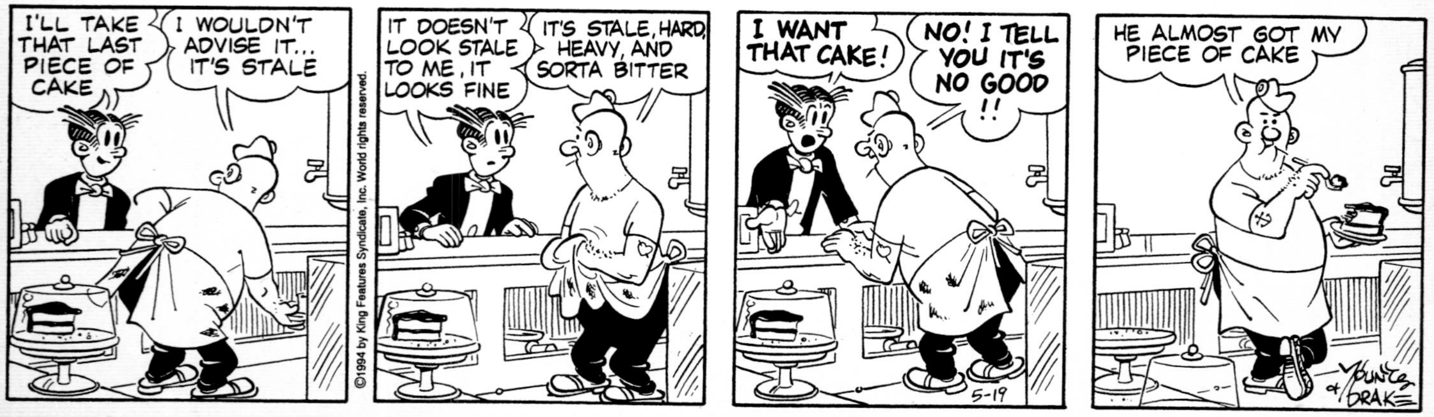
I'LL TAKE THAT LAST PIECE OF CAKE
I WOULDN'T ADVISE IT... IT'S STALE
©1994 by King Features Syndicate, Inc. World rights reserved.
IT DOESN'T LOOK STALE TO ME, IT LOOKS FINE
IT'S STALE, HARD, HEAVY, AND SORTA BITTER
I WANT THAT CAKE!
NO! I TELL YOU IT'S NO GOOD!!
5-19
HE ALMOST GOT MY PIECE OF CAKE
YOUNG & DRAKE

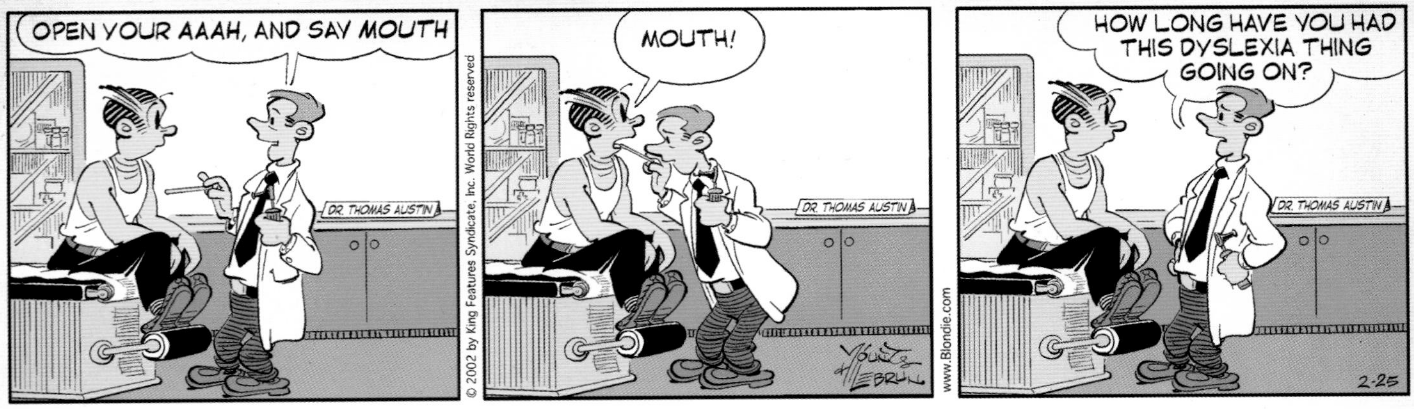
OPEN YOUR AAAH, AND SAY MOUTH
DR. THOMAS AUSTIN
© 2002 by King Features Syndicate, Inc. World Rights reserved
MOUTH!
DR. THOMAS AUSTIN
www.Blondie.com
HOW LONG HAVE YOU HAD THIS DYSLEXIA THING GOING ON?
DR. THOMAS AUSTIN
2-25

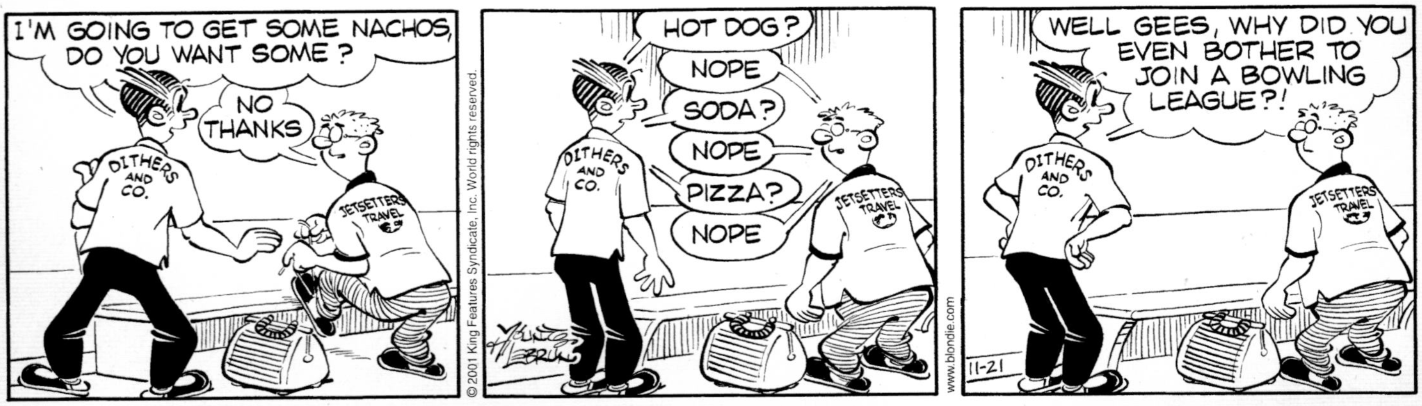
I'M GOING TO GET SOME NACHOS, DO YOU WANT SOME ?
NO THANKS
DITHERS AND CO.
JETSETTERS TRAVEL
© 2001 King Features Syndicate, Inc. World rights reserved.
HOT DOG ?
NOPE
SODA ?
NOPE
PIZZA ?
NOPE
www.blondie.com
WELL GEES, WHY DID YOU EVEN BOTHER TO JOIN A BOWLING LEAGUE ?!
11-21

"I'm happy with my work.
The strip's doing great,
and no man, surely,
could be happier in his work
than I am. I wouldn't want
to be anything other than
a cartoonist."

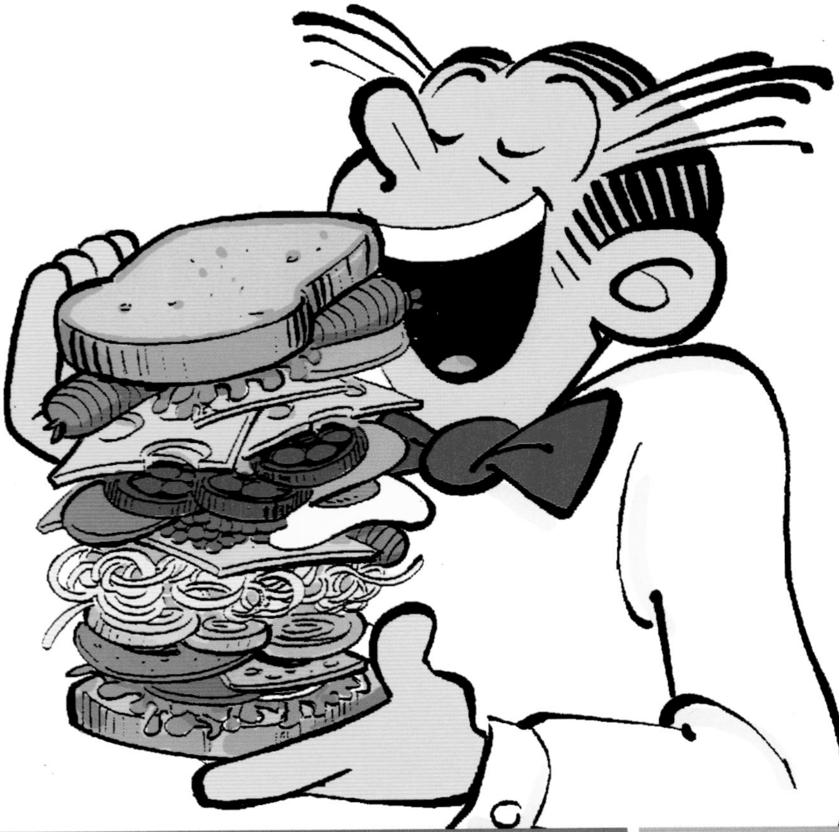

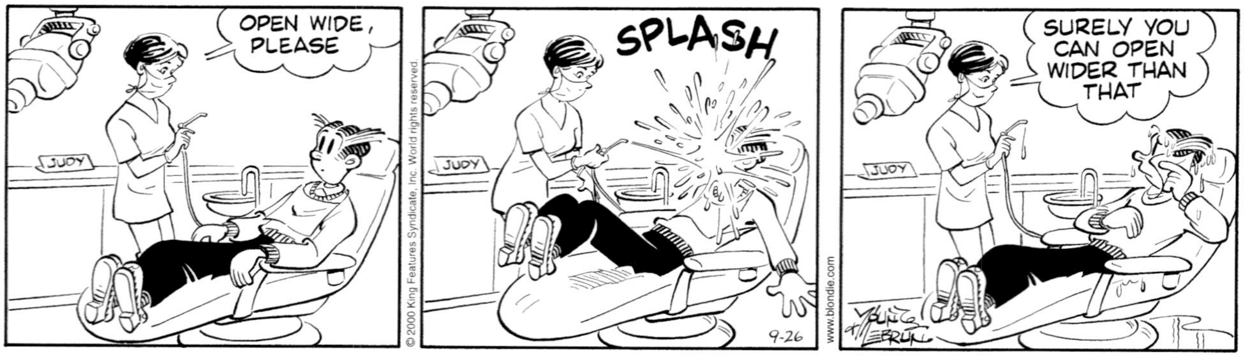
OPEN WIDE, PLEASE
JUDY
SPLASH
© 2000 King Features Syndicate, Inc. World rights reserved
9-26
SURELY YOU CAN OPEN WIDER THAN THAT
www.blondie.com

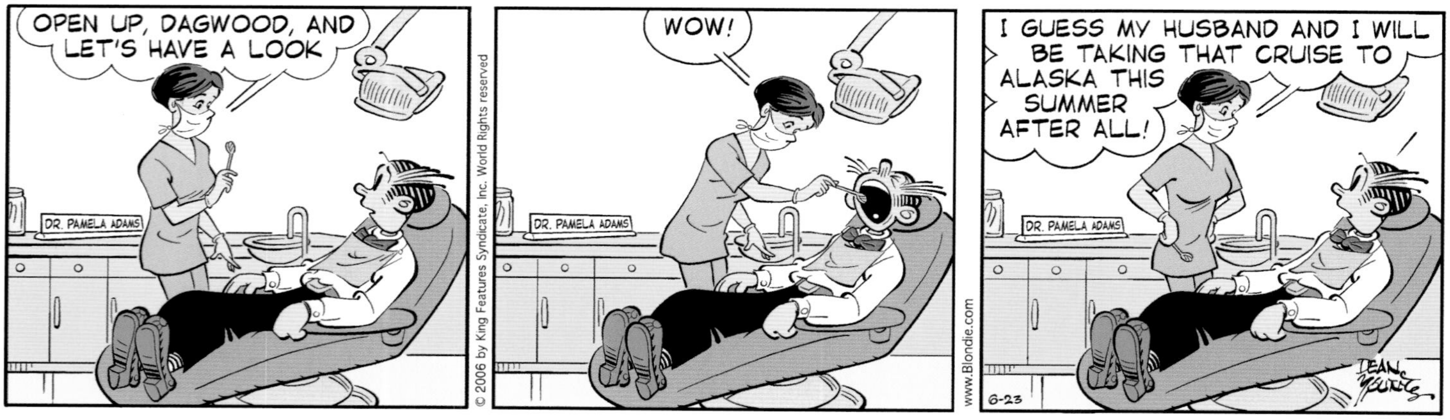
OPEN UP, DAGWOOD, AND LET'S HAVE A LOOK
DR. PAMELA ADAMS
© 2006 by King Features Syndicate, Inc. World Rights reserved
WOW!
I GUESS MY HUSBAND AND I WILL BE TAKING THAT CRUISE TO ALASKA THIS SUMMER AFTER ALL!
www.Blondie.com
6-23

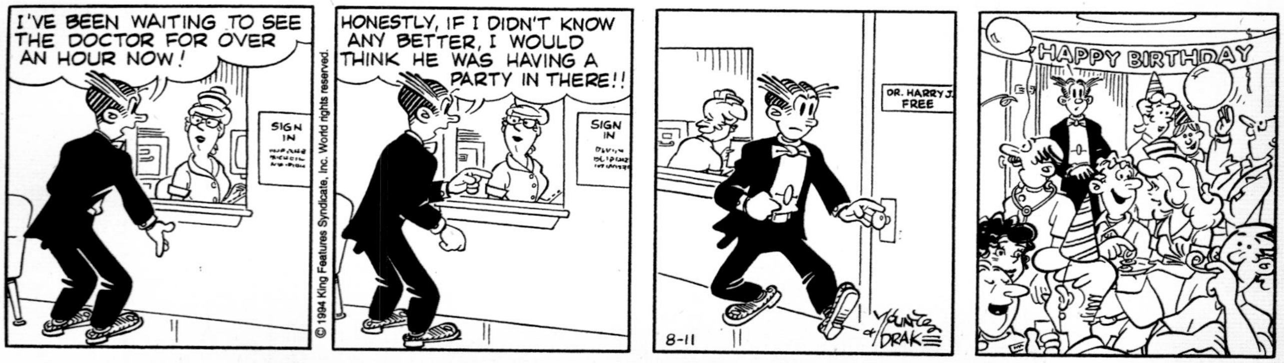
I'VE BEEN WAITING TO SEE THE DOCTOR FOR OVER AN HOUR NOW!
SIGN IN
© 1994 King Features Syndicate, Inc. World rights reserved.
HONESTLY, IF I DIDN'T KNOW ANY BETTER, I WOULD THINK HE WAS HAVING A PARTY IN THERE!!
DR. HARRY J. FREE
8-11
HAPPY BIRTHDAY

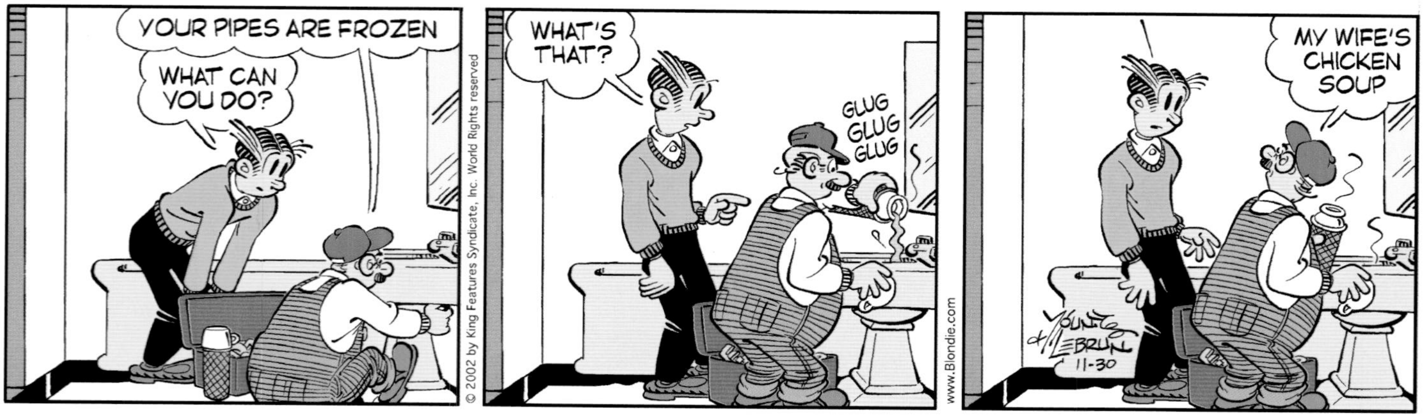
YOUR PIPES ARE FROZEN
WHAT CAN YOU DO?
© 2002 by King Features Syndicate, Inc. World Rights reserved
WHAT'S THAT?
GLUG GLUG GLUG
www.Blondie.com
MY WIFE'S CHICKEN SOUP
11-30

I'VE BEEN WORRYING A LOT ABOUT LOSING MY HAIR LATELY
© 1997 King Features Syndicate, Inc. World rights reserved
OH, THAT'S SILLY! YOU SHOULDN'T WASTE YOUR TIME WORRYING ABOUT THAT
REALLY?
SURE! SIX YEARS FROM NOW THE ONLY THING YOU'LL HAVE TO WORRY ABOUT IS GETTING YOUR HEAD POLISHED
6-16

I'M SORRY I SAID ALL THOSE MEAN THINGS ABOUT YOUR CHOICE FOR OUR NEXT MAYOR
CLIP
CLIP
© 2001 King Features Syndicate, Inc. World rights reserved.
NOT A PROBLEM... THINK NOTHING OF IT
CLIP
CLIP
CLIP
HEY, EVERYONE'S ENTITLED TO HIS OWN OPINION
SNAP
www.blondie.com
6-11

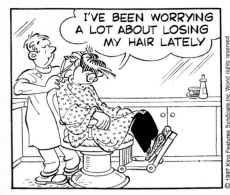

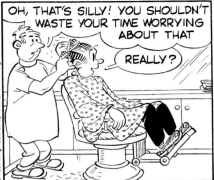

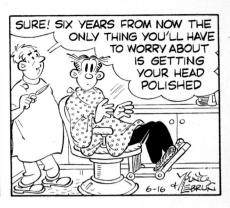

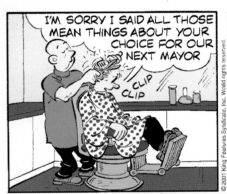

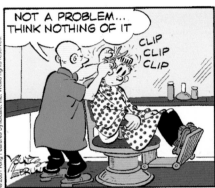

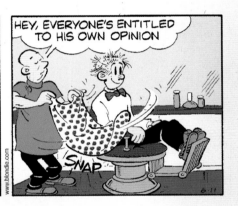

"I've always felt that as a cartoonist, you are allowed to be a teenager forever!"

HOW'S THAT BOOK, HONEY?
IT'S GREAT!
© 2006 by King Features Syndicate, Inc. World Rights reserved
IT'S SO GREAT, I'M GONNA PASS ON MY SNACK SO I CAN FINISH READING IT!
9-25
www.Blondie.com
I THINK I SMELL A PULITZER PRIZE HERE!

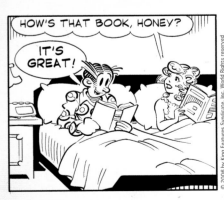

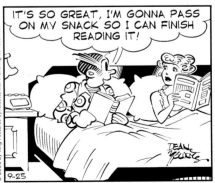

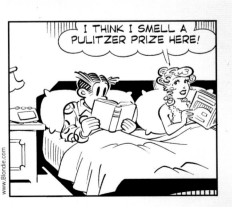

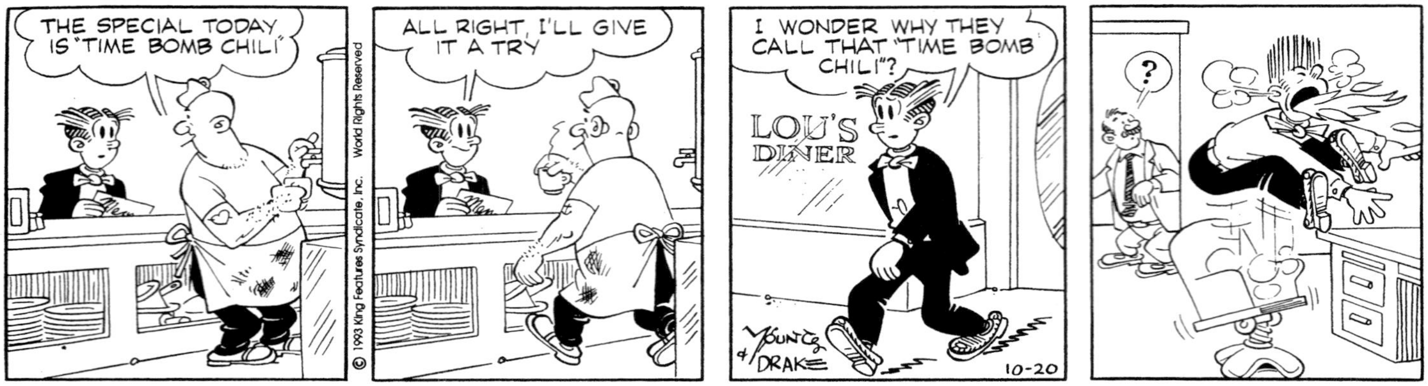
THE SPECIAL TODAY IS "TIME BOMB CHILI"
© 1993 King Features Syndicate, Inc. World Rights Reserved
ALL RIGHT, I'LL GIVE IT A TRY
I WONDER WHY THEY CALL THAT "TIME BOMB CHILI"?
LOU'S DINER
YOUNG & DRAKE
10-20
?

"This is the way we celebrated 70 years—with shenanigans and love."

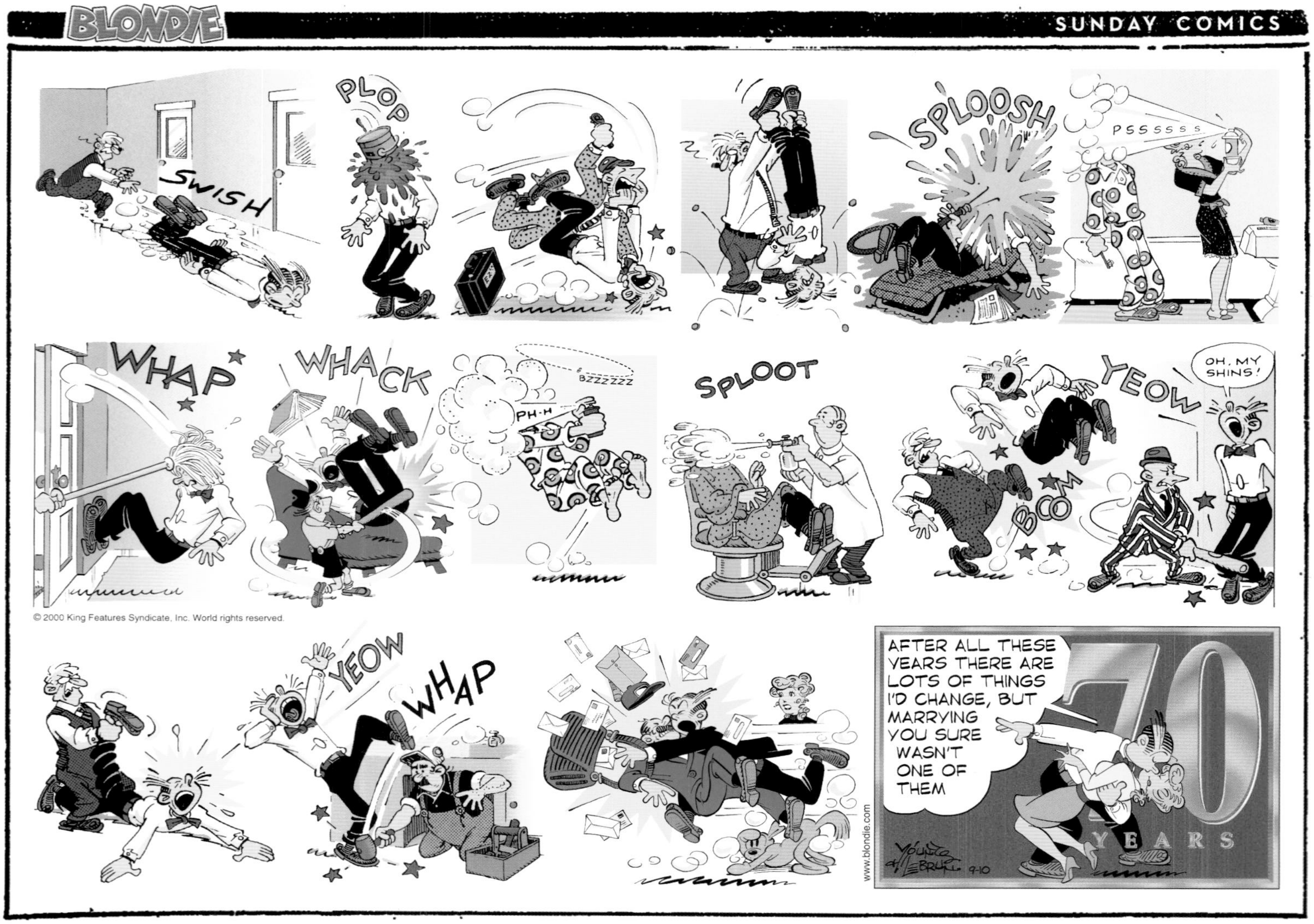
BLONDIE
SUNDAY COMICS
SWISH
PLOP
SPLOOSH
PSSSSSSS
WHAP
WHACK
BZZZZZZ
PH-H
SPLOOT
YEOW
OH, MY SHINS!
BOOM
© 2000 King Features Syndicate, Inc. World rights reserved.
YEOW
WHAP
www.blondie.com
AFTER ALL THESE YEARS THERE ARE LOTS OF THINGS I'D CHANGE, BUT MARRYING YOU SURE WASN'T ONE OF THEM
70 YEARS
9-10

CHAPTER 7

THE 75TH ANNIVERSARY

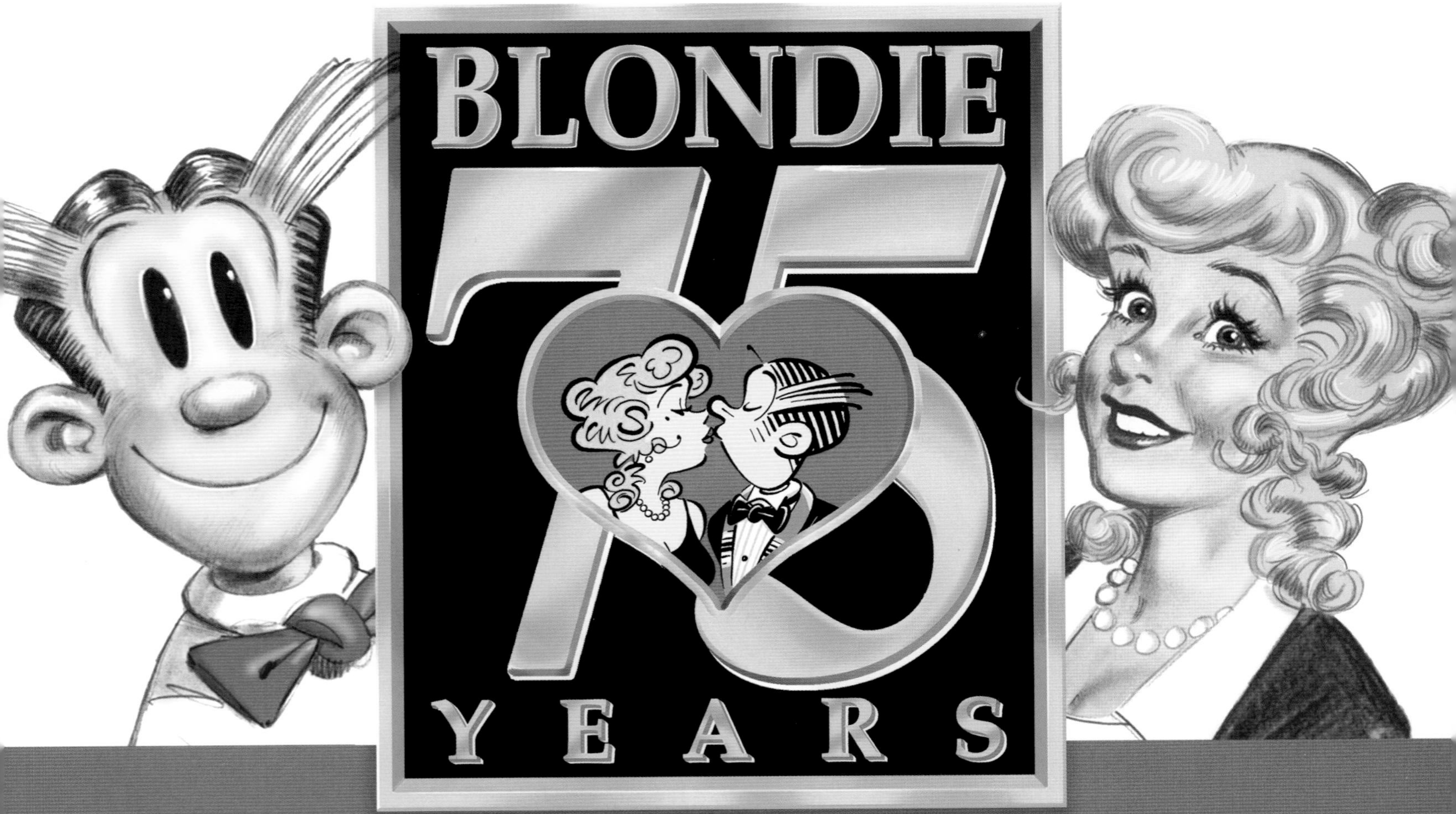
BLONDIE
75
YEARS

Before television and the Internet, before video games and iPods, the Bumsteads were entertaining multiple generations with their good-natured take on family, domesticity, and the American dream. Even today, when all those things and more serve to divide people's attention, *Blondie* enjoys unbelievable popularity. Syndicated to twenty-five hundred newspapers in fifty-five countries and thirty-five languages, devoured by 290 million readers, seven days a week, it is without a doubt the world's most beloved comic strip.

So when it came time to commemorate this classic's seventy-fifth anniversary in 2005, Blondie wanted a real celebration. She clearly deserved it. The party that Dean Young dreamed up for her and the rest of the Bumstead clan was unprecedented; its VIP guests included many of the other beloved characters in the newspaper's funny pages. Even the president of the United States made an appearance, personally congratulating Dean in a letter.

The storyline began two months in advance of the actual anniversary gathering—September 4, 2005—when the Bumsteads started sending invitations to their fellow comic mainstays, from Dilbert to Beetle Bailey to Hagar the Horrible, to come to the bash *chez* Blondie. Making a circuitous journey through the strips of their neighbors-in-newsprint—a trip that was as rare as it was clever, considering the competition among today's cartoonists—they also made personal appearances or were mentioned in dozens of cartoons to promote the occasion.

Blondie wanted a real celebration. She clearly deserved it. And Dean Young dreamed up an unprecedented one.

The anniversary storyline appeared in *Garfield, Rose Is Rose, Wizard of Id, Dick Tracy, B.C., Mother Goose & Grimm, Family Circus, Shoe, Hi & Lois, Sally Forth, Gasoline Alley, Snuffy Smith, Buckles, Baby Blues, Zits, Mutts, Curtis, Marvin, For Better or Worse, Born Loser, Dennis the Menace, Cathy, Thick Thin,* and *Bizarro.* Al Konetzni of Walt Disney and Floyd Johnson also memorialized it in single-panel strips. It worked! The Bumstead anniversary was the most star-studded affair in comic history. Fellow comic artists also paid their own tributes to the strip.

GARFIELD **BY JIM DAVIS**

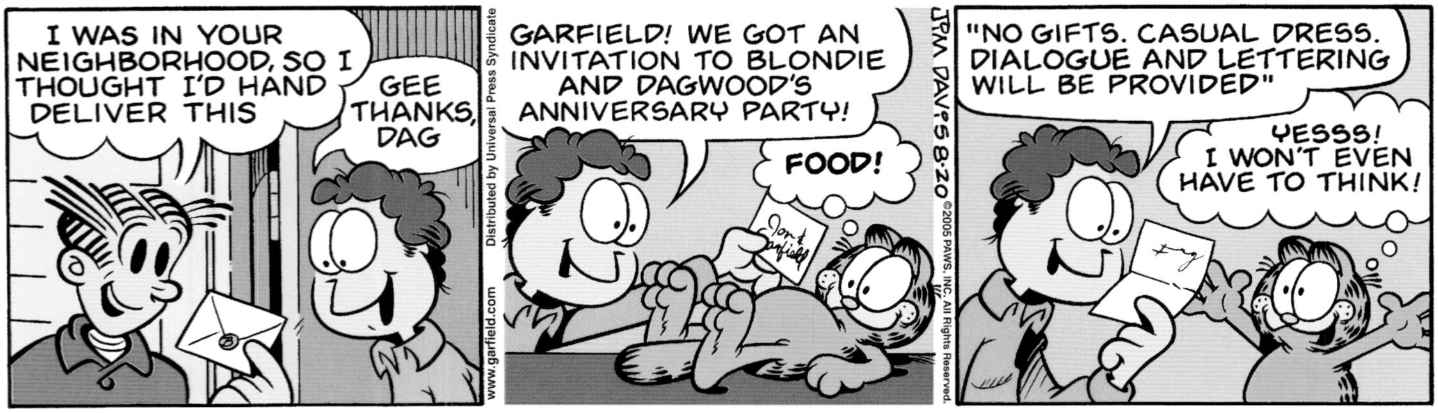

I WAS IN YOUR NEIGHBORHOOD, SO I THOUGHT I'D HAND DELIVER THIS
GEE THANKS, DAG
GARFIELD! WE GOT AN INVITATION TO BLONDIE AND DAGWOOD'S ANNIVERSARY PARTY!
FOOD!
"NO GIFTS. CASUAL DRESS. DIALOGUE AND LETTERING WILL BE PROVIDED"
YESSS! I WON'T EVEN HAVE TO THINK!
Distributed by Universal Press Syndicate
www.garfield.com
JPM DAVIS 8-20
©2005 PAWS, INC. All Rights Reserved.

Garfield © 2005 Paws, Inc. Reprinted by permission of Universal Press Syndicate. All rights reserved.

ROSE IS ROSE **CREATED BY PAT BRADY; BY DON WIMMER**

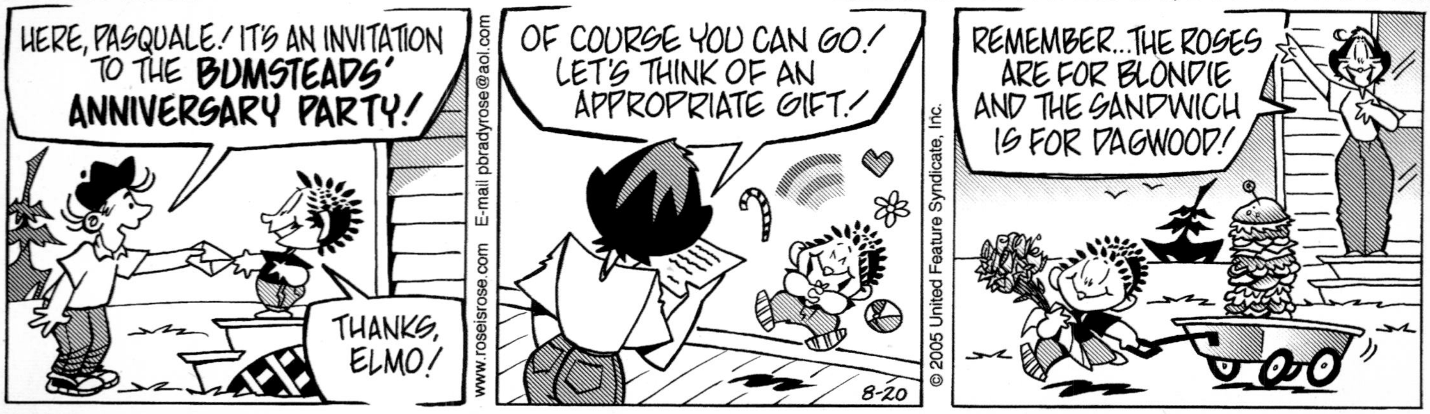

HERE, PASQUALE! IT'S AN INVITATION TO THE BUMSTEADS' ANNIVERSARY PARTY!
THANKS, ELMO!
www.roseisrose.com E-mail pbradyrose@aol.com
OF COURSE YOU CAN GO! LET'S THINK OF AN APPROPRIATE GIFT!
8-20
© 2005 United Feature Syndicate, Inc.
REMEMBER...THE ROSES ARE FOR BLONDIE AND THE SANDWICH IS FOR DAGWOOD!

Rose Is Rose: © United Feature Syndicate, Inc.

SALLY FORTH **BY FRANCESCO MARCIULIANO; DRAWN BY CRAIG MACINTOSH**

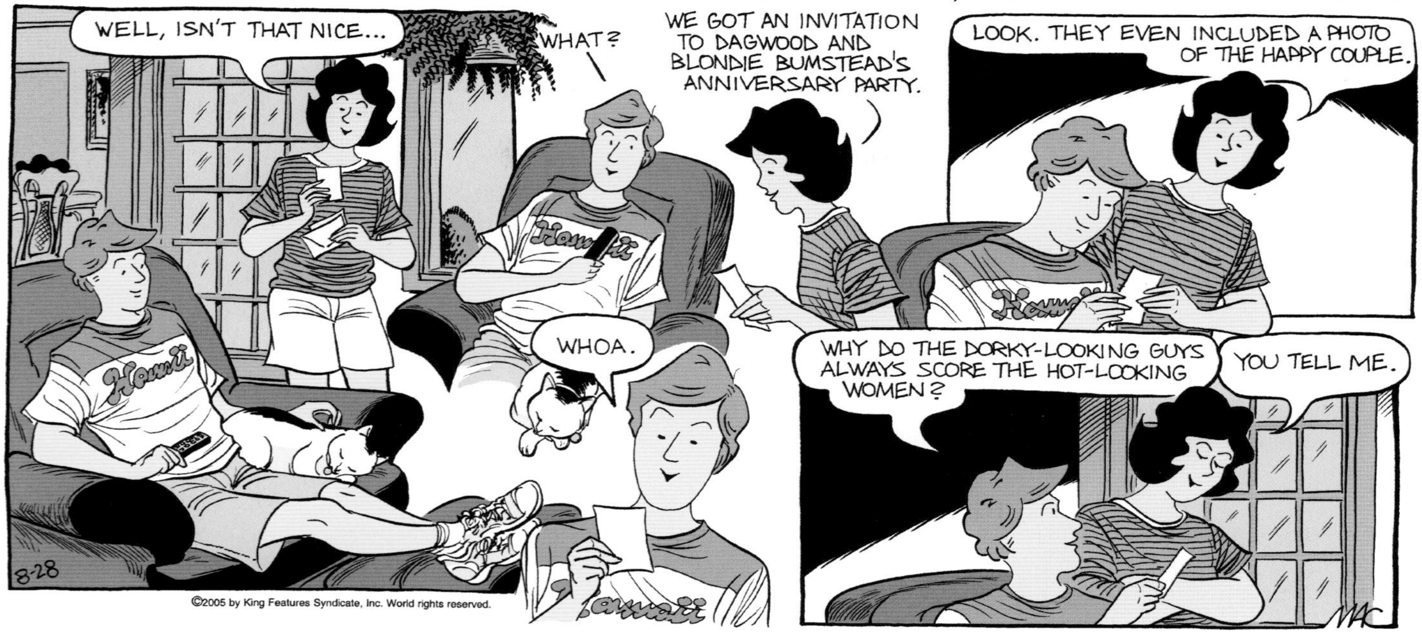
WELL, ISN'T THAT NICE...
WHAT?
WE GOT AN INVITATION TO DAGWOOD AND BLONDIE BUMSTEAD'S ANNIVERSARY PARTY.
LOOK. THEY EVEN INCLUDED A PHOTO OF THE HAPPY COUPLE.
WHOA.
WHY DO THE DORKY-LOOKING GUYS ALWAYS SCORE THE HOT-LOOKING WOMEN?
YOU TELL ME.
8-28
©2005 by King Features Syndicate, Inc. World rights reserved.
MAC

WIZARD OF ID **BY BRANT PARKER & JOHNNY HART**

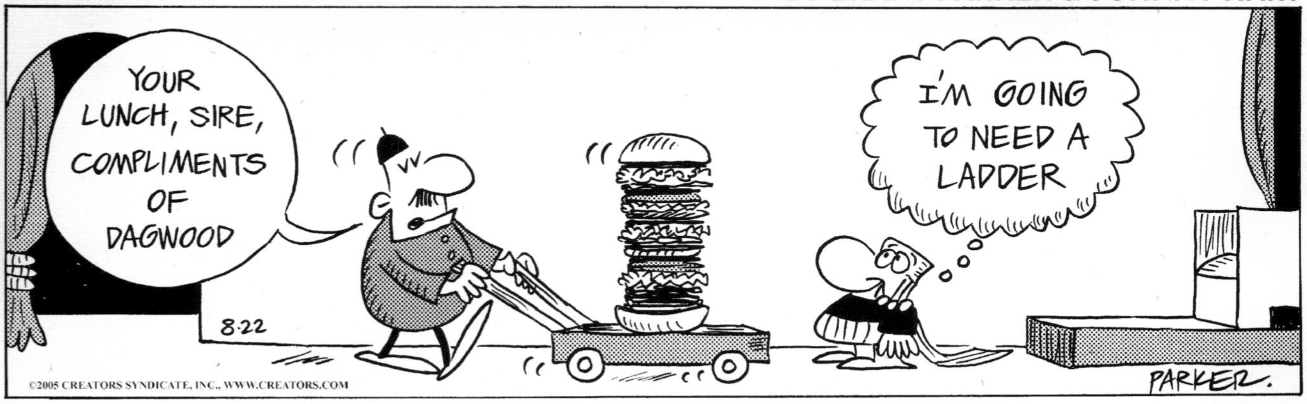
YOUR LUNCH, SIRE, COMPLIMENTS OF DAGWOOD
I'M GOING TO NEED A LADDER
8-22
©2005 CREATORS SYNDICATE, INC., WWW.CREATORS.COM
PARKER.

By permission of John L. Hart FLP and Creators Syndicate, Inc.

MUTTS **BY PATRICK MCDONNELL**

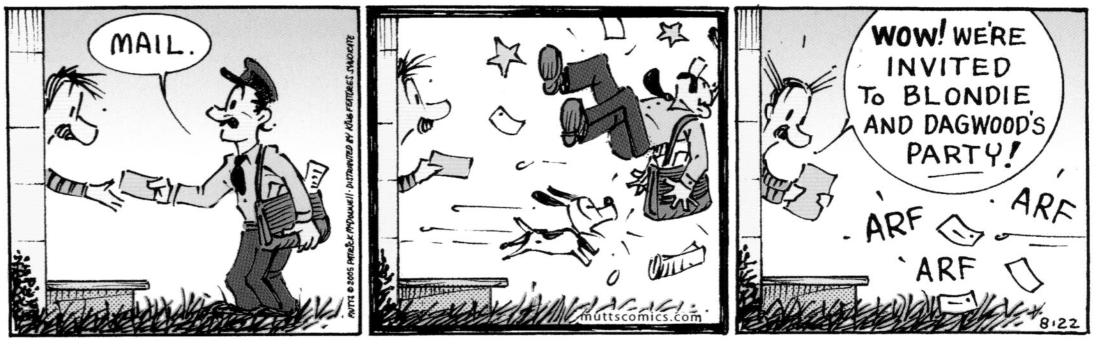
MAIL.
muttscomics.com
WOW! WE'RE INVITED To BLONDIE AND DAGWOOD'S PARTY!
ARF
ARF
ARF
8-22

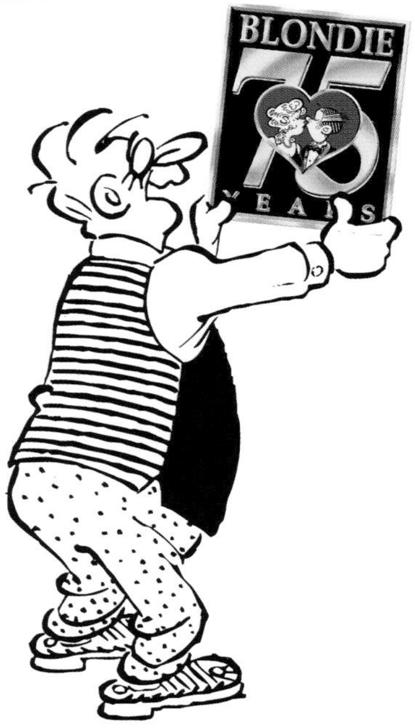
BLONDIE
75
YEARS

BEETLE BAILY — **BY MORT & GREG WALKER**

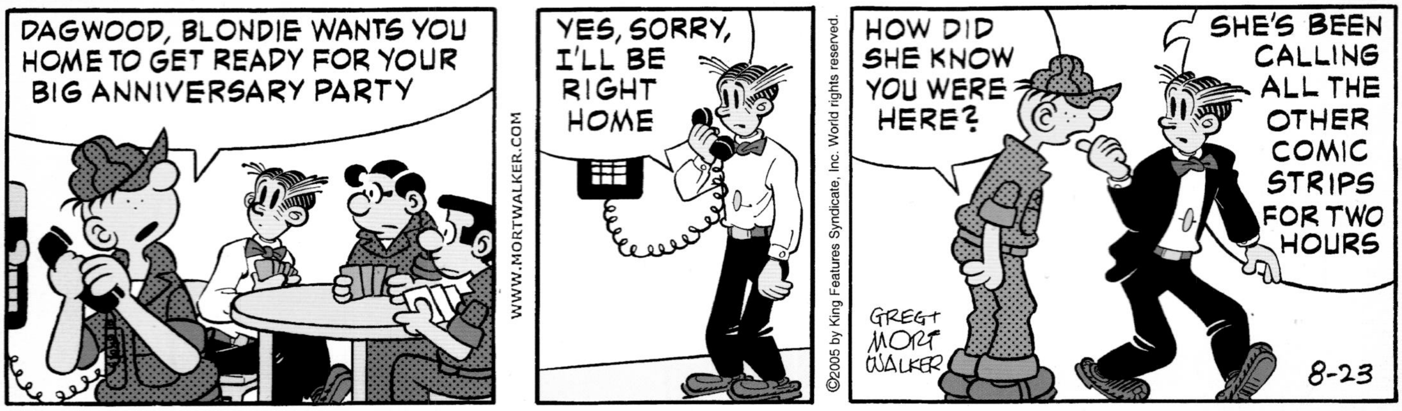
DAGWOOD, BLONDIE WANTS YOU HOME TO GET READY FOR YOUR BIG ANNIVERSARY PARTY
WWW.MORTWALKER.COM
YES, SORRY, I'LL BE RIGHT HOME
©2005 by King Features Syndicate, Inc. World rights reserved.
HOW DID SHE KNOW YOU WERE HERE?
SHE'S BEEN CALLING ALL THE OTHER COMIC STRIPS FOR TWO HOURS
GREG + MORT WALKER
8-23

MOTHER GOOSE & GRIMM — **BY MIKE PETERS**

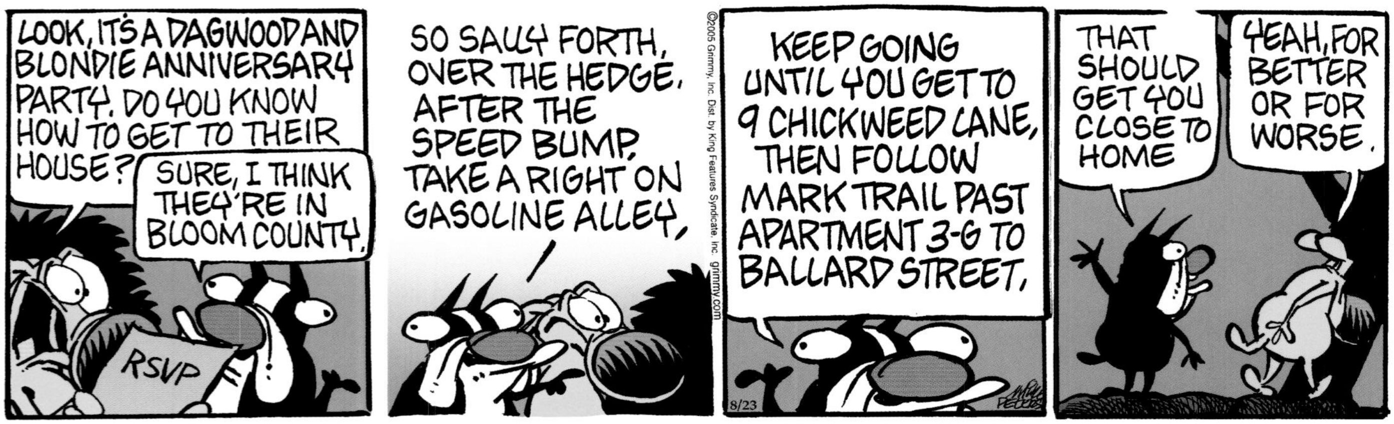
LOOK, IT'S A DAGWOOD AND BLONDIE ANNIVERSARY PARTY. DO YOU KNOW HOW TO GET TO THEIR HOUSE?
SURE, I THINK THEY'RE IN BLOOM COUNTY.
RSVP
SO SALLY FORTH, OVER THE HEDGE, AFTER THE SPEED BUMP. TAKE A RIGHT ON GASOLINE ALLEY,
©2005 Grimmy, Inc. Dist. by King Features Syndicate, Inc. grimmy.com
KEEP GOING UNTIL YOU GET TO 9 CHICKWEED LANE, THEN FOLLOW MARK TRAIL PAST APARTMENT 3-G TO BALLARD STREET,
8/23
THAT SHOULD GET YOU CLOSE TO HOME
YEAH, FOR BETTER OR FOR WORSE.

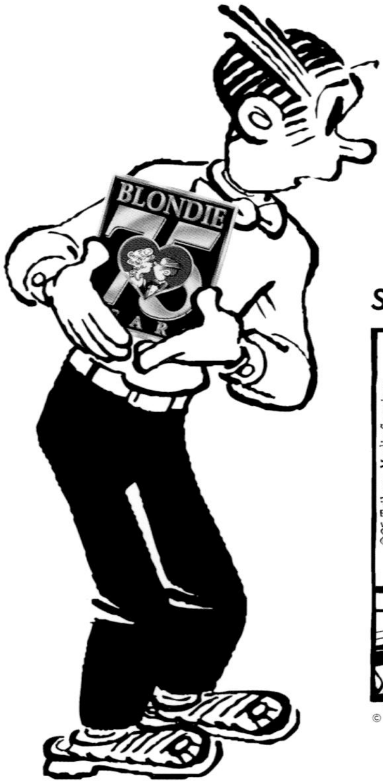
BLONDIE
75
YEARS

The Bumstead anniversary was the most star-studded affair in comic history.

SHOE — **BY CHRIS CASSATT & GARY BROOKINS**

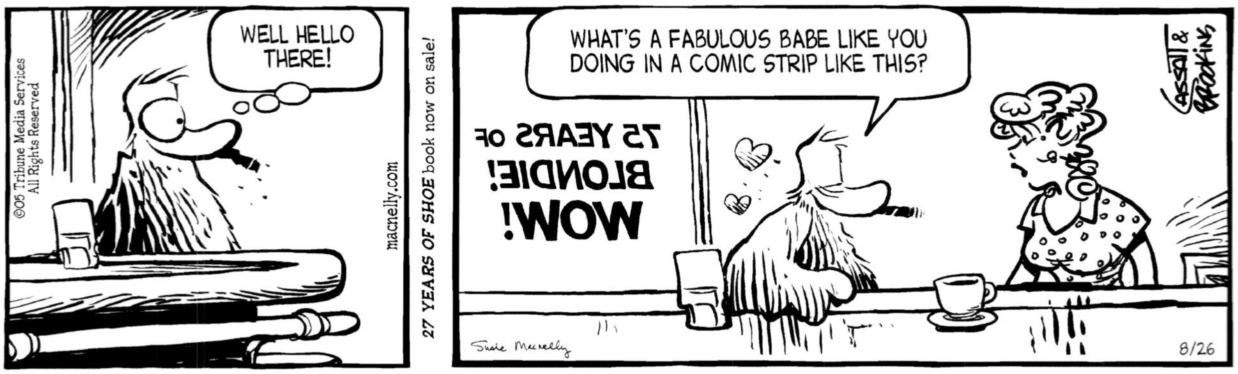
©05 Tribune Media Services All Rights Reserved
WELL HELLO THERE!
macnelly.com
27 YEARS OF SHOE book now on sale!
WHAT'S A FABULOUS BABE LIKE YOU DOING IN A COMIC STRIP LIKE THIS?
75 YEARS OF BLONDIE! WOW!
CASSATT & BROOKINS
8/26

HI AND LOIS

BY BRIAN WALKER, GREG WALKER, & CHANCE BROWNE

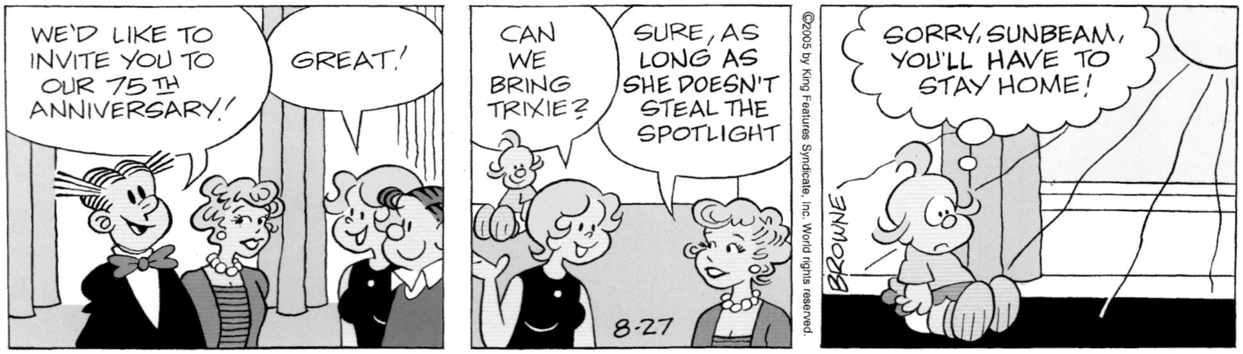

WE'D LIKE TO INVITE YOU TO OUR 75TH ANNIVERSARY!
GREAT!
CAN WE BRING TRIXIE?
SURE, AS LONG AS SHE DOESN'T STEAL THE SPOTLIGHT
8-27
©2005 by King Features Syndicate, Inc. World rights reserved.
SORRY, SUNBEAM, YOU'LL HAVE TO STAY HOME!
BROWNE

FOR BETTER OR FOR WORSE

BY LYNN JOHNSTON

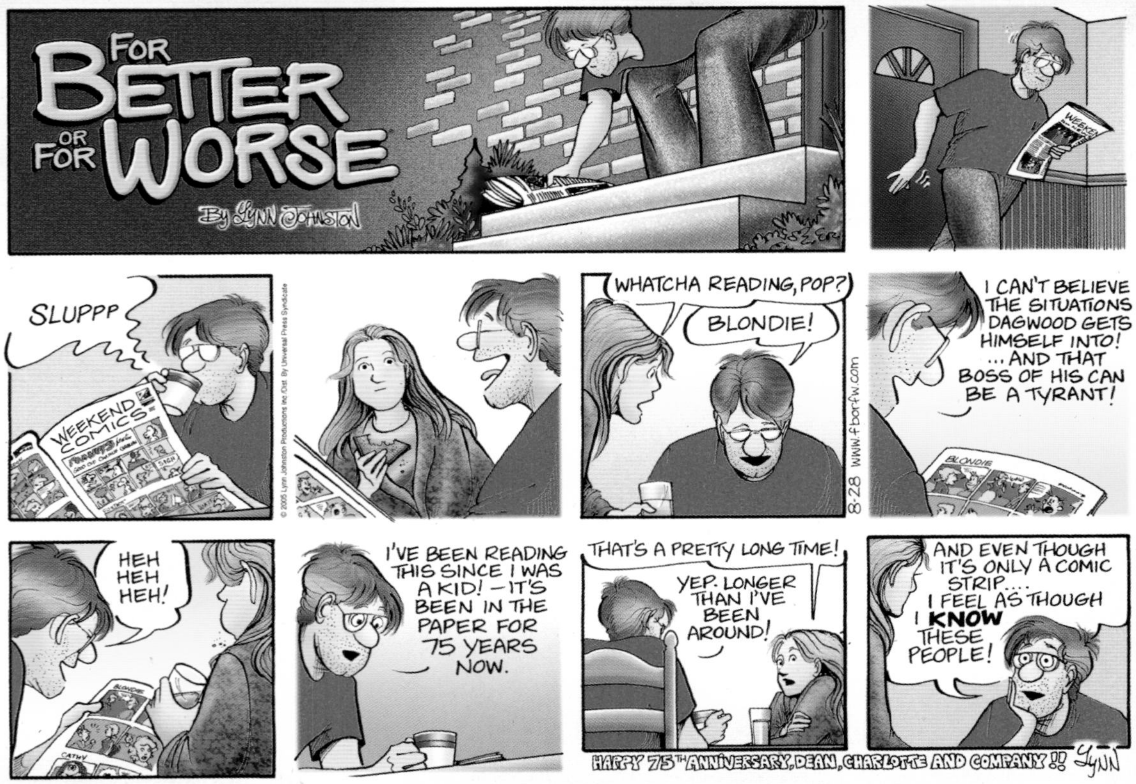

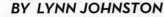

FOR BETTER OR FOR WORSE
By Lynn Johnston
SLUPPP
WEEKEND COMICS
WHATCHA READING, POP?
BLONDIE!
8-28 www.fborfw.com
I CAN'T BELIEVE THE SITUATIONS DAGWOOD GETS HIMSELF INTO! ...AND THAT BOSS OF HIS CAN BE A TYRANT!
HEH HEH HEH!
I'VE BEEN READING THIS SINCE I WAS A KID! —IT'S BEEN IN THE PAPER FOR 75 YEARS NOW.
THAT'S A PRETTY LONG TIME!
YEP. LONGER THAN I'VE BEEN AROUND!
AND EVEN THOUGH IT'S ONLY A COMIC STRIP.... I FEEL AS THOUGH I **KNOW** THESE PEOPLE!
HAPPY 75TH ANNIVERSARY, DEAN, CHARLOTTE AND COMPANY!! LYNN

BARNEY GOOGLE AND SNUFFY SMITH

BY JOHN ROSE

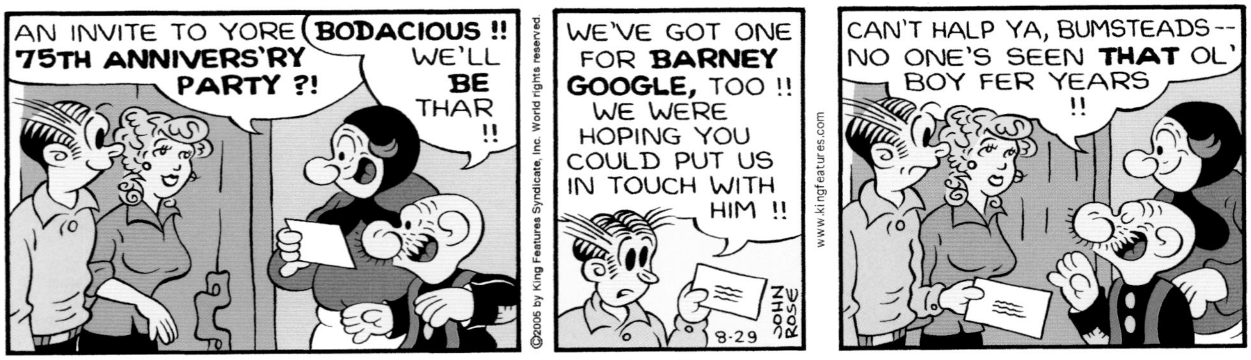

AN INVITE TO YORE **75TH ANNIVERS'RY PARTY?!**
BODACIOUS!! WE'LL **BE** THAR!!
©2005 by King Features Syndicate, Inc. World rights reserved.
WE'VE GOT ONE FOR **BARNEY GOOGLE,** TOO!! WE WERE HOPING YOU COULD PUT US IN TOUCH WITH HIM!!
8-29 JOHN ROSE
www.kingfeatures.com
CAN'T HALP YA, BUMSTEADS-- NO ONE'S SEEN **THAT** OL' BOY FER YEARS!!

BUCKLES

BY DAVID GILBERT

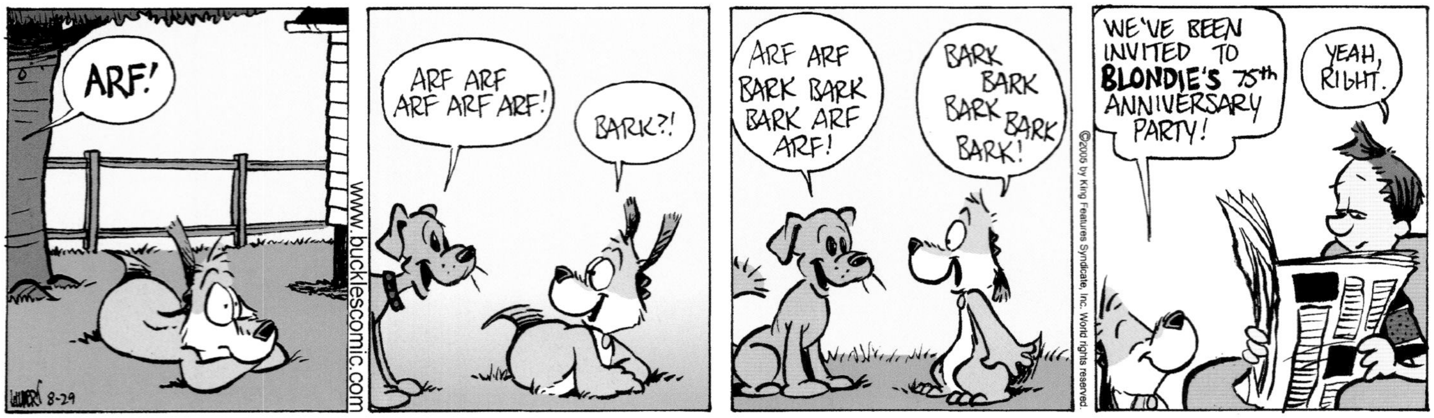

ARF!
www.bucklescomic.com
ARF ARF ARF ARF ARF!
BARK?!
ARF ARF BARK BARK BARK ARF ARF!
BARK BARK BARK BARK BARK!
©2005 by King Features Syndicate, Inc. World rights reserved.
WE'VE BEEN INVITED TO BLONDIE'S 75th ANNIVERSARY PARTY!
YEAH, RIGHT.

BABY BLUES

BY RICK KIRKMAN & JERRY SCOTT

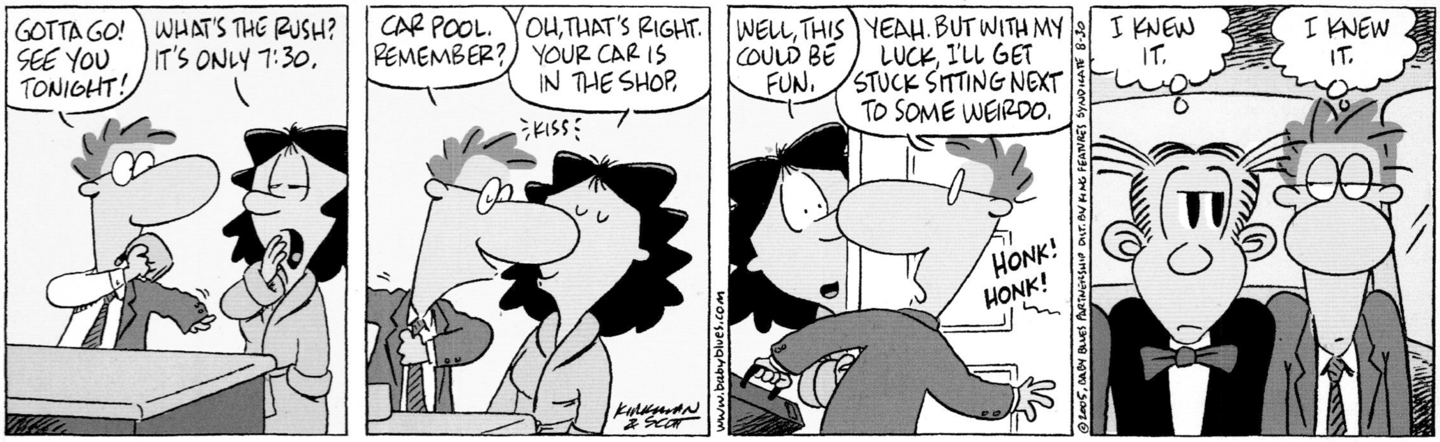

GOTTA GO! SEE YOU TONIGHT!
WHAT'S THE RUSH? IT'S ONLY 7:30.
CAR POOL. REMEMBER?
OH, THAT'S RIGHT. YOUR CAR IS IN THE SHOP.
KISS
KIRKMAN & SCOTT
www.babyblues.com
WELL, THIS COULD BE FUN.
YEAH. BUT WITH MY LUCK, I'LL GET STUCK SITTING NEXT TO SOME WEIRDO.
HONK! HONK!
I KNEW IT.
I KNEW IT.

CURTIS

BY RAY BILLINGSLEY

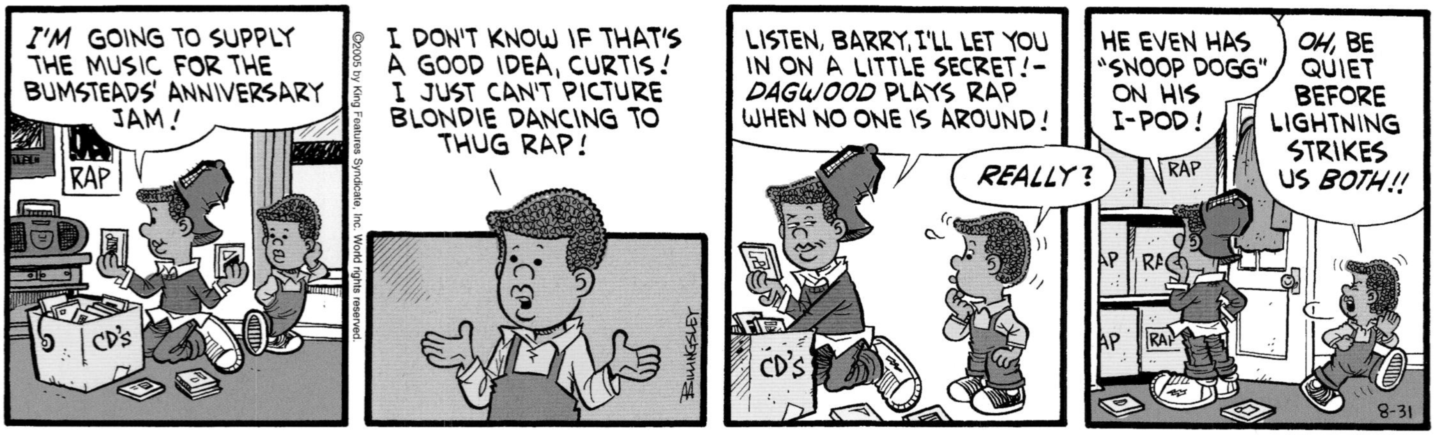

I'M GOING TO SUPPLY THE MUSIC FOR THE BUMSTEADS' ANNIVERSARY JAM!
RAP
CD's
©2005 by King Features Syndicate, Inc. World rights reserved.
I DON'T KNOW IF THAT'S A GOOD IDEA, CURTIS! I JUST CAN'T PICTURE BLONDIE DANCING TO THUG RAP!
BILLINGSLEY
LISTEN, BARRY, I'LL LET YOU IN ON A LITTLE SECRET! - DAGWOOD PLAYS RAP WHEN NO ONE IS AROUND!
REALLY?
CD's
HE EVEN HAS "SNOOP DOGG" ON HIS I-POD!
OH, BE QUIET BEFORE LIGHTNING STRIKES US BOTH!!
RAP
8-31

ZITS — **BY JERRY SCOTT & JIM BORGMAN**

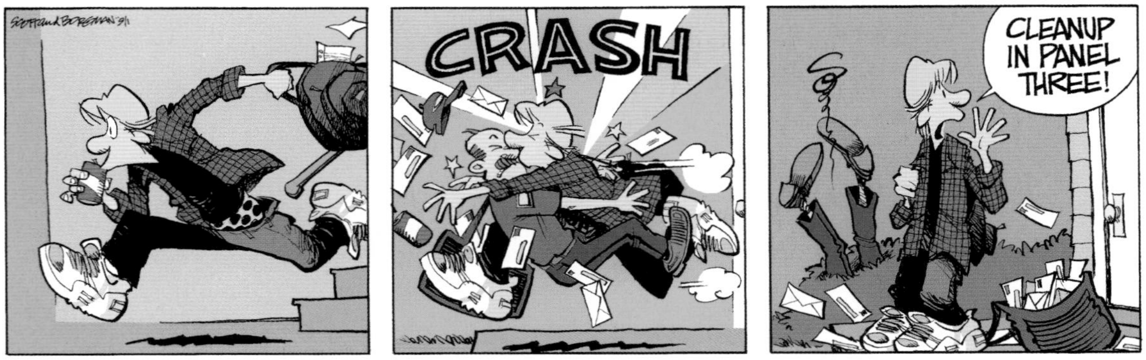
CRASH
CLEANUP IN PANEL THREE!

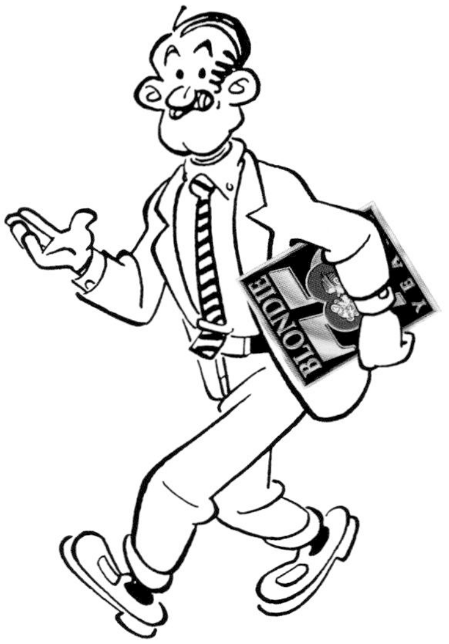

HAGAR THE HORRIBLE — **BY CHRIS BROWNE**

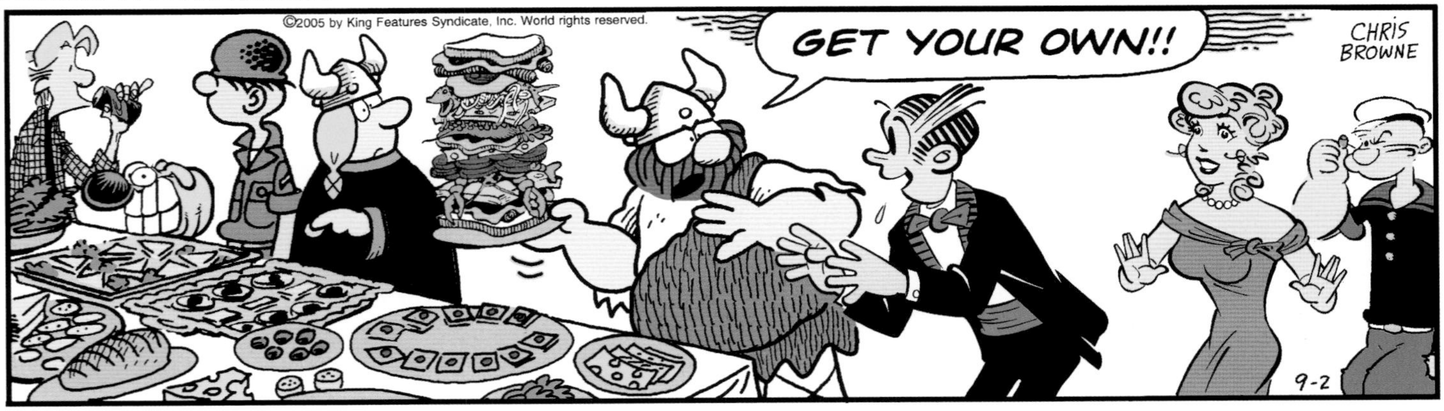
©2005 by King Features Syndicate, Inc. World rights reserved.
GET YOUR OWN!!
CHRIS BROWNE
9-2

MARVIN — **BY TOM ARMSTRONG**

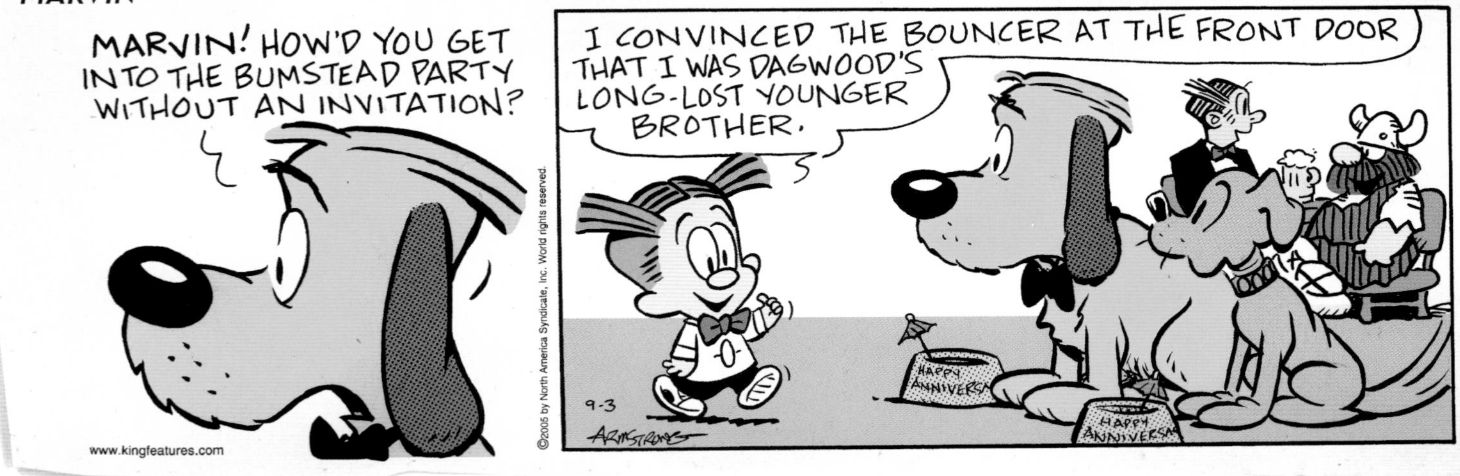
MARVIN! HOW'D YOU GET INTO THE BUMSTEAD PARTY WITHOUT AN INVITATION?
www.kingfeatures.com
©2005 by North America Syndicate, Inc. World rights reserved.
I CONVINCED THE BOUNCER AT THE FRONT DOOR THAT I WAS DAGWOOD'S LONG-LOST YOUNGER BROTHER.
HAPPY ANNIVERSA
HAPPY ANNIVERSA
9-3
ARMSTRONG

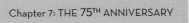

BIZARRO **BY DAN PIRARO**

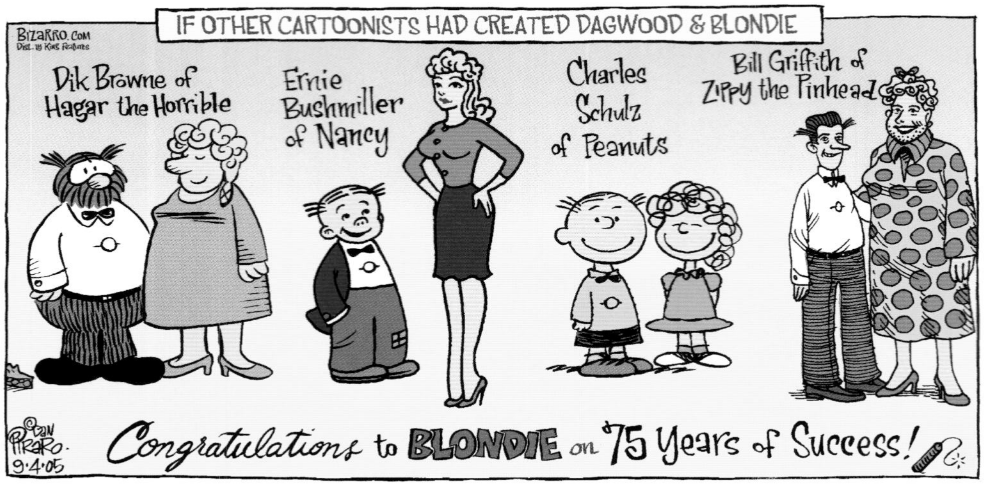
IF OTHER CARTOONISTS HAD CREATED DAGWOOD & BLONDIE
BIZARRO.COM
Dik Browne of Hagar the Horrible
Ernie Bushmiller of Nancy
Charles Schulz of Peanuts
Bill Griffith of Zippy the Pinhead
©DAN PIRARO 9·4·05
Congratulations to BLONDIE on 75 Years of Success!

© Dan Piraro 2005. Distributed by King Features Syndicate.

B.C. **BY JOHNNY HART**

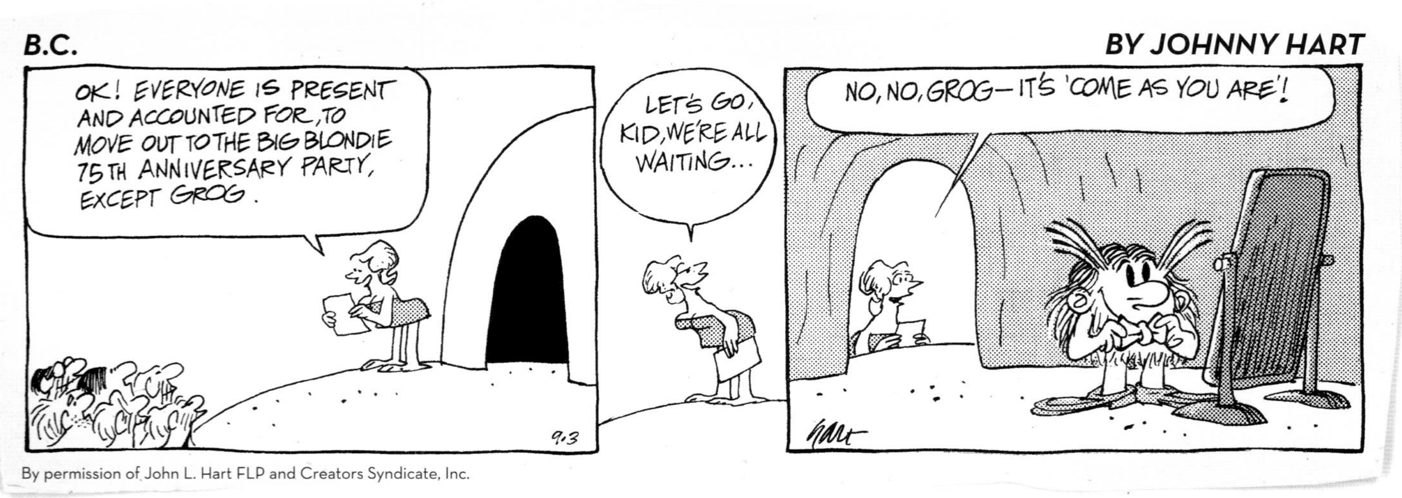
OK! EVERYONE IS PRESENT AND ACCOUNTED FOR, TO MOVE OUT TO THE BIG BLONDIE 75TH ANNIVERSARY PARTY, EXCEPT GROG.
9·3
LET'S GO, KID, WE'RE ALL WAITING...
NO, NO, GROG— IT'S 'COME AS YOU ARE'!
hart

By permission of John L. Hart FLP and Creators Syndicate, Inc.

Blondie is without a doubt the world's most beloved comic strip.

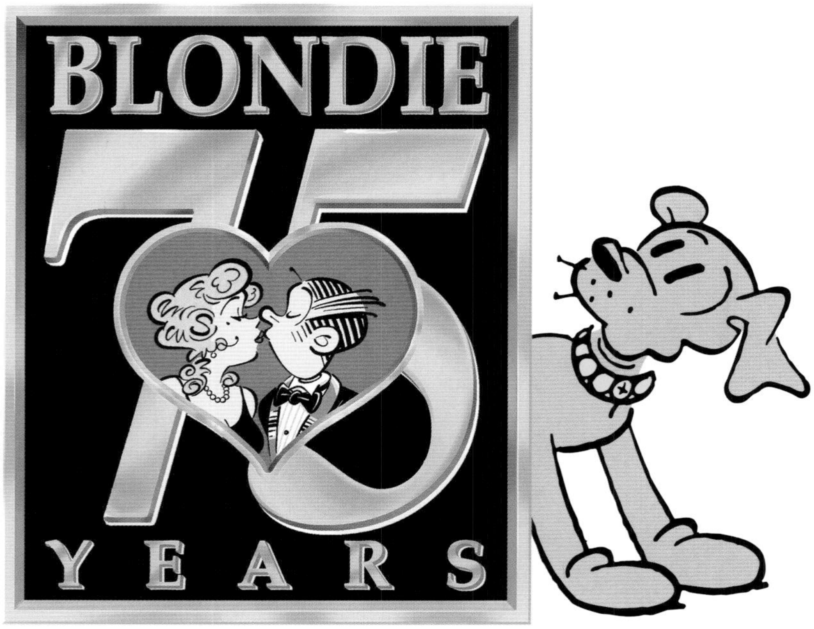
BLONDIE
75
YEARS

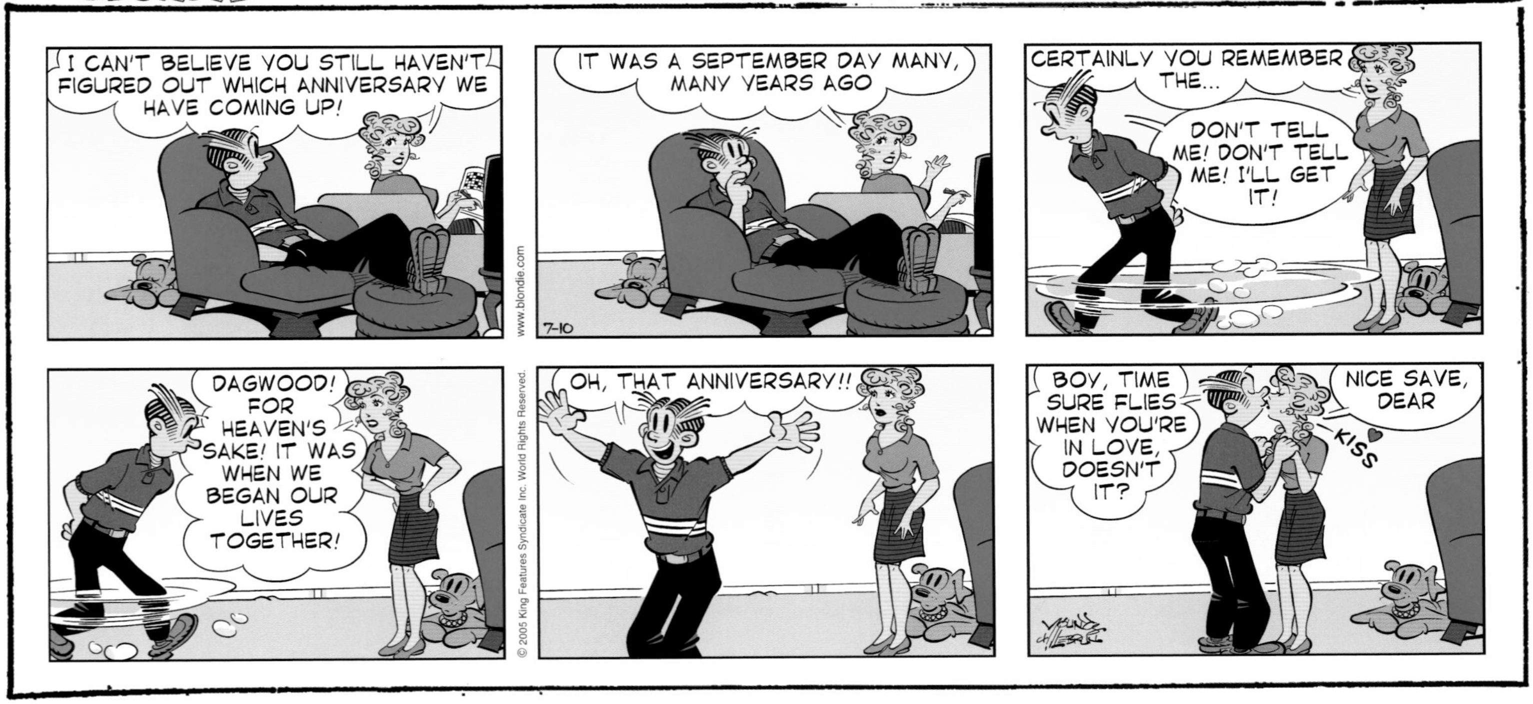
I CAN'T BELIEVE YOU STILL HAVEN'T FIGURED OUT WHICH ANNIVERSARY WE HAVE COMING UP!
IT WAS A SEPTEMBER DAY MANY, MANY YEARS AGO
CERTAINLY YOU REMEMBER THE...
DON'T TELL ME! DON'T TELL ME! I'LL GET IT!
DAGWOOD! FOR HEAVEN'S SAKE! IT WAS WHEN WE BEGAN OUR LIVES TOGETHER!
OH, THAT ANNIVERSARY!!
BOY, TIME SURE FLIES WHEN YOU'RE IN LOVE, DOESN'T IT?
NICE SAVE, DEAR
KISS
www.blondie.com
7-10
© 2005 King Features Syndicate Inc. World Rights Reserved.

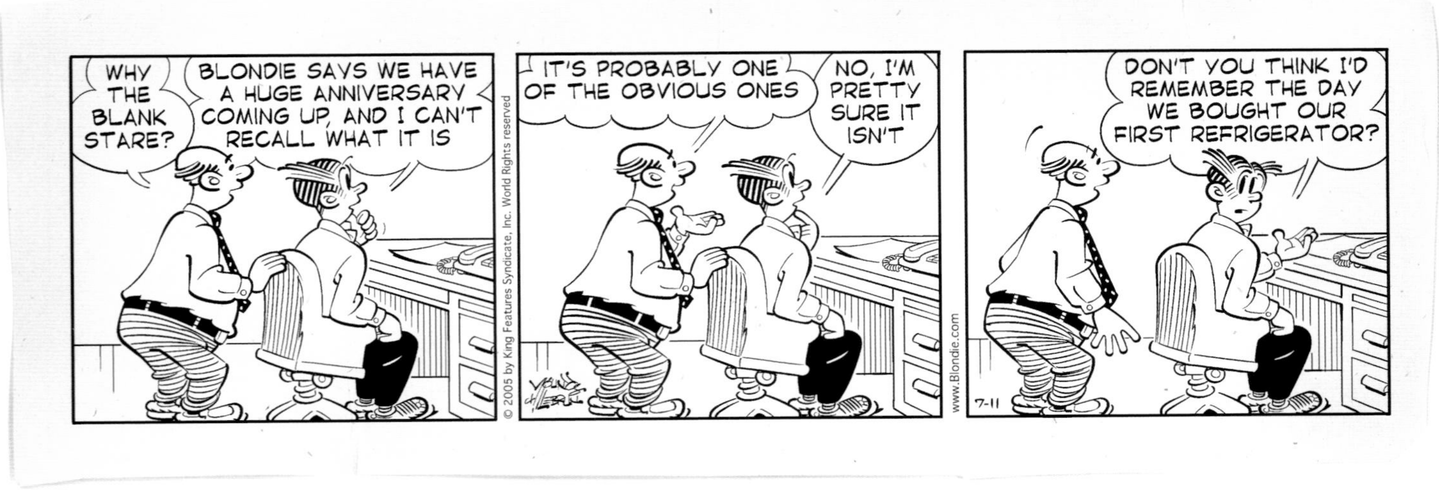
WHY THE BLANK STARE?
BLONDIE SAYS WE HAVE A HUGE ANNIVERSARY COMING UP, AND I CAN'T RECALL WHAT IT IS
IT'S PROBABLY ONE OF THE OBVIOUS ONES
NO, I'M PRETTY SURE IT ISN'T
DON'T YOU THINK I'D REMEMBER THE DAY WE BOUGHT OUR FIRST REFRIGERATOR?
© 2005 by King Features Syndicate, Inc. World Rights reserved
www.Blondie.com
7-11

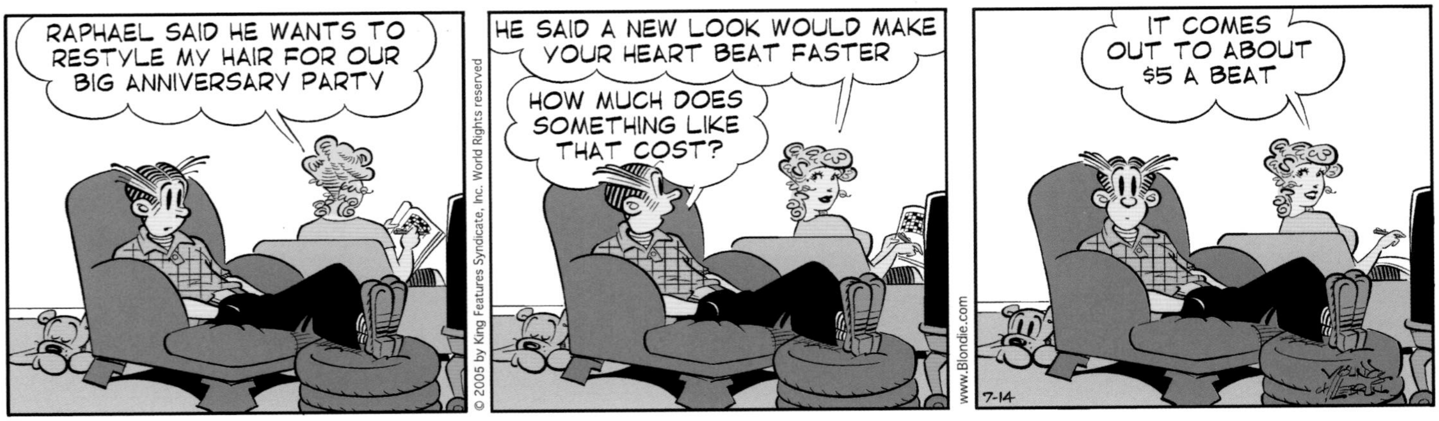
RAPHAEL SAID HE WANTS TO RESTYLE MY HAIR FOR OUR BIG ANNIVERSARY PARTY
HE SAID A NEW LOOK WOULD MAKE YOUR HEART BEAT FASTER
HOW MUCH DOES SOMETHING LIKE THAT COST?
IT COMES OUT TO ABOUT $5 A BEAT
© 2005 by King Features Syndicate, Inc. World Rights reserved
www.Blondie.com
7-14

ARE YOU EXCITED ABOUT OUR PARTY, DEAR?
YES, IT'S ALL I CAN THINK ABOUT LATELY
WELL...THAT, AND THE LEFTOVER PIZZA IN THE KITCHEN
© 2005 by King Features Syndicate, Inc. World Rights reserved
7-20
www.Blondie.com

HOW'S YOUR INVITATION LIST FOR THE PARTY COMING ALONG?
DAGWOOD HAS IT NARROWED DOWN TO JUST THE PEOPLE HE'S CLOSEST TO
THAT MEANS I'M IN!
© 2005 by King Features Syndicate, Inc. World Rights reserved
7-22
www.Blondie.com

MOM, WHAT'S WITH DADDY?!
YEAH, HE'S BEEN IN THE YARD ALL DAY... SITTING AND STARING!
HE'S BUSY THINKING...I ASKED HIM TO PLAN THE MENU FOR OUR PARTY
WELL, HE'S SURE GIVING IT LOTS OF TIME
I'VE GOT IT! I FINALLY DECIDED ON THE APPETIZER!
© 2005 by King Features Syndicate, Inc. World Rights reserved
7-23
www.Blondie.com

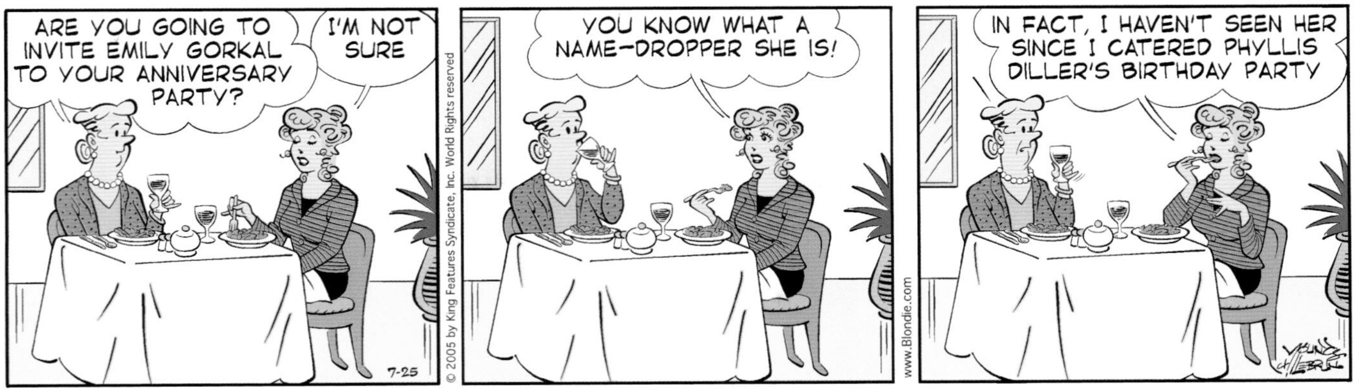
ARE YOU GOING TO INVITE EMILY GORKAL TO YOUR ANNIVERSARY PARTY?
I'M NOT SURE
7-25
© 2005 by King Features Syndicate, Inc. World Rights reserved
YOU KNOW WHAT A NAME-DROPPER SHE IS!
www.Blondie.com
IN FACT, I HAVEN'T SEEN HER SINCE I CATERED PHYLLIS DILLER'S BIRTHDAY PARTY

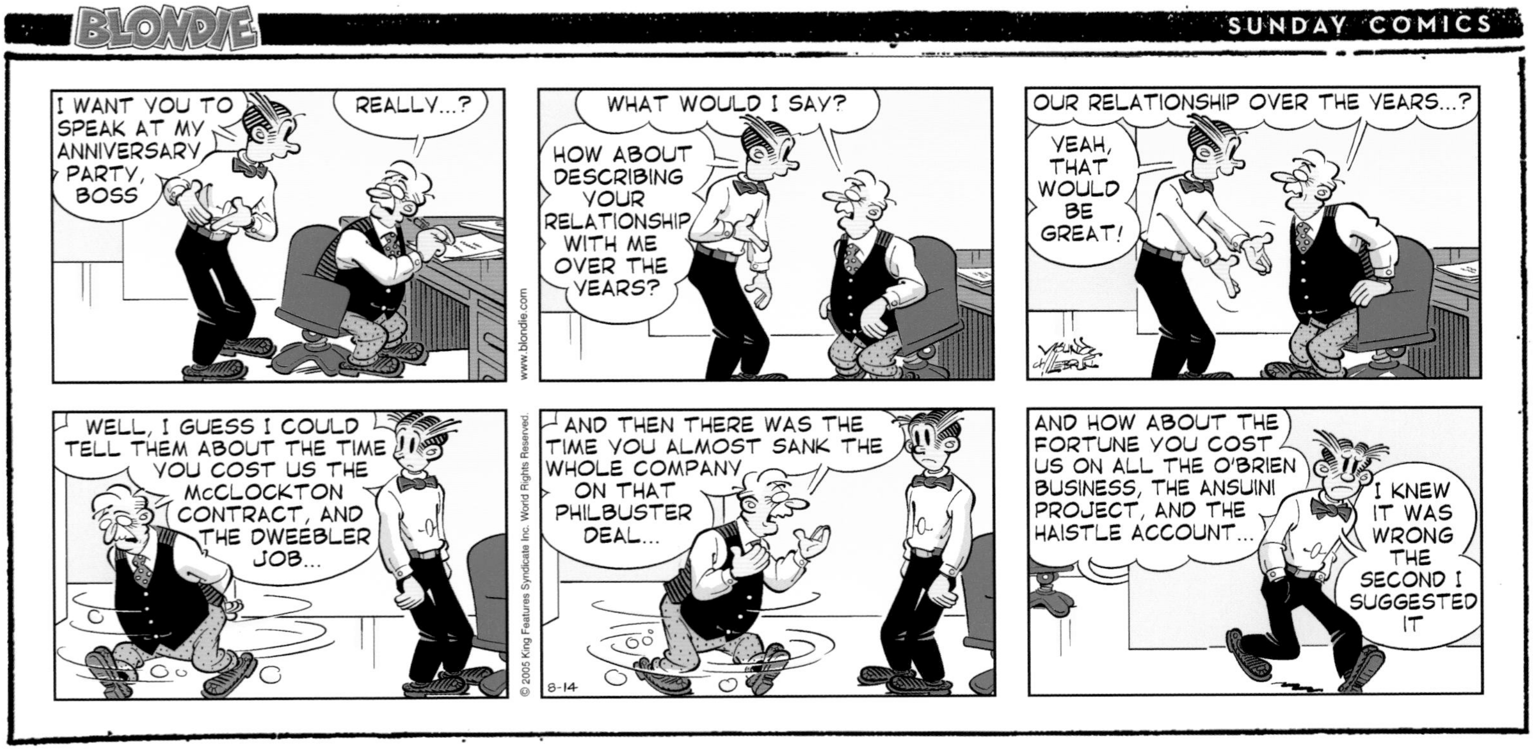
BLONDIE
SUNDAY COMICS
I WANT YOU TO SPEAK AT MY ANNIVERSARY PARTY, BOSS
REALLY...?
www.blondie.com
WHAT WOULD I SAY?
HOW ABOUT DESCRIBING YOUR RELATIONSHIP WITH ME OVER THE YEARS?
OUR RELATIONSHIP OVER THE YEARS...?
YEAH, THAT WOULD BE GREAT!
WELL, I GUESS I COULD TELL THEM ABOUT THE TIME YOU COST US THE McCLOCKTON CONTRACT, AND THE DWEEBLER JOB...
© 2005 King Features Syndicate Inc. World Rights Reserved.
AND THEN THERE WAS THE TIME YOU ALMOST SANK THE WHOLE COMPANY ON THAT PHILBUSTER DEAL...
8-14
AND HOW ABOUT THE FORTUNE YOU COST US ON ALL THE O'BRIEN BUSINESS, THE ANSUINI PROJECT, AND THE HAISTLE ACCOUNT...
I KNEW IT WAS WRONG THE SECOND I SUGGESTED IT

Blondie & Company Celebrate 75 Years

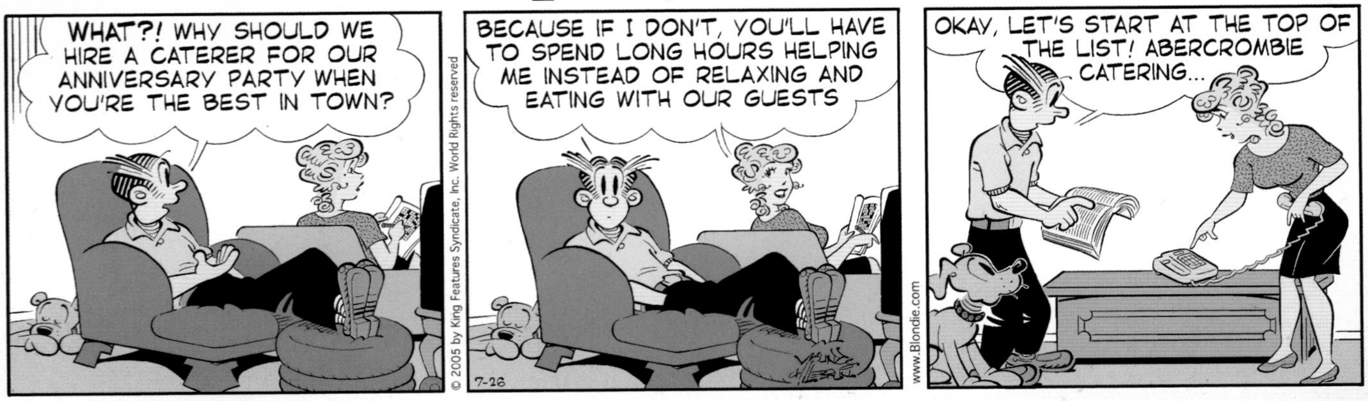
WHAT?! WHY SHOULD WE HIRE A CATERER FOR OUR ANNIVERSARY PARTY WHEN YOU'RE THE BEST IN TOWN?
© 2005 by King Features Syndicate, Inc. World Rights reserved
BECAUSE IF I DON'T, YOU'LL HAVE TO SPEND LONG HOURS HELPING ME INSTEAD OF RELAXING AND EATING WITH OUR GUESTS
7-26
www.Blondie.com
OKAY, LET'S START AT THE TOP OF THE LIST! ABERCROMBIE CATERING...

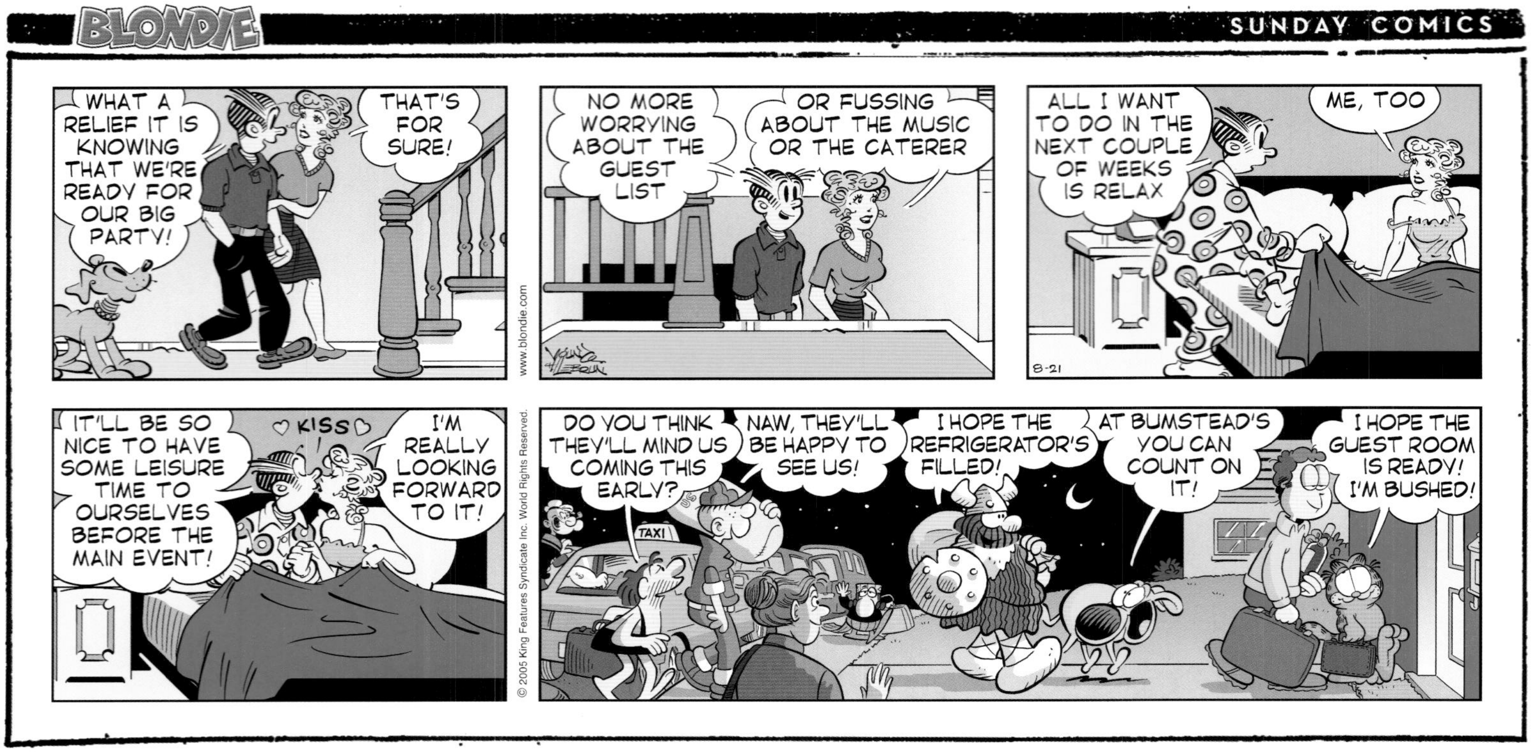
BLONDIE
SUNDAY COMICS
WHAT A RELIEF IT IS KNOWING THAT WE'RE READY FOR OUR BIG PARTY!
THAT'S FOR SURE!
NO MORE WORRYING ABOUT THE GUEST LIST
OR FUSSING ABOUT THE MUSIC OR THE CATERER
ALL I WANT TO DO IN THE NEXT COUPLE OF WEEKS IS RELAX
ME, TOO
8-21
www.blondie.com
IT'LL BE SO NICE TO HAVE SOME LEISURE TIME TO OURSELVES BEFORE THE MAIN EVENT!
KISS
I'M REALLY LOOKING FORWARD TO IT!
© 2005 King Features Syndicate Inc. World Rights Reserved.
DO YOU THINK THEY'LL MIND US COMING THIS EARLY?
NAW, THEY'LL BE HAPPY TO SEE US!
I HOPE THE REFRIGERATOR'S FILLED!
AT BUMSTEAD'S YOU CAN COUNT ON IT!
I HOPE THE GUEST ROOM IS READY! I'M BUSHED!
TAXI

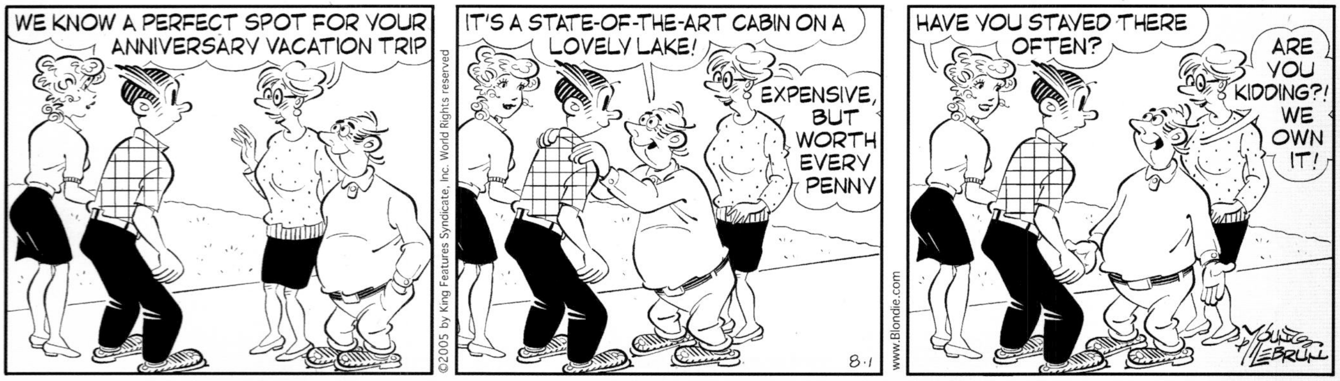
WE KNOW A PERFECT SPOT FOR YOUR ANNIVERSARY VACATION TRIP
©2005 by King Features Syndicate, Inc. World Rights reserved
IT'S A STATE-OF-THE-ART CABIN ON A LOVELY LAKE!
EXPENSIVE, BUT WORTH EVERY PENNY
8-1
www.Blondie.com
HAVE YOU STAYED THERE OFTEN?
ARE YOU KIDDING?! WE OWN IT!

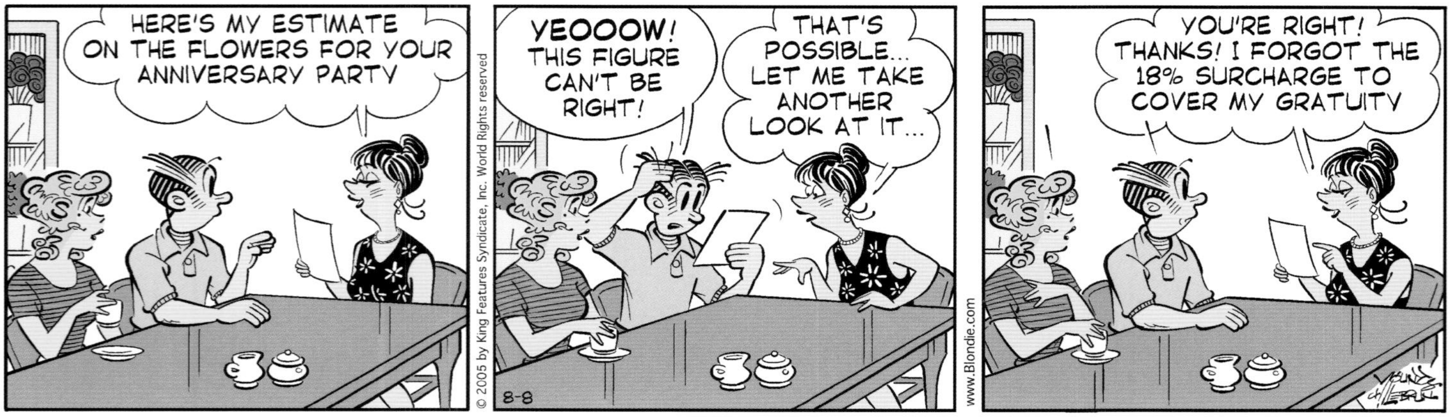
HERE'S MY ESTIMATE ON THE FLOWERS FOR YOUR ANNIVERSARY PARTY
© 2005 by King Features Syndicate, Inc. World Rights reserved
YEOOOW! THIS FIGURE CAN'T BE RIGHT!
THAT'S POSSIBLE... LET ME TAKE ANOTHER LOOK AT IT...
8-8
www.Blondie.com
YOU'RE RIGHT! THANKS! I FORGOT THE 18% SURCHARGE TO COVER MY GRATUITY

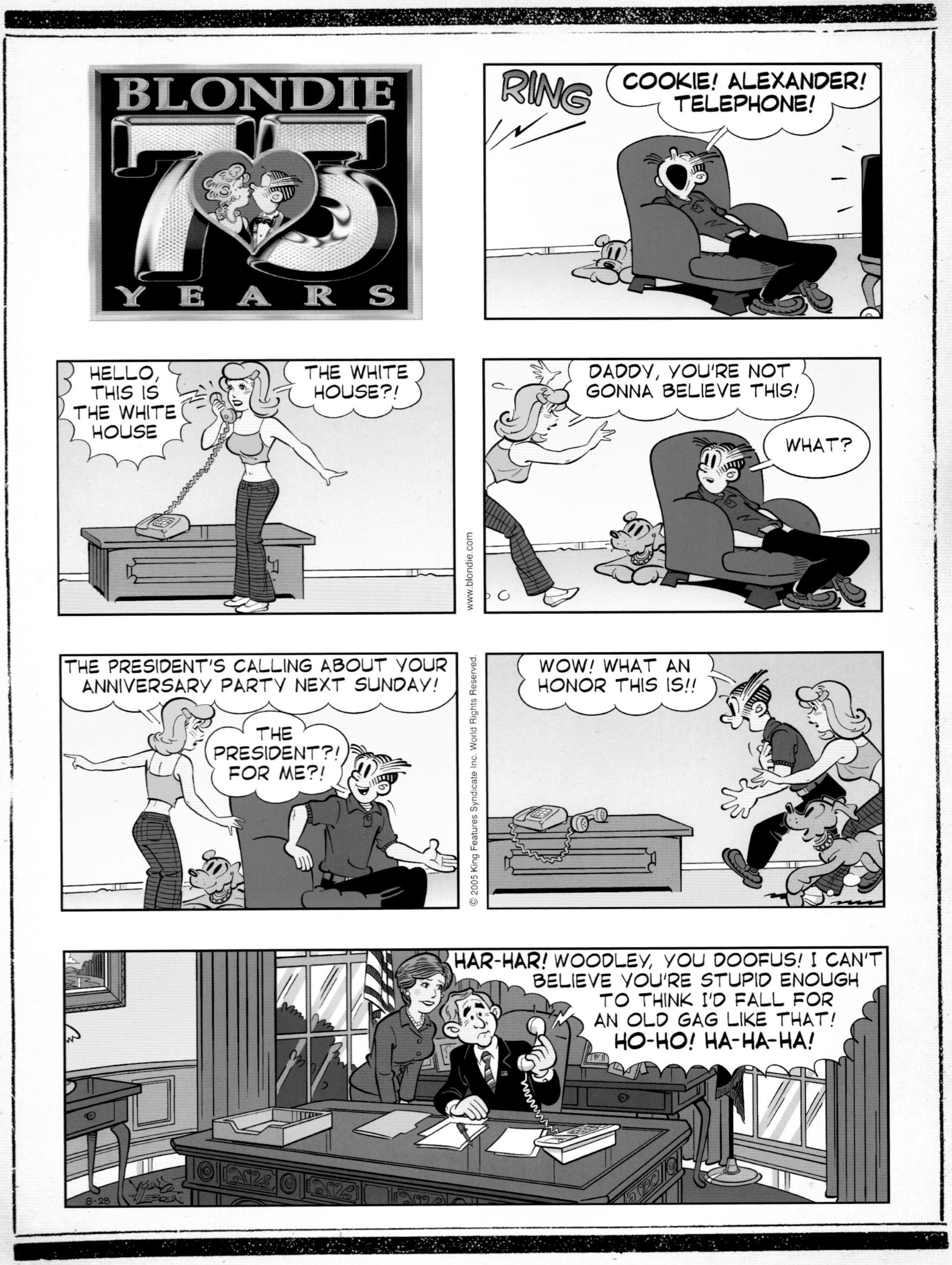
BLONDIE
75
YEARS
RING
COOKIE! ALEXANDER! TELEPHONE!
HELLO, THIS IS THE WHITE HOUSE
THE WHITE HOUSE?!
DADDY, YOU'RE NOT GONNA BELIEVE THIS!
WHAT?
www.blondie.com
© 2005 King Features Syndicate Inc. World Rights Reserved.
THE PRESIDENT'S CALLING ABOUT YOUR ANNIVERSARY PARTY NEXT SUNDAY!
THE PRESIDENT?! FOR ME?!
WOW! WHAT AN HONOR THIS IS!!
HAR-HAR! WOODLEY, YOU DOOFUS! I CAN'T BELIEVE YOU'RE STUPID ENOUGH TO THINK I'D FALL FOR AN OLD GAG LIKE THAT! HO-HO! HA-HA-HA!
8-28

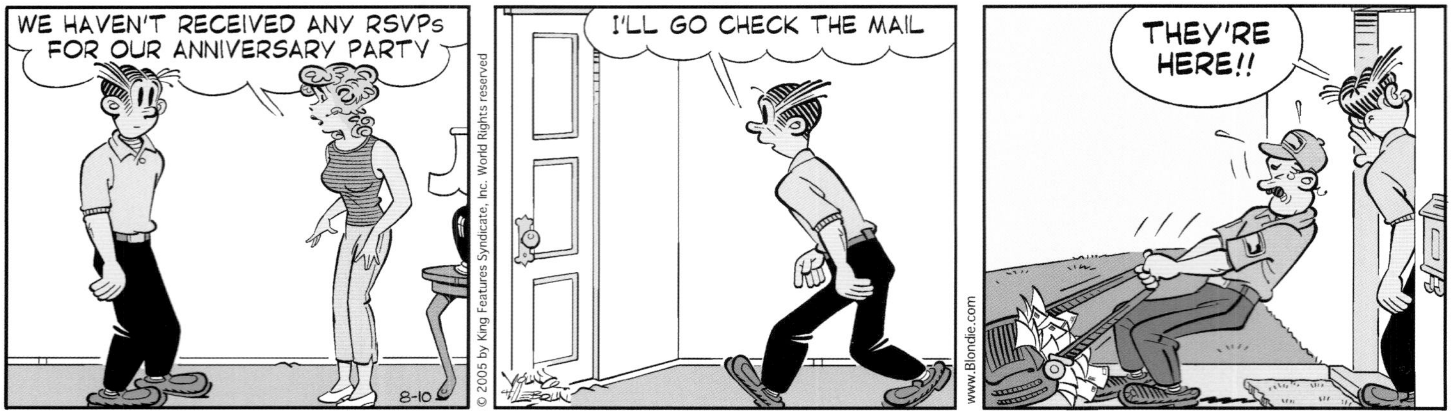
WE HAVEN'T RECEIVED ANY RSVPs FOR OUR ANNIVERSARY PARTY
I'LL GO CHECK THE MAIL
THEY'RE HERE!!
8-10
© 2005 by King Features Syndicate, Inc. World Rights reserved
www.Blondie.com

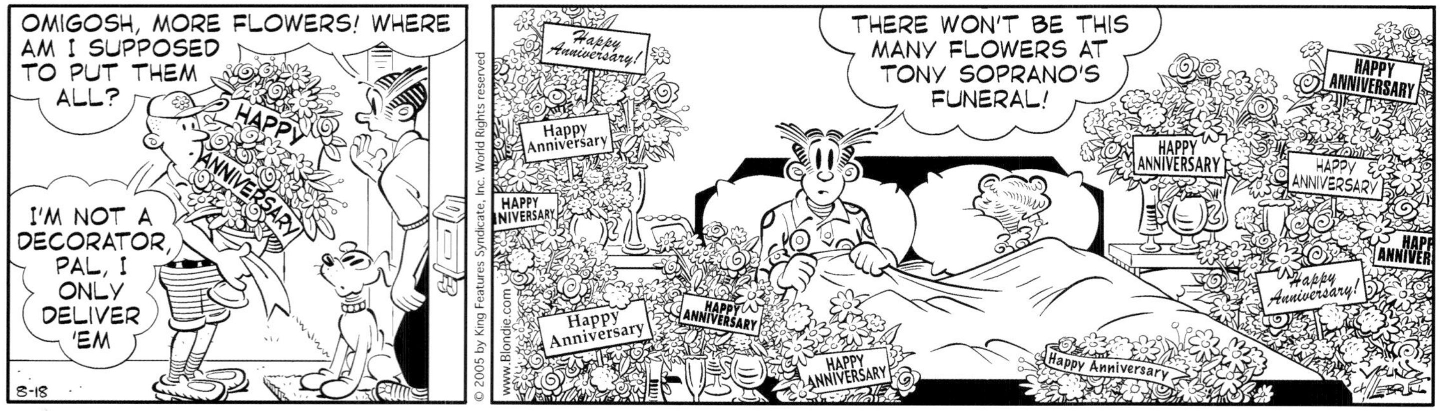
OMIGOSH, MORE FLOWERS! WHERE AM I SUPPOSED TO PUT THEM ALL?
I'M NOT A DECORATOR, PAL, I ONLY DELIVER 'EM
HAPPY ANNIVERSARY
THERE WON'T BE THIS MANY FLOWERS AT TONY SOPRANO'S FUNERAL!
Happy Anniversary!
Happy Anniversary
8-18
© 2005 by King Features Syndicate, Inc. World Rights reserved
www.Blondie.com

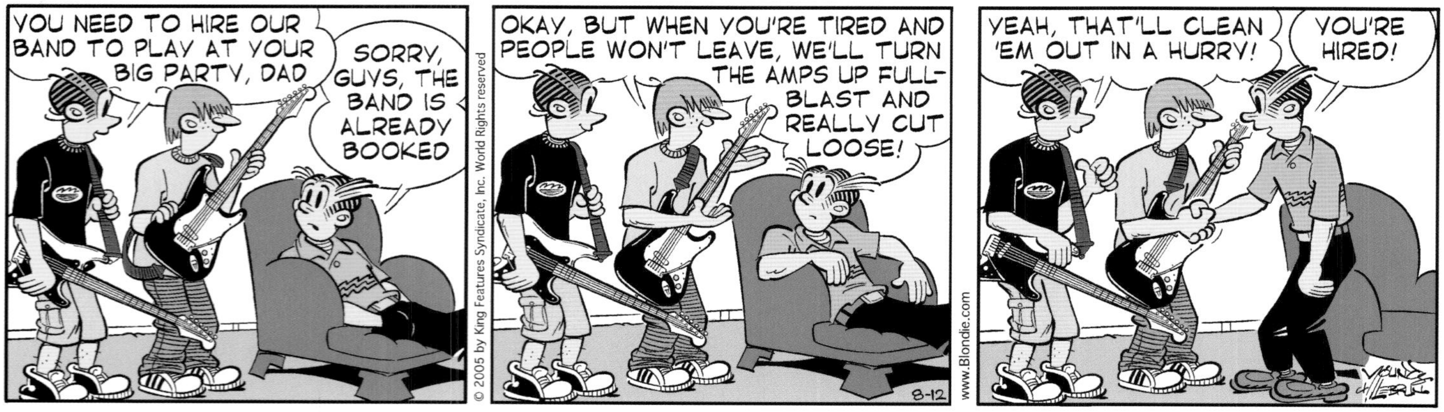
YOU NEED TO HIRE OUR BAND TO PLAY AT YOUR BIG PARTY, DAD
SORRY, GUYS, THE BAND IS ALREADY BOOKED
OKAY, BUT WHEN YOU'RE TIRED AND PEOPLE WON'T LEAVE, WE'LL TURN THE AMPS UP FULL-BLAST AND REALLY CUT LOOSE!
YEAH, THAT'LL CLEAN 'EM OUT IN A HURRY!
YOU'RE HIRED!
8-12
© 2005 by King Features Syndicate, Inc. World Rights reserved
www.Blondie.com

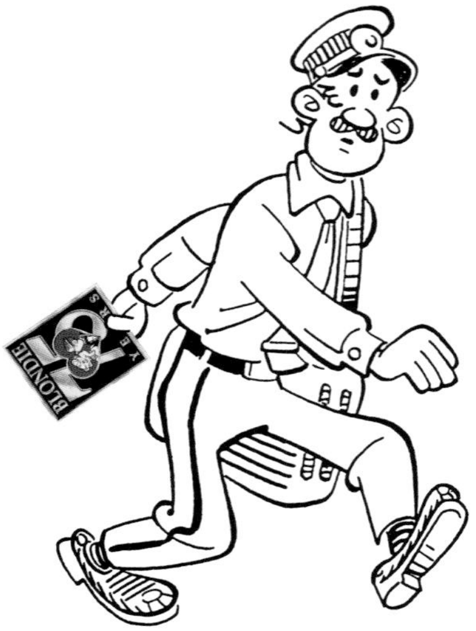
BLONDIE

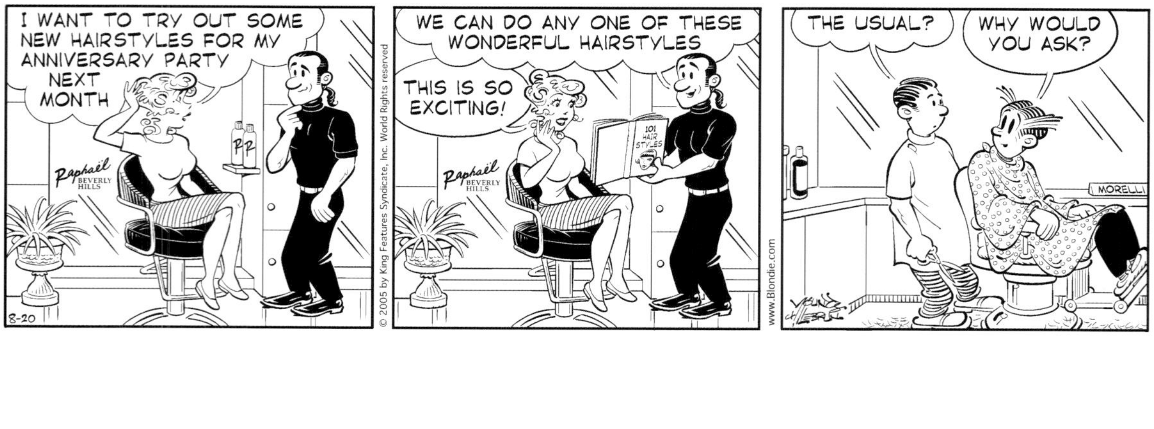
I WANT TO TRY OUT SOME NEW HAIRSTYLES FOR MY ANNIVERSARY PARTY NEXT MONTH
Raphaël BEVERLY HILLS
WE CAN DO ANY ONE OF THESE WONDERFUL HAIRSTYLES
THIS IS SO EXCITING!
101 HAIR STYLES
THE USUAL?
WHY WOULD YOU ASK?
MORELLI
8-20
© 2005 by King Features Syndicate, Inc. World Rights reserved
www.Blondie.com

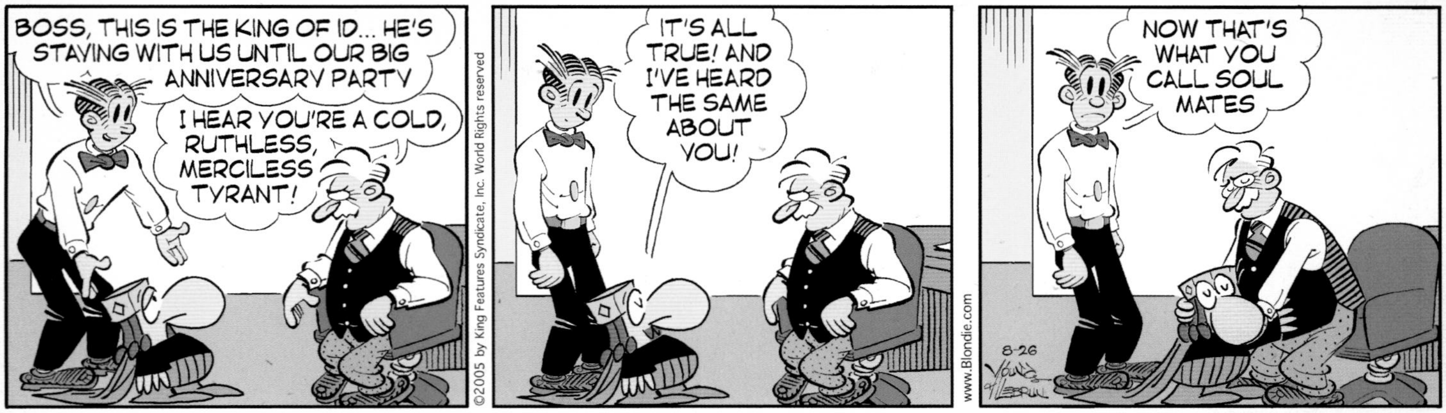
BOSS, THIS IS THE KING OF ID... HE'S STAYING WITH US UNTIL OUR BIG ANNIVERSARY PARTY
I HEAR YOU'RE A COLD, RUTHLESS, MERCILESS TYRANT!
IT'S ALL TRUE! AND I'VE HEARD THE SAME ABOUT YOU!
NOW THAT'S WHAT YOU CALL SOUL MATES
©2005 by King Features Syndicate, Inc. World Rights reserved
www.Blondie.com
8-26

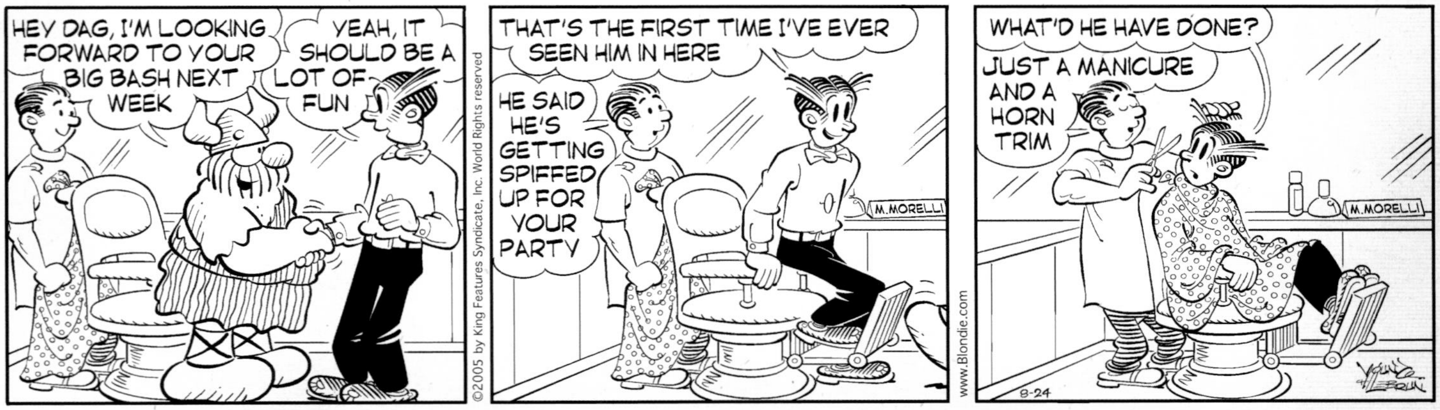
HEY DAG, I'M LOOKING FORWARD TO YOUR BIG BASH NEXT WEEK
YEAH, IT SHOULD BE A LOT OF FUN
THAT'S THE FIRST TIME I'VE EVER SEEN HIM IN HERE
HE SAID HE'S GETTING SPIFFED UP FOR YOUR PARTY
M.MORELLI
WHAT'D HE HAVE DONE?
JUST A MANICURE AND A HORN TRIM
M.MORELLI
©2005 by King Features Syndicate, Inc. World Rights reserved
www.Blondie.com
8-24

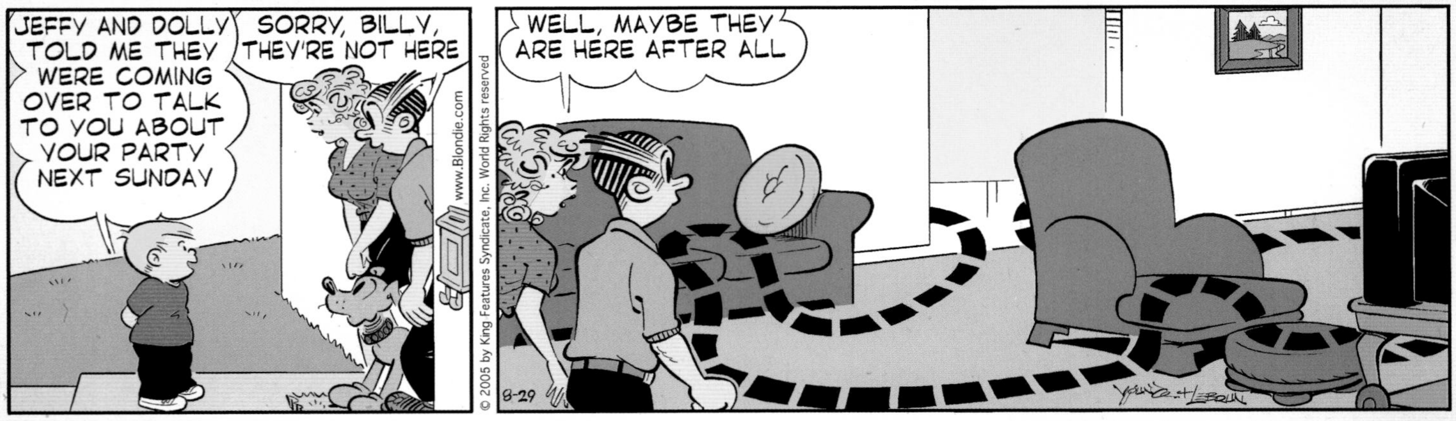
JEFFY AND DOLLY TOLD ME THEY WERE COMING OVER TO TALK TO YOU ABOUT YOUR PARTY NEXT SUNDAY
SORRY, BILLY, THEY'RE NOT HERE
WELL, MAYBE THEY ARE HERE AFTER ALL
© 2005 by King Features Syndicate, Inc. World Rights reserved
www.Blondie.com
8-29

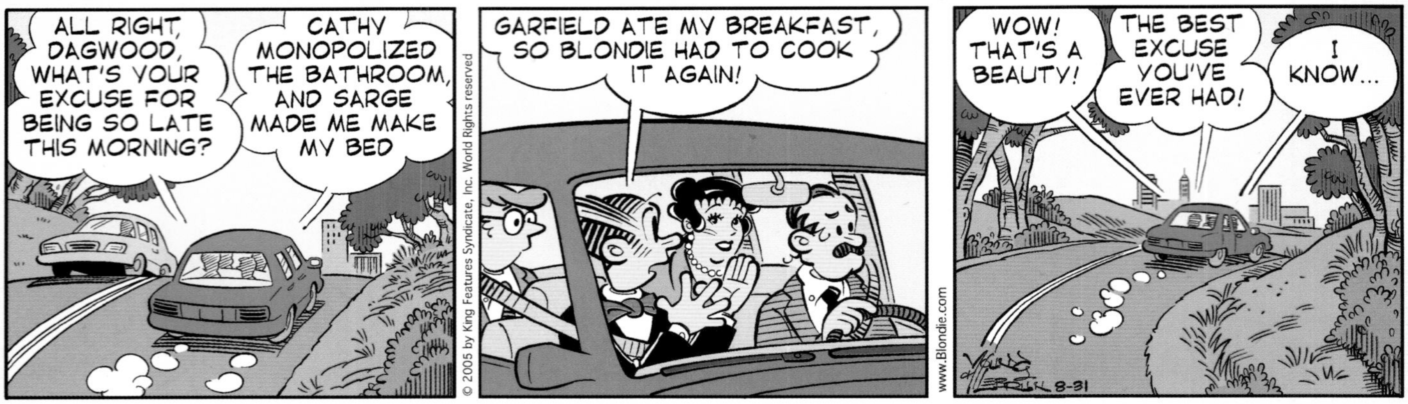
ALL RIGHT, DAGWOOD, WHAT'S YOUR EXCUSE FOR BEING SO LATE THIS MORNING?
CATHY MONOPOLIZED THE BATHROOM, AND SARGE MADE ME MAKE MY BED
GARFIELD ATE MY BREAKFAST, SO BLONDIE HAD TO COOK IT AGAIN!
WOW! THAT'S A BEAUTY!
THE BEST EXCUSE YOU'VE EVER HAD!
I KNOW...
© 2005 by King Features Syndicate, Inc. World Rights reserved
www.Blondie.com
8-31

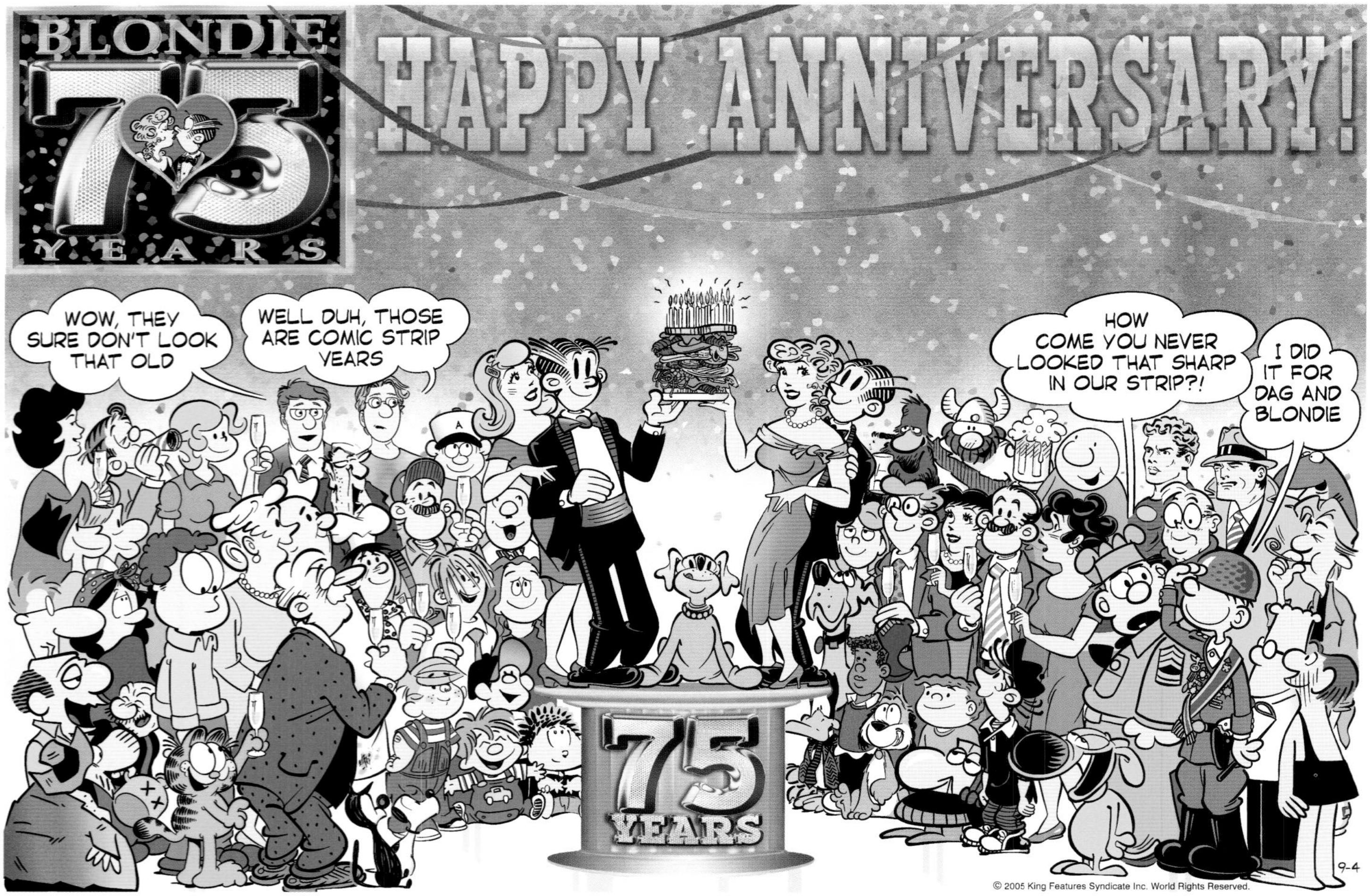
BLONDIE
75
YEARS
HAPPY ANNIVERSARY!
WOW, THEY SURE DON'T LOOK THAT OLD
WELL DUH, THOSE ARE COMIC STRIP YEARS
HOW COME YOU NEVER LOOKED THAT SHARP IN OUR STRIP?!
I DID IT FOR DAG AND BLONDIE
75
YEARS
9-4
© 2005 King Features Syndicate Inc. World Rights Reserved.

WOW, IT'S BEEN A WHILE SINCE WE TRAVELED ANYWHERE
YOU MEAN BECAUSE THEY'RE SO DUSTY?
©2005 by King Features Syndicate, Inc. World Rights reserved
NO, OUR SUITCASES ARE SO OLD THEY DON'T HAVE WHEELS
www.Blondie.com
WHEN DID THEY START PUTTING WHEELS ON SUITCASES?
IT'S BEEN EVEN LONGER THAN I THOUGHT
9·5

CAN YOU BELIEVE WE FORGOT OUR LUGGAGE AND HAD TO GO BACK?
HEARD THAT BEFORE
©2005 by King Features Syndicate, Inc. World Rights reserved
YOU'VE STILL GOT PLENTY OF TIME... I JUST NEED TO SEE I.D. AND TICKETS
9·8
www.Blondie.com
TICKETS?!! I THOUGHT YOU HAD 'EM!!
NO! THEY WERE ON THE KITCHEN TABLE !!

YOUR HUSBAND CAME THROUGH THE INSPECTION OKAY
BUT OUR PLANE IS LEAVING IN A FEW MINUTES!
SECURITY INSPECTION ROOM
9·10
©2005 by King Features Syndicate, Inc. World Rights reserved
I CAN REMEMBER WHEN GENTLEMEN WORE SUITS AND TIES TO THE AIRPORT
LET'S FACE IT, FRIEDA, IT'S A DIFFERENT WORLD!
www.Blondie.com

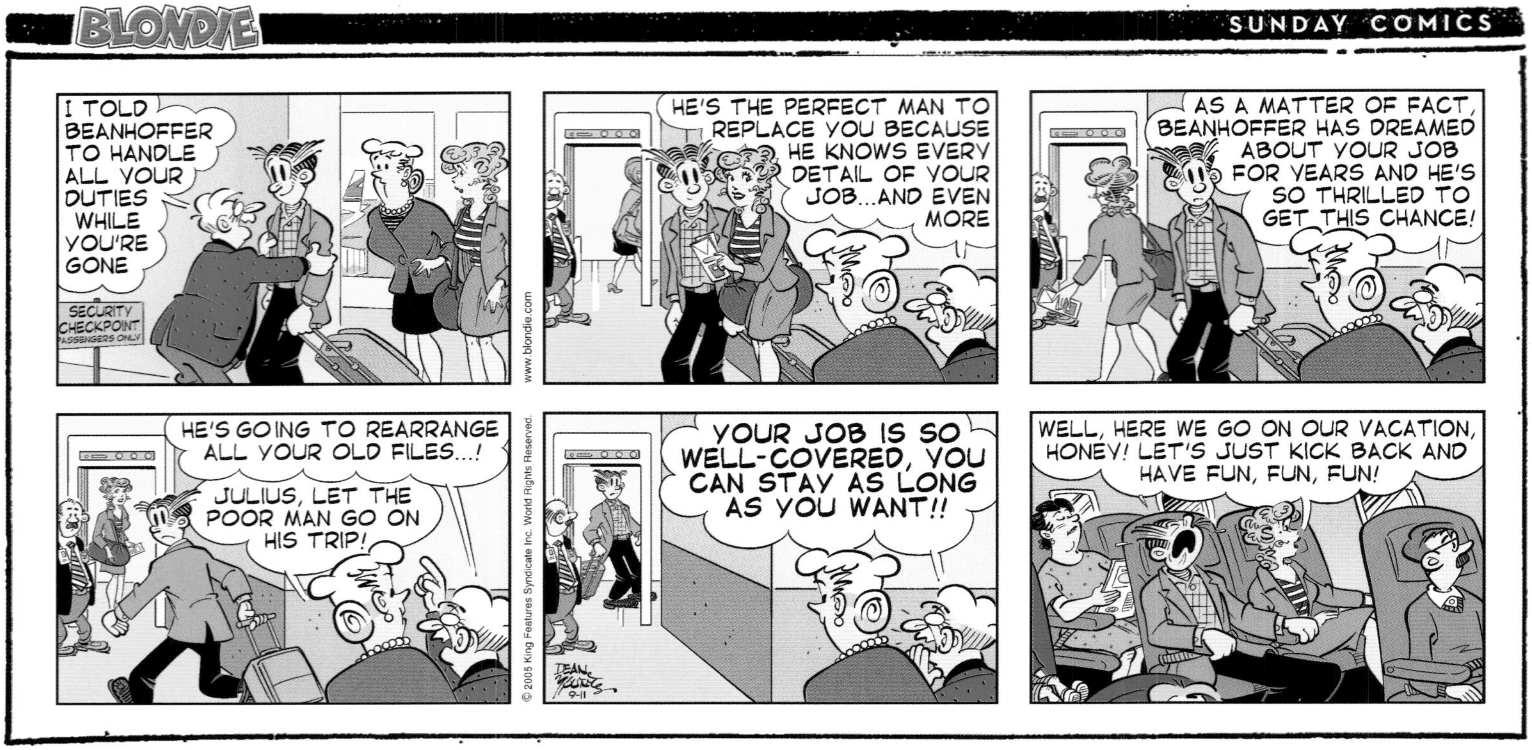
BLONDIE
SUNDAY COMICS
I TOLD BEANHOFFER TO HANDLE ALL YOUR DUTIES WHILE YOU'RE GONE
SECURITY CHECKPOINT PASSENGERS ONLY
HE'S THE PERFECT MAN TO REPLACE YOU BECAUSE HE KNOWS EVERY DETAIL OF YOUR JOB...AND EVEN MORE
www.blondie.com
AS A MATTER OF FACT, BEANHOFFER HAS DREAMED ABOUT YOUR JOB FOR YEARS AND HE'S SO THRILLED TO GET THIS CHANCE!
HE'S GOING TO REARRANGE ALL YOUR OLD FILES...!
JULIUS, LET THE POOR MAN GO ON HIS TRIP!
© 2005 King Features Syndicate Inc. World Rights Reserved.
YOUR JOB IS SO WELL-COVERED, YOU CAN STAY AS LONG AS YOU WANT!!
WELL, HERE WE GO ON OUR VACATION, HONEY! LET'S JUST KICK BACK AND HAVE FUN, FUN, FUN!

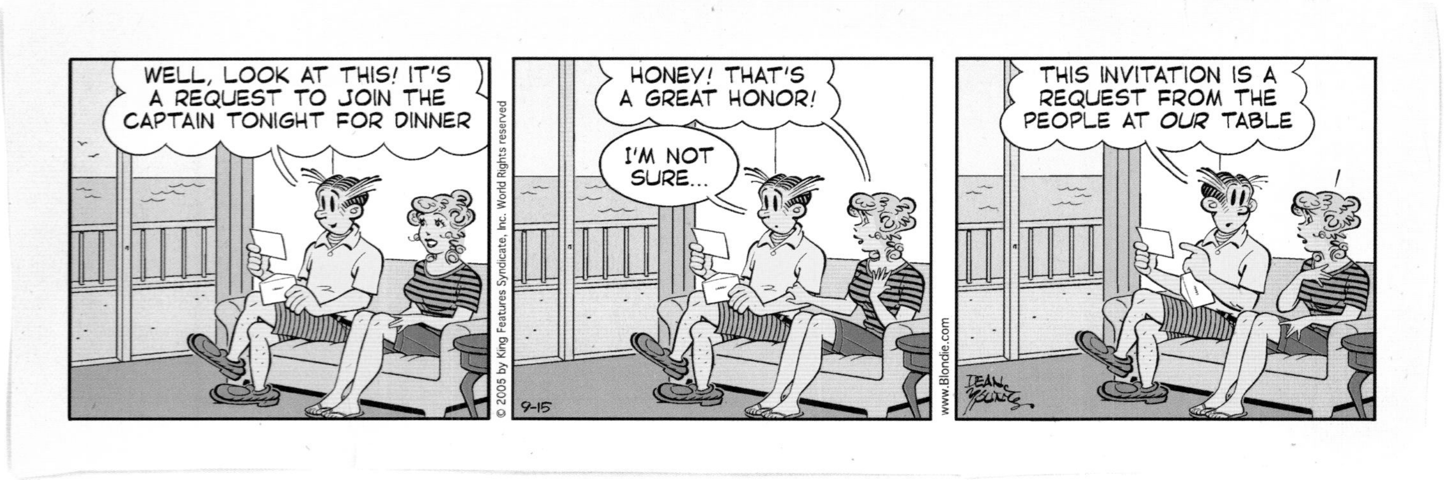
WELL, LOOK AT THIS! IT'S A REQUEST TO JOIN THE CAPTAIN TONIGHT FOR DINNER
© 2005 by King Features Syndicate, Inc. World Rights reserved
HONEY! THAT'S A GREAT HONOR!
I'M NOT SURE...
www.Blondie.com
THIS INVITATION IS A REQUEST FROM THE PEOPLE AT OUR TABLE

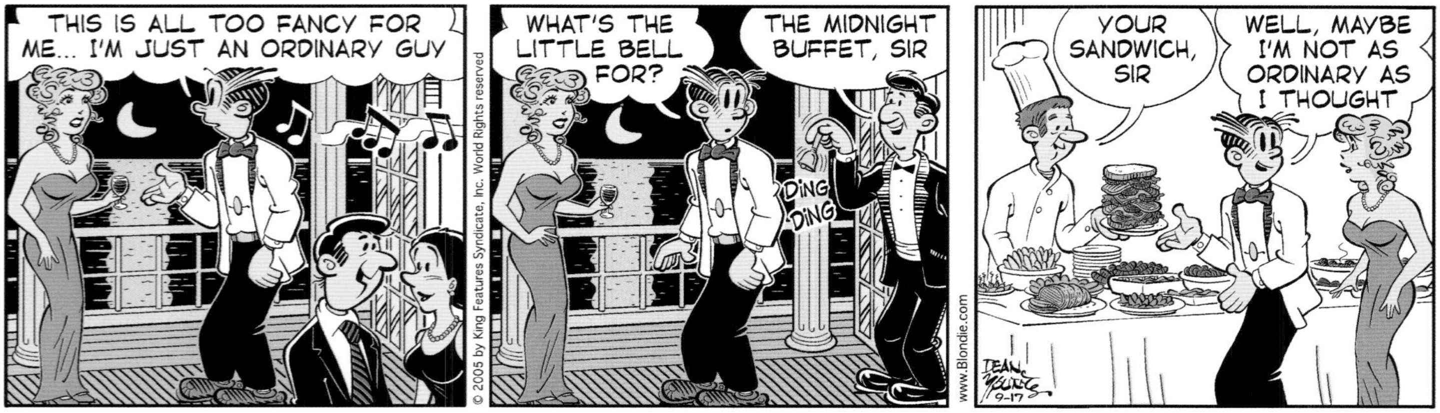
THIS IS ALL TOO FANCY FOR ME... I'M JUST AN ORDINARY GUY
© 2005 by King Features Syndicate, Inc. World Rights reserved
WHAT'S THE LITTLE BELL FOR?
THE MIDNIGHT BUFFET, SIR
DING DING
www.Blondie.com
YOUR SANDWICH, SIR
WELL, MAYBE I'M NOT AS ORDINARY AS I THOUGHT

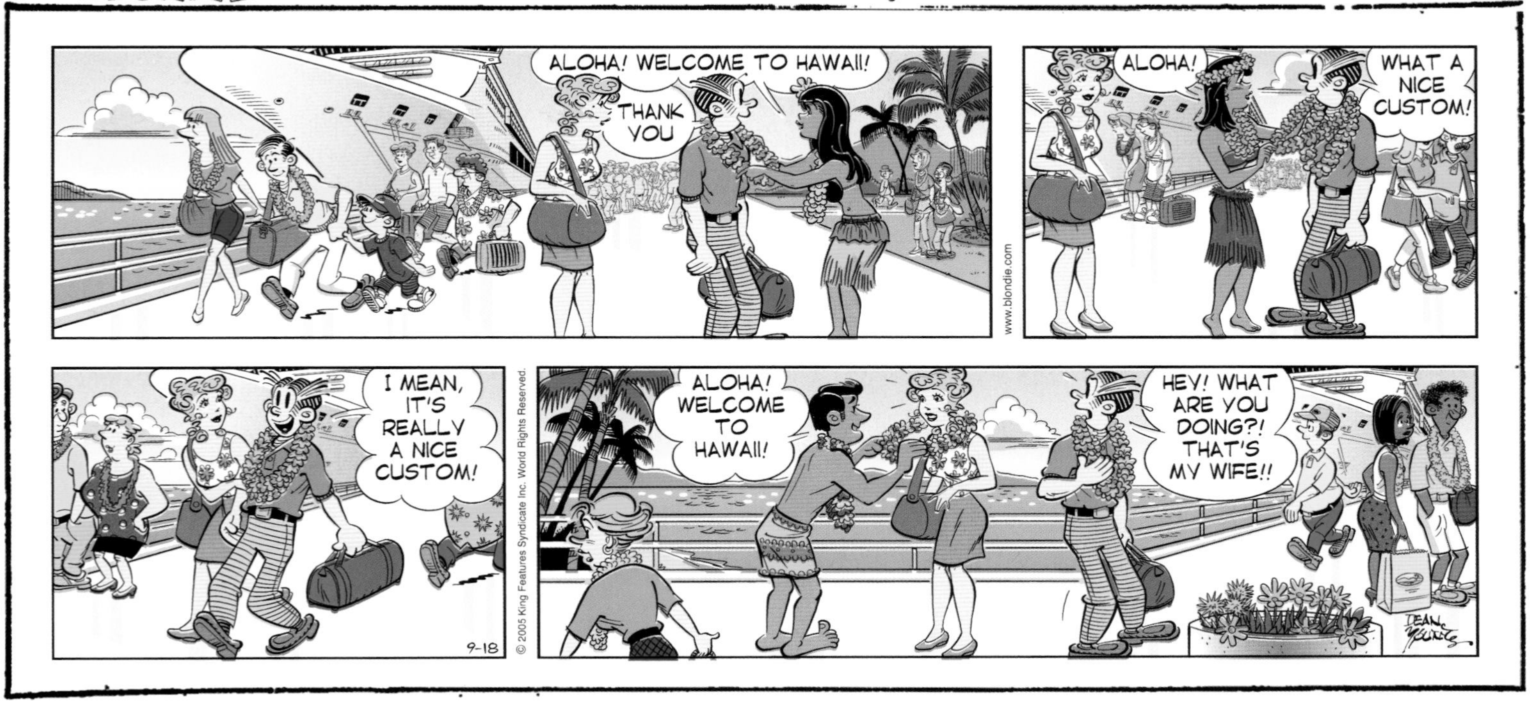
ALOHA! WELCOME TO HAWAII!
THANK YOU
ALOHA!
WHAT A NICE CUSTOM!
I MEAN, IT'S REALLY A NICE CUSTOM!
ALOHA! WELCOME TO HAWAII!
HEY! WHAT ARE YOU DOING?! THAT'S MY WIFE!!
9-18
© 2005 King Features Syndicate Inc. World Rights reserved
www.blondie.com

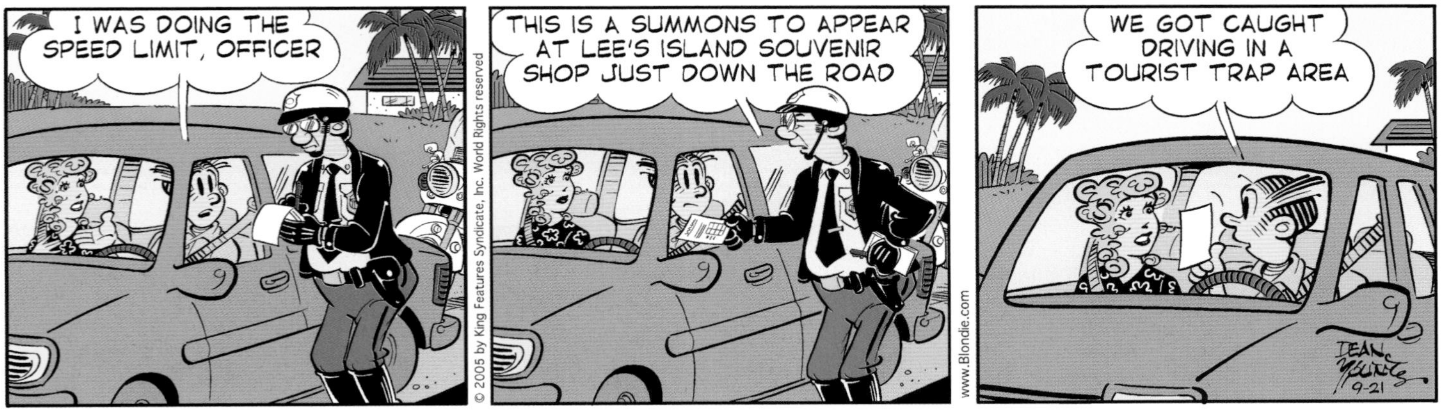
I WAS DOING THE SPEED LIMIT, OFFICER
THIS IS A SUMMONS TO APPEAR AT LEE'S ISLAND SOUVENIR SHOP JUST DOWN THE ROAD
WE GOT CAUGHT DRIVING IN A TOURIST TRAP AREA
9-21
© 2005 by King Features Syndicate, Inc. World Rights reserved
www.Blondie.com

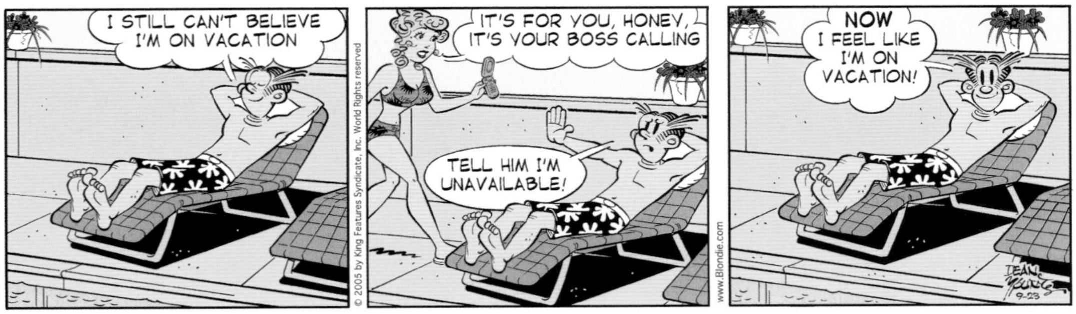
I STILL CAN'T BELIEVE I'M ON VACATION
IT'S FOR YOU, HONEY, IT'S YOUR BOSS CALLING
TELL HIM I'M UNAVAILABLE!
NOW I FEEL LIKE I'M ON VACATION!
© 2005 by King Features Syndicate, Inc. World Rights reserved
www.Blondie.com

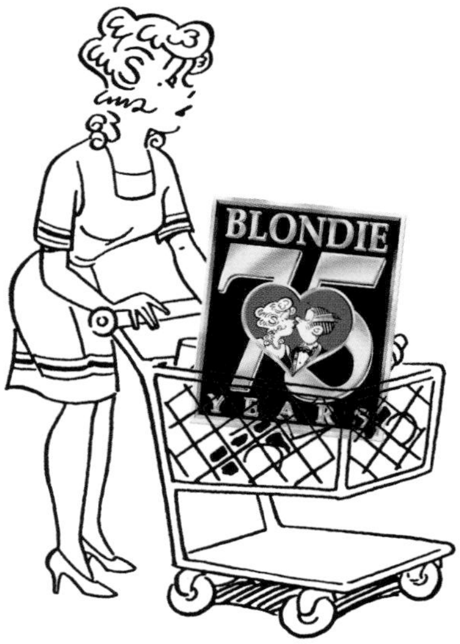
BLONDIE
75
YEARS

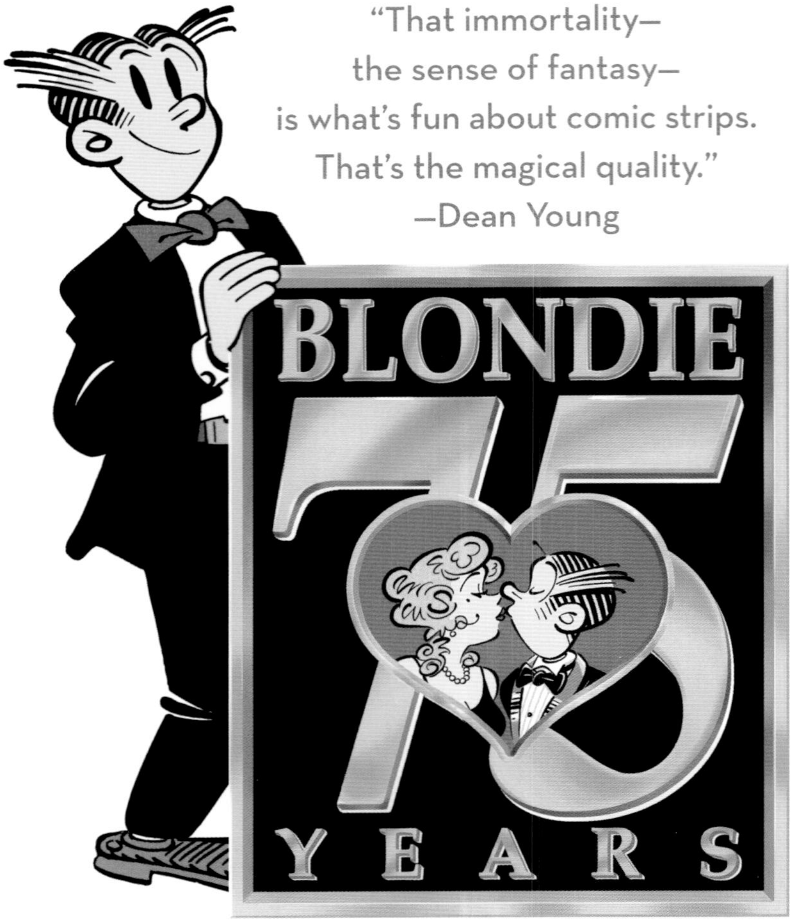
BLONDIE
75
YEARS

"That immortality—
the sense of fantasy—
is what's fun about comic strips.
That's the magical quality."
—Dean Young

Marking more than forty years of his own work on the strip, the event was a highlight for Dean Young. Against all odds, he has managed to extend and even elevate the characters his brilliant father created during the Depression, carrying them through the turn of a century and into another era.

"The Bumsteads' world is pretty steady and nice, and it will stay that way," he says proudly. "That immortality—the sense of fantasy—is what's fun about comic strips. That's the magical quality."

And just as Dean inherited *Blondie* from his father, he is preparing to pass it on to his successor—daughter Dana Coston, who will put her own spin on the characters for decades to come.

Immortality is possible in the comics where the magic, fun, and humor of *Blondie* will carry on.

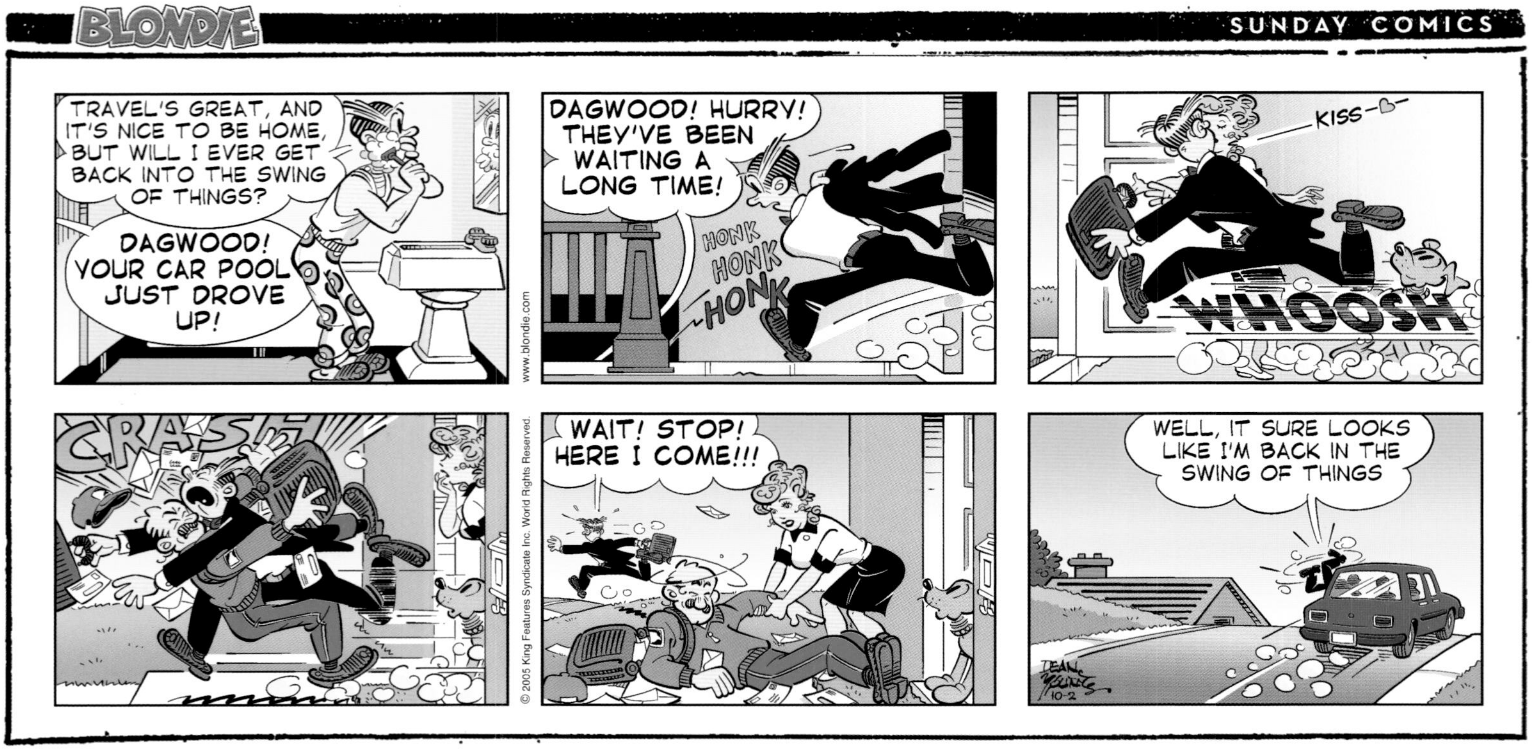
BLONDIE
SUNDAY COMICS
TRAVEL'S GREAT, AND IT'S NICE TO BE HOME, BUT WILL I EVER GET BACK INTO THE SWING OF THINGS?
DAGWOOD! YOUR CAR POOL JUST DROVE UP!
DAGWOOD! HURRY! THEY'VE BEEN WAITING A LONG TIME!
HONK HONK HONK
KISS
WHOOSH
CRASH
WAIT! STOP! HERE I COME!!!
WELL, IT SURE LOOKS LIKE I'M BACK IN THE SWING OF THINGS
www.blondie.com
© 2005 King Features Syndicate Inc. World Rights Reserved.

CHAPTER 8

FOREVER YOUNG

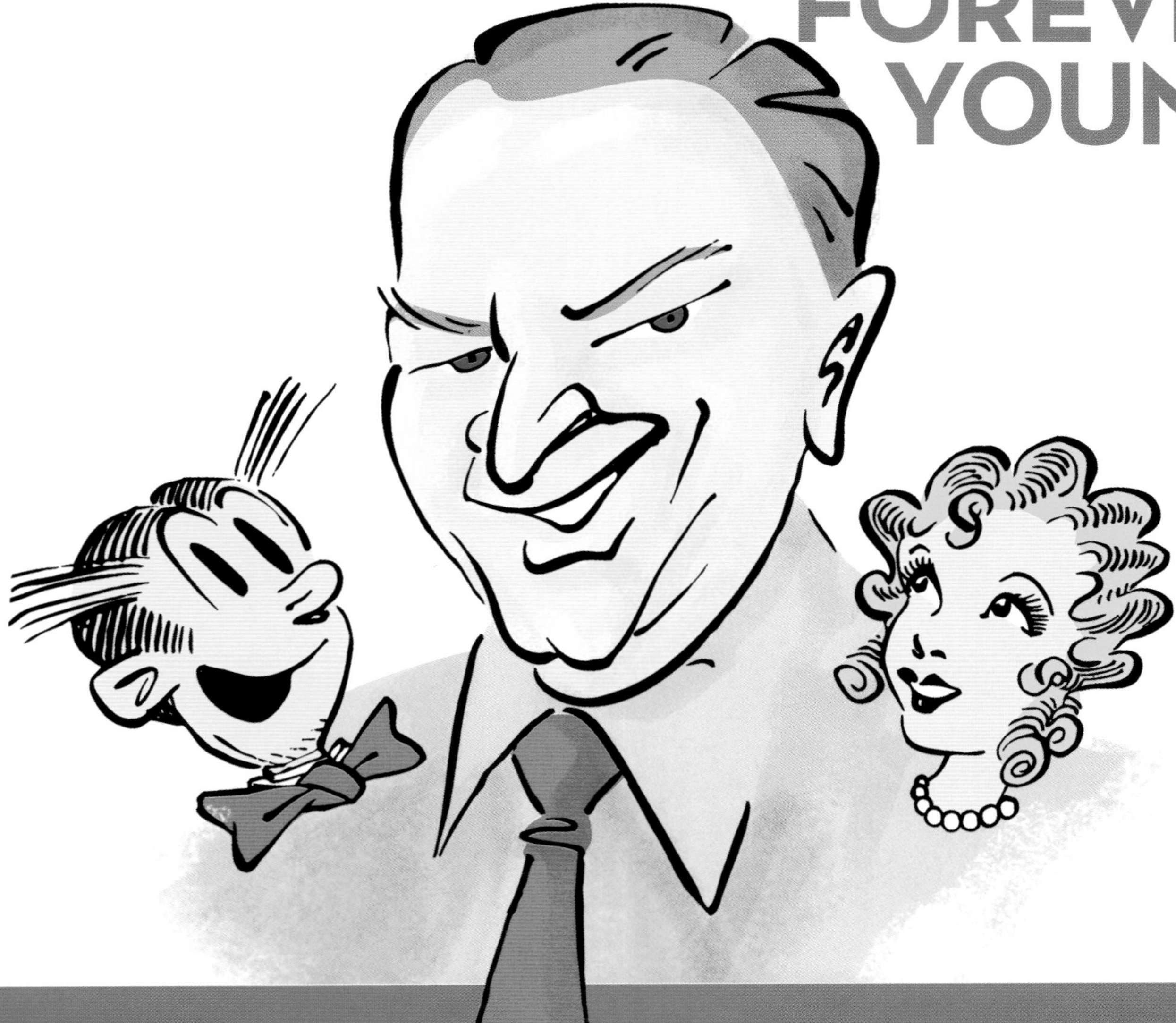

One of the funny pages' longest-lasting and most dynamic storylines began inauspiciously enough, with a man who even his friends and family considered painfully shy.

Murat Bernard Young was born in Chicago, January 9, 1901, and grew up on the south side of St. Louis, a German-Lutheran neighborhood where he inherited typically Teutonic traits like stubbornness, dedication, and frugality, as well as the decidedly un-German nickname "Chic." His father, James, was a shoe salesman who didn't think highly of artists. Of course, this meant that all four of his children were creative types. Son Walter was a painter, daughter Jamar a commercial artist, and Chic's older brother Lyman, the first Young drawn to comics, wound up creating the adventure strip *Tim Tyler's Luck* for King Features Syndicate, where Chic would eventually find a home.

In fact, it was Lyman who cultivated Chic's talent, urging him to draw at every opportunity. Chic worked on his high school yearbook, but with after-school and weekend jobs as a postal clerk and salesman at the family shoe store, he didn't have much time to practice. After high school and a typewriting course, he found a job in Chicago as a stenographer for the vice president of the Illinois

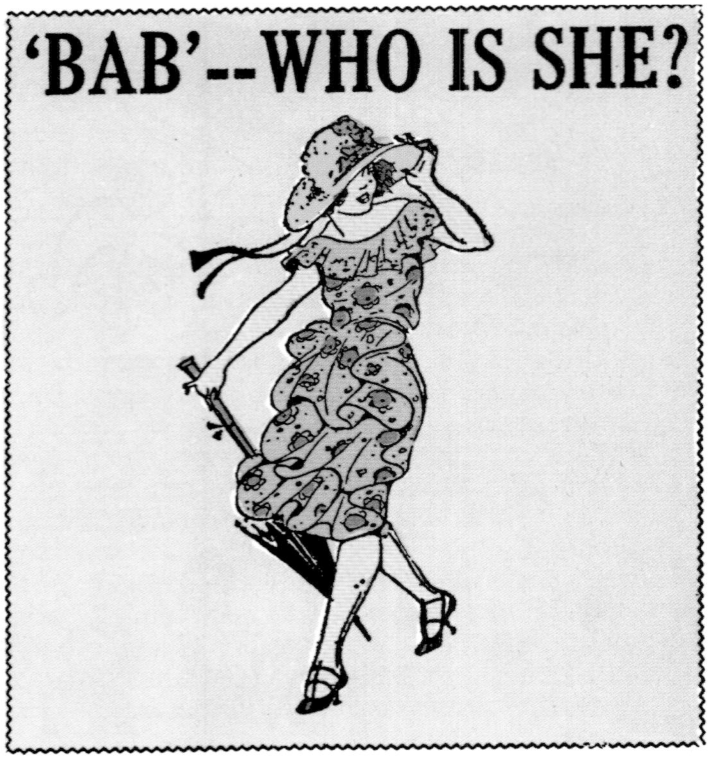
'BAB'--WHO IS SHE?

Central Railroad, who may have served as inspiration for Dagwood's father, railroad tycoon J. Bolling Bumstead. But he didn't neglect his talents entirely; he enrolled in night classes at the Art Institute of Chicago. The classes paid off. When he was only twenty, Chic secured a job as a cartoonist for the Newspaper Enterprise Association

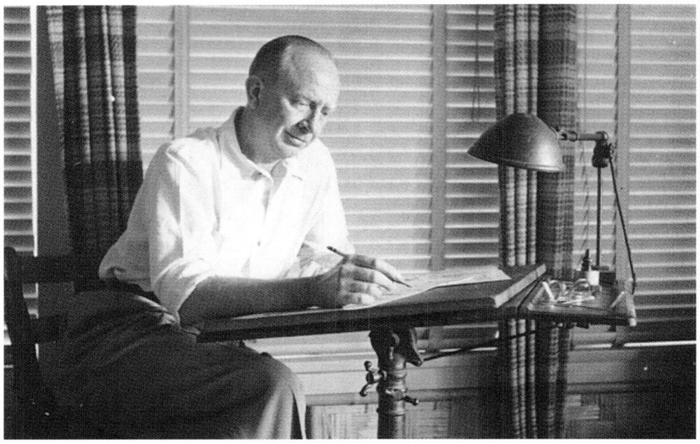

Chic working at his drawing board

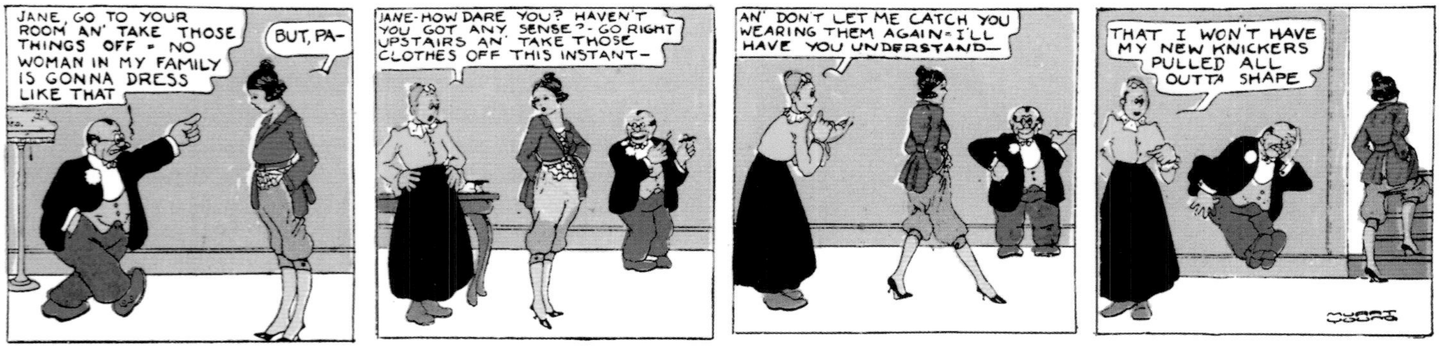
JANE, GO TO YOUR ROOM AN' TAKE THOSE THINGS OFF - NO WOMAN IN MY FAMILY IS GONNA DRESS LIKE THAT
BUT, PA-
JANE-HOW DARE YOU? HAVEN'T YOU GOT ANY SENSE?- GO RIGHT UPSTAIRS AN' TAKE THOSE CLOTHES OFF THIS INSTANT-
AN' DON'T LET ME CATCH YOU WEARING THEM AGAIN-I'LL HAVE YOU UNDERSTAND-
THAT I WON'T HAVE MY NEW KNICKERS PULLED ALL OUTTA SHAPE

The Affairs of Jane, which he drew for the Newspaper Enterprise Association, was Chic's first comic strip.

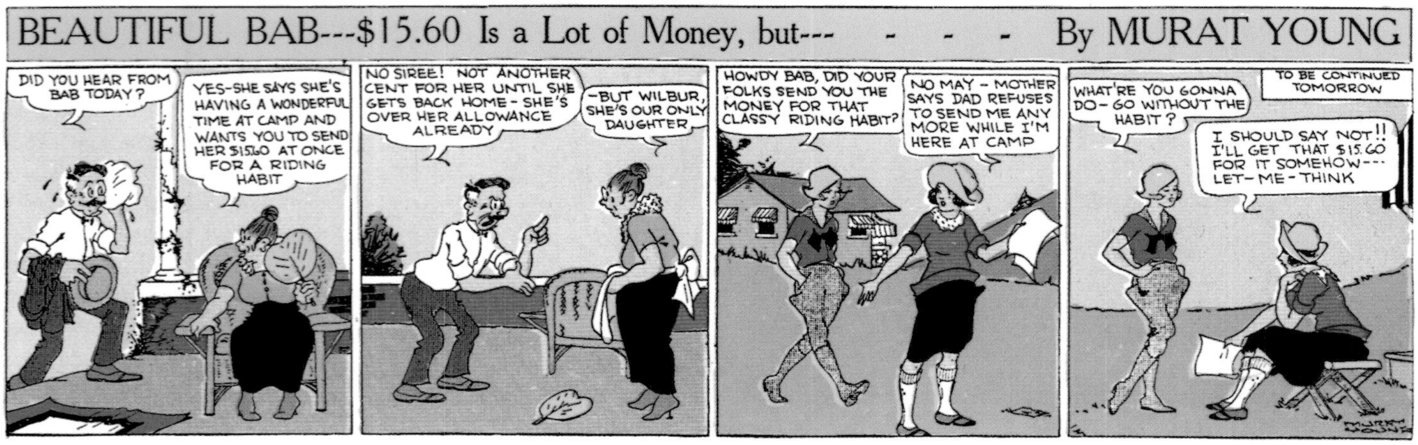
BEAUTIFUL BAB---$15.60 Is a Lot of Money, but--- - - - By MURAT YOUNG
DID YOU HEAR FROM BAB TODAY?
YES-SHE SAYS SHE'S HAVING A WONDERFUL TIME AT CAMP AND WANTS YOU TO SEND HER $15.60 AT ONCE FOR A RIDING HABIT
NO SIREE! NOT ANOTHER CENT FOR HER UNTIL SHE GETS BACK HOME - SHE'S OVER HER ALLOWANCE ALREADY
-BUT WILBUR, SHE'S OUR ONLY DAUGHTER
HOWDY BAB, DID YOUR FOLKS SEND YOU THE MONEY FOR THAT CLASSY RIDING HABIT?
NO MAY - MOTHER SAYS DAD REFUSES TO SEND ME ANY MORE WHILE I'M HERE AT CAMP
TO BE CONTINUED TOMORROW
WHAT'RE YOU GONNA DO- GO WITHOUT THE HABIT?
I SHOULD SAY NOT!! I'LL GET THAT $15.60 FOR IT SOMEHOW--- LET-ME-THINK

Beautiful Bab made its appearance on July 15, 1922 with the Bell Syndicate.

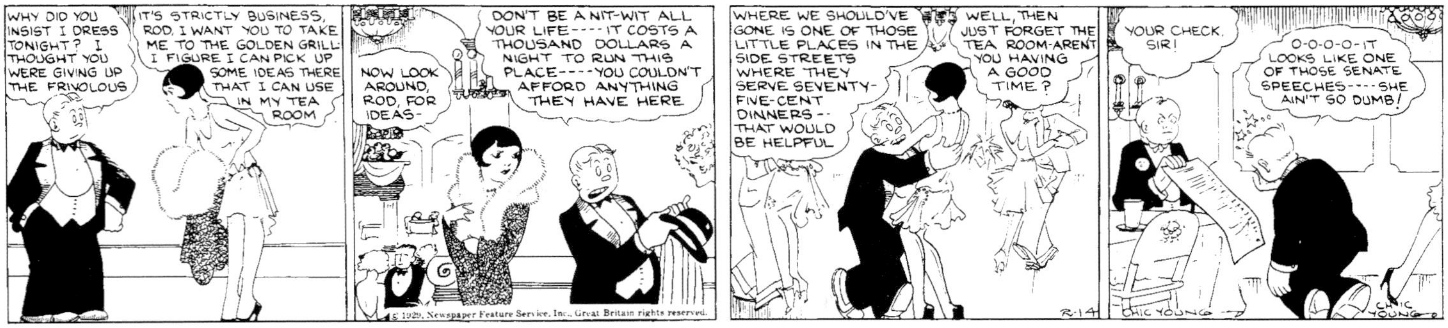
WHY DID YOU INSIST I DRESS TONIGHT? I THOUGHT YOU WERE GIVING UP THE FRIVOLOUS
IT'S STRICTLY BUSINESS, ROD. I WANT YOU TO TAKE ME TO THE GOLDEN GRILL: I FIGURE I CAN PICK UP SOME IDEAS THERE THAT I CAN USE IN MY TEA ROOM
NOW LOOK AROUND, ROD, FOR IDEAS-
DON'T BE A NIT-WIT ALL YOUR LIFE----IT COSTS A THOUSAND DOLLARS A NIGHT TO RUN THIS PLACE----YOU COULDN'T AFFORD ANYTHING THEY HAVE HERE
© 1929, Newspaper Feature Service, Inc., Great Britain rights reserved.
WHERE WE SHOULD'VE GONE IS ONE OF THOSE LITTLE PLACES IN THE SIDE STREETS WHERE THEY SERVE SEVENTY-FIVE-CENT DINNERS--THAT WOULD BE HELPFUL
WELL, THEN JUST FORGET THE TEA ROOM-AREN'T YOU HAVING A GOOD TIME?
R-14
YOUR CHECK, SIR!
O-O-O-O-IT LOOKS LIKE ONE OF THOSE SENATE SPEECHES----SHE AIN'T SO DUMB!
CHIC YOUNG
CHIC YOUNG

An early Dumb Dora strip, which Chic created for King Features Syndicate

(NEA) in Cleveland, where he created the first in a long line of strips centered on pretty girls, *The Affairs of Jane,* which debuted on September 26, 1921.

Though *Jane* only lasted six months, it provided Murat Young, as he then signed his work, with a salary (albeit a meager one, twenty-two dollars a week) and a sounding board for his still-maturing talent. His strengths included an unerring ear for social trends and an equally unerring eye for drawing young women, who in the 1920s were finally coming into their own in the pages of the comics and elsewhere.

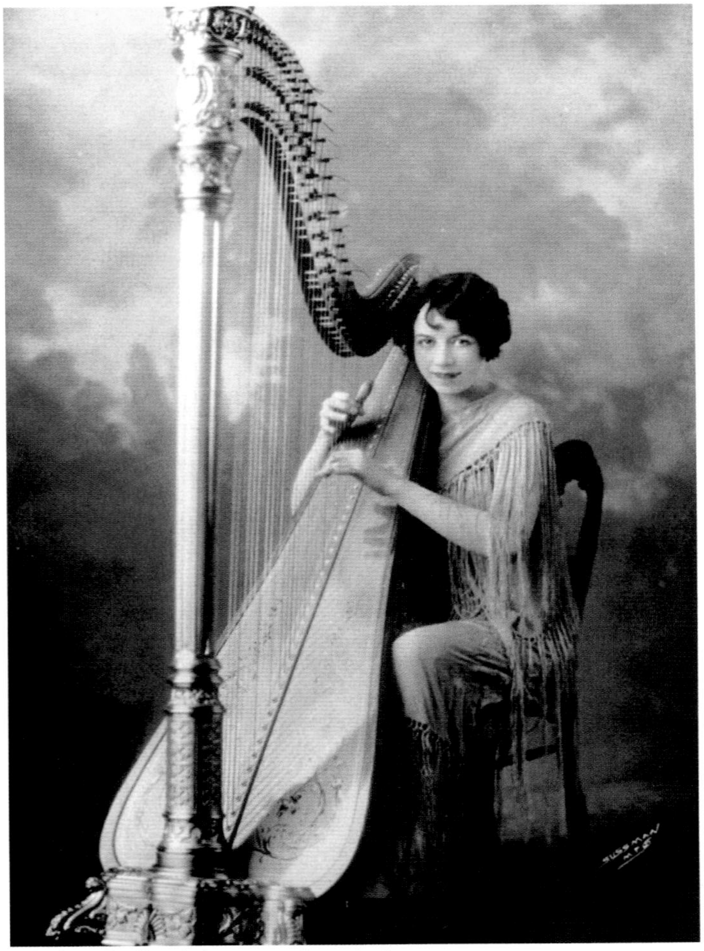

Athel Lindorff at her concert harp, just about the time she met Chic Young.

After his stint with NEA, Chic switched syndicates and created another similarly themed strip, *Beautiful Bab,* which drew the attention of a particularly important fan. William Randolph Hearst was renowned for discovering talent, and now his attention had landed on Chic Young, then still a struggling young Cleveland cartoonist. The offer that Hearst extended—a job in the art department at the King Features "bull-pen" in New York—was technically a step down. But the company was so prestigious for comic artists—many of the cartoonists who were then making it big had started as office boys or touch-up artists there—that Chic gleefully accepted.

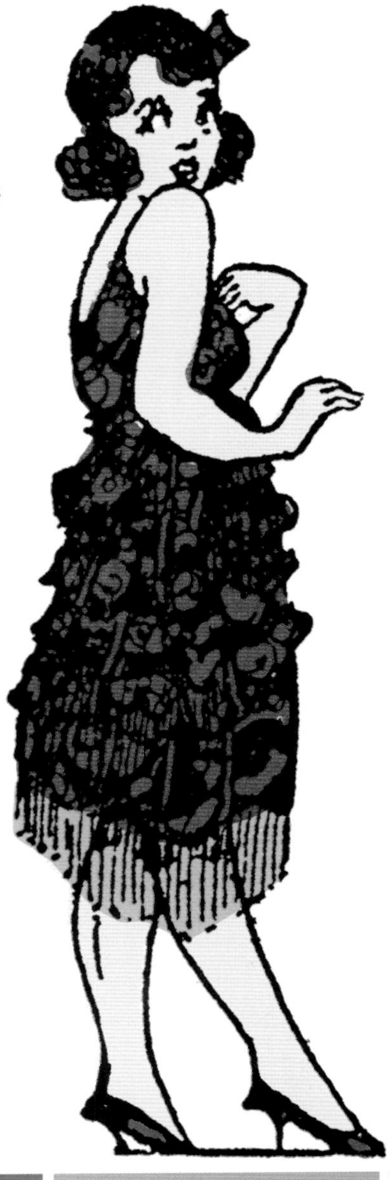

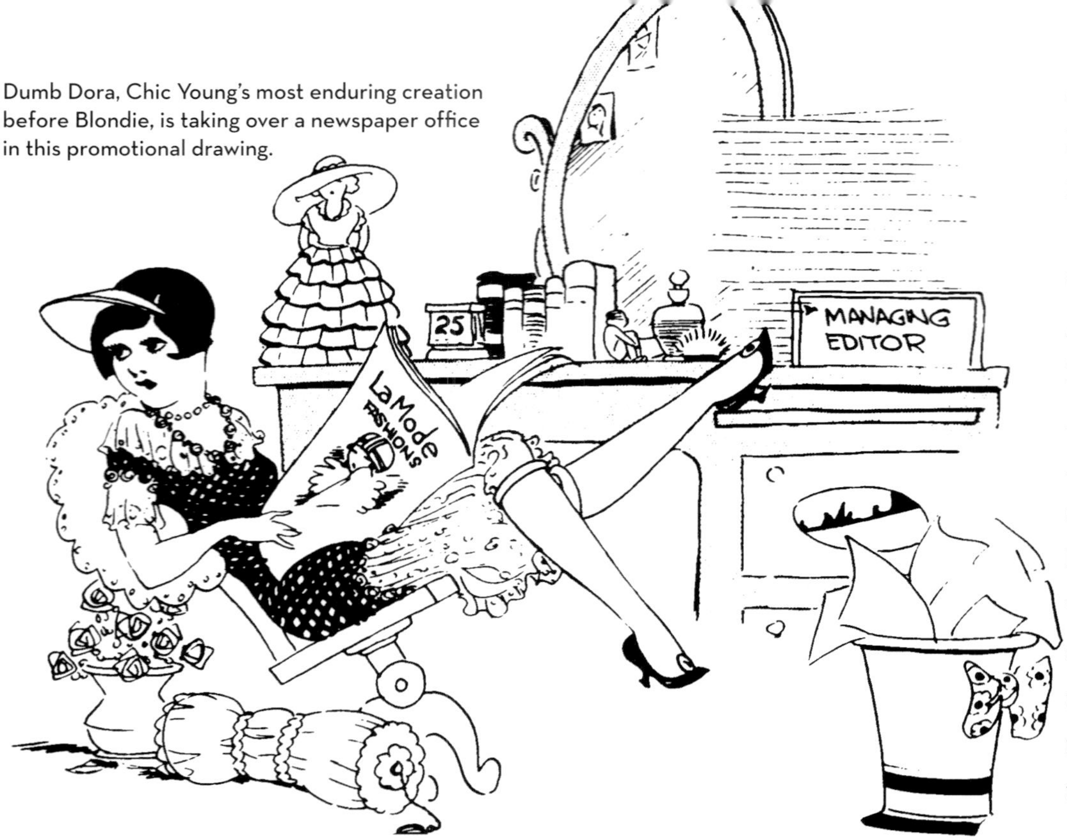
25
LaMode FASHIONS
MANAGING EDITOR

Dumb Dora, Chic Young's most enduring creation before Blondie, is taking over a newspaper office in this promotional drawing.

And after he moved to New York, he realized that he'd had a near miss with King Features more than a year before. A King executive traveling through Cleveland had spotted *The Affairs of Jane* and called NEA. Chic remembered the call; he had answered it himself. But the bullpen at NEA was so full of practical jokers—Chic included—and a call from a King exec to a newbie was so ridiculously unlikely that he simply listened with mock politeness to the request for a meeting with him, made an appointment at a false address, and then hung up, wondering which one of his unsuspecting colleagues was responsible for such a good gag. None of them, it turned out; the offer had been real. But the call he got a year later was at the behest of Hearst himself, so the deal was a better one. Practical jokes, though, were never quite as appealing.

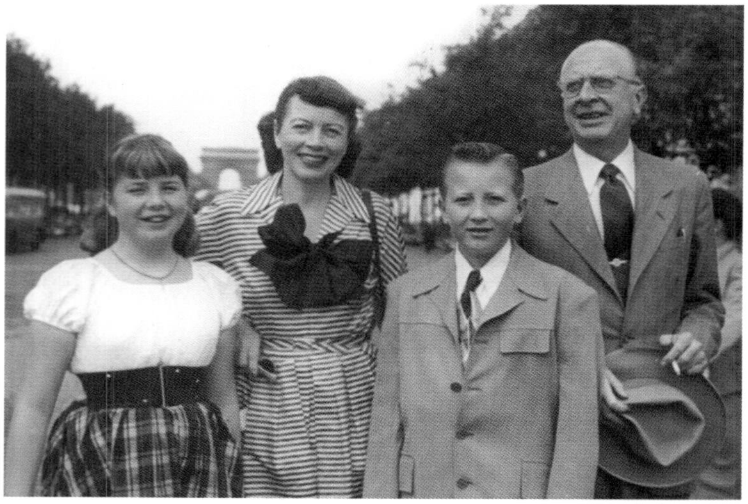

Jeanne, Athel, Dean, and Chic Young visited Paris in the early 1950s.

By 1924, Chic had come up with a more lasting strip, *Dumb Dora* (subtitle: "She's Not So Dumb As She Looks"). A true creature of the Jazz Age, Dora sported miniskirts and a cavalier attitude about her suitors. Soon the strip was appearing in more than one hundred papers. Chic's move to New York had proved fruitful; he was on his way to becoming a success.

In 1927, he made another step in that direction when he met the beautiful, auburn-haired Athel Lindorff, a French-trained concert harpist from Rock Island, Illinois, who was touring New York. Within days of their first date, she found him on the sidewalk beneath her window.

"Why don't you come in out of the cold?" she asked. But he wasn't interested in short-term company.

"I want you to come down," he said. "Let's get married." Surprisingly, she agreed, and the marriage lasted forty-six happy years.

Though "A," as Athel came to be known, gave up her career once she married, she always kept a beautiful gold harp in the Young home, which she played regularly to keep her skills intact. (And to

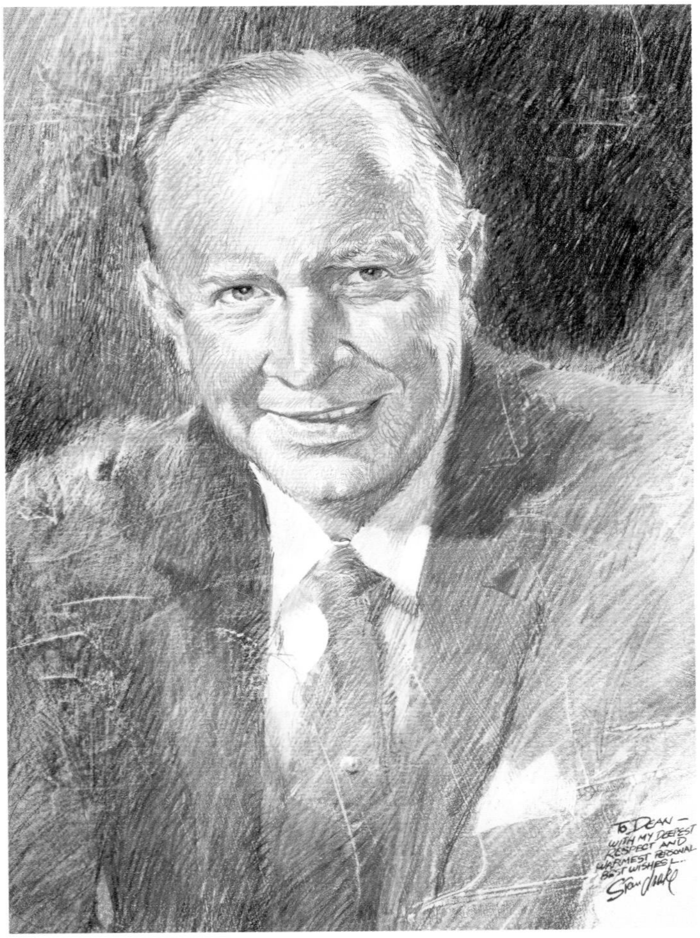
To Dean –
With my deepest respect and warmest personal best wishes...
Stan Drake

Chic Young

allow her husband to make the joke that she was always "harping" on something.) Throughout her life she was an important force in the success of *Blondie,* reading every strip before it was sent to the syndicate, just as Dean's wife Charlotte does to this day.

Personally and professionally, Chic Young now felt set, but it wasn't long until he felt a creative itch again, not to mention a financial one. After the stock market crash of 1929 dissolved his carefully laid out investments, he was more determined than ever to improve his salary. When the management of King Features refused his request for a raise or for the ownership of *Dora,* he left—sailing on a cruise ship to France with A in tow. King blinked first, and Chic returned to the promise that he could do his own strip. Over several weeks in the summer of 1930, in his studio in Great Neck Long Island, he created the last comic strip he would ever work on—*Blondie.*

From her early years as a flapper to her recent incarnation as a business owner, Blondie has maintained a consistent style and tone that has charmed the country, and Chic Young soon was one of the most celebrated cartoonists in

Soon enough, his father offered him the opportunity to work on the strip with him, and Dean jumped at the chance.

the business. He hired assistants—including an artist, Jim Raymond, who became a guiding force in the strip, even taking it over for a year when the Youngs took a sabbatical after their first son, Wayne, died from jaundice at age six.

Raymond, the brother of fellow cartoonist Alex Raymond, who also started on *Blondie* before working on strips such as *Flash Gordon,* worked with Chic Young and his successor Dean, until his death in 1989, helping cement the look and feel of the strip as a valued and trusted contributor.

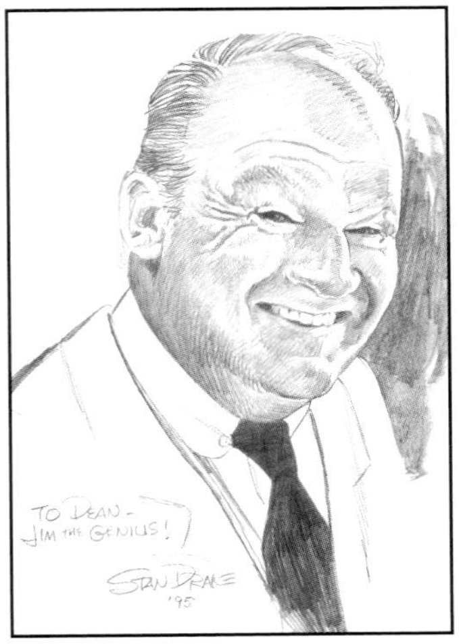
To Dean –
Jim the Genius!
Stan Drake
'95

Jim Raymond

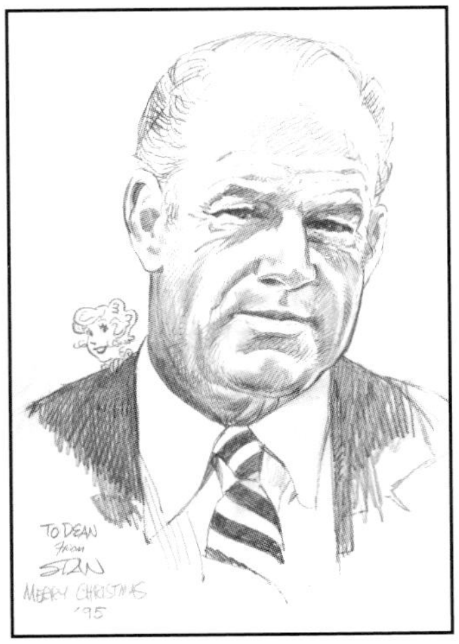
To Dean
from
Stan
Merry Christmas
'95

Stan Drake

He was followed by artists including Stan Drake, Mike Gersher, Denis LeBrun, and most recently, John Marshall and his assistant Frank Cummings, all of whom have

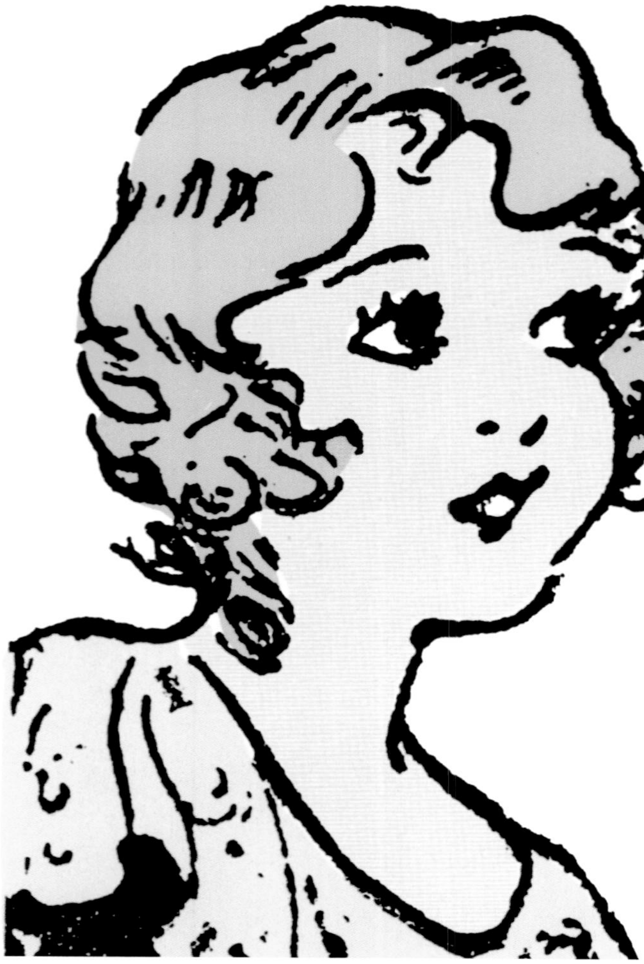

An early rendering of Blondie as a beautiful flapper

remained true to the sense of realism that Chic Young envisioned for the strip. From their full-body depiction to their changing clothing, the characters in *Blondie* resemble anatomically correct people—with just a few features punched up for comic effect.

> "My mom was a guiding force in the comic strip. There was never anything done or sent out from the studio before my mother proofread it."
> – Dean Young

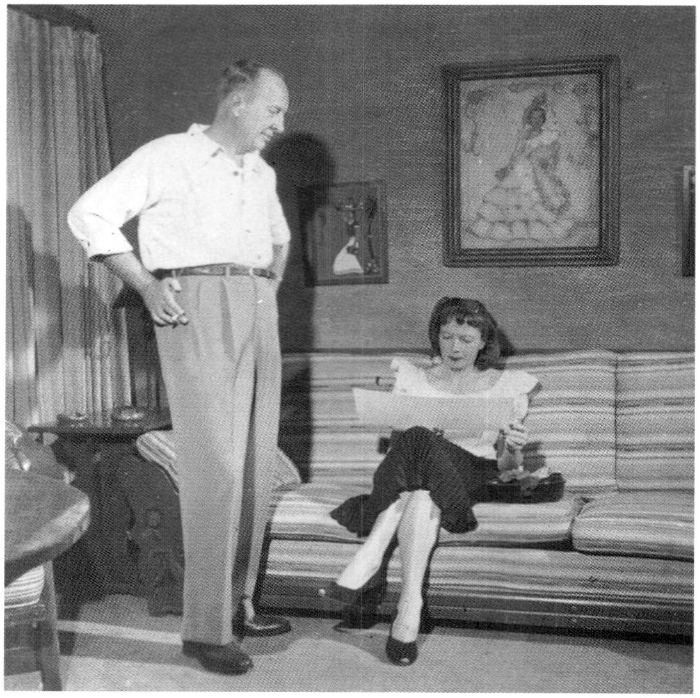

Athel, Chic's wife, reviewed every *Blondie* strip before it was sent to King Features Syndicate.

By the 1940s, *Blondie*'s popularity had surpassed the pages of the newspaper; the characters were reborn in radio plays and in twenty-eight Columbia feature films. The Youngs, along with their one-year-old son Dean, moved to California to be closer to those Hollywood productions. A daughter, Jeanne, was born soon after. (Though Chic remained a shy man who shunned publicity, the family did occasionally get touches of the celebrity life, visiting the set to meet the 3-D version of Blondie and Dagwood, Penny

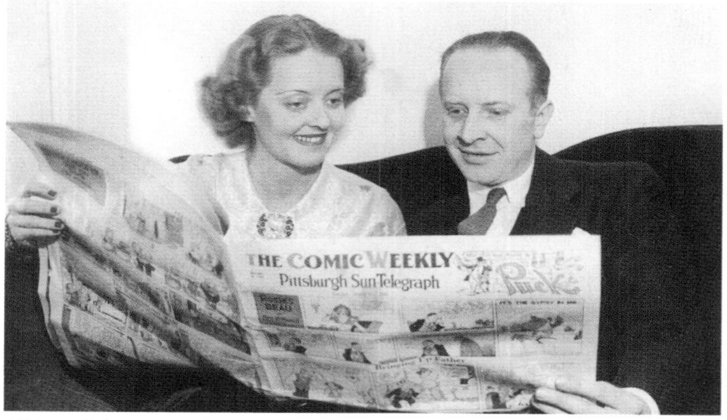
THE COMIC WEEKLY
Pittsburgh Sun-Telegraph

Although he was a shy man, Chic enjoyed this photo-op with Bette Davis in the 1930s.

Singleton and Arthur Lake, who also played Dagwood on the radio shows.) After more than fifteen years in California, though, Chic found he preferred Florida, where his brother Lyman lived. When Dean was a senior in high school, the family moved to Clearwater Beach, Florida, where Dean still resides.

Jim Raymond (right) was Blondie's artist and a guiding force in the strip, working first with Chic and later with Dean (left), until Jim died in 1989.

doubt, of a very long love affair with food.) Soon enough, his father offered him the opportunity to work on the strip with him, and Dean jumped at the chance. The ten years they worked together before Chic's death in 1973 proved instrumental in shaping Dean's understanding of *Blondie.*

Though Dean had displayed some interest in cartooning in his youth, he chose to pursue another career at first. After graduating from college with a business degree, he worked in an advertising agency in Miami, and then as a sales executive for a grocery chain. (The beginnings, no

"My dad was a genius," Dean said. "He put these people, these characters, together, just brilliantly. I mean, how'd he do that?"

Soon enough, Dean figured out how. Though his father crumpled and threw out Dean's first attempt at a Sunday

Chic Young, who created Blondie

Dean Young, who increased Blondie's popularity

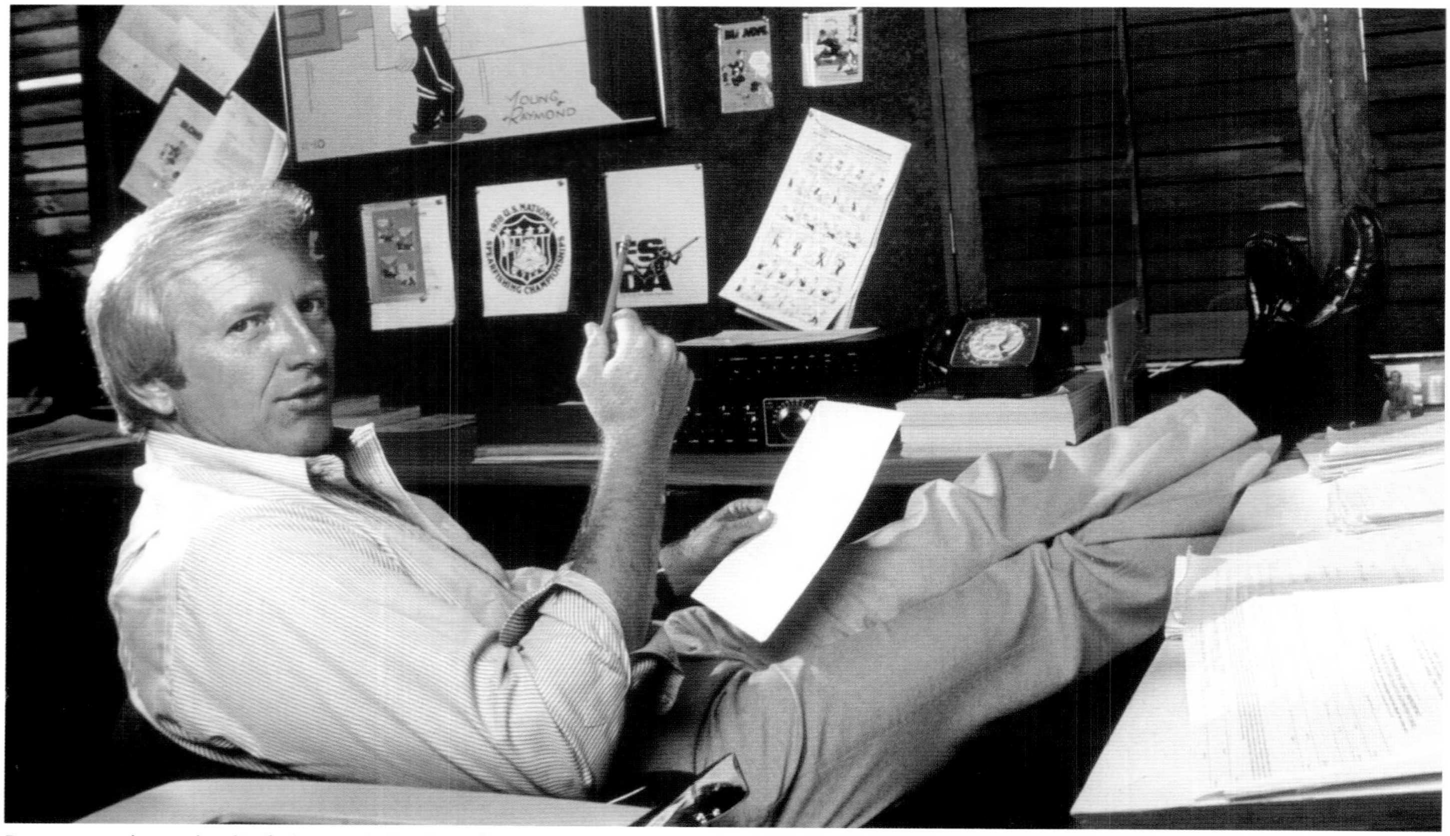

Dean remembers what his father said: do what's funny to you, don't offend anyone, and "make friends, not enemies."

page, the two eventually grew into a rhythm.

"It was great," Dean says of being mentored by his dad. "Thankfully, I have a lot of his DNA, so we think alike."

But in the year after Chic's death, hundreds of newspapers dropped the strip, fearful that without its creator at the helm it would founder. Dean was devastated, but he was also wary about not living up to his father's legacy. "In the beginning, I thought about all the millions of fans—I would try to picture them when I was in a football stadium—and it scared me. I thought: *I need to conquer this fear.*"

He did it by remembering some of the lessons his father had taught him: do what's funny to you, don't offend anyone, and "make friends, not enemies."

"I think of the comics as a refuge, where you can see something that's pleasurable and funny, and not mean-spirited and insulting," he said. "That's my formula, and it seems to be working."

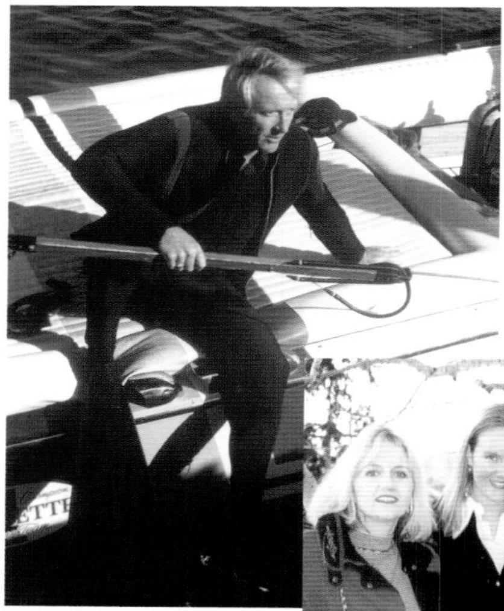

In his spare time, Dean is an award-winning spearfisherman.

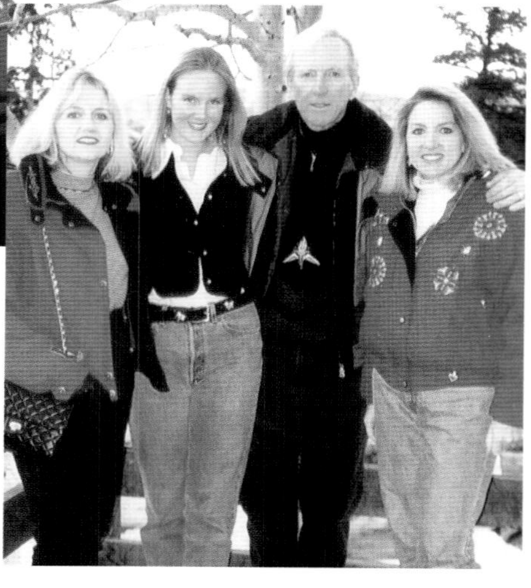

Dean with his three daughters: Lisa, Dianne, and Dana

It certainly does. In the thirty-plus years that Dean has written *Blondie,* the strip has replaced the dropped newspapers and added more than seven hundred to its publication roster. It consistently ranks among the top five most popular comics in newspaper polls around the nation. Part of its success, Dean believes, is because of his continuing efforts to keep it fresh.

Blondie consistently ranks among the top five most popular comics in newspaper polls around the nation.

"I try to read two newspapers and magazines every day," he said. "There needs to be this osmosis thing that goes into me, where I've got what's going on in the world, but I translate that into the comedic thing that happens in the Bumsteads' world."

Of course, inspiration can hit closer to home. When his mother Athel was alive, Dean ran the strips by her for approval; now his wife, Charlotte, fulfills that role of sounding board. His three daughters—Lisa Rogers, Dianne Erwin, and Dana Coston, a lawyer, graphic designer, and cartoonist-in-training, respectively, now all grown up with families of their own—provided plenty of fodder in their teenage years.

"I think they recognize their situations," their dad chuckled.

With retirement still years away, Dean adheres to a regular five-day-a-week schedule in a studio near his home, using two days for creative work and the rest for administrative duties; in his off time he's an avid boater and award-winning spearfisherman. John Marshall, *Blondie*'s artist, lives and works in Binghamton, New York, but the two stay in constant communication, and the relationship runs smoothly.

"More than any other way, I see the strip happening graphically," Dean said. "I see where the characters are, I see exactly where the balloons are. I know which character's going to speak first—that character's going to be on the left side. I see that right away. I don't even have to think about it."

And as to the question he does have to think about, because he gets asked about it most often—whether there are any similarities between Dagwood and him—the answer, of course, is yes.

"We both like naps," Dean laughed. "And I love a good sandwich!"

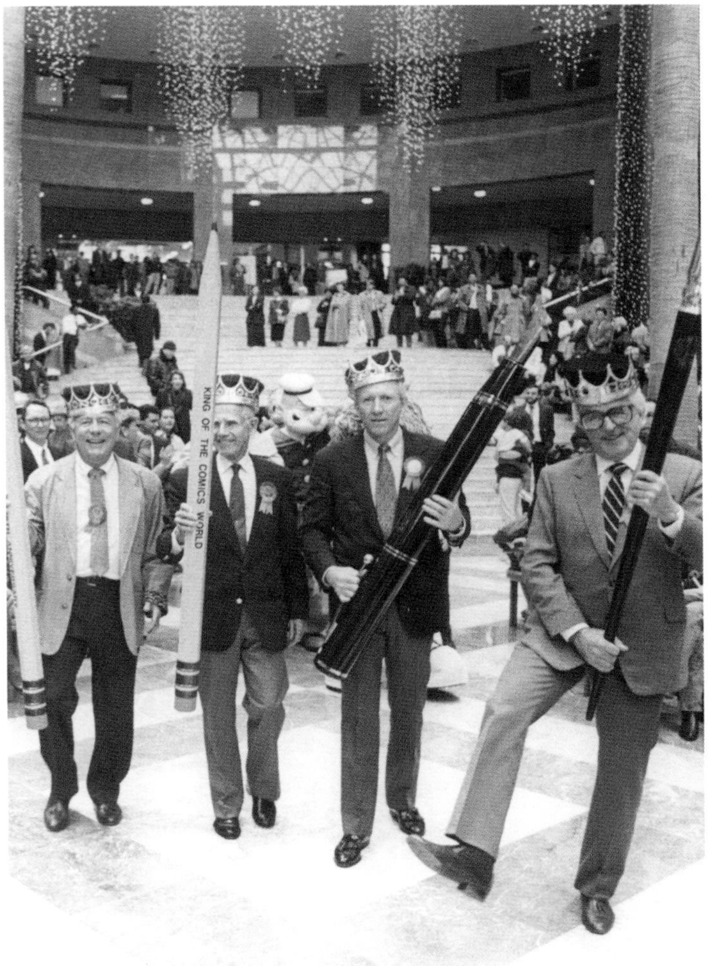
KING OF THE COMICS WORLD

The "Kings of the Comics World" Mort Walker, creator of *Beetle Bailey*, Bill Keane, creator of *Family Circus*, Dean Young, and Hank Ketcham, creator of *Dennis the Menace*, were together for a King Features promotion at the World Financial Center in New York City.

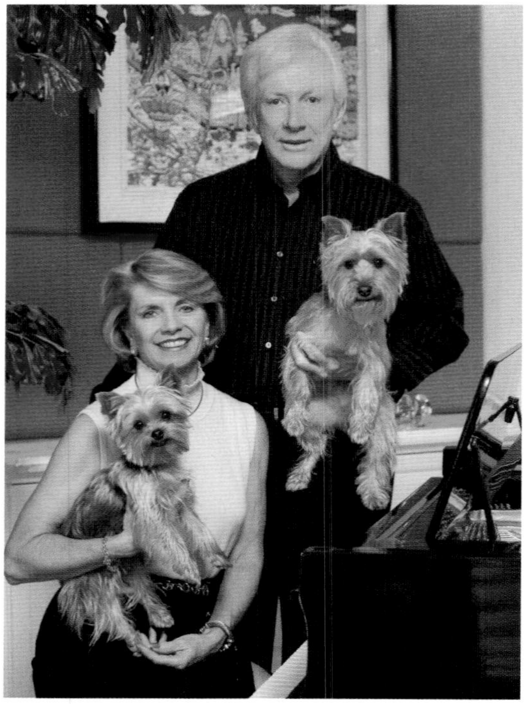

Dean's wife, Charlotte, follows in Athel's footsteps and reviews every strip. Their two dogs are named, appropriately, Blondie and Dagwood.

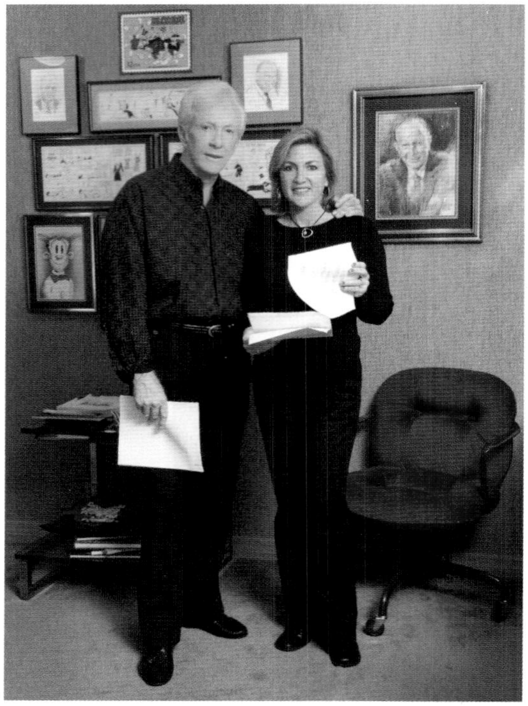

Just as Dean inherited *Blondie* from his father, he plans to pass the strip on to his daughter, Dana Young Coston, who will undoubtedly put her on spin on it.

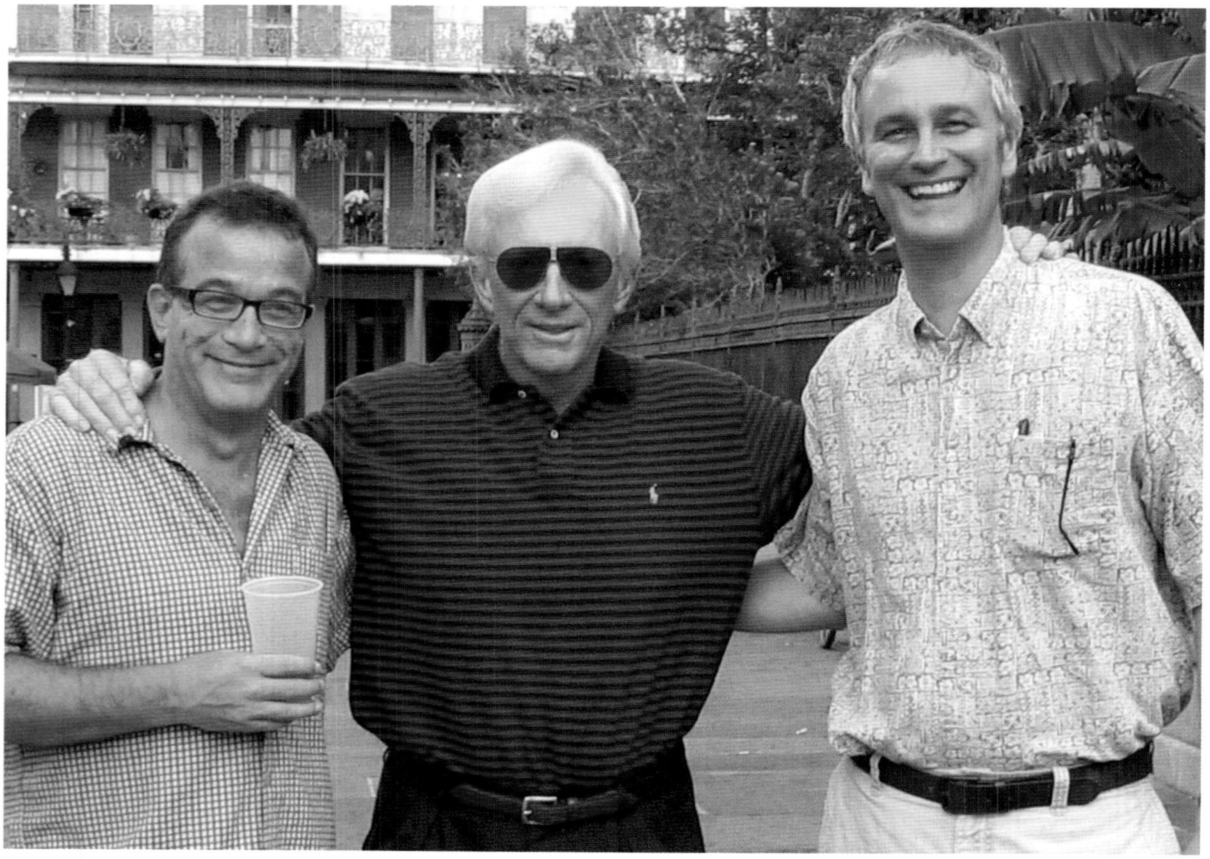

Dean with John Marshall, *Blondie's* artist (on right), and Frank Cummings, his assistant (on left). John and Frank have remained true to the sense of realism that Chic envisioned for *Blondie*.